THE *CONFE*

AND CORRESPONDENCE,
INCLUDING THE LETTERS
TO MALESHERBES

JEAN-JACQUES ROUSSEAU

THE *CONFESSIONS*
AND CORRESPONDENCE,
INCLUDING THE LETTERS
TO MALESHERBES

THE COLLECTED WRITINGS OF ROUSSEAU
Vol. 5

EDITED BY
CHRISTOPHER KELLY, ROGER D. MASTERS,
AND PETER G. STILLMAN

TRANSLATED BY
CHRISTOPHER KELLY

DARTMOUTH COLLEGE
PUBLISHED BY UNIVERSITY PRESS OF NEW ENGLAND
HANOVER AND LONDON

DARTMOUTH COLLEGE

Published by University Press of New England, Hanover, NH 03755

© 1995 by the Trustees of Dartmouth College

First University Press of New England paperback edition 1998

All rights reserved

Printed in the United States of America   5   4   3   2

*This publication has been supported by a grant from
the National Endowment for the Humanities,
an independent federal agency. Support has also
been provided by Pro Helvetia.*

Frontispiece: *Jean-Jacques Rousseau at Montmorency 1757–1762,*
drawing by Houel; used by permission of Musée
Jean-Jacques Rousseau, Montmorency.

Library of Congress Cataloging-in-Publication Data
Rousseau, Jean-Jacques, 1712–1778.
    [Confessions. English]
    The confessions ; and, Correspondence, including the letters to
Malesherbes / Jean-Jacques Rousseau ; edited by Christopher Kelly,
Roger D. Masters, and Peter G. Stillman ; translated by Christopher
Kelly.
        p.   cm. — (The collected writings of Rousseau ; vol. 5)
    Includes bibliographical references and index.
    ISBN 0-87451-707-9 (cl.: alk. paper). — ISBN 0-87451-836-9 (pbk.: alk. paper)
    1. Rousseau, Jean-Jacques, 1712–1778—Biography.   2. Rousseau,
Jean-Jacques, 1712–1778—Correspondence.   3. Malesherbes, Chrétien
Guillaume de Lamoingnon de, 1721–1794—Correspondence.   4. Authors,
French—18th century—Biography.   5. Authors, French—18th century—
Correspondence.   I. Malesherbes, Chrétien Guillaume de Lamoingnon
de, 1721–1794.   II. Kelly, Christopher, 1950–   .   III. Masters,
Roger D.   IV. Stillman, Peter G.   V. Rousseau, Jean-Jacques,
1712–1778. Correspondence. English. Selections.   VI. Title.
VII. Title: Confessions.   VIII. Title: Confessions ; and,
Correspondence, including the letters to Malesherbes.   IX. Title:
Correspondence, including the letters to Malesherbes.   X. Series:
Rousseau, Jean-Jacques, 1712–1778. Works. English. 1990 ; vol. 5.
PQ2034.A3   1990 vol. 5
[PQ2036]
848'.509 s—dc20
[848'.509]   94-47021
[B]
∞

Contents

THE COLLECTED WRITINGS OF ROUSSEAU

Roger D. Masters and Christopher Kelly,
Series Editors

Volume 1
Rousseau, Judge of Jean-Jacques: Dialogues

Volume 2
Discourse on the Sciences and Arts (First Discourse)
and Polemics

Volume 3
Discourse on the Origins of Inequality (Second Discourse),
Polemics, and Political Economy

Volume 4
Social Contract, Discourse on the Virtue Most Necessary for a Hero,
Political Fragments, and Geneva Manuscript

Volume 5
The *Confessions* and Correspondence,
Including the Letters to Malesherbes

Volume 6
Julie, or the New Heloise: Letters of Two Lovers
Who Live in a Small Town at the Foot of the Alps

Volume 7
Essay on the Origin of Languages
and Writings Related to Music

Volume 8
The Reveries of the Solitary Walker,
Botanical Writings, and Letter to Franquières

Preface

Although Jean-Jacques Rousseau is a significant figure in the Western tradition, there is no standard edition of his major writings available in English. Unlike those of other thinkers of comparable stature, moreover, many of Rousseau's important works either have never been translated or have become unavailable. The present edition of the *Collected Writings of Rousseau* is intended to remedy this situation.

Our goal is to produce a series that can provide a standard reference for scholarship that is accessible to all those wishing to read broadly in the corpus of Rousseau's work. To this end, the translations seek to combine care and faithfulness to the original French text with readability in English. Although, as every translator knows, there are often passages where it is impossible to meet both of these criteria at the same time, readers of a thinker and writer of Rousseau's stature deserve texts that have not been deformed by the interpretive bias of translators or editors. Wherever possible, existing translations of high quality have been used, although in some cases the editors have felt minor revisions were necessary to maintain the accuracy and consistency of the English versions. Where there was no English translation (or none of sufficient quality), a new translation has been prepared.

Each text is supplemented by editorial notes that clarify Rousseau's references and citations or passages otherwise not intelligible. Although these notes do not provide as much detail as is found in the critical apparatus of the Pléiade edition of the *Oeuvres complètes*, the English-speaking reader should nevertheless have in hand the basis for a more careful and comprehensive understanding of Rousseau than has hitherto been possible.

Volume 5 contains the first English translation of the *Confessions* based on the definitive French edition, along with most of the variants contained in the different manuscripts of the work. In addition, it includes translations of the letters to and from Rousseau referred to in the body of the *Confessions*. Of special importance are the four letters to Malesherbes, which represent Rousseau's earliest autobiographical effort. The *Confessions* has probably been Rousseau's most consistently popular work in the two centuries since it was first published. It is responsible for giving impetus to the great wave of autobiographies that followed it and had a profound influence on the development of the modern novel. Along with its importance as a personal document and literary work, the *Confessions* is Rousseau's attempt to illustrate the principles of his understanding of human nature by means of a concrete example. Finally, it explores in all their complexity the relations between the attempt to achieve psychological independence and wholeness on the one hand and the effort to live in a complex society on the other.

The translator would like to thank the National Endowment for the Humanities for its support in the form of a summer stipend that assisted in the preparation of the final draft of the translation. Thanks are also due to Jeanne Kelly, Joel Schwarz, Elaine Wolfe, Michael Comenetz, and the anonymous readers for the University Press of New England for their detection of errors and suggestions for improvement as a result of their reading of early drafts. We are also grateful to Robert Thiéry, conservateur of the Musée J.-J. Rousseau in Montmorency for permission to reproduce the sketch by Houel that serves as frontispiece to this volume.

June 1994

C.K.
R.D.M.
P.G.S.

Chronology of Events Reported in the Confessions

Book I
1672
December 28: Birth of Rousseau's father, Isaac Rousseau.

1673
February 6: Birth of Rousseau's mother, Suzanne Bernard.

1704
Marriage of Rousseau's parents.

1705
Birth of Rousseau's brother, François.

1712
June 28: Birth of Jean-Jacques Rousseau.

1722
October: Rousseau's father leaves Geneva after his quarrel with
Captain Gautier, and Rousseau is sent to Bossey to live with the
Lamberciers.

1724
Rousseau returns to Geneva to live with his uncle, Gabriel Bernard.
Rousseau is apprenticed to the city clerk, M. Masseron.

1725
April: Rousseau is apprenticed to the engraver, Abel Du Commun.

1728
March 14: Rousseau decides to run away from Geneva after finding
the city gates locked.

Book II
1728
March 21: Rousseau meets Mme de Warens in Annecy.
April 12: Rousseau enters the hospice for the catechumens in Turin.
April 23: Rousseau is baptized a Catholic.

July: Rousseau enters the service of Mme de Vercellis.
December: Death of Mme de Vercellis.

Book III
1729

February: Probable beginning of Rousseau's employment with the Gouvon family.
Summer: Rousseau returns to Mme de Warens in Annecy.
Summer-Fall: Rousseau studies at the Lazarist Seminary and then begins to study music with M. Le Maître.

1730

April: Rousseau abandons M. Le Maître in Lyon.

Book IV
1730

July: Rousseau escorts Merceret to Fribourg and presents himself as Vaussore de Villeneuve, a French musician, in Lausanne.
Winter: Rousseau teaches music in Neuchâtel.

1731

April: Rousseau becomes the interpreter for the fake Archimandrite of Jerusalem.
June: Rousseau visits Paris for the first time.
September: Rousseau travels to Chambéry by way of Lyon to rejoin Mme de Warens.

Book V
1731

October: Rousseau begins work in the King's survey.

1732

June: Rousseau leaves the survey and begins to teach music.

1733

July: Rousseau travels to Besançon to study with the Abbé Blanchard. (This might have taken place either a year earlier or a year later.)

1734

March: Death of Claude Anet.

1736

Probable date of Rousseau's and Mme de Warens's first stay at Les Charmettes.

Book VI

1737

June: Rousseau is injured in an accident during a chemistry experiment.

July: Rousseau returns to Geneva to receive his share of his mother's estate.

September: Rousseau leaves Chambéry for Montpellier to consult Dr. Fizes.

1738

February: Probable date of Rousseau's return to Chambéry.

1740

April: Rousseau becomes tutor to the children of M. de Mably in Lyon.

1741

May: Rousseau returns to Chambéry.

Book VII

1741

End of December: Earliest possible date for Rousseau's arrival in Paris with his new system of musical notation.

1742

August 22: Rousseau reads his *Project Concerning New Signs for Music* to the Academy of Sciences.

1743

January: Publication of the *Dissertation on Modern Music*.

July 10: Rousseau leaves Paris to begin working as secretary to M. de Montaigu, the French Ambassador to Venice.

September 4: Rousseau arrives in Venice.

1744

August 6: Rousseau leaves the Embassy after a quarrel with M. de Montaigu.

October: Rousseau arrives in Paris.

1745

March: Rousseau meets Thérèse Levasseur.
July: Rousseau completes *The Gallant Muses*.
Fall: Rousseau works on *Ramirro's Festival*.

1746

Winter: Rousseau begins working as a secretary for the Dupin family.
Birth of Rousseau's first child, who is put in the Foundling Hospital.

1747

May: Death of Rousseau's father.
Fall: Rousseau writes *The Reckless Engagement*.

1748

Birth of Rousseau's second child.

1749

January–March: Rousseau writes articles on music for the *Encyclopedia*.
July 24: Diderot is imprisoned in Vincennes.

Book VIII

1749

August: Rousseau meets Grimm.
October: On the way to visit Diderot, Rousseau reads the essay topic proposed by the Academy of Dijon, "Has the restoration of the sciences and arts tended to purify morals?" and immediately begins to write the *Discourse on the Sciences and the Arts*.

1750

July: The *First Discourse* is awarded the prize by the Academy of Dijon.

1751

January: Publication of the *First Discourse*.
February: Rousseau gives up his position with the Dupins and starts to work as a music copyist.
Spring: Birth of Rousseau's third child.
October: Rousseau responds to the King of Poland's attack on the *First Discourse*.
November: Rousseau responds to Gautier's *Refutation* with his *Letter to Grimm*.

1752

April: Rousseau responds to Bordes's attack with his *Response to M. Bordes*.

Spring–Summer: Rousseau composes *The Village Soothsayer*. Performance of *The Village Soothsayer* at Fontainebleau.

December 18: Unsuccessful performance of *Narcissus*.

1753

January: Publication of *Narcissus* along with its Preface.

November: Rousseau begins writing the *Second Discourse*. Publication of the *Letter on French Music*.

1754

June 1: Rousseau leaves Paris for Geneva.

June 12: Rousseau dates the dedication to the *Second Discourse* from Chambéry.

August 1: Rousseau regains his Genevan citizenship.

October: Rousseau returns to Paris.

1755

April 24: Publication of the *Second Discourse*.

Book IX

1756

April 9: Rousseau moves into the Hermitage near Montmorency.

August: Rousseau sends his letter to Voltaire on providence, responding to Voltaire's poems *On Natural Law* and *On the Disaster at Lisbon*.

End of Summer: Rousseau begins writing *Julie*.

1757

March–April: Quarrel and reconciliation of Rousseau and Diderot over Diderot's *The Natural Son*.

Spring: Rousseau falls in love with Sophie d'Houdetot.

End of August: Exchange of notes between Rousseau and Mme d'Epinay over his suspicions of her.

October 10: Publication of Vol. VII of the *Encyclopedia*, containing the article, *Geneva*.

October 25: Mme d'Epinay leaves for Geneva.

November: Grimm breaks with Rousseau.

December 5: Diderot visits Rousseau at the Hermitage.

December 15: Rousseau leaves the Hermitage and moves into the house at Mont-Louis in Montmorency.

Book X
1758

March: Rousseau finishes writing the *Letter to d'Alembert*.

Spring: Diderot informs Saint-Lambert about Rousseau's love for Mme d'Houdetot.

September: Rousseau finishes writing *Julie*.

October: Publication of the *Letter to d'Alembert*, along with an inserted announcement of Rousseau's rupture with Diderot.

October 29: Rousseau has reconciliation dinner with Saint-Lambert and Mme d'Houdetot.

1759

April: Rousseau makes the acquaintance of the Duc de Luxembourg.

May 6: At the invitation of the Duc de Luxembourg, Rousseau moves into the Little Chateau while repairs are made on his house at Mont-Louis.

July: Rousseau returns to Mont-Louis.

1760

July: Rousseau assists in obtaining the Abbé Morellet's release from prison.

Book XI
1761

January: *Julie* goes on sale in Paris one month after going on sale in London.

November: Duchesne begins printing *Emile*.

November: Rousseau expresses his fears of a Jesuit conspiracy against *Emile*.

1762

April: Publication of the *Social Contract*.

May: Publication of *Emile*.

June 9: A Warrant is issued for Rousseau's arrest; he flees Montmorency.

Book XII
1762

June 14: Rousseau arrives at Yverdon.

June 19: *Emile* and the *Social Contract* are burned at Geneva.

July 10: Rousseau is driven out of Yverdon and goes to Môtiers.

July 29: Death of Mme de Warens.

November 18: Rousseau dates the *Letter to Beaumont*.

1763
March: Publication of the *Letter to Beaumont*.
April 17: Rousseau is made a citizen of Neuchâtel.
May 12: Rousseau renounces his Genevan citizenship.

1764
May 18: Death of the Duc de Luxembourg.
December: Publication of the *Letters Written from the Mountain*.
December: Voltaire publishes the *Sentiments of the Citizens*.

1765
Spring: Rousseau is summoned before the Consistory at Môtiers.
September 6–7: Rousseau's house is stoned.
September 12: Rousseau arrives at the Island of St. Pierre.
October 16: Rousseau is expelled from the island.
October 29: Rousseau leaves Bienne for Berlin (although he is
eventually persuaded to go to England).

1770
December: Rousseau completes the *Confessions* and gives his first
readings from them.

1771
Rousseau gives the last of his readings from the *Confessions*, which
cease after Mme d'Epinay protests to the police.

Introduction

At nine o'clock in the morning one day late in 1770, seven guests assembled at the home of the Marquis de Pezay in Paris. Sometime after eleven o'clock in the evening (perhaps as late as two the next morning), Jean-Jacques Rousseau concluded his reading to them from his *Confessions*. Almost immediately after leaving, one of the listeners wrote a letter in which he said that he had been moved to tears by the noble frankness with which Rousseau admitted his faults. Another later commented on the extreme, or even mad, desire for notoriety that must be the source of Rousseau's enterprise. Upon learning about this and subsequent readings, Rousseau's former patroness, Mme d'Epinay wrote to the Lieutenant of Police Sartine to ask him to take action to prohibit future readings.[1] Profound emotion, wonder about Rousseau's motives and sanity, and outrage have continued to mark the responses of readers of the *Confessions* since the publication of Part One in 1782.

One thing that has changed since the original appearance of the *Confessions* is the sense of novelty of the enterprise of openly discussing one's innermost feelings and most shameful deeds. Readers in an age when autobiographies proliferate are more likely to be bemused than shocked by Rousseau's claim of novelty for his attempt to show a man "inside and under the skin." Living in an age in which the genre of autobiography was not well established enough even to have a name, Rousseau's contemporaries were shocked by his self-revelation. Rousseau was far from being the first person to discover that external manifestations of character such as words and deeds can be deceptive, but his emphasis on the internal life of feelings is surely unprecedented and epoch-making. Our unreflective acceptance of such a view is the result of the fact that Rousseau and his numberless imitators have won us over: we accept, as Rousseau's contemporaries and predecessors did not, that feelings are what count, much more so than thoughts, words, or deeds.

In spite of, or perhaps because of, our familiarity with a tradition of autobiography after Rousseau, many features of the *Confessions* are liable to misinterpretation. What follows is an attempt to clarify several of the most contentious issues for interpreting the work: truthfulness, goodness, the split between appearance and reality, and the alleged conspiracy against Rousseau. In each case the discussion will attempt to show the importance of these issues within both the *Confessions* and Rousseau's other works. The goal is to provide a context for the approach to this work, but not to substitute for attempts to understand it on its own terms.

Truthfulness and the *Confessions*

Numerous aims converge in the writing of the *Confessions*. As was frequently the case for Rousseau's works, the original impetus for it came from someone else. Over a period of years, his publisher, Marc-Michel Rey, asked Rousseau for an account of his life suitable to serve as an introduction to a collection of his writings. Rousseau had suddenly emerged out of obscurity into a widespread fame upon the publication of the *First Discourse* in 1751 and the round of disputes that followed this attack on the most universally admired aspects of modern European civilization.[2] Curiosity seekers were hungry for information about this man from the provinces who dared to make a learned and eloquent attack against the learning and eloquence of Paris. Their interest was all the more piqued when he reacted to his new fame by shunning Parisian society and returning to rural solitude. Thus, Rey importuned with a publisher's instinct for what would stimulate sales, but Rousseau failed to commit himself until he decided that an account of his life could serve a larger purpose.

There is considerable evidence that Rousseau discovered a number of different purposes that could be served by the *Confessions* and that their relative importance shifted over the time he worked on his autobiography, although none of them simply disappeared. These purposes can be divided into two apparently different categories. First, he concluded that by writing his life he could do something entirely new and useful: he could give the first accurate account of the genesis of the internal life of feelings in an individual that could subsequently help to lay the foundation for a science of human nature.[3] Second, he decided that it was necessary to preserve an account of his side of his quarrels with his former friends. The *Confessions*, then, combines self-revelation in the service of a general goal with self-justification for reasons that are quite particular to Rousseau.

On the surface, these two purposes have no necessary relation to each other, but after the persecution of Rousseau began with the censorship of *Emile* and the warrant issued for his arrest at the beginning of June 1762, they tended to converge. In mid-November of the same year Rousseau expressed the importance of his account of his life in a letter to Rey in which he says, "Six months ago my life unfortunately became a work of importance that requires time and reflection."[4] Almost from the beginning of his literary career, Rousseau had presented himself as the virtual embodiment of the principles contained in his writings, a living example of the truth of what he said.[5] With the suppression of his books and his being persecuted, he concluded that his personal fate had become virtually identical to the fate of his teaching and that the vindication of his reputation was necessary for the preservation of his message. When he was able to begin his work in earnest a few years later, Rousseau wrote to Rey, "I will do something unique, and I dare say something truly fine. I am making it into such an important object that I am devoting the remainder of my life to it."[6] In the end, self-justification and presentation of the truth about human nature were indistinguishable from each other.

In spite of their convergence, these two dimensions of Rousseau's project raise the question of the truthfulness of the account given in the *Confessions* in rather different ways. The truth of this or that particular fact is not the same thing as the general truth of a fundamental principle of human nature.[7] At times the goal of setting the record straight about the facts of his life in the face of many true and false rumors spread by his enemies makes the *Confessions* read like a legal brief. To counter the rumors, Rousseau attempts to introduce as much counterevidence as possible: he gives names, dates, and places; he appeals to the testimony of witnesses, and he tries to establish his own credentials as a witness by being as open as possible about his faults. Rousseau's frequent appeals to the reader to attempt to verify the truth of his account constantly point beyond the text to the outside world.

This emphasis on factual truth has led to a truly extraordinary scholarly effort over the past two centuries. Almanacs have been consulted for weather records, the registry of deeds in Chambéry has been searched, and police records in Venice have been combed through. As Rousseau himself predicts when he discusses the problems of relying on a faulty memory,[8] many small errors have been found in his account. At the same time other points about which he was once thought to have been mistaken, lying, or exaggerating have been shown to be substantially accurate. By and large, Rousseau's honesty and accuracy of memory are now, or at least deserve to be, more respected than they were 150 years ago. Nevertheless, if learning the factual truth of Rousseau's life were the only reason to read the *Confessions*, the work would be superseded by numerous biographies that have made use of the investigations referred to.[9] For all his insistence on setting the factual record straight, Rousseau was the first to suggest that the importance of his, or any, account of a life stems less from particular facts, about which total certainty is impossible, than from the way those facts relate to one another, the interpretation one gives them, and the lessons one draws from this interpretation.[10] Furthermore, autobiography is not biography, and Rousseau's claim for both the accuracy and importance of the *Confessions* rests much more on his account of his internal life than on his actions or the circumstances in which he found himself.

As stated, Rousseau's claim that people are to be measured by the depth and nature of their feelings is perhaps the most revolutionary aspect of the *Confessions*. Rousseau's willingness to expose what he finds most ridiculous and shameful, along with what he finds most touching or most noble makes him into an entirely new sort of hero, diametrically opposed to the kings, generals, and statesmen whose lives he loved to read about in Plutarch.[11] Rousseau can argue that his life is more worthy of being recorded than that of the greatest king, not simply because he has thought about things a king has not thought about—an argument that philosophers have always used for justifying their activity—but also because he has felt what they have not felt.[12] It is perhaps not so strange as it might seem that Rousseau's insistence on his own uniqueness in this respect has attracted readers to the *Confessions*. Anyone who has ever felt himself to be unique and believed that others did not appreciate his or her depths as they deserved to be appreciated finds a kindred soul in Rousseau. Furthermore, reading the *Confessions* has no doubt caused many people to feel this way for the first time. Thus, in addition to providing an account of the life of an extraordinary figure, the *Confessions* gives a new image of what is important about human life, an image with which apparently ordinary people who feel that they are extraordinary can identify.[13]

Rousseau's insistence that his life has more intrinsic interest than that of any king can be understood in two ways. First, the depth and complexity of his thoughts make his life of virtually unique importance as an example for learning about human nature. Second, these same things make him a model for imitation. If thoughts and feelings are what count, Rousseau is a model of human excellence, even though it is a very peculiar hero who admits and displays such a wide range of flaws.

That Rousseau presents himself as an entirely new sort of hero in the *Confessions* indicates how hard it is not to read the work as a story, fable, or novel, albeit one that constantly beckons the reader beyond the bounds of the book. Rousseau had been perfectly willing to let his readers believe that his novel *Julie* was autobiographical. Frequently he writes his autobiography as if it were a novel. Incidents such as his infatuation with Mademoiselle de Breil in Book III have a formal structure that sets them apart from the rest of the book and makes them read like miniature novels.

At particularly significant moments, such as the account of his life at les Charmettes in Book VI or the description of the events leading up to the breakup with his friends in Book IX, the order of his narration bears little resemblance to the actual chronology of events. Rousseau does not conceal this divergence from chronology and even takes the trouble to point it out. At times he comments on the resemblance between a story he is telling and a novel. It is clear that he has arranged his presentation of events to further this novelistic, if not precisely fictional, aspect of the book.

The presentation of a concrete image of how a human life should be understood is connected with Rousseau's goal of providing an example that can contribute to the understanding of human nature. Rousseau's major philosophic works are devoted to the development of an understanding of human nature more than anything else. It should not be surprising, then, that he uses his comprehensive understanding of human nature to understand himself and that, in turn, he uses his description of his own life to embody his understanding of human nature.[14] This side of the purpose of the *Confessions* can be seen by examining the role important features of this general understanding play in Rousseau's account of his life and how he uses this account to oppose alternative understandings of human nature.

Goodness in the *Confessions*

The major principle of Rousseau's understanding of human nature is his doctrine of natural goodness.[15] The *Confessions* illustrates this doctrine with an exploration of the complex fate of Rousseau's own goodness. The centrality of this issue within the autobiography is indicated by Rousseau's emphatic challenge to any other person to dare to say, "*I was better than that man.*"[16] A proper understanding of the *Confessions* depends on the proper understanding of what it means to claim that no one is better than an individual as flawed as Rousseau admits he is.

The most obvious target of the *Confessions* is its most famous predecessor, the *Confessions* of St. Augustine. At various times Rousseau referred to his autobiography as a memoir, a life, or a portrait, but his ultimate choice of a title indicates his intention to replace his predecessor and make his book into *the* Confessions. One of the features that Rousseau's book shares with Augustine's is its emphasis on childhood, but in these new confessions this emphasis is even greater than it had been in the old one. The reason for this is indicated in the *Letter to Beaumont*, written in 1762, that has an epigraph from St. Augustine. There, Rousseau attacks the doctrine of original sin as it is traditionally interpreted by Christianity and especially by Augustine.[17] A major part of his attack consists in his claim that the traditional doctrine of original sin does not explain what it purports to explain: the origin of human wickedness. He says, "Original sin explains everything except its principle, and it is the principle that is the issue to explain."[18] While original sin offers an explanation of why we sin now, it poses the problem of how Adam and Eve came to sin since they were not affected by original sin in advance.

In Rousseau's view, then, a satisfactory account of the origin of human evil requires a genetic account, but one very different from that found in *Genesis* or its Christian interpretations. Such an account of the passions that make people wicked is what he claims to give in *Emile*.[19] This book on education mainly offers a description of how to prevent these passions from arising or how to channel them in healthy directions once they do arise. Fundamental to this argument are the claims that these passions are unnatural and that humans are therefore in need of nothing beyond their own efforts to prevent their emergence. The *Confessions* offers a complementary account that shows how these same passions—most importantly anger, shame, vanity, and particular forms of sexual desire—first develop in one man.[20] The Jean-Jacques of the *Confessions* could be considered the anti-Emile. He is the exemplar of precisely the civilized corruption avoided in the natural education. Thus, the *Confessions* represents one further demonstration of the truth of Rousseau's systematic understanding of human nature.

This account of the natural goodness of humans and of the genesis of their wickedness is also closely related to the aim of self-justification in the *Confessions*. While Rousseau does present himself as an example of the consequences of the premature stimulation of anger, vanity, peculiar sexual desires, and other unnatural passions, he does not present himself as a wicked man. In some sense he is both a corrupt man and a good man at the same time. A failure to understand either the exact nature of Rousseau's doctrine or the precise charges against which he is defending himself can lead to much confusion.[21] This confusion can be avoided if one pays attention to certain distinctions Rousseau makes and that he follows, sometimes tacitly, but on the whole consistently. Rousseau's distinctions among goodness, virtue, and vice are absolutely central to his thought and occur frequently in his writings. When these distinctions are applied to situations that are prominent in the *Confessions*, further fundamental distinctions emerge: between guilt and innocence, weakness and wickedness, and faults and wrongs. Some of them indicate clear oppositions, but others represent alternative sources of apparently similar behavior.

In the *Second Discourse* Rousseau formulates what he calls the "maxim of natural goodness": "Do what is good for you with the least possible harm to others."[22] The first part of the maxim, "Do what is good for you," is primary. Natural goodness involves following one's own healthy inclinations. In the best circumstances, the second part of the maxim, "with the least possible harm to others," follows almost automatically from the first: in the absence of artificial passions (such as greed, vanity, or anger) that make people wish to harm each other, seeking one's own good will involve harming others very little. In the *Confessions* Rousseau indicates that he has adopted this maxim as a principle for his own behavior. For example, he has refused to allow himself to be put in the position of profiting from a friend's death by being named in his will.[23] As a result of this refusal, Rousseau keeps himself from being in a position in which what is good for himself would lead him to wish for what is bad for his friend.

Of course, in some circumstances this maxim of natural goodness would not only allow, it would require that one harm other people. Very different things can cause this. For example, one's desires can be corrupted so that they lead one to want things that require harming others. Alternatively, one can find oneself in circumstances in which even fundamentally good desires, such as the desire to stay alive, require harming others. In either of these cases natural goodness is compromised and something more than inclination to follow one's own desires is necessary if one is to refrain from harming others. This something is virtue. Virtue can be regarded as a strength that allows one to overcome one's desires rather than to follow them or as a strength that prevents one from forming harmful desires in the first place. Thus, when Rousseau does not follow his desire to continue his affair with Mme de Larnage in Book VI, he is inspired by virtue, or at least something that is very hard to distinguish from it.[24] In sum, however similar they might look in certain circumstances and although they can both be considered as opposites of vice and wickedness, virtue and goodness can be considered as very distinct complements to each other. Goodness allows one to follow one's inclinations without (usually) harming anyone else. Virtue allows one to overcome one's inclinations on those occasions when they would lead to harming someone else. While goodness is a natural quality, virtue is a moral quality made necessary by the complexity of social life.

This distinction between goodness and virtue reveals the significance of Rousseau's declarations of his own goodness. Although Rousseau does claim to be a good man in the *Confessions*, he does not often claim to be a virtuous one. He admires virtue, he loves it, for a while he is intoxicated

by it, but he rarely practices it. Because he is good without being virtuous, he can be guilty of faults,[25] and it is the admission of his faults that
makes up what could be called Rousseau's confessions in the strict sense
of the term. Among the major faults he admits are his false accusation of
Marion in Book II, his abandonment of M. Le Maître in Book III, and
putting his children in the foundling hospital in Book VIII.[26] In each of
these cases Rousseau admits that he was guilty of doing something wrong
and, by implication, that he was not virtuous.

It is at this point that much of the confusion over Rousseau's attempts
at self-justification enters, because he generally follows his admission of
guilt with an explanation that appears to be a more or less feeble attempt
to exonerate himself from blame. The most noteworthy, and most noted,
of these occasions concerns his false accusation of Marion when, after admitting that he falsely accused her of a theft that he committed, he insists
that he had no intention of harming her and, in fact, had been very fond
of her. The virtually simultaneous admission and explanation exemplify
why some readers find the *Confessions* so morally repugnant while others
find them so compellingly human. The former are struck by the thought
that Rousseau is, in effect, retracting his admission of wrongdoing in
the very act of making it, that he is asking for credit for sincerity while
speaking in bad faith. Whatever might ultimately be said about Rousseau's sincerity, it should be noted that in these instances Rousseau never
claims that he is innocent either in some fundamental theological sense
or of the particular wrongdoing that he committed. What he does claim
in the case of admitted wrongdoing is that his lapses were cases of weakness rather than wickedness, that they were faults rather than wrongs.[27]
In sum, Rousseau presents himself as a fundamentally good man, who,
because he is not virtuous, commits faults out of weakness. He is not
a fundamentally wicked man who commits crimes out of a willingness
to harm. He never denies that he is guilty of committing misdeeds for
which he deserves a measure of blame. In short, Rousseau's "excuses" are
frequently the consequences of the application of his doctrine of natural
goodness rather than simple signs of bad faith. Judgment of his behavior
must entail a judgment about his moral doctrine.

Aside from Rousseau himself, the character in the *Confessions* who most
fully embodies both goodness and its weakness is Mme de Warens. In
each of Books III, V, and VI, Rousseau gives a description of her that emphasizes her decency, generosity, and lack of spiteful passions. But in each
of these cases, he also says that she did commit faults. While in Rousseau's
false accusation of Marion, the artificial passion of shame played a major
role in his misdeed, in the case of Mme de Warens it is not passion but

false principles of morality that cause her to act badly on occasion. She is seduced by sophisms not by her passions.[28] Thus, when it is properly understood, her life, which is so scandalous when judged by the standards of either conventional propriety or strict morality, is a monument to her good heart.

Misdeeds can be explained, but they are not entirely excused by weakness that makes one follow inclinations rather than duty or by false principles that make one follow an erroneous notion of duty. Once again, Rousseau makes no claim whatsoever that either he or Mme de Warens is a paragon of virtue or that either of them is innocent of wrongdoing. What he does claim is that their faults do not make them exemplars of wickedness or vice. The character in the *Confessions* who best exemplifies wickedness is Rousseau's false friend, the master of duplicity and leader of the conspiracy against Rousseau's reputation, Friedrich Melchior Grimm. Although Rousseau finds something unfathomable in Grimm's behavior, he clearly presents it as unmitigated wickedness.

Like Rousseau's own behavior, Grimm's is based on a single fundamental maxim. Rousseau says that Mme d'Epinay once informed him that Grimm's "compendium of morality" consisted of the single article, "The sole duty of a man is, to follow the inclinations of his heart in everything."[29] Strangely, Grimm's declared maxim of behavior bears a strong resemblance to Rousseau's maxim of natural goodness. How exactly does it differ and how does this difference qualify it as vicious? While in Rousseau's account goodness must be considered as distinct from and (from a moral standpoint) inferior to virtue, Grimm's maxim blurs this distinction by claiming that one actually has a duty to follow one's inclinations in everything. Thus, on Grimm's view there is no such thing as a genuine virtue that opposes one's inclination in any circumstances. Any talk about such a virtue must be only foolishness or hypocrisy. Furthermore, Grimm's maxim does not contain the qualification found in the maxim of natural goodness, "with the least possible harm to others." Far from avoiding situations that would allow him to profit from harming others, Grimm follows a continuous course of profiting from his ability to take advantage of other people. Grimm's wickedness represents a denaturing of natural goodness that refuses to acknowledge any claims that others might have.

In sum, in the most primitive case, following one's natural inclinations (which will consist solely of moderate desires for food, sleep, and sex[30]) leads to goodness, that is, one's own advantage at little expense to others. The situation is complicated in the case of someone who, living in a social world, has some artificial passions or is led astray by false principles. Those, like Rousseau or Mme de Warens, who preserve some, but not all, of natural goodness, are likely to be generous, compassionate, impulsive people who on occasion commit faults that harm others and themselves. They are good, but in one way or another they are weak. In the case of people like Grimm, the extreme artificial passions and wicked principles completely transform all natural inclinations into vices. Such people not only find themselves in situations in which they inadvertently harm others, they wish to do so. The good seek their own good without concern for others.[31] The wicked seek to dominate others even at the cost of considerable effort on their own part. In the end they tend to define their own good largely in terms of their ability to have power over others, even if the attempt to acquire this ability does themselves no genuine good.

Appearance and Reality

The presentation of Grimm's wickedness helps to illustrate the theme of goodness in the *Confessions*. How he practices wickedness helps to illustrate a related theme: that of the split between appearance and reality in the social world.[32] More than anything else Grimm is the master of manipulating appearances. Ultimately Rousseau presents him as the orchestrator of a great conspiracy to destroy Rousseau's good reputation and replace it with a false image, but his manipulation of appearances shows itself in smaller ways also. Grimm acquires social success by coldly calculating how to present an image of himself as a suffering scorned lover or as a devoted friend.[33] Even more simply, he uses makeup to improve his appearance. Just as his wickedness completes a coherent picture of the moral world in the *Confessions*, his manipulation of appearances represents the culmination of Rousseau's discovery of the ills of the social world. In fact, to the extent that the *Confessions* tells a coherent story, what it tells is how someone falls victim to the split between reality and appearance and how he comes to understand the nature of that split.

This discovery proceeds through a number of stages which, broadly speaking, correspond to an account Rousseau gives of his intellectual development in the *Letter to Beaumont*. He says, "As soon as I was in a position to observe men, I watched them act and I watched them speak; then, seeing that their actions bore no resemblance to their speeches, I looked for the reason for this dissimilarity, and I found that, since for them being and appearing were two things as different as acting and speaking, this second difference was the cause of the other and itself had a cause that I still had to look for." [34] The dramatization of these divergences between word and deed and appearance and being is one of the guiding threads of the plot of the *Confessions*. Rousseau moves from an initial bafflement and rage at his experience of these divergences, to a gradual immersion in the social world where they dominate, to a comprehensive discovery that explains his experience, and finally to the confrontation between his unmasking of the social system and of those, like Grimm, who profit from it.

This development begins in Book I with the young Rousseau's discovery of a literary world of romantic novels and Plutarch's heros that gives him an image of the world that corresponds to no real experience, fills him with unattainable hopes, and prepares him to be deceived by anyone who appeals to the passions instilled in him by books. Also in Book I, he is accused by his tutors of a crime that he did not commit. He has his first experience of the feeling of injustice and sees himself as innocent and his tutors as people who torment him while claiming to be just. He cannot grasp the fact that they have made an innocent mistake because all appearances point to his guilt. As he gets older, he accumulates a range of experiences that teach him that people often present deceptive appearances either wittingly or unwittingly and that one of the ways to succeed in the world is to learn how to manipulate these appearances.

As Rousseau explores the different ways being and appearance are opposed, he alternates between somber examples and ones involving humorous or moving aspects. He shows the consequences of his own ability to present a false appearance of angelic innocence when he accuses Marion, but he also revels in the comic absurdity of his attempt to pass himself off as a composer in spite of his utter ignorance of composition. While his wrestling with the split between what he feels himself to be and the way he appears to others forms the dramatic core of the *Confessions*, Rousseau also provides little vignettes of how this problem manifests itself in other people's lives. Many of these case studies are so captivating that it is easy to ignore their significance for the general theme. It is hard to miss the political significance of the French peasant who must adopt the appearance of abject poverty to avoid ruin by an unjust system of taxation, but one should also pay attention to the touching and comical M. Simon, whose intelligent mind and sensitive heart are concealed by his dwarfish stature, and to the engaging libertine Venture de Villeneuve, who lives by his wits, pretending to know what he does not know and concealing his real talents in order to display them at opportune moments. [35] The opposition between being and appearance can work itself out in an infinite number of ways, and Rousseau's self-education consists of his discovery of the pervasiveness of this split in the social world around him.

The emotional crisis of this discovery occurs at Venice when Rousseau finds himself, not for the first or the last time, a victim of an unjust social order that rewards incompetence in the ascendant class at the expense of talented social inferiors. At the moment of his greatest resentment over his own low standing, Rousseau finds himself with the divinely beautiful courtesan, Zulietta, who lavishes her charms on him even though she has no way of perceiving his genuine merit beneath his status as a lowly secretary. Zulietta herself is a bewildering example of supreme beauty and social ostracism, an incomprehensible object of desire and repulsion. In a passage that Rousseau identifies as the most crucial in the *Confessions*, the encounter with Zulietta focuses the conflict between appearance and being, convention and nature, imagination and truth into a single example that prepares the way for Rousseau's discovery of the principle that explains these oppositions.[36]

He finally grasps this principle clearly on the road to Vincennes while on the way to visit his imprisoned friend, Diderot. Even though the "illumination" on the road to Vincennes takes place well into Part Two of the *Confessions*, it clearly marks the turning point in Rousseau's life. As such, it stands comparison with events such as Paul's conversion on the road to Damascus. Rousseau's discovery happens as a result of reading the question proposed by the Academy of Dijon, "Has the restoration of the sciences and arts tended to purify morals?" Upon his contemplation of this question Rousseau says, "I saw another universe and became another man."[37] Suddenly he is able to see that the ultimate source of the tension between action and speech, being and appearing, that has caused so much confusion in his life can be found in an unjust social order that tyrannizes over nature.[38]

Although Rousseau frequently refers to his discovery of this revolutionary principle as a sudden inspiration, it did not come out of nowhere. The experiences described earlier in the *Confessions* set the stage for this discovery by illustrating in a fragmentary or particular way the effects of the social order on individual life. In the *Confessions* Rousseau's sudden emergence as an important thinker looks, as it did to many of his contemporaries, like the emergence of Athena fully armed from the head of Zeus. What is clear, although not dramatized so visibly, is that in the years leading up to this discovery Rousseau was engaged in an intensive intellectual development. In the years he spent at Chambéry, he devoted himself to studying philosophy, history, mathematics, astronomy, and other subjects. In addition, at the same time he was studying music history and theory leading to his invention of a new system of musical notation, which took him to Paris to try to make his fortune. While he was in Venice as the French ambassador's secretary, he studied the history of diplomacy in order to learn his new profession. When he returned to Paris, he worked as a sort of research assistant for the Dupin family and took thousand of pages of notes and wrote hundreds of pages of drafts of manuscripts on questions of political economy, history, chemistry, and the role of women in society. Finally, during this same time he formed close ties to Diderot and the circle of intellectuals who were about to begin the *Encyclopedia*. In the dozen years before he wrote the *First Discourse* Rousseau had transformed himself from a failed apprentice and naive adventurer into someone with the intellectual resources to stun even an age that prided itself on its learning. The emphasis on feelings in the *Confessions* allows Rousseau to dramatize the emotional effect of the discovery of the source of the split between reality and appearance, while he gives only glimpses of the intellectual preparation for the discovery.

The Conspiracy

Just as the *Confessions* emphasizes the feelings and experiences that led Rousseau to his discovery of his system, it pays special attention to the effect of this discovery on his life. In a corrupt society, what is the fate of a man who to a large extent has preserved his natural goodness and has discovered both the principle of this natural goodness and the social origin of wickedness? The initial result of the publication of the *First Discourse* was to make Rousseau into a public sensation. This effect was multiplied when he composed a new opera containing pleasing tunes and glorifying rustic loves against urban sophistication. He also gained considerable notoriety from his decision to turn his back on the sophistication of Paris, which applauded him as he condemned it. With his adoption of simple dress and eventual move to the country, Rousseau self-consciously made himself into a sort of hero, the embodiment of the qualities praised in his writings.

Rousseau claims that the outcome of all this success was the massive conspiracy formed against him that led to the warrant being issued for his arrest in France and to efforts to drive him out of each place where he sought refuge. Because of the extreme claims that Rousseau makes, the conspiracy is probably the most troubling theme in the *Confessions*. It cannot be denied that the form Rousseau's accusations take is heavily influenced by the acute emotional distress caused by his stormy relations with his friends and the persecution he suffered. Nevertheless, one should also be aware of the fact that many of Rousseau's specific charges, and among them some that appear delusional on their face, are solidly grounded in fact. It is unlikely that there will ever be a reliable diagnosis of Rousseau's emotional or physical illnesses,[39] and the interpretation of the motives of Rousseau's enemies is likely to remain a subject of partisanship among scholars. It is possible, however, to be fairly specific about the role the conspiracy plays within the *Confessions*.

The part of the *Confessions* in which Rousseau's belief in a plot against him is most prominent is the footnotes, which were late additions to the manuscripts.[40] It is in these footnotes that Rousseau makes the widest array of accusations against the greatest numbers of individuals. That the footnotes are so frequently inserted to contradict what is in the text indicates that the version of the conspiracy given in the body of the text is a considerably more moderate one.

The assertion of the existence of a plot against Rousseau does not enter the body of the text of the *Confessions* in an unequivocal way until the beginning of Book X.[41] In this context Rousseau attributes its origin to what appear to be purely personal factors involving his love for Mme d'Houdetot and his suspicions of Mme d'Epinay. Upon closer scrutiny the things that make the conspiracy possible turn out to be a mixture of purely personal and more broadly significant factors. In addition to petty jealousy and conflicts of personality, Rousseau mentions several things that laid the foundation for the conspiracy.

The first thing he notes that caused a cooling off among his friends was the immense popular success of his opera.[42] Rousseau had been supported in his literary endeavors by Diderot, who commissioned him to write articles on music for the *Encyclopedia*, encouraged him to write the *First Discourse*, and offered advice during the writing of the *Second Discourse*. It is clear that during this period, in spite of the increasing clarity of the differences between Rousseau's views and those of his fellow Encyclopedists, they looked at each other as involved in a common enterprise.[43] Nevertheless, as Rousseau had argued as early as in the *First Discourse*, beneath the sense of a common intellectual enterprise lies a desire for personal fame and distinction that manifests itself in petty jealousy. Rousseau's sudden success as a composer gave him a status quite independent of this shared literary life in which all men of letters could succeed and assist each other in succeeding. He claims that his musical success gave him a sort of celebrity that his friends could not hope to share or rival.

If the reaction to Rousseau's musical success reveals the self-interest lying beneath an apparent devotion to reason, the reaction to his moral reform and move to the country indicates another problem in the Enlightenment. Rousseau argues that his moral reform resulted from his attempt to put his conduct into accord with his principles. He also argues that his fellow intellectuals regarded this reform as an implicit reproach to them for following the life of competitiveness, engagement in high society, and currying favor with the powerful.[44] Thus, his very conspicuous stance as a new model for the relation between thought and life was understood and, perhaps even more important, felt as a threat to the prevailing model. Rousseau stands as the intellectual outsider who is the enemy of partisan activity and who insists on a certain moral purity. It is the general significance of his personal decision to abandon Paris that leads to such a personal hatred against Rousseau on the part of those who regard the conquest of Parisian society as the ultimate goal of their activity. In sum, Rousseau's great ability to show himself as embodying fundamental intellectual and human problems is what makes the conspiracy against him such an odd mixture of personal grudges and serious intellectual disputes.

There are a number of reasons for Rousseau's emphasis on the personal side of his persecution. Most important of these is that this personal side was very real. The literary society of Paris in the mid-eighteenth century was a very small world filled with rivalry and intrigue in which everyone knew everyone else. Even the ability to be published could depend on whether a friend of a friend or a friend of a rival was appointed as the government censor of one's book. In addition, however, by emphasizing that his persecution was the outcome of personal resentments, Rousseau can argue that it was not the result of the content of his works. By claiming that attacks on his works are personally motivated, Rousseau can urge his readers to ignore those attacks and pay attention to his thought.

In short, the treatment of the conspiracy reflects the constant tendency of the *Confessions*. Rousseau focuses on the personal and the intimate, but in doing so he claims to gain access to general truths of ultimate significance. Early in the book he uses his very idiosyncratic responses to spankings to raise questions about the origins of sexuality and feelings about justice and injustice. He uses the fact of his father's failure to pursue him beyond Annecy when he ran away from Geneva to reflect on the fundamental maxim of natural goodness.[45] Conversely he reveals apparently general discussions about the moral character of the theatre to be guided by personal desires to curry favor with the powerful and then shows that petty personal rivalries are connected with competing views about the proper place of an intellectual in society. In the *Confessions* every general issue is connected with a personal problem and every personal problem illustrates a general issue.

The fact that the *Confessions* has probably been the most consistently popular of Rousseau's works, maintaining its popularity as other works like *Julie* or the *Social Contract* come into and go out of fashion, indicates that the work stands very well on its own. Nevertheless, the preceding remarks are intended to show that this remarkable book appears even more remarkable if it is seen in the light of the major issues of Rousseau's thought. While philosophers have always been concerned with the communication of their thought, no other approaches Rousseau's attempt to show the connection between his philosophic thought and his feelings. In addition to being a behind-the-scenes look at the private life of a public man, the *Confessions* is at the center of Rousseau's philosophic enterprise.

Translating the *Confessions*

The various purposes that converge in the *Confessions* are reflected in the great diversity of literary styles incorporated in the work. Rousseau says in the Neuchâtel Preface, "For what I have to say it would be necessary to invent a language as new as my project."[46] This style is less a simple invention of something new than an artful use of a combination of classical French literary language, Genevan provincialisms, and other forms.[47] In broad terms the nostalgic account of Part One contrasts with the, at times, frantic tone of Part Two. Within the more polished earlier part, Rousseau moves fluidly from style to style, from the dramatic episode of the broken comb to the mock heroic epic of the aqueduct, from digressions taking the form of essays like the discussion of money in Book I to the "idyll of the cherries" in Book IV.

Among his most striking devices are sudden shifts of tense in a narrative as he alternates between recreating a moment dramatically by writing in the present tense and commenting on it by describing it with a past tense. Rousseau sometimes also moves from addressing the reader in the second person to using an impersonal or passive construction. These sometimes sudden shifts in literary style, voice, and tense are often jarring in French and must become even more so in translation. Nevertheless, they are an essential part of Rousseau's style and can be important indications of his emphasis. Accordingly, we have tried to preserve them even at the cost to elegance.

The care Rousseau took in writing is shown by the minuteness of the changes from one manuscript to another. He changes the choice of a word or the order of terms in a series often apparently to give a poetic rhythm to a prose passage. No doubt some of these changes are connected with the fact that one of the complete manuscripts was intended for publication, while the other was to be used for Rousseau's readings to select audiences. Many of the changes seem trivial, but others raise fascinating questions about important aspects of the autobiographical project. For example, what is indicated about the relation between memory and writing by the fact that in one manuscript the only defect of the beautiful Mlle de Charly is that her hair is too red, while in the other manuscript it is too blonde?[48] We have elected to err on the side of inclusiveness in indicating manuscript variants in the notes.

There is one other area in which we have chosen to preserve Rousseau's variations. That is in his spelling of proper names of people. These spellings vary, not only from manuscript to manuscript, but also within manuscripts. The failure to regularize the spelling may cause a few slight confusions, but these confusions reflect what Rousseau wrote. Efforts to correct the spelling of names would run into the problem that many of the people referred to in the *Confessions* are known to us almost exclusively because he refers to them. While it is possible to correct the spellings of some of these names, these people have become known as characters in Rousseau's book with the names he gave them. Correct or standard spellings are provided in the notes along with other information about the people to whom Rousseau refers. On the other hand, we have standardized and modernized the spelling of the names of cities (for example, Neuchâtel instead of Neufchatel or Neufchâtel). Finally, we have tried to follow, as much as English allows, Rousseau's sentence structure and punctuation, although the irregularities of eighteenth-century punctuation severely strain modern English practice.

It would be desirable to capture all of the aspects of Rousseau's writing style of the *Confessions* in the translation or to find some English equivalent for them. Regrettably this has been far from possible. What we have attempted to achieve is a clear and readable translation that follows the aim of the *Collected Writings* as a whole of allowing the reader to see the relation between this work and Rousseau's other writings. Accordingly we have made an effort to make the translation consistent with the ones in earlier volumes, particularly with regard to more or less technical and recurring terms.

Rousseau after the *Confessions*

An inescapable limitation of the genre of autobiography is the impossibility of the author telling the story to its end. Like other autobiographies the *Confessions* does not tell us about its author's last days. Even beyond this, the incompleteness of the work is signaled by Rousseau's occasional suggestions that he is contemplating a third part. Nevertheless, by the conclusion Rousseau makes it clear that his failure to continue his work resulted from a conscious decision to stop and not merely from externally imposed factors.

There are, in fact, two conclusions to the *Confessions*. The narrative breaks off at October 29, 1765, with Rousseau's departure from Bienne. The following paragraphs describe the reading from the autobiography given by Rousseau in May of 1771. The period between these two events fairly closely corresponds to the period during which the *Confessions* was composed. As Rousseau says, he left Bienne with the intention of going to Berlin, but ended by accepting David Hume's invitation to seek refuge in England. From a personal standpoint, the period Rousseau spent in England was disastrous. His mounting emotional distress, coupled with considerable lack of understanding on both sides, led Rousseau to accuse Hume of a variety of misdeeds and bad intentions. Hume responded by going public with his side of the story in order to preempt what he thought was Rousseau's intention to do the same. This aggravated Rousseau's sense of grievance and created a public sensation that lasted for years. In May of 1767 Rousseau left Wootton in a panic and returned to France under the assumed name of Jean-Joseph Renou. He then spent a year at the home of the Prince de Conti at Trye where he finished Part One of the *Confessions*. He did not begin writing Part Two until late 1769 and finished it in about a year.

In 1770 Rousseau resumed the use of his name and returned to Paris with the tacit permission of the government, although the warrant for his arrest remained in effect. He continued to live in Paris until the last two months of his life. During this time he took his autobiographical project in new directions with the *Dialogues* and *Reveries*. He also wrote *Considerations on the Government of Poland*, developed his interest in botany, and was fairly active as a composer. He died on July 2, 1778, during a visit to the Marquis de Girardin at Ermenonville.

Note on the Text

It is not possible to identify the moment when Rousseau began to work on the *Confessions*.[1] In the work itself Rousseau says that by 1759 his publisher Marc-Michel Rey, whose acquaintance he had made in 1754, had been urging him to write his memoirs for a long time.[2] Rey was hoping for a sketch of Rousseau's life to be included as an introduction to a collection his writings. Rousseau probably began to contemplate the project seriously and to assemble materials for it sometime after his falling-out with Mme d'Epinay at the end of 1757. He wrote a large part of Part One during his stay in England in 1766, although he completed it only after his return to France the following year. After completing Part One Rousseau broke off work. He began Part Two toward the end of 1769. After another break, he finally finished Part Two around December of 1770. In short, Rousseau worked on the *Confessions*, with numerous interruptions, over a period of at least a dozen years.

There are two complete manuscripts of the *Confessions* (the so-called Paris Manuscript [P] and the so-called Geneva Manuscript [G]) as well as another partial manuscript (the so-called Neuchâtel Manuscript [N]) that represents an earlier draft of the first three books and a part of the fourth. The Geneva Manuscript is certainly the one Rousseau intended for publication. He entrusted it to his friend Paul Moultou in 1778, shortly before his death. Rousseau held the Paris Manuscript in reserve in case something happened to the Geneva Manuscript. The relation between these two manuscripts is made more complicated by the fact that some revisions in Part Two of the Paris Manuscript were made after Rousseau made the copy of Part Two in the Geneva Manuscript. As a result, neither manuscript can be regarded as unambiguously definitive.

On several occasions Rousseau made it clear that he wanted the *Confessions* to be published only after his death and was very specific about not wanting Part Two to be published until after 1800 when all the people discussed in it would be dead. Nevertheless, an abridged version of Part One was published (along with the *Reveries of a Solitary Walker*) in 1782, and an abridged version of Part Two was published in 1789. These two versions relied on the Geneva Manuscript. In 1798 a complete edition was published using the Paris Manuscript to fill in the gaps of the earlier editions.[3] English translations of the *Confessions* have relied on this composite version of the text.

For our translation we have relied on the Geneva Manuscript as it is found in Volume I of the *Oeuvres complètes* (Paris: Bibliothèque de la Pléiade, 1958) edited under the direction of Bernard Gagnebin and Marcel Raymond. In the case of apparent copying errors, or damage done to the manuscript by rebinding, the Paris Manuscript has been used to supplement the Geneva Manuscript. These cases have been indicated by the use of brackets. In end notes and in Appendix II, we have provided the variations from both of the alternative manuscripts as they are given in the notes to the Pléiade edition. In addition, we have included some of the other variations from the edition of the *Confessions* edited by Jacques Voisine (Paris: Garnier Frères, 1964). Voisine gives an essentially exhaustive list of the manuscript variations, including very minor ones of punctuation and word order that would be impossible to reproduce in translation.

Neither of the complete manuscripts nor the published editions include the collection of letters that Rousseau originally intended to accompany the *Confessions*. The notebooks that contain these letters would fill a volume equal to the size of the *Confessions* itself. In Appendix I, we have provided translations of the letters to which Rousseau explicitly directs the readers in the body of the *Confessions*. For these letters we have used the *Correspondance complète* (Geneva: Institut et Musée Voltaire, 1965–) except in the case of the four letters to Malesherbes, which are contained in Volume I of the Pléiade edition.

THE CONFESSIONS
OF J.-J. ROUSSEAU[1]

FIRST PART

*took nature exatly
how it was but
spliced it together to
idealizes   idealize*

↑

Here is the only portrait of a man, painted exactly according to nature and in all its truth, that exists and that will probably ever exist. Whoever you may be whom my destiny or my trust has made the arbiter of the fate of this notebook, I entreat you by my misfortunes, by your innermost emotions, and in the name of the whole human species not to destroy a unique and useful work which can serve as the first piece of comparison for the study of men, a study which certainly has not yet begun, and not to take away from the honor of my memory the only accurate monument to my character that has not been disfigured by my enemies. Finally, even if you yourself might be one of these implacable enemies, cease to be so towards my ashes, and do not sustain your cruel injustice up to the time when neither you nor I will be alive any longer; so that at least once you might nobly bear witness to yourself of having been generous and good when you could have been harmful and vindictive. If indeed evil intended for a man who has never done, or wished to do any, can bear the name of vengeance.[2]

*divide between nature &
culture
truth & falsehood
mand kind complex
-exaggeration
- radical subjectivity
- extive truthfulness
- useful to help study mankind*

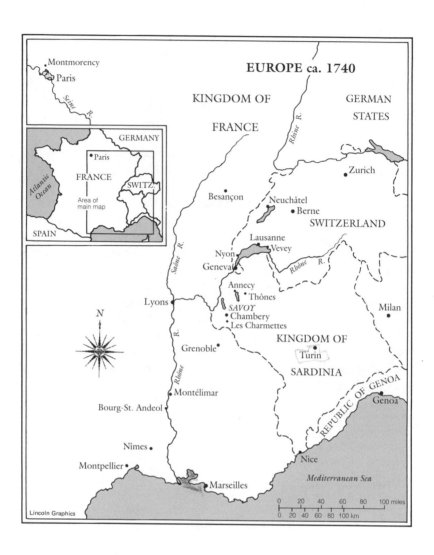

EUROPE ca. 1740

Montmorency
Paris
Seine R.

GERMANY

• Paris

FRANCE
Atlantic Ocean
SWITZ.
Area of
main map

SPAIN

KINGDOM OF

FRANCE

GERMAN
STATES

Rhine R.

• Zurich

Besançon

Neuchâtel
• Berne

SWITZERLAND

Lausanne
Nyon ·Vevey
Geneva
Rhône R.

Annecy
• Thônes
SAVOY
• Chambery
·Les Charmettes

Milan
•

Lyons •

Saône R.

KINGDOM OF

Turin

SARDINIA

Grenoble•

Rhône R.

• Montélimar

Bourg-St. Andeol •

Nîmes •

Montpellier •

Marseilles

Nice

REPUBLIC OF GENOA

Genoa

Mediterranean Sea

Lincoln Graphics

| 0 | 20 | 40 | 60 | 80 | 100 miles |

| 0 | 20 | 40 | 60 | 80 | 100 km |

Book I

Intus, et in Cute[3]

[**1.**][4] 1. I am forming an undertaking which has no precedent, and the execution of which[5] will have no imitator whatsoever. I wish to show my fellows a man in all the truth of nature; and this man will be myself.

2. Myself alone. I feel my heart and I know men. I am not made like any of the ones I have seen; I dare to believe that I am not made like any that exist. If I am worth no more, at least I am different. Whether nature has done well or ill in breaking the mold in which it cast me, is something which cannot be judged until I have been read.[6]

3. Let the trumpet of the last judgment sound when it will; I shall come with this book in my hands to present myself before the Sovereign Judge.[7] I shall say loudly, "Behold what I have done, what I have thought, what I have been. I have told the good and the evil with the same frankness. I have been silent about nothing bad, added nothing good, and if I have happened to use some inconsequential ornament, this has never happened except to fill up a gap occasioned by my lack of memory; I may have assumed to be true what I knew might have been so, never what I knew to be false. I have shown myself as I was, contemptible and low when I was so, good, generous, sublime when I was so: I have unveiled my interior as Thou hast seen it Thyself. Eternal Being, assemble around me the countless host of my fellows: let them listen to my confessions, let them shudder at my unworthiness, let them blush at my woes.[8] Let each of them in his turn uncover his heart at the foot of Thy throne with the same sincerity; and then let a single one say to Thee, if he dares: *I was better than that man.*"

[**2.**] 1. I was born in Geneva in 1712, child of Isaac Rousseau, Citizen, and Susanne Bernard, Citizen.[9] Because a very mediocre property divided among fifteen children had reduced my father's portion to almost nothing, for his livelihood he had only his trade of watchmaker, in which he was, in truth, very skillful. My mother, daughter of the Protestant Minister Bernard,[10] was wealthier; she had prudence and beauty: it was not without difficulty that my father won her. Their love had begun almost with their life: from the age of eight or nine they walked together every

5

night on the Treille;[11] at ten they could no longer be separated. Sympathy, the harmony of souls, strengthened the feeling produced in them by habit. Both, born tender and sensitive, were only waiting for the moment to find the same disposition in someone else, or rather this moment was waiting for them, and each of them threw his heart into the first which opened to receive it. Fate, which seemed to thwart their passion, only enlivened it. Not being able to win his mistress, the young lover was consumed with sorrow; she advised him to travel in order to forget her. He traveled fruitlessly and returned more in love than ever. He found the one he loved still tender and faithful. After this test nothing remained but for them to love each other all their lives; they swore to do so, and Heaven blessed their vow.

2. Gabriel Bernard, my mother's brother, fell in love with one of my father's sisters; but she consented to marry the brother only on the condition that her brother marry the sister. Love arranged everything, and the two marriages took place on the same day.[12] Thus my Uncle was the husband of my aunt, and their children were doubly my first cousins. A child was born to each couple after a year; after which they had to separate again.

3. My uncle Bernard was an Engineer: he went to serve in the empire and in Hungary under Prince Eugene. He distinguished himself at the siege and battle of Belgrade.[13] After the birth of my only brother, my father left for Constantinople, where he had been summoned, and became watchmaker to the seraglio. During his absence, my mother's beauty, her mind, her talents,* attracted admirers to her. M. de la Closure, Resident of France,[15] was among the most eager to offer tributes to her. His passion must have been deep; for thirty years[16] later I saw him moved when speaking to me about her. For defending herself my mother had more than virtue, she loved her husband tenderly;[17] she urged him to return: he left everything and returned. I was the unhappy fruit of that return. Ten months later, I was born feeble and sickly; I cost my mother her life, and my birth was the first of my misfortunes.[18]

4. I did not know how my father bore this loss; but I know that he

---

* She had too many brilliant ones for her station because her father, the Minister, who adored her had taken great care over her education. She drew, she sang, she accompanied herself on the Theorbo, she was well read and composed passable poems. Here is one she composed impromptu while walking with her sister-in-law and their two children during the absence of her brother and her husband upon a remark that someone made to her about them.

> *Ces deux Messieurs qui sont absens*
> *Nous sont chers de bien des manieres;*
> *Ce sont nos amis, nos amans;*
> *Ce sont nos maris et nos fréres,*
> *Et les péres de ces enfans.*[14]

never consoled himself for it. He believed he saw her again in me, without being able to forget that I had deprived him of her; he never hugged me without me feeling from his sighs, from his convulsive embraces, that a bitter regret was mixed with his caresses; they were all the more tender on this account. When he said to me, "Jean-Jacques, let's talk about your mother"; I said to him, "Very well, father, then we are going to cry," and this word alone would already draw tears from him. "Ah!" he said moaning, "Give her back to me, console me for her; fill the void she has left in my soul. Would I love you this way if you were only my son?" Forty years[19] after having lost her, he died in the arms of a second wife, but with the name of the first on his lips, and her image at the bottom of his heart.

5. Such were the authors of my life. Of all the gifts which Heaven had bestowed on them, a sensitive heart is the only one they left to me; but it had brought about their happiness, and brought about all the misfortunes of my life.

[**3.**] 1. I was born almost dying; they had little hope of saving my life. I bore the seed of a discomfort which the years have reinforced, and which now sometimes gives me respite only to let me suffer more cruelly in another manner.[20] One of my father's sisters, a lovable and sensible girl, took such great care of me that she saved me.[21] At the moment I am writing this she is still alive, at the age of eighty nursing a husband who is younger than herself, but worn out by drink. Dear aunt, I forgive you for having made me live, and I grieve that at the end of your days I cannot return to you the tender cares you lavished on me at the beginning of mine. My nurse Jacqueline is also still alive, healthy and robust.[22] The hands which opened my eyes at my birth will be able to close them for me at my death.

2. I felt before thinking; this is the common fate of humanity. I experienced it more than others. I am not aware of what I did up to the age of five or six: I do not know how I learned to read;[23] I remember only my first readings and their effect on me. This is the time from which I date the uninterrupted consciousness of myself. My mother had left behind some Novels. My father and I began to read them after supper. At first it was only a matter of giving me practice at reading by means of amusing books; but soon our interest became so lively that we read in turn without respite, and passed the nights in this occupation. We could never stop before the end of the volume. Sometimes, hearing the morning song of the swallows, my father said, completely ashamed, "Let's go to bed; I am more of a child than you are."

3. By this dangerous method[24] I acquired in a short time not only

an extraordinary facility in reading and understanding, but also an intelligence about the passions that was unique for my age. I had no idea whatsoever about matters whose feelings were all known to me already. I had conceived nothing; I had felt everything.[25] These confused emotions which I experienced one after the other did not at all impair my reason which I did not yet have: but they formed one of a different stamp in me, and gave me bizarre and romantic concepts about human life, from which experience and reflection have never been able to cure me completely.

4. The Novels ended with the summer of 1719. The following winter brought something else. Since my mother's library had been exhausted, we had recourse to the portion of her father's that had fallen to us. Fortunately there were some good books in it; and it could hardly be otherwise; since this library had been formed by a Minister, in truth, and even a learned one (for that was the fashion then), but also a man of taste and intelligence. *The History of the Church and the Empire* by Le Sueur, the discourse of Bossuet on universal history, the illustrious men of Plutarch, the *History of Venice* by Nani, Ovid's *Metamorphoses*, la Bruyère, the worlds of Fontenelle, his *Dialogues of the Dead*, and some volumes of Molière,[26] were carried into my father's workshop, and I read them to him every day during his work.[27] There I developed a taste that was rare and perhaps unique for that age. Above all Plutarch became my favorite reading. The pleasure I took in rereading him ceaselessly cured me a little of the Novels;[28] and I soon preferred Agesilaus, Brutus, and Aristides to Orondates, Artamenes, and Juba.[29] From these interesting readings, from the discussions they occasioned between my father and myself, was formed that free and republican spirit, that indomitable and proud character, impatient with the yoke and servitude which has tormented me my whole life in situations least appropriate for giving vent to it. Ceaselessly occupied with Rome and Athens; living, so to speak, with their great men, myself born the Citizen of a Republic, and son of a father whose love of the fatherland was his strongest passion, I caught fire with it from his example; I believed myself to be Greek or Roman; I became the character whose life I read. the account of the traits of constancy and intrepidity[30] which had struck me made my eyes sparkle and my voice strong. One day while I was recounting the adventure of Scaevola at table,[31] they were frightened to see me stretch forward and hold my hand over a chafing-dish to represent his deed.[32]

5. I had a brother seven years older than myself.[33] He was learning my father's trade. The extreme affection they had for me caused him to be a little neglected and I do not approve of this. His education felt the effect of this negligence. He adopted the way of life of libertinism, even before

he was old enough to be a true libertine. He was placed with another master, where he had his escapades as he had had in the paternal house. I hardly saw him at all: I can barely say that I had made his acquaintance: but I did not fail to love him tenderly, and he loved me, as much as a rascal can love anything. I remember that once when my father was beating him harshly and angrily, I impetuously threw myself between the two of them, embracing him closely. I covered him with my body this way, receiving the blows aimed at him, and I persevered so well in this posture, that finally my father had to pardon him, either because he was disarmed by my cries and my tears or so as not to treat me worse than him. Finally my brother became so bad that he ran away and completely disappeared. Some time later we learned he was in Germany. He did not write once. We had no more news about him after that, and that is how I was left an only child.

6. If that poor boy was brought up negligently, it was not the same for his brother, and the children of Kings could not have been cared for with greater zeal than I was during my earliest years, idolized by all who surrounded me, and—which is much more rare—always treated as a darling child, never as a spoiled child. Up to my departure from the paternal house, never once did they allow me to run alone in the street with the other children: never did they have to repress in me or satisfy any of those fantastic moods which are attributed to nature, and which are all born from education alone. I had the flaws of my age; I was a babbler, a glutton, sometimes a liar. I would have stolen fruits, candies, food; but I never took pleasure in doing harm, damage, in accusing others, in tormenting poor animals. I do, however, remember once having pissed into the cooking pot of one of our neighbors named Mme Clot, while she was at church. I even admit that this memory still makes me laugh, because Mme Clot, a good woman on the whole, was easily the most peevish old woman I have known in my life. That is the short and veracious history of all my childish misdeeds.[34]

7. How could I have become wicked, since under my eyes I had only examples of gentleness, and around me only the best people in the world? My father, my aunt, my nurse, my relatives, our friends, our neighbors, all who environed[35] me did not obey me it is true, but they loved me; and I likewise loved them. My wishes were excited so little and contradicted so little that it did not enter my mind to have any. I can swear that until my apprenticeship under a master, I did not know what a whim was. Except for the time I passed reading or writing with my father and when my nurse took me for a walk, I was always with my aunt, watching her embroider, listening to her sing, sitting or standing beside her, and

I was content. Her sprightliness, her sweetness, her pleasant face, have left such strong impressions on me, that I still see her manner, her look, her attitude; I remember her little caressing remarks: I could say how she was dressed and how she wore her hair, without forgetting the two curls made by her black hair on her temples, in accordance with the fashion of that time.

8. I am persuaded that it is to her I owe the taste or rather the passion for music that completely developed in me only a long time afterward. She knew a prodigious number of tunes and songs which she sang with a very sweet thin voice. This excellent girl's serenity of soul drove reverie and sadness from her and from everyone around her. Her singing had such an attraction for me that not only have several of her songs always remained in my memory; but, today when I have lost her, some of them still come back to me, which—totally forgotten since my childhood—come to mind again to the extent that I age, with a charm that I cannot express. Would anyone say that I, an old dotard, gnawed by cares and troubles, sometimes catch myself weeping like a child muttering these little tunes with a voice already broken and trembling? There is one especially which has completely come back to me, as for the tune; but the second half of the words has constantly resisted all my efforts to recall it, although the rhymes come back to me in a confused way. Here is the beginning, and what I can recall of the rest.

> Tircis, je n'ose
> Ecouter ton Chalumeau
> sous l'Ormeau;
> Car on en cause
> Déja dans nôtre hameau.
> . . . .
> [. . .] un berger
> [. . .] s'engager
> [. . .] sans danger;
> Et toujours l'épine est sous la rose.[36]

I seek the touching charm my heart finds in this song: it is a caprice about which I understand nothing; but it is completely impossible for me to sing it to the end, without being stopped by my tears. A hundred times I have planned to write to Paris to have the rest of the words sought out, if there is anyone who still knows them. But I am almost certain that the pleasure I take in recalling this tune would partially vanish, if I had proof that other people besides my poor aunt Suson have sung it.

9. Such were the first affections from my entrance into life; in this way there began to be formed in me, or to show itself, that heart, at the same time so proud and so tender, that effeminate but nevertheless indomi-

table character, which—always floating between weakness and courage, between softness and virtue—has put me in contradiction with myself to the bitter end, and has caused abstinence and enjoyment, pleasure and wisdom, equally to escape me.

10. This course of education was interrupted by an accident whose consequences have influenced the rest of my life. My father had a quarrel with a M. Gautier, a captain in the French army who had relations in the Council. This Gautier, an insolent and cowardly man, got a bloody nose, and to get revenge accused my father of having drawn his sword in the City. My father, whom they wanted to send to prison, persisted in wanting the accuser to be imprisoned along with him in accordance with the law. Since he could not accomplish this, he preferred to leave Geneva and be expatriated for the rest of his life, rather than to give way on a point in which honor and freedom appeared to him to be compromised.[37]

11. I stayed under the guardianship of my Uncle Bernard who was then employed on the fortifications of Geneva. His oldest daughter had died, but he had a son my age.[38] Together we were sent to Bossey to the Minister Lambercier's home, to learn, along with Latin, all the trifling rubbish which accompanies it under the name of education.[39]

1.[40] Two years spent in the village softened my Roman harshness a little, and brought me back to the state of childhood. At Geneva where nothing was imposed on me, I loved application, reading, it was almost my only amusement. At Bossey work made me love the games which served as relaxation from it. The country was so new to me that I could not grow weary of enjoying it. The taste I acquired for it was so lively that it could never be extinguished. During all the periods of my life until the one that brought me back to it the remembrance of the happy days I passed there made me mourn for my stay there, and its pleasures. M. Lambercier was a very reasonable man, who, without neglecting our instruction, did not burden us at all with extraordinary duties. The proof that he acted well in this is that, in spite of my aversion for constraint, I never recall my hours of study with distaste, and that, even if I did not learn much from him, what I did learn I learned without difficulty, and have never forgotten.

2. The simplicity of that rural life did me a good of inestimable value by opening my heart to friendship. Until then I had known only elevated but imaginary feelings. The habit of living together in a peaceful condition united me tenderly to my cousin Bernard. In a short time I had feelings for him more affectionate than the ones I had had for my brother, and which have never been erased. He was a tall boy, very thin, very slender, as gentle in spirit as he was weak in body, and who did not abuse too much

the preference they had for him in the house as the son of my guardian. Our labors, our amusements, our tastes were the same; we were alone; we were the same age; each of us needed a comrade: to separate us was in a manner to annihilate us. Although we had few occasions to test our attachment for each other, it was extraordinary, and not only could we not live for an instant when separated, but we did not imagine that we would ever be able to. Since we both had a spirit that easily gave way to blandishments, complaisant when they did not wish to constrain us, we always agreed about everything. If, by the favor of those who governed us, he had some ascendancy over me in their eyes; when we were alone I had one over him that restored equilibrium. In our studies, I prompted him in his lesson when he hesitated; when my theme was written I helped him to do his, and in our amusements my more active taste always served as his guide. In sum our two characters harmonized so well, and the friendship that united us was so true, that in the more than five years that we were almost inseparable whether at Bossey or Geneva, we often fought, I admit; but we never had to be separated, our quarrels never lasted longer than a quarter of an hour, and never once did either of us accuse the other of anything. These remarks are puerile, if you wish, but nevertheless from them there results a possibly unique example, since children have existed.

3. The manner in which I lived at Bossey suited me so well that if it had only lasted longer it would have absolutely fixed my character. Tender, affectionate, peaceful feelings formed its foundation. I believe that no individual of our species has ever naturally had less vanity than I did. By spurts I raised myself up to sublime impulses, but just as quickly I fell back into my languor. To be loved by everyone who approached me was my keenest desire. I was gentle, so was my cousin; so were those who brought us up. For two whole years I was neither witness nor victim of a violent feeling. Everything nourished the inclinations which my heart received from nature. I knew nothing as charming as to see the whole world content with me and with everything. I will always remember that, when I responded at catechism at the Temple, nothing bothered me more when I happened to hesitate, than to see signs of uneasiness and pain on Mlle Lambercier's face. This alone afflicted me more than the shame of failing in public, which nevertheless affected me extremely: for although little sensitive to praise I was always very much so to shame,[41] and I can say here that the expectation of Mlle Lambercier's reprimands gave me less anxiety than the fear of annoying her.

4. Nevertheless neither she nor her brother lacked severity when it was needed; but since this severity, almost always just, was never short-tempered, it distressed me, but I did not mutiny against it at all. I was

more sorry about displeasing than about being punished, and the sign of dissatisfaction was more cruel to me than the corporal punishment. It is embarrassing to explain myself better, but nevertheless I must. How methods with Young People would be changed if the remote effects of the one used—always indiscriminately and often indiscreetly—were better seen! The great lesson that can be drawn from an example as common as it is fatal, makes me resolve to give it.[42]

1. Just as Mlle Lambercier had the affections of a mother for us, she also had the authority of one, and sometimes carried it to the point of inflicting children's punishments on us, when we deserved it. For a rather long time she confined herself to the threat, and this threat of a punishment that was completely new to me seemed very frightening; but after its execution, I found the experience of it less terrible than the expectation had been, and what is most bizarre in this is that this punishment increased my affection even more for the one who had inflicted it on me. It even required all the truth of that affection and all my natural gentleness to keep me from seeking the repetition of the same treatment by deserving it: for I had found in the suffering, even in the shame, an admixture of sensuality which had left me with more desire than fear to experience it a second time from the same hand. It is true that, doubtless some precocious sexual instinct was mixed in this, the same punishment received from her brother did not appear at all pleasant to me. But with his disposition, this substitution was hardly to be feared, and if I abstained from deserving correction, it was solely out of fear of making Mlle Lambercier angry; for such is the ascendancy of benevolence in me, and even of the type of benevolence which the senses have caused to be born, that in my heart it always gives the law to the senses.

2. This second offense, which I postponed without fearing, happened without it being my fault, that is to say the fault of my will, and I took advantage of it, I can say, in security of conscience. But this second time was also the last: because, having doubtless perceived by some sign that this punishment was not serving its purpose, Mlle Lambercier declared that she was abandoning it and that it tired her too much. Until then we had slept in her room, and in winter even in her bed sometimes. Two days later they made us sleep in another room, and from that time I had the honor, with which I could very well have dispensed, of being treated by her as a big boy.

3. Who would believe that this childhood punishment received at eight years of age from the hand of a woman of thirty[43] determined my tastes, my desires, my passions, myself for the rest of my life, and this, precisely

in the opposite sense to the one that ought to follow naturally? At the same time that my senses were inflamed, my desires were so well put off the track, that—being limited to what I had experienced—they did not venture to look for anything else. With a blood burning with sensuality almost from my birth I preserved myself pure from all stain up to the age at which the coldest and most backward temperaments develop. Tormented for a long time without knowing by what, I devoured beautiful women with an ardent eye; solely to make use of them in my fashion, and to make so many Mlle Lamberciers out of them.

4. Even after the age of puberty, this bizarre taste always persisted and carried to the point of depravity, to the point of madness, preserved in me the decent[44] morals which it might seem that it should have deprived me of. If ever an education was modest and chaste, the one I received surely was. My three aunts were not only persons of exemplary good behavior, but also of a reserve that women have not known for a long time. In the presence of the women he loved most, my father—a man of pleasure, but gallant in the old fashion—never made a remark that could make a virgin blush, and the respect owed to children has never been pushed farther than in my family and in front of me. I did not find any less attention given to the same point at M. Lambercier's, and an extremely good servant was dismissed there because of a slightly too saucy remark she uttered in front of us. Not only did I not have any distinct idea of the union of the sexes before my adolescence; but also that confused idea never offered itself to me except in an odious and disgusting image. I had a horror of street walkers that has never worn off; I could not see a debauched person without disdain, even without fright: for my aversion to debauchery went that far, ever since the day, while going to Little Sacconex[45] by a sunken road, on both sides I saw the holes in the ground where I was told that these people copulated. Also what I had seen of the couplings of dogs always came back to mind when I thought of these debauched people, and this memory alone made me sick to my stomach.

5. These prejudices of education, by themselves fit for delaying the first explosions of a combustible temperament, were aided, as I have said, by the diversion the first barbs of sensuality caused me to make. Since I imagined only what I had felt; in spite of very uncomfortable effervescences of the blood, I knew about bringing my desires only toward the sort of voluptuousness I had known, without ever proceeding to the sort that had been rendered hateful to me, and that stood so close to the other, without my suspecting it at all. In my foolish whims, in my erotic furies, in the extravagant acts to which they sometimes carried me,[46] I imagina-

tively borrowed the help of the opposite sex, without ever thinking that it was suited for any other use than the one I was burning to draw from it.

6. Thus even with a very ardent, very lascivious, very precocious temperament, not only did I nevertheless go through the age of puberty without desiring, without knowing any other pleasures of the senses than those about which Mlle Lambercier had very innocently given me the idea; but also, when the passage of years finally made me a man, what ought to have ruined me still preserved me. Instead of vanishing, my old childhood taste was so much associated with the other one that I never could detach it from the desires inflamed by my senses; and this madness, joined to my natural timidity, has always made me very unenterprising with women, either from not daring to say everything or from not being able to do everything; the sort of enjoyment (for me, the other was only the final consummation) could not be usurped by the one who desired it, nor guessed by the woman who could grant it. Thus, I have passed my life coveting and being silent near the women I loved the most. Not ever daring to declare my taste, at least I beguiled it through relationships which preserved my idea of it. To be on my knees before an imperious mistress, to obey her orders, to ask her for forgiveness, were very sweet enjoyments for me, and the more my lively imagination inflamed my blood, the more I had the appearance of a faint-hearted lover. It can be imagined that this way of making love does not lead to very rapid progress, and is not extremely dangerous to the virtue of those who are its object. Thus, I have possessed extremely few, but I have not failed to enjoy many in my manner; that is to say, by imagination. This is how my senses, in harmony with my timid disposition and my romantic spirit, have preserved pure feelings and decent morals for me, by means of the same tastes which might possibly have plunged me into the most brutal sensuality if I had had a little more effrontery.

7. I have made the first and most painful step in the obscure and miry labyrinth of my confessions. It is not what is criminal that costs the most to tell, it is what is ridiculous and shameful. From now on I am sure of myself, after what I have just dared to say, nothing can stop me any more. One can judge what similar admissions might have cost me, from the fact that never in the course of my life—even though sometimes next to the ones I loved I was carried away by the furies of a passion that deprived me of the faculty of seeing and of hearing, out of my senses, and seized with a convulsive trembling in my whole body—have I been able to take it upon myself to declare my madness to them, and, while in the most intimate familiarity, to implore from them the only favor that was missing. This

happened to me only once, in childhood, with a child of my own age; furthermore it was she who made the first proposition.

1. While going back this way to the first traces of my sensitive being, I find elements which, although they sometimes seem incompatible, have not failed to unite forcefully to produce a uniform and simple effect, and I find others, in appearance the same, which through the concurrence of certain circumstances have formed such different combinations that one would never imagine there was any relation between them. For example, who would believe that one of the most vigorous springs of my soul was steeped in the same source from which lewdness and softness flowed into my blood? Without leaving the subject about which I have just been speaking, one will see a very different impression coming from it.

One day I was studying my lesson alone in the room next to the kitchen. The maid had put Mlle Lambercier's[47] combs in the chimney niche to dry. When she came back to get them, one was found in which a whole row of teeth was broken. Who was to blame for this damage? No one but myself had entered the room. I was interrogated; I denied that I had touched the comb. M. and Mlle Lambercier combined; exhorted me, pressed me, threatened me; I stubbornly persisted; but the proof was too strong, outweighed all my protestations, even though this was the first time I was found to have so much audacity in lying. The matter was taken seriously; it deserved to be. The wickedness, the lying, the obstinacy appeared equally deserving of punishment: but this time it was not inflicted on me by Mlle Lambercier. They wrote to my uncle Bernard; he came. My poor Cousin was charged with another offense that was not less serious: we were wrapped up in the same execution. It was terrible. If, seeking the remedy in the evil itself, they wished to stifle my depraved senses forever, they could not have taken a better course.[48] Consequently my senses left me in peace for a long time.

They could not extract the admission they demanded from me. Reprimanded several times, and reduced to the most frightful condition, I was unshakable. I would have suffered death and I was resolved to do so. Even force had to give way before the diabolical wilfulness of a child; for they did not call my constancy anything else. Finally I emerged from this cruel test in pieces, but triumphant.

It has now been more than fifty years since this adventure, and today I have no fear of being punished a second time for the same deed. Well, I state before Heaven that I was innocent, that I had neither broken nor touched the comb, that I had not gone near the niche, and that I had not even thought of doing so. Do not ask me how the damage was done; I do not know, and cannot understand it; what I know very certainly is that I was innocent of it.

Imagine a character that is timid and docile in ordinary life, but ardent, proud, indomitable when in a passion; a child always governed by the voice of reason, always treated with gentleness, equity, kindness; who did not even have the idea of injustice, and who suffers such a terrible one for the first time from precisely the people he loves and respects the most. What a reversal of ideas! what disorder of feelings! what an upheaval in his heart, in his brain,[49] in all his little intellectual and moral being! I say, imagine all that if it is possible to do so; because as for me, I do not feel myself capable of unraveling, of following, the smallest trace of what happened in me at that time.

I did not yet have enough reason to feel how much appearances condemned me, and to put myself in the place of the others. I kept to my own place, and all I felt was the severity of a dreadful punishment for a crime I had not committed. Although it was severe, I hardly felt the bodily pain, I felt only indignation, rage, despair. My Cousin was in a nearly similar case, and since he had been punished for an involuntary fault as if it had been a premeditated action, became enraged following my example, and worked himself up in unison with me so to speak. Both being in the same bed we embraced each other with convulsive outbursts, we were suffocated; and when our young hearts, a little eased, could vent their rage, we sat up, and both began to shout a hundred times with all our strength: "*Carnifex, Carnifex, Carnifex.*"[50]   *reproach, a torment*

While writing this I feel my pulse beat faster again; these moments will always be present to me if I live a hundred thousand years. This first feeling of violence and injustice has remained so deeply engraved on my soul, that all the ideas related to it give me back my first emotion; and this feeling, relating to myself in its origin, has taken such a consistency in itself, and has been so much detached from all personal interest, that my heart is inflamed at the spectacle or narrative of all unjust actions— whatever their object might be and wherever they are committed—just as if their effect fell on me. When I read the cruelties of a ferocious tyrant, the crafty foul deeds of a cheat of a priest, I would willing set off in order to stab those wretches, even if I were obliged to perish a hundred times in doing so. I have often gotten myself bathed in perspiration, by pursuing at a run or by throwing stones at a rooster, a cow, a dog, an animal that I saw tormenting another one, solely because it felt itself to be stronger. This impulse may be natural to me, and I believe it is; but the profound remembrance[51] of the first injustice that I suffered has been tied to it for too long and too strongly, not to have reinforced it a lot.[52]

There was the end of the serenity of my childlike life. From that moment I ceased to enjoy a pure happiness, and even today I feel that the remembrance of the charms of my childhood stops there. We remained at Bossey for several months. We were there as the first man is represented to us in the terrestrial paradise, but we had ceased to enjoy it.[53] In appearance it was the same situation, and in fact a completely different manner of being. Attachment, respect, intimacy, confidence no longer tied the students to their guides; we no longer regarded them as Gods who read in our hearts: we were less ashamed of doing wrong, and more fearful of being accused: we began to hide ourselves, to mutiny, to lie. All the vices of our age corrupted our innocence and disfigured our games. In our eyes even the countryside lost that attraction of sweetness and simplicity that goes to the heart. It seemed deserted and somber to us; it was as if it had been covered by a veil that hid its beauties from us. We ceased to cultivate our little gardens, our herbs, our flowers. We no longer went to scrape the earth lightly and to shout with joy when we discovered the shoot of grain we had sown. We grew tired of this life; they grew tired of us; my uncle took us away, and we were separated from M. and Mlle Lambercier, each of us sated with the others, and regretting little[54] our leaving.

Almost thirty years passed after my departure from Bossey without me recalling the stay in a pleasant manner with remembrances that were at all coherent: but since I have passed middle age and am declining toward old age, I feel that these same remembrances are reborn while others fade away, and are imprinted on my memory with features whose charm and strength increase day by day; as if, already feeling life slipping away, I am trying to seize it again at its beginnings. The smallest facts from that time please me by the mere fact that they are from that time. I recall all the circumstances of places, people, times. I see the maid or the valet working in the room, a swallow coming in the window, a fly alighting on my hand, while I was reciting my lesson: I see the whole arrangement of the room in which we were; M. Lambercier's study on the right, an engraving representing all the popes, a barometer, a big calendar; raspberry bushes which, from a very elevated garden into which the house sank toward the back, shaded the window, and sometimes came inside. I know very well that the reader does not have a great need of knowing all this; but I myself have a need to tell it to him. If only I dared to recount in the same way all the little anecdotes of that happy age, which still make me shiver with joy when I recall them. Especially five or six . . . let us compromise. I will spare you five, but I want one of them, only one; as long as I am allowed to recount it for as long as I can, in order to prolong my pleasure.

If I was seeking only your pleasure, I could choose the anecdote about Mlle Lambercier's rear end, which, through an unfortunate tumble at the bottom of the meadow, was displayed in full view in front of the King of Sardinia as he was passing by:[55] but the one about the walnut tree on the terrace is more amusing for me since I was an actor whereas I was only a spectator of the tumble, and I acknowledge that I did not find the slightest humor in an accident which, although comic in itself, alarmed me on behalf of a person whom I loved as a mother, and perhaps more.

Oh you, readers curious about the great history of the walnut tree on the terrace, listen to its horrible tragedy, and refrain from shuddering, if you can.

Outside the gate to[56] the Courtyard there was a terrace to the left upon entering, where[57] we often went to sit in the afternoon, but which had no shade whatsoever. To give it some, M. Lambercier had a walnut tree planted there. The planting of this tree was done with solemnity. The two boarders were its Godfathers, and while the trough was being filled, we each held the tree with one hand with songs of triumph. To water it they made a sort of basin all around its foot. Ardent spectators of this watering, every day my cousin and I were confirmed in the very natural idea that it was finer to plant a tree on the terrace than a flag in the breach; and we resolved to procure this glory for ourselves without sharing it with anyone whatsoever.

To do so, we went to cut a slip from a young willow, and we planted it on the terrace, eight or ten feet from the majestic walnut tree. We did not forget to make a trough around our tree also: the difficulty was to obtain something with which to fill it; for the water came from rather far away, and they did not let us run to get any. Nevertheless it was absolutely necessary for our willow. For several days we used all sorts of ruses to supply it with some, and we succeeded so well that we saw it sprout and put out little leaves whose growth we measured from hour to hour; persuaded that it would not take long to give us shade although it was not a foot high.

Since our tree occupied us completely, it left us incapable of any application, any study, so that we were as if in a delirium, and since they did not know its cause, they kept a tighter hold on us than before; we foresaw the fatal instant when water would fail us, and we grieved while we waited to see our tree perish from drought. Finally necessity, the mother of industry, suggested to us an invention to save the tree and ourselves from a certain death: this was to make a trench under the earth which secretly conveyed to the willow a part of the water with which they watered the walnut tree. Although it was executed with ardor, this undertaking nevertheless did not succeed right away. We had made the slope so poorly that the water did not flow. The earth caved in and blocked the trench; the entrance became filled with rubbish; everything met with setbacks. Nothing discouraged us. *Omnia vincit labor improbus.*[58] We burrowed deeper into the earth for our basin to let the water flow; we cut the bottoms of boxes into little narrow planks, of which some were set flat in a row, and placing the others at an angle on the two sides, we made a triangular canal for our conduit.[59] At the entrance we planted small scraps of thin wood and lattice-work which, making a sort of grillwork or toad-catcher,[60] held back the mud and stones, without blocking the passage to the water. We carefully covered our work with well-packed earth, and the day everything was completed, trembling with hope and fear, we waited for time for the watering. After centuries of waiting the time came at last: according to his custom M. Lambercier also came to help in the operation during which we both kept behind him to hide our tree, to which he very fortunately turned his back.

They had hardly finished pouring the first pail of water before we began to see it flowing into our basin. At this sight prudence abandoned us; we began shouting cries of joy which made M. Lambercier turn around, and this was a pity: for he was taking great pleasure in seeing how good the earth around the walnut tree was and how avidly it was drinking his water. Struck by seeing it divided between two basins, he shouted in turn, looked, perceived the knavish trick, brusquely had a pickaxe brought over, gave a blow, set flying two or three slivers of our planks, and shouting as loud as he could, *"An aqueduct, an aqueduct,"* he struck pitiless blows everywhere, each of which landed in the middle of our hearts. In an instant the boards, the conduit, the basin, the willow, everything was destroyed, everything was dug up; without any other word being pronounced during this terrible expedition, except the exclamation that he repeated ceaselessly. *"An aqueduct,"* he cried while shattering everything, *"An aqueduct, an aqueduct!"*

It will be thought that the adventure finished badly for the little architects. That would be a mistake: everything was over. M. Lambercier did not say a single reproachful word to us, did not give us a dirty look, and did not say any more about it to us; we even heard him a little later roaring with laughter with his sister, for M. Lambercier's laughter could be heard a long way off; and what was still more surprising, is that, after the first shock, we ourselves were not very troubled. We planted another tree somewhere else, and we often recalled the catastrophe of the first, while repeating between ourselves emphatically: *"An aqueduct, an aqueduct!"* Until then I had had fits of pride at intervals when I was Aristides or Brutus. This was my first well-marked movement of vanity.[61] To have been able to construct an aqueduct with our hands, to have put a cutting into competition with a big tree seemed to me the supreme degree of glory. At ten I judged about it better than Caesar did at thirty.

The idea of this walnut tree and the little story relating to it stayed with me or came back so well, that one of my most pleasant plans on my trip to Geneva in 1754[62] was to go to Bossey to see the monuments of my childhood games again, and above all the dear walnut tree which by then should already have been a third of a century old.[63] I was so continuously besieged, so little master of myself, that I could not find a moment to satisfy myself. It is not very likely that this opportunity ever will arise for me again. Nevertheless, I have not lost the desire to do it along with the hope; and I am almost sure, that if I ever found my dear walnut tree still existing when I returned to those dear places, I would water it with my tears.

Having returned to Geneva, I passed two or three years at my Uncle's home while waiting for them to decide what could be done with me.[64] Since he intended his son to be an engineer, he made him learn a little drawing and taught him Euclid's elements. I learned all of that out of companionship, and I acquired a taste for it, particularly for drawing.[65] Nevertheless they deliberated about whether they would make me a watchmaker, lawyer, or minister. I preferred to be a Minister, for I found it very fine to preach. But the small income from my mother's property which was to be divided between my brother and myself was not enough for furthering my studies. Since my age did not make this choice very pressing yet, I stayed in my uncle's home while I waited, almost wasting my time, and not failing to pay a rather large fee for room and board, as was just.

Like my father, my uncle was a man of pleasure, but my uncle was unable to subject himself to his duties as my father did and took rather little care of us. My aunt was a devout woman who was a bit of a pietist and preferred to sing psalms than to look after our education.[66] They left us an almost complete freedom which we never abused. Always inseparable, we sufficed for each other, and because we were not at all tempted to frequent the rascals of our age, we acquired none of the libertine habits that idleness could have inspired in us. I am even wrong to imply that we were idle, because we were never less so in our lives, and what is lucky was that all the amusements with which we became successively impassioned kept us occupied together in the house without us even being tempted to go out into the street. We made cages, flutes, kites, drums, houses, *popguns*, crossbows. We ruined my good old grandfather's[67] tools by making watches in imitation of him. Above all our preferred taste was for smearing paper, drawing, painting washes, coloring, making a mess of colors. An Italian mountebank named *Gamba-Corta* came to Geneva; we went to see him once, and then we no longer wanted to go: but he had marionettes, and we began to make marionettes; his marionettes acted sorts of plays, and we wrote plays for ours. From lack of practice we mimicked Punch's voice in our throats, in order to perform these charming plays which our poor good relatives had the patience to watch and listen to. But one day after my uncle Bernard read a very fine sermon of his own composition to the family, we abandoned plays, and began composing sermons. I admit that these details are not very interesting; but they show how well directed our earliest education was, so that, almost masters of our time and at such a tender age, we were so little tempted to abuse it. We had so little need of making comrades for ourselves, that we even neglected opportunities to do so. When we went for a walk we looked at their games in passing without longing, without even thinking of taking part in them. Friendship filled our hearts so well that it was sufficient for us to be together for the simplest tastes to bring us joy.

As a result of seeing us inseparable they took notice of us; all the more so because, since my Cousin was very tall and I very short, we made a rather amusingly contrasting couple. His long slender figure, his small face like a baked apple, his soft expression, his nonchalant gait roused the children to make fun of him. In the dialect of the country they gave him the nickname *Barnâ bredanna*,[68] and as soon as we went outside, we heard nothing but "*Barnâ bredanna*" all around us. He bore this more tranquilly than I did. I got angry, I wanted to fight; that is what the little rascals wanted. I fought, I was beaten. My poor cousin helped me the best he could; but he was weak, he was knocked down with one punch. Then I became furious. Nevertheless, although I took many punches, they did not want to give them to me, they wanted to give them to *Barnâ Bredanna*: but with my unruly anger I made things so much worse that we no longer dared to go out except when they were in class, for fear of being hooted at and followed by the schoolboys.

Behold me already a righter of wrongs. To be a Paladin[69] in due form I needed only to have a Lady; I had two of them. From time to time I went to see my father at Nyon, a small city in the Pays de Vaud where he had settled. My father was well liked, and his son benefited from this benevolence. During the short stay I made with him the issue was who would entertain me the most. Above all a Mme de Vulson gave me a thousand caresses, and to add the finishing touch, her daughter took me for her favorite. One feels what a twelve-year-old favorite is for a girl of twenty-two. But all those minxes are so fond of putting forward little dolls this way in order to hide the big ones, or in order to tempt them with the image of a game they know how to make attractive. As for myself who saw no disparity at all between us, I took things seriously; I abandoned myself with all my heart, or rather with all my head; for it was almost only through it that I was in love, even though I was so to the point of madness, and how my outbursts, my agitations, my rages made scenes suited to convulsing anyone with laughter.

I know two sorts of love which are very distinct, very real, and which have almost nothing in common, although both are very lively and both different from tender friendship.[70] The whole course of my life has been divided between these two loves of such different natures, and I have even experienced both of them at the same time. For example, at the moment about which I am speaking, while I was taking possession of Mlle de Vulson so publicly and so tyrannically that I could not allow anyone to approach her, with a little Mlle Goton I had rather short but rather lively tête-à-têtes, in which she condescended to play the school mistress, and that was all; but this all, which in fact was everything to me, seemed to me to be the supreme happiness. Already feeling the value of mystery—although I knew how to make use of it only in a childish way—I paid back Mlle de Vulson, who hardly suspected it, for the care that she took to use me to hide other loves. But to my great regret my secret was discovered or less well kept on the part of my little school mistress than on my part; for they did not delay in separating us, and sometime afterwards when I had returned to Geneva, while passing through Coutance[71] I heard little girls crying out to me in an undertone, "*Goton tic tac Rousseau.*"[72]

In truth this little Mlle Goton was a singular person. Without being beautiful she had a face which was hard to forget, and which I still recall, often too much for an old fool. Neither her stature, nor her bearing, nor above all her eyes belonged to her age. She had an imposing and proud little manner, very fitting for her role, and which brought about the first idea between us. But the most bizarre thing about her was a mixture of audacity and reserve difficult to conceive. She allowed herself the greatest familiarities with me without ever allowing me any with her; she treated me exactly like a child. This makes me believe either that she had already ceased to be one, or on the contrary that she was still enough of one herself to see nothing but a game in the danger to which she exposed herself.

I belonged completely so to speak to each of these two persons, and so perfectly that when I was with either of the two I never happened to think of the other. But otherwise, there was nothing similar in what they caused me to experience. I would have passed my entire life with Mlle de Vulson without dreaming of leaving her; but my joy in approaching her was tranquil and did not reach the point of emotion. Above all I loved her in a large company; pleasantries, teasing, even jealousy attracted me, interested me; with pride I triumphed from her preference in front of great rivals whom she seemed to mistreat. I was tormented, but I loved this torment. Applause, encouragement, laughter inflamed me, enlivened me. I had outbursts of anger, flashes of wit: I was carried away with love in a social circle. In a tête-à-tête I would have been constrained, cold, possibly bored. Nevertheless, I was tenderly concerned with her, I suffered when she was sick: I would have given up my health to restore hers, and take notice that I knew very well from experience what sickness was, and what health was. When absent from her I thought about her, I missed her; when present, her caresses were sweet to my heart, not to my senses. I was familiar with her with impunity; my imagination asked only for what she granted me: nevertheless I would not have been able to bear to see her grant as much to others. I loved her as a brother; but I was as jealous as a lover with her.

With Mlle Goton I would have been as jealous as a Turk, as a wild man, as a Tiger, if I had only imagined that she could grant someone else the same treatment she granted me; for even this was a favor for which one had to ask on one's knees. I approached Mlle de Vulson with a very lively pleasure, but without being troubled; whereas by merely seeing Mlle Goton, I no longer saw anything; all my senses were disrupted. I was familiar with the former, without having familiarities; on the contrary I was equally trembling and agitated before the latter, even in the heat of the greatest familiarities. I believe that if I had stayed with her for too long I would not have been able to live; the palpitations would have stifled me. I feared displeasing them equally; but I was more obliging with the one and more obedient with the other. I would not have wanted to make Mlle de Vulson angry for anything in the world, but if Mlle Goton had ordered me to throw myself into the flames, I believe I would have obeyed her instantly.

My love-making or rather my assignations with the latter lasted for a short time, very fortunately for her and for me. Although my relations with Mlle de Vulson might not have had the same danger, they did not fail to have their catastrophe also, after having lasted a little longer. The end of all such relations always ought to have a slightly romantic air and give occasion for exclamations. Although my dealings with Mlle de Vulson were less lively, they were perhaps more binding. We never separated without tears, and it is singular what an overwhelming void I felt myself plunged into after I left her. I could speak about nothing but her and think about nothing but her; my regrets were true and lively; but I believe that at bottom these heroic regrets were not all for her, and that, without me having noticed it, the amusements of which she was the center had their fair share in them. To moderate the pain of absence, we wrote each other letters of a pathos that could make rocks split. Finally I had the glory of her not being able to keep herself away and of her coming to see me at Geneva. This time my head was completely turned; I was drunk and mad for the two days she stayed there. When she left, I wanted to throw myself in the water after her, and I filled the air with my cries for a long time. A week later, she sent me candies and gloves; which might have seemed extremely courteous to me, if I had not learned at the same time that she had married, and that this trip with which she was pleased to honor me, was to buy her wedding clothes.[73] I will not describe my rage; it may be conceived. In my noble wrath I swore never to see the perfidious one again, not imagining a more terrible punishment for her. Nevertheless, she did not die from it; for twenty years afterwards, having gone to see my father and sailing with him on the lake, I asked who the Ladies were whom I saw in a boat close to ours. "What," my father said to me smiling, "doesn't your heart tell you? It is your old love; it is Mme Cristin, it is Mlle de Vulson." I trembled at this almost forgotten name: but I told the boatmen to change direction; even though I had a fine enough chance to take my revenge, not judging it to be worth the trouble of forswearing myself, and of renewing a twenty-year-old quarrel with a woman of forty.[74]

In this way the most precious time of my childhood was lost in foolishness before my destination had been decided. After long deliberations about following my natural aptitude, they finally made the choice for which I had the least, and placed me with M. Masseron the City registrar, to learn under him, as M. Bernard said, the useful profession of pettifogger. This nickname supremely displeased me; the hope of earning plenty of money by ignoble means did not gratify my haughty disposition very much; the occupation appeared boring, unbearable to me; assiduousness, subjection completed my repulsion for it, and I never entered the office with anything but a horror[75] that increased from day to day. Not being very satisfied with me on his side, M. Masseron treated me with disdain, ceaselessly reproaching me for my dullness, my stupidity; repeating to me every day that my uncle had assured him, *"that I knew, that I knew,"* whereas in truth I knew nothing; that he had promised him a fine boy, and that he had given him only an ass. Finally I was ignominiously dismissed from the office for my ineptitude, and M. Masseron's clerks declared that I was not good for anything but handling a watchmaker's file.

Now that my vocation was settled this way, I was placed in appren-

ticeship; not however with a watchmaker, but with an engraver.[76] The
registrar's scorn had extremely humiliated me, and I obeyed without a
murmur. My master, named M. Ducommun, was a loutish and violent
young man, who in a very short time completely tarnished all the brilliance of my childhood, brutalized my loving and lively character, and
reduced me in mind as well as fortune to my genuine station as an apprentice. My Latin, my antiquities, my history, everything was forgotten
for a long time: I did not even remember that there had been Romans in
the world. When I went to see him, my father no longer found his idol in
me; I was no longer the gallant Jean-Jacques for the ladies, and I myself
felt so well that M. and Mlle Lambercier would no longer have recognized their pupil in me, that I was ashamed to present myself to them, and
have not seen them again since then. The vilest tastes, the most base tricks
replaced my amiable amusements, without leaving me even the slightest
idea of them. Despite the most decent education, I must have had a great
penchant to degenerate; because it happened very rapidly, without the
slightest difficulty, and never did such a precocious Caesar so promptly
become Laridon.[77]

In itself the trade did not displease me; I had a keen taste for drawing; using the chisel rather amused me, and since the talent required of
an engraver for watchmaking is very limited, I hoped to attain perfection
in it. Perhaps I would have succeeded in it if my master's brutality and
the excessive restraint had not repelled me from the work. I stole time
from him, to use it in occupations of the same type, but which had the
attraction of freedom for me. I engraved sorts of medals to serve as orders
of chivalry for myself and my comrades.[78] My master surprised me in this
contraband work, and thrashed me, saying that I was practicing to make
counterfeit money, because our medals had the coat of arms of the Republic. I can swear that I had no idea of counterfeit money, and very little
of the genuine sort. I knew better how the Roman As was made than our
three sous pieces.[79]

My master's tyranny ended by making unbearable to me work that I
would have loved, and by giving me vices that I would have hated, such as
lying, laziness, theft. Nothing has taught me the difference between filial
dependence and servile slavery better than the memory of the changes
produced in me by this period. Naturally timid and bashful, I never had
more aversion for any flaw than I had for impudence. But I had enjoyed
a decent freedom which had been restrained until then only by degrees,
and which finally vanished completely. I was bold at my father's home,
free at M. Lambercier's, discreet at my uncle's; I became fearful at my
master's, and from then on I was a lost child. I had been accustomed to a

perfect equality with my superiors in the manner of living, not to know a pleasure that was not within my reach, not to see a dish of which I did not have my share, not to have a desire which I did not express, in sum to put all the emotions of my heart upon my lips; judge what I had to become in a house where I did not dare open my mouth, where I had to leave the table a third of the way through the meal,[80] and the room as soon as I had nothing more to do there, where—ceaselessly chained to my work—I saw objects of enjoyment only for others and privations for me alone, where the image of the master's and journeyman's freedom added weight to my subjugation, where I did not dare open my mouth in disputes about the things I knew the most, finally where everything I saw became an object of covetousness for my heart solely because I was deprived of everything. Farewell to ease, gaiety, and happy expressions which previously had often caused me to escape punishment for my faults. I cannot recall without laughing that one night at my father's, being condemned to go to bed without supper because of some piece of mischief, and passing by the kitchen with my sorry piece of bread, I saw and smelled the joint turning on the spit. They were around the fire; I had to greet everyone while passing. When the rounds had been made, looking out of the corner of my eye at that joint which looked and smelled so good, I could not abstain from making a bow to it also and from saying to it, *"farewell joint."* This outburst of naivete seemed so pleasant that they made me stay to dine. Perhaps it would have had the same luck at my master's house, but it certainly would never have occurred to me, or I would never have dared to deliver the outburst there.

That is how I learned how to covet in silence, to hide myself, to dissimulate, to lie, and finally to steal; a whim that had not come to me until then, and of which I have not been able to cure myself very well since. Covetousness and powerlessness always lead to this. That is why all lackeys are knaves, and why all apprentices ought to be: but in an equal and tranquil condition, where all they see is within their reach, the latter lose this shameful penchant when they grow up. Not having had the same advantage, I could not draw the same profit from it.

It is almost always good feelings badly directed that make children take the first step toward evil. In spite of continuous privations and temptations, I remained with my master for more than[81] a year without being able to make up my mind to take anything, not even things to eat. My first theft was a matter of the desire to be obliging; but it opened the door to others, which did not have such a praiseworthy goal.

At my master's there was a journeyman named M. Verrat, whose house in the neighborhood had a garden that was rather far off which produced very fine asparagus. M. Verrat, who did not have much money, took it into his head to steal some early asparagus from his mother, and to sell it in order to buy several good lunches. Since he did not want to take the risk himself and because he was not terribly nimble, he chose me for this expedition. After some preliminary coaxing which won me over all the better because I did not see its goal, he proposed it to me as an idea that had occurred to him on the spot. I argued a lot; he insisted. I have never been able to resist blandishments; I gave way. Every morning I went to harvest the finest asparagus; I brought it to the Molard,[82] where some old woman, who saw that I had just stolen it, told me so in order to get it at a better price. In my fright I took what she chose to give me; I brought it to M. Verrat. It was promptly converted into a lunch of which I was the provider, and which he shared with another comrade; for, as for me, very content to have some scraps from it, I did not even touch their wine.

This little arrangement lasted for several days, without it even entering my mind to rob the robber, and to take a tithe of the product of his asparagus from M. Verrat. I performed my piece of knavishness with the greatest fidelity;[83] my only motive was to please the one who was making me do it. Nevertheless, if I had been surprised, what blows, what injuries, what cruel treatment would I not have suffered; whereas the wretch would have been believed at his word when he gave me the lie, and I doubly punished for having dared to accuse him; seeing that he was a journeyman, and that I was only an apprentice. This is how in every condition the guilty strong person saves himself at the expense of the innocent weak one.

Thus, I learned that it was not as terrible to steal as I had thought, and I soon turned my science to such account that nothing I coveted was safely out of my reach. I was not absolutely badly fed in my master's home, and sobriety was not troublesome to me except for seeing him keep it so poorly. The practice of making young people leave the table when what tempts them the most is served seems to me very capable of making them into both gluttons and knaves. In a short time I became both, and I found that for me being both usually went very well, sometimes very badly, when I was surprised.

One remembrance that still makes me both shudder and laugh at the same time, is of a hunt for apples that cost me dearly. These apples were at the bottom of a Pantry, which received light from the kitchen through blinds. One day when I was alone in the house, I climbed onto the bin to look at this precious fruit in the garden of the Hesperides[84] to which I was unable to gain access. I went to find the spit to see if it could reach: it was too short. I lengthened it with another little spit that was used for small game birds; for my master loved hunting. I struck unsuccessfully several times; finally with rapture I felt that I was pulling up an apple. I pulled very gently; already the apple touched the blinds; I was ready to seize it. Who will speak my sorrow? The apple was too wide; it could not fit through the hole. How many inventions did I not put[85] into practice to pull it through. It was necessary to find supports to hold the spit still, a knife long enough to split the apple, a slat to hold it up. By virtue of skill and time I succeeded in dividing it, hoping to pull the pieces up next one after the other. But hardly were they separated than they both fell into the pantry. Compassionate reader, share my affliction.

I did not lose my courage at all; but I had lost a great deal of time. I was afraid of being surprised; I postponed a more fortunate attempt to the next day, and I went back to work as tranquilly as if I had done nothing, without thinking about the two indiscreet witnesses that were testifying against me in the pantry.

Finding the opportunity fine the next day, I make a new attempt. I climb onto my stand, I lengthen the spit, I adjust it, I was ready to strike . . . unfortunately the dragon was not asleep. Suddenly the pantry door opens; my master comes through it, crosses his arms, looks at me, and says to me, "Bravo. . . ." The pen falls from my hands.

Soon as a result of suffering bad treatment, I became less sensitive to it; in sum it seemed to me a sort of payment for theft, which gave me the right to continue it. Instead of turning my eyes back to the rear and looking at the punishment, I brought them forwards and looked at the vengeance. I judged that being beaten like a rogue authorized me to be one. I found that stealing and being beaten went together, and in some way made up a single condition, and that by fulfilling the part of that condition that depended on me, I could leave the care of the other part to my master. From this idea, I set out to steal more calmly than before. I said to myself, "What will come of it in the end? I will be beaten. So be it: that's what I am made for."

Although I am not greedy, I love to eat; I am sensual and not a glutton. Too many other tastes distract me from that one. I have never concerned myself with my mouth except when my heart was idle, and this has so rarely happened to me in my life that I have hardly had time to think about tasty morsels. This is why I did not limit my knavery to foodstuffs for very long, I soon extended it to everything that tempted me, and if I did not become a regular thief, it is because I have never been tempted very much by money. Inside the common workshop my master had another separate workshop, which could be locked; I found the way to open its door and to close it again without it appearing to have been done. There

I pressed into service his good tools, his better drawings, his impressions, everything that excited my envy and he affected to keep away from me. At bottom these thefts were quite innocent, since they were committed only to be used in his service: but I was carried away with joy at having these bagatelles in my power; I believed I was stealing his talent along with his productions. Besides, in boxes there were chips of gold and silver, small jewels, valuable pieces, coins. If I had four or five sous in my pocket, that was a lot: nevertheless, far from touching any of the boxes, I do not remember even having cast a covetous look at them in my life. I saw it with more fright than pleasure. I very much believe that this horror of stealing money and what produces it comes in great part from my education. Mixed with it are secret ideas of infamy, prison, punishment, the gallows which would have made me shudder if I had been tempted; whereas my tricks seemed to me to be only acts of mischief, and in fact were nothing else. All of them could be worth nothing but a thrashing from my master, and I prepared myself for that in advance.

But once again, I did not even covet enough to have to abstain; I felt nothing to combat. A single sheet of fine drawing paper tempted me more than the money to pay for a ream of it. This peculiarity is derived from one of the singular features of my character. It has had so much influence on my conduct, that it is important to explain it.

I have very ardent passions, and as long as they are disturbing me nothing equals my impetuousness; I know neither discretion, nor respect, nor fear, nor decorum; I am cynical, brazen, violent, intrepid: There is no shame that stops me nor danger that frightens me. Aside from the sole object that engages me the universe no longer means anything to me: but all this lasts only for a moment and the following moment throws me into annihilation. Take me in periods of calm I am indolence and timidity themselves: everything scares me, everything disheartens me, a housefly in flight frightens me; a word to be said, a gesture to be made terrifies my laziness, fear and shame subjugate me to such an extent that I would like to disappear from the eyes of all mortals. If I must act I do not know what to do; if I must speak I do not know what to say; if they look at me I am disconcerted. When I am impassioned, I can sometimes find what I must say; but in ordinary conversations I find nothing, nothing at all; they are unbearable for me because I am obliged to speak.

Add to this that none of my dominant tastes consists in things that can be bought. I require only pure pleasures, and money poisons them all. For example, I love those of the table; but not being able to bear either the bother of good company nor the debauchery of the tavern, I can taste them only with a friend, for alone, I cannot do so: then my imagination is occupied with something else, and I get no pleasure from eating. If my aroused blood demands women, my tender heart also demands love even more. Women who can be bought with money would lose all their charms for me; I doubt whether I would even have it in me to take advantage of them. It is the same way with all the pleasures within my reach: if they are not free I find them insipid. I love only the goods that belong to nobody but the first one who knows how to taste them.[86]

To me money has never seemed to be as precious a thing as it is usually found to be. Further; to me it has never seemed very convenient; it is good for nothing by itself; one must transform it in order to enjoy it; one must buy, haggle, often be a dupe, pay well, in order to be poorly served. I would like something of good quality; with my money I am sure of having one of bad quality. I buy a fresh egg dearly, it is old; a fine fruit, it is green; a girl, she is tainted. I love good wine; but where is it to be found? At a wine merchant's? Whatever I might do he will poison me. Do I absolutely want to be well served? How many cares, what bother! to have friends, correspondents, to give commissions, to write, to go, to come, to wait, and often in the end still to be fooled. How much trouble with my money! I fear it more than I love good wine.

A thousand times, during my apprenticeship and since, I have gone out with the plan of buying some delicacy. I approach a pastry shop: I notice some women at the counter; I believe I already see them laughing and joking among themselves about the little glutton. I pass in front of a fruit vendor, I cast a glance out of the corner of my eye at some fine pears, their odor tempts me; very nearby two or three young people are looking at me; a man who knows me is in front of his shop; from afar I see a girl coming; isn't she the maid of the house? My near-sightedness causes me a thousand illusions. I take everyone who passes for someone of my acquaintance: everywhere I am intimidated, held back by some obstacle: my desire increases with my shame, and I finally return like a fool, devoured by covetousness, having enough in my pocket to satisfy it, and not having dared to buy anything.

I would enter into the most insipid details, if I followed the bother, the shame, the repugnance, the inconveniences, the distasteful things of every sort I have always suffered in the use of my money, either from myself or others. To the extent that the reader gains knowledge of my disposition as he advances in my life, he will feel all this without my dwelling on telling it to him at too great a length.

This being understood, one of my supposed contradictions will be understood without difficulty; that of joining an almost sordid avarice with the greatest disdain for money. For me it is so inconvenient a movable good, that I do not even take it into my head to desire it when I do not have it, and when I have some I keep it for a long time[87] without spending it, for lack of knowing how to use it at my whim; but does a convenient and pleasant opportunity present itself? I take advantage of it so well that my purse empties itself before I notice it. Besides, do not look in me for the miser's quirk of spending for ostentation; completely on the contrary, I spend in secret and for pleasure: far from making a glory for myself in spending, I hide it. I feel so strongly that money is of no use to me, that I am almost ashamed of having any, still more of making use of it.

If I had ever had an income sufficient for living comfortably, I would not have been at all tempted to be a miser, I am very sure of it. I would spend all my income without seeking to increase it; but my precarious situation keeps me in fear. I adore freedom: I abhor bother, trouble, subjugation. As long as the money I have in my purse lasts, it ensures my independence, it spares me from maneuvering to find more of it; a necessity for which I have always had a horror: but out of fear of seeing it end I coddle it. The money one possesses is the instrument of freedom; that which one pursues is the one[88] of servitude. This is why I squeeze very tight and covet nothing.

Thus my disinterestedness is only laziness; the pleasure of having is not worth the pain of acquiring: and my dissipation is also only laziness; when the occasion to spend agreeably presents itself, it is impossible to take too much advantage of it. I am less tempted by money than by things, because there is always an intermediary between money and the desired possession, whereas there is none between the thing itself and its enjoyment. I see the thing, it tempts me; if I see only the means for acquiring it, it does not tempt me. Thus I have been a knave, and sometimes I still am with bagatelles that tempt me and which I would rather take than ask for. But, small or big, I do not remember having taken a cent from anyone in my life; aside from one single time, fifteen years ago, when I stole seven livres, ten sous. The adventure is worth the trouble of relating, because it contains a priceless combination of effrontery and stupidity, which I would have trouble believing myself if it concerned anyone but me.

It was at Paris. I was taking a walk with M. de Francueil at the Palais Royal around five o'clock.[89] He takes out his watch, looks at it, and says to me, "Let's go to the Opera." I am very willing. We go. He takes two tickets for the Amphitheater, gives me one, and goes ahead first with the other; I follow him, he enters. Entering after him, I find the door blocked. I look; I see everyone standing up. I judge that I will be able to lose myself very well in that crowd, or at least allow M. de Francueil to suppose that I was lost there. I leave, I take back my ticket stub, then my money, and I go out, without dreaming that as soon as I reached the door everyone sat down, and then M. de Francueil clearly saw that I was no longer there.

Since nothing is further from my disposition than this deed, I mention it to show that there are moments of a sort of delirium, in which men must not be judged by their actions. It was not precisely stealing this money, it was stealing its use: the less it was a theft, the more it was a disgrace.

I would not end these details if I wanted to follow all the paths by which I passed from the sublimity of heroism to the baseness of a good-for-nothing during my apprenticeship. Nevertheless, while adopting the vices of my condition I could not adopt its tastes completely. I was bored with my comrades' amusements, and when excessive restraint had also repelled me from work I was bored with everything. That brought me back to the taste for reading which I had lost for a long time. These readings, taken away from my work, became a new crime, which attracted new punishments to me. Irritated by constraint, this taste became a passion, soon a rage. La Tribu, a famous book lender furnished me with all sorts. Good and bad, all were acceptable, I did not choose at all; I read them all with equal voracity. I read at the workbench, I read while going to do my errands, I read on the toilet and in this way forgot whole hours, my head turned by the reading, I could do nothing but read. My master spied on me, surprised me, beat me, took my books. How many volumes were torn up, burned, thrown out of windows! How many works were left with volumes missing at la Tribu's! When I no longer had anything to pay her I gave her my shirts, my ties, my togs;[90] my three sous of pocket money were brought to her regularly every Sunday.

Here then, I will be told, money became necessary. That is true; but that was when reading deprived me of all activity. Having abandoned myself completely to my new taste I did nothing but read, I did not want anything more. This is yet again one of my characteristic differences. At the height of a certain habit of being a trifle distracts me, changes me, attaches me, finally impassions me, and then I forget everything. I think about nothing but the new object that occupies me. My heart beat with impatience to leaf through the new book I had in my pocket; I took it out as soon as I was alone and no longer thought about rummaging through my master's workshop. I even have trouble believing I would have stolen even if I had had more costly passions. Limited as I was to the present moment, it was not within my turn of mind to organize myself for the future that way. La Tribu gave me credit, the advances were small, and when I had pocketed my book, I no longer thought about anything. The money that came to me naturally passed in the same way to that woman, and when she became pressing, nothing was in my hand more quickly than my own belongings. To steal in advance was too much foresight, and to steal to pay was not even a temptation.

As a result of quarrels, blows, furtive and poorly chosen readings, my disposition became taciturn, wild, my head began to be spoiled, and I lived like a true werewolf. Nevertheless, if my taste did not preserve me from flat and insipid books, my good fortune preserved me from obscene and licentious books; not that la Tribu, a woman who was accommodating in every respect, had any scruples about lending them to me. But to enhance them she named them to me with an air of mystery which precisely forced me to refuse them, as much out of disgust as out of shame, and chance seconded my modest disposition so well, that I was more than thirty years old[91] before I had cast my eyes on any of those dangerous books that a fine Lady in high society finds inconvenient, in that one can, she says,[92] read them only with one hand.[93]

In less than a year I exhausted la Tribu's slender stock, and then I found myself cruelly unoccupied during my leisure time. Cured of my childish and roguish tastes by the one for reading, and even by my readings, which—although they were chosen unselectively and were often bad— nevertheless led my heart back to nobler feelings than the ones given to me by my station. Disgusted with everything within my grasp, and feeling everything that might have tempted me to be too far from me, I saw nothing possible that could gratify my heart. For a long time my agitated senses demanded from me an enjoyment whose object I could not even imagine. I was as far from the genuine one as if I had had no sex at all, and already pubescent and sensitive, I sometimes thought about my follies, but I saw nothing beyond them. In this strange situation my restless imagination made a choice that saved me from myself and calmed my nascent sensuality. This was to nourish itself on the situations which had interested me in my readings, to recall them, to change them, to combine them, to appropriate them to myself so much that I became one of the characters I imagined, that I always saw myself in the most agreeable positions in harmony with my taste, that finally the fictive condition into which I had just thoroughly placed myself made me forget my real condition with which I was so discontent. This love of imaginary objects and this facility at occupying myself with them disgusted me completely with everything that surrounded me, and determined that taste for solitude, which has always remained with me since then. More than once in what follows one will see the bizarre effects of this inclination, in appearance so misanthropic and so somber, but which in fact comes from a too affectionate, too loving, too tender heart which—for lack of finding existing ones that resemble it—is forced to feed itself with fictions. For the present, it is enough for me to have pointed out the origin and first cause of a penchant that has modified all my passions, and which, repressing them by themselves, has always rendered me lazy in acting because of too much ardor in desiring.

Thus I reached my sixteenth year, restless, discontent with everything and with myself, without the tastes of my station, without the pleasures of my age, devoured by desires whose object I did not know, crying without any reason for tears, sighing without knowing what for; in sum, tenderly indulging my chimeras for lack of seeing anything around me worthy of them. On Sundays my comrades came to find me after service to go frolic with them. I would have willingly slipped away from them if I could: but once in the spirit of their games, I was more ardent and I went farther than anyone else; difficult both to start and to hold back. That was always my constant inclination. In our walks outside the city I always went forward without thinking about returning, unless others thought about it for me. Twice I was caught; the gates were closed before I could reach them. One can imagine how I was treated the next day, and the second time I was promised such a welcome for the third, that I resolved not to expose myself to it. Nevertheless, this third time which was dreaded so much did happen.[94] My vigilance was made worthless by an accursed Captain named M. Minutoli, who always closed the gate at which he was on watch a half hour before the others.[95] I was returning with two comrades. Half a league from the City I hear the tattoo being sounded; I double my pace; I hear the drum beat, I run as fast as my legs can take me: I arrive out of breath, bathed in sweat: my heart beats; from afar I see the soldiers at their post; I run up, I shout with a choking voice. It was too late. Twenty steps from the advance guard, I see the first bridge raised. I shudder upon seeing those horns in the air, terrible, sinister and fatal omen of the inevitable fate that was beginning for me at that moment.

In the first outburst of my sorrow I threw myself on the bank, and bit the ground. Laughing at their misfortune, my comrades instantly made their choice. I also made mine, but it was in a different manner. On the very spot I swore never to return to my master; and the next day, when they returned to the city at the opening of the gates, I said farewell to them forever, asking them only to inform my cousin Bernard in secret of the resolution I had made, and of the place where he could see me one more time.

Being more separated from him at my entrance into apprenticeship, I saw him less. Nevertheless for some time we got together on Sundays: but insensibly each of us acquired other habits, and we saw each other more rarely. I am persuaded that his mother contributed a lot to this change. He was a boy from the high city: I, a paltry apprentice, I was no longer anything but a child of St. Gervais.[96] There was no longer equality between us in spite of our birth; to frequent my company was to fall beneath his rank. Nevertheless, the connections between us did not cease completely, and since he was a boy with a good natural disposition, sometimes he followed his heart rather than his mother's lessons. Having learned about my resolution, he hastened, not to dissuade me from it or to share it with me, but to put some pleasantness into my flight by means of some small gifts; for my own resources could not take me very far. Among other things he gave me a little sword with which I was very much taken, which I carried as far as Turin, where need made me get rid of it, and where I passed it, as they say, through my body.[97] The more I have reflected since then at the way he behaved with me in this critical moment, the more I am persuaded that he was following his mother's and perhaps his father's instructions; for it is impossible that, left to himself, he would not have made some effort to keep me there, or that he would not have been tempted to follow me: but nothing of the sort. He encouraged me in my plan rather than dissuading me from it: then when he saw me well resolved, he left me without many tears. We never wrote or saw each other again; it is a shame. He had an essentially good character: we were made to love each other.

Before abandoning myself to the fatality of my destiny, permit me to turn my eyes for a moment onto the one that naturally awaited me, if I had fallen into the hands of a better master. Nothing was more suited to my disposition nor more fit to make me happy, than the tranquil and obscure condition of a good artisan, above all in undisputed classes, such as the engraver's is at Geneva. This condition, lucrative enough to give an easy subsistence, and not enough to lead to wealth, would have limited my ambition for the rest of my days, and leaving me a decent leisure for cultivating moderate tastes, it would have kept me in my sphere without offering me any means for leaving it. Having an imagination rich enough to adorn all conditions with its chimeras, powerful enough to transport me, so to speak, at my will from one to another, it mattered little to me in which I was in fact. It could not have been so far from where I was to the first castle in Spain that I could not have easily settled there. From this alone it followed that the simplest condition, the one that gave the least worry and fewest cares, the one that left the mind the most free, was the one that suited me best, and that was precisely my own. In the bosom of my religion, my fatherland, my family and my friends, I would have passed a peaceful and sweet life, such as my character needed, in the uniformity of a labor to my taste, and of a society in harmony with my heart. I would have been a good Christian, good citizen, good father of a family, good friend, good worker, good man in everything. I would have loved my station; perhaps I would have honored it, and after having passed a simple and obscure, but even and sweet life, I would have died peacefully in the bosom of my own people. Doubtless soon forgotten, at least I would have been missed for as long as I might be remembered.

Instead of that . . . what picture am I going to draw? Ah! Let us not anticipate the miseries of my life! I will be occupying my readers only too much with this sad subject.[98]

Book II[1]

The moment I executed the project of flight appeared just as charming to me as the moment when fear suggested it to me had appeared sad. While I was still a child, to leave my country, my relatives, my protection, my resources, to leave a half-finished apprenticeship without knowing my profession well enough to live from it; to abandon myself to the horrors of poverty without seeing any means of leaving it; to expose myself to all the temptations of vice and despair in the age of weakness and innocence; to seek from afar evils, errors, snares, slavery, and death, under a yoke much more inflexible than the one I had not been able to bear; that was what I was going to do, that is the perspective I should have envisaged. How different was the one I depicted for myself! The independence which I believed I had acquired was the only feeling that influenced me. Free and master of myself, I believed I could do everything, attain everything: I had only to leap in order to soar and fly[2] through the air. I would enter safely into the vast space of the world; my merit was going to fill it: at each step I was going to find feasts, treasures, adventures, friends ready to serve me, mistresses eager to please me: by merely showing myself I was going to occupy the universe with me: not however the whole universe; I would exempt it to some degree, I did not need that much. A charming social circle was enough for me without bothering myself with the rest. My moderation inscribed me inside a narrow but delightfully chosen sphere, where I was assured of reigning. A single Castle circumscribed my ambition. Favorite of the Lord and Lady, lover of the Damsel, friend of the brother, and protector of the neighbors, I was content; I needed nothing more.

While waiting for this modest future, I wandered around the City for several days, lodging with peasants of my acquaintance, who all received me with more kindness than city dwellers would have. They welcomed me, lodged me, fed me too kindly to take any credit for it. This could not be called giving charity; they did not put enough of an air of superiority into it.

As a result of traveling and wandering around the world, I went as far as Confignon, territory of Savoy two leagues from Geneva. The curate was named M. de Pontverre. This name, famous in the history of the Republic, struck me very much. I was curious to see how the descendants of the Gentlemen of the spoon were formed.[3] I went to see M. de Pont-verre. He received me well, spoke to me about the heresy of Geneva, the authority of the Holy Mother Church, and gave me dinner. I found little to answer to arguments that ended this way, and I judged that curates at whose home one dined so well were worth at least as much as our Ministers. I was certainly more learned than M. de Pontverre, Gentleman though he was;[4] but I was too good a guest to be as good a theologian, and his wine from Frangi—which seemed excellent to me—argued so victoriously for him, that I would have blushed to shut the mouth of such a good host. Thus, I gave way, or at least I did not openly resist. To see the discretion I made use of one would have believed me to be false; one would be mistaken. I was only decent, that is certain. Flattery, or rather condescension, is not always a vice, it is more often a virtue, especially in young people. The kindness with which a man treats us attaches us to him; one does not give way to him in order to deceive him, one does so in order not to make him sad, not to return him harm for good. What interest did M. de Pontverre have in welcoming me, in treating me well, in wishing to convince me? None other than my own. My young heart told itself that. I was touched with gratitude and respect for the good Priest. I felt my superiority;[5] I did not want to harass him as the reward for his hospitality. There was no hypocritical motive at all in this conduct: I did not dream of changing religion; and very far from growing accustomed so quickly to that idea, I envisaged it only with a horror that ought to have kept it away from me for a long time; I only wanted not to anger these people who were cajoling me with that intention; I wanted to cultivate their benevolence and to leave them the hope of success by appearing less well armed than I was in fact. My fault in that resembled the coquetry of decent women, who to succeed in their goals sometimes know how to raise hopes for more than they wish to carry out without permitting anything or promising anything.

Reason, pity, love of order assuredly demanded that, far from lending themselves to my folly, people should keep me away from the ruin to which I was running, by sending me back to my family. That is what every truly virtuous man would have done or attempted to do. But although M. de Pontverre was a good man, he was assuredly not a virtuous man. On the contrary he was a devout man who knew no other virtue than worshipping images and saying the rosary; a sort of Missionary who imagined nothing better for the good of the faith, than to make libels against the ministers of Geneva. Far from thinking of sending me home he took advantage of the desire I had to get away from it, to make it impossible for me to return there even if I acquired the desire to do so.[6] There was every chance that he was sending me to perish from misery or to become a good-for-nothing. That was not what he saw. He saw a soul removed from heresy and restored to the Church. Decent man or good-for-nothing, what did that matter as long as I went to Mass? It should not be thought, moreover, that this manner of thinking is peculiar to Catholics; it is that of every dogmatic religion in which belief is made into the essential thing rather than deeds.

"God calls you," M. de Pontverre said to me, "Go to Annecy; there you will find a very charitable good Lady, whom the good deeds of the King put into a position to save other souls from the error from which she herself has departed." This was Mme de Warens, a new convert, whom the priests in effect forced to share with the mob that came to sell its faith, a pension of two thousand francs given to her by the King of Sardinia. I felt myself very humiliated to need a very charitable good Lady. I would have much preferred that they give me necessities, but not that they give me charity, and a devout woman was not extremely attractive to me. Nevertheless, hastened by M. de Pontverre, by the hunger that spurred me on; also delighted to make a trip and to have a goal, I made my decision, although with difficulty, and I left for Annecy. I could have been there easily in a day; but I did not hurry, I took three. I did not see a chateau to the right or left without going to seek the adventure that I was sure was waiting for me there. I did not dare to enter the chateau or knock; for I was very timid. But I sang under the window that seemed most promising, very surprised, after having shouted myself out of breath for a long time, not to see either Ladies or Damsels appear attracted by the beauty of my voice or the piquancy of my songs; considering that I knew admirable ones which my comrades had taught me, and which I sang admirably.

Finally I arrive; I see Mme de Warens. This epoch of my life determined my character; I cannot resolve to pass over it lightly. I was in the middle of my sixteenth year. Without being what is called a handsome boy, I had a fine little figure; I had a pretty foot, a fine leg, an open manner, an animated physiognomy, a delicate mouth,[7] black eyebrows and hair, eyes that were small and even deep-set, but which forcefully cast forth the fire with which my blood was inflamed. Unfortunately I knew nothing about all that, and in my life I have happened to think about my appearance only when it was too late to take advantage of it. Thus I had the timidity both of my age and of a very loving natural disposition, always troubled by the fear of displeasing. Moreover, although I had a sufficiently cultivated mind, since I had never seen the world I was totally lacking in manners, and my knowledge, far from compensating for them, served only to intimidate me further by making me feel how much I lacked them.

Fearing thus that my bearing did not predispose in my favor, I made use of other expedients, and I wrote a fine letter in the style of an Orator, in which, stitching together bookish sentences with an apprentice's idiom, I deployed all my eloquence to win over Mme de Warens's benevolence.[8] I enclosed M. de Pontverre's letter inside of mine, and I set out for that terrible audience. I did not find Mme de Warens in; they tell me that she has just left to go to Church. It was Palm Sunday of the year 1728. I run to follow her: I see her, I overtake her, I speak to her. . . . I ought to remember the place; since that time I have often watered it with my tears and covered it with my kisses. Why can I not surround that happy place with a golden railing![9] Why can I not attract the homages of the whole earth to it! Whoever loves to honor the monuments of men's salvation ought to approach it only on his knees.

It was a passageway behind her house, between a stream on the right hand which separated it from the garden, and the courtyard wall on the left, leading to the Church of the Franciscans by means of a blind door. About to enter this door, Mme de Warens turns around at the sound of my voice. What becomes of me at that sight! I had drawn for myself a very sullen devout old woman: M. de Pontverre's good Lady could be nothing else in my opinion. I see a face full of charms, beautiful blue eyes full of sweetness, a dazzling complexion, the outline of an enchanting breast. Nothing escaped the rapid glance of the young proselyte; for I became hers at that moment; certain that a religion preached by such missionaries could not fail to lead to paradise. Smiling, she takes the letter I present to her with a trembling hand, opens it, casts a glance at the one by M. de Pontverre, comes back to mine which she reads completely, and which she would have read again if her lackey had not informed her that it was time to enter. "Ah! my child," she said to me in a tone that made me tremble, "You are very young to be roving around the country; it is truly a shame." Then without waiting for my answer, she added, "Go wait for me at my house; say that they are to give you something to eat. After the Mass I will come to chat with you."

Louise Eleonor de Warens was a Mlle de la Tour de Pil, a noble and ancient family of Vevey, a City in the Pays de Vaud.[10] When very young she had married M. de Warens of the house of Loys, eldest son of M. de Villardin of Lausanne. This marriage, which produced no children, was not very successful; pushed by some domestic distress, Mme de Warens took the opportunity of King Victor Amadeus being at Evian to cross the

lake and come to throw herself at the feet of this Prince; thus abandoning her husband,[11] her family and her country, by means of a giddiness
rather similar to my own, and about which she too had time enough to
cry. The King, who loved to play the Catholic zealot, took her under his
protection, gave her a pension of fifteen hundred Piedmontese Livres,[12]
which was a lot for a Prince who was so little lavish, and seeing that he
was thought to be in love with her because of that welcome, he sent her
to Annecy, escorted by a detachment of his Guards, where, under the direction of Michel Gabriel de Bernex titular Bishop of Geneva, she made
her abjuration at the Convent of the Visitation.

She had been there for six years[13] when I came, and she was then
twenty-eight, having been born with the century. She had the sort of
beauty that preserved itself, because it is more in the physiognomy than
in the features; also hers was still in all its first radiance.[14] She had a caressing and tender manner, a very sweet glance, an angelic smile, a mouth in
the same proportion as mine, ash-blonde hair of an uncommon beauty,
and to which she gave a careless turn which rendered it very piquant. She
was small of stature, even short, and a little plump in the waist, although
without deformity. But it was impossible to see a more beautiful head,
a more beautiful bosom, more beautiful hands and more beautiful arms.

Her education had been very mixed. Like me she had lost her mother
from her birth and, indiscriminately receiving instruction as it was presented to her, she had learned a little from her governess, a little from her
father, a little from her teachers,[15] and much from her lovers; above all
from a M. de Tavel,[16] who, having some taste and knowledge, adorned
the person he loved with them. But so many different sorts of instruction
harmed each other, and the paucity of order that she put into them prevented her diverse studies from extending her mind's natural soundness.
Thus, although she had some principles of philosophy and physics, she
did not fail to acquire the taste her father had for empirical medicine[17]
and for alchemy; she made elixirs, dyes, balms, medical precipitates, she
claimed to have secrets. Taking advantage of her weakness, charlatans fell
upon her, plagued her, ruined her and in the midst of furnaces and drugs
used up her mind, her talents and her charms, with which she could have
brought delight to the best societies.

But if some vile rogues abused her poorly directed education in a way
that obscured the enlightenment of her reason, her excellent heart was
proof against them and always remained the same: her loving and gentle
character, her sensitivity toward the unfortunate, her inextinguishable
kindness, her gay, open, and frank mood never changed; and even at the
drawing near of old age, in the bosom of indigence, ills, diverse calami-

ties, the serenity of her beautiful soul preserved all the gaiety of her finest days until the end of her life.

Her errors came to her from a fund of inexhaustible activity which ceaselessly required occupation. It was not women's intrigues that she needed, it was enterprises to perform and direct. She was born for great affairs. In her place Mme de Longueville would have been only a busy-body; in Mme de Longueville's place she would have governed the State.[18] Her talents had been misplaced, and what would have brought about her glory in a more elevated situation brought about her ruin in the one in which she lived. In things that were within her grasp she always laid out her plan in her head and always saw her object in large scale. As a result, using means proportioned to her aims more than to her strength, she failed through the fault of other people, and when her project happened to fail she was ruined where others would have lost almost nothing. This taste for business that did her so much harm, did her at least one great good in her monastic retreat, by keeping her from settling there for the rest of her days as she had been tempted to do. The uniform and simple life of Nuns, their little babbling in the parlor, all that could not gratify a mind always in motion, which, each day forming new systems, needed freedom in order to abandon itself to them. The good Bishop de Bernex, with less intelligence than François de Sales, resembled him on numerous points, and Mme de Warens, whom he called his daughter and who re-sembled Mme de Chantal in many other points, could have still resembled her in her retirement, if her taste had not turned her from the idleness of a convent.[19] If this lovable woman did not abandon herself to the tri-fling practices of devotion that seemed to suit a new convert living under the direction of a Prelate, it was not at all from lack of zeal. Whatever the motive for her change of religion might have been, she was sincere in the one she had embraced. She might repent having committed the fault, but she did not desire to return from it. She not only died a good Catholic, she lived as one in good faith, and I—who thinks he has read in the depths of her soul—dare to affirm that it was solely from aversion for pretension that she did not play the pious woman at all in public. She had too solid a piety to affect devotion. But this is not the place to enlarge upon her principles; I will have other occasions to speak about them.

Let those who deny the sympathy of souls explain, if they can, how from the first interview, from the first word, from the first glance, Mme de Warens inspired me with, not only the most lively attachment, but a perfect confidence that was never disappointed. Let us assume that what I felt for her was genuinely love; which will appear at least doubtful to anyone who follows the history of our relations; how did it happen that from its birth this passion was accompanied by the feelings it inspires least; peace of heart, calm, serenity, security, certainty? How did it happen that upon approaching for the first time a lovable, cultured, dazzling woman;[20] a Lady of a station superior to mine, whose like I had never encountered, the one upon whom my fate in some manner depended from the greater or lesser interest that she would take in it; how, I say, with all that did I find myself instantaneously as free, as much at my ease, as if I had been perfectly sure of pleasing her? How did it happen that I did not have a moment of embarrassment, timidity, discomfort? Naturally bashful, disconcerted, having never seen the world, how did I take with her from the first day, from the first instant easy-going manners, tender language, the familiar tone I had ten years later, when the greatest intimacy made them natural? Does one have love, I do not say without desires— I had them[21]—but without restlessness, without jealousy? Does one not wish at least to learn from the object one loves whether one is loved? This is a question which it no more entered my mind to ask her once in my life, than to ask myself whether I loved myself, and she was never any more curious with me. There was certainly something singular in my feelings for this charming woman, and in what follows one will find peculiarities that one does not expect.

The question was what I would become, and to chat about this more at leisure she kept me to dine. This was the first meal in my life in which I lacked an appetite, and her chambermaid, who also served us, said that I was the first traveler of my age and mettle that she had seen lacking one. This remark, which did not harm me in her mistress's mind, fell a little directly on a fat boor who was dining with us, and who devoured a decent meal for six people all by himself. As for me, I was in a rapture that did not allow me to eat. My heart fed itself on a completely new feeling with which it occupied my whole being: it did not leave me wits for any other function.

Mme de Warens wanted to know the details of my little story; in order to tell them to her I found again all the fire[22] I had lost at my master's. The more I interested this excellent soul in my favor, the more she pitied the fate to which I was going to expose myself. Her tender compassion was marked in her manner, in her glance, in her gestures. She did not dare to exhort me to return to Geneva. In her position that would be a crime of treason against Catholicism, and she did not forget how much she was under surveillance and how much her speeches were weighed. But she spoke to me about my father's affliction in such a touching tone, that it could easily be seen that she would have approved of my going to console him. She did not know how much she was pleading against herself without meaning to. Aside from the fact that my resolution was formed as I believe I have said; the more eloquent and persuasive I found her, the more her speeches went to my heart, the less I could resolve to remove myself from her. I felt that to return to Geneva was to put an almost insurmountable barrier between her and me. At least it was to take back the step I had taken, and to which it was better to hold myself once and for all. Thus I held myself to it. When she saw that her efforts were useless Mme de Warens did not push them far enough to compromise herself, but she said to me with a look of commiseration, "Poor little one, you must go where God calls you, but when you are grown you will remember me." I believe that she herself did not think that this prediction would be so cruelly fulfilled.

The difficulty remained in its entirety. How to live outside my country when I was so young? Barely half-way through my apprenticeship I was very far from knowing my profession. Even if I had known it, I would not have been able to live from it in Savoy, a country too poor to have arts. Being forced to make a pause to rest his jaws, the Boor who was dining for[23] us proposed the opinion which he said came from Heaven, and which—to judge from the consequences—came much sooner from the opposite side. It was that I should go to Turin, where, in a Hospice established for the instruction of catechumens, I would have, he said, temporal and spiritual sustenance, until, having entered into the bosom of the Church, I found a place that suited me through the charity of good souls. "With regard to the expenses for the trip," continued my man, "If Madame proposes this holy work to him, His Grace Monseigneur the Bishop, will not fail to wish to provide for it charitably, and Madame the Baronne who is so charitable," he said bowing over his plate, "will surely be prompt to contribute also."

I found all this charity very harsh; I was sick at heart, I said nothing, and although she did not seize this project with as much ardor as it was offered, Mme de Warens was content to respond that each should contribute to the good according to his power and that she would speak of it to Monseigneur: but my Devil of a man, who feared that she might not speak about it in accordance with his taste, and who had his little interest in this business, ran to warn the chaplains and taught the good priests so well what to say, that when Mme de Warens—who feared this trip for me—wished to speak to the Bishop about it, she found that it was a settled business, and he instantly gave her the money destined for my little viaticum. She did not dare to insist upon making me stay: I was nearing the age at which a woman of her age could not modestly want to keep a young man near her.

Since my trip was managed in this way by the people who were taking charge of me, it was very necessary for me to submit, and I even did so without much repugnance. Although Turin was farther than Geneva, I judged that being the capital,[24] it had closer connections with Annecy than a city foreign to the State and Religion, and then, leaving in order to obey Mme de Warens, I looked at myself as still living under her direction; that was even more than living near her. Finally the idea of a great journey gratified my mania for strolling which already was beginning to break out. To me it seemed fine to cross the mountains at my age,[25] and to raise myself above my comrades by all the height of the Alps. To see the country is a bait which a Genevan hardly resists: thus I gave my consent. My boor was leaving in two days with his wife. I was entrusted and commended to them. My purse was given to them reinforced by Mme de Warens who in addition secretly gave me a little gratuity to which she added ample instructions, and we left on Holy Wednesday.

The day after my departure from Annecy, my father arrived there following my trail with a M. Rival his friend, a watchmaker like him, a man of intelligence, even fine intelligence, who wrote better poems than La Motte[26] and spoke almost as well as he, and furthermore a perfectly decent man, but his misplaced literary activity ended only by making one of his sons into an actor.[27]

These Gentlemen saw Mme de Warens, and contented themselves with weeping over my fate along with her, instead of following me and catching me, as they could have done easily, since they were on horse and I was on foot. The same thing had happened to my Uncle Bernard. He had come to Confignon, and, knowing that I was at Annecy, he returned from there to Geneva. It seemed that my family conspired with my star to abandon me to the destiny that awaited me. My brother had been lost[28] by a similar negligence, and so well lost that it was never learned what had become of him.

My father was not only a man of honor; he was a man of an unfailing probity and he had one of those strong souls which make great virtues. Furthermore, he was a good father,[29] above all for me. He loved me very tenderly but he also loved his pleasures, and other tastes had cooled paternal affection a little since I was living far from him. He had remarried at Nyon, and although his wife was no longer young enough to give me brothers, she had relatives: that made another family, other objects, a new household, which no longer recalled my memory so often. My father was growing old and had no property to sustain his old age. My brother and I had some property from my mother, the revenue of which was to belong to my father during our absence. This idea did not offer itself to him directly and did not prevent him from doing his duty, but it acted secretly without his being aware of it himself, and sometimes lessened his zeal, which he might have pushed farther without it. This is, I believe, why, having come at first to Annecy on my trail, he did not follow me to Chambéry where he was morally certain of catching me. This is again why, although I often went to see him after my flight, I always received a father's caresses from him, but without great efforts to detain me.

This behavior from a father whose tenderness and virtue I knew so well has caused me to make reflections about myself, which have contributed not a little to keeping my heart healthy. From them I have drawn this great maxim of morality, perhaps the only one of use in practice, to avoid situations that put our duties in opposition with our interests, and which show us our good in the harm of someone else: certain that whatever sincere love of virtue one brings to such situations, sooner or later one weakens without being aware of it, and one becomes unjust and bad in fact, without having ceased to be just and good in the soul.[30]

This maxim—strongly impressed in the depths of my heart and put into practice, although a bit late, in all my behavior—is one of those that have given me the most bizarre and crazy manner in public and above all among my acquaintances. The wish to be original and to act differently from others has been imputed to me. In truth I hardly was thinking about acting either as others do or otherwise. I sincerely desired to do what was good. With all my strength I avoided situations that might give me an interest contrary to the interest of another man, and as a consequence a secret although involuntary desire for the harm of that man.

Two years ago[31] My Lord Marshal wanted to put me in his will.[32] I opposed it with all my strength. I informed him that nothing in the world could make me want to know that I was in the will of anyone at all, and much less in his. He yielded; now he wants to give me a life pension, and I do not oppose it. It will be said that I find my advantage in this change: that may be. But oh my benefactor and my father, if I have the misfortune to survive you I know that in losing you I have everything to lose and nothing to gain.

In my view that is good philosophy, the only one truly suited to the human heart. Each day I am more and more filled with its profound solidity, and I have examined it in different ways in all of my latest writings; but the public which is frivolous has not been able to notice it in them. After I finish this undertaking, if I live long enough to take up another, I propose to give such a charming and striking example of this same maxim in the sequel to *Emile* that my reader will be compelled to pay attention to it.[33] But this is enough of reflections for a traveler; it is time to take up my route again.

I took it up more pleasantly than I ought to have expected, and my

Boor was not as surly as he appeared to be. He was a middle-aged man who wore his graying black hair in a tail; he had a grenadier's manner, a strong voice, rather gay, walking well, eating better, and was a Jack of all trades for lack of being master of any. I believe he had proposed to establish some kind of factory or other at Annecy. Mme de Warens had not failed to give in to the project, and he was making the well-defrayed trip to Turin in order to try to get it approved by the Minister. Our man had the talent of intriguing by always positioning himself with the priests, and, from playing at being eager to serve them, he had acquired from their school a certain devout jargon which he used ceaselessly, priding himself on being a great preacher. He even knew a Latin passage from the Bible, and it was as if he had known a thousand of them, because he repeated it a thousand times a day. For the rest, he rarely lacked money if he knew it was in someone else's purse. Nevertheless, he was more clever than knavish, and when he declaimed his tirades in the tone of a recruiting sergeant he resembled Peter the Hermit,[34] preaching the crusade with his sword at his side.

As for Mme Sabran his wife, she was a good enough woman, more tranquil during the day than at night. Since I always slept in their room, her noisy insomnia often awakened me, and would have awakened me even more if I had understood the reason for it. But I did not even suspect it, and on this score my stupidity left all the care for my education to nature alone.

I proceeded gaily with my devout guide and his sprightly companion. No accident troubled my journey; I was in the most fortunate situation of body and mind in which I have been in my life. Young, vigorous, full of health, security, confidence in myself and in others, I was in that short but precious moment of life in which its expansive fullness extends our being through all our sensations so to speak, and in our eyes embellishes all of nature with the charm of our existence. My sweet restlessness had an object that rendered it less[35] wandering and settled my imagination. I looked at myself as the product, student, friend, almost the lover of Mme de Warens. The obliging things she had said, the little caresses she had given me, the so tender interest she had seemed to take in me, her charming glances which to me seemed full of love because they inspired me with it; all this nourished my ideas during the walk, and caused me to dream delightfully. No fear, no doubt about my fate troubled these reveries. In my view to send me to Turin was to engage herself to provide for my living there, to acquire a suitable position for me there. I no longer had any concern about myself; others had burdened themselves with this care. Thus I walked lightly, relieved of this weight; young desires, enchanting hope, brilliant projects filled my soul. All the objects I saw seemed to me to be guarantees of my impending happiness. In the houses I imagined rustic feasts, in the fields frolicsome games, along the waterways, bathing, outings, fishing, on the trees delicious fruits, under their shadows voluptuous tête-à-têtes, on the mountains tubs of milk and cream, a charming idleness, peace, simplicity, the pleasure of going along without knowing where. In sum, nothing struck my eyes without carrying some attraction to my heart for enjoyment. The grandeur, the variety, the real beauty of the spectacle made this attraction worthy of reason; even vanity mixed its barb into it. So young, to go to Italy, to have seen so many countries already, to follow Hannibal across the mountains seemed to me a glory beyond my age.[36] Join to all this frequent and good stops, a big appetite and enough to satisfy it: for in truth it was not worth the trouble for me to do without, and in comparison to M. Sabran's dinner mine appeared to be nothing.

In the whole course of my life I do not remember having had an interval more perfectly exempt from care and trouble, than the one of seven or eight days we put into this trip;[37] for Mme Sabran's pace—upon which it was necessary to govern ours—made it into nothing but a long stroll. This remembrance left me the keenest taste for everything relating to it, above all for mountains and for pedestrian trips. Only during my heyday did I travel on foot, and always with delight. Soon duties, business, baggage to carry forced me to play the Gentleman and take carriages; gnawing cares, bothers, inconvenience got into them along with me, and since then—unlike previously in my travels when I felt only the pleasure of going—I have no longer felt anything but the need to arrive. In Paris for a long time I looked for two comrades with the same taste as myself, who each wanted to devote fifty Louis of his purse and a year of his time to making a tour of Italy on foot together, without any other retinue than a boy who would carry a bag with our necessities for us. Many people showed themselves enchanted with this project in appearance: but at bottom all of them took it for a pure Castle in Spain about which one chatted in conversation without wanting to execute it in fact. I remember that by speaking with passion about this project with Diderot and Grimm, I finally gave them a fancy for it. Once I believed the business settled; but it all came down to wanting to make a trip in writing, in which Grimm found nothing so pleasant as to cause Diderot to commit many impieties, and to cause me to be imprisoned by the Inquisition in his place.[38]

My regret at arriving at Turin so quickly was tempered by the pleasure of seeing a large city, and by the hope of soon cutting a figure worthy of myself there: for the fumes of ambition were already rising to my head;

I already looked at myself as infinitely above my former station as an apprentice; I was very far from foreseeing that in a short time I was going to be very far beneath it.[39]

Before going further I owe the reader my excuse or my justification both for the minute details into which I have just entered and for those into which I will enter in what follows, and which have no interest in his eyes. In the undertaking I have made of showing myself completely to the public, nothing of me must remain obscure or hidden to him; I must hold myself ceaselessly before his eyes, so that he might follow me in all the aberrations of my heart, in all the recesses of my life; so that he might not lose me from view for a single instant, for fear that, finding the smallest lacuna in my narrative, the smallest gap, and asking himself, what did he do during that time, he might accuse me of not having wanted to say everything. I am exposing myself enough to the malignity of men by my narratives without exposing myself even more by my silence.

My little savings were gone; I had babbled, and my indiscretion was not a pure loss for my guides. Mme Sabran found a way to pluck me all the way down to a little ribbon glazed with silver that Mme de Warens had given me for my little sword and which I missed more than all the rest: even the sword would have stayed in their hands if I had been less stubborn.[40] They had faithfully paid my expenses on the route, but they had left me nothing. I arrive at Turin without clothes, without money, without linen, and leaving all the honor of the fortune I was going to make very precisely to my merit alone.

I had some letters, I delivered them, and right away I was brought to the hospice of the catechumens,[41] to be instructed there in the religion for which I had been sold my sustenance. Upon entering I saw a big door with iron cross-bars, which was closed and double locked on my heels as soon as I entered. To me this commencement seemed more imposing than pleasant and was beginning to give me something to think about, when they made me enter a rather big room. The only furnishing I saw there was a wooden Altar mounted with a big crucifix at the far end of the room, and scattered around, four or five chairs also wooden which seemed to have been polished, but which were glossy only because of use and rubbing. In this assembly room were four or five hideous scoundrels, my comrades in instruction, and who seemed more like the Devil's bodyguard than aspirants for making themselves into children of God. Two of these rascals were Slavs who called themselves Jews and Moors, and who, as they admitted to me, spent their life crossing Spain and Italy embracing Christianity and having themselves baptized, everywhere that the profit was worth the trouble. Another iron door was opened, which divided in two a large balcony reigning over the Courtyard. From this door entered our sisters the catechumens, who like me had come to be regenerated, not by baptism, but by a solemn abjuration. They were certainly the greatest sluts and the nastiest looking[42] trollops who had ever infected the Lord's fold. Only one seemed pretty to me and rather interesting. She was about my age, perhaps one or two years older. She had roguish eyes which sometimes met mine. This gave me some desire to make her acquaintance; but during the almost two months that she still remained in that house (where she had already been for three) it was absolutely impossible for me to approach her; she was so guarded by our old wardress and plagued by the Holy missionary who worked on her conversion with more zeal than speed. She must have been extremely stupid, although she did not have the air of being so; for never were instructions so long. The holy man always found her in no condition to abjure; but she became bored with her cloister, and said she wanted to leave, Christian or not. It was necessary to take her at her word while she still consented to become a Christian, for fear that she might mutiny and no longer want to do so.

The little community was assembled in honor of the newcomer. They made us a short exhortation, to me to pledge myself to respond to the grace God gave me, to the others to invite them to grant me their prayers and to edify me by their examples. After which, when our virgins had returned to their cloister, I had the time to marvel completely at my ease at the one in which I found myself.

The next morning they assembled us anew for instruction, and it was then that I began to reflect for the first time on the step that I was going to make, and on the proceedings that had led me to it.

I have said, I am repeating, and perhaps I will repeat again, a thing of which I am more convinced every day; that is that if ever a child received a reasonable and sound education, it was I. Born into a family distinguished from the common people by its morals, I had received only lessons of wisdom and examples of honor from all my relatives. Although he was a man of pleasure, my father had, not only a reliable probity, but much religion. A man of gallantry in the social world and a Christian inside, early on he had inspired me with the feelings with which he was filled. Of my three aunts, all prudent and virtuous, the two elder were devout, and the third, a girl all at once full of graces, wit, and sense, was perhaps even more so than they were, although with less ostentation. From the bosom of this estimable family I passed to M. Lambercier, who, although a man of the Church and preacher, was a believer on the inside, and acted almost as well as he spoke. By means of gentle and judicious teachings his sister and he cultivated the principles of piety they found in my heart. These worthy people used such true, such cautious, such reasonable means for this, that far from being bored with the sermon, I never left it without being touched inside and without making resolutions to live well which I rarely failed to keep when I thought about them. At my aunt Bernard's home the devoutness bored me a little more because she made a trade of it. With my master I hardly thought about it any more, without nevertheless thinking differently. I did not find any young people who perverted me. I became a young rascal, but not a libertine.

Thus of religion I had all that a child of my age could have. I even had more of it, for why disguise my thought here? [43] My childhood was not at all that of a child. I always felt, I thought as a man. It was only in growing up that I returned into the ordinary class, upon being born I had left it. One will laugh to see me modestly present myself as a prodigy. So be it; but when one has laughed well, find a child who at six years of age is attached to novels, interested, carried away to the point of weeping hot tears at them; then I will feel my ridiculous vanity, and I will acknowledge that I am wrong.

Thus when I said that one must not speak to children at all about religion if one wants them to have some someday, and that they were incapable of knowing God even in our manner, I drew my sentiment from my observations, not from my own experience: I knew that it settled nothing for others.[44] Find a J.-J. Rousseau at six years old, and speak to him about God at seven, I assure you that you are running no risk.

It is felt, I believe, that for a child, and even for a man, to have some religion is to follow the one in which he is born. Sometimes one subtracts from it; one rarely adds to it;[45] dogmatic faith is a fruit of education. Other than this common principle that attaches me to the observances of my forefathers, I have the aversion peculiar to our city[46] for Catholicism, which is presented to us as an abominable idolatry, and whose Clergy are depicted under the blackest colors. This feeling went so far in me that at the beginning I never caught a glimpse of the inside of a Church, I never met a priest in a surplice, I never heard the bell of a procession without a shuddering of terror and fright which soon left me in cities, but which has often returned to me in country parishes, more similar to the ones in which I had first experienced it. It is true that this impression contrasted singularly with the memory of the blandishments which the curates of the area around Geneva willingly make to the children of the city.[47] At the same time that the bell of the viaticum scared me, the bell for the Mass or vespers reminded me of a dinner, a snack, fresh butter, fruits, dairy products. M. de Pontverre's good dinner had also produced a big effect. Thus I was easily made dizzy on all that. Only envisaging papism through its connections with amusements and love of good food, I had become familiar with the idea of living in it without difficulty; but that of entering solemnly into it was present to me only for a fleeting moment and in a distant future.[48] At that moment there was no longer a way to put myself off the track: I saw the sort of commitment I had made and its inevitable consequence with the most lively horror. The future neophytes I had around me were not suitable for sustaining my courage by their example, and I could not dissimulate to myself that the Holy work that I was going to perform was at bottom only the action of a scoundrel. Still very young I felt that whichever religion might be the true[49] one I was going to sell mine, and that, even if I chose well, I was going to lie to the Holy Spirit at the bottom of my heart and deserve the scorn of men. The more I thought about it, the more indignant I became against myself, and I bemoaned the fate that had led me there, as if this fate had not been my doing. There were moments in which these reflections became so strong that if I had found the gate open for an instant, I would certainly have escaped; but this was not possible for me, and this resolution did not maintain itself terribly strongly either.

Too many secret desires fought against it not to vanquish it. Moreover the obstinacy of the plan I had formed of not returning to Geneva; shame, even the difficulty of recrossing the mountains; the perplexity of seeing myself far from my country, without friends, without resources; all this combined to make me look at the remorse of my conscience as a tardy repentance; I pretended to reproach myself for what I had done in order to excuse what I was going to do. By aggravating the wrongs of the past, I looked at the future as their necessary consequence. I did not say to myself, "Nothing has been done yet and you can be innocent if you wish"; but I said to myself, "Bemoan the crime of which you have made yourself guilty, and which you have made it necessary to complete."

In fact, what rare strength of soul would have been necessary at my age to revoke everything I had been able to promise or to allow hope for up to then, in order to break the chains I had given myself, to declare intrepidly that I wanted to remain in the religion of my fathers, at the risk of everything that might happen? Such vigor did not belong to my age, and it is hardly probable that it would have succeeded. Things were too far along for them to let me contradict them, and the greater my resistance might have been, the more they would have made it into a law for themselves to overcome it one way or another.

The sophism that ruined me is the one made by the majority of men, who complain about lacking strength when it is already too late to make use of it. Virtue costs us only through our own fault, and if we always wanted to be wise, we would rarely need to be virtuous. But inclinations that would be easy to overcome sweep us away without resistance: we give way to slight temptations whose danger we scorn. Insensibly we fall into perilous situations from which we could easily have protected ourselves, but from which we can no longer extricate ourselves without heroic efforts that frighten us, and finally we fall into the abyss, while saying to God, "Why did You make me so weak?" But in spite of us He answers to our consciences, "I made you too weak to leave the chasm, because I made you strong enough not to fall into it."

I did not precisely form the resolution to make myself a Catholic; but seeing the end still distant, I took the time to become used to this idea, and while waiting I imagined some unforeseen event which would get me out of the perplexity. To gain some time I resolved to make the finest defense I could. Soon my vanity excused me from pondering my resolution, and as soon as I noticed that sometimes I perplexed those who wanted to instruct me, I needed nothing more to seek to overcome them completely. I even put a very ridiculous zeal into this enterprise: for while they worked on me I wanted to work on them. I naively believed that it was necessary only to convince them in order to induce them to become Protestants.

Thus they did not find quite as much facility in me as they expected, either with respect to enlightenment or with respect to will. Protestants are generally better educated than Catholics. This ought to be so: the doctrine of the former requires discussion, that of the latter submission. The Catholic ought to adopt the decision he is given, the Protestant ought to learn to decide for himself. They knew that; but they did not expect great difficulties for experienced people from either my station or my age. Moreover, I had not yet made my first communion, nor received the instruction related to it: they already knew this; but they did not know that on the other hand I had been well taught at M. Lambercier's, and that further I had in my possession a little armory very inconvenient to these Gentlemen in the *History of the Church and Empire*[50] which I had almost learned by heart with my father, and since then just about forgotten, but which came back to me, to the extent that the dispute became heated.

An old priest, short, but rather venerable, gave us the first meeting in common. For my comrades this meeting was a catechism rather than a controversy, and he had more to do in instructing them than in resolving their objections. It was not the same with me. When my turn came, I stopped him on everything, I did not spare him any of the difficulties[51] I could make for him. That made the meeting very long, and very boring for the participants. My old priest talked a lot, became heated, beat around the bush, and withdrew from the business by saying that he did not understand French very well. The next day, out of fear that my indiscreet objections might scandalize my comrades, they took me aside into another room with another priest who was younger, a fine talker, that is to say a maker of long phrases, and self-satisfied if ever a Doctor of the Church was. However I did not let myself be too overwhelmed by his imposing appearance, and feeling that I was holding my own after all, I began to answer him with enough assurance and to batter him on all sides the best I could. He thought he could knock me down with St. Augustine, St. Gregory, and the other fathers, and with unbelievable surprise he found that I handled all those fathers almost as nimbly as he did; it was not that I had ever read them, nor perhaps had he; but I had remembered many passages drawn from my Le Sueur; and as soon as he cited one to me, without disputing about his citation I retorted with another from the same father, and which often perplexed him very much. He prevailed in the end, however, for two reasons. First, he was the stronger, and feeling myself at his mercy so to speak, I judged very well that however young I might be I must not push him to the limit; for I saw well enough that the little old priest had not taken a liking either to my erudition or to me. The other reason was that the young priest had studied some and I had not done so at all. That meant that he put into his manner of arguing a method that I could not follow, and, as soon as he felt himself assailed with an unforeseen objection, he put it off to the next day, saying that I was straying from the present subject. Sometimes he even rejected all my citations maintaining that they were false, and offering to go find the book for me, challenged me to find them. He felt that he was not risking very much, and that with all my borrowed erudition, I was too little experienced in handling books, and too poor a Latinist to find a passage in a fat volume, even if I was assured it was there. I even suspect him of having practiced the unfaithfulness of which he accused the Ministers, and of having sometimes fabricated passages in order to extricate himself from an objection that inconvenienced him.

While these little quibbles went on, and the days passed in disputing, muttering prayers, and playing the good-for-nothing; a rather disgusting nasty little adventure happened to me that almost ended very badly for me.

There is no soul so base and heart so barbarous that it is not susceptible to some sort of attachment. One of those two scoundrels who called themselves Moors acquired an affection for me. He approached me willingly, chatted with me in his rank gibberish, did me some small services, sometimes shared his portion with me at table, and above all gave me frequent kisses with an ardor that was very uncomfortable to me. Whatever fright I might naturally have of this gingerbread face decorated with a long scar, and this lustful glance which seemed more furious than tender, I endured these kisses saying to myself inside, "The poor man has conceived a very lively friendship for me, I would be wrong to rebuff him." By degrees he passed to freer manners and made such peculiar remarks that sometimes I believed that his head had turned. One night he wanted to come to sleep with me; I opposed this saying that my bed was too small: he pressed me to get into his; I still refused him; for this wretch was so filthy and stank so strongly of chewing tobacco that he made me sick to my stomach.

The next day rather early in the morning the two of us were alone in the assembly room. He began his caresses again, but with such violent motions that they made him frightful. Finally he wanted to pass by degrees to the most filthy[52] liberties, and to force me to do the same by making use of my hand. I vehemently shook myself free uttering a cry and making a leap backwards, and without showing either indignation or anger, for I did not have the slightest idea what it was all about; I expressed my surprise and my distaste with so much energy that he left me there: but while he was finishing tossing about,[53] I saw flying off toward the chimney and falling to the ground something sticky and whitish that turned my stomach. I darted onto the balcony more upset, more troubled, even more frightened than I had ever been in my life, and ready to faint.

I could not understand what this wretch had done. I believed he had been seized with epilepsy or some even more terrible frenzy, and truly I know nothing more hideous for someone in cold blood to see than that obscene and filthy bearing, and that horrible face inflamed with the most brutal concupiscence. I have never seen another man in such a state; but if we are like this in our raptures around women, their eyes must be very fascinated for them not to be horrified at us.

I had no more urgent business than to go tell everyone what had just happened to me. Our old mother superior told me to be quiet, but I saw that this account had affected her strongly, and I heard her muttering between her teeth, "*Can maledet, brutta bestia.*"[54] Since I did not understand why I should be quiet, I kept on my way in spite of the prohibition and I chattered so much that early in the morning the next day one of the administrators came to deliver a rather lively remonstrance to me, accusing me of making a lot of noise over little harm and of compromising the honor of a holy house.

He prolonged his censure by explaining to me many things I did not know, but which he did not believe he was teaching me, since he was persuaded that I had defended myself while knowing what was wanted of me, and not wishing to consent to it. He gravely told me that this was a forbidden action like lewdness, but as for the rest the intention was not insulting to the person who was its object, and that there was nothing to become so very annoyed about in having been found lovable. He told me straightforwardly that he himself had had the same honor in his youth, and that having been surprised in no position to resist, he had found nothing so cruel in it. He pushed his impudence to the point of using exact terms and, imagining that the cause of my resistance was the fear of pain, he assured me that this fear was idle, and that one must not get alarmed over nothing.

I listened to this disgraceful man with all the more astonishment because he was not speaking at all for himself; he seemed to be teaching me only for my good. His speech appeared so simple to him that he had not even sought the secrecy of a tête-à-tête, and as a third we had an Ecclesiastic who was not any more shocked by this than he was. This natural manner made such an impression on me that I came to believe that this was doubtless a practice allowed in the world of society, and about which I had not had the occasion to be taught earlier. This made me hear about it without anger but not without disgust. The image of what had happened to me, but above all of what I had seen, remained so strongly imprinted on my memory that my stomach turned again when I thought about it. Without my knowing any more about it my aversion for the thing extended to the apologist, and I was not able to hold myself back well enough to keep him from seeing the bad effect of his lessons. He cast me a glance that was not very affectionate, and after that he spared nothing to render my stay in the hospice unpleasant. He succeeded so well in this that, perceiving only a single way to leave, I hurried to take it just as much as I had struggled to put it off until then.

This adventure protected me for the future against the undertakings of the Knights of the cuff,[55] and since they recalled to me the manner and gestures of my dreadful Moor, the sight of people who were looked upon as being such has always inspired me with so much horror that I have barely been able to conceal it. On the contrary women gained much in my mind in this comparison:[56] it seemed to me that for the offenses of my sex I owed them reparation in tenderness of feelings, in the homage of my person, and at the memory of this false African, the ugliest hag became an adorable object to my eyes.

As for him, I do not know what they might have said to him. It did not seem to me that anyone other than Lady Lorenza regarded him less favorably than before. Nevertheless, he neither accosted me nor spoke to me any more. A week later he was baptized with great ceremony, and dressed in white from head to toe to represent the innocence of his regenerated soul. The next day he left the hospice and I never saw him again.

My turn came a month later; for all that time was necessary to give my Directors the honor of a difficult conversion, and they made me pass all the dogmas in review to triumph over my new docility.

Finally, well enough instructed and well enough disposed for my masters' taste, I was led in a procession to the metropolitan Church of St. John to make a solemn abjuration there, and to receive the accessories of baptism, although they did not really baptize[57] me; but as these were almost the same ceremonies, this served to persuade the people that Protestants are not Christians. I was clothed in a certain gray robe decorated by white frogging and used for this sort of occasion. In front of and behind me two men carried copper basins upon which they struck with a key, and into which each put his alms to the extent of his devotion or the interest he took in the new convert. In sum no Catholic display was omitted to render the solemnity more edifying for the public and more humiliating for me. The only thing missing was the white clothing, which would have been very useful to me, and which they did not give me as they did the Moor, considering that I did not have the honor of being a Jew.

That was not all. Afterwards I had to go to the Inquisition to receive absolution for the crime of heresy and to return into the bosom of the Church with the same ceremony to which Henri IV was subjected through his Ambassador.[58] The air and the manners of the very Reverend Father Inquisitor were not fit to dissipate the secret terror that had seized me upon entering this house. After several questions about my faith, about my condition, about my family, he abruptly asked me if my mother was damned. Fright made me repress my first movement of indignation; I was content to answer that I wished to hope that she was not, and that God had been able to enlighten her in her final hour. The Monk was silent, but he made a grimace that did not appear to me to be at all a sign of approbation.[59]

When all this had been done; at the moment in which I thought I was finally to be placed in accordance with my hopes; they put me out of the door with a little more than twenty francs in small change which my collection had produced. They urged me to live as a good Christian, to be faithful to grace; they wished me good luck, they closed the door on me, and everyone disappeared.

Thus all my great hopes were eclipsed in an instant, and from the self-interested step that I had just made nothing was left for me except the remembrance of having been an apostate and a dupe at the same time.

It is easy to judge what a sudden revolution should have been made in my ideas, when from my brilliant projects of fortune, I saw myself fall into the most complete misery, and when, after having deliberated in the morning over the choice of the palace in which I would live, I saw myself in the evening reduced to sleeping in the street. It will be believed that I began by abandoning myself to a despair all the more cruel since the regret for my faults must be inflamed when I reproached myself that all my misfortune was my own work. Not at all. For the first time in my life I had just been shut up for more than two months.[60] The first feeling I tasted was that of the freedom I had recovered. Having become master of myself and my actions again after a long slavery, I saw myself in the middle of a big city abundant in resources, full of people of rank, by whom my talents and my merit could not fail to make me welcomed as soon as I became known to them. I had, moreover, plenty of time to wait, and to me the twenty francs I had in my pocket seemed a treasure that could not be exhausted. I could dispose of it at my whim, without accounting to anyone. This was the first time I had seen myself so rich. Far from surrendering to discouragement and tears, I only changed hopes, and amour-propre[61] lost nothing by it. I never felt so much confidence and security: I believed my fortune already made, and I found it a fine thing to be obliged to no one but myself for it.

The first thing I did was to satisfy my curiosity by wandering around the whole City, even though this might only have been to perform an act of freedom. I went to see the mounting of the guard; the military instruments pleased me very much. I followed the processions; I liked the flat drone of the priests. I went to see the King's Palace: I approached it with fear; but seeing other people enter, I did as they did, I was allowed to do so. Possibly I owed this favor to the little package I had under my arm. However that might have been, upon finding myself in this Palace I formed a great opinion of myself: already I looked at myself almost as a resident of it.[62] At last as a result of going and coming, I got tired, I was hungry, it was hot; I entered the shop of a dairy merchant: they gave me some Giuncà, some curdled milk, and along with two *grisses* of that excellent bread from Piedmont that I love more than any other, for five or six sous I had one of the best dinners I have had in my life.[63]

I needed to look for lodging. Since I already knew enough Piedmontese to make myself understood, it was not hard for me to find it, and I had the prudence to choose it more in accordance with my purse than with my taste. Someone informed me that in the Via di Po a soldier's wife took in servants out of service for one sou a night. At her home I found an empty pallet and I established myself there. She was young, and newly married, although she already had five or six children. We all slept in the same room, the mother, the children, the guests, and it went on in this manner for as long as I stayed with her. On the whole she was a good woman, swearing like a trooper, always half-dressed and uncombed, but with a gentle heart, a busybody, who acquired a friendship for me, and who was even useful to me.

I passed several days by abandoning myself solely to the pleasure of independence and curiosity. I went wandering inside and outside the City, nosing about, visiting everything that appeared curious and new to me, and everything was so to a young man leaving his niche who had never seen a capital. Above all I was very exact in paying my court and every morning I regularly assisted at the King's Mass. I found it fine to see myself in the same Chapel with this Prince and his attendants: but my passion for music, which began to declare itself, had more of a share in my assiduousness than the pomp of the Court which was not striking for very long because it was quickly seen and always the same. At that time the King of Sardinia had the best symphony in Europe. Somis, Desjardins, the Bezuzzis shone there one after the other.[64] That much was not required to attract a young man who was easily sent into rapture by the playing[65] of the slightest instrument, as long as it was accurate. For the rest, I had only a stupid admiration without covetousness for the magnificence that struck my eyes. The only thing that interested me in all the brilliance of the Court was to see whether there might not be some young Princess there who deserved my homage, and with whom I could have a romance.

I nearly began one in a less brilliant station, but where I would have found pleasures a thousand times more delightful if I had brought it to a conclusion.

Although I lived with much economy, my purse was gradually running out. Besides, this economy was less the effect of prudence than of a simplicity of taste that even today has not changed at all from frequenting the tables of the great. I did not know and I still do not know any better fare than that of a rustic meal. You are always sure to entertain me very well with dairy products, eggs, herbs, cheese, whole wheat bread and some passable wine:[66] my good appetite will do the rest if the steward and lackeys around me do not cloy me with their importunate appearance. At that time I made much better meals with six or seven sous of expense than I have made since with six or seven francs. Thus I was sober for lack of being tempted not to be so; still I am wrong to call all that sobriety; for I put all the sensuality possible into it. My pears, my Giuncà, my cheese, my loaves, and several glasses of a strong wine from Montferrat that could be cut with a knife made me the happiest of gourmands. But even with all that the end of twenty Livres could be seen. I perceived it more palpably day by day, and in spite of the heedlessness of my age, my anxiety about the future soon reached the point of fright. Of all my Castles in Spain the only one I had left was that of seeking an occupation that might make a living for me, and that was not easy to achieve. I thought of my former profession; but I did not know it well enough to go to work with a master, and masters were not even abundant at Turin. Then, while waiting for something better, I made the decision to go offer myself from shop to shop to engrave initials or coats of arms on tableware, hoping to tempt people with the low price by letting them set it for me at their discretion. This expedient was not very lucky. I was sent packing almost everywhere, and I found so few things to do that I barely earned several meals from it. One day, however, passing through the Contrà Nova rather early in the morning, through a shop window I saw a young tradeswoman of such good grace and with such an attractive manner, that in spite of my timidity around Ladies, I did not hesitate to enter and offer her my small talent. She did not rebuff me at all, had me sit down, tell my little story, pitied me, told me to take courage, and that good Christians would not abandon me: then, while she sent to a goldsmith in the neighborhood for the tools I had said I needed, she showed me into her kitchen and provided me with something for breakfast herself. This beginning appeared auspicious to me; what followed did not contradict it. She appeared content with my small work; still more with my small babble when I was a little reassured: for she was brilliant and well dressed, and in spite of her gracious manner that radiance had impressed me. But her very kind welcome, her compassionate tone, her gentle and caressing manners soon put me at my ease. I saw that I was succeeding and this made me succeed further.[67] But although she was Italian, and too pretty not to be a little coquettish, she was nevertheless so modest, and I so timid that it was hard for anything to happen quickly. We were not allowed enough time to complete the adventure. I only recall the short moments I passed near her with more charm, and I can say that I tasted the sweetest as well as the purest pleasures of love there in their first fruits.

She[68] was an extremely lively brunette, but whose good natural disposition, which was depicted on her pretty face, rendered her vivacity touching.[69] She was called Madame Basile. During his trips her husband, who was older than she and fairly jealous, left her under the guard of a clerk who was too surly to be seductive, and who did not fail to have pretensions on his own account which he barely showed except by his ill humor. He formed a lot of ill humor against me, although I loved to listen to him play the flute, which he played rather well. This new Aegis-thus[70] always grunted when he saw me enter his Lady's house: he treated me with a disdain which she returned to him very well. It even seemed that she was pleased to caress me in his presence in order to torment him, and this sort of vengeance, although very much to my taste, might have been even more so in a tête-à-tête. But she did not push it to that point or at least not in the same way. Either she found me too young, or she could not make the advances, or she seriously wanted to be chaste; at that time she had a sort of reserve that was not repellent, but which intimidated me without me knowing why. Although I did not feel for her that respect as true as it was tender that I had for Mme de Warens, I felt more fear and much less familiarity. I was bothered, trembling, I did not dare look at her. I did not dare breathe near her; nevertheless, I feared leaving her more than death. With an avid eye I devoured everything I could see without being perceived: the flowers of her dress, the tip of her pretty foot, the interval of a firm white arm that appeared between her glove and her cuff, and the one that was sometimes made between her throat and her handkerchief. Each object added to the impression of the others. As a result of looking at what I could see and even beyond, my eyes became blurred, my chest was constricted, I had much difficulty regulating my breathing which became more constrained from moment to moment, and all I could do was to heave very inconvenient noiseless sighs in the silence we were in rather often. Fortunately it seemed to me that Mme Basile did not notice it since she was occupied at her work. Nevertheless I sometimes saw her scarf swell up rather frequently as if in a sort of sympathy. This dangerous sight completed my ruin, and when I was ready to give way to my rapture, she addressed some word to me in a tranquil tone that made me return to myself instantly.

Several times I saw her alone in this manner without a word, a gesture, even a too expressive glance ever marking the least intelligence between us. This condition, very tormenting for me, nevertheless delighted me, and in the simplicity of my heart it was hard for me to imagine why I was so tormented. It seemed that these little tête-à-têtes did not displease her either; at least she made the occasions for them fairly frequent; a care assuredly very gratuitous on her part for the use she made, and which she allowed me to make of them.

One day, being bored by the clerk's foolish talk, she had gone up to her room; in the back of the shop where I was I hurried to finish my little task and I followed her. Her room was half open; I entered it without being perceived. She was embroidering near a window facing the side of the room opposite the door. She could neither see me enter, nor hear me, because of the noise the wagons were making in the street. She was always well dressed: that day her adornment approached coquetry. Her posture was graceful, her head—being a little lowered—allowed the whiteness of her neck to be seen, her hair—elegantly done up on top of her head—was decorated with flowers. In her whole form there reigned a charm that I had time to consider,[71] and that sent me outside of myself. I threw myself on my knees at the entrance of the room while stretching my arms toward her with an impassioned motion, certain that she could not hear me, and not thinking that she could see me: but there was a mirror on the mantle that betrayed me.[72] I do not know what effect this rapture had on her; she did not look at me at all, did not speak to me at all: but half turning her head, with a simple motion of[73] a finger she indicated to me the mat at her feet. To shiver, to utter a cry, to throw myself at the place she had indicated to me were only a single thing for me: but what one might find hard to believe is that while in this position I did not dare undertake anything beyond it, nor to say a single word, nor to raise my eyes to her, nor even to touch her in such a constrained posture, to rest on her knees for an instant. I was dumb, immobile, but certainly not tranquil: everything showed my agitation, joy, gratitude, ardent desires uncertain in their object and held back by the fear of displeasing about which my young heart could not reassure itself.

She did not appear either more tranquil or less timid than I was. Troubled at seeing me there, bewildered at having attracted me, and beginning to feel all the consequences of a sign doubtless given before any reflection, she neither welcomed me nor repulsed me; she did not move her eyes from her work; she tried to act as if she had not seen me at her feet; but all my stupidity did not keep me from judging that she shared my confusion, perhaps my desires, and that she was held back by a shame similar to mine, without this giving me the strength to surmount it.[74] In my view the five or six years that she was older than me should have put all the boldness on her side, and I told myself that since she was not doing anything to excite my boldness she did not want me to have any. Even today I find that I thought accurately, and certainly she had too much intelligence not to see that a novice like me needed, not only to be encouraged, but to be taught.

I do not know how this lively and mute scene might have ended, nor how much time I would have remained immobile in this ridiculous and delightful position, if we had not been interrupted. At the height of my agitation I heard the door of the kitchen (which adjoined the room we were in) open and Mme Basile, alarmed, said to me with a lively voice and gesture, "Get up, there is Rosina." While getting up hastily I seized a hand that she offered me, and I applied two burning kisses to it, at the second of which I felt that charming hand press itself a little against my lips. In my whole life I have not had such a sweet moment: but the occasion I had lost did not return, and our young loves stopped there.

It is perhaps because of this very thing that the image of that lovable woman has stayed imprinted at the bottom of my heart with such charming features. It has even become more beautiful as I have become better acquainted with the world and women. If only she had had experience, she would have set about animating a little boy differently: but if her heart was weak it was decent; she involuntarily surrendered to the penchant that swept it away; according to all appearances it was her first infidelity, and perhaps I would have had to do more to vanquish her shame than my own. I tasted inexpressible sweetness [75] with her without having arrived at that point. Nothing of all the feelings caused in me by the possession of women is worth the two minutes I spent at her feet without even daring to touch her dress. No, there are no enjoyments like the ones that can be given by a decent woman whom one loves: everything is a favor with her. A little sign of the finger, a hand lightly pressed against my mouth are the only favors that I ever received from Mme Basile, and the remembrance of such slight favors still carries me away when I think about them.

The two following days I watched out for a new tête-à-tête, it was impossible for me to find the moment for it, and I did not notice an effort to arrange it on her part. Her bearing was even, not colder, but more reserved than normal, and I believe she avoided my glances out of fear of not being able to govern her own well enough. Her cursed Clerk was more provoking than ever. He even began to banter, to jeer; he told me that I would make my way with the Ladies. I trembled at having committed some indiscretion, and—already regarding myself as having an understanding with her—I wanted to cover with mystery a taste that did not need it very much until then. This made me more circumspect at grasping occasions to satisfy it, and as a result of wanting them to be safe, I did not find any at all.

This is another romantic folly of which I have never been able to cure myself, and which, joined to my natural timidity, has very much belied the Clerk's predictions. I loved too sincerely, too perfectly, I dare say, to be capable of being happy easily. Never have passions been at the same time more lively and more pure than mine; never has love been more tender, more true, more disinterested. I would have sacrificed my happiness a thousand times for that of the person I loved; her reputation was dearer to me than my life, and never would I have wished to compromise her repose for a moment for all the pleasures of enjoyment. This has caused me to put so many cares, so much secrecy, so many precautions into my undertakings that none of them has ever been able to succeed. My lack of success with women has always come from loving them too much.

To return to Aegisthus the flute player, what was peculiar was that while becoming more unbearable, the traitor seemed to become more obliging. From the first day that his Lady had taken an affection for me she had thought about making me useful in the shop. I knew arithmetic passably; she had proposed to him to teach me how to keep the books: but my curmudgeon received the proposition very poorly, fearing perhaps that he might be supplanted. Thus all my work, after my engraving, was to transcribe some accounts and memoranda, to make a fair copy of some books, and to translate some business letters from Italian into French. All of a sudden my man took it into his head to return to the proposition that had been made and rejected, and said that he would teach me double-entry accounts, and that he wanted to put me in a position to offer my services to M. Basile when he returned. There was an indefinable some-thing false, cagey, ironic in his tone, in his manner that did not give me confidence. Without waiting for my response, Mme Basile drily told him that I was obliged to him for his offers, that she hoped that in the end fortune would favor my merit, and that it would be a great shame that with so much intelligence I might be only a Clerk.

Several times she had told me that she wished to make me acquainted with someone who could be useful to me. She was prudent enough to feel that it was time to detach me from her.[76] Our mute declarations had been made on a Thursday. On Sunday she gave a dinner at which I was present, and at which I also found a pleasant-looking Jacobin to whom she introduced me. The monk treated me very affectionately, congratu-lated me on my conversion, and told me several things about my story which showed me that she had related it to him in detail; then, giving me two little slaps on the cheek with the back of his hand, he told me to be well-behaved, to keep up my spirits, and to go to see him, that we would chat together more at leisure. I judged by the respect everyone had for him that he was a man of distinction, and—from the paternal tone he took with Mme Basile—that he was her Confessor. I also recall very well that his modest familiarity was mixed with marks of esteem and even of respect for his penitent that made less impression on me at that time than they do today. If I had had more intelligence, how touched I might have been at having rendered sensitive a young woman who was respected by her Confessor!

The table was not large enough for all of us. A little one was necessary at which I had a pleasant tête-à-tête with Monsieur the Clerk. There I lost nothing on the side of attentions and good cheer; many dishes were sent to the little table that were certainly not intended for him. Everything went very well up to that point; the women were very gay, the men very gallant, Mme Basile did her honors with a charming grace. In the middle of the dinner a carriage is heard stopping at the door, someone comes up; it is M. Basile. I see him as if he were coming in now, in a scarlet suit with gold buttons; a color for which I have had an aversion since that day. M. Basile was a big and handsome man, who presented himself very well. He enters with a roar, and with the air of someone who is surprising his company, although only his friends were there. His wife throws her arms around his neck, takes his hands, gives him a thousand caresses that he receives without returning them to her. He salutes the company, he is given a place setting, he eats. Hardly had they begun to talk about his trip, when casting his eyes on the little table, he asks in a severe tone who the little boy is whom he notices there. Mme Basile tells him completely ingenuously. He asks whether I lodge in the house? He is told no. "Why not," he continues coarsely, "since he possesses it during the day, he might as well stay there at night." The monk begins to speak, and after a serious and true commendation of Mme Basile, he makes one of me in a few words; adding that far from blaming his wife's pious charity, he ought to hurry to take part in it; since nothing in it passed the limits of discretion. The husband replied in an angry tone half of which he hid (being held back by the monk's presence) but which sufficed to make me feel that he was informed about me, and that the clerk had served me in his manner.

No sooner were we away from the table, than the clerk came in triumph to notify me on his boss's behalf to leave his house immediately and never set foot in it again in my life. He seasoned his commission with everything that could make it insulting and cruel. I left without saying anything, but cut to the quick, less from leaving that lovable woman, than from leaving her prey to her husband's brutality. He was right, doubtless, not to want her to be unfaithful; but although chaste and of a good family, she was Italian, that is to say sensitive and vindictive, and he was wrong, it seems to me, to use with her the means best suited for attracting the unhappiness he feared.

Such was the success of my first adventure. I wanted to try to pass by in the street two or three times, in order at least to see again the one for whom my heart ceaselessly mourned; but instead of her I saw only her husband and the vigilant Clerk, who, when he noticed me, made a gesture with the shop's measuring stick that was more expressive than enticing. Seeing myself so well watched I lost courage and no longer passed by. I at least wanted to go to see the patron she had arranged for me. Unfortunately, I did not know his name. Several times I prowled uselessly around the monastery to try to meet him. Finally some other events deprived me of the charming memories of Mme Basile, and in a little while I forgot her so well that—as simple and as much a novice as before—I did not even remain tempted by pretty women.

Nevertheless, her generosity had replenished my little outfit a bit; although very modestly and with the foresight of a prudent woman, who regarded propriety more than display, and who wished to keep me from suffering, and not to make me shine. My suit which I had brought from Geneva was good and still wearable; she added only[77] a hat and some linen to it. I had no cuffs; she did not want to give me any, although I would have liked them very much. She was content to put me in a position to keep myself clean, and this was a care that it was unnecessary to recommend to me as long as I was appearing in front of her.

A few days after my catastrophe, my landlady who, as I have said, had formed a friendship for me, told me that she had perhaps found a place for me, and that a Lady of rank wanted to see me. At this word, I believed I was well on the way to high adventures, for I always returned to them. This one did not turn out to be as brilliant as I had pictured it. I went to this Lady's house with the servant who had spoken to her about me. She questioned me, examined me; I did not displease her; and right away I entered her service, not exactly as a favorite, but as a lackey. I was dressed in her livery: the only distinction was that her people wore a shoulder knot, and I was not given one: since there was no gold braid in her livery, this made up just about bourgeois clothing. This was the unexpected conclusion to which all my great hopes came at last.

Madame the Comtesse de Vercellis, into whose house I entered, was a widow and had no children.[78] Her husband was Piedmontese; as for her, I have always believed her to be Savoyard, not being able to imagine that a Piedmontese could speak French so well and have such a pure accent. She was middle aged, had a very noble countenance, a well-adorned mind, loving French literature, and being well acquainted with it. She wrote much, and always in French. Her letters had the turn of expression and almost the grace of Mme de Sévigné's; some of them could have been mistaken for hers.[79] My principal employment, which did not displease me, was to write them under her dictation; since a breast cancer, which made her suffer very much, did not permit her to write by herself any longer.

Mme de Vercellis had not only much intelligence, but a very elevated and strong soul. I followed her last illness, I saw her suffer and die without ever showing an instant of weakness, without making the slightest effort to constrain herself, without departing from her role as a woman, and without suspecting that in this there might be philosophy; a word that was not yet in fashion, and that she did not even know in the sense it carries today.[80] That strength of character sometimes went to the point of coldness. She always appeared to me as little sensitive to others as to herself, and when she did good for the unfortunate, it was to do what was good in itself rather than out of a genuine commiseration.[81] I experienced this insensitivity a little during the three months I passed with her. It was natural that she acquire an affection for a young man of some promise whom she had ceaselessly under her eyes and, feeling herself to be dying, that she consider that he would need help and support after her: nevertheless, either because she did not judge me worthy of particular attention, or because the people who were badgering her did not permit her to consider anyone but them, she did nothing for me.

I recall very well, however, that she had shown some curiosity to get to know me. Sometimes she questioned me; she was very glad for me to show her the letters I wrote to Mme de Warens, for me to report my feelings. But, by never showing me her own, she assuredly did not behave very well for getting to know mine. My heart loved to pour itself out provided it felt that it was with another one. Dry and cold interrogations without any sign of approbation or blame for my answers did not give me any confidence. When nothing informed me whether my babble was pleasing or displeasing I was always afraid, and I sought less to show what I thought than to say nothing that could do me harm. I have noticed since [82] that this dry manner of questioning people in order to know them is a rather common habit among women who pride themselves on intelligence. They imagine that by not allowing their feeling to appear at all they will see into yours better; but they do not see that in this way they take away the courage to show it. From that alone a man who is being questioned begins to put himself on guard, and if he believes that one wants only to make him chatter without taking a genuine interest in him, he lies, or is silent, or redoubles his attentiveness to himself, and prefers to pass for a fool rather than to be the dupe of your curiosity. In sum, to affect to hide one's own heart is always a bad way to read other people's.

Mme de Vercellis never said a word to me that expressed affection, pity, benevolence. She questioned me coldly, I answered with reserve. My answers were so timid that she must have found them low and been bored by them. Toward the end she no longer asked me questions, no longer talked to me except for her service. She judged me less upon what I was than upon what she had made me, and as a result of seeing nothing but a lackey in me, she prevented me from appearing as anything else to her.

I believe that from that time I experienced that malicious play of hidden interests that has crossed me all my life, and that has given me a very natural aversion for the apparent order that produces them. Having no children, Mme de Vercellis had as heir her nephew the Comte de la Roque[83] who assiduously paid her his Court. Aside from that, her principal domestic servants who saw her drawing near her end did not forget themselves, and there were so many bustling around her that it was difficult for her to have time to think about me. At the head of her household was one named M. Lorenzy, a clever man, whose wife, even more clever, had insinuated herself so much into her mistress's good graces that she was more on the footing of a friend with her than of a woman in her employ. She had given her as a chambermaid one of her nieces, named Mlle Pontal, a sly minx, who gave herself the airs of a Young Lady in waiting and helped her aunt so well in obsessing their mistress that she saw only through their eyes and acted only with their hands. I did not have the good fortune to please these three persons: I obeyed them, but I did not serve them; I did not imagine that aside from the service of our shared mistress I ought also to be the valet of her valets. Furthermore I was a disconcerting sort of fellow for them.[84] They saw very well that I was not in my place; they feared that Madame also saw it, and that what she might do to put me there might reduce their shares; for these sorts of people, too greedy to be just, regarded all bequests for others as taken from their own property. Thus they joined together to keep me away from her eyes. She loved to write letters; it was an amusement for her in her condition; they made her dislike it and caused her to be diverted from it by the doctor persuading her that it was tiring. Under the pretext that I did not understand service they employed two fat boors of chair carriers around her instead of me: in sum, they acted so well that when she made her will it had been eight days since I had entered her room. It is true that after that I entered there as before, and I was even more assiduous than anyone else: for that poor woman's suffering tore me apart, the constancy with which she bore it made her extremely worthy of respect and dear to me, and I shed very sincere tears in her room, without it being noticed by her or anyone.

Finally we lost her. I saw her expire. Her life had been that of a woman of intelligence and sense; her death was that of a sage. I can say that she made the Catholic religion lovable to me through the serenity of soul with which she fulfilled its duties, without negligence and without affectation. She was naturally serious. At the end of her illness she acquired a sort of gaiety that was too even to be feigned, and that was only a counterweight given by reason itself against the sadness of her condition. She kept to her bed only for the last two days and did not stop conversing peacefully with everyone. Finally no longer speaking, and already in the throes of agony, she made a big fart. "Good," she said turning over, "a woman who farts is not dead." These were the last words she pronounced.

She had bequeathed one year's wages to her underservants; but not being set down in the estate as part of her house I had nothing. Nevertheless, the Comte de la Roque had thirty livres given to me and left me the new suit I had on, and of which M. Lorenzy wished to deprive me.[85] He even promised to seek to place me and permitted me to come to see him. I went there two or three times without being able to speak to him. I was easy to rebuff, I no longer went back. It will soon be seen that I was wrong.

Why have I not finished everything I had to say about my stay at Mme de Vercellis's![86] But, although my apparent situation remained the same, I did not leave her house as I had entered it. I carried away from it the long remembrances of crime and the unbearable weight of remorse with which my conscience is still burdened after forty years, and the bitter feeling of which, far from growing weaker, becomes inflamed as I grow older. Who would believe that the fault of a child could have such cruel consequences? My heart does not know how to console itself over these more than probable consequences. I have perhaps caused a lovable, decent, estimable girl, who was surely worth much more than I was, to die in disgrace and misery.

It is very difficult for the dissolution of a household not to involve a little confusion in the house, and for many things not to be mislaid. Nevertheless, such was the faithfulness of the domestic servants, and the vigilance of M. and Mme Lorenzy, that nothing was found missing in the inventory. Only Mlle Pontal lost a little pink and silver colored ribbon that was already old. Many other better things were within my reach; only this ribbon tempted me, I stole it, and since I scarcely hid it they soon found it on me. They wanted to know from where I had taken it. I faltered, I stammered, and finally, blushing, I said that it was Marion who gave it to me. Marion was a young girl from the Maurienne whom Mme de Vercellis had made her cook, when—ceasing to give dinners—she had dismissed hers, since she needed good broths more than fine ragouts. Not only was Marion pretty, but she had a freshness of coloring that is found only in the mountains, and above all an air of modesty and sweetness that made it impossible to see her without liking her. Besides she was a good girl, well behaved, and of a completely reliable fidelity. That is what surprised them when I named her. They had hardly less confidence in me than in her, and they judged it important to verify which of the two was the rascal. They made her come; the gathering was numerous, the Comte de la Roque was there. She arrives, they show her the ribbon, I charge her brazenly; she remains astonished, is silent, casts a glance at me that would have disarmed demons and that my barbarous heart resisted. Finally she denies with self-assurance, but without anger, apostrophizes me, exhorts me to return to myself, not to dishonor an innocent girl who has never done me any harm; and I confirm my declaration with an infernal impudence and maintain in front of her that she gave me the ribbon. The poor girl begins to cry, and says to me only these words, "Ah Rousseau! I believed you had good character. You are making me very unhappy, but I would not want to be in your place." That is all. She continued to defend herself with as much simplicity as firmness, but without ever allowing herself the slightest invective against me. Compared to my resolute tone this comparative moderation did her harm. It did not seem natural to assume such a diabolical audacity on one side, and such an angelic sweetness on the other. They did not appear to decide absolutely, but the presumptions were for me. In the bustle they were in they did not give themselves time to examine the matter thoroughly, and in dismissing the two of us the Count de la Roque was content to say that the conscience of the guilty one would sufficiently avenge the innocent. His prediction was not empty, there is not a single day in which it fails to come true.[87]

I do not know what became of that victim of my calumny; but it does not appear that she could have found it easy to place herself well after this. She carried off an imputation that was cruel to her honor in every way. The theft was only a bagatelle, but in the end it was a theft, and what is worse, used to seduce a young boy; finally lying and obstinacy did not leave anything to hope for from the one in whom so many vices were joined. I do not even look at poverty and abandonment as the greatest danger to which I exposed her. Who knows, at her age, where the discouragement of dishonored innocence might have carried her. Ah! if the remorse for having been capable of making her unhappy is unbearable, judge about that for having been capable of making her worse than myself.[88]

This cruel remembrance troubles me sometimes and upsets me so much that during my sleepless nights I see that poor girl come to reproach me for my crime as if it had been committed only yesterday. As long as I lived tranquilly it tormented me less, but in the midst of a stormy life it deprives me of the sweetest consolation of persecuted people who are innocent: it makes me feel very much what I believe I have said in some work, that remorse sleeps during a prosperous fate and grows sour in adversity.[89] Nevertheless, I have never been able to take it upon myself to unburden my heart of this admission in the bosom of a friend. The closest intimacy has never caused me to make it to anyone, not even to Mme de Warens. All I was able to do was to admit that I had an atrocious action for which to reproach myself, but I never said what it consisted in.[90] Thus this weight has remained on my conscience without relief up to this day, and I can say that the desire to free myself from it in some measure has contributed very much to the resolution I have made to write my confessions.

I have proceeded straight to the point in the confession I just made, and it will surely not be found that I have palliated the foulness of my heinous crime. But I would not fulfill the goal of this book[91] if I did not expose my internal inclinations at the same time, and if I feared to excuse myself in what agrees with the truth. Never has wickedness been farther from me than in that cruel moment, and when I accused that unfortunate girl, it is bizarre but true that my friendship for her was the cause. She was present to my thought, I excused myself on the first object that offered itself. I accused her of having done what I wanted to do and of having given me the ribbon because my intention was to give it to her. When I saw her appear afterwards my heart was torn apart, but the presence of so many people was stronger than my repentance. I did not fear the punishment very much, I feared only the shame; but I feared it more than death, more than crime, more than everything in the world. I would have wished to bury myself, suffocate myself in the center of the earth: invincible shame outweighed everything, shame alone caused my impudence, and the more criminal I became, the more intrepid I was made by the fear[92] of acknowledging it. I saw only the horror of being detected, declared publicly—with myself present—a thief, liar, calumniator. A universal agitation deprived me of all other feeling. If they had allowed me to return to myself, I would have infallibly declared everything. If M. de la Roque had taken me aside, if he had said to me, "Don't ruin this poor girl. If you are guilty admit it to me," I would have thrown myself at his feet instantly; I am perfectly sure of it. But they only intimidated me when it was necessary to give me courage.[93] It is also just to consider my age. I had hardly left childhood, or rather I was still in it. In youth genuinely heinous acts are even more criminal than in maturity; but what is only weakness is much less so, and at bottom my fault was hardly anything else. Therefore its remembrance afflicts me less because of the evil in itself, than because of the one it must have caused. It has even done me the good of protecting me for the rest of my life from every act tending to crime because of the terrible impression that has remained from the only one I have ever committed. Furthermore I believe I feel that my aversion for lying comes to me in great part from the regret of having been capable of committing such a black one. If this is a crime that can be expiated, as I dare to believe it is, it ought to be by so many misfortunes that overwhelm the end of my life, by forty years of uprightness and honor in difficult circumstances; poor Marion finds so many avengers in this world, that however great my offense against her might have been, I am not very afraid of carrying off the guilt with me to the next one.[94] This is what I had to say on this article. May I be permitted never to speak of it again.[95]

Book III [1]

Having left Mme de Vercellis's in almost the same condition as I had entered it, I returned to my former landlady's, and stayed there for five or six weeks, during which health, youth, and idleness often rendered my temperament importunate. I was restless, heedless, a dreamer; I wept, I sighed, I desired a happiness about which I had no idea, and the deprivation of which I felt nevertheless. This condition cannot be described, and few men can even imagine it; because most of them have anticipated this simultaneously tormenting and delightful plenitude of life which gives a foretaste of enjoyment in the intoxication of desire.[2] My inflamed blood continuously filled my brain with girls and women, but—since I was unaware of the genuine use—in a bizarre way I made use of them at my whim in my mind's eye without knowing how to do anything more with them, and these ideas kept my senses in a very uncomfortable activity from which they fortunately did not teach me to relieve myself. I would have given my life to find a Mlle Goton again for a quarter of an hour. But this was no longer the time when the games of childhood went in that direction as if by themselves. Along with years had come shame, the companion of the consciousness of evil; it had increased my natural timidity to the point of rendering it invincible, and never—either at that time or since—have I been able to succeed in making a lascivious proposal unless the one to whom I was making it had in a way compelled me to do so by her advances, even when I knew that she was not scrupulous and I was almost certain of being taken at my word.

My agitation grew to the point that, not being able to satisfy my desires, I stirred them up by the most extravagant maneuvers. I sought out dark alleys, hidden nooks where I could expose myself from afar to persons of the opposite sex in the condition in which I would have wished I could be near them. What they saw was not the obscene object, I did not even dream of that, it was the ridiculous object; the foolish pleasure I had in displaying it to their eyes cannot be described. There was only one step to take from that to feeling the desired treatment, and I do not doubt that some bold one would have given me this amusement while passing by, if I had had the audacity to wait. This madness had a catastrophe that was just about as comic, but a little less pleasant for me.

One day I went to take my position at the far end of a courtyard where there was a well where the girls of the house often came to seek water. In this far end there was a little stairway that led to some cellars by means of several passageways. I explored these underground passageways in the darkness, and, since I found them to be long and dark I judged that they were endless, and that if I were seen and surprised, I would find a sure refuge in them. In this confidence, I offered to the girls who came to the well a sight more laughable than seductive; the most prudent pretended to see nothing, others began to laugh, still others believed they were being insulted and made a commotion. I escaped into my retreat; I was followed. I hear a man's voice, which I had not counted on and which alarmed me: I plunged into the underground at the risk of getting lost there; the noise, the voices, the man's voice always followed me; I had counted on darkness, I saw light. I shuddered; I plunged farther down; a wall stopped me, and not being able to go any farther I had to await my destiny there. In a moment I was reached and seized by a big man wearing a big mustache, a big hat, a big sabre, escorted by four or five old women each armed with a broomstick, among whom I perceived the little hussy who had betrayed me, and who doubtless wanted to see me face to face.

Taking me by the arm the man with the sabre brusquely asked me what I was doing there. One realizes that I did not have a ready answer. I pulled myself together, however, and exerting myself in this critical moment I drew out of my head a novelistic expedient that succeeded. In a supplicating tone I told him to have pity on my age and my condition; that I was a young foreigner of high birth whose brain was deranged; that I had escaped from my paternal house because they wanted to shut me up, that I was lost if he made me known; but that if he would let me go I would perhaps be able to show my gratitude for this favor one day. Against all expectation, my speech and my manner had an effect. The terrible man was touched by them, and after a rather short reprimand, he gently let me go without questioning me further. From the manner in which the young and old women saw me leave, I judged that the man whom I had feared so much was very useful to me, and that with the women alone I would not have gotten off so cheaply. I heard them murmuring something or other that I hardly cared about; for as long as the sabre and the man did not become mixed up in it,[3] I was very certain, nimble and vigorous as I was, of soon saving myself from both their cudgels and themselves.

Several days later, while I was walking in a street with my neighbor, a young abbé, I bumped into the man with the sword. He recognized me, and mimicking me in a railing tone, he said to me, "I am a Prince, I am a

Prince; and I, I am a coward, but don't let his Highness come back." He added nothing more, and I sneaked away lowering my head and thanking him in my heart for his discretion. I judged that those cursed old women had made him ashamed of his credulity. Be that as it may, Piedmontese though he was, he was a good man, and I never think of him without a stirring of gratitude: for the story was so amusing, that anyone else in his place would have shamed me merely out of a desire to get a laugh. Although it did not have the consequences I might have feared from it, that adventure did not fail to make me reasonable for a long time.[4]

My stay with Mme de Vercellis had procured me several acquaintances whom I maintained in the hope that they might be useful to me. Among others sometimes I went to see a Savoyard abbé named M. Gaime, tutor of the Comte de Mellarède's children.[5] He was still young, and moved very little in society, but he was full of good sense, probity, enlightenment and one of the most decent men I have known. He was of no help at all to me for the object that drew me to him: he did not have enough influence to place me; but with him I found more precious advantages that have profited me for my whole life; lessons of sound morality, and maxims of right reason. In the succession of my tastes and ideas I had always been too high or too low; Achilles or Thersites, sometimes a hero and some-times a good-for-nothing.[6] M. Gaime took the care to put me in my place and show me myself without either sparing me or discouraging me. He spoke very honorably about my natural disposition[7] and my talents; but he added that he saw obstacles born from them that would prevent me from taking advantage of them, so that, according to him, they ought to serve me less as steps for climbing to fortune than as resources for doing without it. He drew me a true picture of human life about which I had only false ideas; he showed me how, in an adverse destiny, the wise man can always attain happiness and tack close to the wind to reach it, how there is no true happiness without wisdom, and how there is wisdom in every station. He very much subdued my admiration for greatness by proving to me that those who dominated others were neither wiser nor happier than they. He told me something that has often returned to my memory, which is that if each man could read in the hearts of all the others, there would be more people who would want to descend than to rise. This reflection—the truth of which is striking and which is not at all exaggerated—has been of great use to me in the course of my life by making me keep peacefully in my place. He gave me the first true ideas about what is decent, which my bombastic genius had grasped only in its extremes. He made me feel that enthusiasm for sublime virtues was of little use in society; that by aiming too high one was subject to falls; that the continuity of small duties always well fulfilled did not require any less strength than heroic actions; that one could turn them to better account for honor and for happiness; and that it was worth infinitely more always to have men's esteem than sometimes to have their admiration.

To establish the duties of man one must go back to their principle. Furthermore the step I had just made, and which my present condition was the consequence of, led us to speak about religion. One already realizes that the decent M. Gaime is at least in great part the original of the Savoyard Vicar.[8] Only, since prudence obliged him to speak with more reserve, he explained himself less openly on certain points; but for the rest his maxims, his feelings, his opinions were the same, even including his advice to return to my fatherland; everything was just as I have rendered it since to the public. Thus, without enlarging upon the conversations whose substance can be seen by anyone, I will say that his lessons, wise, but at first without effect, were a seed of virtue and religion in my heart that was never smothered, and that was only waiting for the care of a dearer hand in order to bear fruit.

Although my conversion was not very solid up to that time, I did not fail to be moved. Far from being bored with his conversations, I acquired a taste for them, because of their clarity, their simplicity, and above all a certain interest of the heart with which I felt they were full. I have a loving soul, and I have always been devoted to people, less in proportion to the good they have done for me than to that which they have wanted to do for me, and my sense of discrimination hardly ever fools me on this. Also I genuinely became attached to M. Gaime, I was his second disciple so to speak, and for the moment that brought me even the inestimable good of turning me away from the downward slope to vice onto which my idleness was drawing me.

One day when I least expected it, someone came to find me on behalf of the Comte de la Roque. As a result of going and not being able to talk to him, I had become bored, I did not go any longer: I believed he had forgotten me or that bad impressions of me had stayed with him. I was wrong. More than once he had witnessed the pleasure with which I fulfilled my duty with respect to his aunt; he had even said so to her, and he talked to me about it again when I no was longer thinking about it myself. He received me well, told me that instead of amusing me with vague promises he had sought to place me; that he had succeeded, that he had set me on the path to become something; that it was up to me to do the rest; that the house into which he was having me enter was powerful and esteemed; that I had no need of any other protectors in order to advance; and that, although treated at first as a simple domestic servant, as I had just been, I could be assured that if they judged me to be above that station because of my feelings and behavior, they were disposed not to leave me there. The end of this speech cruelly belied the brilliant hopes given to me by the beginning. "What, always a lackey?" I said to myself with a bitter disdain that confidence soon erased. I felt myself too little made for that place to fear that they would leave me there.

He took me to the Comte de Gouvon, the Queen's First Equerry and head of the illustrious house of Solar.[9] This respectable old man's air of dignity made the affability of his welcome more touching to me. He questioned me with interest and I answered him with sincerity. He said to the Comte de la Roque that I had a pleasant physiognomy and one that promised intelligence, that it seemed to him in fact that I was not lacking in it, but that this was not everything, and that the rest remained to be seen. Then, turning toward me, he said to me, "My child, in almost everything the beginnings are rough; however yours will not be very much so. Be prudent, and seek to please everyone here; at present this is your sole business. For the rest, have courage; we want to take care of you." Immediately he went to his daughter-in-law the Marquise de Breil, and presented me to her, then to the Abbé de Gouvon his son.[10] This beginning seemed auspicious to me. I already knew enough[11] to judge that people did not make so much fuss over the reception of a lackey. In fact they did not treat me as such. I sat at the Steward's table. They did not make me wear livery at all, and when the Comte de Favria,[12] a young feather-brain, wanted to make me mount behind his carriage, his grandfather forbade me to mount behind any carriage and to attend anyone outside of the house.[13] Nevertheless I served at table, and inside I performed almost the service of a lackey; but to some extent I did so freely, without being explicitly attached to anyone. Aside from some letters dictated to me, and some pictures that the Comte de Favria had me cut out, I was almost the master of all my time during the day. This test, which I did not notice, was certainly very dangerous; it was not even very humane; for this great idleness might have caused me to contract vices that I would not have had otherwise.

But very fortunately that is not at all what happened. M. Gaime's lessons had made an impression on my heart, and I acquired so much taste for them that I sometimes slipped away to go hear them again. I believe that those who saw me leave furtively this way hardly guessed where I was going. Nothing could be more sensible than the advice he gave me about my behavior. My beginning was admirable, I had an assiduousness, an attentiveness, a zeal that charmed everyone. The Abbé Gaime had wisely warned me to moderate this first fervor, out of fear that it would relax and that they would notice it.[14] "Your beginning," he said to me, "is the rule of what will be required of you: seek to behave so as to do more afterwards, but watch out never to do less."

Since they had hardly examined me about my little talents and they assumed I had only the ones given me by nature, it did not seem that they were thinking of making any use of me in spite of what the Comte de Gouvon had told me. Some things got in the way, and I was almost forgotten. The Marquis de Breil, the Comte de Gouvon's son, was Ambassador to Vienna at that time. Events occurred at Court which made themselves felt in the family, and for several weeks it was in an agitation that hardly left time for thinking about me. Nevertheless, up to then I had relaxed very little.[15] One thing did me both good and harm by distancing me from all external dissipation, but by making me a little more distracted in my duties.

Mademoiselle de Breil was a young person of about my age,[16] well formed, rather beautiful, very fair with very black hair, and, although a brunette, on her face she wore that air of gentleness of blondes that my heart has never been able to resist. The clothing of the Court, so favorable to young people, showed off her pretty figure, exposed her breasts and shoulders, and rendered her complexion still more dazzling from the mourning they were wearing at that time.[17] It will be said that a servant should not notice such things; doubtless I was wrong to do so, but I noticed them all the same, and I was not the only one. The steward and the valets de chambre sometimes spoke about them at table with a coarseness that made me suffer cruelly. Nevertheless, my head was not turned to the point of being altogether in love. I did not forget myself at all; I kept to my place, and even my desires did not get out of control. I liked to see Mlle de Breil, to hear her make some remarks that showed intelligence, sense, decency; my ambition, limited to the pleasure of serving her, did not go at all beyond my rights. At table I was attentive in seeking occasions for making them worthwhile. If her lackey left her chair for a moment, instantly I was seen standing there: otherwise I kept myself across from her; I sought in her eyes for what she was going to ask, I spied out the moment for changing her plate. What would I not have done for her to deign to order me to do something, to look at me, to say a single word to me; but no; I had the mortification of being nothing for her; she did not even notice I was there. Nevertheless, when her brother—who sometimes addressed a word to me at table—said something or other to me that was not very gracious, I gave him an answer so sharp and well turned that she paid attention to it and cast her eyes upon me.[18] This look which was brief did not fail to carry me away. The next day the occasion to obtain a second one presented itself and I took advantage of it. A great dinner was given that day, at which I was very astonished to see for the first time the steward serve with his sword by his side and hat on his head. By chance they happened to speak of the motto of the house of Solar which was on the tapestry along with the coat of arms. *Tel fiert qui ne tue pas.* As the Piedmontese are not ordinarily accomplished in the French language, someone found a spelling mistake in this motto, and said that there should be no *t* in the word *fiert*.

The old Comte de Gouvon was going to answer, but having cast his eyes on me, he saw that I was smiling without daring to say anything: he ordered me to speak. Then I said that I did not believe that the *t* was superfluous; that *fiert* was an old French word which did not come from the substantive *ferus* proud (*fier*), threatening; but from the verb *ferit*, he strikes (*il frappe*), he wounds. That thus the motto did not appear to me to say such a one threatens, but *such a one wounds who does not kill.*[19]

Everyone looked at me and looked at each other without saying anything. Such astonishment has never been seen. But what gratified me even more was to see an air of satisfaction clearly on Mlle de Breil's face. This person who was so disdainful deigned to cast a second glance at me which was worth at least as much as the first; then turning her eyes toward her grandpapa, with a sort of impatience she seemed to be waiting for the praise he owed me, and which in fact he gave me so fully and completely and with such a satisfied manner that the whole table rushed to join in the chorus. This moment was brief, but delightful in every respect. This was one of those too rare moments that put things back into their natural order and avenge debased merit for the insults of fortune. Several minutes later, once again raising her eyes to me, in a tone of voice as timid as it was affable, Mlle de Breil asked me to give her something to drink. One can judge that I did not keep her waiting, but upon drawing near I was seized with such a trembling that having filled the glass too full,[20] I spilled some of the water onto the plate and even over her. Her brother thoughtlessly asked me why I was trembling so strongly. This question did not serve to steady me, and Mlle de Breil blushed to the whites of her eyes.

Here ended the romance;[21] from which it will be noticed, as with Mme Basile and all the rest of my life, that I am not lucky in the conclusion of my loves. I attached myself to Mme de Breil's antechamber in vain; I did not obtain another mark of attention from her daughter. She came and went without noticing me, and I hardly dared to cast my eyes on her. I was even so stupid and so lacking in skill that one day when she let her glove fall while passing; instead of throwing myself upon this glove which I would have wished to cover with tears, I did not dare leave my place, and I allowed the glove to be picked up by a fat lout of a valet whom I would have throttled willingly. To complete my intimidation I noticed that I did not have the good fortune of pleasing Mme de Breil. Not only did she give me no orders, but she never accepted my service, and two times[22] finding me in her antechamber she asked me with an extremely sharp tone whether I had nothing to do. I had to renounce this dear antechamber: at first I regretted it; but distractions intervened, and soon I no longer thought about it.

I had enough to console myself for the disdain of Madame de Breil in the kindnesses of her father-in-law, who finally realized I was there. On the evening of the dinner about which I have spoken he had a conversation with me for half an hour, with which he seemed content and with which I was enchanted. This good old man, although intelligent, was less so than Mme de Vercellis, but he had deeper emotions, and I succeeded better with him. He told me to attach myself to his son the Abbé de Gouvon, who had taken a liking to me, that this liking could be useful to me if I took advantage of it, and could make me acquire what I lacked for the prospects they had for me. The next morning I immediately flew to M. the Abbé. He did not receive me at all as a servant; he had me sit at the corner of his fire, and questioned me with the greatest gentleness, he soon saw that my education, begun on so many things, had not been completed in any. Finding in particular that I had little Latin, he undertook to teach me more. We agreed that I would report to him every morning, and I began immediately the next day. Thus by one of those peculiarities that will often be found in the course of my life, at the same time above and beneath my station, I was pupil and valet in the same house, and in my servitude I nevertheless had a preceptor whose birth made him suitable to be one only for the children of Kings.

M. the Abbé de Gouvon was a younger son destined by his family for a bishopric, and for this reason his studies had been pushed more than is ordinarily the case for children of quality. He had been sent to the university at Siena, where he had stayed several years, and from which he had brought back a strong enough dose of Cruscantism to be at Turin almost what the Abbé de Dangeau formerly was at Paris.[23] Distaste for theology had thrown him into belles lettres, which is very common in Italy for those who enter the career of prelacy. He had read the poets well; he composed Latin and Italian verses passably. In a word he had the taste needed for forming mine, and for introducing some selectivity into the rubbish with which I had stuffed my head. But either because my babbling had given him some illusion about my knowledge, or because he could not bear the boredom of elementary Latin, at first he put me much too high, and no sooner had he made me translate several of Phaedrus' fables than he threw me into Virgil of which I understood almost nothing. As will be seen in what follows, I was destined to relearn Latin often, and never to know it. Nevertheless, I worked with enough zeal, and M. the Abbé lavished his efforts with a kindness the remembrance of which still moves me. I passed a good part of the morning with him, both for my instruction and for his service: not for that of his person, for he never tolerated me doing him any, but for writing under his dictation, and for copying, and my function of secretary was more useful to me than that of student. Not only did I learn Italian in its purity this way, but I acquired the taste for literature and some discernment about good books that was not to be acquired from la Tribu,[24] and that was very useful to me later when I began to work by myself.

This was the one time in my life when, without romantic projects, I could most reasonably abandon myself to the hope of succeeding. Being very satisfied with me, the Abbé told everyone so, and his father had taken such a singular liking to me that the Comte de Favria informed me that he had spoken to the King about me. Mme de Breil herself had dropped her scornful manner with me. In sum, I became a sort of favorite in the house, to the great jealousy of the other domestics, who,[25] seeing me honored with instruction from their master's son, felt very well that this was not happening in order to keep me their equal for very long.

As much as I could judge about the prospects they had for me from some words dropped at random, and upon which I reflected only afterwards, it seemed to me that, wanting to enter the career of embassies, and perhaps to open from afar that of government minister, the house of Solar would have been very glad to form in advance a subject who had merit and talents, and who, while depending solely on them, could obtain their confidence and serve them usefully in the course of events. This project of the Comte de Gouvon was noble, judicious, magnanimous, and truly worthy of a great, benevolent, and farsighted Lord: but aside from the fact that I did not see its whole extent at that time, it was too sensible for my head, and demanded too long a subjection. My mad ambition sought fortune only through adventures; and not seeing any women in all this, this manner of succeeding seemed slow, painful, and sad to me; although I should have found it all the more honorable and safe since women were not at all mixed up in it, since the sort of merit they protect is certainly not worth as much as the sort I was assumed to have.

Everything was proceeding wonderfully. I had obtained everyone's esteem almost by storm: the tests had ended, and in the house I was generally regarded as a young man of the greatest promise, who was not in his place and whom one expected to see reach it. But my place was not the one that had been assigned to me by men, and I had to attain it by very different paths. I am touching on one of those characteristic features that belong to me, and which it suffices to present to the reader without adding any reflections to it.

Although there were many new converts of my sort at Turin, I did not like them, and had not wished to see any of them. But I had seen several Genevans who were not converts; among others a M. Mussard nicknamed wry-yap, a painter of miniatures and a distant relative of mine.[26] This M. Mussard unearthed my residence with the Comte de Gouvon, and came to see me with another Genevan named Bâcle, whose comrade I had been during my apprenticeship.[27] This Bâcle was a very amusing boy, very gay, full of farcical sallies which his age made agreeable.[28] Behold me all at once crazy about M. Bâcle, but crazy to the point of not being able to leave him. He was soon going to depart to return to Geneva. What a loss this would be for me! I felt its whole magnitude very well. In order at least to take advantage of the time left to me, I did not leave him, or rather he did not leave me, for at first my head was not turned to the point of going out of the House to pass the day with him without leave: but soon, seeing that I was completely obsessed with him, they forbade him the door, and I became so irritated that, forgetting everything aside from my friend Bâcle, I went to neither M. the Abbé nor to M. the Comte, and I was no longer seen in the house. They gave me reprimands to which I did not listen. They threatened to dismiss me. This threat was my ruin; it made me see that it was possible that Bâcle would not go by himself. From that time I no longer saw any other pleasure, any other fate, any other happiness than that of making a similar trip, and in it I saw only the ineffable felicity of a trip, at the end of which, in addition, I glimpsed Mme de Warens, but at an immense distance; as for returning to Geneva, I never considered it. The mountains, the fields, the woods, the streams, the villages followed each other endlessly and ceaselessly with new charms; this blissful journey seemed as if it ought to absorb my entire life. I recalled with delight how charming this same trip had seemed to me when coming. What must it be when, to all the attraction of independence, was joined that of traveling with a comrade of my age, of my taste and good humored, without bother, without duty, without constraint, without obligation to go or to stay except as we pleased? One would have to be mad to sacrifice such a fortune to ambitious projects of a slow, difficult, uncertain execution, and which—assuming them to be realized someday—in all their brilliance were not worth a quarter of an hour of true pleasure and freedom in youth.

Full of this bright whim, I behaved so well that I managed to get my-self thrown out, and in truth this was not accomplished without difficulty. One evening as I was returning, the steward notified me of my dismissal on behalf of M. the Comte. This was precisely what I was asking for: for, since I felt the extravagance of my behavior in spite of myself, I added injustice and ingratitude to it in order to excuse myself, believing that I could put others in the wrong this way, and so as to justify to myself[29] a decision made out of necessity. On behalf of the Comte de Favria I was told to go speak to him the next morning before my departure, and since they saw that my head had turned and that I was capable of not doing it, the steward put off until after this visit giving me some money they had intended for me and that surely I had very badly earned: for, since they had not wanted to leave me in the station of a valet, they had not settled my wages.

Young and giddy though he was, on this occasion the Comte de Favria gave me the most sensible and I would almost dare to say, the most tender speech; in so flattering and touching a manner did he put before me his uncle's care and his grandfather's intentions. Finally, after having vividly set before my eyes everything I was sacrificing in order to run to my ruin, he offered to make my peace, demanding as the only condition that I no longer see that little wretch who had seduced me.

It was so clear that he was not saying all of this on his own that, in spite of my stupid blindness, I felt all the kindness of my old master and I was touched by it: but this beloved trip was too much imprinted on my imagination for anything to counter its charm. I was completely out of my senses, I stiffened, I hardened myself, I played the proud man, and I answered arrogantly that since they had given me my dismissal I had taken it, that it was too late to withdraw it, and that, whatever might hap-pen to me in my life, I was strongly resolved never to get myself ejected twice from one house. Then this young man, justly irritated, called me the names I deserved, put me out of his room by the shoulders and shut the door on my heels. As for me, I left triumphing as if I had just carried off the greatest victory, and, for fear of having a second battle to undergo, I had the baseness to leave without going to thank M. the Abbé for his kindness.

In order to conceive how far my delirium went at that moment, one would have to know how much my heart is subject to flare up over the smallest things and with what force it plunges itself into imagining the ob-ject that attracts it, however vain this object might sometimes be. The most bizarre, the most infantile, the craziest plans come to caress my favorite idea and show me some plausibility for abandoning myself to it. Would it be believed that at almost nineteen years of age someone could base the sustenance of the rest of his days on an empty bottle? Well, listen.

Several weeks earlier the Abbé de Gouvon had given me as a present a very pretty little Hiero-fountain, with which I was enraptured.[30] As a result of making this fountain work and of speaking about our trip, the wise Bâcle and I thought that the former could serve the latter very well and prolong it. What was there in the world as curious as a Hiero-fountain? This principle was the foundation upon which we built the edifice of our fortune. In each village we would assemble the countryfolk around our fountain, and there meals and good cheer would fall on us with all the more abundance since we were both persuaded that provisions cost nothing to those who gather them, and that if they did not stuff passers-by with them, it was out of pure ill will on their part. Everywhere we imagined nothing but feasts and wedding receptions, reckoning that without spending anything but the wind of our lungs and the water of our fountain, it could defray our expenses in Piedmont, in Savoy, in France, and all over the world. We made plans for traveling that did not end, and we first directed our path to the north, more for the pleasure of crossing the Alps, than for the assumed necessity of finally stopping somewhere.

Such was the plan on which I set to work, abandoning without regret my protector, my teacher, my studies, my hopes, and the expectation of an almost assured fortune, in order to begin the life of a true vagabond.[31] Farewell to the capital, farewell to the Court, ambition, vanity, love, the beauties, and all the great adventures the hope for which had led me the year before. I leave with my fountain and my friend Bâcle, with my purse lightly garnished, but my heart saturated with joy and thinking of nothing except enjoying this ambulatory happiness to which I had suddenly limited my brilliant projects.

I made this extravagant trip almost as pleasantly as I had expected, however, but not exactly in the same manner; for although our fountain amused the hostesses and their waitresses in the taverns for a few moments, it was no less necessary to pay upon leaving. But that hardly bothered us, and we thought of making real use of this resource only when money failed. An accident saved us the trouble; the fountain broke near Bramant, and it was time for it; for, without daring to say it to ourselves, we felt that it was beginning to bore us. This misfortune made us more gay than before, and we laughed a lot about our heedlessness, for having forgotten that our clothes and shoes would wear out, or for having believed we would renew them with the playing of our fountain. We continued our trip as buoyantly as we had begun it, but we were drawing a little more directly toward the conclusion that our emptying purse made it necessary for us to reach.

At Chambéry I became pensive, not about the foolishness I had just committed: never did a man so soon or so well resign himself over the past; but about the welcome that awaited me with Mme de Warens: for I envisaged her house exactly as my paternal house. I had written to her about my entrance at the Comte de Gouvon's; she knew what footing I was on, and upon congratulating me about it she had given me very wise lessons about the way I ought to respond to the kindness they had for me. She looked at my fortune as assured if I did not destroy it through my own fault. What was she going to say when she saw me arrive? It did not even enter my mind that she might shut her door to me; but I feared the grief I was going to give her; I feared her reproaches which would be harsher than misery for me. I resolved to endure everything in silence, and to do everything to appease her. I saw nothing in the universe but her alone: to live in her disgrace was a thing that could not be.

What troubled me the most was my traveling companion with whom I did not want to burden her, and whom I feared I would not be able to get rid of easily. I prepared that separation by living rather coolly with him the last day. The scamp understood me; he was more crazy than foolish. I believed that he would be grieved by my inconstancy; I was wrong; my friend Bâcle was grieved by nothing. Upon entering Annecy we had barely set foot in the city when he said to me, "You are home," embraced me, said farewell, made a pirouette, and disappeared. I have never heard anything about him since. Our acquaintance and our friendship lasted about six weeks in all, but their consequences will last as long as I do.[32]

How my heart beat as I approached Mme de Warens's house! My legs trembled under me, my eyes were covered by a veil, I saw nothing, I heard nothing, I would have recognized no one; I was obliged to stop several times to breathe and recover my senses. Was it fear of not obtaining the help I needed that troubled me to this extreme? At the age I was does the fear of dying of hunger cause such alarm? No, no, I say it with as much truth as pride; never at any time in my life has either self-interest or indigence been able to brighten up or oppress my heart. In the course of a life that has been uneven and memorable for its vicissitudes, often without refuge and without bread, I have always seen opulence and misery in the same way. Out of need I could have begged or stolen like someone else, but I could not bother myself about being reduced to that point. Few men have groaned as much as I have, few have shed as many tears in their life, but never has poverty or the fear of falling into it made me heave a sigh or drop a tear. Proof against fortune, my soul has known no true good or true ills except those that do not depend on it, and it is when I have lacked nothing by way of necessities that I have felt myself to be the most unfortunate of mortals.

Hardly had I appeared before Mme de Warens's eyes than her manner reassured me. I shivered at the first sound of her voice, I threw myself at her feet, and in the raptures of the liveliest joy I pressed my mouth to her hand. As for her, I do not know whether she had received news about me, but I saw little surprise on her face, and I saw no grief there. "Poor little one," she said to me in an affectionate tone, "you are back again then? I knew very well that you were too young for that trip; I am very relieved at least that it did not turn out as badly as I had feared." Then she made me tell my story, which was not long, and which I gave her very faithfully, nevertheless suppressing several articles, but for the rest without either sparing or excusing myself.

There was the question of my lodging. She consulted her chamber-maid.[33] I did not dare to breathe during this deliberation; but when I heard that I would sleep in the house I could barely contain myself, and I saw my little bundle carried into the room destined for me almost as St. Preux saw his carriage put up at Mme de Wolmar's home.[34] In addition I had the pleasure of learning that this favor would not be at all temporary, and at a moment when they thought I was paying attention to something completely different, I heard her say, "They will say what they want, but since providence has sent him back to me, I am determined not to abandon him."

Behold me then finally established in her home. Nevertheless, this establishment was not yet the one from which I date the happy days of my life, but it served to prepare for it. Although that sensitivity of heart that makes us truly enjoy ourselves is the work of nature and perhaps a product of physical organization, it needs situations that develop it. Without these precipitating causes[35] a man who was born very sensitive would feel nothing, and he would die without having known his being. I had almost been that way until then, and possibly I would always have been so, if I had never known Mme de Warens, or even if, having known her, I had not lived near her long enough to contract the sweet habit of the affectionate feelings with which she inspired me. I will dare to say it; whoever feels only love does not feel what is sweetest in life. I am acquainted with another feeling, less impetuous perhaps, but a thousand times more delightful, which sometimes is joined to love and which is often separate from it. This feeling is not friendship alone either; it is more voluptuous, more tender; I do not imagine that it can take effect for someone of the same sex; at least I have been a friend, if ever a man has been, and I have never experienced it with any of my male friends. This is not clear, but it will become so in what follows; feelings are described well only through their effects.

She lived in an old house, but big enough to have a fine spare room which she made her reception room and which was the one in which I was lodged. This room was over the passageway about which I have spoken where our first interview took place, and beyond the stream and the gardens one could glimpse the country. This view was not an inconsequential matter for the young inhabitant. It was the first time since Bossey that I had some green outside my windows. Always masked by walls, I had had only roofs or the grey of the streets under my eyes. How touching and sweet this novelty was for me! It very much increased my disposition to tenderness. I made this charming countryside into yet another one of the benefits from my dear patroness: it seemed to me that she had put it there expressly for me; I took my place peacefully near her; I saw her everywhere among the flowers and greenery; her charms and those of the springtime were mingled in my eyes. My heart, compressed until then, found itself more at large in that space, and my sighs were breathed more freely among these orchards.

The magnificence I had seen at Turin was not found at Mme de Warens's, but[36] cleanliness, modesty, and a patriarchal[37] abundance with which ostentation is never united were found there. She had few silver dishes, none at all of porcelain, neither game in her kitchen, nor foreign wines in her cellar; but both were well stocked for the use of everyone, and she served excellent coffee in crockery cups. Whoever came to see her was invited to dine with her or in her home, and never did a worker, a messenger, or a traveler leave without eating or drinking.[38] Her household was made up of a rather pretty chambermaid from Fribourg named Merceret,[39] a valet from her country named Claude Anet about whom more will be said in what follows,[40] a cook, and two chair carriers for when she went visiting, which she rarely did. This is a lot for two thousand livres of income; nevertheless, if it had been managed well her little revenue could have sufficed for all that, in a country where the earth is very good and money very rare. Unfortunately economy was never her favorite virtue; she went into debt, she paid; money shuttled back and forth, and everything went along.

The manner in which her household was conducted was precisely the one I would have chosen; one can believe that I took advantage of it with pleasure. What pleased me less was that it was necessary to stay at table for a long time. She could hardly bear the first smell of the soup and meats.

This smell made her almost fall into a faint, and this distaste would last for a long time. She recovered little by little, chatted, and did not eat at all. It was only after half an hour that she tried the first piece. I would have dined three times in that interval: my meal was done long before she began hers.[41] I began again so as to be company; thus I ate enough for two, and did not find myself any the worse for it. In the end I abandoned myself all the more to the sweet feeling of well-being I experienced near her, since this well-being I enjoyed was mixed with no uneasiness about the means of maintaining it. Not yet being in close confidence about her affairs, I assumed that they were in a condition to go along on the same footing forever. Later I found the same pleasures in her house; but, better informed about her real situation, and seeing that they encroached upon her income, I did not taste them so tranquilly any longer. Foresight has always spoiled enjoyment for me. I have foreseen the future in vain: I have never been able to avoid it.

From the first day the sweetest familiarity[42] was established between us to the same degree at which it continued all the rest of her life. *Little one* was my name, *Mamma* was hers,[43] and we always remained *Little one and Mamma*, even when the number of years had almost effaced the difference between us. I find that these two names marvelously give the idea of our tone, the simplicity of our manners and above all the relationship of our hearts. For me she was the most tender of mothers who never sought her own pleasure but always my good; and if the senses entered into my attachment for her, this did not change its nature, but only rendered it more exquisite, intoxicated me with the charm of having a young and pretty mamma whom it was delightful for me to caress; I say, to caress in the literal sense; for never did she think of depriving me of kisses or of the most tender maternal caresses, and never did it enter my heart to abuse them. It will be said that in the end we had relations of another sort, however; I acknowledge it, but it is necessary to wait; I cannot say everything at once.

The first glance of our first interview was the only truly passionate moment she ever made me feel; and even that moment was the work of surprise. My indiscreet glances never went ferreting about under her handkerchief, even though a poorly concealed plumpness in that place might well have attracted them there. I had neither raptures nor desires around her: I was in a ravishing calm, enjoying without knowing what. I would have passed my life and even eternity in this way without being bored for an instant. She is the only person with whom I never felt that dryness of conversation that makes the duty of maintaining it a torture for me. Our tête-à-têtes were less discussions than an inexhaustible babble which did not end unless it was interrupted. Far from making it a law for myself to speak, I much more needed to make it one to be quiet. As a result of meditating about her projects she often fell into reverie. Very well, I let her dream; I was quiet, I contemplated her, and I was the happiest of men. I still had a very peculiar quirk. Without claiming the favors of a tête-à-tête, I sought it ceaselessly, and I enjoyed it with a passion that degenerated into rage if importunate people came to interrupt it. As soon as someone arrived, man or woman, it did not matter which, I left muttering, not being able to bear staying around her as a third. I went away to count the minutes in her antechamber, cursing these eternal visitors a thousand times, and not being able to conceive how they had so much to say, because I had even more to say.

I felt all the strength of my attachment for her only when I did not see her. When I saw her I was only content; but my uneasiness in her absence went so far as to be painful.[44] My need for living with her gave me outbursts of tenderness which often went as far as tears. I will always remember that one high holiday, while she was at vespers, I went for a walk outside the city, my heart full of her image and of the ardent desire to pass my days near her. I had enough sense to see that at present this was not possible, and that a happiness that I was tasting so well would be brief. That gave my reverie a sadness that however had nothing somber about it and that was tempered by a flattering hope. The sound of bells which has always particularly affected me, the song of the birds, the beauty of the day, the gentleness of the countryside, the scattered and rural houses in which my ideas placed our common residence; all that struck me so much with a lively, tender, sad, and touching impression that I saw myself carried away as if in ecstasy to that happy time and into that happy abode, where my heart—possessing all the felicity that could please it—tasted it in inexpressible raptures, without even thinking about the voluptuousness of the senses. I do not remember ever launching myself into the future with more force and illusion than I did then; and what struck me most in the remembrance of this reverie when it came true, is that I found objects so exactly as I had imagined them. If ever the dream of a man awake had the air of a prophetic vision, it was surely that one. I was deceived only in its imaginary duration; for in it days and years and my entire life passed in an unchangeable tranquillity, whereas in fact all that lasted only for a moment. Alas! my most constant happiness was but a dream. Its accomplishment was almost immediately followed by waking up.[45]

I would not finish if I entered into detail about all the foolish things the memory of that dear Mamma made me commit, when I was no longer under her eyes. How many times did I kiss my bed while thinking that she had slept in it, my curtains, all the furniture of my room while thinking that they belonged to her, that her beautiful hand had touched them, even the floor upon which I prostrated myself while thinking that she had walked on it. Sometimes even in her presence some extravagances that only the most violent love seemed capable of inspiring burst out of me. One day at table, at the moment that she had put a morsel in her mouth, I exclaim that I see a hair on it: she spits it out onto her plate, I seize it greedily and swallow it. In a word, there was only one single difference between me and the most passionate lover, but this was an essential one, and renders my condition almost inconceivable to reason.

I had come back from Italy not altogether as I had gone there; but perhaps as no one of my age has ever come back from it. I had brought back not my virginity, but my maidenhead. I had felt the progress of the years; my restless temperament had finally declared itself, and its first, very involuntary, eruption, had given me alarms about my health that depict the innocence in which I had lived until then better than anything else. Soon reassured, I learned that dangerous supplement [46] that fools nature and saves young people of my disposition from many disorders at the expense of their health, their vigor, and sometimes their life. This vice, which shame and timidity find so convenient, furthermore has a great attraction for lively imaginations; it is, so to speak, to dispose of the whole opposite sex at their whim, and to make the beauty who tempts them serve their pleasures without needing to obtain her consent. Seduced by this fatal advantage, I labored to destroy the good constitution that nature had reestablished in me, and to which I had given time to form itself well. Add to this inclination the locality of my present situation, lodged in the home of a pretty woman, caressing her image at the bottom of my heart, ceaselessly seeing her during the day; at night surrounded by objects that recalled her to me, sleeping in a bed in which I know she has slept. How many stimulants! any reader who represents them to himself regards me as already half dead. Completely to the contrary; what ought to have ruined me was precisely what saved me, at least for a time. Intoxicated with the charm of living near her, with the ardent desire to pass my days there, absent or present I always saw in her a tender mother, a dear sister, a delightful friend, and nothing more. I always saw her that way, always the same, and never saw anything but her. Always present to my heart, her image left no room there for any other; for me she was the only woman in the world, and since the extreme sweetness of the feelings she inspired in me did not leave my senses time to awaken for others, it protected me from her and from her whole sex. In a word, I was chaste because I loved her. From these effects which I relate poorly, let anyone who can do so tell what sort of attachment mine was for her. As for me all I can say about it is that if it already appears very extraordinary, it will appear much more so in what follows.

I passed my time in the most agreeable manner in the world, occupied with things that pleased me the least. There were projects to draw up, memoranda to make fair copies of, receipts to transcribe; there were herbs to pick out, drugs to pound, stills to supervise. Into the midst of all this came crowds of passers-by, beggars, visits of all sorts. It was necessary to entertain a soldier, an apothecary, a Canon, a fine Lady, a lay brother all at the same time. I cursed, I grumbled, I swore, I sent all that cursed throng to the devil. As for her who took everything gaily, my rages made her laugh to the point of tears, and what made her laugh even more was to see me all the more furious at not being able to keep myself from laughing. These little intervals in which I had the pleasure of growling were charming, and if a new pest arrived unexpectedly during the quarrel, she knew how to take further advantage of it for the amusement by maliciously prolonging the visit, and casting glances at me for which I would willingly have beaten her. She had trouble keeping herself from bursting out while seeing me strained and held back by decorum while I gave her the looks of a man possessed, although at the bottom of my heart, and even in spite of myself, I found all this very comical.

Without pleasing me in itself, all this nevertheless amused me because it formed a part of a manner of being that was charming for me. Nothing that happened around me, nothing they made me do agreed with my taste, but everything agreed with my heart. I believe that I would have come to love medicine, if my distaste for it had not furnished sprightly scenes that ceaselessly cheered us up: it is perhaps the first time that this art produced a similar effect. I claimed to know a book of medicine from its odor, and what is pleasant is that I was rarely mistaken. She made me taste the most detestable drugs. I ran away or wanted to defend myself in vain; in spite of my resistance and my horrible grimaces, in spite of me and my teeth; when I saw those pretty smeared fingers approaching my mouth, I had to end by opening it and sucking. When all her little household was assembled in the same room, to hear us run and shout in the midst of bursts of laughter, one would have believed that some farce was being played, and not that some opiate or elixir was being made.

Nevertheless my time did not pass entirely in these childish pranks. I had found several books in the room I occupied: the *Spectator*, Pufendorf, St. Evremond, the *Henriade*.[47] Although I no longer had my former rage for reading, from inactivity I read a little from all these. Above all

The Spectator pleased me very much and did me some good. M. the Abbé de Gouvon had taught me to read less avidly and with more reflection; I read to greater advantage. I accustomed myself to reflect on elocution, on elegant constructions; I practiced discerning pure French from my provincial idioms. For example, I was corrected of a spelling mistake that I made along with all our Genevans by these two verses from *The Henriade*:

> Soit qu'un ancien respect pour le sang de leurs maitres
> Parlât encor pour lui dans le coeur de ces traitres.[48]

This word *parlât*, which struck me, taught me that a *t* is needed in the third person of the subjunctive; instead of which I formerly wrote and pronounced *parla*, as in the present of the indicative.[49]

Sometimes I chatted with Mamma about my readings; sometimes I read to her; I took great pleasure in it; I practiced reading well, and that was useful to me also. I have said that she had a cultivated mind. At that time it was in full flower.[50] Numerous literary people had been eager to please her, and had taught her to judge about works of the mind. She had, if I can speak this way, a slightly Protestant taste: she spoke only of Bayle[51] and made much of St. Evremond, who had long been out of favor in France. But that did not keep her from being acquainted with good literature and from speaking about it extremely well. She had been brought up in select society, and since she had come into Savoy while still young, in the charming company of the nobility of the country she had lost that mannered tone of the Pays de Vaud where women take fine wit for worldly intelligence, and know how to speak only in epigrams.

Although she had seen the Court only in passing, she had cast a rapid look at it which had been enough for her to know it. She always preserved some friends there, and in spite of secret jealousies, in spite of the muttering excited by her behavior and her debts, she never lost her pension. She had experience of the world of high society, and the spirit of reflection that profits from this experience. This was the favorite subject of her conversations, and, given my chimerical ideas, this was precisely the sort of instruction I needed most. Together we read La Bruyére: she preferred him to La Rochefoucauld, a sad and distressing book, especially when one is young and does not like to see man as he is.[52] When she moralized, she sometimes wandered off into the distance; but by kissing her mouth or hands from time to time I kept my patience, and her longwindedness did not bore me.

This life was too sweet to be able to last. I felt this, and the uneasiness of seeing it end was the only thing that troubled my enjoyment of it. Even while she was being playful Mamma studied me, observed me, questioned me, and built up many projects for my fortune that I would have done very well without. Fortunately it was not enough to know my inclinations, my tastes, my little talents, it was necessary to find or cause to be born occasions for taking advantage of them, and all that was not the business of a day. Even the prejudices the poor woman had conceived in favor of my merit pushed back the moments for putting it into practice by making her more demanding about the choice of means; in sum, everything went according to the whim of my desires, thanks to the good opinion she had of me; but it had to be lowered, and from that time, farewell tranquillity.[53] One of her relatives named M. d'Aubonne came to see her.[54] He was a man of much intelligence, scheming, like her a genius at projects, but who did not ruin himself in them, a sort of adventurer. He had just proposed to Cardinal Fleury a very well-designed lottery plan, which had not been approved.[55] He was going to propose it at the Court of Turin where it was adopted and put into execution. He stopped for some time at Annecy and fell in love with the Intendant's wife, who was an extremely amiable person, very much to my taste, and the only one I saw with pleasure at Mamma's house. M. d'Aubonne saw me, his kinswoman spoke to him about me, he took it upon himself to examine me, to see what I was fit for, and—if he found any mettle in me—to seek to place me.

Mme de Warens sent me to him two or three mornings in a row, under the pretext of some commission, and without warning me about anything. He succeeded very well in making me chatter, familiarized himself with me, set me at my ease as much as possible, spoke to me about nonsense and about all sorts of subjects. All this without appearing to observe me, without the least affectation, and as if, being pleased with me, he wanted to converse without constraint. I was enchanted with him.[56] The result of his observations was that, in spite of what my exterior and animated physiognomy promised, I was—if not completely inept—at least a boy of little intelligence, without ideas, almost without accomplishments, in a word very limited in all respects; and that the honor of some day becoming a village Curate was the highest fortune to which I ought to[57] aspire. Such was the account he rendered of me to Mme de Warens. This was the second or third time I was judged this way; it was not the last, and M. Masseron's verdict[58] has often been upheld.

The cause of these judgments is too much connected to my character not to require some explanation here: for in conscience, one feels[59] very well that I cannot sincerely subscribe to it, and that with all the impartiality possible, whatever M. Masseron, M. d'Aubonne, and many others might have said, I cannot take their word for it.

Two almost incompatible things are joined in me[60] without me being able to conceive how: a very ardent temperament, lively, impetuous passions, and ideas that are slow to be born, confused, and that never offer themselves until after the event. One would say that my heart and my mind[61] do not belong to the same individual. Feeling comes to fill my soul quicker than lightning, but instead of enlightening me it sets me on fire and dazzles me. I feel everything and I see nothing. I am fiery but stupid: I need to be cool in order to think. What is surprising in this is that I nevertheless have reliable enough discrimination, penetration, even finesse as long as one waits for me: I make excellent impromptu remarks at leisure; but I have never done or said anything worthwhile on the spur of the moment. I would carry on an extremely pretty conversation by post, as they say the Spaniards play chess. When I read the striking event of a Duke of Savoy who, while on his journey, turned around to shout, "*You* stuff it, Paris merchant," I said, "That is I."[62]

It is not only in conversation that I have this slowness in thinking joined with this liveliness in feeling, I have it even when I am alone and when I am working. My ideas arrange themselves in my head with the most incredible difficulty. They circulate there dumbly; they ferment there to the point of rousing me, heating me up, giving me palpitations, and in the midst of all this emotion I do not see anything clearly; I cannot write a single word, I have to wait. Insensibly this great motion subsides, this chaos sorts itself out; each thing comes to put itself in its place, but slowly and after a long and confused agitation. Have you ever seen the Opera in Italy? In the changes of scene in these large theaters, there reigns an unpleasant disorder, which lasts a rather long time: all the backdrops are mixed up together; from every direction there is a pushing and pulling which is painful to see; one believes that everything is going to turn upside down. Nevertheless little by little everything is arranged, nothing is lacking, and one is completely surprised to see a ravishing spectacle follow this long tumult. That maneuvering is almost the same as the one that goes on in my brain when I want to write. If I had known how, first to wait, and then to render in their beauty the things that depicted themselves there, few Authors would have surpassed me.

From this comes the extreme difficulty I find in writing. My scratched out, blotted, mixed up, indecipherable manuscripts attest to the trouble they have cost me. There is not one of them that I have not had to transcribe four or five times before giving it to the press. I have never been able to do anything with pen in hand in front of a table and my paper. It is while walking in the midst of rocks and woods, it is at night in my bed and during my insomnias that I compose in my brain, one can judge how slowly, above all for a man absolutely devoid of[63] verbal memory, and who has never in his life been able to retain six verses by heart. I have turned and re-turned some of my passages for five or six nights in my head before they have been in a condition to be set down on paper. From this it happens again that I succeed better in works that demand some labor than in those that require a certain lightness, such as letters; a genre whose tone I have never been able to grasp, and occupation with which puts me to torture. Even writing letters on the most trivial subjects costs me hours of fatigue, or if I want to write successively what comes to me, I can neither begin nor end,[64] my letter is a long and confused verbiage that is barely intelligible when it is read.

Not only does it give me pain to render ideas, it even gives me pain to receive them. I have studied men and I believe myself to be a rather good observer.[65] Nevertheless I do not know how to see anything of what I am seeing; I see well only what I recall, and I have intelligence only in my memories. Out of everything that is said, everything that is done, everything that happens in my presence, I feel nothing, I penetrate nothing. The exterior sign is all that strikes me. But later everything comes back to me: I recall the place, the time, the tone, the look, the gesture, the circumstance, nothing escapes me. Thus based on what has been done or said I find what has been thought, and I am rarely mistaken.

So little master of my mind when I am all by myself, one can judge what I must be in conversation, where, in order to speak to the point one must think about a thousand things simultaneously and on the spot. The mere idea of so many social conventions, at least one of which I am certain to forget, is enough to intimidate me. I do not understand how one even dares to speak in a social circle: for at each word one would have to pass in review all the people who are there: one would have to be acquainted with all their characters, know[66] their histories in order to be sure of saying nothing that might offend someone. On this point those who live in the world of high society have a great advantage: knowing better what one should be quiet about, they are more sure about what they are saying: even so blunders often escape them. Judge then about someone who falls into it from the clouds! it is almost impossible for him to speak for a minute with impunity. In a tête-à-tête there is another inconvenience that I find worse; the necessity of always talking. If someone talks to you, you must answer, and if not a word is said, you must revive the conversation. This unbearable constraint alone would have disgusted me with society. I find no bother more terrible than the obligation of talking on the spot and always.[67] I do not know if this depends on my mortal aversion for all subjugation: but I must only be absolutely required to speak in order to say something stupid without fail.

What is more fatal is that, instead of knowing how to be quiet when I have nothing to say, that is when I have the frenzy to want to speak so as to pay my debt the sooner. I hurry promptly to stammer some words without ideas, only too happy if they mean nothing at all. By wanting to conquer or hide my ineptness, I rarely fail to show it. Among a thousand examples that I could cite of this I take one that is not from my youth, but from a time at which, since I had lived in the world of high society for several years, I would have acquired its facility and tone if it had been possible to do so. One evening I was with two great Ladies and a man whose name can be given; it was M. the Duc de Gontaut.[68] No one else was in the room, and I struggled to provide some words, God knows which ones, for a conversation among four people three of whom certainly did not need my supplement. The mistress of the house had an opiate brought to her which she took two times every day for her stomach. Seeing her make a grimace the other Lady said while laughing, "Is that M. Tronchin's opiate?" "I don't believe so," answered the first in the same tone. "I believe it's hardly any different," gallantly added the spiritual Rousseau.[69] Everyone stopped amazed. Not the slightest word nor the slightest smile escaped, and the next instant the conversation took another turn. With regard to someone else the blunder might have been merely a pleasantry, but addressed to a woman too lovable not to have made herself talked about a little, and whom assuredly I did not intend to offend, it was terrible, and I believe that the two witnesses, man and woman, had a lot of difficulty refraining from bursting out.[70] This is one of those strokes of wit that escape me because I want to talk without having anything to say. It will be hard for me to forget that one; for, aside from the fact that it is very memorable in itself, I have it in my head that it had consequences that remind me of it only too often.

I believe this is enough to make it sufficiently understood how, although I am not a fool, I have nevertheless often passed for one, even among people in a position to judge well: all the more unfortunate since my physiognomy and my eyes promise more,[71] and since it makes my stupidity more shocking to others when that expectation has been frustrated. This detail, which has arisen from a particular occasion, is not useless to what is to follow. It contains the key to many extraordinary things I have been seen to do, which are attributed to a savage mood that I do not have at all. I would love society as much as anyone else if I was not sure of showing myself, not only to my disadvantage there, but com-

pletely different from the way I am. The decision I have made to write
and hide myself is [72] precisely the one that suits me. If I had been present,
no one would ever have known what I am worth, they would not even
have suspected it; and this is what happened to Mme Dupin, even though
she is an intelligent woman, and although I lived in her house for several
years.[73] She herself has told me so numerous times since then. Besides,
there are certain exceptions to all this, and I will return to it later on.

Since the measure of my talents had been settled this way and the station that suited me was thus marked out for the second time, there was
no other question except to fulfill my vocation. The difficulty was that I
had not completed my studies and that I did not know even enough Latin
to be a priest. Mme de Warens planned to have me taught for some time
at the seminary. She spoke about it to the Superior; this was a Lazarist
called M. Gros, a good little man, half blind, thin, grey-haired, the most
spiritual and the least pedantic Lazarist that I have known; although, to
tell the truth, that is not saying very much.[74]

He sometimes came to Mamma's house where she welcomed him, ca-
ressed him, even provoked him, and sometimes had him lace her up, an
occupation [75] that he took upon himself willingly enough. When he had
taken up his duty, she ran from one side of the room to another, sometimes doing one thing sometimes another. Pulled by the lace, Monsieur
the Superior followed while scolding, and saying at every moment, "But,
Madame hold still then." This made a rather picturesque subject. M. Gros
lent himself good-heartedly to Mamma's project. He was content with a
very moderate fee, and took charge of the instruction. There was only the
question of the consent of the Bishop, who not only granted it, but who
wanted to pay the fee.[76] He also permitted me to remain in lay clothing,
until a trial allowed them to judge what success they should hope for.

What a change! I had to submit to it. I went to the seminary as I would
have gone to torture.[77] What a sad house a Seminary is, especially for
someone who leaves that of a lovable woman. I brought a single book
which I had asked Mamma to lend me, and which was a great support
for me. One will not guess what sort of book this was: a book of music.
Among the talents she had cultivated, music had not been forgotten. She
had a voice, sang passably, and played the Harpsichord a little. She had
had the kindness to give me some singing lessons, and it was necessary to
begin from the beginning, for I hardly knew the music of our Psalms. Far
from putting me in a condition to sol-fa, eight or ten very much interrupted lessons from a woman did not teach me a quarter of the signs of
music. Nevertheless, I had such a passion for this art that I wanted to try
to practice by myself. The book that I carried off was not even one of the

easiest ones; it was the *Cantatas* of Clerambault.[78] You will conceive what my application and my obstinacy were, if I say that without knowing either transposition or quantity I succeeded at deciphering and singing the first recitative and the first air of the Cantata of *Alpheus and Arethusa* without a mistake; and it is true that this air is so exactly scanned, that one need only recite the verses in their measure to catch the phrasing of the air.

At the Seminary there was a cursed Lazarist who took me in hand and who made me acquire a horror of Latin which he wanted to teach me. He had flat, greasy black hair, a gingerbread face, the voice of a buffalo, the looks of a screech-owl, bristles of a wild boar instead of a beard; his smile was sardonic;[79] his limbs played like the pulleys of a mannequin: I have forgotten his odious name; but his frightful and sickly sweet face has remained very much with me, and I have trouble recalling him without shuddering. I believe I am meeting him again in the corridors, holding out his filthy square cap to make me a sign to enter his room, which frightened me more than a prison cell. Judge about the contrast of such a master, for the pupil of a Court Abbé!

If I had remained at the mercy of this monster for two months[80] I am persuaded that my head would not have put up with it. But the good M. Gros who noticed that I was sad, that I did not eat, that I was growing thin, guessed the subject of my sorrow; that was not hard. He removed me from the clutches of my beast, and by a still more marked contrast put me into the hands of the most gentle of men. This was a young Abbé from Faucigny, called M. Gâtier who was studying at the seminary and who out of the desire to be obliging for M. Gros, and I believe, out of humanity, wanted to take from his own studies the time he gave to direct mine.[81] I have never seen a more touching physiognomy than M. Gâtier's. He was blond and his beard tended toward red. He had the ordinary bearing of the people of his province, all of whom hide much intelligence underneath a dense look; but what was truly marked in him was a sensitive, affectionate, loving soul: in his large blue eyes he had a mixture of gentleness, tenderness, and sadness, which made it impossible to see him without taking an interest in him. From the looks, from the tone of this poor young man, one might have said that he foresaw his destiny, and that he felt himself born to be unhappy.

His character did not belie his physiognomy. Full of patience and the desire to be obliging, he seemed rather to study with me than to teach me. It did not require that much to make me love him, his predecessor had made that very easy. Nevertheless, in spite of all the time he gave me, in spite of all the good will we both put into it, and although he went about it in a very good way, I progressed little while working a lot. It is peculiar that, even with a sufficient faculty for comprehending, I have never been able to learn anything with masters except my father and M. Lambercier. The little I know in addition I have learned alone, as will be seen below. Impatient with any sort of yoke, my mind cannot submit itself to the law of the moment. Even the fear of not learning keeps me from being attentive. From fear of making the person speaking to me impatient, I pretend to understand; he goes forward and I understand nothing. My mind wants to go at its own tempo, it cannot submit to anyone else's.

When the time for ordinations came, M. Gâtier returned to his province as a Deacon. He carried with him my regrets, my attachment, my gratitude. I made prayers for him that were not heard any more than the ones I made for myself. Several years later I learned that, being a Vicar in a parish, he had had a child by a girl, the only one with whom he had ever been in love, although he had a very tender heart. This was a dreadful scandal in a very severely administered Diocese. As a good rule, Priests should have children only by married women. For having failed to observe this law of social convention he was put in prison, defamed, expelled. I do not know whether he was able to reestablish his affairs afterwards; but since it was profoundly engraved on my heart, the feeling of his misfortune came back to me when I wrote *Emile*, and joining M. Gâtier with M. Gaime, from these two worthy priests I made the original of the Savoyard Vicar.[82] I flatter myself that the imitation did not dishonor its models.

While I was at the seminary M. d'Aubonne was obliged to leave Annecy. M. the Intendant took it into his head to object to him making love to his wife. That was acting like the gardener's dog;[83] for although Mme Corvezy was amiable, he got along extremely badly with her; ultra-montane tastes made her useless to him, and he treated her so brutally that there was a question of separation.[84] M. Corvezi was a nasty-looking man, black as a mole, knavish as an owl, who ended by getting himself dismissed because of his vexatious measures. They say that people from Provence avenge themselves on their enemies with songs; M. D'Aubonne avenged himself on his with a play; he sent this piece to Mme de Warens who had me look at it. It pleased me and caused to be born in me the whim of writing one in order to test whether I was in fact as stupid as the Author had declared: but it was only at Chambéry that I executed this project by writing *The Lover of Himself*. Thus when I said in the preface to that piece that I had written it at eighteen years of age, I lied by several years.[85]

About this time there occurred an event hardly important in itself, but which has had consequences for me, and which caused a commotion in the world when I had forgotten it. Every week I had permission to go out once. I do not need to say what use I made of it. One Sunday when I was at Mamma's a fire broke out in one of the Franciscan friars' buildings adjoining the house she occupied. This building, where their oven was, was full to the roof with dried faggots. In a very short time everything was ablaze. The house was in great peril and covered by flames carried there by the wind. We hastily set about removing the furniture and carrying it into the garden, which was across from my former windows and above the stream about which I have spoken. I was so upset that I indiscriminately threw everything that fell into my hands out of the window, even a large stone mortar that I would have had trouble lifting at any other time. I was ready to throw out a big mirror in the same way, if someone had not held me back. The good Bishop who had come to see Mamma that day did not remain idle either. He led her into the garden where he began to pray with her and everyone who was there, so that arriving some time after, I saw them all on their knees and began to pray like the others. During the Holy man's prayer,[86] the wind changed, but so abruptly and so opportunely that the flames that covered the house and were already entering through the windows were carried to the other side of the Courtyard, and the house had no damage whatsoever. Two years later, after M. de Bernex had died, his old brethren the Antonines,[87] began to collect evidence that could be used for his beatification. At the request of Father Boudet[88] I added to these pieces an attestation of the fact that I just reported, in which I acted well; but I acted badly by presenting this fact as a miracle. I had seen the Bishop in prayer, and during his prayer I had seen the wind change, and even very opportunely: that is what I could say and certify: but that one of these two things was the cause of the other, that is what I ought not to have attested, because I could not know it. Nevertheless, as far as I can recall my ideas, which were sincerely Catholic at that time, I was in good faith. The love of the marvelous so natural to the human heart, my veneration for this virtuous Prelate, the secret pride at having perhaps contributed to the miracle myself, helped to seduce me, and what is certain is that if this miracle were the effect of the most ardent prayers, I would have been very capable of attributing a part of it to myself.

More than thirty years later, when I published the *Letters from the Mountain*, M. Freron somehow or other unearthed this certificate and made use of it in his pamphlet.[89] It must be admitted that the discovery was fortunate, and its apt use appeared very humorous even to me.

I was destined to be the outcast from all stations. Although M. Gâtier gave the least unfavorable account of my progress that he could, they saw that it was not proportionate to my work, and that was not encouraging for making me push my studies forward. Also the Bishop and the Superior were discouraged, and[90] they sent me back to Mme de Warens as a subject who was not even good enough to be a priest; otherwise a good enough boy, they said, and not at all vicious; this caused her not to abandon me in spite of so many discouraging prejudices on my account.

In triumph I brought back her book of music of which I had made such good use. My tune of Alpheus and Arethusa was almost all I had learned at the seminary. My marked taste for this art gave rise to the thought of making me into a musician.[91] The occasion was convenient. Music was performed at her house at least once a week, and the music master of the Cathedral who directed this little concert came to see her very often. He was a Parisian named M. Le Maître,[92] a good composer, extremely lively, extremely gay, still young, rather well built, with little intelligence, but on the whole a very good man.[93] Mamma had me make his acquaintance; I attached myself to him, I did not displease him: a fee for lodging was spoken of; it was agreed to. In short I entered his house, and I passed the winter there all the more agreeably since, because the master's residence was not twenty steps from mamma's house, we were there in a moment and we ate together there very often.

One will judge very readily that the life of the master's residence—always singing and gay, with musicians and children of the choir—pleased me more than that of the seminary with the Lazarist fathers. Nevertheless, although more free, that life was not any less even and regulated. I was made to love independence and never to abuse it. For six whole months, I did not go out a single time except to go to mamma's or to Church, and I was not even tempted to do so. This interval is one of those in which I lived in the greatest calm, and which I recall with the most pleasure. Of the diverse situations in which I have found myself, several have been marked by such a feeling of well-being that in remembering them I am affected by them as if I were still there. Not only do I recall the times, the places, the people, but all the surrounding objects, the temperature of the air, its smell, its color, a certain local impression that makes itself felt only there, and the lively remembrance of which transports me there anew. For example, everything that was rehearsed at the master's residence, everything that was sung in the Choir, everything that was done there, the fine and noble dress of the Canons, the Priests' chasubles, the choristers' miters, the faces of the Musicians, an old lame carpenter who played the counterbass, a little fair-haired abbé who played the violin, the tattered cassock which M. le Maître put on over his lay clothes after having laid down his sword, and the fine beautiful surplice with which he covered its rags to go to choir: the pride with which I went, holding my little flute, to settle myself in the orchestra on the platform, for a little bit of a solo that M. Le Maître had written expressly for me: the good dinner that awaited us afterwards, the good appetite we brought to it; this combination of objects, vividly retraced, has charmed me a hundred times in my memory, as much as and more than in reality. I have always kept a tender affection for a certain tune of *Conditor alme Syderum* which proceeds in iambics, because one Sunday in Advent from my bed I heard this hymn sung before daybreak on the Cathedral steps, in accordance with a rite of that Church. Mlle Merceret, mamma's chambermaid[94] knew a little music: I will never forget a little motet *Afferte* that M. le Maître had me sing with her, and to which her mistress listened with so much pleasure. In sum, everything down to the good servant girl Perrine, who was such a good girl and whom the choirboys got so irritated, everything[95] in the remembrances of these times of happiness and innocence often come back to enrapture and sadden me.

I lived at Annecy almost a year without the slightest reproach; everyone was content with me. Since my departure from Turin I had not done anything stupid, and I did not do so as long as I was under mamma's eyes. She led me, and always led me well; my attachment for her had become my only passion, and what proves that it was not a foolish passion is that my heart formed my reason. It is true that a single feeling, absorbing all my faculties so to speak, made it impossible for me to learn anything; not even music, even though I put all my efforts into it. But this was not at all my fault; good will was completely there, assiduousness was there. I was distracted, a dreamer, I sighed; what could I do? Nothing that depended on me was lacking for my progress; but in order for me to commit some new follies, only a subject was needed that might come to inspire me. This subject presented itself; chance arranged things, and, as will be seen in what follows, my unruly head took advantage of it.

One night in the month of February when it was very cold, as we were all gathered around the fire, we heard a knock at the street door. Perrine takes her lantern, goes down, opens: a young man enters with her, comes up, presents himself with an easy manner, and pays a short and well-turned compliment to M. le Maître, giving himself out as a French musician the bad condition of whose finances forced him to offer his services from town to town to make his way. At the words, "French musician," the good Le Maître's heart leapt with joy; he passionately loved his country and his art. He welcomed the young itinerant, offered him the board for which he appeared to have great need and which he accepted without much ceremony. I examined him while he warmed himself up and chattered while waiting for supper. He was short of stature, but broad shouldered; he had an indefinable something malformed in his shape without any particular deformity; he was a hunchback with flat shoulders so to speak, but I believe he limped a little. He had a black coat more worn out than old, which was falling to pieces, a very fine and very dirty shirt, beautiful fringed ruffles, gaiters in each of which he could have put both his legs, and to protect himself from the snow a little hat to carry under his arm. Nevertheless, in this comic outfit he had something noble that his bearing did not belie; his physiognomy had something delicate and pleasing, he spoke easily and well, but not very modestly. Everything about him indicated a debauched young man who had some education and who did not go begging as a beggar, but as a fool. He told us that he was called Venture de Villeneuve, and that he came from Paris, that he had strayed from his route, and forgetting his role as a musician a little, he added that he was going to Grenoble to see a relative he had in the parlement.[96]

During supper we talked about music, and he spoke about it well. He knew all the great virtuosi, all the famous works, all the actors, all the actresses, all the pretty women, all the Great Lords. He appeared to be acquainted with everything that was said; but hardly had a subject been broached when he jumbled up the conversation with some racy joke which made us laugh and forget what had been said. It was a Saturday; the next day there was music at the Cathedral. M. le Maître proposes that he sing there. "*Very willingly*"; asks him what his part is? "*Counter-tenor*," and he speaks of something else. Before going to the Church he was offered his part to look over in advance; he did not cast his eyes on it. This boasting surprised Le Maître: he whispered in my ear, "You will see that he doesn't know a note of music." "I am very much afraid so," I answered him. Very uneasy, I followed them. When they began, my heart beat with a terrible strength; for I was very much concerned for him.

I was soon well enough reassured. He sang his two solos with all the accuracy and all the taste imaginable, and what is more with a very pretty voice. I have hardly ever had a more pleasant surprise. After Mass M. Venture received endless compliments from the Canons and the Musicians to which he responded by making lewd remarks, but always with much grace. M. Le Maître embraced him wholeheartedly; I did so also: he saw that I was very glad, and that appeared to give him pleasure.

I am sure it will be agreed that after having become infatuated with M. Bâcle, who everything considered was only a boor, I was capable of becoming infatuated with M. Venture who had education, talents, wit, experience of the world, and who could pass for an amiable debauched fellow. That is also what happened to me, and would have happened, I think, to any other young man in my place, even all the more easily if he had had a better sense of discrimination for feeling merit, and a better taste for attaching himself to it: for without contradiction Venture did have some, and above all he had one very rare at his age; that of not being at all in a hurry to show off his learning. It is true that he boasted about many things that he did not know at all; but as for those he did know, which were rather numerous, he said nothing about them: he waited for the occasion to show them; then he availed himself of them without haste, and that caused a greater effect. Since he stopped after each thing without speaking about the rest, one did not know when he had shown everything. Playful, frolicsome, irrepressible, seductive in conversation, always smiling and never laughing, he said the coarsest things in the most elegant tone and made them pass. Even the most modest women were surprised at what they put up with from him. They felt very well that they had to get angry, but they did not have the strength. He required only fallen girls, and I do not believe that he was made to have good luck with women, but he was made to give an infinite pleasure to the society of people who did. It would have been hard for him to stay in the sphere of musicians for very long, since he had so many agreeable talents, in a country were they were known and where they were liked.

My taste for M. Venture, more reasonable in its cause than the one I had acquired for M. Bâcle, was also less extravagant in its effects, even though it was more lively and more durable. I loved to see him, to listen to him; to me everything he did appeared charming, to me everything he said seemed to be oracles: but my infatuation did not reach the point of making me incapable of being separated from him. Nearby I had a good preservative against that excess.[97] Moreover, finding his maxims to be very good for him, I felt that they were not intended for me; I needed another sort of sensual delight about which he had no idea, and about which I did not even dare to speak to him, certain that he would make fun of me. Nevertheless, I would have liked to combine this attachment with the one that dominated me. I spoke to Mamma about him with rapture. Le Maître spoke to her about him with praise. She consented to his being introduced; but this interview did not succeed at all: he found her affected; she found him to be a libertine, and being alarmed about such a bad acquaintance for me, not only did she forbid me to bring him back but she depicted to me the dangers I was running with this young man so strongly that I became a little more circumspect about abandoning myself to them, and, very fortunately for my morals and for my head, we were soon separated.

M. le Maître had the tastes of his art; he loved wine. Nevertheless, at table he was sober; but while working in his study he had to drink. His serving-girl knew him so well that, as soon as he was preparing his paper for composing and he took up his cello, his jug and his glass arrived the instant afterwards, and the jug was replenished from time to time. Without ever being absolutely drunk, he was almost always under the influence of wine, and in truth it was a shame; for he was an essentially good chap,[98] and so gay that mamma called him nothing but *kitten*. Unfortunately he loved his talent, worked a lot, and drank a lot. That influenced his health and at last his mood; sometimes he was touchy, and easy to offend. Incapable of coarseness, incapable of overlooking anyone who was coarse, he never said a harsh word, even to one of the children of the Choir. But one must not fail to be respectful toward him, and that was just. The bad thing was that, since he was not very intelligent, he did not discern tones and characters, and often flew into a temper over nothing.

The ancient Chapter of Geneva into which formerly so many Princes and Bishops did themselves honor by entering, lost its former splendor in its exile, but it preserved its pride. To be capable of being admitted to it, one still had to be a gentleman or doctor of the Sorbonne, and if there is a pardonable pride after that drawn from personal merit, it is that drawn from birth. Moreover all Priests who have lay people in their employ usually treat them rather haughtily. It is thus that the Canons often treated the poor Le Maître. Above all the Precentor, called M. the Abbé de Vidonne,[99] who otherwise was a very gallant man, but too full of his nobility, did not always have the consideration for him that his talents deserved, and Le Maître did not put up with this disdain willingly. That year during holy week they had a more lively quarrel than ordinary at the customary dinner that the Bishop gave for the Canons, and to which Le Maître was always invited. The Precentor did him some injustice and said some harsh word to him, which he could not stomach. On the spot he formed the resolution of running away the following night, and nothing could make him let go of it, although Mme de Warens, to whom he went to make his farewell, spared nothing to appease him. He could not renounce the pleasure of avenging himself on his tyrants, by leaving them at a loss at the Easter holidays, the time when they needed him most.[100] But what put him at a loss himself was his music which he wanted to carry off, which was not easy. It made up a rather large and extremely heavy chest, which could not be carried under one's arm.

Mamma did what I would have done and what I would still do in her place. After many useless efforts to hold him back, seeing him resolved to leave whatever might happen, she made the decision to help him in so far as it depended on her. I dare to say that she was obliged to. Le Maître had dedicated himself to her service so to speak. In what depended on either his art or his efforts he was entirely at her disposal, and the heart with which he obeyed her gave an additional value to his complaisance. Thus she was only doing in return for a friend in an essential occasion what he did for her bit by bit for three or four years; but she had a soul that did not need to think of such things as duties in order to fulfil them. She had me come, ordered me to follow M. Le Maître at least as far as Lyon, and to attach myself to him for as long as he might need me. Since then she has admitted to me that the desire to separate me from Venture had entered very much into that arrangement. She consulted her faithful servant Claude Anet about transportation for the chest. He was of the opinion that instead of taking a beast of burden at Annecy, which would infallibly cause us to be discovered, we must carry the chest in our arms for a certain distance when it was night and afterwards rent an ass in a village to transport it as far as Seyssel, where—being on French soil—we would have nothing more to risk. This advice was followed: we left the same night at seven o'clock, and under the pretext of paying my expenses Mamma increased the poor kitten's little purse with an addition that was not useless to him. Claude Anet the gardener and I carried the chest as best we could as far as the first village, where an ass relieved us, and the same night brought us to Seyssel.

I believe I have already remarked that there are times when I am so little like myself that I would be taken for another man of a completely opposite character. An example of this is going to be seen. M. Reyde-let the Curate of Seyssel was a Canon of St. Pierre, consequently one of M. Le Maître's acquaintances, and one of the men from whom he ought to hide himself the most.[101] My advice was on the contrary to go present ourselves to him, and ask him for lodging under some pretext, as if we were there with the consent of the chapter. Le Maître approved of this idea which rendered his vengeance mocking and humorous. Thus we im-pudently went to M. Reydelet's, who received us very well. Le Maître told him that he was going to Bellay at the request of the Bishop to direct his music for the Easter holiday, that he planned on coming back in a few days, and in support[102] of this lie I strung together a hundred others so natural that M. Reydelet, finding me to be a nice boy, formed a friendship for me and gave me a thousand endearments. We were well entertained, well lodged, M. Reydelet could not make enough of us; and we sepa-rated the best friends in the world, with our promise to stop longer on our return. We were barely able to wait until we were alone to begin our bursts of laughter, and I admit that they seize me again in thinking about it; for one cannot imagine a better sustained or more fortunate piece of mischief. It would have kept us merry during the whole route, if M. Le Maître, who did not stop drinking and raving, had not been attacked two or three times by a seizure to which he was becoming very subject, and which resembled epilepsy very much. That threw me into a quandary that frightened me, and from which I soon thought about extracting myself any way I could.

We went to Bellay to pass the Easter holidays as we had told M. Reydelet, and although we were not at all expected there, we were received by the Music Master and welcomed by everyone with great pleasure. M. Le Maître was highly regarded in his art and deserved to be. The Music master of Bellay did himself honor with his best works and sought to obtain the approbation of such a good judge: for aside from being a connoisseur le Maître was equitable, not at all jealous, and not at all a flunkey. He was so superior to all these provincial music masters, and they felt it so well themselves, that they regarded him less as their colleague than as their chief.

After having passed five or six days very pleasantly at Bellay, we left again and continued our route, without other accident than the ones about which I have just spoken. Having arrived at Lyon we were lodged at *Notre Dame de Pitié*, and while waiting for the chest, which under cover of another lie we had shipped on the Rhone through the efforts of our good host M. Reydelet, M. le Maître went to see his acquaintances, among others Father Caton, a Franciscan friar, who will be spoken of later on, and Abbé Dortan the Comte de Lyon.[103] Both received him well, but they betrayed him, as will soon be seen;[104] his good luck had been exhausted with M. Reydelet.

Two days after our arrival at Lyon, as we were passing through a little street not far from our inn, Le Maître was surprised by one of his seizures, and this one was so violent that I was seized with fright by it. I shouted, called for help, gave the name of his inn and begged them to carry him there; then while they were gathering and hurrying around a man who had fallen senseless and foaming at the mouth in the middle of the street, he was deserted by the only friend on whom he ought to have counted. I took the instant in which no one was thinking about me, I turned the corner of the street and I disappeared. Thank Heaven I have finished this third painful admission; if many similar ones remained for me to make, I would abandon the labor that I have begun.[105]

Some traces of everything I have said up to the present have remained in the places I have lived; but what I have to say in the following book is almost entirely unknown. These are the greatest extravagances of my life, and it is fortunate that they did not turn out worse. Since my head was tuned to the tone of a foreign instrument, it was out of its diapason;[106] it returned to it by itself, and then I ceased my follies, or at least I committed ones more attuned to my natural disposition. This epoch of my youth is the one about which I have the most confused idea. Almost nothing happened in it interesting enough to my heart to retrace its remembrance in a lively way, and in so many goings and comings, in so many successive displacements, it is hard for me not to make some transpositions of time or place. I write absolutely from memory, without monuments, without materials that could recall it for me. There are events of my life that are as present to me as if they had just happened; but there are lacunae and voids that I cannot fill except with the help of accounts as confused as the remembrance of them that has stayed with me. Thus I have been capable of making errors sometimes and I will be capable of doing so again on trifles, up to the time where I have more certain information about myself; but in what truly bears on the subject I am assured of being exact and faithful, as I will always attempt to be in everything: one can depend on that.

As soon as I left M. Le Maître my resolution was made, and I departed for Annecy. The cause and the mystery of our departure had given me a great interest for the safety of our withdrawal; and by occupying me completely that interest diverted me for several days from the one that called me back: but as soon as security left me more tranquil the dominant feeling took back its place. Nothing gratified me, nothing tempted me, I had no desire for anything except to return near Mamma. The tenderness and truth of my attachment for her had uprooted all imaginary projects, all the follies of ambition from my heart. I no longer saw any other happiness than that of living near her, and I did not make a step without feeling that I was separating myself from this happiness. Thus I returned to it as soon as I could. My return was so prompt and my mind so distraught that, although I recall all my other trips with so much pleasure, I do not have the slightest remembrance of this one. I do not recall anything at all about it except my departure from Lyon and my arrival at Annecy. Judge whether that last period above all should have left my memory! Upon arriving I no longer found Mme de Warens: she had left for Paris.[107]

I have never known the secret of this trip very well. She would have told it to me, I am very sure of it, if I had pressed her about it; but never has a man been less curious than I about his friends' secret. Solely occupied with the present,[108] my heart fills up all its capacity, all its space with it; and, aside from past pleasures, which from now on cause my only enjoyment, there is not an empty corner left in it for what no longer exists.

All I believed I have glimpsed in the little she told me about it is that in the revolution caused at Turin by the abdication of the King of Sardinia, she feared to be forgotten and wanted, under the cover of M. d'Aubonne's intrigues, to seek the same advantage at the French Court, where she often told me she would have preferred it, because the multitude of great affairs makes it so that one is not so disagreeably watched over there. If that is true, it is very surprising that upon her return they did not give her a cooler welcome, and that she always enjoyed her pension without any interruption. Numerous people believed that she had been charged with some secret errand, either on behalf of the Bishop who then had business at the French Court, where he was himself obliged to go; or on behalf of someone still more powerful, who could arrange a happy return for her. What is certain, if that is true, is that the ambassadress was not poorly chosen, and that, still young and beautiful, she had all the talents necessary for coming off well in a negotiation.[109]

Book IV[1]

I arrive and find her there no longer. Judge my surprise and my pain! That is when regret at having abandoned M. Le Maître in a cowardly manner began to make itself felt. It was even sharper when I learned the misfortune that had befallen him. Upon arriving at Lyon his music chest, which contained his whole fortune, that precious chest—saved with so much toil—had been seized through the efforts of Comte Dortan to whom the Chapter had written in order to warn him about this furtive abduction. In vain had Le Maître claimed his property, his livelihood, his whole life's work. The ownership of this chest was at least subject to litigation; there was none. The matter was decided at the very instant by the law of the stronger, poor Le Maître thus lost the fruit of his talents, the work of his youth, and the support of his old age.[2]

Nothing was lacking to make the blow I received overwhelming. But I was at an age when great troubles have little hold, and I soon forged consolations for myself. I counted on having news about Mme de Warens in a while, although I did not know her address, and she did not know that I had come back; and as for my desertion, everything considered, I did not find it so blameworthy. I had been useful to M. Le Maître in his withdrawal; that was the only service that depended on me. If I had stayed with him in France, I would not have cured him of his illness, I would not have saved his chest; I would only have doubled his expenses without being able to do any good for him. That is how I saw things then; I see them differently today. It is not when a nasty deed has just been committed that it torments us; it is when we recall it a long time afterwards; for its remembrance does not die out at all.[3]

The only decision I had to make in order to have news about mamma was to wait for it: for where could I go to look for her in Paris, and with whom could I make the trip? There was no place more certain than Annecy to learn sooner or later where she was. So I stayed there. But I behaved rather badly. I did not go to see the Bishop who had protected me and who might have protected me again. I no longer had my patroness near him and I feared reprimands about our evasion. Still less did I go to the seminary. M. Gros was no longer there.[4] I saw none of my acquaintances: I would have wanted very much, however, to go see Madame the wife of the Intendant,[5] but I never dared. I did worse than all that. I found M. Venture again, about whom I had not even thought since my departure in spite of my enthusiasm. I found him brilliant and celebrated throughout Annecy; he was all the rage among the Ladies. This success turned my head completely. I no longer saw anything but M. Venture, and he almost made me forget Mme de Warens. To take advantage of his lessons more at my ease, I proposed that he share his lodging with me; he consented to do so. He boarded with a Cobbler, a pleasant and farcical personage who in his jargon did not call his wife anything but *slut*; a name which she rather deserved. He had fights with her which Venture was careful to keep going on while appearing to want to do the opposite. In a cold tone and in his Provençal accent he said words to them that caused the greatest effect; they were scenes fit to make one convulse with laughter. The mornings passed in this way without anyone thinking about it. At two or three o'clock we ate a bite. Venture left to go into his social circles where he ate, and I went to walk alone, meditating upon his great merit, admiring, coveting his rare talents,[6] and cursing my dull star which did not call me to that happy life. Oh how poorly I knew myself! Mine might have been a hundred times more charming if I had been less stupid and if I had known how to enjoy it better.

Mme de Warens had taken only Anet along with her; she had left Merceret, her chambermaid about whom I have spoken. I found her still occupying her mistress's apartment. Mademoiselle Merceret was a girl a little older than I, not pretty but pleasant enough; a good girl from Fribourg without malice, and in whom I knew no flaw other than sometimes being a little rebellious with her mistress. I went to see her rather often; she was an old acquaintance, and the sight of her reminded me of a dearer one that made me love her. She had several friends, among others a Mlle Giraud, a Genevan, who for my sins took it into her head to acquire a taste for me.[7] She always pressed Merceret to bring me to her home; I let myself be led there because I rather liked Merceret, and there were other young persons there whom I saw willingly. As for Mlle Giraud, who flirted with me in all sorts of ways, nothing could increase my aversion for her. When she brought her dry and black snout smeared with snuff near my face,[8] I had trouble keeping myself from spitting in it. But I was patient; except for that, I was very pleased to be in the midst of all those girls, and either to pay their court to Mlle Giraud, or for my own sake, all of them celebrated me as much as I wanted. I saw only friendship in all that. Since then I have thought that it depended only on me to see more in it: but I did not take it into my head, I did not think about it.[9]

Moreover, dressmakers, chambermaids, little tradeswomen hardly tempted me. I needed young Ladies. Each has his whims; that has always been mine, and I do not think as Horace did on this point.[10] However, it is not at all vanity of status and rank that attracts me; it is a better preserved complexion, more beautiful hands, a more graceful adornment, an air of delicacy and cleanliness in the whole person, more taste in the manner of dressing and expressing herself, a more delicate and better made dress, a daintier shoe, ribbons, lace, better adjusted hair. I would always prefer the less pretty one who had more of all that. I myself find this preference very ridiculous; but my heart bestows it in spite of me.

Very well, this advantage offered itself again, and it was only up to me to profit from it. How do I love to fall upon the pleasant moments of my youth from time to time? They were so sweet for me; they were so short, so rare, and I tasted them so cheaply! Ah their remembrance alone still gives my heart a pure pleasure that I need in order to reawaken my courage, and to endure the vexations of the rest of my years.

One morning the dawn appeared so beautiful to me that, after dressing hurriedly, I hastened to reach the country to see the sunrise. I tasted this pleasure in all its charm; it was the week after the feast of St. John.[11] In its greatest adornment, the earth was covered with grass and flowers; almost at the end of their warbling the nightingales seemed to take pleasure in intensifying it: bidding their farewell to Spring in concert, all the birds sang the birth of a fine summer day, one of those fine days that one no longer sees at my age, and which have never been seen in the sad land where I live today.[12]

I had imperceptibly gone farther away from the City, the heat increased, and I was walking under the shady spots in a small valley alongside a stream. I hear behind me the steps of horses and the voices of girls who seemed perplexed, but who did not laugh any less wholeheartedly because of it. I turn around, I am called by my name, I draw near, I find two young persons of my acquaintance, Mademoiselle de Graffenried and Mademoiselle Galley,[13] who—not being excellent riders—did not know how to force their horses to cross the stream. Mlle de Graffenried was an extremely amiable young Bernoise, who—having been thrown out of her country for some youthful folly—had imitated Mme de Warens, at whose house I had seen her sometimes; but not having a pension as she did, she had been very fortunate to attach herself to Mlle Galley, who, having formed a friendship for her, had urged her mother to let her be her companion, until she could be placed in some way. Mlle Galley, one year younger than she, was even prettier; she had an indefinable something that was more delicate, finer; she was very dainty and very shapely at the same time, which is the most beautiful moment for a girl. They loved each other tenderly, and the good character of each could do nothing but maintain this union for a long time, unless some lover happened to disturb it. They told me that they were going to Toune, an old chateau belonging to Madame Galley; they implored my help to make their horses cross, since they could not manage it by themselves: I wanted to whip the horses but they were afraid of kicks for me and sudden leaps for themselves. I had recourse to another expedient. I took Mlle Galley's horse by the bridle, then, pulling it after me, I crossed the stream with water half way up my legs, and the other horse followed without difficulty. That done, like a simpleton I wanted to say goodbye to these young Ladies and to depart; they whispered several words to each other, and addressing herself to me, Mlle de Graffenried said, "No, no, one does not slip away from us that way. You got yourself wet in our service; in conscience we ought to take care of drying you: you must come with us if you please, we are taking you prisoner." My heart beat,[14] I looked at Mlle Galley: "Yes, yes," she added, laughing at my bewildered look, "Prisoner of war, get up and ride behind her, we want to take care of you." "But Mademoiselle, I do not have the honor of being acquainted with Madame your mother; what will she say to me when she sees me arrive?" "Her mother," resumed Mlle de Graffenried, "is not at Toune, we are alone; we are coming back tonight, and you will come back with us."

Electricity does not have a quicker effect than the one these words had on me. Throwing myself on Mlle de Graffenried's horse, I trembled with joy, and when I had to hug her to hold myself on, my heart beat so hard that she noticed it; she told me that hers was beating also from fear of falling; in my position this was almost an invitation to verify the fact; I never dared, and during the whole journey my two arms served her as a belt, in truth a very tight one; but without shifting for a moment. Some woman who is reading this would willingly slap my face, and she would not be wrong.

The gaiety of the trip and the babble of these girls sharpened mine so much, that until the evening and as long as we were together we did not stop talking for a moment. They had put me so much at ease that my tongue spoke as much as my eyes, although it did not say the same things. The conversation was a little awkward only for several instants when I found myself tête-à-tête with one or the other; but the absent one came back very quickly, and did not leave us time to clarify that awkwardness.

Having arrived at Toune, and I being well dried, we ate breakfast. Next it was necessary to proceed to the important business of preparing dinner. Cooking all the while, from time to time the two young Ladies kissed the tenant farmer's children, and the poor cook's helper champed at the bit while he watched them do it.[15] Provisions had been sent from the city, and there was enough to make a very good dinner, above all of sweets; but unfortunately they had forgotten wine. This omission was not surprising for girls who hardly drank any: but I was sorry about it, for I had counted a little on this aid to embolden me. They were also sorry about it, perhaps for the same reason, but I do not believe it at all. Their lively and charming gaiety was innocence itself, and furthermore what could they have done with me between the two of them? They sent everywhere in the neighborhood to look for wine; none was found, so sober and poor are the countryfolk of that canton. Since they showed me their regret about this, I told them not to let it bother them so much and that they did not need wine to intoxicate me. That was the only gallantry I dared to say to them the whole day, but I believe that the minxes saw plainly that this gallantry was a truthful one.

We dined in the tenant farmer's kitchen, the two friends sitting on benches on the two sides of the long table and their guest between the two of them,[16] on a three-legged stool. What a dinner! what remembrance full of charms! Since one can taste such pure and such true pleasures at such little cost, how could one seek others? Never did a supper in the little houses of Paris approach that meal, I do not say only for gaiety, for sweet joy, but I say, for sensuality.

After dinner we made an economy. Instead of having the coffee that was left from lunch we kept it to sip with the cream and the cakes they had brought, and to keep our appetite at its peak we went into the orchard to finish our dessert with cherries. I climbed up the tree and I threw them bunches whose stones they returned to me through the branches. One time Mlle Galley, putting forward her pinafore and pushing back her head, presented herself so well, and I aimed so accurately, that I made a bunch fall in her bosom; and what laughter. I said to myself, "Why are my lips not cherries! How wholeheartedly would I throw them there?"

The day passed in that sort of playfulness with the greatest freedom, and always with the greatest modesty. Not a single equivocal word, not a single joke ventured; and this modesty was not imposed on us at all; it came by itself, we adopted the tone that our hearts gave us. In sum my bashfulness, others will say my stupidity, was such that the greatest undue familiarity that escaped me was to kiss Mlle Galley's hand one time. It is true that the circumstances gave some value to that slight favor.[17] We were alone, I had trouble breathing, her eyes were lowered. Instead of finding words my mouth dared to cling to her hand, which she gently drew back, after it was kissed, while looking at me in a manner that was not irritated. I do not know what I could have said to her: her friend entered, and appeared ugly to me at that moment.

Finally they remembered that they should not wait until night to return to the city. We had only just enough time to arrive in daylight, and we hurried to leave, arranging ourselves as we had come. If I had dared I would have transposed that order; for Mlle Galley's look had keenly touched my heart; but I did not dare to say anything, and it was not up to her to propose it. While walking we said that it was wrong of the day to end, but far from complaining that it had been short, we found that we had had the secret of making it long with all the amusements with which we had been able to fill it.

I left them almost in the same spot where they had met me. With what regret did we separate! With what pleasure did we plan to see each other again! Twelve hours spent together were worth centuries of familiarity to us. The sweet remembrance of that day cost nothing to these lovable girls; the tender union that reigned among us three was worth as much as livelier pleasures and could not have existed along with them: we loved each other without mystery and without shame, and we wished to love each other that way forever. Innocence of morals has its pleasure which is worth as much as the other, because it has no interruption and because it acts continuously. As for me, I know that the remembrance of such a beautiful day touches me more, charms me more, returns more to my heart than that of any pleasures I have tasted in my life. I did not know very well what I wanted from these two charming persons, but both appealed to me very much. I do not say that my heart would have been divided if I had been the master of my arrangements; I felt a slight preference. I would have secured my happiness in having Mlle de Graffenried for my mistress, but by choice I believe that I would have preferred her as a confidante. However it might be, upon leaving them it seemed to me that I would not be able to live any longer without either of them. Who could have told me that I would never see them again in my life, and that our ephemeral love would end there?

Those who read this will not fail to laugh at my gallant adventures, remarking that after many preliminaries, the most advanced ended with a kiss of the hand. Oh my readers, do not deceive yourselves. Perhaps I have had more pleasure in my loves which ended with that kissed hand, than you will have in yours, which begin with that at the very least.

Venture, who had gone to bed very late the night before, returned a short time after me. This time I did not see him with the same pleasure as usual, and I kept myself from telling him how I had passed my day. These young Ladies had spoken to me about him with little esteem, and had appeared dissatisfied to learn that I was in such bad hands: this harmed him in my mind: moreover, everything that distracted me from them could only be unpleasant to me. Nevertheless, he soon reminded me of himself and of me by speaking to me about my situation. It was too critical to be able to last. Although I spent very little, my small savings ended by being exhausted; I was without means. No news about Mamma; I did not know what would become of me, and I felt a cruel pang of the heart at seeing Mademoiselle Galley's friend reduced to begging.

Venture told me that he had spoken about me to M. the Civil Magistrate,[18] that he wanted to take me to dine with him the next day, that he was a man in a position to assist me through his friends, furthermore a good acquaintance to make, a man of intelligence and learning, very pleasant company, who had talents and who loved them; then, as usual mixing the most unimportant frivolity with the most serious things, he had me look at a pretty stanza that had arrived from Paris on a tune of an Opera by Mouret that was being played then.[19] This stanza had pleased M. Simon[20] so much (that was the Civil Magistrate's name) that he wanted to write another to the same tune in response: he had told Venture also to write one, and the latter seized the folly of having me write a third; so that, he said, the stanzas would be seen to arrive the next day like the sedan chairs in the *Roman comique*.[21]

Not being able to sleep that night, I wrote my stanza the best I could; for the first verses I had done they were passable, even better, or at least done with more taste than they would have been the day before, since the subject turned upon a very tender situation to which my heart was already completely disposed. In the morning I showed my stanza to Venture, who, finding it pretty, put it into his pocket without telling me whether he had composed his own. We went to dine with M. Simon, who received us well. The conversation was pleasant; it could not fail to be so between two men of wit who had profited from reading. As for me, I played my part; I listened and I was silent. Neither one spoke about the stanzas; I did not speak about them either, and never, that I know of, did they talk about mine.

M. Simon appeared content with my demeanor: that is just about all he saw of me in that interview. He had already seen me several times at Mme de Warens's home without paying much attention to me. Thus it is from this dinner that I can date his acquaintance, which was useless to me for the object that had caused me to make it, but from which I drew other advantages later on which make me remember him with pleasure.

It would be wrong of me not to speak about his appearance, which— based on his capacity as a magistrate, and on his fine wit upon which he prided himself—one would not imagine if I said nothing about it. M. the Civil Magistrate Simon was assuredly not two feet tall.[22] His legs, straight, slender, and even rather long, would have made him taller if they had been vertical; but they lay askew as if they were those of a very open compass. His body was not only short, but thin and in every sense of an inconceivable smallness. He must have looked like a grasshopper when he was naked. His head, of a natural size with a very well-formed face, noble manner, rather fine eyes, seemed like a false head that one would have set up on a stump. He could have saved himself the expense of adornment; because his periwig alone dressed him perfectly from head to foot.

He had two completely different voices that ceaselessly intermingled in his conversation with a contrast that was very pleasant at first but soon very disagreeable. One was deep and sonorous; it was, if I dare to speak this way, his head's voice. The other—thin, sharp and piercing—was his body's voice. If he coddled himself very much, if he spoke very deliberately, if he saved his breath, he could always speak in his big voice; but if he ever grew heated and a more lively accent occurred, this accent became like the whistling of a key, and he had all the trouble in the world resuming his bass.

With the figure I have just depicted, which is not at all exaggerated, M. Simon was gallant,[23] a great flirter, and pushed concern for his attire to the point of coquetry. As he sought to be at an advantage, he gladly gave his morning audiences in his bed; for if a fine head was seen on the pillow, no one was going to imagine that that was all. This sometimes gave occasion to some scenes that I am sure all Annecy still remembers. One morning while he was waiting for litigants in or rather on this bed, in a very delicate and very white beautiful nightcap ornamented with two big tassels of pink colored ribbon, a peasant arrives, knocks at the door. The servant had gone out. M. the Civil Magistrate, hearing it repeated, shouts, "*Come in,*" and that, since it is said a little too loudly, comes from his sharp voice. The man comes in, he looks for where this woman's voice comes from, and seeing in this bed a coif, a top-knot of ribbons, he wants to go back out making great apologies to Madame. M. Simon gets angry and only shouts more thinly. Confirmed in his idea and believing himself insulted,[24] the peasant hurls abuse at him, tells him that apparently she is nothing but a slut, and that M. the Civil Magistrate is hardly setting a good example at home. The Civil Magistrate, furious, and having his chamber pot as his only weapon, was going to throw it at this poor man's head when his housekeeper arrived.

This little dwarf, so disfavored by nature in his body, had made up for it on the side of mind: he had a naturally agreeable one, and he had been careful to adorn it. Although he was, from what they said, a good enough jurisconsult, he did not like his profession. He had thrown himself into fine literature, and he had succeeded in it. From it he had acquired above all that superficial brilliance, that flower that casts pleasantness in company, even with women. He knew by heart all the little striking events from the *anas*[25] and other similar things: he had the art of making the most of them, by telling with interest, with mystery and as an anecdote of the day before, what had happened sixty years ago. He knew music and sang pleasantly in his man's voice: in sum he had enough fine talents for a magistrate. As a result of cajoling the Ladies of Annecy, he had put himself into fashion among them; they had him in their train like a little monkey. He even claimed some amorous successes and that amused them very much. A Madame d'Epagny said that for him the ultimate favor was to kiss a woman on the knee.

Since he was acquainted with good books and he willingly spoke about them, his conversation was not only amusing but instructive. Later, when I had acquired the taste for study I cultivated his acquaintance and I benefited from it very much. I sometimes went to see him from Chambéry where I was at that time. He praised, stirred up my emulation, and gave me good advice for my reading of which I often took advantage. Unfortunately a very sensitive soul lived in this body that was so thin. Several years later he had some bad business or other that grieved him, and he died from it. That was a shame; he was assuredly a good little man, with whom one began by laughing, and whom one ended by loving. Although his life was only slightly tied to mine, since I received some useful lessons from him, I believed I might dedicate a little memorial to him out of gratitude.

As soon as I was free, I ran to Mlle Galley's street, imagining I might see someone enter or leave or at least open some window. Nothing; not even a cat appeared, and the whole time I was there the house remained as closed as if it were not inhabited at all. The street was small and unfrequented, a man would be noticed there: from time to time someone passed by, entered, or left in the neighborhood. I was extremely embarrassed by my appearance; it seemed to me that they guessed why I was there, and this idea put me to the torture: for I have always preferred the honor and repose of those who were dear to me to my own pleasures.

Finally, growing tired of playing the Spanish lover[26] and not having a guitar, I decided to write to Mlle de Graffenried. I would have preferred to write to her friend, but I did not dare, and it was suitable to begin with the one to whom I owed the other's acquaintance and with whom I was better acquainted. Once my letter was written, I went to carry it to Mlle Giraud, as I had agreed with those young Ladies when we separated. It was they who gave me this expedient. Mlle Giraud was a seamstress, and since she sometimes worked for Mme Galley, she had access to the house. Nevertheless, to me the messenger did not appear to be very well chosen; but I was afraid that if I made difficulties about this one they would not propose another to me. Furthermore, I did not dare to say that she wanted to work on her own behalf. I felt myself humiliated that she dared to believe herself to be of the same sex for me as these young Ladies were. In sum, I preferred that depository to none at all, and I held on to it at all hazards.

At the first word Giraud found me out: that was not difficult. Even if a letter to bring to some young girls had not spoken by itself, my foolish and embarrassed manner alone would have betrayed me. One can believe that this commission did not give her much pleasure to perform: still she took it on and faithfully executed it. The next morning I ran to her home and I found my answer there. How I hurried to leave in order to go read and kiss it at my leisure! That does not need to be said; but what does need to be said in addition is the decision made by Mlle Giraud, in which I found more delicacy and moderation than I would have expected from her. Having enough good sense to see that with her thirty-seven years, her hare's eyes, her smeared nose, her harsh voice and her black skin, she did not stand a chance against two young persons full of grace and in all the glow of beauty, she wished neither to betray nor to serve them, and she preferred to lose me than to make arrangements with me for them.

Already for some time Merceret had been thinking of returning to Fribourg since she had no news whatsoever from her mistress; Mlle Giraud led her to decide absolutely. She did more; she caused her to understand that it would be good for someone to accompany her to her father's house, and proposed me. Little Merceret, to whom I also was not displeasing, found it extremely good to put this idea into effect.[27] They spoke to me about it from that same day as a settled business, and since I found nothing that displeased me in this manner of disposing of me I consented to it, looking at this trip as a matter of a week at most. Giraud, who was not thinking the same way, arranged everything. I had to admit the condition of my finances. They were provided for: Merceret took it upon herself to pay my expenses, and to gain back on one side what she spent on the other, at my request it was decided that she would send her little baggage ahead, and that we would go on foot in short stages. This was done.

I am sorry to make so many girls in love with me. But since there is scarcely anything to be very vain about in the advantage I acquired from all these loves, I believe I can tell the truth without scruple.[28] Merceret, who was younger than Giraud and had lost less of her innocence, never made such lively advances to me; but she imitated my tone of voice, my accent, repeated my words, had the attentiveness for me that I should have had for her, and always took great care, as if she was extremely fearful, that we sleep in the same room: an intimacy which is rarely restrained to that on a trip, between a boy of twenty and a girl of twenty-five.[29]

Nevertheless, this time it was restrained to that. My simplicity was such that, although Merceret was not unpleasant, there did not even enter my mind during the whole trip, I do not say the slightest gallant temptation, but even the slightest idea related to it, and if this idea had come to me, I was too foolish to know how to take advantage of it. I did not imagine how a girl and a boy could come to sleep together; I believed that centuries were needed to prepare this terrible arrangement. If poor Merceret counted on some equivalent for paying my expenses, she was duped, and we arrived at Fribourg exactly as we had left Annecy.

When passing through Geneva I went to see no one; but I was ready to faint on the bridges. Never have I seen the walls of that happy city, never have I entered it without feeling a certain sinking of the heart that came from an excess of emotion. At the same time that the noble image of freedom raised up my soul, those of equality, union, gentleness of morals touched me to the point of tears and inspired me with a lively regret at having lost all these benefits. What a mistake I made, but how natural it was! I believed I saw all that in my fatherland because I bore it in my heart.

It was necessary to pass through Nyon. To pass through without seeing my good father! If I had had the courage to do that, I should have died from regret about it. I left Merceret at the inn and I went to see him at all hazards. Oh! how wrong I had been to fear him! At my approach his soul was opened to the paternal feelings with which it was full. How many tears did we shed in embracing! At first he believed that I was coming back to him. I told him my story, and I told him my resolution. He combatted it weakly. He made me see the dangers to which I was exposing myself, told me that the shortest follies were the best. For the rest, he was not even tempted to keep me back by force, and in that I find that he was right: but it is certain that he did not do everything that he could have done to bring me back, either because—after the step I had taken— he himself judged that I ought not to return from it, or perhaps because he was at a loss to know what he could make of me at my age. I have learned since that he had an opinion of my traveling companion that was very unjust, and very far from the truth, but otherwise natural enough. My step-mother, a good woman, a little mealy-mouthed,[30] pretended to want to keep me to dine. I did not stay, but I told them that I was counting on stopping with them for a longer time when I returned, and I left them with custody of my little parcel which I had had come by the boat, and which I found to be an encumbrance. The next day I left early in the morning, well satisfied at having seen my father and at having dared to do my duty.

We arrived at Fribourg without incident. Toward the end of the trip Mlle Merceret's eagerness diminished a little. After our arrival she showed me nothing but coldness, and her father, who was not swimming in opulence, did not give me a very big welcome either; I went to board at a tavern. I went to see them the next day; they offered me dinner, I accepted. We separated from each other without tears, I returned to my hash house in the evening, and I left two days after my arrival, without knowing very well where I planned to go.

Here again is a circumstance of my life in which providence offered me precisely what I needed to glide through happy days. Merceret was a very good girl, not at all brilliant, not at all beautiful, but not at all ugly either; hardly lively, extremely reasonable aside from a little moodiness, which was gotten over by crying, and which never had stormy consequences. She had a real taste for me; I could have married her without trouble, and followed her father's profession.[31] My taste for music would have made me like it. I would have settled at Fribourg, a small city that was hardly pretty, but populated with very good people. Doubtless I would have lost great pleasures, but I would have lived in peace up to my final hour; and I ought to know better than anyone that there was nothing to hesitate about in that bargain.

I went back, not to Nyon, but to Lausanne. I wanted to feast myself on the view of that beautiful lake which is seen there in its greatest extent. The majority of my secret determining motives have not been any more solid. Distant prospects rarely have enough strength to make me act. The uncertainty of the future has always made me look at projects of long execution as bait for a dupe. I abandon myself to hope just like anyone else, as long as it costs me nothing to nourish; but if I must take trouble for a long time, I do not follow it any longer. The smallest little pleasure that offers itself at my door tempts me more than the joys of Paradise. I make an exception, however, for the pleasure that must be followed by pain; that does not tempt me because I love only pure enjoyments, and one never has that sort when one knows that one is preparing repentance for oneself.

I very much needed to reach any destination at all and the closest was the best; for having gone astray on my route I found myself at Moudon in the evening, where I spent the little I had left, aside from ten kreutzers,[32] which departed the next day at dinner, and having arrived in the evening at a little village near Lausanne, I entered a tavern without a sou to pay for my room and board, and without knowing what would happen. I was very hungry; I put on a good face and I asked to dine as if I had had something with which to pay. I went to sleep without thinking about anything, I slept tranquilly, and after having eaten breakfast in the morning and having added up the bill with the proprietor, I wanted to leave him my jacket as security for the seven batz[33] to which my expenses amounted. This worthy man refused it; he told me that thanks to Heaven he had never stripped anyone, that he did not want to begin for seven batz, that I might keep my jacket, and that I would pay him when I could. I was touched by his goodness, but less than I should have been and than I have been since then when I have thought it over. Without delay I sent him his money with thanks[34] by means of a trustworthy man: but when I passed through Lausanne again upon returning from Italy fifteen years later, I had real regret at having forgotten the name of the tavern and the proprietor. I would have gone to see him. It would have given me a true pleasure to remind him of his good deed, and to prove to him that it had not been ill placed. Some services doubtless more important, but rendered with more ostentation, have not appeared so worthy of gratitude to me as the humanity of that decent man which was simple and without display.

Upon drawing near Lausanne I re-examined the poverty in which I found myself, the means to remove myself from it without going to show my wretchedness to my step-mother, and in this pedestrian pilgrimage I compared myself to my friend Venture arriving at Annecy. I warmed up so well from this idea, that, without thinking that I had neither his engaging manner nor his talents, I took it into my head to play the little Venture at Lausanne, to teach music which I did not know, and to say I was from Paris where I had never been. As a consequence of this fine project, since there was no music school there where I might be able to be an assistant, and furthermore since I took care not to stick myself among people who were accomplished in the art, I began by inquiring about a little inn where one could live well enough and cheaply. I was directed to someone named Perrotet, who kept boarders. This Perrotet happened to be the best man in the world, and received me extremely well. I told him my little lies as I had hatched them. He promised to talk about me and to try to procure students for me; he told me that he would ask me for money only when I had earned some. His charge for room and board was five white écus;[35] which was very little for the thing, but very much for me. He advised me to begin at first with only half board, which consisted in a good soup and nothing more for dinner but a good supper in the evening. I agreed to this. This poor Perrotet made me all these advances with the best heart in the world,[36] and spared nothing to be useful to me. Why must it be that having found so many good people in my youth I find so few of them in an advanced age, has their race dried up? No, but the class in which I need to look for them today is no longer the same one in which I found them then. Among the people, where great passions speak only occasionally, the feelings of nature make themselves heard more often. In the more elevated stations they are absolutely stifled, and beneath the mask of feeling nothing but interest or vanity ever speaks there.

From Lausanne I wrote to my father who sent me my parcel and pointed out some excellent things to me of which I could have taken better advantage. I have already noted some moments of inconceivable delirium in which I was no longer myself: here is yet another of the most clear-cut instances of this. To understand to what point my head had turned at that time, to what point I was *venturized* so to speak, it is necessary only to see how many extravagances I heaped up all at the same time. Behold me a singing master without knowing how to make out a tune; for even if the six months I had spent with Le Maître had profited me, they could never have been enough; but aside from that I learned from a master and that was enough for me to learn badly. A Parisian from Geneva and a Catholic in a Protestant country, I believed I ought to change my name as well as my religion and my fatherland. I always came as close to my great model as I could. He had called himself Venture de Villeneuve; I made an anagram of the name Rousseau in that of Vaussore, and I called myself Vaussore de Villeneuve. Venture knew composition, although he said nothing about it; without knowing it I boasted about it to everyone and without being able to take down the slightest popular song I gave myself out as a composer. That is not all: having been presented to M. de Treytorens,[37] a law professor who loved music and gave concerts in his home, I wanted to give him a sample of my talent, and I began to compose a piece for his concert as brazenly as if I had known how to set about it. I had the steadfastness to work for fifteen days on this beautiful work, to make a fair copy of it, to write out the parts and to distribute them with as much self-assurance as if it had been a masterpiece of harmony. Finally, what will hardly be believed, and which is very true, to crown this sublime production worthily, at its conclusion I put a pretty minuet which was making the rounds, and which perhaps everyone still remembers from these words so well-known at that time.

> *Quel caprice!*
> *Quelle injustice!*
> *Quoi, ta Clarice*
> *Trahiroit tes feux?* etc.[38]

Venture had taught me this tune along with the bass and using other, filthy words, with the aid of which I had retained it. Thus I put this Minuet and his bass at the end of my composition while suppressing the words, and I gave it out as my own, all as resolutely as if I had been speaking to the inhabitants of the moon.

They gather to execute my piece. I explain to everyone the type of tempo, the taste of execution, the repetitions of the parts; I was extremely busy. They tune up for five or six minutes that were five or six centuries for me. Finally everything being ready, with a fine roll of paper I beat on my magisterial music stand the five or six[39] beats of the *Attention*. They become silent, I gravely begin to beat the measure, they begin. . . . no, since French Operas have existed, you have not in your life heard a similar din.[40] Whatever they might have thought of my pretended talent, the effect was worse than anything they seemed to expect. The musicians stifled laughs; the listeners opened their eyes wide and would have very much liked to close their ears, but they had no way to do it. My torturers of musicians, who wanted to have some fun, scraped so as to rupture the eardrum of a patient at the *Quinze-Vingt*.[41] I was steadfast enough to keep going at my pace, sweating big drops it is true, but held in place by shame, not daring to flee and entirely stuck there. For my consolation, around me I heard the audience speaking into each other's ears or rather into mine. One, "Nothing in it is bearable"; another, "What rabid music?" another, "What an infernal racket?" Poor Jean-Jacques; at that cruel moment you would hardly hope that one day in front of the King of France and all his court your sounds would excite murmurs of surprise and applause, and that in all the boxes around you the most lovable women would say to themselves in a low voice, "What charming sounds! what enchanting music! all these songs go to the heart."[42]

But what put everyone in a good mood was the minuet. Hardly had they played several measures of it when I heard bursts of laughter coming from every side. Everyone congratulated me on my pretty taste for a song; they assured me that this minuet would make me talked of, and that I deserved to be sung everywhere. I do not need to depict my anguish, nor to admit that I very much deserved it.

The next day one of my symphonists, called Lutold, came to see me, and was a good enough man not to congratulate me on my success. The profound feeling of my foolishness, shame, regret, despair over the condition into which I was reduced, the impossibility of keeping my heart closed in these great difficulties, made me open it to him; I pulled the plug on my tears, and instead of being content to admit my ignorance to him, I told him everything,[43] while asking him for secrecy, which he promised me, and which he kept as one can believe. From that very night

all Lausanne knew who I was, and what is remarkable, no one showed
this to me, not even the good Perrotet, who in spite of all that did not
balk at lodging and feeding me.

I lived, but very sadly. The consequences of such a debut did not make
Lausanne an extremely pleasant stay for me. Students did not present
themselves in a crowd; not a single schoolgirl, and no one from the city.
I had two or three fat Swiss-Germans, as stupid as I was ignorant, who
bored me to death and who did not become great note-scrapers in my
hands. I was called into only one house where a little serpent of a girl gave
herself the pleasure of showing me a lot of music not a note of which I
could read, and which she had the malice to sing afterwards in front of
Monsieur the teacher, to show him how it was performed. I was in so
poor a condition to sight-read a tune that in the brilliant concert of which
I have spoken I could not follow the execution for a moment in order
to know whether they were playing well what I had before my eyes, and
which I had composed myself.

In the midst of so many humiliations I had some very sweet consolations in the news I received from time to time from the two charming
friends. I have always found a great comforting virtue in the opposite sex,
and nothing softens my afflictions in my disgraces more than feeling that
a lovable person is taking an interest in them. This correspondence, however, ceased soon afterwards, and was never renewed, but that was my
fault. When changing location I neglected to give them my address, and
since necessity forced me to think of myself continuously, I soon forgot
them entirely.

I have not spoken about my poor mamma for a long time; but if you
believe that I also forgot her, you are very much mistaken. I did not stop
thinking about her and desiring to find her again, not only for the need of
my sustenance, but even more for the need of my heart. My attachment
for her, however lively and however tender it might be, did not keep me
from loving others, but not in the same way. All equally owed my tenderness to their charms, but with others it depended solely on their charms
and did not survive them; whereas mamma could become old and ugly
without me loving her any less tenderly. My heart had fully transferred
to her person the homage that it gave to her beauty at first, and whatever change she underwent, as long as she always remained herself, my
feelings could not change. I know well that I owed her gratitude; but in
truth I did not think about it. Whatever she might have done or not done
for me, it would always have been the same thing. I loved her neither out
of duty nor out of interest nor out of convenience; I loved her because I
was born to love her. When I fell in love with someone else, that was a

distraction, I admit it, and I thought about her less often, but I thought about her with the same pleasure, and never, in love or not, did I give my attention to her without feeling that there could be no true happiness for me in life, as long as I was separated from her.

Even though I had not had any news at all about her for such a long time, I never believed that I had completely lost her, nor that she could have forgotten me. I said to myself, "Sooner or later she will know that I am wandering, and will give me some sign of life; I will find her again, I am certain." While waiting it was a comfort to me to live in her country, to walk in the streets in which she had walked, in front of the houses in which she had resided, and all by conjecture; for one of my inept peculiarities was not to dare to inform myself about her, nor to pronounce her name without the most absolute necessity. It seemed to me that by naming her I was telling everything she inspired in me, that my mouth was revealing the secret of my heart, that I was compromising her in some way. I even believe that some fear that I would be told something ill of her was mixed up in this. Her step had been much talked of and her behavior a little. From fear that I would not be told what I wanted to hear, I preferred that she not be spoken about at all.

Since my students did not occupy me very much, and her native city was only four leagues from Lausanne, I took an excursion of two or three days there, during which the sweetest emotion did not leave me at all. The view of Lake Geneva and of its wonderful banks always had a particular attraction for my eyes, which I cannot explain, and which does not depend only on the beauty of the spectacle, but on something indefinable which is more interesting that affects me and touches me. Every time I draw near the Pays de Vaud I experience an impression made of the remembrance of Mme de Warens who was born there, of my father who lived there, of Mlle de Vulson who had the first fruits of my heart there, of several pleasure trips I made there in my childhood, and, it seems to me, of some other cause in addition, more secret and stronger than all that. When the ardent desire for that happy and sweet life which flees from me and for which I was born comes to enflame my imagination, it always settles itself in the Pays de Vaud, near the lake, in the charming countryside. I absolutely need an orchard by the side of this lake and no other; I need a firm friend, a lovable woman, a cow, and a little boat. I will not enjoy a perfect happiness on earth until I have all that. I laugh at the simplicity with which I have gone to that country several times solely to seek this imaginary happiness. I have always been surprised to find the inhabitants there, above all the women, of a completely different character from the one I seek. How ill-matched it seemed to me![44] To me, the country and the people with whom it is covered have never appeared to be made for each other.

While following that beautiful shore on this trip to Vevey I abandoned myself to the sweetest melancholy. My heart ardently leapt at a thousand innocent felicities;[45] I was touched, I sighed and wept like a child. Stopping to weep at my ease, seated on a big rock, how many times did I amuse myself by seeing my tears fall into the water?[46]

I went to Vevey to take lodging at the Key, and during the two days that I stayed there without seeing anyone I acquired a love for that City which has followed me in all my travels, and which finally caused me to settle the Heroes of my novel there. I would willingly say to those who have some taste and who are sensitive, "Go to Vevey, visit the country, look over the landscape, take an excursion on the lake, and say whether nature has not made this fine country for a Julie, a Claire, and a St. Preux; but do not look for them there."[47] I return to my story.

Since I was Catholic and gave myself out as such, I followed the worship I had embraced without mystery and without scruples. On Sundays when the weather was good I went to mass at Assens two leagues from Lausanne. Ordinarily I made this journey with other Catholics, above all with a Parisian embroiderer, whose name I have forgotten. He was not a Parisian like me, he was a true Parisian from Paris, God's own arch-Parisian, a good man like someone from Champagne.[48] He loved his country so much that he never wished to doubt that I was from it out of fear of losing this occasion to speak about it. M. de Crouzas[49] the lieutenant-governor had a gardener also from Paris, but less obliging, who found the glory of his country compromised by someone who dared to pass himself off as being from it when he did not have that honor. He questioned me in the manner of a man sure of catching me in a mistake, and then smiled maliciously. Once he asked me what was remarkable at the new market.[50] I beat around the bush, as can be believed. After having spent twenty years in Paris, I ought to know that city at present. Nevertheless, if I was asked a similar question today, I would be no less perplexed to answer it, and from this perplexity one could also very well conclude that I have never been in Paris. How much one is subject to rely on deceptive principles even when one meets the truth.

I cannot say exactly how much time I stayed at Lausanne. I did not carry away very striking memories of that city. I know only that,[51] not finding a means of livelihood there, I went from there to Neuchâtel where I passed the winter. I succeeded better in the latter city; I had some students, and I earned enough to pay my debt to my good friend Perrotet, who had faithfully sent me my little luggage, although I still owed him rather a lot of money.

Insensibly I learned music by teaching it. My life was rather comfortable; a reasonable man could have been content with it: but my restless heart asked me for something else. Sundays and the days when I was free I went to rove about the countryside and the woods of the surrounding area, always wandering, dreaming, sighing, and once I had left the city I did not come back until night. One day, being at Boudry, I entered a tavern to dine: there I saw a man with a long beard with a violet outfit in the Greek style, a fur cap, rather noble appearance and manner, and who often had trouble making himself understood, speaking only an almost incomprehensible jargon, but resembling Italian more than any other language. I understood almost everything he said and I was the only one who did; with the proprietor and the people of the country he could express himself only with signs. I said several words to him in Italian which he understood perfectly; he got up and came to embrace me effusively. The relationship was soon formed, and from that moment I served him as interpreter. His dinner was good, mine was less than mediocre; he invited me to take a share of his, I did not stand much on ceremony. While drinking and jabbering we completed familiarizing ourselves with each other, and from the end of the meal we became inseparable. He told me that he was a Greek Prelate, and Archimandrite of Jerusalem;[52] that he was commissioned to make a collection in Europe for the reestablishment of the Holy Sepulchre. He showed me some fine letters patent from the Czarina and the Emperor; he had some from many other sovereigns. He was satisfied enough with what he had amassed until then, but he had had unbelievable difficulties in Germany, not understanding a word of German, of Latin nor of French, and reduced to his Greek, to Turkish and to lingua franca[53] for his only resort; which did not procure him much in the country into which he was rushing. He proposed that I accompany him to serve as secretary and interpreter. In spite of my newly bought little violet suit which did not square badly with my new post, my manner was sufficiently lacking in substance that he did not believe that I would be hard to win over and he was not at all mistaken. Our agreement was soon concluded; I asked for nothing, and he promised a lot. Without security, without guarantee, without knowledge, I abandoned myself to his good guidance, and from the next day there I was on the way to Jerusalem.

We began our tour with the Canton of Fribourg, where he did not accomplish very much. Episcopal dignity did not permit him to play the beggar and make a collection among private citizens, but we presented his commission to the Senate, which gave him a small sum. From there we went to Berne. More ceremony was necessary here and the examination of his credentials was not the business of a day. We lodged at the Falcon, a good inn at that time, where good company was found. Numerous people were at the table and it was well served. For a long time I had fared badly; I very much needed to recuperate; I had the opportunity to do so, and I took advantage of it. Monseigneur the archimandrite was himself a man of good company, rather liking a well-stocked table, gay, speaking well for those who understood him, not lacking in knowledge of certain subjects, and displaying his Greek erudition pleasantly enough. One day while cracking some hazelnuts at dessert he cut his finger very deeply, and as his blood flowed abundantly, he showed his finger to the company, and said while laughing: *mirate, Signori, questo è sangue Pelasgo*.[54]

At Berne my functions were not useless to him, and I did not come off as badly from it as I had feared. I was much more bold and spoke better than I would have for myself. Things did not happen so simply as at Fribourg. Long and frequent conferences with the first men of the State were necessary, and the examination of his credentials was not the business of a day.[55] Finally everything was in proper order, he was admitted to an audience with the Senate. I entered with him as his interpreter and was told to speak. There was nothing that I expected less, and it had not entered my mind that after having conferred with the members at length it would be necessary to address the body as if nothing had been said. Judge my perplexity! For a man who was so bashful, to speak—not only in public, but before the Senate of Berne—and to speak impromptu without having a single minute to prepare myself; this was enough to reduce me to nothing. I was not even intimidated. I set out the Archimandrite's commission succinctly and plainly. I praised the piety of the Princes who had contributed to the collection he had come to make. Using emulation to spur on their Excellencies' piety, I said that no less was to be hoped from their accustomed munificence, and then, seeking to prove that this good deed was equally one for all Christians without distinction of sect, I finished by promising the blessings of heaven for those who would like to take part in it. I will not say that my speech had an effect, but it is certain that it was appreciated, and that upon leaving the audience the archimandrite received an extremely decent presentation, and moreover, some compliments upon his secretary's intelligence of which I had the agreeable employment of being the interpreter, but which I did not dare to render to him literally. That is the only time in my life that I have spoken in public and before a sovereign, and also the only time, perhaps, that I have spoken boldly and well. What a difference in the aptitude of the same man! Three years ago, when I went to see my old friend M. Roguin at Iverdun, I received a deputation to thank me for some books I had given to the library of that city.[56] The Swiss are great speechifiers; these Gentlemen gave me a great speech. I believed that I was obliged to respond; but I was so perplexed[57] in my response and my head became so confused that I stopped short and made myself a laughing-stock. Although I am naturally timid, sometimes in my youth I was bold, but never in my advanced age. The more I have seen the world, the less I have been able to adapt myself to its tone.

Having left Berne, we went to Soleure; for the Archimandrite's plan was to get back on the route to Germany, and to go back through Hungary or Poland, which made an immense route; but since his purse filled up more than it emptied on the road, he feared detours very little. As for me, who was almost as happy on horseback as on foot, I would not have asked for anything better than to travel this way for my whole life: but it was written that I would not go so far.

The first thing we did upon arriving at Soleure was to go greet M. the Ambassador of France.[58] Unfortunately for my Bishop this ambassador was the Marquis de Bonac who had been ambassador to the Porte,[59] and who must have known all about everything concerning the Holy Sepulchre. The Archimandrite had an audience of a quarter of an hour into which I was not admitted, because M. the Ambassador understood the lingua franca and spoke Italian at least as well as I did. When my Greek was leaving, I wanted to follow him; they kept me back: it was my turn. Having passed myself off as Parisian, as such I was under his Excellency's jurisdiction. He asked me who I was, exhorted me to tell him the truth; I promised him I would do so while asking him for a private audience which I was granted. M. the Ambassador led me into his office the door of which he closed on us, and there, throwing myself at his feet, I kept my word to him. I would not have said less if I had promised nothing; for a continuous need of outpouring puts my heart upon my lips at every moment, and after having opened myself without reserve to the musician Lutold, I was not careful to play the mysterious man with the Marquis de Bonac. He was so satisfied with my little story and with the effusion of heart with which he saw that I had told it, that he took me by the hand, entered the room of Madame his wife, and presented me to her while giving a summary of my narrative. Mme de Bonac welcomed me with kindness and said that I must not be left with the Greek Monk. It was resolved that I would stay at the mansion while waiting for them to see what they could make of me. I wanted to go to say my farewell to my poor Archimandrite, for whom I had conceived an attachment: I was not allowed to. They sent to notify him of my detainment, and a quarter of an hour afterwards, I saw my little sack arrive. M. de la Martiniére, the Secretary of the Embassy, was in a way put in charge of me.[60] While leading me into the room that had been assigned to me, he told me, "Under the Comte du Luc this room was occupied by a famous man, with the same name as you. It is up to you alone to supersede him in every way and someday to make it said Rousseau the first, Rousseau the second."[61] This resemblance, for which I hardly hoped at that time, might have flattered my desires less, if I had been able to foresee at what price I would purchase it one day.

What M. de la Martiniére had told me made me curious. I read the works of the man whose room I was occupying, and based on the compliment I had been given, believing I had some taste for poetry, I wrote a cantata in praise of Madame de Bonac for my first attempt. This taste did not last. From time to time I have written some mediocre verses; this is a rather good exercise for getting used to elegant inversions and for learning to write better in prose; but I have never found enough attraction in French poetry to abandon myself to it completely.[62]

M. de la Martiniére wanted to see my style and asked me to write the same detailed account I had made to M. the Ambassador. I wrote him a long letter which I am informed has been preserved by M. de Marianne, who was attaché for the Marquis de Bonac for a long time and who since has succeeded M. de la Martiniére under the Ambassadorship of M. de Courteille.[63] I asked M. de Malesherbes to seek to procure a copy of this letter[64] for me. If I can get it from him or from anyone else, it will be found in the collection that ought to accompany my confessions.

The experience that I was beginning to acquire, moderated my romantic projects little by little, and for example not only did I not fall in love with Mme de Bonac, but from the first I felt that I could not make a great path in her husband's house. With M. de la Martiniére in place, and M. de Marianne being next in the line of succession, so to speak, I was not allowed to hope for anything more fortunate than employment as an under secretary which did not tempt me infinitely. This made me show a great desire to go to Paris when they consulted me about what I wanted to do. M. the Ambassador approved of this idea which at least tended to rid him of me.[65] M. de Merveilleux,[66] secretary interpreter of the embassy, said that his friend M. Godard,[67] a Swiss Colonel in the service of France, was looking for someone to place with his nephew who was entering the service very young, and thought that I might suit him. My departure was resolved based on this rather lightly taken idea, and I, who saw a trip to make and Paris at the end, was in heartfelt joy over it. They gave me some letters, a hundred francs for my trip accompanied by many good lessons, and I left.

For this trip I took two weeks which I can count among the happy days of my life. I was young, I was in good health, I had enough money, much hope, I was traveling, I was traveling on foot, and I was traveling alone. One might be surprised to see me recount such an advantage, if one had not already been obliged to become familiar with my disposition. My sweet chimeras kept me company, and never did the heat of my imagination beget more magnificent ones. When I was offered some empty place in a carriage, or when someone accosted me on the road, I balked at seeing reversed the fortune whose edifice I was building while walking. This time my ideas were martial. I was going to attach myself to a military man and become a military man myself: for they had arranged that I would begin by being a cadet. I already believed I saw myself in an officer's uniform with a fine white plume. My heart swelled at this noble idea. I had some tincture of geometry and of fortifications; I had an engineer uncle; to a certain extent I had been born to the profession. My nearsightedness offered a bit of an obstacle, but one that did not bother me, and I counted very much on compensating for this flaw by dint of coolness and intrepidity. I had read that Maréchal Schomberg was very nearsighted;[68] why might Maréchal Rousseau not be? I warmed up so much from these follies that I no longer saw anything but troops, ramparts, gabions, batteries, and myself in the middle of the fire and smoke tranquilly giving my orders, field glasses in my hand. Nevertheless when I crossed pleasant countryside, when I saw groves and streams; this touching sight made me sigh with regret; in the midst of my glory I felt that my heart was not made for so much uproar, and soon, without knowing how, I found myself again in the middle of my dear sheepfolds, renouncing forever the labors of Mars.

How much did the first sight of Paris give the lie to the idea that I had of it! The exterior decoration I had seen at Turin, the beauty of the streets, the symmetry and alignment of the houses made me seek something quite different at Paris. I had drawn for myself a city as beautiful as it was big, of the most imposing aspect, where one saw only superb streets, palaces of marble and gold. Entering by the Faubourg St. Marceau I saw only filthy and stinking little streets, nasty-looking black houses, the air of dirtiness, poverty, beggars, carters, cobblers, vendors of rotgut and old hats. From the first all this struck me to such a point that all the real magnificence that I have seen since in Paris has not been able to destroy that first impression, and I have always kept a secret disgust for living in that capital. I can say that all the time I lived there afterwards was employed only in seeking the resources to put me in a condition to live far away from it. Such is the fruit of a too active imagination which exaggerates beyond the exaggeration of men, and always sees more than it is told. Paris had been so vaunted to me that I had drawn it for myself like ancient Babylon, where, if I had seen it, I would find just as much to rebuild perhaps, as a result of the portrait I had made of it for myself. The same thing happened to me at the Opera where I rushed to go the day after my arrival; the same thing happened to me afterwards at Versailles, again afterwards when I saw the sea, and the same thing will always happen to me when I see the sights that have been too much heralded to me: for it is impossible for men and difficult for nature itself to surpass my imagination in wealth.

From the manner I was received by all the people for whom I had letters, I believed my fortune made. The one to whom I was the most recommended and who fawned on me the least was M. de Surbeck, who was retired from the service and living philosophically at Bagneux, where I went to see him several times and where he never even offered me a glass of water.[69] I had a better welcome from Madame de Merveilleux, the Interpreter's sister-in-law, and from his nephew an officer in the Guards.[70] Not only did the mother and the son receive me well, but they offered me their table of which I often took advantage during my stay at Paris. Mme de Merveilleux appeared to me to have been beautiful, her hair was a beautiful black and done up in the old fashion with a curl on the temples. She retained what does not perish along with attractiveness, a very pleasant wit.[71] She appeared to approve of mine, and did all she could to assist me; but no one seconded her, and I was soon disabused about all this great interest they had appeared to take in me. Nevertheless, one must do the French justice; they do not wear themselves out as much as is said in making protestations, and those they do make are almost always sincere; but they have a way of appearing to be interested in you that deceives more than words do. The gross compliments of the Swiss can impose only on fools. The manners of the French are more seductive in this even though they are more simple; one would believe that they are not telling you everything they want to do, so as to surprise you more pleasantly. I will say more; they are not at all false in their demonstrativeness; they are naturally obliging, humane, benevolent, and even, whatever might be said about it, more truthful than any other nation; but they are flighty and fickle. In fact they do have the feeling of which they bear witness to you; but this feeling goes as it came. While they are talking to you they are filled with you; when they no longer see you, they forget you. Nothing is permanent in their heart: everything is the work of the moment for them.

Thus I was very much flattered and little served. This Colonel Godard to whose nephew I had been given turned out to be a nasty old miser, who, although wallowing in gold, wanted to have me for nothing when he saw my distress. He claimed that with his nephew I was a sort of valet without wages rather than a true tutor.[72] Continuously attached to him, and dispensed from the service because of that, I must live from my pay as a cadet, that is to say, as a soldier, and he barely consented to give me the uniform; he would have wanted me to be content with the one from the regiment. Indignant with his propositions, Mme de Merveilleux herself discouraged me from accepting them; her son felt the same way. Something else was sought, and nothing was found. Nevertheless I began to be pressed, and the hundred francs upon which I had made my trip could not carry me very far. Fortunately I received another little remittance from M. the Ambassador which did me a lot of good, and I believe that he would not have abandoned me if I had had more patience: to languish, to wait, to solicit are impossible for me. I became discouraged, I no longer put in an appearance, and everything was finished. I had not forgotten my poor mamma; but how to find her? or to seek her. Mme de Merveilleux, who knew my story, had helped me in that search, and uselessly for a long time. Finally she informed me that Mme de Warens had left more than two months before, but that it was not known whether she had gone to Savoy or Turin, and that several persons said that she had returned to Switzerland.[73] I needed nothing more to settle upon following her, very certain that in whatever spot she might be I would find her in the provinces more easily than I had been able to do in Paris.

Before leaving I practiced my new poetic talent in an epistle to Colonel Godard in which I lampooned him the best I could. I showed this scribbling to Mme de Merveilleux who, instead of censuring me as she should have done, laughed very much at my sarcasms, as did her son also, who, I believe, did not like M. Godard, and it must be admitted that he was not likable. I was tempted to send him my verses, they encouraged me to do so: I sent them to his address in a package, and since at that time there was no local post at Paris, I put it in my pocket, and sent it to him from Auxerre as I passed through. Sometimes I laugh again while thinking about the grimaces he must have made reading this panegyric where he was depicted stroke for stroke. It began this way:

> *Tu croyois, vieux Penard, qu'une folle manie*
> *D'élever ton neveu m'inspireroit l'envie.*[74]

This little piece, badly written, in truth, but which did not lack saltiness, and which announced some talent for satire, is nevertheless the only satirical writing that has come from my pen. My heart is too little filled with hate for such a talent to dominate in me; but I believe that one can judge from several polemical writings done at one time or another for my defense, that, if I had had a quarrelsome disposition, my aggressors would have rarely had the laughers on their side.[75]

The thing I regret most about the details of my life the memory of which I have lost is that I did not make journals of my travels. Never have I thought so much, existed so much, lived so much, been myself so much, if I dare to speak this way, as in these travels I have made alone and on foot. Walking has something that animates and enlivens my ideas: I almost cannot think when I stay in place; my body must be in motion to set my mind in motion. The sight of the countryside, the succession of pleasant views, the open air, the big appetite, the good health that I gain while walking, the freedom of the tavern, the distance from every-thing that makes me feel my dependence, from everything that recalls my situation to me, all this disengages my soul, gives me a greater audacity in thinking, throws me in some manner into the immensity of beings in order to combine them, choose them, appropriate them at my whim without effort and without fear. I dispose of all nature as its master; wan-dering from object to object my heart unites, identifies with the ones that gratify it, surrounds itself with charming images, makes itself drunk with delightful feelings. If I amuse myself by describing them to myself in order to stabilize them, what vigor of brushwork, what freshness of coloring, what energy of expression I give them! It is said that all this has been found in my works, although they have been written toward my declining years. Oh if those of my earliest youth had been seen, those I made up during my travels, those I composed and I never wrote. . . . "Why not write them?" you will say; "And why write them," I will answer you, "Why deprive myself of the present charm of enjoyment in order to tell other people that I had enjoyed?" What did readers, a public and the whole world matter to me, while I soared in Heaven? Besides did I carry paper, pens with me? If I had thought of all that nothing would have come to me. I did not foresee that I would have ideas; they came when they pleased, not when I pleased. They did not come at all, or they came in a crowd, they overwhelmed me with their number and their strength. Ten volumes a day would not have been enough. Where to take the time to write them? Upon arriving I thought only of dining well. Upon leaving I thought only of walking well. I felt that a new paradise was waiting for me at the door; I thought only of going to look for it.

Never have I felt all this so much as in the trip back about which I am speaking. In coming to Paris I had limited myself to ideas relating to what I was going to do there: I had thrown myself into the career into which

I was going to enter, and I had flashed through it with glory enough: but that career was not the one to which my heart called me, and real beings clouded over imaginary beings. Colonel Godard and his nephew appeared badly along with a hero like me. Thanks to Heaven I was now set free from all these obstacles: I could bury myself at my whim in the country of chimeras, for only that remained before me. Also I wandered about in it so much that I really lost my way several times, and I would have been extremely angry to go straighter; for—feeling that I was going to find myself on the earth again at Lyon—I would have wished never to arrive there.

One day in particular, having turned aside on purpose to see close up a place that appeared admirable to me; I was so extremely pleased with it and I made so many turns that I finally became completely lost. After several hours of useless walking, tired and dying of thirst and hunger, I entered a peasant's property, the house of which did not have a fine appearance, but it was the only one that I saw in the surrounding area. I believed that this was just like Geneva or Switzerland, where all the well-off inhabitants are in a condition to exercise hospitality. I asked this one to give me something to eat for which I would pay. He offered me skimmed milk and coarse barley bread while telling me that that was all he had. I drank this milk with delight and I ate this bread, crust and all; but that was not extremely restoring for a man drained from fatigue. This peasant, who was examining me, judged the truth of my story from my appetite. Right away after having told me that he saw very well* that I was a good decent young man who had not come to sell him out, he opened a little trap door next to his kitchen, went down, and came back a moment afterward with a good pure wheat brown bread, a very appetizing ham (although it was pretty deeply cut into), and a bottle of wine the sight of which warmed my heart more than all the rest. Joined to that was a rather thick omelette, and I made a dinner of the sort that no one but a traveller on foot has ever known. When the moment came to pay, his uneasiness and his fears were reestablished again; he did not want my money at all; he pushed it way with an extraordinary agitation, and what was amusing was that I could not imagine what he was afraid of. Finally, shuddering, he pronounced these terrible words of Clerks and Cellar-rats. He made me understand that he hid his wine because of the excise, that he hid his bread because of the *taille*, and that he would be a ruined man if it were suspected that he was not dying of hunger.[77] Everything

---

*Apparently at that time I did not yet have the physiognomy that I have been given since in my portraits.[76]

he told me on this subject, about which I did not have the slightest idea, made an impression on me that will never be blotted out. That was the seed of that inextinguishable hatred that has developed in my heart since then against the vexations suffered by the unfortunate people and against its oppressors. This man, although well-off, did not dare to eat the bread he had earned with the sweat of his brow, and could not avoid his ruin except by showing the same poverty that reigned around him. I left his house as indignant as I was touched and deploring the lot of these beautiful regions upon which nature has lavished its gifts only to make them the prey of barbarous publicans.

This is the only very distinct remembrance I have left of what happened to me during this trip. In addition I recall only that upon drawing near Lyon I was tempted to prolong my route to go to see the banks of the Lignon; for among the novels I had read with my father *Astrée* had not been forgotten, and it was this one that most frequently came back to my heart.[78] I asked the route to Forez, and while chatting with a landlady, was informed by her that that was a good country for supporting workers, that there were many forges there, and that they worked iron extremely well there. With one stroke this eulogy calmed my romantic curiosity, and I did not think fit to go look for Diane and Sylvandre among a people of blacksmiths. The good woman who encouraged me this way surely took me for a locksmith's boy.

I did not go to Lyon entirely without a purpose. Upon arriving I went to les Chasottes to see Mademoiselle du Châtelet, a friend of Mme de Warens, and for whom she had given me a letter when I came with M. Le Maitre: thus this was an already formed acquaintance.[79] Mlle du Châtelet informed me that in fact her friend had passed through Lyon, that she did not know if she had pushed her route all the way to Piedmont, and that upon leaving she herself was uncertain whether she would not end her trip in Savoy: that if I wished she would write to have some news from her, and that the best decision I could make was to wait for news at Lyon. I accepted the offer: but I did not dare to tell Mlle du Châtelet that I was in a hurry for the response, and that my little exhausted purse did not leave me in a condition to wait very long for it. I was not held back because she had given me a poor reception. On the contrary, she had given me many caresses, and treated me on a footing of equality that deprived me of the courage to let her see my condition, and to descend from the role of good company to that of an unfortunate beggar.

I seem to see rather clearly the sequence of everything I have noted in this book. Nevertheless, I believe I recall another trip to Lyon in the same interval whose place I cannot mark and in which I already found myself in very straitened circumstances.[80] A little anecdote that is rather difficult to tell will never allow me to forget it. One night I was sitting in Bellecour after a very scanty supper dreaming about the means to extract myself from the predicament when a man in a cap came to sit down next to me; this man had the manner of one of those silk workers who are called taffeta men at Lyon. He spoke to me, I answered him: thereby a conversation was struck up. We had hardly been chatting for a quarter of an hour when, still with the same coolness and without changing his tone, he proposed that we amuse ourselves together. I waited for him to explain to me what this amusement was; but without adding anything he began to set about giving an example of it. We were almost touching each other, and the night was not dark enough to keep me from seeing what exercise he was preparing himself for. He wanted nothing from me personally, at least nothing announced that intention, and the place would not have favored it. He wanted only, as he had told me, to amuse himself, and for me to amuse myself, each on his own behalf, and that appeared so simple to him, that he had not even assumed that it might not appear the same to me as to him. I was so frightened by this impudence that I hurriedly got up without answering him and began to run away as fast as my legs could carry me, believing that this wretch was at my heels. I was so troubled that instead of reaching my lodging by means of rue St. Dominique, I ran on the side of the docks, and stopped only beyond the wooden bridge, trembling as if I had just committed a crime. I was subject to the same vice; this remembrance cured me of it for a long time.

On this same trip I had another adventure of almost the same sort, but which put me in greater danger. Feeling my cash drawing to its end, I husbanded the puny remnant. I took meals less often at my inn, and soon I did not take them at all anymore, being able to satisfy myself just as well for five or six sous at the tavern as I did there for twenty-five. Since I was not eating there any longer, I did not know how I could go to sleep there; not that I owed very much, but I was ashamed to occupy a room without earning anything for my landlady. The season was fine; one night when it was extremely hot, I decided to pass the night in the square, and I was already settled on a bench, when an Abbé who was passing by saw me lying down that way, came up to me, and asked if I had no lodging; I admitted my circumstances to him, he appeared touched by them; he sat down beside me, and we chatted. He spoke pleasantly; everything he said to me gave me the best opinion in the world of him. When he saw that I was well disposed, he said that he did not have an extremely large lodging, that he had only a single room; but that assuredly he would not leave me to sleep in the square this way; that it was late for finding me lodging, and that he offered me half his bed for that night. I accept the offer, already hoping to make a friend who could be useful to me. We go; he strikes the flint. His room appeared clean to me in its smallness; he did me the honors extremely politely. From an armoire he took out a glass pot in which there were brandied cherries; we each ate two of them, and we went to bed.

This man had the same tastes as my Jew of the hospice, but he did not manifest them so brutally. Either because he feared to force me to defend myself since he knew I could be heard, or because in fact he was less confirmed in his projects, he did not dare to propose their execution openly to me, and sought to excite me without making me anxious. Better informed than the first time, I soon understood his plan, and I shuddered at it; not knowing either in what house or in whose hands I was, I feared to pay with my life for making noise. I pretended not to know what he wanted from me, but appearing very bothered by his caresses and very firm about not enduring their continuation, I acted so well that he was obliged to hold himself back. Then I spoke to him with all the gentleness and all the firmness of which I was capable, and without appearing to suspect anything, I excused myself for the uneasiness I had shown him, based upon my former adventure, which I affected to tell him in terms so full of disgust and horror, that I believe I made him sick to his stomach himself, and he completely renounced his filthy plan. We passed the rest of the night tranquilly. He even told me many very good, very sensible things, and was assuredly not a man without merit, although he was a very nasty fellow.

In the morning, M. the Abbé, who did not want to have a discontented manner, spoke about breakfast, and asked one of the daughters of his landlady who was pretty[81] to have some brought in. She told him that she did not have the time: he addressed himself to her sister, who did not condescend to answer him. We still waited; no breakfast whatsoever. Finally we went into the room of these young Ladies. They received M. the Abbé in a very unaffectionate manner; I had even less upon which to congratulate myself in their welcome. While turning around the elder pressed her pointed heel into the end of my foot, where an extremely painful corn had forced me to cut a hole in my shoe; the other came abruptly to remove from behind me a chair upon which I was ready to sit; their mother sprayed me in the face with some water she was throwing out the window; wherever I put myself they made me move so they could find something, I had not had such treatment in my life. In their insulting and mocking looks I saw a secret rage about which I was stupid enough to understand nothing. Dumbfounded, stupefied, ready to believe them all possessed, I began to be seriously frightened, when the Abbé—who did not seem to see or understand—judging well that there was no breakfast to hope for, decided to go out, and I rushed to follow him, extremely satisfied to escape these three furies. While walking he proposed to me to go breakfast at a café. Although I was very hungry I did not accept this offer upon which he did not insist very much, either, and we separated from each other at the third or fourth street corner; I, charmed to lose sight of everything that belonged to that cursed house, and he, extremely glad, as I believe, to have gotten me far enough away for it not to be easy for me to recognize it. Since nothing similar to these two adventures has ever happened to me either in Paris or in any other city, I have kept an impression from them that is hardly advantageous to the people of Lyon, and I have always regarded that city as the one in Europe in which the most horrible corruption reigns.

The remembrance of the extremities to which I was reduced also does not contribute to my recalling its memory pleasantly. If I had been made like anyone else, if I had had the talent for borrowing, and of putting myself into debt at my tavern, I would have easily extricated myself from the business; but my ineptitude equaled my repugnance for that; and to imagine how far both proceeded, it suffices to know that, after having passed almost all my life in being badly off, and often prepared to lack bread, never once have I been asked for money by a creditor without giving it back to him at the very instant.[82] I have never known how to contract nagging debts, and I have always preferred suffering to owing.

To be reduced to passing the night in the street is assuredly to suffer, and it happened to me several times at Lyon. I preferred to use whatever sous I had left to pay for my bread rather than my lodging, because after all I ran less of a risk of dying of sleepiness than of hunger. What is surprising is that I was neither uneasy nor sad in this cruel condition. I did not have the slightest care about the future, and I waited for the answers that Mme du Châtelet should be receiving, lying under the stars, and sleeping stretched out on the ground or on a bench as tranquilly as on a bed of roses. I even remember having passed a delightful night outside the city on a path that skirted the Rhône or the Saone, I do not recall which. Gardens rising in terraces bordered the path on the opposite side. It had been very hot that day; the evening was charming; the dew moistened withered grass; no wind at all, a tranquil night; the air was cool without being cold; after setting, the sun left in the sky red vapor the reflection of which colored the water pink; the trees of the terraces were filled with nightingales who were responding to each other. I strolled in a sort of ecstasy, abandoning my senses and my heart to the enjoyment of all this, and sighing only a little out of regret at enjoying it alone. Absorbed in my sweet reverie I prolonged my stroll far into the night without noticing that I was tired. Finally I noticed it. I lay down voluptuously on the shelf of a sort of niche or blind door[83] set deep into a wall of the terrace: the canopy of my bed was formed by the tops of trees, a nightingale was precisely above me; I fell asleep to its song: my sleep was sweet, my awakening was even more so. It was broad daylight: upon opening, my eyes saw[84] the water, the greenery, an admirable countryside. I got up, shook myself, was overtaken by hunger, I proceeded gaily toward the city resolved to put the two pieces of six blancs[85] I still had left toward a good breakfast. I was in such a good mood that I went singing the whole length of the path, and I even remember that I sang a Cantata by Batistin[86] entitled *the Baths of Thoméry* which I knew by heart. Blessed be the good Batistin and his good cantata which was worth an even better breakfast for me than the one I was counting on, and a dinner that was even better, which I had not counted on at all. In my best pace of going along and singing I hear someone behind me, I turn around; I see an Antonine monk who was following me, and who appeared to be listening to me with pleasure. He accosts me, greets me, asks me if I know music. I answer, "*A little*," so as to make it understood, "a lot." He continues to question me; I tell him a part of my story. He asks me if I have ever copied music? "Often," I say to him, and that was true; my best way of learning was to copy it. "Good," he says to me, "Come with me; I will be able to keep you busy for several days during which you will lack nothing, as long as you consent not to leave the room." I acquiesced very willingly, and I followed him.

This Antonine was called M. Rolichon;[87] he loved music; he knew it, and sang in little concerts that he gave with his friends. This is only innocent and decent; but this taste apparently degenerated into a mania a part of which he was obliged to hide. He led me into a little room that I occupied where I found a lot of music he had copied. He gave me more to copy, particularly the cantata I had been singing, which he was supposed to sing himself in several days. I stayed there three or four days, copying all the time when I was not eating; for never in my life have I been so famished or better nourished. He brought my meals from their kitchen himself, and it must have been a good one, if their ordinary meals were as good as mine. Never in my life have I had so much pleasure in eating, and it must be admitted also that these mouthfuls came to me very opportunely, for I was as dry as a piece of wood. I worked almost as wholeheartedly as I ate, and that is saying more than a little. It is true that I was not as correct as I was diligent. Several days later M. Rolichon, whom I met in the street, informed me that my scores had rendered the music unperformable; since they had been found to be so full of omissions, duplications, and transpositions. I must admit that later on I chose in this profession the one in the world for which I was least suited.[88] Not that my notes were not fine, and that I did not copy very clearly; but the boredom of a long work makes me so absent-minded that I pass more time in scratching out than in noting, and that if I do not bring the greatest attention to collating[89] my scores, they always cause the performance to fail. Thus I did very poorly while wishing to do well, and to go fast I went exactly the opposite. That did not keep M. Rolichon from treating me well up to the end, and from giving me again a petit écu[90] when I left, which I hardly deserved and which put me completely back on my feet; for a few days later I received news from Mamma who was at Chambéry, and money to go join her, which I did with rapture. Since then my finances have often been extremely limited, but never enough to oblige[91] me to fast. I take note of this epoch with a heart sensitive to the care of providence. It is the last time in my life that I felt poverty and hunger.

I stayed at Lyon seven or eight more days to wait for the commissions with which Mamma had entrusted Mlle du Châtelet, whom I saw during this time more assiduously than before, having the pleasure of talking with her about her friend, and no longer being distracted by those cruel reflections on my situation that forced me to hide it. Mlle du Châtelet was neither young nor pretty, but she did not lack grace; she was sociable and familiar, and her intelligence gave value to this familiarity. She had that taste for observational morality that leads to studying men, and it is from her that this same taste came to me in its first origin. She loved Le Sage's novels, and particularly *Gil Blas*; she spoke to me about it, loaned it to me, I read it with pleasure; but I was not yet ripe for that sort of reading; I needed novels of great feelings.[92] I thus passed my time at the grill of Mlle du Châtelet's convent with as much pleasure as profit, and it is certain that interesting and sensible conversations with a woman of merit are more fit for forming a young man than all the pedantic philosophy of books. At les Chasotes I made the acquaintance of other boarders and their friends; among others with a young person who was fourteen years old called Mademoiselle Serre, to whom I did not pay great attention at that time, but whom I became passionately fond of eight or nine years later, and with reason; for she was a charming girl.[93]

Occupied with waiting to see my good mamma again soon I made a bit of a truce with my chimeras, and the real happiness that was waiting for me spared me from looking for it in my visions. Not only was I finding her again, but I was finding a pleasant condition near her and through her again; for she noted that she had found me an occupation that she hoped would suit me, and which would not take me away from her. I wore myself out with conjectures to divine what this occupation could be, and in fact it would have been necessary to divine in order to guess right. I had enough money to make the journey comfortably. Mlle du Châtelet wanted me to take a horse; I could not consent to this and I was right: I would have lost the pleasure of the last pedestrian trip I have made in my life; for I cannot give this name to the excursions that I often made in my neighborhood, while I resided at Môtiers.[94]

It is a very peculiar thing that my imagination never shows itself more agreeably than when my condition is the least agreeable, and that, on the contrary, it is less cheerful when everything is cheerful around me. My unruly head cannot subject itself to things. It cannot embellish, it wants to create. Real objects are depicted in it at most as they are; it knows how to adorn only imaginary objects. If I want to depict the Spring I must be in the winter; if I want to describe a beautiful countryside I must be inside walls, and I have said a hundred times that if I were ever put in the Bastille, I would paint the tableau of freedom there. In leaving Lyon I saw only an agreeable future; I was also content, and I had every reason to be so, just as I had few reasons to be when I left Paris. Nevertheless, during this trip I did not at all have those delightful reveries that had followed me in the other one. I had a serene heart, but that was all. With emotion I drew near the excellent friend whom I was going to see again. I tasted in advance, but without intoxication, the pleasure of living around her: I had always expected it; it was as if nothing new had happened to me. I was uneasy about what I was going to do, as if that had been extremely disquieting. My ideas were peaceful and sweet, not celestial and ravishing. All the objects I passed struck my view; I paid attention to the countryside, I noticed the trees, the houses, the streams, I deliberated at the crossroads, I was afraid of getting lost and I did not get lost at all. In a word I was no longer in the empyrean, sometimes I was where I was, sometimes where I was going, never farther away.

In recounting my travels I am as I was while making them; I do not know how to conclude. My heart beat with joy upon drawing near my dear mamma and I did not go any faster because of it. I love to walk at my ease, and to stop when I please. The ambulatory life is the one I need. To travel on foot in fine weather in a fine country without being rushed, and to have an agreeable object at the end of my journey; of all the ways of living, that is the one most in accordance with my taste. For the rest, what I understand by a fine country is already known. Never has a flat country, however beautiful it might be, appeared that way to my eyes. I need torrents, rocks, fir trees, dark woods, mountains,[95] rugged paths to climb and descend, on all sides of me precipices that scare me very much. I had this pleasure and I tasted it in all its charm while drawing near Chambéry. Not far from a jagged mountain called the Pas de l'Echelle,[96] under the big path cut in the rock, at the place called Chailles, there runs and seethes in dreadful abysses a little river which appears to have been hollowing them out for thousands of centuries. The path has been bordered with a parapet to prevent misfortunes: that made it so I could contemplate deeply and get dizzy at my ease; for what is funny in my taste for craggy places is that they make my head spin, and I like this spinning very much as long as I am in safety. Well supported on the parapet I put my nose forward, and I stayed there for whole hours, from time to time catching a glimpse of that froth and that blue water whose roaring I heard through the cries of the crows and birds of prey[97] that flew from rock to rock and from bush to bush a hundred fathoms beneath me. In the spots where the slope was smooth enough and the underbrush clear enough to let stones pass through, I went far away to find some as big as I could carry, I gathered them in a pile on the parapet; then throwing one after the other, I took delight in seeing them roll, bounce, and fly into a thousand slivers before reaching the bottom of the precipice.

Closer to Chambéry I had a similar spectacle in the opposite sense. The path passed the foot of the most beautiful waterfall I have seen in my life. The mountain is so steep that the water breaks cleanly away from it and falls in an arc far enough away so that one can pass between the waterfall and the rock, sometimes without getting wet. But if one does not take one's precautions well, one is easily fooled, as I was: for, because of the extreme height, the water divides and falls in a spray, and when one draws a little too close to this cloud, without noticing at first that one is getting wet, instantly one is completely soaked.

At last I arrive, I see her again. She was not alone. M. the Intendant General was at her house at the moment I entered.[98] Without speaking to me she takes me by the hand and presents me to him with that grace that opened all hearts to her, "Here he is, Monsieur, this poor young man; deign to protect him as long as he deserves it, I am no longer at a loss about him for the rest of his life." Then addressing her words to me, "My child," she says to me, "you belong to the King: thank M. the Intendant who gives you bread." I opened my eyes wide without saying anything, without being able to do very much except to imagine: little was needed for nascent ambition to turn my head, and for me to make myself a little Intendant already. My fortune turned out to be less brilliant than I had imagined based on this beginning; but as for the present it was enough to live, and for me that was a lot. Here is how things stood.

Judging from the outcome of the preceding wars and from the condition of the ancient patrimony of his fathers that it would escape him someday, King Victor Amadeus sought only to use it up. Having resolved to put the nobility under the *taille* a few years earlier, he had ordered a general survey of the whole country, so that, making the imposition on real estate, it could be apportioned with greater equity.[99] This work, begun under the father, was completed under the son. Two or three hundred men—both surveyors who were called geometers, and writers who were called secretaries—were employed in this work, and it was among these last that mamma had had me inscribed. Without being extremely lucrative, the post gave enough to live liberally in that country. The problem was that this employment was only temporary, but it put me in a position to seek and wait, and it was by foresight that she tried to obtain a particular protection for me from the Intendant so I could pass on to some more solid employment when the time for this one was finished.

I took up my duties a few days after my arrival. There was nothing difficult in this work, and I soon knew all about it. It is thus that after four or five years of wandering, of follies, and of suffering since my departure from Geneva I began for the first time to earn my bread with honor.

These long details about my earliest youth will have appeared very puerile and I am sorry about it: although born a man in certain respects, I was a child for a long time and I am still one in many others. I have not promised to offer a great personage to the public;[100] I have promised to depict myself as I am and in order to know me in my advanced age, it is necessary to have known me well in my youth. Since in general objects make less of an impression on me than their remembrance does and since all my ideas are in images, the first features that were engraved in my head have remained there, and those that have been imprinted there afterwards have combined with them rather than effaced them. There is a certain succession of affections and ideas that modify those that follow them and which one must know in order to judge them well. In order to make the chain of effects felt I apply myself above all to developing the first causes. I would like to be able to render my soul transparent to the eyes of the reader in some fashion, and to do so I seek to show it to him under all points of view, to clarify it by all lights, to act in such a way that no motion occurs in it that he does not perceive so that he might be able to judge by himself about the principle which produces them.

If I took responsibility for the result and I said to him; such is my character, he would be able to believe, if not that I am fooling him, at least that I am fooling myself. But by relating to him in detail with simplicity everything that has happened to me, everything I have done, everything

I have thought, everything I have felt, I cannot lead him into error unless I want to, even if I wanted to I would not succeed easily in this fashion. It is up to him to assemble these elements and to define the being made up of them; the result ought to be his work, and if he is deceived then, all the error will be of his making. Now for this end it is not enough for my accounts to be faithful; they must also be exact. It is not up to me to judge the importance of the facts, I ought to tell them all, and leave to him the care of choosing. This is what I have applied myself to with all my courage up to this point, and I will not slacken in what follows. But the remembrances of middle age are always less vivid than those of the first youth. I have begun by drawing from the latter the best part I could. If the others come back to me with the same strength, impatient readers will perhaps be bored, but I will not be dissatisfied with my work. I have only one thing to fear in this enterprise; that is not to tell too much or to tell lies; no, it is not to tell everything, and to be silent about things that are true.[101]

Book V[1]

It seems to me that it was in 1732[2] that I arrived at Chambéry as I have just said, and that I began to be employed[3] on the survey in the King's service. I had passed twenty years, almost twenty-one. I was formed well enough for my age on the side of mind, but my judgment was hardly formed, and I very much needed the hands into which I was falling in order to learn how to conduct myself: for several years of experience had not yet been able to cure me radically of my romantic visions, and in spite of all the ills I had suffered, I knew the world and men as little as if I had not purchased[4] this instruction.

I stayed at my home, that is to say at Mamma's; but I did not find my room at Annecy again. No more garden, no more stream, no more countryside. The house she occupied was somber and sad, and my room was the most somber and sad one in the house. A wall for a view, a cul-de-sac for a street, little air, little light, little space, crickets, rats, rotten boards, all that did not make up a pleasant habitation. But I was in her home, near her, ceaselessly at my desk or in her room, I hardly noticed the ugliness of my own, I did not have time to dream there. It will appear bizarre that she had established herself at Chambéry intentionally to live in that nasty house: this was even a skillful stroke on her part about which I should not keep silent. She went to Turin reluctantly, since she felt very much that this was not the moment for presenting herself there after the still very recent revolutions and the agitation they still were in at the Court. Nevertheless, her affairs demanded that she show herself there; she feared being forgotten or ill served. Above all she knew that the Comte de St. Laurent, the Intendant General of finances, did not favor her.[5] At Chambéry he had an old, poorly constructed house in such a nasty position that it always remained empty; she rented it and settled in there. That succeeded for her better than a trip; her pension was not suppressed, and from then on the Comte de St. Laurent was always one of her friends.

There I found her household set up just about as before, and the faithful Claude Anet still with her. He was, as I believe I have said, a peasant from Montreux who in his childhood went botanizing in the Jura to make Swiss tea,[6] and whom she had taken into her service because of her drugs,

148

finding it convenient to have an herbalist as her lackey. He became so enthusiastic for the study of plants, and she fostered his taste so well that
he became a true botanist, and if he had not died young, he would have
made a name for himself in that science, just as he deserved one among
decent people. Since he was serious, even grave, and since I was younger
than he was, he became a sort of governor for me who saved me from
many follies; for he commanded my respect, and I did not dare forget
myself in front of him. He even commanded the respect of his mistress
who knew his great sense, his uprightness, his inviolable attachment for
her, and who very much reciprocated it. Without contradiction, Claude
Anet was a rare man, and even the only one of his sort that I have ever
seen. Slow, composed, reflective, circumspect in his conduct, cold in his
manners, laconic and sententious in his conversation, he had in his passions an impetuosity which he never allowed to appear, but which ate
him up inside, and which caused him to commit only one stupidity in
his life, but a terrible one; that is to have taken poison. This tragic scene
happened shortly after my arrival, and without it I would not have been
informed about this boy's intimacy with his mistress; for if she had not
told me herself, I would never have suspected it. Assuredly if attachment,
zeal, and faithfulness can deserve such a recompense, it was very much
owed to him, and what proves that he was worthy of it is that he never
abused it. They rarely had quarrels, and the ones they did have always
finished well. However, one did occur that finished badly: in anger his
mistress said something insulting to him that he could not stomach. He
consulted only his despair, and finding a vial of Laudanum ready to hand
he swallowed it, then lay down tranquilly counting on never waking up.
Fortunately Mme de Warens, herself uneasy, agitated, roaming around
the house, found the empty vial and guessed the rest. Flying to his aid
she cried out in a way that drew my attention; she admitted everything
to me, implored my assistance, and with much difficulty succeeded in
making him vomit the opium. As a witness to this scene, I wondered at
my stupidity at never having had the slightest suspicion concerning the
relationship about which she informed me. But Claude Anet was so discreet that the most clear-sighted people could have been mistaken. The
reconciliation was such that I was vividly touched by it myself, and from
that time, adding respect to esteem for him, I became his student in some
manner, and did not find myself any the worse for it.

It was not, however, without pain that I learned that someone could
live with her in greater intimacy than I did. I had not even dreamed of
desiring that place for myself, but it was hard for me to see it filled by
someone else; that was extremely natural. Nevertheless, instead of ac-

quiring an aversion for the one who had done me out of it, I felt the attachment I had for her substantially extend itself to him. Above all I desired her to be happy, and since she needed him to be so, I was content that he be happy also. On his side, he entered perfectly into his mistress's views, and took into sincere friendship the friend whom she had chosen for herself. Without putting on the authority that his post gave him the right to take on with me, he naturally took on the authority that his judgment gave him over mine. I did not dare to do anything he appeared to disapprove of, and he disapproved only of what was bad. Thus we lived in a union that made us all happy, and which death alone was able to destroy. One of the proofs of the excellence of character of this lovable woman is that all those who loved her loved each other. Jealousy, rivalry even gave way to the dominant feeling she inspired, and I have never seen any of the people around her wish for the harm of another. Let those who are reading me suspend their reading for a moment at this praise, and if in thinking about it they find some other woman about whom they can say as much, let them attach themselves to her for the sake of the repose of their life, even if she is in other respects the worst of Whores.

Here begins an interval of eight or nine years from my arrival at Chambéry to my departure for Paris in 1741, during which I will have few events to tell, because my life was as simple as it was sweet, and this uniformity was precisely what I needed most to finish forming my character, which continual disorder kept from being settled. It is during this precious interval that my mixed and incoherent education acquired some consistency so as to make me what I have never again ceased to be through the storms that were waiting for me. This progress was imperceptible and slow, burdened with few memorable events; but it nevertheless deserves to be followed and developed.

At the beginning I was hardly occupied except with my work; the constraint of the office did not allow me to think about anything else. The little time I had free was passed with the good mamma, and—since I did not even have any for reading—I was not seized by the whim for it. But when my job, having become a sort of routine, occupied my mind less, it became uneasy again, reading became necessary for me again, and, just as if this taste was always inflamed by the difficulty of abandoning myself to it, it would have become a passion again as it was at my master's, if other tastes had not diverted me from it by running counter to it.

Although our operations did not need a very transcendent arithmetic, they required one that was sufficiently so to perplex me sometimes. To overcome this difficulty I bought arithmetic books and I learned it well, for I learned it by myself. Practical arithmetic extends farther than is

thought, when one wants to put exact precision into it. It has extremely
long operations, in the middle of which I have sometimes seen good
geometers go astray. Reflection joined to practice gives clear ideas, and
then one finds shortcut methods whose invention flatters amour-propre,
whose exactness satisfies the mind, and which make a work that is disagreeable in itself be done with pleasure. I buried myself so deeply in
it that there was no question at all soluble by numbers alone that perplexed me, and now that everything I have known is daily erased from
my memory, this acquisition still remains there in part, after thirty years
of interruption. Several days ago in a trip I made to Davenport to my
landlord's house, while I was helping in his children's arithmetic lesson,
I did one of the most complicated operations without a mistake with an
unbelievable pleasure.[7] While I was writing down my numbers[8] it seemed
to me that I was still at Chambéry in my happy days. This was returning
back on my footsteps from afar.

The tinting of our geometers' maps had also given me a taste for drawing. I bought some colors and I began to draw flowers and the countryside. It is a shame that I found so little talent in myself for that art; the
inclination was completely there. I would have passed whole months in
the midst of my pencils and my brushes without leaving. Since this occupation became too interesting for me, they were obliged to tear me away
from it. It is that way with all the tastes to which I begin to abandon myself, they increase, become a passion, and soon I no longer see anything
in the world but the amusement with which I am occupied. Age has not
cured me of this flaw; it has not even diminished it, and now as I am
writing this, there I am like an old dotard, fascinated by another useless
study about which I understand nothing, and which even those who have
abandoned themselves to it in their youth are forced to give up at the age
at which I want to begin it.

It was then that it might have been in its place. The occasion was fine,
and I had some temptation to take advantage of it. Two or three times
the contentment I saw in Anet's eyes upon coming back burdened with
new plants brought me to the point of going herborizing with him. I am
almost sure that if I had done so a single time it would have won me over,
and perhaps I would be a great botanist today: for I know no study in
the world that mixes better with my natural tastes than that of plants, and
the life that I have been leading for the past ten years in the country is
hardly anything but a continuous herborization, in truth without object
and without progress; but since I did not have any idea of botany at that
time, I had acquired a sort of disdain and even disgust for it; I looked at
it as a sort of Apothecary's study.[9] Mamma, who loved it, did not make

any other use of it herself; she looked for nothing but the usual plants so as to apply them to her drugs. Thus botany, chemistry, and anatomy—mixed up in my mind under the name of medicine—served only to furnish me with playful sarcasms all day long, and to attract me some boxes on the ears from time to time.[10] Moreover a taste that was different from and too contrary to that one was growing by degrees, and soon absorbed all others. I am speaking about music. I surely must have been born for that art, because I began to love it from my childhood, and it is the only one I have loved constantly at all times. What is surprising is that an art for which I was born should nevertheless have cost me so much pain to learn, and with such slow success that after lifelong practice, I have never been able to sing surely by sight reading. Above all what made this study pleasant for me at that time was that I could do it with Mamma. While in other respects we had tastes that were extremely different, music was a meeting point for us which I loved to make use of. She did not resist it; by then I was almost as advanced as she was; in two or three tries we deciphered a tune. Sometimes seeing her busy around the furnace, I said to her, "Mamma, here is a charming duet[11] which appears to me to be just the thing to make your drugs smell from burning." "Ah by my faith," she said to me, "if you make me burn them I will make you eat them." Even while disputing I dragged her away to her harpsichord: we forgot ourselves in it; the extract of juniper or absinthe was charred, she smeared my face with it, and all that was delightful.

One sees that with little time left over, I had many things upon which to use it. Nevertheless, one further amusement came to me, which very much enhanced all the others.

We occupied such a suffocating cell that we sometimes needed to go take the air in the country. Anet engaged Mamma to rent a garden in the suburbs to put some plants there. To this garden was joined a rather pretty little country house that was furnished with the bare necessities. We put a bed there; we often went there to dine, and sometimes I slept there. Insensibly I became infatuated with this little retreat; I put some books there, many prints; I passed a part of my time in decorating it and preparing some pleasant surprise for Mamma when she came to walk there. I left her to come to occupy myself with her, to think about her with more pleasure; another caprice that I neither excuse nor explain, but which I admit because that is the way it was. I remember that one time Mme de Luxembourg was speaking to me, while mocking, about a man who left his mistress in order to write to her. I told her that I might very much have been that man, and I could have added that I had been him sometimes.

Near Mamma, however, I never felt this need for leaving her in order to love her more: for in tête-à-tête with her I was as perfectly at my ease as if I had been alone, and that has never happened to me around anyone else, neither man nor woman, whatever attachment I might have had for them. But she was so often surrounded, and by people who pleased me so little, that spite and boredom chased me into my refuge, where I had her as I wanted her, without fearing that importunate people might come to follow us.

While I was living in the sweetest repose divided in this way among work, pleasure, and instruction, Europe was not as tranquil as I was. France and the Emperor declared war on each other: the King of Sardinia had entered into the quarrel, and the French army went off into Piedmont to enter Milanese territory.[12] A Column passed through Chambéry and among others the Regiment of Champagne whose Colonel was M. the Duc de la Trimouille,[13] to whom I was presented, who promised me many things, and who surely has never thought about me since. Our little garden was precisely at the edge of the suburb by which the troops entered, so that I gorged myself on the pleasure of going to see them pass, and I became impassioned for the success of this war, as if it concerned me very much. Until then I had not yet taken it into my head to think about public matters, and I began to read the gazettes for the first time, but with such a partiality for France that my heart beat with joy at its slightest advantages, and its reverses afflicted me as if they had fallen on me. If that madness had only been transient I would not deign to speak about it; but without any reason it became so rooted in my heart, that when I later played the antidespot and proud republican at Paris, in spite of myself I felt a secret predilection for that same nation that I found to be servile, and for that government which I affected to criticize. What was funny was that, since I was ashamed of an inclination so contrary to my maxims, I did not dare to admit it to anyone, and I scoffed at the French for their defeats, while my heart bled more than theirs. I am surely the only one who, living in a nation that treated him well and that he adored, among them gave himself a false air of despising them.[14] Finally, this inclination has been so disinterested on my part, so strong, so constant, so invincible, that even since my departure from the kingdom, since the government, the magistrates, the authors have broken loose vying with each other against me, since it has become good form to heap me with injustices and outrages, I have not been able to cure myself of my madness. I love them in spite of myself even though they mistreat me. In seeing the beginning of the decadence of England that I predicted in the midst of

its triumphs, I let myself nurse the foolish hope that the French Nation—
victorious in its turn—will possibly come one day to deliver me from the
sad captivity in which I live.[15]

For a long time I have sought the cause of this partiality, and I can
find it only in the occasion that saw it born. A growing taste for literature attached me to French books, to the Authors of these books, and
to the country of these Authors. At the very moment the French army
was marching under my eyes, I was reading Brantome's great Captains.
My head was full of Clisson, Bayard, Lautrec, Coligny, Montmorenci,
La Trimouille, and I delighted in their descendants as the heirs of their
merit and their courage.[16] With each Regiment that passed I believed I
saw again those famous black bands which formerly had performed so
many exploits in Piedmont. In sum I applied the ideas I drew from books
to what I saw; my continued readings always drawn from the same nation
nourished my affection for it, and finally gave me a blind passion for it that
nothing was able to overcome. Since then I have had occasion to remark
in my travels that this impression is not peculiar to me, and that—acting
to a greater or lesser degree in all countries on that part of the Nation
that loves reading and that cultivates letters—it counterbalances the general hatred inspired by the conceited manner of the French. Novels attach
the women of all countries to them more than the men, their dramatic
masterpieces make the young take delight in their theaters. The fame of
the one in Paris attracts crowds of foreigners there who return from it as
enthusiasts: In sum, the excellent taste of their literature subjects to them
all minds who have any taste, and in the very unfortunate war that they
have·just left, I have seen their Authors and their philosophers maintain
the glory of the French name tarnished by their warriors.[17]

Thus I was an ardent Frenchman, and that made me a seeker of news.
I went to the public square with the crowd of gulls[18] to wait for the arrival of the couriers, and more stupid than the ass in the fable I became
very anxious to know which master's pack I would have the honor of
carrying:[19] for at that time it was claimed that we belonged to France,
and that the Milanese territory was being traded for Savoy. It must be
acknowledged nevertheless that I had some reason for fear; for if this war
had turned out badly for the allies mamma's pension would be at great
risk. But I was full of confidence in my good friends, and this time, in
spite of M. de Broglie's surprise, this confidence was not mistaken, thanks
to the King of Sardinia about whom I had never thought.[20]

While they were fighting in Italy they were singing in France. Rameau's
Operas began to cause a stir and called attention to his theoretical works
whose obscurity put them over the heads of all but a few. By chance, I

heard his treatise on harmony spoken of, and I had no rest until I had acquired this book.[21] By another chance, I fell ill. The illness was inflammatory: it was intense and short; but my convalescence was long, and for a month I was in no condition to go out. During this time I outlined, I devoured my treatise on harmony; but it was so long, so diffuse, so poorly arranged that I felt I needed a considerable time to study it and sort it out. I suspended my application and I diverted my eyes with music. Bernier's Cantatas, which I practiced on, did not leave my mind.[22] I learned four or five by heart, among others *Sleeping Loves*, which I have not seen again since that time, and which I still know almost entirely, the same as *Love Stung by a Bee*, a very pretty Cantata by Clerambault, which I learned at about the same time.[23]

To finish me off there arrived from Valdosta a young organist called Abbé Palais, a good musician, a good man, who accompanied very well on the Harpsichord.[24] I made his acquaintance; we were inseparable. He was the student of an Italian monk, a great Organist. He spoke to me about his principles; I compared them with those of my Rameau, I filled my head with accompaniment, concords, harmony. To do all this, I had to form my ear: I proposed to mamma a little Concert every month; she consented to it. Behold me so full of this Concert that day or night I was occupied with[25] nothing else, and it truly did keep me busy and very much so, to assemble the music, the Participants, the instruments, to draw up the parts, etc.[26] Mamma sang, Father Caton (about whom I have already spoken and about whom I am going to speak again) also sang; a dance instructor called Roche and his son played violin; Canavas a Piedmontese musician who worked at the Survey and who since has gotten married at Paris played the Cello;[27] the Abbé Palais accompanied on the Harpsichord: I had the honor of conducting the music, without forgetting the woodcutter's baton.[28] You can judge how fine all this was! not exactly as at M. de Treytorens's, but not far from it.

The little concert of Mme de Warens the new convert who, it was said, was living from the King's charity, made the devout crowd mutter, but it was a pleasant amusement for numerous decent people. You would not guess whom I put at their head on this occasion? a Monk; but a monk who was a man of merit, and even amiable, whose misfortunes affected me very keenly later on, and whose memory, linked to that of my heyday, is still dear to me. This was Father Caton, a Franciscan who together with the Comte D'Ortan had had the poor Kitten's music seized at Lyon, which is not the finest deed of his life.[29] He received a degree from the Sorbonne: he had lived for a long time at Paris in the highest society, and was very well connected above all with the Marquis d'Antremont, then

Ambassador from Sardinia.[30] He was a tall man, well formed, a full face, bug-eyed, black hair that swerved without affectation near his brow, a manner at the same time noble, open, modest, presenting himself simply and well; having neither the sanctimonious or brazen bearing of monks, nor the cavalier aspect of a fashionable man, although he was one, but the assurance of a decent man who is proud of himself without blushing about his robe and always feels that he is in his place among decent people. Although Father Caton might not have had much learning for a Scholar, he had a lot for a man of the world, and—not being at all in a hurry to show his accomplishments—he placed them so opportunely that he appeared even more accomplished. Having lived much in society he was more devoted to pleasing talents than to solid knowledge. He had intelligence, wrote verses, spoke well, sang better, had a fine voice, played the organ and Harpsichord a little. It did not require that much to make him sought after, and so he was; but this made him neglect the concerns of his position so little that, in spite of very jealous Rivals, he succeeded in being elected Definitor for his province, or as is said, one of the great Necklaces[31] of the order.

This Father Caton made Mamma's acquaintance at the Marquis d'Antremont's home. He heard our concerts talked about, he wanted to be in them, he was in them, and made them shine. We were soon tied together by our shared taste for music, which was a very lively passion in each of us, with this difference that he was truly a Musician, and I was only a dabbler. We went with Canavas and the Abbé Palais to play music in his room, and sometimes at his Organ on feast days. We often dined at his informal supper; for what is still more surprising for a Monk is that he was generous, liberal, and sensuous without coarseness. On the days of our concerts he dined at mamma's. These suppers were very gay, very pleasant; we told risqué stories, we sang duos: I was at my ease, I had wit, sallies, Father Caton was charming, Mamma was adorable, with his bull's voice the Abbé Palais was the butt of all the jokes. Such sweet moments of frolicsome youth, how long you have been gone!

Since I will not have anything more to say about this poor Father Caton, let me complete his sad story here in two words. The other monks, jealous or rather furious at seeing a merit and an elegance of morals in him that had nothing of monastic scum, acquired a hatred for him, because he was not as hateful as they were. The Leaders conspired against him and roused up the young monks who envied his place, and who previously did not dare to look at it. They gave him a thousand affronts, they dismissed him from office, they deprived him of his room (which he had furnished with taste although with simplicity), they banished him somewhere or other; finally these wretches heaped so many outrages on him that his decent and justifiably proud soul could no longer resist; and after having been the delight of the most amiable social circles, he died of sorrow on a lowly pallet, in some hole of a cell or prison, regretted, wept for by all the decent people who knew him, and who found no flaw in him except that he was a Monk.[32]

With this little pattern of life I did so well in very little time that, absorbed entirely by music, I found myself in no condition to think about anything else. I no longer went to my Office except unwillingly, the bother and the constant application at work were an unbearable torture for me, and I finally came to wish to leave my job in order to abandon myself totally to music. One can believe that this folly did not get by without opposition. To leave a decent post with a fixed revenue in order to run after uncertain students was too senseless a decision to please Mamma. Even assuming my future progress to be as great as I portrayed it to myself, reducing myself for life[33] to the station of Musician was to limit my ambition very modestly. It was with pain that she, who formed only magnificent projects and who no longer took me entirely at M. d'Aubonne's word,[34] saw me seriously occupied with a talent that she found so frivolous, and often repeated to me this provincial proverb, which is a little less just at Paris, that *he who sings and dances well does not have a profession that advances well.* On another side she saw me swept away by an irresistible taste; my passion for music was becoming a rage, and it was to be feared that, if my work felt the effect of my distractions, it might draw a dismissal for me which it was much better to take on my own initiative. I pointed out again that this job would not last very long, that I needed a talent in order to live, and that this would be accomplished more surely by acquiring through practice the talent to which my taste carried me and which she had chosen for me, than by putting me at the mercy of protection, or by making new attempts that might succeed badly, and leave me without a way to earn my bread after I had passed the age for learning. Finally, I extorted her consent more as a result of importunities and blandishments than from reasons that might satisfy her. At once I ran proudly to thank M. Coccelli the Director General of the survey, as if I had performed the most heroic act, and I voluntarily left my job without cause, without reason, without pretext, with as much and even more joy than I had had when I took it not even two years before.[35]

Foolish though it was, this step drew me a sort of consideration in the country that was useful to me. Some assumed I had resources that I did not have; others, seeing me abandoning myself completely to music, judged my talent by my sacrifice, and believed that with such a passion for that art I must possess it to a superior degree. In the Kingdom of the blind the one-eyed are Kings; I passed for a good teacher because there were only bad ones. Moreover, because I did not lack a certain taste for singing and, furthermore, was favored by my age and my appearance, I soon had more students than I needed to replace my pay as a secretary.

It is certain that for pleasantness of life one could not pass more rapidly from one extreme to the other. At the survey, occupied eight hours a day in the most gloomy work with still gloomier people, closed up in a sad Office stinking with the breath and sweat of all these boors, the majority extremely unkempt and extremely dirty, I sometimes felt myself overpowered to the point of dizziness by the attention, the smell, the bother and the boredom.[36] Instead of that there I was all at once thrown into the fine social world, admitted, sought after in the best houses; everywhere a gracious, affectionate welcome, the atmosphere of a party: lovable well-dressed Young Ladies waited for me, greeted me eagerly; I saw only charming objects, I smelled nothing but roses and orange blossoms; we sing, we chat, we laugh, we amuse ourselves; I depart only to go somewhere else to do the same things: it will be acknowledged that, with the monetary benefits being equal, there was nothing to compare in the choice. Also I was so satisfied with my choice that it never occurred to me to regret it, and I do not regret it even at this moment, when I weigh the actions of my life in the scale of reason, and when I am freed from the senseless motives that carried me away to it.

This is almost the only time that I have not seen my expectations deceived when I listened only to my inclinations. The easy welcome, the amiable spirit, the easy-going mood of the country's inhabitants made the company of the social world amiable, and the taste I acquired for it then has proven to me very well that if I do not like to live among men, it is less my fault than theirs.

It is a shame that the Savoyards are not rich, or perhaps it would be a shame if they were; for as they are they are the best and the most sociable[37] people I know. If there is a little City in the world where one tastes the sweetness of life in a pleasant and reliable company, it is Chambéry. The nobility of the province who gather there have only enough property to live, they do not have enough to rise, and since they cannot abandon themselves to ambition, by necessity they follow the advice of Cineas.[38] They devote their youth to the military station, then come back to grow old peacefully at home. Honor and reason preside over this division. The women are beautiful and could dispense with being so; they all have the things that can give value to beauty, and even substitute for it. It is peculiar that although I was called by my station to see many young girls, I do not recall having seen a single one at Chambéry who was not charming. It will be said that I was disposed to find them so, and that might be correct; but I did not need to add anything of my own for it to be true. In truth I cannot recall the remembrance of my young students without pleasure. Why can I not, by naming the most lovable ones here, call them back and myself with them to the happy age we were at the time, a time of moments as sweet as they were innocent which I passed near them! The first was Mademoiselle de Mellarede my neighbor, the sister of M. Gaime's student.[39] She was a very lively brunette, but with an affectionate vivacity, full of graces, and without giddiness. She was a little thin, as most girls are at her age; but her shining eyes, her slender waist and her inviting manner did not need filling out in order to please. I went there in the morning, and she was usually still in dishabille, without any other dressing for her hair than having it done up carelessly, adorned with some flower that was put in at my arrival and removed at my departure. I fear nothing in the world as much as a pretty person in dishabille; I would dread her a hundred times less dressed up. Mademoiselle de Menthon, to whose house I went in the afternoon, was always dressed up and made just as sweet an impression on me, but a different one.[40] Her hair was ash-blond: she was very dainty, very timid, and very pale; a clear, exact, and flute-like voice, but which did not dare to stretch out. On her breast she had a scar from a scalding with boiling water that a blue silk neckerchief did not entirely hide. This mark sometimes attracted to that location my attention, which was soon attracted by something other than the scar. Another of my neighbors, Mademoiselle de Challes[41] was a completely developed girl; tall, fine breadth of shoulder, filled out; she had been very pretty. She was no longer a beauty; but she was a person to cite for good grace, for an even temper, for a good nature. Her sister, Madame de Charly, the most beautiful woman in Chambéry, did not learn music, but she had it taught to her daughter who was still very young, but whose nascent beauty promised to equal her mother's if unfortunately she had not been a little redheaded.[42] At the Visitation I had a little young French Lady whose name I have forgotten, but who deserves a place in the list of my preferences. She had acquired the slow and drawling tone of the Nuns, and in this drawling tone she said very risqué things, which did not seem to go with her bearing. For the rest she was lazy, did not like to take the trouble to show her wit, and it was a favor that she did not accord to everyone. It was only after a month or two of lessons and of negligence that she took this expedient into her head to make me more assiduous; for I have never been able to force myself to be so. I enjoyed my lessons when I was there, but I did not like to be obliged to show up at them or to be commanded by the clock. In everything bother and subjugation are unbearable to me; they would make me acquire a hatred for pleasure itself. It is said that among the Moslems a man passes in the streets at daybreak to order husbands to do their duty to their wives. I would be a bad Turk at those hours.

I also had several students among the Bourgeoisie, and one of them was the indirect cause of a change of relationship about which I must speak, since after all I must tell everything. She was a Grocer's daughter, and was named Mademoiselle Lard, a true model of a Greek statue and I would cite her as the most beautiful girl I have ever seen, if there were any genuine beauty without life and without soul.[43] Her indolence, her coldness, her insensitivity reached an unbelievable degree. It was equally impossible to please or to anger her, and I am persuaded that if someone had made an attempt on her she would have allowed it, not out of liking, but out of stupidity. Her mother, who did not wish to run the risk, did not move a step away from her. By making her learn to sing, by giving her a young teacher, she did her best to excite her, but that did not succeed at all. While the teacher was provoking the daughter, the mother was provoking the teacher, and that did not succeed much better. Madame Lard added to her natural vivacity everything her daughter should have had. She had a little sprightly wrinkled face marked by smallpox. Her eyes were very ardent and slightly red, because they were almost always sore. Every morning when I arrived I found[44] my coffee and cream ready, and the mother never failed to welcome me with a kiss applied directly to the mouth, which I would have liked to give to the daughter out of curiosity, to see how she would have taken it. Moreover all this was done so simply and with so little importance that when M. Lard was there the flirting and[45] the kisses did not go any less on their course. He was a good soul of a man, the true father of his daughter, and his wife did not deceive him, because there was no need for it.

I lent myself to all these blandishments with my usual doltishness, naively taking them for marks of pure friendship. I was, however, bothered by them sometimes; for the lively Mme Lard did not stop being demanding, and if during the day I had passed the shop without stopping by there would have been a fuss. When I was in a rush I had to take a detour to go by another street, knowing very well that it was not as easy to leave her place as it was to enter it.

Mme Lard gave me too much attention for me not to give her any. Her attentions touched me very much; I talked about them to mamma as a thing without mystery, and if there had been any I would not have talked about them any less; for I would have been incapable of keeping a secret from her about anything whatsoever: my heart was open before her as before God. She did not take it at all with the same simplicity as I did. She saw advances where I had seen only friendly gestures; she judged that Mme Lard would succeed in making herself understood one way or another because she would make it a point of honor to leave me less of a fool than she had found me, and aside from the fact that it would not be right for another woman to burden herself with the instruction of her student, she had motives more worthy of her, to protect me from the traps to which my age and my status were exposing me. At the same time one of a more dangerous sort was set for me that I escaped, but which made her feel that the dangers that ceaselessly threatened me rendered necessary all the precautions she could bring to bear.

Madame the Comtesse de Menthon, the mother of one of my students, was a woman of much wit and passed for having no less malice. She had been the cause, from what was said, of many imbroglios, one of which had had fatal consequences for the House of Antremont.[46] Mamma had been connected with her enough to be acquainted with her character; having very innocently inspired a liking in someone on whom Mme de Menthon had pretensions, she was charged by her with the crime of this preference, even though she had neither sought nor accepted it, and from that time Mme de Menthon sought to play several tricks on her rival, none of which succeeded. I will report one of the most comic as a sort of sample. They were together in the country with several Gentlemen of the neighborhood, and among others the aspirant in question. One day Mme de Menthon said to one of these gentlemen that Mme de Warens was nothing but a woman of affectation, that she had no taste at all, that she dressed badly, that she covered her breast like a bourgeoise. As for this last point, the man—who was a joker—said to her, "She has her reasons, and I know that she has a nasty-looking fat rat marked on her bosom, but so lifelike that you would say it is running." Like love, hate makes one credulous. Mme de Menthon resolved to take advantage of this discovery, and one day when mamma was playing cards with the ingrate favored by the Lady, the latter seized the occasion to pass behind her rival, then half turning over her chair she skillfully uncovered her neckerchief. But instead of the large rat, the Gentleman saw only an extremely different object which was not easier to forget than to see, and this was not to the Lady's advantage.

I was not a personage to occupy Mme de Menthon, who wanted only brilliant people around her. Nevertheless, she paid some attention to me, not for the sake of my looks (about which she surely did not care at all), but for the wit I was assumed to have, and which might have made me useful for her tastes. She had a rather lively one for satire. She loved to write songs and verses about people who displeased her. If she had found me talented enough to help her write her verses and accommodating enough to write them, between us we would soon have turned Chambéry upside down. These libels would have been traced back to the source: Mme de Menthon would have extricated herself from the business by sacrificing me, and I would possibly have been locked up for the rest of my days for teaching myself to play Phoebus[47] with the Ladies.

Fortunately none of that happened. Mme de Menthon kept me to dine two or three times to make me chat, and found that I was only a fool. I felt it myself and I bemoaned it, envying my friend Venture's talents, whereas I should have thanked my stupidity for saving me from peril. For Mme de Menthon I remained her daughter's singing master and nothing more: but I lived tranquilly and always well regarded in Chambéry. That was worth more than being a fine wit for her, and a serpent for the rest of the country.

However that might be, Mamma saw that to rescue me from the perils of my youth it was time to treat me as a man, and that is what she did, but in the most peculiar manner any woman ever took into her head on a similar occasion. I found her manner more grave and her conversation more moral than usual. To the frolicsome gaiety that she usually intermingled with her teaching, all at once there succeeded an always sustained tone that was neither familiar nor severe, but which seemed to be paving the way for an explanation. After I had looked into myself in vain for the reason for this change I asked her for it; that was what she was waiting for. She proposed a walk to the little garden for the next day: we were there from the morning on. She had taken her measures so that we would be left alone the whole day; she used it to prepare me for the kindnesses she wished to give me, not by stratagem and flirtations like another woman; but by conversations full of feeling[48] and reason, made more to instruct me than to seduce me, and which spoke more to my heart than to my senses. Nevertheless, however excellent and useful the speeches she made me were, and although they were anything but cold and sad, I did not pay them all the attention they deserved, and I did not engrave them in my memory as I would have done at any other time. Her beginning, this air of preparation, had made me uneasy: dreaming and distracted in spite of myself while she was speaking, I was less occupied with what she was saying than with looking for what she was driving at, and as soon as I understood it (which was not easy for me) the novelty of this idea—which had not come into my mind a single time since I had been living with her—occupied me completely, no longer leaving me master of thinking about what she was saying to me. I thought only about her, and I did not listen to her.

Wishing to make young people attentive to what one wants to say to them by showing them an object that is very interesting for them at the end, is a very common misconception among teachers, and one that I did not avoid myself in my *Emile*. Struck by the object presented to him, the young man is occupied solely with it, and takes a standing jump over your preliminary speech to go directly to where you are leading him too slowly for his taste. When you want to make him attentive you must not let yourself be seen through in advance, and this is where Mamma was unskillful. By a peculiarity that was based on her systematic spirit she took the very vain precaution of making her conditions; but as soon as I saw the prize I did not even hear them, and I hurried to agree to everything. I even doubt that in a similar case there is on the entire earth a man frank enough or courageous enough to dare to haggle, and a single woman who could pardon him for having done so. As a consequence of the same peculiarity she put the gravest formalities into this agreement, and gave me eight days to think about it which I falsely assured her that I did not need: for to crown the singularity I was very glad to have them, so much had the novelty of these ideas struck me, and I was feeling such an upheaval in my own ideas, which demanded time for me to arrange them!

It will be believed that these eight days lasted eight Centuries for me. Completely on the contrary; in fact I would have wanted them to last that long. I do not know how to describe the condition in which I found myself, full of a certain fright mixed with impatience, dreading what I desired, to the point of sometimes seriously looking in my head for some decent means of avoiding being happy. Let anyone represent to himself my ardent and lascivious temperament, my inflamed blood, my heart drunk with love, my vigor, my health, my age; let him think that in this condition, perturbed by the thirst for[49] women, I had not yet approached any, that imagination, need, vanity, curiosity joined together to devour me with the ardent desire to be a man and to appear to be one. Above all let him add—for this must not be forgotten—that, far from cooling, my lively and tender attachment for her had only increased from day to day, that I was well off only near her, that I went away from her only to think about her, that my heart was full, not only with her kindnesses, her lovable character, but also with her sex, with her appearance, with her person, in a word with her, from all the relations by which she could be dear to me; and let him not imagine that she was old or appeared to me to be so because I was ten or twelve years younger than she. In the five or six years since I had experienced such sweet transports at the first sight of her, she had really changed very little, and to me did not appear to have changed at all. She had always been charming for me, and was still so for everyone. Only her waist had acquired a little more roundness. For the rest it was the same eye, the same complexion, the same bosom, the same features, the same beautiful blond hair, the same gaiety, all the way to the same voice, that silvery voice of youth which always made such an impression on me, so that even today I cannot hear the sound of a girl's pretty voice without emotion.

Naturally what I had to fear in the expectation of the possession of such a dear person was to anticipate it, and not to be able to govern my desires and imagination enough to remain master of myself. It will be seen that in an advanced age merely the idea of some slight favors that were waiting for me near the beloved person set my blood on fire to such a point that I could not make the short journey that separated me from her with impunity.[50] How, by what prodigy could I have so little eagerness for the first enjoyment in the flower of my youth? How could I see its time approach with more pain than pleasure? How instead of delights that should have intoxicated me did I feel almost repugnance and fears? It is not to be doubted that if I had been able to slip away from my happiness with decorum, I would have done so with all my heart. I have promised peculiarities in the story of my attachment for her; surely here is one that was not expected.

Already shocked, the reader judges that, since she was possessed by another man, she was degrading herself in my eyes by sharing herself, and that a feeling of disesteem cooled those she had inspired in me: he is wrong. This sharing, it is true, caused me a cruel pain, as much from an extremely natural delicacy, as because in fact I found it hardly worthy of her and of me; but as for my feelings for her, it did not change them at all, and I can swear that never did I love her more tenderly than when I desired to possess her so little. I knew her chaste heart and her temperament of ice too well to believe for a moment that the pleasure of the senses had any part in this abandonment of herself: I was perfectly sure that only the concern to extract me from otherwise almost inevitable dangers, and to preserve me entirely for myself and my duties made her transgress one that she did not look at with the same eye as other women, as will be said below. I felt sorry for her, and I felt sorry for myself. I would have liked to say to her, "No mamma, it is not necessary; I answer to you for myself without that," but I did not dare; first because that was not a thing to say, and then because at the bottom I felt that it was not true, and that in fact there was only one woman who could protect me from other women and make me proof against temptations. Without desiring to possess her,

I was very glad that she removed from me the desire to possess others; so much did I regard everything that could distract me from her as a misfortune.

Far from weakening my feelings for her, the long habit of living together and of doing so innocently had reinforced them, but at the same time it had given them a different direction that rendered them more affectionate, more tender perhaps, but less sensual. As a result of calling her mamma, as a result of making use of the familiarity of a son with her I was accustomed to regarding myself as such. I believe that this is the genuine cause of the little eagerness I had to possess her even though she was so dear to me. I remember very well that my first feelings were more voluptuous without being any more lively. At Annecy I was intoxicated, at Chambéry I no longer was. I always loved her as passionately as possible, but I loved her more for herself and less for me, or at least I looked more for my happiness than my pleasure with her: for me she was more than a sister, more than a mother, more than a friend, even more than a mistress, and it was for that reason that she was not a mistress.[51] In sum, I loved her too much to covet her: that is what is clearest in my ideas.

Dreaded rather than being looked forward to, the day came at last. I have promised everything and I did not lie. My heart confirmed my pledges without desiring their reward. I obtained it nevertheless. For the first time I saw myself in a woman's arms, and in those of a woman I adored. Was I happy? No, I tasted pleasure. I do not know what invincible sadness poisoned its charm. I was as if I had committed an act of incest. Two or three times while squeezing her in my arms I soaked her bosom with my tears. As for her, she was neither sad nor lively; she was affectionate and tranquil. Since she was hardly sensual and had not at all sought sensual pleasure, she did not have its delights, and never had remorse about it.

I repeat it: all her faults came to her from her errors, never from her passions. She was wellborn, her heart was pure, she loved decent things, her inclinations were upright and virtuous, her taste was delicate, she was made for an elegance of morals that she always loved and never followed; because instead of listening to her heart which led her well, she listened to her reason which led her badly. If her false principles led her astray, her true feelings always contradicted them: but unfortunately she prided herself on philosophy, and the morality she constructed for herself spoiled the one her heart dictated to her.

M. de Tavel, her first lover, was her philosophy teacher, and the principles he gave her were the ones he needed to seduce her. Finding her attached to her husband, to her duties, always cold, reasoning, and unassailable by means of the senses, he attacked her by means of sophisms, and succeeded in showing her the duties to which she was so attached as a prattle of catechism, made solely to amuse children, the union of the sexes as an act the most indifferent in itself, conjugal fidelity as an obligatory appearance whose entire morality concerned opinion, the peace of mind of husbands as the only rule of women's duty, so that unknown infidelities—nonexistent for the one they offend—were also nonexistent for the conscience; in sum, he persuaded her that the thing in itself was nothing, that it acquired existence only from the scandal, and that every woman who appeared chaste was so in fact from that alone. This way the wretch succeeded in his goal by corrupting the reason of a child whose heart he had been unable to corrupt. He was punished for it by the most consuming jealousy, persuaded that she was treating him as he had taught her to treat her husband. I do not know whether he was mistaken on this point. Minister Perret was looked on as his successor.[52] What I do know, is that the cold temperament of that young woman, which might have protected her from this system, was what kept her from renouncing it later on. She could not conceive that so much importance was given to something that had none for her. She never honored an abstinence that cost her so little with the name of virtue.

Thus she hardly abused this false principle for her own sake; but she did abuse it for others, and did so out of another maxim almost as false, but more in accord with the goodness of her heart. She always believed that nothing attached a man to a woman as much as possession, and although she loved her friends only with friendship, it was with such a tender friendship that she used all the means that depended on her to attach them more strongly. What is extraordinary is that she almost always succeeded. She was really so lovable that, the greater the intimacy in which one lived with her, the more one found new reasons for loving her. Another thing worth noticing is that after her first weakness she hardly favored anyone but unfortunates; brilliant people all wasted their effort with her: but a man whom she began by feeling sorry for had to be very unlovable for her not to end by loving him. If she made choices unworthy of her, far from that being from base inclinations which never approached her noble heart, it was solely from her too generous, too humane, too compassionate, too sensitive character, which she did not always govern with enough discernment.

If some false principles led her astray, how many admirable ones did she have from which she never swerved? With how many virtues did she not make up for her weaknesses, if one can call by this name errors in which the senses had so little share. This same man who deceived her on one point taught her excellently on a thousand others; and since her passions, which were not fiery, always allowed her to follow her enlightenment, she proceeded well when her sophisms did not lead her astray. Her motives were praiseworthy even in her faults; she could do evil while deceiving herself, but she could not want anything that was evil. She abhorred duplicity, lying; she was just, equitable, humane, disinterested, faithful to her word, to her friends, to her duties that she recognized as such, incapable of vengeance and of hatred, and it did not even occur to her that there could be the slightest merit in pardoning. In sum, to return to what was least excusable in her, although she did not esteem her favors for what they were worth, she never made a low transaction of them; she lavished them but she did not sell them; even though she was ceaselessly reduced to expedients in order to live, and I dare say that if Socrates could esteem Aspasia, he would have respected Mme de Warens.[53]

I know in advance that by attributing to her a sensitive character and a cold temperament I will be accused of contradiction as usual and with as much reason. It might be that nature was wrong, and that this combination should not have been; I know only that it was. Everyone who knew Mme de Warens (and such a large number of them still exist) was able to know that she was this way. I even dare to add that she knew only one true pleasure in the world; that was to give it to those she loved. Still, anyone is permitted to argue against this completely at his convenience and to prove in a learned way that it is not true. My function is to tell the truth, but not to make it believed.

I learned everything I have just said little by little in the conversations that followed our union, and which alone made it delightful. She had been right to hope that her kindness would be useful to me; I drew great advantages from it for my instruction. Until then she had spoken to me about myself only as if to a child. She began treating me as a man and spoke to me about herself. Everything she told me was so interesting, I felt myself so touched by it that, withdrawing into myself, I applied her confidences more to my advantage than I had applied her lessons. When we truly feel that the heart speaks, ours opens itself to receive its effusions, and all the moral philosophy of a pedagogue will never be worth the affectionate and tender chatter of a sensible woman to whom one is attached.

Because the intimacy in which I lived with her had allowed her to appreciate me more advantageously than she had, she judged that it was worth the effort to cultivate me for the social world in spite of my awkward manner, and that if one day I could show myself on a certain footing there, I would be in a position to make my way in it. Based on this idea she applied herself, not only to forming my judgment, but my exterior, my manners, to making me amiable as well as estimable, and if it is true that one can blend success in the world with virtue—which as for me I do not believe—at least I am sure that there is no other route for this than the one she had taken and which she wished to teach me. For Mme de Warens knew men and knew to a superior degree the art of dealing with them without lying and without imprudence, without tricking them, and without getting them angry. But this art was in her character very much more than in her lessons, she knew how to put it into practice better than how to teach it, and I was the man in the world least suited to learning it. Also everything she did in this regard was, very nearly, wasted effort, the same as the care she took to give me teachers for dancing and for arms. Although nimble and well made, I could not learn to dance a minuet. Because of my corns I had so much acquired the habit of walking on my heels that Roche could not break me of it, and even with a spry enough manner I was never able to leap a medium-sized ditch. It was even worse in the fencing room. After three months of lessons I was still practicing parrying, in no condition to make an attack, and I never had a supple enough wrist or a firm enough arm to hold onto my foil when it pleased my teacher to knock it away. Add that I had a mortal disgust for this exercise and for the teacher who tried to teach it to me. I would never have believed that one could be so proud of the art of killing a man. To put his vast genius within my grasp he explained himself only by means of comparisons drawn from music, which he did not know at all. He found striking analogies between thrusts of tierce and carte and the musical intervals of the same name. When he wanted to make a feint he told me to watch out for this sharp, because formerly sharps were called *feints*: when he had knocked my foil out of my hand, he said while sneering that it was *a pause*. In sum, I have never in my life seen a more unbearable pedant than this poor man, with his plume and his breast-plate.

Thus I made little progress in my exercises which I soon quit out of pure disgust; but I made more in a more useful art, that of being content with my lot and of not desiring a more brilliant one, for which I began to feel that I was not born. Abandoned entirely to the desire to make Mamma's life happy, I was always more pleased near her, and when I had to go away from her to roam around the City, I began to feel the bother of my lessons in spite of my passion for music.

I do not know whether Claude Anet noticed the intimacy of our relations. I have reason to believe that it was not hidden from him. He was a very clear-sighted but very discreet chap who never spoke contrary to his thought, but who did not always say it. Without showing me in the least that he was informed, his behavior made him appear to be, and this behavior assuredly did not come from baseness of soul, but from the fact that, since he had entered into his mistress's principles, he could not disapprove of her acting consistently with them. Although he was as young as she was, he was so mature and so serious that he looked at us almost as two children worthy of indulgence, and we both looked at him as a respectable man whose esteem we had to take into consideration. It was not until after she was unfaithful to him that I became well-acquainted with all the attachment she had for him. Since she knew that I thought, felt, and breathed only through her, she showed me how much she loved him so that I might love him as much, and spoke favorably even less of her friendship for him than of her esteem, because that was the feeling that I could share most fully. How many times did she touch our hearts and make us embrace with tears, by telling us that we were both necessary for the happiness of her life; and let the women who read this not smile maliciously. With her temperament this need was not ambiguous: it was solely that of her heart.

In this way there was established among us three a society without another example perhaps on the earth.[54] All our wishes, our cares, our hearts were in common. Nothing of them passed outside this little circle. The habit of living together and of living exclusively this way became so great that if one of the three was missing at our meal or a fourth came everything was disordered, and, in spite of our private relations, tête-à-têtes were less sweet to us than reunion. What prevented trouble among us was an extreme reciprocal confidence, and what prevented boredom was that we were all extremely busy. Always forming projects and always active, Mamma hardly left either of us idle, and each of us still had enough to fill up our time well on our own account. In my view, lack of occupation is no less the scourge of society than of solitude. Nothing narrows the mind more, nothing engenders more trifles, malicious tales, sly tricks, teasing, lies, than being eternally shut up face to face with one another in a room, reduced to the necessity of continually babbling as one's only occupation. When everyone is occupied, one speaks only when one has something to say,[55] but when one is doing nothing it is absolutely necessary to speak all the time, and that is the most inconvenient and dangerous of all bothers. I dare to go even further, and I maintain that to make a social circle truly agreeable it is necessary that each not only does something, but something that demands a little attention. To knit is to do nothing, and just as much effort is needed to amuse a woman who is knitting as one who keeps her arms crossed. But if she is embroidering, it is a different matter; she is sufficiently occupied to fill the intervals of silence.

What is shocking, ridiculous, is in the meantime to see a dozen clods get up, sit down, go, come, pirouette on their heels, turn the porcelain figures on the mantel around two hundred times, and rack their brains to keep up an inexhaustible flow of words: a fine occupation! Such people, whatever they may do, will always be a burden to others and to themselves. When I was at Môtiers I went to make laces at my neighbors' houses; if I returned into the world, I would always have a cup-and-ball in my pocket, and I would play with it all day long to be dispensed from speaking when I had nothing to say. If everyone did as much men would become less wicked, their dealings would become more reliable and, I think, more agreeable. In sum, let the jokers laugh if they wish, but I maintain that the only morality within the reach of the present age is the morality of the cup-and-ball.

Moreover we were hardly left the trouble of avoiding boredom by ourselves; importunate people gave us too much of it with their influx to leave us any when we remained alone. The impatience they formerly caused me had not diminished, and the only difference was that I had less time to abandon myself to it. Poor Mamma had not at all lost her former whim for undertakings and systems. On the contrary, the more pressing her domestic needs became, the more she abandoned herself to her visions in order to provide for them. The fewer resources she had present, the more she fabricated for herself in the future. The progress of the years did nothing but increase that mania in her, and to the extent that she lost the taste for the pleasures of the world and of youth, she replaced it by that for secrets and projects. The house was always full of charlatans, manufacturers, alchemists, entrepreneurs of every sort, who, dispensing riches by the millions, ended by needing an écu.[56] None left her house empty-handed, and one of the things I am astonished by is that she was able to support so many extravagances for so long without exhausting the source, and without wearing out her creditors.

The project with which she was most occupied at the time about which I am speaking and which was not the most unreasonable one she might have formed was to have a Royal Garden of plants established at Chambéry with an appointed demonstrator, and one understands in advance for whom that place was destined. That city's position in the middle of the Alps was favorable to Botany, and Mamma, who always facilitated[57] one project with another, joined to it that of a college of pharmacy, which genuinely appeared very useful in such a poor country, where Apothecaries are almost the only Doctors. The retirement of Premier Doctor Grossy to Chambéry after the death of King Victor appeared to assist this idea very much, and perhaps suggested it to her. However that might be, she began to cajole Grossy, who nevertheless was not excessively cajolable; for he was certainly the most caustic and the most brutal Gentleman I have ever known.[58] One will judge about this from two or three deeds that I am going to cite as a sample.

One day he was in consultation with some other doctors, one of whom had been brought from Annecy, who was the sick man's usual doctor. This young man, still poorly instructed for a Doctor, dared not to be of the same opinion as Monsieur the Premier. As his only response the latter asked him when he was going back, where he was passing through, and what vehicle he was taking? After having satisfied him the other asks him in his turn if there was something he could do for him. "Nothing, nothing," says Grossi, "I only want to go put myself at a window while you pass by, to have the pleasure of seeing an ass riding a horse." He was as miserly as he was rich and harsh. One day one of his friends wanted to borrow some money from him on good security. "My friend," he said to him while shaking his arm and gnashing his teeth; "if St. Peter came down from Heaven to borrow ten pistoles[59] from me and he would give the Trinity as guarantee, I would not lend them to him." One day having been invited to dine with M. the Comte Picon, governor of Savoy and very devout,[60] he arrives early, and His Excellency, being busy saying the rosary at that time, proposes this same amusement to him. Not knowing very well how to respond he makes a frightful grimace and puts himself on his knees. But hardly had he recited two *Aves*, being unable to hold back any longer, he gets up abruptly, takes his cane, and leaves without saying a word. Comte Picon runs after him, and shouts to him, "M. Grossy, M. Grossy, stay then; there is an excellent Partridge on the spit for you." "M. the Comte!" responds the other turning around; "you could give me a roasted Angel and I would not stay." That is M. the Premier Doctor Grossy, whom Mamma tackled and whom she succeeded in taming. Even though he was extremely busy, he became accustomed to come to her house very often, acquired a friendship for Anet, showed that he made much of his knowledge, spoke of him with esteem, and, what one would not have expected from such a Bear, applied himself to treating him with consideration in order to efface the impressions of the past. For although Anet was no longer on the footing of a servant, it was known that he had been one, and nothing less than the example and authority of M. the Premier Doctor was needed to set the tone with regard to him that would not have been taken on from anyone else. With a black suit, a well-combed wig, a serious and decent bearing, a wise and circumspect behavior, extensive enough knowledge in medical matters and in botany, and the favor of head of the faculty, Claude Anet could have reasonably hoped to fill the place of royal Demonstrator of plants with applause if the projected establishment had taken place, and really Grossy had approved of the plan, had adopted it, and to propose it to the Court he was only waiting for the moment when peace would permit thinking about useful things, and would allow disposing of some money to provide for it.

But this project, the execution of which would probably have thrown me into botany for which it seems I was born, failed because of one of those unexpected blows that overthrow the best laid plans. I was destined to become by degrees an example of human miseries. One would say that providence, which called me to these great trials, brushed aside with its hand everything that might have prevented me from reaching them. In a walk that Anet had made high into the mountains to go look for some *Genipi*, a rare plant that grows only on the Alps, which M. Grossi had needed, this poor chap became so heated that he caught a pleurisy from which the Genipi could not save him, although it is, they say, a specific for it, and in spite of all the art of Grossi, who certainly was a very skillful man, in spite of the infinite cares his good mistress and I took of him, on the fifth day he died in our hands [61] after the cruelest agony, during which mine were the only exhortations he had, and I lavished them on him with bursts of sorrow and zeal which, if he was in a condition to understand me, ought to have been of some consolation for him. That is how I lost the most solid friend I had in my whole life, an estimable and rare man, in whom nature took the place of education, who nourished in servitude all the virtues of great men, who perhaps lacked only the chance to live and be placed to show himself that way to the whole world. [62]

The next day I was speaking about him with Mamma with the most lively and most sincere affliction, and suddenly in the middle of the conversation I had the low and unworthy thought that I might inherit some of his togs and above all a fine black suit whose looks I had a taste for. I thought it, consequently I said it; for with her they were the same things for me. Nothing made her feel the loss she had suffered more than this craven and odious statement, disinterestedness and nobility of soul being the qualities that the deceased had eminently possessed. Without answering anything the poor woman turned in the other direction and began to cry. Dear and precious tears! They were understood, and ran straight into my heart; they cleansed it of a base and indecent feeling down to the last traces; it has never entered it since that time.

This loss caused Mamma as much injury as sorrow. From that moment her affairs did not cease to go into decline. Anet was a precise and steady chap who maintained order in his mistress's house. His vigilance was feared, and less was wasted. She herself feared his censure and held herself back more in her dissipations. His attachment was not enough for her, she wanted to preserve his esteem, and she dreaded the just reproach he sometimes dared to make her when she squandered someone else's property as well as her own. I thought as he did, I even said so; but I did not have the same ascendancy over her and my speeches did not make an impression on her as his did. When he was no longer, I was forced to take his place, for which I had as little aptitude as taste. I filled it badly. I was not very careful, I was extremely timid, scolding to myself all the while, I let everything go along as it was. In other respects I had very much obtained the same confidence, but not the same authority. I saw the disorder, I bemoaned it, I complained about it, and I was not heeded. I was too young and too lively to have the right to be reasonable, and when I wanted to dabble in playing the censor, Mamma gave me endearing little slaps in the face, called me her little Mentor, and forced me to take back the role that suited me.

The deep feeling of the distress into which her poorly restrained expenses were bound to throw her sooner or later made an impression on me that was all the stronger since, now that I had become the overseer of her house, I judged the inequality of the balance between the *owed* and the *have* by myself. I date from that epoch the inclination to avarice that I have always felt since then. I have never been foolishly prodigal except by fits and starts, but until then I had never troubled myself much whether I had little or much money. I began to pay attention to this and to acquire some concern about my purse. I became miserly from a very noble motive; for in truth I thought only of saving some resource for Mamma in the catastrophe I foresaw. I feared that her creditors might seize her pension, that it might be completely withheld, and, in accordance with my narrow views, I imagined that my little hoard would be a great help to her then. But to build it and above all to conserve it, I had to hide it from her; for it would not be suitable for her to know that I had ready money while she was being driven to expedients. Thus I went here and there looking for little hiding places where I stuffed some louis [63] as a safe deposit, counting on continuously increasing this deposit up to the moment of laying it at her feet. But I was so clumsy in the choice of my hiding places that she always discovered them; then to show me that she had found them, she removed the gold [64] I had put there, and put in more of a different specie. Completely ashamed I came to bring my little treasure to the common purse and she never failed to use it for togs or furnishings for my advantage, such as a silver sword, watch, or other similar thing.

Well convinced that I would never be successful in accumulating and that this would be a slender resource for her, at last I felt that I had no other resort against the misfortune I feared[65] than to put myself in a condition to provide for her subsistence by myself, when, ceasing to provide for mine, she would find herself at the point of lacking bread. Unfortunately, casting my projects on the side of my tastes, I foolishly persisted in seeking my fortune in music, and, since I felt ideas and songs born in my head, I believed that as soon as I was in a condition to take advantage of them I was going to become a famous man, a modern Orpheus whose sounds should attract all the silver of Peru. Since I was beginning to read music passably, the question was how to learn composition. The difficulty was to find someone to teach it to me; for with my Rameau alone I did not hope to succeed in it by myself, and since M. Le Maitre's departure, there was no one in Savoy who understood anything about harmony.

Here again one is going to see one of those inconsistencies with which my life is full, and which have so often caused me to go against my goal, even though I thought I was tending directly to it. Venture had spoken to me very much about the Abbé Blanchard, his composition teacher, a man of merit and great talent, who at that time was music master at the Cathedral of Besançon, and who is now at the Chapel of Versailles.[66] I took it into my head to go to Besançon to take lessons from the Abbé Blanchard, and this idea appeared so reasonable to me that I succeeded in making Mamma find it the same. She began working on my little outfit, and did so with the profusion she put into everything. Thus, although I still had the project of preventing a bankruptcy and of restoring the work of her dissipation in the future, I began right away by causing an expense of eight hundred francs for her: I accelerated her ruin so as to put myself in a condition to remedy it. However foolish this behavior might have been, the illusion was complete on my part and even on hers. We were both persuaded, I that I was working usefully for her, she that I was working usefully for me.

I had counted on finding Venture still at Annecy and on asking him for a letter for the Abbé Blanchard. He was no longer there. As my only information, I had to be content with a Mass in four parts of his composition and in his hand which he had left for me. With this recommendation I go to Besançon, passing through Geneva where I saw my relatives, and Nyon where I saw my father, who received me in his normal way, and took charge of the arrival of my trunk which was only coming after me, because I was on horseback. I arrive at Besançon. The Abbé Blanchard receives me well, promises me his instruction, and offers me his services. We were ready to begin when I learn by a letter from my father that my trunk has been seized and confiscated at *les Rousses*, France's Custom Office on the Swiss border. Frightened by this news I use the acquaintances I had made at Besançon to learn the motive for this confiscation; for since I was certain that I did not have any contraband, I could not conceive on what pretext they could have based it. At last I learn: it must be told, for it is a curious fact.

At Chambéry I used to see an old man from Lyon, an extremely good man, called M. DuVivier, who had worked at the *Passport Office* under the Regency, and for lack of employment had come to work on the survey. He had lived in the world; he had some talents, some knowledge, gentleness, politeness, he knew music, and since I shared a Room with him, we made friends with each other by preference in the midst of the poorly licked Bears who surrounded us. He had correspondents at Paris who furnished him with those little trifles, those ephemeral novelties that circulate, no one knows why, which die no one knows how, without anyone ever thinking about them again when they have ceased to be talked about. Since I sometimes brought him to dine at mamma's house, he paid me his court to some extent, and to make himself agreeable he tried to make me like this twaddle, for which I always had such a distaste that never in my life have I happened to read any by myself. To gratify him I took these precious rags,[67] I put them in my pocket, and I did not think of them again except for the only use for which they were any good. Unfortunately one of these cursed papers remained in the coat pocket of a new suit I had worn two or three times so as to be in proper order with the customs Clerks. This paper was a rather insipid Jansenist parody of the beautiful scene in Racine's *Mithridates*.[68] I had not read ten lines of it and left it in my pocket out of forgetfulness. This is what caused my outfit to be confiscated. At the head of the inventory of that trunk the customs Clerks put a magnificent official statement, in which—supposing that this writing came from Geneva to be printed and distributed in France—they expatiated in holy invectives against the enemies of God and the Church, and in praises of their pious vigilance which had stopped the execution of this infernal project. They doubtless found that my shirts also smelled of heresy; for in virtue of this terrible paper everything was confiscated, without me ever being able to obtain either a reason for it or news about my poor shoddy belongings. The tax-farmer's people to whom I addressed myself demanded so many instructions, information, certificates of testimonials, that losing myself in this Labyrinth a thousand times, I was constrained to abandon everything. I truly regret not having preserved the official statement of the office at les Rousses. It was a piece fit to appear with distinction among the ones whose collection is to accompany this writing.

This loss made me return to Chambéry right away without having done anything with the Abbé Blanchard, everything taken into consideration, seeing misfortune follow me in all my undertakings, I resolved to attach myself solely to Mamma, to share her fortune, and no longer worry myself uselessly over a future about which I could do nothing. She received me as if I had brought back treasures, replenished my small wardrobe little by little, and my misfortune, big enough for both of us, was forgotten almost as soon as it happened.

Even though this misfortune might have cooled me off about my musical projects, I did not give up forever studying my Rameau, and as a result of efforts I finally succeeded in understanding it, and in making some little attempts at composition whose success encouraged me. The Marquis d'Antremont's son, the Comte de Bellegarde,[69] had returned from Dresden after the death of King Augustus. He had lived in Paris for a long time, he loved music extremely and had acquired a passion for Rameau's. His brother, the Comte de Nangis[70] played violin, their sister Mme the Comtesse de la Tour sang a little. All that put music in fashion at Chambéry, and they established a sort of public concert the direction of which they wanted to give to me at first; but they soon perceived that it was beyond my strength, and they arranged it otherwise. I did not stop presenting some little pieces of my composition there, and among others a Cantata that pleased very much. It was not a well-written piece, but it was full of new songs and effects, which they were not expecting from me. Since I read music so poorly, these Gentlemen could not believe that I could be in a condition to compose any that was passable, and they did not doubt that I had had myself given the honor for someone else's work. To verify this M. de Nangis came to find me one morning with one of Clerambault's cantatas which he said he had transposed for the voice's convenience, and for which it was necessary to write a different bass, since the transposition rendered Clérambault's impracticable on the instrument.[71] I answered that that was a considerable work which could not be done on the spot. He believed that I was looking for a way out and urged me to write him at least the bass for one recitative. I did it then, badly without a doubt, because to do well in anything I need my comfort and freedom; but at least I did it according to the rules, and since he was present, he could not doubt that I knew the elements of composition. In this way I did not lose my students, but I cooled off a little about music, seeing that they put on a concert and that they could do it without me.

It was just about at that time that, peace having been concluded, the French army crossed the mountains again.[72] Several Officers came to see Mamma; among others M. the Comte de Lautrec, Colonel of the Orléans

Regiment, since then plenipotentiary at Geneva, and finally Maréchal of France, to whom she introduced me. Based on what she told him, he appeared to be very interested in me, and promised me many things, which he did not remember until the last year of his life, when I no longer needed him. The young Marquis de Sennecterre, whose father was then Ambassador to Turin, passed through Chambéry at the same time.[73] He dined at Mme de Menthon's; I also dined there that day. After the dinner it was a question of music; he knew it very well. The Opera *Jephtha* was new at that time;[74] he spoke about it, they had it brought in. He made me tremble by proposing to me that the two of us perform this Opera, and while opening the book he chanced upon this famous piece for two choruses:

> La terre, l'enfer, le Ciel même,
> Tout tremble devant le Seigneur.[75]

He said to me, "How many parts do you want? I will do these six for my share." I was not yet accustomed to this French impetuousness, and although I might sometimes stumble through some scores, I did not understand how the same man could do six parts at the same time or even two. Nothing has cost me more in the practice of music than to leap so lightly from one part to the other, and to have my eye on a whole score at the same time. From the manner in which I extricated myself from this undertaking M. de Sennecterre must have been tempted to believe that I did not know music. It was perhaps to verify this suspicion that he proposed that I note down a song he wanted to give to Mlle de Menthon. I could not protest against it. He sang the song; I wrote it, even without making him repeat very much. He read it next, and found, as was true, that it had been very correctly noted down. He had seen my embarrassment, he took pleasure in making the most of this little success. However, it was a very simple thing. At bottom I knew music extremely well, I lacked only that liveliness at the first glance that I have never had with anything, and which is acquired in music only by a consummate practice. However that might be, I was grateful for the decent effort he took to blot out the little shame I had had both in the mind of the others and in my own; and when I met him in several houses in Paris twelve or fifteen years afterwards, several times I was tempted to recall this anecdote for him, and to show him that I still remembered it. But he had lost his sight since that time. I feared to renew his regret by recalling to him the use he had been able to make of it, and I was silent.

I am touching the moment that begins to link my past existence with the present. Some friendships from that time prolonged up to this time have become very precious to me. They have often made me regret that happy obscurity when those who called themselves my friends were so and liked me for myself, out of pure benevolence, not out of vanity at having connections with a well-known man, or out of the secret desire to find more occasions to harm him in this way. It is from here that I date my first acquaintance with my old friend Gauffecourt who has always remained with me, in spite of the efforts that have been made to take him away from me. Always remained! No. Alas! I have just lost him.[76] But he did not stop loving me except when he stopped living, and our friendship ended only with him. M. de Gauffecourt was one of the most amiable men who have ever existed. It was impossible to see him without liking him, and to live with him without attaching oneself completely to him. Never in my life have I seen a more open, more affectionate physiognomy, which had more serenity, which showed more feeling and intelligence, which inspired more confidence. However reserved one might be, one could not protect oneself from being as familiar with him after the first sight as if one had known him for twenty years, and I was so with him from the first moment, I who had so much trouble being at my ease with new faces. His tone, his accent, his talk went perfectly together with his physiognomy. The sound of his voice was clear, full, very sonorous; a fine ample trilling bass voice which filled the ear and resounded in the heart. It is impossible to have a more even and sweeter gaiety, truer and simpler graces, more natural and more tastefully cultivated talents. Add to that a loving heart, but loving everyone a little too much, an over-obliging character with little selectivity, serving his friends with zeal, or rather making himself the friend of people he could serve, and knowing how to conduct his own business very skillfully while very warmly conducting someone else's. Gauffecourt was the son of a simple watchmaker and had been a watchmaker himself. But his appearance and his merit called him into another sphere which he entered without delay. He made the acquaintance of M. de la Closure, the French Resident at Geneva,[77] who acquired a friendship for him. He procured other acquaintances for him at Paris who were useful to him, by which he succeeded in obtaining the furnishing of salt for Valais, which was worth twenty thousand livres of revenue to him. His fortune, fine enough, was limited to that on the side of men, but on the side of women there was a throng; he could have his choice, and did what he wanted to.[78] What was more rare, and more honorable for him was that having connections in all stations, he was cherished everywhere, sought after by everyone without ever being envied or hated by anyone, and I believe that he died without having had a single enemy in his life. Lucky man! Every year he went to the baths at Aix where the good company of the neighboring countries assembled. Connected with all the nobility of Savoy, he went from Aix to Chambéry to see the Comte de Bellegarde and his father the Marquis d'Antremont, at whose house mamma made and had me make his acquaintance. This acquaintance, which it seemed should have led to nothing and was interrupted for a number of years, was renewed upon the occasion that I will speak of and became a genuine attachment.[79] This is enough to authorize me to speak about a friend with whom I have had such close relations: but even if I did not take any personal interest in his memory, he was such a lovable man and so fortunately born that for the honor of the human race I would always believe it good to preserve it. That man who was so charming nevertheless had his flaws, just as others do, as will be seen below;[80] but if he did not have them perhaps he might have been less lovable. To render him as interesting as possible, it was necessary that one have something for which to pardon him.

Another connection from the same time has not been extinguished, and still lures me with that hope for temporal happiness that dies with such difficulty in man's heart. M. de Conzié, a Savoyard gentleman, at that time young and amiable, had the whim of learning music, or rather of making the acquaintance of the person who taught it.[81] Along with wit and taste for fine knowledge, M. de Conzié had a sweetness of character that rendered him very winning, and I was very much the same myself for the people in whom I found it. The connection was soon made.[82] The seed of literature and philosophy, that began to ferment in my head and which awaited only a little cultivation and emulation to be completely developed, found them in him. M. de Conzié had little inclination for music; that was a good thing for me: the hours of the lessons passed in anything but in sol-faing. We lunched, we chatted, we read some of the latest books, and not a word about music. Voltaire's correspondence with the Crown Prince[83] of Prussia was causing a stir at that time; we often conversed about these two famous men: the latter of whom in the short time he had been on the throne already gave promise of what he would show himself to be in a little while and the former of whom, as disparaged as he is now admired, made us sincerely sorry about the misfortune that seemed to pursue him, which is so often seen to be the portion of great talents.[84] The Prince of Prussia had not been very happy in his youth, and Voltaire seemed destined never to be so. The interest we took in both of them extended to everything that related to them. Nothing that Voltaire wrote escaped us. The taste I acquired for these readings inspired me with the desire to learn to write elegantly, and to try to imitate the beautiful coloring of this author with whom I was enchanted. Some time afterward his *Philosophic Letters* appeared; although they were assuredly not his best work, it was this one that attracted me most toward study, and this nascent taste has not died out since that time.

But the moment had not come to abandon myself to it entirely. I still had a slightly fickle mood,[85] a desire to come and go that had been constrained rather than extinguished, and which was nourished by the way of life in Mme de Warens's house, too noisy for my solitary mood. This crowd of unknown people who daily flocked to her from all directions and the persuasion I had that each of these people sought only to dupe her in his own manner, made a true torment for me in the place I lived. Since I had succeeded Claude Anet in his mistress's confidence, I followed the state of her business more closely; in it I saw a progress toward the bad that frightened me. A hundred times I had remonstrated, begged, pressed, entreated, and always uselessly. I had thrown myself at her feet, I had strongly represented to her the catastrophe that menaced her, I had sharply exhorted her to retrench her expenses beginning with me, to suffer a little while she was still young rather than, by always multiplying her debts and her creditors, to expose herself in her old age to their vexations and to misery. Sensitive to the sincerity of my zeal she became tender with me, and promised me the finest things in the world. Did some wretch arrive? Instantly everything was forgotten. After a thousand proofs of the uselessness of my remonstrances, what was left for me to do but to turn my eyes away from the evil I could not prevent? I went away from the house whose door I could not guard; I made little trips to Nyon, to Geneva, to Lyon, which numbed me to my secret pain, while at the same time increasing the subject through my expense. I can swear that I would have suffered all retrenchments of them with joy, if Mamma had truly profited from these savings; but certain that whatever I refused myself passed over to some rogues, I abused her desire to be obliging in order to share with them, and like the dog who came back from the slaughterhouse, I carried off my bit of the piece that I had been unable to save.

I did not lack pretexts for all these trips, and Mamma alone would have furnished me with a surplus of them, she had so many connections, negotiations, business, commissions everywhere to give to someone reliable. These trips put me in a position to make several good acquaintances who were agreeable or useful to me later on: among others at Lyon that of M. Perrichon, whom I reproach myself for not having cultivated enough, in light of the kindness he had for me; that of the good Parisot[86] about whom I will speak in his time: at Grenoble those of Madame Deybens and Madame de Bardonanche, the President's wife, a woman of much intelligence, who might have acquired a friendship for me if I had been in a position to see her more often:[87] at Geneva that of M. de la Closure, the French Resident, who often spoke to me about my mother from whom his heart had not been able to free itself in spite of death and time; that of the two Barrillots, of whom the father, who called me his grandson, was very amiable company and one of the worthiest men I have ever known.[88] During the troubles of the Republic these two Citizens threw themselves into two opposite parties; the son into that of the bourgeoisie, the father in that of the Magistrates, and since I was at Geneva when arms were taken up in 1737, I saw the father and the son leave the same house armed, the one to go up to the City Hall, the other to proceed to his district, certain of finding themselves face to face with each other two hours later, in danger of slaughtering each other. This horrible spectacle made such a keen impression on me that I swore never to be a party to any civil war, and never to uphold domestic freedom with arms, or my person, or my assent if I ever returned to my rights as a citizen. I bear witness to myself of having kept this oath on a delicate occasion,[89] and it will be found—at least I think so—that this moderation had some value.

But I was not yet at that first fermentation of patriotism that Geneva in arms excited in my heart. How far from it I was will be judged from a very serious deed chargeable to me that I forgot to put in its place and which ought not to be omitted.

Several years earlier my uncle Bernard had gone to Carolina to build the city of Charlestown, the plan of which he had given.[90] He died there a little later; my poor cousin had also died in the King of Prussia's service, and thus my aunt lost her son and her husband almost at the same time. These losses rekindled a little her friendship for the closest relative she had left, who was myself. When I went to Geneva I lodged with her, and I diverted myself by nosing about and[91] leafing through the books and papers my uncle had left. There I found many curious pieces and letters which assuredly one would not suspect. My aunt, who attached little importance to these old papers, would have let me carry them all away if I had wanted to. I was satisfied with two or three books commented on by the hand of my grandfather Bernard the Minister, and among others the *Posthumous Works* of Rohault in quarto, the margins of which were full of excellent glosses that made me love mathematics.[92] This book remained among those of Mme de Warens; I have always been angry that I did not keep it. To these books I joined five or six manuscript memoranda, and a single printed one, which was by the famous Micheli Ducret, a man of great talent, learned, enlightened, but too much of an agitator, who was treated very cruelly by the magistrates of Geneva, and who recently died in the fortress[93] of Arberg where he was imprisoned for long years, for having, it is said, had a hand in the conspiracy at Berne.[94]

This memorandum was a rather judicious critique of that great and ridiculous plan for fortifications that has been partially executed at Geneva, to the great derision of people of the profession who do not know the secret goal the Counsel had in the execution of this magnificent undertaking. Having been excluded from the chamber of fortifications for having blamed this plan, M. Micheli had believed, as a member of the Two Hundred, and even as a Citizen, he could state his opinion more at length, and that was what he had done by means of this memorandum which he had imprudently had printed, but not published; for he had obtained only the number of copies that he sent to the Two Hundred, which were all intercepted in the mail by order of the Small Council. I found this memorandum among my Uncle's papers, with the response he had been charged to make to it, and I took away both. I had made this trip a little after my departure from the Survey, and I had remained in some connection with the lawyer Coccelli who was its leader. Some time later the Director of Customs took it into his head to ask me to stand as godfather for his child, and gave me Madame Coccelli as godmother.[95] The honors turned my head, and proud to be so closely connected to Monsieur the Lawyer, I tried to play the important man in order to show myself worthy of that glory.

With that idea I believed I could do nothing better than to have him see my Memorandum printed by M. Micheli, which really was a rare item, to prove to him that I was connected to the notables of Geneva who knew State secrets. Nevertheless, out of a half-restraint for which it would be hard for me to give a reason, I did not show him my uncle's response to this memorandum, perhaps because it was in manuscript and something printed was needed for M. the Lawyer. Nevertheless, he so much felt the value of the writing that I had the stupidity to entrust to him that I was never able to get it back or see it again, and, very convinced of the uselessness of my efforts, I made a merit of the matter for myself and transformed this theft into a present. I do not doubt for a moment that he made the very most of this piece, more curious than useful, at the Court of Turin, and that he took great care to get himself reimbursed in one manner or another for the money it should have cost him to acquire it. Fortunately of all the possible futures one of the least probable is that some day the King of Sardinia will besiege Geneva. But since the thing is not impossible, I will always reproach my stupid vanity for having shown the greatest flaws of that place to its oldest enemy.

I passed two or three years in this manner between music, medical potions, projects, trips, floating ceaselessly from one thing to another, seeking to settle myself without knowing upon what, but nevertheless induced by degrees toward study, seeing literary people, hearing literature spoken about, sometimes joining in speaking about it myself, and acquiring rather the jargon of books than the knowledge of their contents. In my trips to Geneva from time to time, in passing I went to see my former good friend M. Simon who fomented my newly born emulation very much with very fresh news about the Republic of Letters drawn from Baillet or Colomiés.[96] At Chambéry I also saw a lot of a Jacobin Professor of physics, a good man of a monk whose name I have forgotten, who often performed little experiments that amused me very much. From his example[97] I wanted to make some sympathetic ink.[98] For that effect after having filled a bottle more than half way with quicklime, yellow arsenic, and water I corked it well. Almost instantly the effervescence began very violently. I ran to the bottle to uncork it but I was not in time; it blew up in my face like a bomb. I swallowed some arsenic, some lime, I almost died from it. I stayed blind for more than six weeks, and in this way I learned not to meddle in experimental physics without knowing the elements.[99]

This adventure happened inopportunely for my health, which had been noticeably deteriorating for some time. I do not know how it happened that I visibly declined even though I was well formed in my constitution and practiced no sort of excess. I had a good enough breadth of shoulder, a large chest, my lungs ought to have operated easily in it; nevertheless, I had shortness of breath; I felt myself oppressed: I sighed involuntarily, I had palpitations, I spat up blood; a slow fever set in and I never got rid of it completely. How can one fall into this condition in the prime of life without having any corrupted internal organ, without having done anything to destroy one's health?

The sword wears out the scabbard, it is sometimes said. That is my story. My passions have made me live, and my passions have killed me. What passions you will say? Trifles: the most puerile things in the world; but which affected me as if it were a question of the possession of Helen or of the throne of the universe. First women. When I had one, my senses were tranquil, but my heart never was. The needs of love devoured me[100] in the bosom of enjoyment. I had a tender mother, a dear friend but I needed a mistress. I imagined one in her place; I created her for myself in a thousand ways in order to mislead myself. If I had believed I held mamma in my arms when I was holding her there, my embraces would not have been less lively, but all my desires would have been extinguished; I would have sobbed with tenderness, but I would not have enjoyed. Enjoyed? Is that fate made for man? Ah if ever a single time in my life I had tasted all the delights of love in their fullness,[101] I do not imagine that my frail existence would have been able to bear it; I would have died in the act.

Thus I was burning up with love without any object, and this is perhaps how it is most draining. I was anxious, tormented with my poor mamma's bad state of affairs and with her imprudent conduct, which could not fail to bring about her total ruin in a short time. My cruel imagination, which always runs ahead of misfortunes, showed me this one ceaselessly in all its extent and in all its consequences. In advance I saw myself necessarily separated by poverty from her to whom I had consecrated my life and without whom I could not enjoy it. This is how I always had an agitated soul. Desires and fears alternately devoured me.

Music was another passion for me, less impetuous but not less consuming from the ardor with which I abandoned myself to it, from the stubborn study of Rameau's obscure books, from my invincible obstinacy in wanting to load them into my memory which always rejected them, from my continuous running around, from the immense compilations that I heaped up, very often passing entire nights copying. And why stop with permanent things, when all the follies that passed in my inconstant head—the fleeting tastes of a single day, a trip, a concert, a supper, a walk to take, a novel to read, a play to see, everything that was the least premeditated in the world among my pleasures or among my business— became so many violent passions for me, which gave me the truest torment in their ridiculous impetuosity. I believe that reading—with fury and often interrupted—the imaginary misfortunes of Cleveland caused me more distress than my own misfortunes did.[102]

There was a Genevan named M. Bagueret,[103] who had been employed under Peter the Great at the court of Russia; one of the nastiest-looking men[104] and greatest fools I have ever seen, always full of projects as foolish as he was, who made millions fall like the rain and for whom zeros cost nothing. Having come to Chambéry for some trial at the Senate, this man[105] seized hold of mamma as might be expected and for his treasures of zeros that he generously lavished on her, he took her little écus from her one by one. I did not like him at all, he saw it; with me that is not difficult: there is no sort of baseness that he did not use to cajole me. He took it into his head to propose that I learn chess which he played a little. I tried, almost in spite of myself, and after having more or less learned the moves, my progress was so rapid that before the end of the first sitting I gave him the rook which he had given me at the beginning. I needed nothing more: Behold me wild about chess. I buy a chess board; I buy the Calabrian;[106] I close myself up in my room, I spend days and nights there wanting to learn all the elements by heart, to stuff them in my head willy-nilly, to play alone without relaxation and endlessly. After two or three months of this fine labor and unimaginable efforts I go to the café, skinny, yellow, and almost stupefied. I try my skill, I play with M. Bagueret again: he beats me one time, two times, twenty times; so many combinations had gotten mixed up in my head, and my imagination had so weakened itself that I no longer saw anything but a cloud in front of me. Every time I wanted to practice studying the elements with Philodor's book or Stamma's the same thing has happened to me, and after having exhausted myself with fatigue I found myself weaker than before.[107] Furthermore, whether I have given up chess, or whether in playing I have again made myself breathless, I have never advanced a notch since that first sitting, and I have always found myself at the same point I was at its end. I might practice for thousands of centuries and I would end by being able to give a rook to Bagueret, and nothing more. There is time well employed, you will say! and I have employed more than a little in it. I did not end this first attempt until I no longer had the strength to continue. When I went to show myself after leaving my room I had the appearance of an exhumed body, and if I had continued on the same course I would not have remained exhumed for very long. It will be agreed that it is difficult, above all in the ardor of youth, for such a head to leave the body always in health.

The impairment of my health acted on my mood and tempered the ardor of my whims. Feeling myself grow weaker I became more tranquil and lost the rage for trips a little. Being more sedentary I was overtaken, not by boredom, but by melancholy; the vapors [108] followed after the passions; my languor became sadness; I wept and sighed over nothing, I felt life escaping me without having tasted it; I bewailed the condition in which I was leaving my poor mamma, the one into which I saw her ready to fall; I can say that to depart from her and to leave her to be pitied was my only regret. At last I fell completely ill. She looked after me as no mother has ever looked after her child, and that did her some good by diverting her from projects and keeping the projectors away. What a sweet death, if it had come then! If I had tasted the good things of life little, I had felt its misfortunes little. My peaceful soul could leave without the cruel feeling of the injustice of men which poisons life and death. I had the consolation of living on in my better half; that was hardly to die. Without the anxiety I had about her fate I would have died as I might have gone to sleep, and even this anxiety had an affectionate and tender object which tempered its bitterness. I said to her, "You are the depository of my whole being; act so that it might be happy." Two or three times when

I was most ill, I happened to get up in the night and drag myself to her room, to give her advice about her conduct, advice which I dare say was full of soundness and sense, but in which the interest I took in her fate was more noticeable than anything else. As if tears were my nourishment and my remedy, I fortified myself with the ones I shed near her, with her, sitting on her bed, and holding her hands in mine. The hours flowed by in these nocturnal conversations, and I returned from them in a better condition than I had come; content and calm in the promises she had made me, in the hopes she had given me, upon that I slept with peace of heart and resignation to providence. May it please God that after so many reasons to hate life, after so many storms that have agitated mine and which have made it nothing but a burden to me, death—which must end it—might be as little cruel for me as it would have been at that moment.

As a result of cares, vigilance, and incredible efforts she saved me, and it is certain that she alone could have saved me.[109] I have little faith in the medicine of doctors, but I have a lot in that of true friends: the things upon which our happiness depends are always done much better than all others. If there is a delightful feeling in life, it is the one we experienced at being returned to each other. Our mutual attachment did not increase from it, that was not possible; but it acquired an indefinable something that was more intimate, more touching in its great simplicity. I became completely her work, completely her child and more than if she had been my true mother. Without thinking about it we began not to separate from each other any more, so as to put our whole existence in common in some way, and feeling that we were reciprocally not only necessary but sufficient for each other, we accustomed ourselves to thinking about nothing that was foreign to us any longer, to limiting our happiness and all our desires absolutely to that possession that was mutual and perhaps unique among humans, which was not at all, as I have said, that of love; but a more essential possession which—without depending on the senses, on sex, on age, on looks—depended on everything by which one is oneself, and which one cannot lose without ceasing to be.

How did it happen that this precious crisis did not lead to the happiness of the rest of her days and mine? It was not because of me, I bear this consoling witness for myself. It was not because of her either, at least not because of her will. It was written that invincible natural disposition [110] would soon take back its ascendancy. But this fatal return did not happen suddenly. There was, thanks to Heaven, an interval (a short and precious interval!) [111] that did not end through my fault, and which I will not reproach myself with having taken poor advantage of.

Although I had been cured of my great illness, I had not gotten back my vigor. My chest had not recovered; a remnant of fever still remained, and kept me in languor. I no longer had any taste for anything but for ending my days near the one who was dear to me, to sustain her in her good resolutions, to make her feel in what the true charm of a happy life consisted, to make hers happy to the extent that it depended on me. But I saw, I even felt that in a somber and sad house the continuous solitude of the tête-à-tête would also become sad in the end. The remedy for that presented itself as if by itself. Mamma had prescribed milk for me and wanted me to go into the country to take it. I consented to this, on the condition that she come there with me. Nothing more was needed to make her decide; there was no longer any question except the choice of the spot. The garden in the suburb was not strictly in the country; surrounded by houses and other gardens, it did not have the attractions of a rustic retreat. Furthermore after Anet's death we had left this garden for reasons of economy, no longer having our hearts set on maintaining plants there, and other aims making us regret this reduction very little.

Taking advantage now of the distaste for the city that I found in her, I proposed that we abandon it completely, and that we establish ourselves in an agreeable solitude, in some little house distant enough to put off importunate people. She might have done it, and this decision which her good angel and mine suggested to me might very likely have guaranteed happy and tranquil days, up to the moment at which death should separate us. But this condition was not the one to which we were called. Mamma was obliged to undergo all the pains of indigence and illness after having passed her life in abundance, so as to make her leave it with less regret; and I, by means of a collection of ills of every sort, was obliged one day to be an example to anyone who, inspired only by the love of the public good and justice, dares—strong in his innocence alone—to tell the truth openly to men without being supported by cabals, without forming parties for himself to protect him.

One unfortunate fear held her back. She did not dare to leave her nasty house, from fear of angering the owner. "Your project of retirement is charming," she said to me, "and extremely to my taste; but in that retirement we must live. If I leave my prison I risk losing my bread, and when we no longer have any in the woods it will be very necessary to return to the city to seek it. So as to have less need of coming to this, let us not leave completely. Let us pay that little pension to the Comte de St. Laurent so that he will leave me my own. Let us look for some retreat far enough from the City to live in peace, and close enough to return whenever we have to." Thus it was done. After having looked a little, we settled on les Charmettes, M. de Conzié's land just outside Chambéry, but secluded and solitary as if it was a hundred leagues away. Between two rather high hills is a little dale running north and south, at the bottom of which runs a channel among the stones and trees. Along this dale halfway up the hill are some scattered houses, extremely pleasant for whoever loves a refuge that is a little wild and secluded. After having tried two or three of these houses, we finally chose the prettiest one, belonging to a Gentleman who was in the service, called M. Noiret.[112] The house was very suitable for occupation. A terraced garden in front, a vineyard above, an orchard below, opposite a little copse of Chestnut trees, a fountain within reach, higher up the mountain fields for grazing cattle; in sum, everything that was needed for the little rustic household we wanted to establish. As near as I can recall the times and the dates, we took possession of it near the end of the summer of 1736.[113] I was in raptures, the first day we slept there. "O Mamma!" I said to that dear friend while embracing her and inundating her with tears of emotion and joy, "this is the abode of happiness and innocence. If we do not find both of them here, we must not look for them anywhere."[114]

Book VI[1]

Hoc erat in votis: modus agri non ita magnus,
Hortus ubi, et tecto vicinus aqua fons;
Et paululum sylva super his foret.[2]

I cannot add: *auctius atque Dî melius fecere*: but no matter; I did not need anything more; I did not need even the property: the enjoyment of it was enough for me; and for a long time I have said and felt that the owner and the possessor are often two very different persons; even leaving aside husbands and lovers.

Here begins the short happiness of my life; here come the peaceful but quickly passing moments which have given me the right to say that I have lived. Precious and regretted moments, ah begin your lovable course for me again; flow more slowly in my remembrance, if it is possible, than you really did in your fleeting passage. What can I do to prolong this very touching and simple narrative at my pleasure; to say the same things over and over again, and in repeating them not to bore my readers more than I bore myself by endlessly beginning them over again? Besides if all that consisted in deeds, in actions, in words, I could describe it and render it in some fashion: but how can I say what was neither said, nor done, nor even thought, but tasted,[3] but felt, without my being able to express any object of my happiness except this very feeling. I rose with the sun and I was happy; I took a walk and I was happy, I saw mamma and I was happy, I left her and I was happy,[4] I roamed through the woods, the hills, I wandered in the valleys, I read, I was idle, I worked in the garden, I gathered fruits, I helped with the housekeeping, and happiness followed me everywhere; it was not in any definable thing, it was entirely in me, it could not depart from me for a single instant.

Nothing that happened to me during this cherished epoch, nothing I did, said, and thought all the time it lasted has escaped my memory. The times that precede and follow come back to me intermittently. I re-call them unevenly and confusedly; but I recall this one completely as if it were still going on. My imagination, which always went forward in my youth and now goes backward, makes up for the hope I have lost forever by means of these sweet remembrances. I no longer see anything in the future that tempts me; only returns to the past can soothe me, and these returns, so lively and so true in the epoch about which I am speaking, often make me live happily in spite of my misfortunes.

I will give a single example of these remembrances which will enable one to judge their strength and truth. The first day that we went to sleep at Les Charmettes, Mamma was in a sedan chair, and I followed her on foot. The road climbs, she was rather heavy, and, being afraid of tiring her porters too much, she wanted to get out about halfway there to go the rest on foot. While walking she sees something blue in the hedge and says to me, "There is some periwinkle still in bloom." I had never seen periwinkle, I did not bend over to examine it, and I am too near-sighted to distinguish plants on the ground from my full height. I cast a glance at that one only in passing, and almost thirty years went by without me seeing periwinkle, or without me paying attention to it. In 1764 while I was at Cressier with my friend M. du Peyrou,[5] we climbed a little mountain on the summit of which he has a pretty trellised enclosure that he justly calls Belle-vue. Then I began to herbalize a little. While climbing and looking among the bushes I let out a shout of joy, *"Ah, there is some periwinkle"*; and in fact it was so. Du Peyrou noticed the outburst, but he did not know its cause; he will learn it, I hope when he reads this some-day. From the impression of such a little object the reader can judge about the one made on me by all those that relate to the same epoch.

Nevertheless, the country air did not give me back my former health at all. I was languishing; I became worse. I could not bear milk, I had to give it up. At that time water was in fashion as the remedy for everything; I applied myself to water, and so indiscriminately that it almost cured me, not of my ills, but of life. Every morning when I got up I went to the fountain with a big goblet, and I drank the equivalent of two bottles one right after the other while walking around. I gave up wine altogether at my meals. The water that I drank was a little hard and difficult to pass, as are most mountain waters. In short I did so well that in less than two months I totally destroyed my stomach, which had been very good until then. Now that I could no longer digest anything, I understood that I must no longer hope for a cure. At this same time an accident happened to me as peculiar in itself as in its consequences, which will end only when I do.

One morning when I was not any sicker than usual, while putting a little table on its legs, I felt a sudden and almost inconceivable revolution in my whole body. I cannot do better than to compare it to a sort of storm that arose in my blood and instantly reached all my members. My arteries set themselves beating with such a great force that not only did I feel their beating, but I even heard it and above all that of the carotids. A great noise in the ears was joined to this, and this noise was triple or rather quadruple, namely: a deep and rumbling buzzing, a murmur clearer than running water, a very sharp whistling, and the beating I just mentioned and whose strokes I could easily count without feeling my pulse or touching my body with my hands. This internal noise was so great that it deprived me of the subtlety of hearing that I had before, and made me, not completely deaf, but hard of hearing, as I have been since that time.

One can judge of my surprise and my fright. I believed I was dead; I put myself to bed; the doctor was called; I told him my case while shuddering and judging it to have no remedy. I believe that he thought the same way about it, but he played his profession. He strung together long chains of reasoning about which I understood nothing at all; then in consequence of his sublime theory he began *in anima vili*,[6] the experimental cure that it pleased him to try. It was so painful, so disgusting, and worked so little that I soon quit it, and when I saw that I was neither better nor worse after several weeks, I left my bed and resumed my ordinary life, with the beating of my arteries and my buzzings which have not left me for a minute since that time, that is to say for thirty years.

Until then I had been a great sleeper. The total privation of sleep that was joined to all these symptoms and which has constantly accompanied them until now, succeeded in persuading me that I had little time left to live. For a time this persuasion calmed me from the effort to cure myself. Not being able to prolong my life, I resolved to draw all the advantage possible from the little I had left, and that was possible because of a singular favor of nature,[7] which exempted me from the suffering that it seemed it should have brought me in such a distressing condition. I was troubled by this noise, but I did not suffer from it: it was accompanied by no other habitual inconvenience whatsoever except insomnia during the nights, and at all times a shortness of breath that did not reach the point of asthma, and only made itself felt when I wanted to run or act a little vigorously.

This accident which ought to have killed my body killed only my passions, and I bless heaven every day for the fortunate effect it produced on my soul. I can very well say that I did not begin to live until I looked at myself as a dead man.[8] Giving their genuine value to the things I was going to leave, I began to occupy myself with more noble efforts, as if out of anticipation of the ones I would soon have to fulfill, which I had very much neglected until then. I had often travestied religion in my way but I had never been completely without religion. It cost me less to return to this subject which is so sad for so many people, but so sweet for anyone who makes it into an object of consolation and hope. On this occasion

Mamma was much more useful to me than all the theologians would have been.

Since she put everything into a system, she had not failed to do so with religion also, and this system was composed of very disparate ideas (some very sound others very foolish) of feelings connected to her character, and of prejudices that came from her education.[9] In general, believers make God as they are themselves, the good make him good, the wicked make him wicked; the devout who are spiteful and choleric see only Hell because they would like to damn the whole world: loving and gentle souls hardly believe in it, and one of the astonishing things from which I cannot recover is to see the good Fenelon speak about it in his *Telemachus*, as if he truly believed in it: but I hope that he was lying then; for in the end however truthful one may be, one certainly must lie sometimes when one is a Bishop.[10] Mamma did not lie to me, and that soul without bitterness, which could not imagine God as vindictive and always wrathful, saw only clemency and mercy where the devout saw only justice and punishment. She often said that it would not be justice at all for God to be just with regard to us, because—since he had not given us what we needed to be just—it would be asking for a return of more than he had given. What was bizarre was that, although she did not believe in Hell, she did not fail to believe in Purgatory. This came from her not knowing what to do with the souls of the wicked, since she could not either damn them or put them with the good until they had become such; and one must admit that in fact the wicked are always very vexing both in this world and in the other.

Another peculiarity. One sees that the whole doctrine of original sin and redemption is destroyed by this system, and the basis of vulgar Christianity is shaken by it, and that at least Catholicism cannot subsist. Nevertheless Mamma was a good Catholic or claimed to be one, and it is certain that she claimed it in very good faith. It seemed to her that Scripture was explained too literally and too harshly. To her everything that one reads there about eternal torments appeared comminatory or figurative. To her the death of Jesus Christ appeared as an example of truly divine charity to teach men to love God and to love each other in the same way. In a word, faithful to the religion she had embraced, she sincerely accepted its profession of faith as a whole; but when one came to the discussion of each article, it happened that she saw completely differently from the Church, even while always submitting to it. On that point she had a simplicity of heart, a frankness more eloquent than quibbling, which often troubled even her confessor; for she hid nothing from him. "I am a good Catholic," she said to him. "I want always to be so; I adopt the decisions of the Holy Mother the Church with all the power of my soul. I am not mistress of my faith, but I am of my will, I submit it without reserve, and I want to believe everything. What more do you ask of me?"

Even if there had not been any Christian morality I believe that she would have followed it, so well was it adapted to her character. She did everything that was commanded, but she would have done it the same if it had not been commanded. In things of no consequence she loved to obey, and if it had not been permitted, even prescribed, to her to eat meat, she would have fasted between God and herself, without prudence needing to enter into it at all. But all this morality was subordinate to M. de Tavel's principles, or rather she claimed to see nothing contradictory in it. She might have slept with twenty men everyday with an easy conscience, and even without having any more scruple than desire. I know that any number of devout people are no more scrupulous [11] on this point, but the difference is that they are seduced by their passions, and she was so only by her sophisms. In the most touching and I dare say the most edifying conversations, she came upon this point without changing either manner or tone, without believing she was contradicting herself. If need be she could even interrupt the conversation for the deed, and then take it up again with the same serenity as before: so deeply was she persuaded that all this was nothing but a maxim of social order, about which every sensible person could make his own interpretation, application, exception according to the spirit of the thing, without the slightest risk of offending God. Although I was assuredly not of her opinion on this point, I admit that I did not dare to combat it, being ashamed of the ungallant role that I would have to play in doing so. I would have tried very hard to establish the rule for others while trying to exempt myself from it; but aside from the fact that her temperament prevented the abuse of her principles well enough, I know that she was not a woman to be led astray and that to lay claim to the exception for myself was to leave it for everyone who pleased her. Nevertheless, I add this inconsistency along with the others, although it always had little effect on her behavior and at that time it had none at all; but I have promised to expose her principles faithfully, and I want to keep that engagement: I return to myself.

Finding in her all the maxims I needed to protect my soul from the terrors of death and its consequences, I imbibed from this source of confidence with security. I attached myself to her more than I had ever done; I would have wished to transport completely into her my life which I felt ready to abandon me. From this doubling of attachment for her, from the persuasion that I had little time left to live, from my profound security about my future fate, resulted a very calm and even sensual habitual state, in that it let me enjoy the few days left to me without uneasiness and without disturbance because it deadened all the passions that carry our fears and our hopes into the distance. One thing contributed to making these days more pleasant; that was the effort to nourish her taste for the country by means of all the amusements I could summon up. By making her love her garden, her poultry yard, her pigeons, her cows, I myself delighted in all that, and these little occupations that filled my day without troubling my tranquillity were worth more to me than milk and all the remedies for preserving my poor machine, and even making it recover, to the extent that was possible.

The grape harvest, the gathering of the fruits amused us the rest of that year, and attached us more and more to the rustic life in the midst of the good people by whom we were surrounded. We saw the winter arrive with great regret and we returned to the City as if we were going into exile. Above all myself, who believed that he was bidding farewell to les Charmettes forever because he doubted he would see Spring again. I did not leave it without kissing the ground and the trees, and without turning around several times while moving away. Having given up my students long before, having lost the taste for the amusements and social circles of the city, I no longer went out, I no longer saw anyone, except Mamma, and M. Salomon who had become her Doctor and mine a short time before: a decent man, an intelligent man, a great Cartesian, who spoke rather well about the system of the world, whose agreeable and instructive conversations were worth more to me than all his prescriptions.[12] I have never been able to bear that foolish and silly padding of ordinary conversations; but useful and solid conversations have always given me great pleasure and I have never shunned them. I acquired a great taste for M. Salomon's; it seemed to me that with him I got an advance on that exalted knowledge that my soul was going to acquire when it lost its shackles. The taste I had for him extended to the subjects he treated, and I began to seek out the books that could help me understand him[13] better. Those that mixed devoutness with the sciences suited me best; such as those of the Oratory and of Port-Royal in particular.[14] I began to read them or rather to devour them. One by Father Lamy fell into my hands, entitled *Conversations on the Sciences*.[15] This was a sort of introduction to acquaintance with the books that treat of them. I read it and reread it a hundred times; I resolved to make it my guide. Finally, little by little, I felt myself being carried away toward study with an irresistible force in spite of my condition, or rather because of my condition, and all the while looking at each day as the last one of my life, I studied with as much ardor as if I must live forever. They said that it was doing me harm; I myself believe that it did me good, and not only for my soul, but for my body; since that application for which I was impassioned became so delightful to me, that, no longer thinking of my illnesses, I was much less affected by them. It is nevertheless true that nothing procured me a real relief; but since I did not have any sharp pains, I accustomed myself to languishing, to not sleeping, to thinking instead of acting, and finally to looking at the successive and slow withering away of my machine as an inevitable progress that my death alone could stop.

Not only did this opinion detach me from all the vain cares of life, but it freed me from the importunity of cures, to which they had subjected me in spite of myself until then. Convinced that his drugs could not save me, Salomon spared me their aftertaste, and was content to amuse my poor Mamma's suffering with some of those indifferent prescriptions that entice[16] the hope of the sick and maintain the doctor's credit. I stopped the strict regimen, I returned to the use of wine and, in proportion to my strength, to the whole course of life of a man in health, sober with regard to everything but abstaining from nothing. I even went out and began to go see my acquaintances again, above all M. de Conzié whose company pleased me very much. Finally, either because it appeared fine to me to learn up until my final hour, or because a remnant of hope to live was hidden at the bottom of my heart, the expectation of death, far from lessening[17] my taste for study, seemed to enliven it, and I hurried to amass a few accomplishments for the other world, as if I believed that I would have only the ones I brought there with me. I acquired an affection for the shop of a book dealer called Bouchard where some literary people gathered,[18] and since the Spring—which I had believed I would not see again—was near, I provided myself with several books for les Charmettes, in case I had the good fortune to return there.

I did have that good fortune and I took advantage of it the best I could.[19] The joy with which I saw the first buds is inexpressible. For me, seeing the spring again was to come to life again in paradise. The snow had hardly begun to melt when we left our dungeon, and we were at les Charmettes early enough to have the first songs of the nightingale there. After that I no longer believed I was going to die; and really it is peculiar that I have never had great illnesses in the country. I have often suffered very much, but I have never been bedridden there. Often when I have felt myself sicker than usual, I have said, "When you see me ready to die, carry me to the shadow of an oak;[20] I promise you that I will recover."

Although I was weak I returned to my rustic functions, but in a manner proportionate to my strength. I was truly annoyed at not being able to do the gardening all alone; but when I had given six blows with a spade, I was out of breath, sweat streamed down me, I could not do any more. When I bent over, my beating redoubled and the blood rushed to my head with such force that I had to straighten up very quickly. Constrained to limiting myself to less fatiguing concerns, I undertook that of the pigeon house among others, and I became so fond of it that I often passed several hours in succession there without being bored for a moment. Pigeons are extremely timid and difficult to tame. Nevertheless, I succeeded in inspiring mine with such confidence that they followed me everywhere and let themselves be caught whenever I wanted. I could not appear at the garden or in the courtyard without having two or three of them instantly on my arms, on my head, and at last—in spite of the pleasure I took there—this retinue became so inconvenient to me that I was obliged to deprive them of this familiarity. I have always taken a singular pleasure in taming animals, above all those that are fearful and wild. It appeared charming to me to inspire them with a confidence that I never abused. I wanted them to love me in freedom.

I have said that I brought some books. I made use of them; but in a manner less suited to instructing me than overwhelming me. The false idea I had of things persuaded me that in order to read a book fruitfully it was necessary to have all the knowledge it assumed, very far from thinking that often the author did not have it himself, and that he borrowed it from other books to the extent that he needed it. With this mad idea I had stopped at every instant, forced to run ceaselessly from one book to another, and sometimes I would have had to exhaust libraries before reaching the tenth page of the book I wanted to study. Nevertheless, I persisted so well in this extravagant method that I lost an infinite amount of time in it, and nearly jumbled up my head to the point of not being able to see anything or know anything any more. Fortunately I perceived that I was going down a wrong path that was leading me astray in an immense labyrinth, and I got out of it before getting completely lost.

If one has the slightest true taste for the Sciences, the first thing one feels when one devotes oneself to them is their connection which causes them to attract, help, mutually clarify each other, so that one cannot get along without the other. Although the human mind cannot suffice for all,[21] and it might always be necessary to prefer one as the principal, if one does not have some notion of the others, one often finds oneself in obscurity even in one's own. I felt that what I had undertaken was good and useful in itself, that only the method had to be changed. First taking the encyclopedia[22] I had been proceeding by dividing it into its branches; I saw that it was necessary to do exactly the opposite; to take each of them separately, and pursue each separately up to the point where they rejoined each other. Thus I arrived at the ordinary synthesis; but I arrived there as a man who knows what he is doing.[23] Meditation took the place of knowledge for me in this, and a very natural reflection helped to guide me well. Whether I lived or died, I had no time to lose. To know nothing at nearly twenty-five years of age and to wish to learn everything is to commit oneself to taking good advantage of time. Not knowing at what point chance or death might stop my zeal, I wanted to acquire some ideas about everything in any event, as much to probe my natural aptitude as to judge for myself about what most deserved to be cultivated.

In the execution of this plan I found another advantage which I had not thought about; that of putting a great deal of time to profit. I must not have been born for study; for a long application tires me out to such a point that it is impossible for me to occupy myself with strength on the same subject for an entire half-hour, above all while following someone else's ideas: for it has sometimes happened that I abandoned myself for a longer time to my own and even rather successfully. If I have followed an author who must be read with application for several pages, my mind abandons him and loses itself in the clouds. If I persist I exhaust myself uselessly; bewilderment takes over me, I no longer see anything. But let different subjects follow each other, even without interruption, one re-freshes me from the other, and I follow them more easily without needing relaxation. I took advantage of this observation in my plan of studies, and I intermingled them so much that I was occupied all day long and never tired myself out.[24] It is true that rustic and domestic concerns made useful diversions; but in my increasing fervor I soon found the means to spare time from them for study, and to occupy myself with two things at the same time, without dreaming that each of them proceeded less well.

In so many little details which charm me and with which I often weary my reader I nevertheless use a discretion that he would hardly suspect if I did not take care to notify him of it. Here for example I recall with delight[25] all the different attempts I made to distribute my time so that I might find in it as much pleasure and usefulness as possible all together, and I can say that this period of time when I lived in seclusion and always sick was the one in my life in which I was the least idle and the least bored. Two or three months went by in this way testing the inclination of my mind and enjoying, in the most beautiful season of the year and in a place that it rendered enchanting, the charm of life whose value I felt so well, that of a society as free as it was sweet (if one can give the name society to such a perfect union), and that of the fine knowledge that I proposed to acquire for myself; since for me it was as if I had already possessed it; or rather it was even better, since the pleasure of learning contributed a great deal to my happiness.

I must pass over those attempts which all were enjoyments for me, but too simple to be capable of being explained. Once again true happiness cannot be described, it is felt, and is felt all the better when it can be described least, because it does not result from a combination of facts, but is a permanent condition. I repeat myself often, but I would repeat myself still more, if I said the same thing as many times as it comes to my mind. When my way of life—which had frequently changed—had at last taken a uniform course, here is just about how it was distributed.

I got up every morning before the sun. I went up through a neighboring orchard into a very pretty road that was above the vineyard and followed the side of the hill to Chambéry. There, still walking, I said my prayer, which did not consist in a vain stammering of the lips, but in a sincere elevation of the heart to the author of this lovable nature whose beauties were under my eyes. I have never liked praying in a room: it seems to me that walls and all these little works of men interpose themselves between God and me. I love to contemplate him in his works while my heart raises itself to him. My prayers were pure, I can say it, and worthy of being granted because of that. For myself and for the one who was never separated from my wishes I asked only an innocent and tranquil life; exempt from vice, from suffering, from painful needs; the death of the just; and their lot in the future. Otherwise this act was passed more in admiration, and in contemplation than in requests, and I knew that with the dispenser of true goods the best means of obtaining the ones we need is less to ask for them than to deserve them. I returned while walking, by means of a rather long route, occupied with considering with interest and sensual pleasure the rustic objects with which I was surrounded, the only ones with which the eye and the heart never grow tired. From afar I looked to see if it was day for mamma; if I saw her shutters open, I leapt for joy and I ran up. If they were closed I went into the garden while waiting until she had awakened, amusing myself by thinking over what I had learned the day before or by gardening. The shutters opened; I went to embrace her in her bed—often while she was still half asleep—and this embrace, as pure as it was tender, drew from its very innocence a charm that is never attached to the voluptuousness of the senses.

We usually breakfasted with café au lait. It was the time of the day at which we were most tranquil, at which we chatted the most at our ease. These sittings, ordinarily rather long, left me with a keen taste for breakfasts, and I infinitely prefer the practice of England and Switzerland—in which breakfast is a true meal which brings everyone together—to that of France in which each breakfasts alone in his room, or most often, does not breakfast at all. After an hour or two of chatting, I went to my books until dinner. I began with some book of philosophy, such as the *Logic* of

Port-Royal, Locke's *Essay*, Malebranche, Leibnitz, Descartes, and so on.[26] I soon noticed that all these authors were in almost perpetual contradiction with each other, and I formed the chimerical project of reconciling them, which tired me out very much and made me lose a lot of time. I confused my head, and made no progress at all. Finally renouncing this method also, I acquired an infinitely better one, to which I attribute all the progress I have been able to make, in spite of my lack of capacity; for it is certain that I have always had extremely little for study. While reading each Author, I made it a law for myself to adopt and follow all his ideas without mixing in my own or those of anyone else, and without ever disputing with him. I said to myself, "Let's begin by giving myself a storehouse of ideas, true or false, but clear, while waiting for my head to be well enough equipped to be able to compare and choose them." This method is not without inconvenience, I know, but for me it succeeded in the object of instructing myself. At the end of several years passed in not exactly thinking except through others, without reflecting, so to speak, and almost without reasoning, I found myself with a big enough fund of acquisitions to suffice for myself and to think without anyone else's help. Then when trips and business deprived me of the means of consulting books, I amused myself by thinking over and comparing what I had read, by weighing each thing in the scale of reason, and sometimes by judging my masters. I did not find that my faculty of judging had lost its vigor because it had been put into use late, and when I published my own ideas, I was not accused of being a servile disciple, and of swearing *in verba magistri*.[27]

From that I passed to elementary Geometry; for I have never gotten any farther, persisting in wanting to overcome my lack of memory by dint of retracing my steps hundreds of times over and of ceaselessly beginning the same route again. I did not relish that of Euclid who sought the chain of demonstrations rather than the connection of ideas; I preferred the geometry of Father Lamy, who from that time became one of my favorite Authors, whose works I still reread with pleasure.[28] Algebra followed and it was still Father Lamy whom I took for a guide; when I was more advanced I acquired *The Science of Calculus* by Father Reynaud, then his *Analysis Demonstrated* which I only skimmed.[29] I have never gotten far enough to feel the application of algebra to geometry very well. I do not at all like that manner of operating without seeing what you are doing, and it seemed to me that to resolve a problem of Geometry by equations was to play a tune by turning a crank. The first time I found by means of calculation that the square of a binomial was composed of the square of each of its parts and of the double product of the one times the other, I did not want to believe any of it until I had drawn the figure, in spite of the accuracy of my multiplication. It was not that I did not have a great taste for algebra considering it only as abstract quantity, but applied to extension I wanted to see the operation on lines, otherwise I no longer understood anything.[30]

After that came Latin. It was my most painful study, and one in which I have never made great progress. At first I began the Latin method of Port-Royal, but fruitlessly. Those Ostrogothic verses made me sick to my stomach and could not enter my ear. I got lost in those crowds of rules, and upon learning the last, I forgot everything that had preceded it. A study of words is not what is required for a man without a memory, and it was precisely to force my memory to acquire some capacity that I persisted in this study. I had to give it up in the end. I understood construction well enough to be able to read an easy author with the aid of a Dictionary. I followed that route and it was lucky for me. I applied myself to translation—not in writing, but mentally—and I stopped there. As a result of time and practice I have succeeded in reading Latin authors fluently enough, but never to be able either to speak or write in that language; which has often caused me embarrassment when I found myself, I know not how, enlisted among literary people. Another inconvenience following from this manner of learning is that I have never known prosody, still less the rules of versification. Since I desired nevertheless to feel the harmony of the language in verse and in prose, I made many efforts to succeed in it; but I am convinced that that is almost impossible without a teacher. Having learned the composition of the easiest of all the verses, which is the hexameter, I had the patience to scan almost all of Virgil and to mark the feet and quantity in it; then when I was in doubt whether a syllable was long or short, I went to consult my Virgil. One feels that this caused me to make many mistakes, because of the alterations permitted by the rules of versification. But if there is an advantage in studying alone, there are also great inconveniences, and above all an unbelievable difficulty. I know that better than anyone.

Before noon I left my books, and if dinner was not ready, I went to make a visit to my friends the pigeons or to work in the garden while waiting for the time. When I heard myself called I ran up extremely content, and supplied with a big appetite; for it is worth noticing that however sick I might be I never lack an appetite. We dined very agreeably, chatting about our business while waiting for mamma to be able to eat. Two or three times a week when the weather was good, we went behind the house to take coffee in a cool and leafy arbor which I had trimmed with hops, and which gave us great pleasure during the heat; there we passed a short hour visiting our vegetables, our flowers, in conversations relating to our manner of living which caused us to taste[31] its sweetness better. I had another little family at the end of the garden: it was some bees. I hardly ever failed to pay them a visit and often Mamma came with me; I was very interested in their work, I was infinitely amused to see them return from plundering, their little thighs sometimes so burdened that they had trouble walking. In the first days, curiosity made me indiscreet, and they stung me two or three times; but afterwards we became so well acquainted that however close I came they let me do it, and however full the hives might be, ready to swarm, I was sometimes surrounded by them, I had them on my hands, on my face, without any ever stinging me. All animals mistrust man and are not wrong to do so; but once they are sure that he does not want to harm them, their confidence becomes so great that one must be more than barbarous to abuse it.

I returned to my books: but my afternoon occupations should bear the name of work and study less than that of recreations and amusement. I have never been able to bear the application of study after my dinner, and in general all effort costs me during the heat of the day. Nevertheless, I was occupied, but without restraint and almost without rule, in reading without studying. The things I followed most regularly were history and geography, and since these demanded no application of the mind whatsoever, I made as much progress in them as my lack of memory allowed. I wanted to study Father Petau,[32] and I buried myself in the obscurities of chronology; but I became disgusted with the critical part which has neither bottom nor shore, and I preferred the exact measurement of time and the path of the celestial bodies. I would have even acquired a taste for astronomy if I had had the instruments; but I had to content myself with some elements taken from books, and some rough observations made with a spy-glass, only in order to know the general situation of the Sky: for my nearsightedness does not allow me to distinguish the stars clearly enough with the naked eye.[33] On this subject, I recall an adventure the remembrance of which has often made me laugh. I had bought a celestial planisphere to study the constellations. I had attached this planisphere to a frame, and on the nights when the Sky was clear I went into the garden to put my frame on four stakes of my height, the planisphere turned upside down, and in order to light it without the wind blowing my candle out, I put the candle in a pail on the ground between the four stakes; then looking alternately at the planisphere with my eyes, and the stars[34] with my telescope I practiced recognizing the stars and discerning the constellations. I believe I have said that M. Noiret's garden was terraced; from the road one saw everything that happened there. One night some peasants, passing by rather late, saw me in a grotesque outfit busy with my operation. The light which played on my planisphere whose source they did not see because the candle was hidden from their eyes by the sides of the pail, these four stakes, this big paper scrawled with figures, this framework and the play of my telescope which they saw move back and forth gave this object an air of a magician's book of spells which frightened them. My attire was not suited to reassuring them: a flapped hat over my cap, and a short padded night-gown of mamma's which she had obliged me to put on offered the image of a true sorcerer to their eyes, and since it was almost midnight they had no doubt whatsoever that this was the beginning of the witches' sabbath. Not very curious to see any more of it, they ran away very alarmed, woke up their neighbors to tell them about their vision, and the story circulated so well that from the next day everyone in the neighborhood knew that the sabbath had been held at M. Noiret's house. I do not know what this rumor might have produced, if one of the peasants who was a witness to my conjurations had not brought his complaint about them the same day to two Jesuits who came to see us, and who provisionally undeceived them without knowing what it was about. They recounted the story to us, I told them its cause, and we laughed a lot. Nevertheless, for fear of a relapse it was resolved that from then on I would observe without light and that I would go to consult the planisphere in the house. I am sure that those who have read about my magic in Venice in the *Letters from the Mountain* [35] will find that I have had a long-standing great vocation for being a sorcerer.

Such was my course of life at les Charmettes when I was not occupied with any rustic cares; for they always took preference, and in what did not exceed my strength, I worked like a peasant; but it is true that at that time my extreme weakness left me hardly anything but the merit of good will on that score. Moreover I wanted to do two tasks at the same time, and because of that I did not do either of them well. I had taken it into my head to give myself some memory by force; I persisted in wanting to learn a lot by heart. For that purpose I always carried with me some book which I studied and ran through with an unbelievable effort, working all the while. I do not know how the obstinacy of these vain and continuous efforts did not make me stupid in the end. A good twenty times I must have learned and relearned the eclogues of Virgil, of which I do not know a single word. I lost or broke up a set of multitudes of books, from the habit I had of carrying them with me everywhere, to the dove-cot, to the garden, to the orchard, to the vineyard. When I was occupied with something else, I set my book at the foot of a tree or on the hedge; I always forgot to pick it up again, and often at the end of two weeks I found it again moldy or gnawed upon by ants and snails. This ardor for learning became a mania that stupefied me, incessantly and totally occupied as I was with muttering something between my teeth.

Since the Writings of Port Royal and the Oratory were the ones I read most frequently, they had made me a half Jansenist, and their harsh theology scared me sometimes in spite of all my confidence. The terror of Hell, which I had feared very little until then, troubled my security little by little, and if mamma had not soothed my soul, that frightening doctrine might have completely bowled me over in the end. My confessor, who was also hers, contributed his share in maintaining me in a good state. This was Father Hemet, a Jesuit, a good and wise old man whose memory I will always hold in veneration.[36] Although a Jesuit, he had the simplicity of a child, and his morality—less lax than gentle—was precisely what I needed to counterbalance the sad impressions of Jansenism. This good man and his companion Father Coppier[37] often came to see us at les Charmettes, although the road was extremely rough, and rather long for people of their age. Their visits did me much good: may it please God to give the same to their souls in return, for they were too old then for me to presume them to be still alive today. I also went to see them at Chambéry, I familiarized myself little by little with their house; their library was at my service; the remembrance of that happy time is linked with that of the Jesuits, to the point of making me love the latter because of the former, and—although their doctrine has always appeared dangerous to me—I have never been able to find it in myself to hate them sincerely.

I would like to know whether there sometimes pass in the hearts of other men puerilities similar to those that sometimes pass in mine. In the midst of my studies and a life as innocent as one can lead, and in spite of everything they had been able to say to me, the fear of Hell still troubled me often. I asked myself, "In what state am I? If I died at this very instant would I be damned?" According to my Jansenists the thing was indubitable; but according to my conscience it seemed to me that it was not. Always fearful, floating in that cruel uncertainty, in order to leave it I had recourse to the most laughable expedients, for which I would willingly shut a man away if I saw him do the same. One day, while dreaming about this sad subject, I exerted myself mechanically by throwing rocks against the trunks of trees, and did so with my usual skill, that is to say, almost without hitting any of them. Right in the middle of this fine exercise, I took it into my head to make it into a sort of prognostic for myself in order to calm my anxiousness. I tell myself, "I am going to throw this rock against the tree which is across from me. If I hit it, sign of salvation; if I miss it, sign of damnation." While speaking this way I throw my rock with a trembling hand and with a horrible beating of the heart, but so luckily that it strikes right in the middle of the tree; which, to tell the truth, was not difficult; for I had been careful to choose one that was extremely big and extremely close. After that time I never doubted my salvation again. Recalling this stroke I do not know whether I ought to laugh or moan over myself. You other great men who certainly are laughing, congratulate yourselves, but do not insult my misery; for I swear to you that I feel it very well.[38]

Besides, these troubles, these alarms which are perhaps inseparable from devoutness, were not a permanent condition. Usually I was calm enough, and the impression made on my soul by the idea of an imminent death was less one of sadness than of a peaceful languor which even had its sweetness. Among some old papers I have just found a sort of exhortation that I made to myself in which I congratulate myself upon dying at an age at which one finds enough courage in oneself to envisage death, without having experienced great evils either of the body or of the mind during my life. How right I was! A presentiment made me fear living in order to suffer. It seems that I foresaw the fate that was waiting for me in my old age. I have never been so close to wisdom as during that happy epoch. Without great remorse about the past; liberated as I was from cares about the future, the feeling that constantly dominated in my soul was to enjoy the present. The devout ordinarily have a very lively little sensuality that makes them savor with delight the innocent pleasures that they are allowed. I do not know why the worldly make this into a crime for them, or rather I know it well. It is because they envy in others the enjoyment of simple pleasures the taste for which they themselves have lost. I had this taste, and I found it charming to satisfy it in safety of conscience. My heart, which was still new, abandoned itself over to everything with the pleasure of a child, or rather if I dare to say it, with the sensual pleasure of an angel: for in truth these calm enjoyments have the serenity of the ones of paradise. Dinners on the grass at Montagnole, suppers under the bower, the harvest of the fruits, the grape harvests, the evenings of stripping hemp with our people, all this made up so many festivals for us from which Mamma took the same pleasure as I did. Some more solitary walks had an even greater charm, because the heart unbosomed itself more in freedom. Among others we made one on a St. Louis Day,[39] which was Mamma's name day, which forms an epoch in my memory. We left together and by ourselves early in the morning after the mass which a Carmelite had come to say for us at daybreak in a chapel adjoining the house.[40] I had proposed to go wandering about the hillside opposite the one where we were, which we had not yet visited at all. We had sent our provisions in advance, for the walk was supposed to last the whole day. Although Mamma was a little round and plump, she walked pretty well; we went from hill to hill and from woods to woods, sometimes in the sun and often in the shade; resting from time to time, and forgetting ourselves for whole hours; chatting about ourselves, about our union, about the sweetness of our lot, and making wishes for its duration which were not granted. Everything seemed to conspire toward the happiness of that day. It had rained a little before; no dust at all, and streams running well. A little cool breeze rustled the leaves, the air was pure, the horizon cloudless; serenity reigned in the Sky as in our hearts. We had our dinner at a peasant's house and shared with his family who blessed us wholeheartedly. These poor Savoyards are such good people! After dinner we reached the shade under tall trees where, while I was gathering twigs of dry wood to make our coffee, mamma amused herself by herbalizing among the undergrowth, and with the flowers of the bouquet which I had gathered for her while we made our way she made me notice a thousand curious things in their structure which amused me very much and should have given me a taste for botany, but the moment had not come; I was distracted by too many other studies. An idea that happened to strike me diverted me from the flowers and plants. The situation of soul in which I found myself, everything we had said and done that very day, all the objects that had struck me recalled to me the sort of dream I had had while wide awake at Annecy seven or eight years before of which I have given an account in its place.[41] The relations to it were so striking that I was moved to the point of tears in thinking about it. In a transport of emotion I embraced that dear friend. "Mamma, mamma," I said to her with passion, "this day has been promised to me for a long time, and I see nothing surpassing it. Thanks to you my happiness is at its summit, if only it might not decline henceforward! if only it could last as long as I preserve the taste for it! it will end only with me."

In this way my happy days flowed by, and all the happier, because, since I perceived nothing that might trouble them, in fact I did not envisage their end except with my own. It was not that the source of my cares was absolutely suppressed; but I saw it take another course which I directed the best I could toward useful objects, so that it might bring its remedy along with it. Mamma naturally loved the country and this taste did not cool with me. Little by little she acquired the taste for rustic concerns; she loved to turn the land to account and she had knowledge about it that she made use of with pleasure. Not content with the land belonging to the house she had taken, sometimes she rented a field sometimes a meadow. Finally, bringing her entrepreneurial disposition to agricultural objects instead of remaining idle in her house, she took the path of soon becoming a big farmer. I did not very much like seeing her extend herself that way and I opposed it as much as I could; very certain that she would always be deceived, and that her liberal and prodigal disposition would always bring expense beyond the product. Nevertheless, I consoled myself by thinking that this product at least would not be nothing and would help her live. Of all the undertakings she could form this one appeared to me the least ruinous, and without envisaging an object of profit in it as she did, I envisaged in it a continuous occupation that would protect her from bad businesses and swindlers. In that idea I ardently desired to recover as much strength and health as I needed to look after her affairs, to be overseer of her workers or her foremost worker, and naturally the exercise this caused me to do often tore me away from my books, and by distracting me from my condition must have rendered it better.

Upon returning from Italy the following winter Barrillot brought me some books, among others the Bontempi and Father Banchieri's *Cartella per Musica* which gave me some taste for the history of Music and for theoretical researches in this fine art.[42] Barrillot stayed with us for some time and since I had reached my age of majority several months before,[43] it was agreed that I would go to Geneva the following spring to ask for my mother's property again or at least the part of it which fell to me, while waiting to learn what had become of my brother. That was executed as it had been resolved. I went to Geneva, my father came there on his side. For a long time he had been going back without anyone seeking a quarrel with him, although his warrant had never been purged: but since his courage was esteemed and his probity respected, they pretended to have forgotten his affair, and the Magistrates—occupied with the great project that burst out a little afterwards—did not want to alarm the bourgeoisie prematurely by inopportunely reminding it of their former bias.[44]

I was afraid that they would make difficulties for me about my change of religion; they did not make any. In that regard the laws of Geneva are less harsh than those of Berne, where anyone who changes religion loses not only his status but his property. Thus mine was not disputed with me, but somehow or other was found to be reduced to an extremely small amount.[45] Although they were almost certain that my brother was dead, there was no legal proof of it. I lacked sufficient title to lay claim to his portion, and without regret I left it to help maintain my father, who enjoyed it as long as he lived. As soon as the formalities of justice were done and I received my money, I put some portion of it into books,[46] and I flew to bring the rest to mamma's feet. My heart beat with joy during the journey, and the moment I put that money into her hands was a thousand times sweeter to me than the one it entered my own. She received it with that simplicity of beautiful souls who, because they do such things without effort, see them without wonder. That money was employed almost entirely for my use, and that with an equal simplicity. Its use would have been exactly the same if it had come to her from somewhere else.

Meanwhile my health was not restored at all. On the contrary, to the naked eye I was wasting away. I was as pallid as a dead man and thin as a skeleton. My beating of the arteries was terrible, my palpitations more frequent, I was continuously oppressed, and my weakness finally became so great that I had trouble moving; I could not walk quickly without suffocating, I could not bend over without becoming dizzy, I could not lift up the lightest load; I was reduced to the most tormenting inaction for a man as restless as I am. It is certain that the vapors were very much mixed up with all this. The vapors are the malady of happy people; it was mine: the tears I shed (often without any reason for crying), the lively frights at the noise of a leaf or a bird; the unevenness of mood in the calm of the sweetest life, all these are marks of that boredom of well-being that takes sensitivity to the point of extravagance so to speak. We are so little made to be happy here below that either the soul or the body must necessarily suffer when both of them are not suffering, and the good condition of one almost always injures the other.[47] When I might have been able to enjoy life delightfully my machine in decay prevented me from doing so, without me being able to say where the cause of the illness had its true seat. Later on, in spite of the decay of years[48] and very real and very serious illnesses, my body seems to have reacquired strength in order to feel my misfortunes better, and now when I am writing this, infirm and almost a sexagenarian; overpowered with suffering of every sort, I feel more vigor and life in myself for suffering, than I had for enjoying at the flower of my age and in the bosom of the truest happiness.[49]

To finish me off, having made a little physiology enter into my readings, I began to study anatomy, and passing in review the multitude and the action of the pieces that made up my machine, I expected to feel all of it become unhinged twenty times a day; far from being astonished at finding myself dying I was astonished that I could still live, and I did not read the description of any malady without believing I had it. I am certain that if I had not been sick, I would have become so from that fatal study. Finding some symptoms of mine in every malady, I believed I had them all, and from that I caught in addition an even crueler one from which I had believed myself freed: the fantasy of being cured; this is a difficult one to avoid when one begins to read books of medicine. As a result of seeking, reflecting, comparing, I came to imagine that the basis of my illness was a polyp on the heart, and Salomon himself appeared struck by that idea. Reasonably I should have gone from that opinion to confirm myself in my former resolution. I did not do so at all. I strained all the springs of my mind to find out how one could cure a polyp on the heart, resolved to undertake that wondrous cure. In a trip that Anet had made to Montpellier to go to see the plant garden and the demonstrator M. Sauvages, he had been told that M. Fizes had cured a similar polyp.[50] Mamma remembered this and spoke to me about it.[51] Nothing more was needed to inspire me with the desire to go consult M. Fizes. The hope for a cure made me find courage and strength to undertake this trip. The money that had come from Geneva furnished the means. Far from discouraging me, mamma exhorted me to it; and there I was leaving for Montpellier.

I did not need to go that far to find the doctor I needed. Because the horse tired me out too much, I had taken a carriage at Grenoble. At Moirans five or six other carriages arrived in file after mine. This time it was truly the adventure of the sedan chairs.[52] Most of these carriages were the procession of a newlywed called Madame du Colombier.[53] With her was another woman called Madame de Larnage (less young and less beautiful than Mme du Colombier, but not less lovable) who was supposed to follow her route from Romans, where the latter stopped, up to Bourg St. Andéol near the Pont du St. Esprit.[54] With the timidity one knows I have, one will expect that I did not soon make an acquaintance with brilliant ladies and the attendants who surrounded them: but finally, since we were following the same route, lodging in the same inns, and, since I was forced to present myself at the same table, under penalty of passing for a werewolf, it was inevitable that I would make this acquaintance; thus it was made, and even sooner than I would have wished; for all this crush hardly suited a sick man and above all a sick man of my disposition. But curiosity makes these hussies of women so insinuating that in order to succeed in becoming acquainted with a man they begin by turning his head. Thus it happened to me. Being too much surrounded by her young puppies, Mme du Colombier hardly had time to provoke me, and furthermore it was not worth the effort, because we were going to leave each other; but being less importuned, Mme de Larnage had to make provisions for her route: thus, it was Mme de Larnage who took me in hand, and farewell the poor Jean-Jacques, or rather farewell the fever, the vapors, the polyp, all of them left while I was with her, aside from certain palpitations which remained with me and of which she did not want to cure me. The bad state of my health was the first text of our acquaintance. It was seen that I was sick, it was known that I was going to Montpellier, and it must be that my air and my manners did not announce a debauched man, for it was clear in what followed that I had not been suspected of going there to be treated for venereal disease.[55] Although for a man the condition of sickness is not a great recommendation with Ladies, it nevertheless made me interesting to these. In the morning they sent to inquire about me and to invite me to take chocolate with them; they asked how I had passed the night. One time, in accordance with my praiseworthy custom of speaking without thinking, I answered that I did not know. This answer made them believe that I was mad; they examined me further and this examination did not harm me. One time I heard Mme du Colombier say to her friend, "He lacks experience of the world, but he is amiable." This expression reassured me very much, and caused me to become amiable in fact.

In getting to know one another, one must speak of oneself, say where one came from, who one was. That perplexed me; for I felt very well that among good company and with gallant women[56] the expression "new convert" was going to kill me. I do not know what peculiarity made me take it into my head to pass for an Englishman. I gave myself out as a Jacobite,[57] I was taken for such; I called myself Dudding, and I was called M. Dudding. A cursed Marquis de Torignan who was there, sick like me, old on top of everything, and rather ill-humored, took it into his head to strike up a conversation with M. Dudding.[58] He spoke to me about King James, about the Pretender, about the former Court of Saint Germain. I was on thorns. About all that, I knew only the little I had read in Count Hamilton and in the gazettes;[59] nevertheless I made such good use of this little that I extricated myself from the business: fortunate that they did not take it into their heads to question me about the English language, of which I did not know a single word.

The whole company got along and saw the moment for separating with regret. We made our stages at a snail's pace. One Sunday we found ourselves at St. Marcellin; Mme de Larnage wanted to go to mass, I went with her; that almost spoiled my business. I behaved as I always did.[60] From my modest and meditative countenance, she believed I was devout and acquired the worst opinion in the world of me, as she admitted to me two days later. I needed much gallantry afterwards to efface that bad impression, or rather Mme de Larnage—as a woman of experience and one who was not easily rebuffed—wished very much to run the risk of her advances to see how I would extricate myself from them. She made many to me, and such that, very far from presuming on my appearance, I believed that she was making fun of me. Based on this madness, I committed every possible sort of stupidity; it was worse than the Marquis of *The Legacy*.[61]

Mme de Larnage held fast, flirted with me so much and said such tender things to me, that a much less stupid man might have had a lot of trouble taking all that seriously. The more she did, the more she confirmed me in my idea, and what tormented me still more was that I was on the verge of falling completely in love. I said to myself and I said to her while sighing, "Ah! if only all this were true! I would be the happiest of men." I believe that my simplicity as a novice only inflamed her whim; she did not want to have to disappoint it.

We had left Mme du Colombier and her retinue at Romans. We continued our route in the slowest and most agreeable way in the world, Mme de Larnage, the Marquis de Torignan, and I. Although he was sick and a grumbler, M. de Torignan was a good enough man, but one who did not much like eating bread when others were having a roast. Mme de Larnage hid her taste for me so little that he noticed it sooner than I did myself, and his mischievous sarcasms at least ought to have given me the confidence I did not dare to take from the Lady's kindnesses, if—from a failing of the mind of which I alone was capable—I had not imagined that they were cooperating in order to make fun of me. That foolish idea completely confused my head and made me play the lowest personage in a situation in which my heart, being really smitten, could have set down a rather brilliant one for me. I do not conceive how Mme de Larnage was not put off by my sullenness and did not dismiss me with utter scorn. But she was an intelligent woman who knew how to discern her world, who saw very well that there was more stupidity than indifference in my actions.

Finally she succeeded in making herself understood, and it was not without difficulty that she did so. At Valence we had arrived for dinner, and according to our praiseworthy custom we passed the rest of the day there. We were lodged outside the City at St. Jacques; I will always remember that inn as well as the room Mme de Larnage occupied there. After dinner she wanted to take a walk; she knew that M. de Torignan was not a lively man: this was the way to manage a tête-à-tête for herself that she had very much resolved to turn to account: for there was no more time to lose in order to have some left to take advantage of. We walked around the City along the moats. There I took up again the long history of my complaints, to which she responded with such a tender tone, sometimes pressing against her heart my arm which she held in such a way that a stupidity such as mine was required to prevent me from verifying that she was speaking seriously. What was priceless was that I was excessively agitated myself. I have said that she was lovable; love rendered her charming; it returned to her all the glow of the earliest youth, and she planned her flirting with so much art that she would have seduced a man who was immune to it. Thus I was extremely ill at ease and always on the point of casting off all restraint. But the fear of offending or of displeasing; the still greater fear of being hooted at, hissed, hoodwinked, of furnishing an anecdote for the dinner table, and of being complimented on my undertakings by the pitiless Torignan, held me back to the point of being indignant at my foolish shame myself, and at not being able to vanquish it even while reproaching myself for it. I was on the rack; I had already abandoned my Celadonian[62] remarks, all the ridiculousness of which I felt now that I was well on the way; no longer knowing what countenance to maintain or what to say, I kept quiet; I had a sullen manner; in sum, I did everything necessary to attract the treatment I had dreaded. Fortunately Mme de Larnage arrived at a more humane decision. She brusquely interrupted this silence by putting an arm around my neck, and instantly her mouth spoke too clearly upon mine to leave me in my error. The crisis could not have happened more opportunely. I became lovable. It was time for it. She had given me that confidence the lack of which has almost always kept me from being myself. I was so at that time. Never have my eyes, my senses, my heart and my mouth spoken so well; never have I so fully redressed my wrongs, and if that little conquest had cost Mme de Larnage some effort, I have reason to believe that she did not regret it.

If I live a hundred years I would never recall the remembrance of that charming woman without pleasure. I say charming, although she was neither beautiful nor young; but not being ugly or old either, she had nothing in her appearance that kept her wit and her graces from having all their effect. Completely contrary to other women, what was least fresh about her was her face, and I believe that rouge had spoiled it. She had her reasons for being of easy virtue: it was the way to be valued for her whole worth. One could see her without loving her, but not possess her without adoring her, and that proves, it seems to me, that she was not always as prodigal of her kindnesses as she was with me. She had been seized by a taste too prompt and too lively to be excusable, but into which the heart entered at least as much as the senses, and during the short and delightful time I passed near her I have reason to believe from the compulsory precautions she imposed on me, that, although she was sensual and voluptuous, she preferred my health even to her pleasures.

Our understanding did not escape the Marquis de Torignan. He did not fire on me any less because of it; on the contrary he treated me more than ever as a poor bashful lover, a martyr of the rigors of his Lady. Never did a word, a smile, a look escape him that could make me suspect that he might have found us out, and I would have believed him our dupe, if Mme de Larnage—who saw better than I—had not told me that he was not, but that he was a gallant man; and in fact one could not have more decent thoughtfulness nor comport oneself more politely than he always did, even with regard to me, aside from his jokes, especially after my success: perhaps he attributed the honor to me, and assumed I was less foolish than I had appeared; as has been seen he was mistaken, but no matter; I took advantage of his error, and it is true that, now that the laugh was on my side, I lay myself open wholeheartedly and with good enough grace to his epigrams, and I returned them sometimes even happily, quite proud of doing myself honor in front of Mme de Larnage with the wit she had given me. I was no longer the same man.

We were in a country and a season of good cheer. We enjoyed it excellently everywhere, thanks to M. de Torignan's good efforts. Nevertheless, I would have done without his extending them to our rooms; but he sent his lackey ahead to reserve them, and, either on his own authority or by his master's order, the rascal always lodged him beside Mme de Larnage, and stuck me at the other end of the house; but that hardly vexed me and our assignations were only more piquant because of it. That delightful life lasted four or five days during which I gorged myself, I intoxicated myself with the sweetest pleasures. I tasted them pure, lively, without any mixture of pain, they are the first and only ones I have tasted this way, and I can say that I owe it to Mme de Larnage that I did not die without having known pleasure.

If what I felt for her was not precisely love, it was at least such a tender return for the love she showed me, it was a sensuality so burning in pleasure and an intimacy so sweet in conversations, that it had all the charm of passion without having its delirium which turns the head and causes one not to know how to enjoy. I have felt true love only a single time in my life, and it was not with her. I did not love her as I had loved and as I did love Mme de Warens either; but, for that very reason, I possessed her a hundred times better. With mamma, my pleasure was always troubled by a feeling of sadness, by a secret shrinking of the heart that I overcame[63] only with difficulty; instead of congratulating myself for possessing her, I reproached myself for debasing her. With Mme de Larnage on the contrary, proud of being a man and of being happy I abandoned myself to my senses with joy, with confidence, I shared the impression I made on hers; I was sufficiently myself to contemplate my triumph with as much vanity as voluptuousness, and from that to draw the wherewithal to redouble it.

I do not remember the spot where we left the Marquis de Torignan, who was from that country, but we found ourselves alone before we arrived at Montélimar, and after that Mme de Larnage settled her Chambermaid in my carriage, and I moved over into hers with her. I can assure you that the route did not bore us in this manner, and it would be very difficult for me to say what the country we ran through was like. At Montélimar she had some business which kept her there for three days during which, nevertheless, she left me for only a quarter of an hour for a visit that attracted to her tiresome importunities and invitations that she was careful not to accept. She gave as a pretext an indisposition that nevertheless did not prevent us from going to take a walk every day[64] tête-à-tête in the most beautiful country and under the most beautiful sky in the world. Oh, those three days! I ought to regret them sometimes; I have not known their like since.

Love affairs on journeys are not made to last. It was necessary for us to separate, and I admit that it was time for it; not that I was sated or ready to be; I became more attached every day; but in spite of all the Lady's discretion, I hardly had anything left but good will, and before we separated I wanted to venture this last remainder, which she put up with as a precaution against the girls of Montpellier. We distracted our regrets by means of plans for our reunion. It was decided that since this regimen did me good I would make use of it, and that I would go to pass the winter at Bourg St. Andéol under Mme de Larnage's direction. I should stay at Montpellier for only five or six weeks, to allow her time to prepare things so as to forestall the gossips. She gave me ample instructions about what I should know, about what I should say, about the manner in which I should comport myself. While waiting we were supposed to write to each other. She spoke to me at length and seriously about the care of my health; exhorted me to consult skillful people, to be very attentive to everything they prescribed for me; and undertook to make me carry out their prescription no matter how severe it might be for as long as I was with her. I believe that she spoke to me sincerely, for she loved me: she gave me a thousand proofs of it more certain than favors. She judged from my attire that I was not swimming in opulence; although she was not rich herself, at our separation she wanted to force me to share her purse which she was carrying back from Grenoble rather well-lined, and I had much difficulty keeping myself from sharing it. Finally I left her with my heart full of her, and leaving her, it seems to me, with a genuine attachment for me.

I finished my route by beginning it all over again in my remembrances, and this time very content to be in a good carriage so as to dream about the pleasures I had tasted, and about those promised to me more at my ease. I thought only about Bourg St. Andéol and about the charming life

that awaited me there. I saw only Mme de Larnage and her surroundings. All the rest of the universe was nothing for me, even Mamma had
been forgotten. I occupied myself by combining in my head all the details
into which Mme de Larnage had entered to give me in advance an idea
of her residence, her neighborhood, her social circles, her entire manner
of living. She had a daughter about whom she had spoken to me very
often as an idolizing mother. This girl had passed fifteen years; she was
lively, charming, and had an amiable character. I had been promised that
I would be fawned upon, I had not forgotten that promise and I was
extremely curious to imagine how Mademoiselle de Larnage would treat
her mother's good friend. Such were the subjects of my reveries from
Pont St. Esprit to Remoulin. I had been told to go to see the Pont du
Gard; I did not fail to do so. After a breakfast of excellent figs, I took a
guide and I went to see the Pont du Gard. It was the first work of the
Romans I had seen. I expected to see a monument worthy of the hands
that had constructed it. This time the object surpassed my expectation,
and this was the only time in my life. It belongs only to the Romans
to produce this effect. The sight of this simple and noble work struck
me all the more since it is in the middle of a wilderness where silence
and solitude render the object more striking and the admiration more
lively; for this so-called bridge was only an aqueduct. One asks oneself
what force transported these enormous rocks so far from any quarry, and
brought together the arms of so many thousands of men in a place where
none of them live. I wandered about the three stories of this superb edifice although my respect for it almost kept me from daring to trample it
underfoot. The reverberation of my steps on these immense vaults made
me believe I heard the strong voices of those who had built them. I lost
myself like an insect in that immensity. While making myself small, I felt
an indefinable something that raised up my soul, and I said to myself
while sighing, "Why was I not born a Roman!" I remained there several
hours in a ravishing contemplation. I returned from it distracted and a
dreamer, and this reverie was not favorable to Madame de Larnage. She
had thought of forearming me against the girls of Montpellier, but not
against the Pont du Gard. One never thinks of everything.

At Nîmes I went to see the Arena. It is a much more magnificent work
than the Pont du Gard, and one that made much less of an impression
on me, either because my admiration exhausted itself on the first object
or because the situation of the other in the middle of a city was less
suited to exciting it. This vast and superb circus is surrounded by small
nasty-looking houses, and other houses that are even smaller and more
nasty-looking fill the arena; so that the whole produces only a disparate

and confused effect, in which regret and indignation stifle pleasure and surprise. Since then I have seen the circus of Verona, infinitely smaller and less beautiful than the one at Nîmes, but kept up and conserved with all possible modesty and propriety, which by that very fact made a stronger and more agreeable impression on me. The French do not take care of anything and do not respect any monument. They have all fire for undertaking things and cannot finish or preserve anything.

I was changed to such a point and my sensuality, set into motion, had so well awakened that I stopped for a day at the Pont de Lunel to enjoy good cheer with the company that was found there. This tavern, the most esteemed in Europe, at that time deserved to be so. Those who were keeping it had known how to turn its fortunate location to account for keeping it supplied abundantly and with quality. It was really a curious thing to find, in a house alone and isolated in the middle of the countryside, a table furnished with fresh and salt-water fish, with excellent game, with fine wines, served with that attentiveness and care that are found only in the homes of the noble and the rich, and all that for your thirty-five sous. But the Pont de Lunel did not remain on this footing very long, and as a result of using up its reputation, finally completely lost it.

During my journey I had forgotten that I was sick; I remembered it upon arriving at Montpellier. My vapors were very well cured, but all my other ills remained with me, and although habit rendered me less sensitive to them, there were so many of them that anyone who suddenly found himself attacked by them would believe he was dead. In fact they were less painful than frightening, and made the mind suffer more than the body whose destruction they seemed to announce. That made it so that when I was distracted by lively passions I no longer thought about my condition; but since it was not imaginary, I felt it as soon as I was in cold blood. Thus I thought seriously about Mme de Larnage's advice and about the goal of my trip. I went to consult the most illustrious practitioners, above all M. Fizes, and, from superabundance of precaution, for room and board I established myself with a doctor. He was an Irishman called Fitz-Moris who kept a rather numerous table of medical students,[65] and it was convenient for a sick man to establish himself there, because M. Fitz-Moris was content with a modest charge for food and took nothing from his boarders for his efforts as a Doctor. He took it upon himself to execute M. Fizes's prescriptions and to look after my health. He performed this function very well as for the regimen; one did not get indigestion at that boarding house, and although I am not extremely sensitive to privations of that sort, objects of comparison were so close that I could not keep from noting to myself sometimes that M. de Torignan was a better provider than M. Fitz-Moris. Nevertheless, since we were not dying of hunger, either, and since all those young men were extremely gay; that manner of living really did me some good and kept me from falling back into my languors. I passed the morning by taking drugs, some waters or other, I believe the waters from Vals, and by writing to Mme de Larnage, for the correspondence went on its way, and Rousseau took it upon himself to pick up his friend Dudding's letters. At noon I went to take a walk to La Canourgue with one of our young beginning students who were all very good fellows; we got together again, we went to dine. After dining, an important business occupied most of[66] us until evening: that was to go outside the city to play for the afternoon snack in two or three games of mall. I did not play; I had neither the strength nor the skill for it, but I wagered, and—out of interest from the wager— following our players and their balls across roads that were uneven and full of rocks, I had a pleasant[67] and healthful exercise that entirely suited me. We snacked in a tavern outside the city. I do not need to say that these snacks were gay, but I will add that they were quite modest, even though the girls of the tavern were pretty. Being a great player of mall, M. Fitz-Moris was our president, and I can say that in spite of the bad reputation of students, I found more morals and modesty among all that youth, than it would be easy to find in the same number of grown men. They were more noisy than foul, and more gay than libertines, and I lend myself so easily to a course of life when it is voluntary that I would not have asked for anything better than to see that one last forever. Among these students there were several Irishmen with whom I attempted to learn some English words as a precaution for Bourg St. Andéol; for the time for making my way there was approaching. Mme de Larnage urged me to it with each courier, and I was preparing to obey her. It was clear that my doctors, who had understood nothing about my illness, looked at me as a hypochondriac and treated me on this footing with their china-root, their waters, and their whey. Completely contrary to Theologians, doctors and philosophers admit as true only what they can explain, and make their intelligence the measure of possibilities. These Gentlemen knew nothing about my illness; thus I was not sick: for how can anyone suppose that Scholars do not know everything? I saw that they were seeking only to humor me and make me eat up my money, and judging that their substitute at Bourg St. Andéol would do that fully as well as they did but more pleasantly, I resolved to give preference to her and I left Montpellier with that wise intention.

I left toward the end of November after a stay of six weeks or two months in that city,[68] where I left a dozen Louis without any profit for my health or for my instruction, aside from a course of anatomy begun under M. Fitz-Moris, which I was obliged to abandon because of the horrible stench of the cadavers that were dissected, which I could not bear.

Being ill at ease inside myself about the resolution I had made, I reflected on it while I advanced toward the Pont St. Esprit which was the route to both Bourg St. Andéol and Chambéry. The remembrances of Mamma and her letters, although less frequent than those of Mme de Larnage, awoke in my heart the remorse that I had suppressed during my first journey.[69] While I was returning it became so lively that, counterbalancing the love of pleasure, it put me in a condition to listen to reason alone. First, in the role of an adventurer (which I was going to take up again) I might be less fortunate than the first time; in order to unmask me, in all of Bourg St. Andéol there needed to be only a single person who might have been in England, who was acquainted with the English, or who knew their language. Mme de Larnage's family might become badly disposed toward me, and treat me in a hardly decent manner. Her daughter, about whom I thought more than necessary in spite of myself, made me even more anxious. I trembled at falling in love with her and that fear already accomplished half the job. As the reward for the mother's kindnesses, was I, then, going to corrupt the daughter, enter into the most detestable commerce, bring dissension, dishonor,[70] scandal, and hell into her house? This idea horrified me; I made the firm resolution to combat myself and to vanquish myself if this unfortunate inclination happened to declare itself. But why expose myself to this combat? What a wretched position to live with the mother with whom I would have been sated, and to burn for the daughter without daring to show her my heart? What need was there to go to look for that position, and to expose myself to misfortunes, affronts, remorse for the pleasures whose greatest charm I had exhausted in advance: for it is certain that my whim had lost its first vivacity. The taste for pleasure was still there, but the passion no longer was. To this were mixed reflections relative to my situation, to my duties, to that mamma so good so generous, who—already burdened with debts—was even more burdened with my foolish expenses, who exhausted herself for me and whom I was deceiving so unworthily. This reproach became so lively that it won out in the end. While drawing near St. Esprit, I formed the resolution to go through Bourg St. Andéol without stopping and pass straight on. I executed it[71] courageously, with some sighs, I admit; but also with that internal satisfaction that I tasted for the first time in my life of saying to myself, "I deserve my own esteem, I know how to prefer my duty to my pleasure." This is the first genuine obligation that I had from studying. It was studying that had taught me to reflect, to compare. After such pure principles that I had adopted such a short time before; after the rules of wisdom and virtue that I had made for myself and which I had felt myself so proud of following; the shame of being so little consistent with myself as to give the lie to my own maxims so soon and so emphatically won out over voluptuousness: pride might perhaps have as great a part in my resolution as virtue; but if this pride is not virtue itself it has such similar effects that it is pardonable to mistake it for virtue.[72]

One of the advantages of good actions is to raise up the soul and to dispose it to perform better ones: for such is human weakness that one ought to number among the good actions abstinence from the evil one is tempted to commit. As soon as I had made my resolution I became another man, or rather I became again the one I had been before whom this moment of intoxication had made disappear. Full of good feelings and good resolutions I continued my route with the good[73] intention of expiating my fault; thinking only of regulating my conduct upon the laws of virtue from now on, of dedicating myself without reserve to the service of the best of mothers, of swearing as much fidelity to her as I had attachment for her, and of no longer listening to any other love than that of my duties. Alas! the sincerity of my return to good seemed to promise me a different destiny; but mine was written and already begun, and if my heart—full of love for good and decent things—no longer saw anything but innocence and happiness in life, I was touching the fatal moment that must drag the long chain of my misfortunes after it.

Haste to arrive caused me to make more speed than I had counted on. From Valence I had indicated to her the day and hour of my arrival. Having gained a half day on my calculation, I stayed at Chaparillan for that much time, in order to arrive just at the moment I had noted. I wanted to taste the pleasure of seeing her again in all its charm. I preferred to put it off a little so as to join to it the charm of being expected. That precaution had always succeeded for me. I had always seen my arrival marked by a sort of little holiday: I did not expect one any less this time, and these attentions, which were so gratifying to me, were well worth the trouble of arranging.

Thus I arrived exactly at the time. From far away I looked to see if I might not see her on the road; my heart beat more and more as I drew near. I arrive out of breath, for I had left my carriage in the city: I see no one in the courtyard, at the door, at the window; I begin to get flustered; I dread some accident. I enter; everything is calm; some workers were snacking in the kitchen; otherwise no preparations. The maid appeared surprised to see me, she did not know that I was supposed to arrive. I go upstairs, at last I see her, that dear Mamma so tenderly, so keenly, so purely loved; I run up I throw myself at her feet. "Ah! here you are little one!" she says to me while embracing me, "Have you had a good trip? How are you?" This welcome bewildered me a little. I asked her if she had not received my letter. She told me yes. "I would have thought not," I said to her; and explanation ended there. A young man was with her. I knew him because I had already seen him in the house before my departure: but this time he appeared established there, indeed he was. In short I found my place taken.

This young man was from the Pays de Vaud. His father, called Vintzenried, was caretaker or so-called Captain of the Chateau of Chillon.[74] The son of Monsieur the Captain was a wig-maker's boy and was wandering around the world in that position when he came to present himself to Mme de Warens, who received him well, as she did all those passing through and above all those from her country. He was a big mawkish blonde well enough put together, featureless face, mind the same, speaking like the handsome Liander,[75] mixing all the tones, all the tastes of his station with the long history of his happy conquests; naming only half the Marquises with whom he had slept, and claiming not to have dressed the hair of any pretty women whose husbands he had not also dressed with cuckold's horns. Vain, foolish, ignorant, insolent; for the rest the best fellow in the world. Such was the substitute given for me during my absence, and the partner offered to me after my return.

Oh if souls disengaged from their earthly shackles still see what happens among mortals from the bosom of the eternal light, pardon me dear and respectable shade, if I give no more mercy to your faults than to my own, if I unveil both equally to the readers' eyes. I must be, I want to be truthful for you as for myself; you will always lose much less from it than I will. Ah! how many weaknesses (if the wrongs of your reason alone can be called this) are redeemed by your lovable and sweet character, your inexhaustible kindness of heart, your frankness and all your excellent virtues. You had errors and not vices; your conduct was reprehensible, but your heart was always pure. Put the good and the bad in the scale and be equitable. What other woman, if her secret life was shown like yours, would ever dare compare herself to you.

The newcomer had shown himself zealous, diligent, exact for all those little commissions that were always very numerous; he had made himself the supervisor of her workers. As noisy as I was quiet, he made himself seen and above all heard at the plow, at the hay, in the woods, in the stable, in the Poultry yard all at the same time. He neglected only the garden because it was too peaceful a labor and made no noise at all. His great pleasure was to pick up and carry, to saw or split wood, one always saw him with an axe or pick in his hand; one heard him running, thumping, shouting at the top of his lungs. I do not know how many men's work he did, but he always made the noise of ten or twelve. All this racket made an impression on my poor mamma; she believed this young man was a treasure for her business. Wanting to attach him to herself she used all the means she believed fit for it, and did not forget the one on which she counted the most.

One must know my heart, its most constant, truest feelings, above all the ones that brought me back to her at that moment. What a sudden and complete upheaval in all my being! Put oneself in my place to judge about it. In one moment I saw the whole future of happiness I had depicted for myself vanish forever. All the sweet ideas that I cherished so affectionately disappeared; and I—who since my childhood could see my existence only with hers—I saw myself alone for the first time. This moment was dreadful: the ones that followed it have always been somber. I was still young: but that sweet feeling of enjoyment and hope that invigorates youth left me for ever. Since that time my sensitive being has been half dead. I no longer saw before me anything but the sad remnants of an insipid life, and if sometimes an image of happiness still came into my desires, this happiness was not the one suited to me, I felt that I would not be truly happy if I obtained it.

I was so stupid and my confidence was so full that in spite of the newcomer's familiar tone (which I looked at as an effect of that easy-going disposition of Mamma who drew everyone to her) I would not have taken it into my head to suspect its genuine cause, if she had not told it to me herself; but she hastened to make that admission to me with a frankness capable of adding to my rage, if my heart could have been turned in that direction; finding the thing completely simple herself, reproaching me for my negligence in the house, and citing my frequent absences, as if she had been of a temperament extremely hard-pressed to fill the voids. "Ah, Mamma," I said to her, heartsick with suffering, "of what do you dare to inform me? What reward for an attachment like mine? Have you preserved my life so many times only to deprive me of everything that makes it dear to me? I will die from it, but you will miss me." She answered me in a tone tranquil enough to make me crazy that I was a child, that one does not die at all from such things; that I would lose nothing, that we would not be less good friends because of it, not less intimate in all senses, that her tender attachment [76] for me could diminish or end only with her. In a word, she had me understand that all my rights remained the same, and that, while sharing them with someone else, I was not being deprived of them.

Never have the purity, the truth, the strength of my feelings for her, never the sincerity, the decency of my soul made themselves better felt to me than in that moment. I hurled myself at her feet, I embraced her knees while shedding torrents of tears. "No, mamma," I said to her with rapture, "I love you too much to debase you; your possession is too dear to me to share it: the regrets that accompanied it when I acquired it have increased with my love; no, I cannot preserve it at the same price. You will always have my adorations;[77] always be worthy of them: it is even more necessary for me to honor you than to possess you. It is to yourself, oh Mamma, that I give you up; it is to the union of our hearts that I sacrifice all my pleasures. Might I be able to perish a thousand times, before tasting any pleasures that degraded what I love."

I kept this resolution with a constancy worthy, I dare to say it, of the feeling that had made me form it. From that moment I no longer saw that so dear mamma except with the eyes of a genuine son; and it is to be noted that, although my resolution did not have her secret approbation at all, as I perceived only too well, in order to make me renounce it she never used either insinuating remarks, or blandishments, or any of that skillful flirting that women know how to use without committing themselves, which rarely fails to succeed for them. Reduced to seeking for myself a lot independent of her, and not even being able to imagine one, I soon passed to the other extreme and sought it completely within her. I sought it there so perfectly that I succeeded in almost forgetting myself. The ardent desire to see her happy whatever the cost might be absorbed all my affections: she might well have separated her happiness from mine, I saw it as mine, in spite of her.

Thus began to germinate, along with my misfortunes, the virtues whose seeds were at the bottom of my soul, which study had cultivated, and which awaited only the ferment of adversity in order to bloom. The first fruit of this very disinterested inclination was to draw away from my heart every feeling of hatred and envy against the one who had supplanted me. On the contrary I wanted, and I wanted sincerely, to attach myself to this young man, to form him, to work at his education, to make him feel his happiness, to render him worthy of it if that was possible, and—in a word—to do for him everything that Anet had done for me on a similar occasion. But parity between the persons was lacking. With greater gentleness and enlightenment I did not have Anet's coolness and firmness, nor that strength of character that makes an impression, and which I would have needed to succeed. I found even less in the young man the qualities that Anet had found in me; docility, attachment, gratitude; above all the feeling of the need I had for his efforts and the ardent desire to render them useful. All that was lacking here. The one I wanted to form saw in me only an importunate Pedant who did nothing but babble. On the contrary, he admired himself as an important man in the house, and measuring the services he believed he rendered there by the noise he made, he regarded his axes and his picks as infinitely more useful than all my old books. In a way he was not wrong; but he went from that to giving himself airs that made one die from laughing. With the peasants he set himself up as the country Gentleman, soon he did the same with me, and finally with mamma herself. Since his name of Vintzenried did not appear noble enough to him, he gave it up for that of Monsieur de Courtilles, and it is under this latter name that he has been known since at Chambéry, and in the Maurienne where he married.

In sum, the illustrious personage did so much that he was everything in the house and I nothing. Since it was Mamma and not me whom he scolded when I was unlucky enough to displease him, the fear of exposing her to his brutalities rendered me docile to everything he desired, and every time he split wood—an activity that he performed with a pride without equal—I had to be the idle and tranquil spectator, the admirer of his prowess. This boy, however, was not absolutely of a bad natural disposition; he loved Mamma because it was impossible not to love her; he did not even have an aversion for me, and when the pauses in his impetuous activity allowed us to talk to him, he sometimes listened to us docilely enough, frankly acknowledging that he was nothing but a fool, after which he did not commit any fewer new foolish acts. Besides he had such a limited intelligence and such low tastes that it was difficult to talk reason to him and almost impossible to be pleased with him. To the possession of a woman full of charms, he added the relish of an old chambermaid, redheaded, toothless, whose disgusting service Mamma had the patience to endure, although she made her sick to her stomach. I became aware of this new household arrangement and I was furious with indignation at it: but I became aware of another thing that even affected me much more keenly, and which threw me into a deeper discouragement than everything that had happened up until then. This was Mamma's cooling off with respect to me.

The privation which I had imposed on myself, which she had made a pretense of approving, is one of those things that women do not pardon at all, whatever show they might make, less from the privation that results from it for themselves than from the indifference they see in it for their possession. Take the woman who is most sensible, most philosophic, least attached to her senses: the most irremissible crime that the man whom moreover she desires the least can commit with regard to her, is to be able to possess her and not to do it. There must not be any exceptions to this, since such a natural and such a strong sympathy was impaired in her by an abstinence that had only motives of virtue, attachment, and esteem. From that time I ceased to find in her that intimacy of hearts that always caused the sweetest enjoyment of my own. She no longer unburdened herself with me except when she had to complain about the newcomer; when they got along well together I entered little into her confidences. Finally little by little she took on a manner of being in which I no longer took part. My presence still gave her pleasure, but she no longer needed it, and I might have passed entire days without seeing her, and she would not have noticed it.

Insensibly I felt myself isolated and alone in this same house of which formerly I was the soul and where I lived doubly so to speak. Little by little I got used to separating myself from everything that was done there, even from those who lived there, and to spare myself continuous disturbances, I closed myself up with my books, or else I went to sigh and weep at my ease in the middle of the woods. This life soon became completely unbearable to me. I felt that the personal presence and withdrawal of heart of a woman who was so dear to me aggravated my suffering, and that by ceasing to see her I would feel myself less cruelly separated from her. I formed the project of leaving her house; I told it to her, and far from opposing it she favored it. At Grenoble she had a friend called Madame Deybens whose husband was a friend of M. de Mably, Grand Provost at Lyon.[78] M. Deybens proposed the education of M. de Mably's children to me: I accepted, and I departed for Lyon without leaving or almost feeling the slightest regret at a separation of which the idea alone previously would have given us the pangs of death.

I had just about enough knowledge to be a Tutor and I believed I had the talent. During the year that I passed at M. de Mably's home I had the time to disabuse myself. The gentleness of my natural disposition might have made me fit for this profession if anger did not mix its storms up with it. As long as everything went well and I saw my cares and my efforts succeed then I did not stint at all, I was an angel. I was a Devil when things went amiss. When my students did not understand me I raved, and when they showed mischievousness I would have killed them: this was not the way to make them learned and well-behaved. I had two of them; they had very different dispositions. One, eight or nine years old called *Ste. Marie*, had a pretty face, rather open mind, rather lively, giddy, playful, mischievous, but of a gay mischief. The Younger called *Condillac*[79] appeared almost stupid, dawdling, stubborn as a mule, and not able to learn anything. One can judge that between these two subjects I did not do a good piece of work. With patience and coolness perhaps I might have been able to succeed; but for lack of both I did nothing worthwhile and my students turned out very badly. I did not lack assiduousness, but I lacked evenness, above all prudence. With them I knew how to use only three instruments that are always useless and often pernicious with children, feeling, reasoning, anger.[80] Sometimes with Ste. Marie I became softened to the point of crying; I wanted[81] to soften him himself as if childhood were susceptible to a genuine emotion of the heart: sometimes I wore myself out speaking reason to him as if he could understand me, and since he sometimes made me very subtle arguments, I took him as entirely reasonable, because he was a reasoner. Little Condillac was even more vexing; because—understanding nothing, answering nothing, moved by nothing, and of an unwearying obstinacy—he never triumphed over me better than when he had put me in a rage; then it was he who was the wise man and it was I who was the child. I saw all my faults, I felt them; I studied the mind of my students, I entered into them very well, and I do not believe that I was ever the dupe of their ruses a single time: but what good did it do me to see the evil, without knowing how to apply the remedy? While seeing through everything, I prevented nothing, I succeeded in nothing, and all I did was precisely what it was necessary not to do.

I hardly succeeded better for myself than for my students. I had been recommended to Mme de Mably by Mme Deybens. She had asked her to form my manners and to give me the tone of the social world; she made some efforts in this and wanted me to learn to do the honors of her house; but I set about it so clumsily, I was so bashful, so foolish that she became discouraged and left me in the lurch. This did not prevent me from falling in love with her in accordance with my custom. I did so enough for her to notice it, but I never dared to declare myself; she did not feel in the mood to make the advances, and I was in the mood for my sidelong glances and my sighs, with which soon even I was bored[82] seeing that they were not leading to anything.

At mamma's house I had completely lost the taste for little knavish tricks, because since everything was mine, I had nothing to steal. Moreover the elevated principles that I had constructed for myself ought to have rendered me henceforth very superior to such base acts, and it is certain that since then I have ordinarily been so: But this is less from having learned to vanquish my temptations than from having cut their root, and

I would be in great fear of stealing as in my childhood if I were subject to the same desires. I had the proof of that at M. de Mably's house.[83] Surrounded by little things that would have been easy to steal which I did not even look at, I took it into my head to covet a certain very nice little white wine from Arbois, to which I bad become attracted as a result of several glasses of it that I had drunk at table from time to time. It was a little cloudy; I believed I knew how to clarify wine very well, I boasted about it; they entrusted that one to me; I clarified it and spoiled it, but only to the eyes. It still remained pleasant to drink, and the occasion made me appropriate several bottles from time to time to drink at my ease in my little private quarters. Unfortunately I have never been able to drink without eating. What to do to have some bread? It was impossible for me to put some aside. To have the lackeys buy some was to betray myself and almost to insult the master of the house. I never dared to buy any myself. A fine Gentleman with a sword at his side go into a bakery to buy a piece of bread, could that be done? In the end I remembered the makeshift of a great Princess to whom it was said that the peasants had no bread, and who answered, "Let them eat cake."[84] I bought some cake. Still what a fuss to achieve that! Having gone out alone with this plan, I sometimes wandered around the whole city and passed in front of thirty pastry shops before entering one. There had to be only a single person in the shop, and her physiognomy had to attract me very much for me to dare to cross the threshold. But also, once I had my dear little cake and was well closed up in my room, I went to find my bottle at the bottom of a closet, what good little drinking bouts I had there all alone while reading some pages of a novel. For to read while eating has always been my whim for lack of a tête-à-tête. It is the compensation for the society I lack. I alternately devour a page and a bite: it is as if my book was dining with me.

I have never been dissolute or crapulous, and have never been drunk in my life. Thus my little thefts were not extremely indiscreet: nevertheless they were discovered; the bottles betrayed me. They did not let on to me; but I no longer had the management of the cellar. In all this M. de Mably behaved decently and prudently. He was a very gallant man, who, under an appearance as harsh as his job, had a genuine gentleness of character and a rare kindness of heart. He was judicious, equitable, and, what one would not expect from an officer in the Mounted Constabulary, even very humane. In feeling his indulgence I became more attached to him because of it, and that made me prolong my stay in his house more than I would have done otherwise. But at last, disgusted with a profession for which I was not fit and with a very bothersome situation that had nothing pleasant for me, after a year of trying during which I did not spare my efforts at all, I decided to leave my disciples, very convinced that I would never succeed at bringing them up well. M. de Mably himself saw that fully as well as I did. Nevertheless, I believe that he might never have taken it upon himself to send me back if I had not spared him the trouble, and I assuredly do not approve of such an excess of accommodativeness in such a case.

What rendered my condition more unbearable was the continuous comparison that I made between it and the one I had left; it was the remembrance of my dear les Charmettes, of my garden, my trees, my fountain, my orchard, and above all of her for whom I had been born and who gave a soul to all that. In thinking about her again, about our pleasures, about our innocent life, I was struck by pangs of the heart, suffocation that deprived me of the courage to do anything. A hundred times I had been violently tempted to leave at the instant and on foot to return to her; I would have been content to die at the very instant on condition that I see her again one more time. In the end I could not resist these very tender remembrances which called me back to her whatever the cost might be. I told myself that I had not been patient enough, accommodating enough, affectionate enough, that I could still live happily in a very sweet friendship by putting more of myself into it than I had done. I form the most beautiful plans in the world, I burn to execute them. I desert everything, I renounce everything; I leave; I fly, I arrive in all the same raptures of my first youth, and I find[85] myself at her feet once more. Ah, I would have died of joy there if I had once again found in her welcome,[86] in her caresses, in sum in her heart, a quarter of what I had found there before, which I still brought back to it.

Horrible illusion of human things! She still received me with her excellent heart which could die only with her: but I was coming to look for the past which was no longer and which could not be reborn. I had hardly stayed with her for half an hour when I felt my former happiness to be dead forever. Again I found myself in the same distressing situation I had been forced to flee, and that, without me being able to say that it was anyone's fault; for at bottom Courtille was not bad, and appeared to see me again with more pleasure than sorrow. But how could I allow myself to be a supernumerary near her for whom I had been everything, and who could not cease being everything for me? How could I live as a stranger in the house whose child I was? The sight of objects that witnessed my past happiness rendered the comparison more cruel for me. I would have suffered less in another dwelling place. But to see myself ceaselessly recalling so many sweet remembrances was to irritate the feeling of my losses. Consumed by vain regrets, abandoned to the blackest melancholy, I reacquired the way of life of staying alone aside from meal-times. Closed up with my books, I sought useful distractions in them, and feeling the peril I had formerly feared so much to be imminent, I tormented myself once again by seeking within myself for means to provide for the time when mamma would no longer have any resources. I had put things in her house on a footing to go on without growing worse; but since I had left everything had changed. Her Household-manager was a spendthrift. He wanted to shine: a good horse, good outfit, he loved to display himself nobly to the neighbors' eyes; he made continuous undertakings in things about which he understood nothing. The pension was eaten up in advance, its quarterly payments were committed, the rents were in arrears, and the debts went along on their course. I foresaw that the pension would be seized before long[87] and perhaps suppressed. In sum, I envisaged nothing but ruin and disasters, and to me the moment for them seemed so close that I felt all its horrors in advance.

My dear Study was my only distraction. As a result of looking there for remedies against the trouble of my soul I took it into my head to look there for some against the ills I foresaw, and returning to my former ideas, behold me building new Castles in Spain to extricate that poor Mamma from the cruel extremities into which I saw her ready to fall. I did not feel myself learned enough and did not believe myself to have enough intelligence to shine in the republic of letters and make a fortune by that method. A new idea that presented itself inspired me with the confidence that the mediocrity of my talents could not give me. I had not abandoned music when I had ceased to teach it. On the contrary, I had studied its theory enough to be able to regard myself at least as learned in that portion. By reflecting on the trouble I had had in learning to decipher notes, which I still had in singing by sight reading, I came to think that this difficulty might very well come from the thing as much as from me, knowing above all that in general learning music was not an easy thing for anyone. While examining the constitution of the signs I often found them extremely badly invented. A long time earlier I had thought of noting the scale by numbers in order to avoid having always to trace the lines and staffs when I needed to note down the slightest little Tune. I had been stopped by the difficulty of the octaves, and by that of the measure and quantities. That old idea returned into my mind, and when I thought about it again I saw that these difficulties were not insurmountable. I pondered them with success and I succeeded in noting any music whatsoever by my numbers with the greatest simplicity. From that moment I believed my fortune made, and in the ardor to share it with her to whom I owed everything, I thought only of leaving for Paris, not doubting that I would cause a revolution by presenting my project to the Academy. I had brought back some money from Lyon; I sold my books. In fifteen days my resolution was made and executed. At last, full of the magnificent ideas that had inspired me with it, and always the same at all times, I left Savoy with my System of music, as I had formerly left Turin with my Hiero-fountain.[88]

Such have been the errors and faults of my youth. I have narrated their history with a fidelity with which my heart is content. If in what followed I honored my mature age with some virtues, I would have told them with the same frankness and that was my plan. But I must stop here. Time can lift many veils. If my memory reaches posterity, perhaps one day it will learn what I had to say. Then it will be known why I am silent.

END [89]

These notebooks which are full of errors of every sort and which I have not even had the time to reread are enough to put every friend of the truth onto its track, and to give him the means of making sure of it by his own investigations. Unfortunately it appears to me difficult and even impossible for them to escape the vigilance of my enemies. If they fall into the hands of an honest man [even if he is one of M. de Choiseul's friends, even if they reach M. de Choiseul himself, I do not believe that the honor of my memory still has no resort.[1] But oh Heaven, protector of innocence, defend these last pieces of information about my innocence from the hands of the Ladies de Boufflers, de Verdelin, from those of their friends.[2] Rescue at least from these two furies the memory of an unfortunate man whom you abandoned to them during his life.][3]

THE CONFESSIONS
OF J.-J. ROUSSEAU

Intus, et in Cute[4]

SECOND PART

Book VII

[**1.**]1.[5] After two years of silence and patience, in spite of my resolutions, I am taking up the pen again.[6] Reader, suspend your judgment about the reasons that have forced me to do it. You can judge about them after you have read me.

2. My peaceful youth has been seen to flow by in an even life that was sweet enough, without great setbacks or great prosperity. That ordinariness was in large part the work of my ardent but feeble natural character, even less prompt to undertake than it was easy to discourage, leaving repose as a result of jolts, but returning to it out of lassitude and taste, and which, always leading me back—far from great virtues and still farther from great vices—to the idle and tranquil life for which I felt myself born, never allowed me to attain anything great, either for good or for evil.

3. What a different picture I will soon have to develop![7] Fate, which favored my inclinations for thirty years, contradicted them for another thirty, and from this continuous opposition between my situation and my inclinations, one will see born enormous faults, unparalleled misfortunes, and all the virtues, except strength, which can honor adversity.[8]

4. My first part was written entirely from memory and I must have made many errors in it. Forced to write the second from memory also, I will probably make many more. The sweet remembrances of my fine years which passed with both tranquillity and innocence,[9] left me a thousand charming impressions which I love to recall ceaselessly. It will soon be seen how different are the ones from the remainder of my life. To recall them is to renew their bitterness. Far from sharpening the bitterness of my situation by these sad recollections, I ward them off as much as I can, and often I succeed in doing so to such an extent that I cannot find them again when I need to. This facility of forgetting evils is a consolation which Heaven has arranged for me amidst those which fate was to heap up on me one day. My memory, which retraces only pleasant objects, is the happy counterweight to my frightened imagination, which makes me foresee only cruel futures.

5. Because they have passed into other hands, all the papers I had assembled to supplement my memory and guide me in this undertaking will not return into mine again. I have only one faithful guide upon which I

can count; that is the chain of feelings which have marked the succession of my being, and,[10] by means of them, the succession of events which have been their cause or effect. I easily forget my misfortunes, but I cannot forget my faults, and I forget my good feelings even less. Their remembrance is too dear to me ever to be effaced from my heart. I can make omissions in the facts, transpositions, errors of dates; but I cannot deceive myself about what I have felt, or about what my feelings have made me do; and that is what is principally at issue. The particular object of my confessions is to make my interior known exactly in all the situations of my life. It is the history of my soul I have promised, and to write it faithfully I need no other memories: it is enough for me to return inside myself, as I have done up to this point.

6. Nevertheless, and very fortunately, there is an interval of six or seven years for which I have reliable information in a transcribed collection of letters the originals of which are in the hands of M. du Peyrou.[11] This collection, which ends in 1760, covers the whole time of my stay at the Hermitage, and of my big falling out with my self-proclaimed friends: a memorable epoch in my life and one which was the source of all my other misfortunes. With regard to more recent original letters which I have left, and of which there are very few, instead of transcribing them after the collection, which is too voluminous for me to be able to hope to shield from the vigilance of my Arguses,[12] I will transcribe them in this very writing, when they appear to me to furnish some enlightenment,[13] either to my advantage or against me: for I do not fear that the reader will ever forget that I am making my confessions and thereby believe that I am making my apology;[14] but[15] he ought not to expect me to keep silent about the truth either, when it speaks in my favor.

7. Moreover this second part does not have anything in common with the first except this same truth, nor any advantage over it but through the importance of things. Aside from that, it can only be inferior to it in every way. I wrote the first with pleasure, willingly, at my ease, at Wootton or in the Chateau of Trye:[16] all the remembrances I had to recall were so many new enjoyments.[17] I returned to them endlessly with a new pleasure, and I was able to shape my descriptions without bother until I was satisfied with them. Today my weakened memory and head render me almost incapable of any labor; I pay attention to this one only by force and am sick at heart from distress. It offers me nothing but misfortunes, betrayals, perfidies, saddening, and heart-rending remembrances. I would give anything in the world to be able to shroud in the night of time what I have to say, and, now that I am forced to speak in spite of

myself, I am still reduced to hiding myself, to resorting to trickery, to try-ing to lead astray, to lowering myself to things for which I was least born; the ceiling under which I live has eyes, the walls that encircle me have ears, surrounded by spies and malevolent and vigilant watchers, anxious and distraught I hastily [18] throw on to the paper some interrupted words which I barely have time to reread, still less to correct. I know that, in spite of the immense barriers that are heaped up endlessly around me, it is always feared that the truth will escape through some fissure. How can I go about making it pierce through? I am attempting to do so with little hope of success. Judge whether there is enough in this to make agreeable pictures and give them a very attractive coloration! Thus I warn those who would like to begin this reading that as they pursue it nothing can protect them against boredom, unless it is the desire to finish knowing a man, and the sincere love of justice and truth.[19]

[**2.1.**][20] In my First Part I left myself reluctantly departing for Paris, leaving my heart at les Charmettes, building my last Castle in Spain there, planning some day to return to Mamma's feet having brought back to her the Treasures I would have acquired, and counting on my system of music as an assured fortune.

[**2.**] I stopped at Lyon for some time to see my acquaintances there, to procure some recommendations for myself for Paris, and to sell my Geometry books which I had brought with me.[21] Everyone made me wel-come. M. and Mme de Mably showed some pleasure at seeing me again, and had me to dinner several times. At their home I became acquainted with the Abbé de Mably, as I had already done with the Abbé de Condil-lac, who both had come to see their brother.[22] The Abbé de Mably gave me some letters for Paris, among others one for M. de Fontenelle and one for the Comte de Quailus.[23] Both were very pleasant acquaintances for me, above all the former who, until his death, did not cease showing me [24] friendship and in our tête-à-têtes giving me advice of which I should have taken better advantage.

[**3.**] I saw M. Bordes again, with whom I had been acquainted for a long time, and who had often obliged me wholeheartedly and with the truest pleasure.[25] On this occasion I found him still the same. It was he who had me sell my books, and he gave me by himself or procured for me some good recommendations for Paris.

[**4.**][26] I saw M. the Intendant again, whose acquaintance I owed to M. Bordes, and to whom I owed that of M. the Duc de Richelieu who passed through Lyon at that time.[27] M. Pallu introduced me to him. M. de

Richelieu received me well and told me to go see him at Paris; which I did several times, nevertheless that high acquaintance, about which I will often speak in what follows, was never useful to me for anything.[28]

[5.] I saw the Musician David who had done me a service in my distress during one of my previous trips.[29] He had loaned or given me a cap and some stockings which I have never returned to him and which he has never asked me to give back, although we have often seen each other again since that time.[30] However, later on I gave him a gift that was just about equivalent. I would say more than this if the question here were what I should have done; but it is what I have done, and unfortunately that is not the same thing.

[6.] I saw the noble and generous Perrichon again, and not without experiencing his ordinary magnificence, for he made me the same gift he had formerly made to the noble Bernard, by defraying my place in the stage coach.[31] I saw the Surgeon Parisot again, the best and the best-acting of men; I saw his dear Godefroi whom he kept for ten years, and whose sweetness of character and kindness of heart made up just about her only merit; but whom one could not meet without taking an interest in, nor leave without being moved; for she was in the final period of a consumption from which she died a little after. Nothing shows a man's true inclinations better than the sort of attachments he forms.* When one had seen the sweet Godefroi, one knew the good Parisot.

[7.] I had an obligation to all these decent people. Later on I neglected all of them. Certainly not out of ingratitude, but out of that invincible laziness which has often given me its appearance. The feeling of their services has never left my heart; but it would have cost me less to prove my gratitude to them than to bear witness to it assiduously. Exactitude in writing has always been beyond my strength;[33] as soon as I begin to slacken, shame and embarrassment at making up for my fault make me aggravate it, and I no longer write at all. Thus, I have been silent and I have appeared to forget them. Parisot and Perrichon have not even paid attention to it, and I have always found them the same; but it will be seen twenty years afterwards in M. Bordes to what point the amour-propre of a fine wit can carry vengeance when he believes himself neglected.

---

*Unless he was mistaken in his choice at first, or the one to whom he was attached changed her character by a conjunction of extraordinary causes; which is not absolutely impossible. If one wanted to accept this consequence without modification it would thus be necessary to judge Socrates by his wife Xanthippe and Dion by his friend Calippus, which would be the most iniquitous and false judgment one could ever make. Moreover, set aside here any application injurious to my wife. She is, it is true, very limited and easier to fool than I had believed; but as for her character, pure, excellent, without malice, it is worthy of all my esteem, and will have it as long as I live.[32]

[8.] Before leaving Lyon I ought not to forget a lovable person whom I saw there again with more pleasure than ever and who left very tender remembrances in my heart. It is Mlle Serre about whom I spoke in my First Part[34] and with whom I had renewed my acquaintance while I was at M. de Mably's. Having more leisure on this trip, I saw her more; my heart was captured, and very keenly. I had some grounds for thinking that hers was not against me; but she granted me a confidence which removed from me the temptation to abuse it. She did not have anything; neither did I; our situations were too similar for us to be able to be united, and in the intention that occupied me I was very far from thinking of marriage. She informed me that a young merchant[35] called M. Genève[36] appeared to want to be attached to her. I saw him at her house once or twice; he appeared to me to be a decent man, he passed for one. Persuaded that she would be happy with him, I wanted him to marry her, as he did afterwards; and in order not to trouble their innocent loves I hastened to leave, making prayers for the happiness of that charming person which, alas, were granted here below for only a very short time: for I learned afterward that she had died at the end of two or three years of marriage.[37] Occupied by my tender regrets during my whole route I felt, and I have often felt when I have thought it over since then, that if the sacrifices one makes to duty and virtue are costly to make, one is well paid for them by the sweet remembrances they leave at the bottom of the heart.

[3.] 1.[38] Just as I had seen the unfavorable side of Paris on my previous trip, on this one I saw its brilliant side, although not with regard to my lodging; for, based on an address that M. Bordes had given me, I went to lodge at the hotel St. Quentin rue des Cordiers near the Sorbonne, a nasty street, nasty hotel, nasty room; but where nevertheless men of merit had lodged, such as Gresset,[39] Bordes, the Abbés de Mably, de Condillac, and several others unfortunately none of whom I found there any longer; but I did find a M. de Bonnefond, a country squire, lame, litigious, playing the purist, to whom I owed the acquaintance of M. Roguin, now the Eldest of my friends, and through him that of the philosopher Diderot, about whom I will have much to say in what follows.

2. I arrived at Paris in the autumn of 1741 with fifteen silver louis ready money, my Play *Narcissus* and my musical project as my only resources, and consequently having little time to lose to try to profit from them. I hurried to turn my recommendations to account. A young man who arrives in Paris with a passable appearance and who is heralded for his talents is always sure of being welcomed. I was; that procured me pleasures without leading me to anything great. Of all the people to whom I

was recommended only three were useful to me. M. Damesin, a Savoyard Gentleman, then equerry and I believe favorite of Mme the Princesse de Carignan; M. de Bose, secretary of the academy of inscriptions and keeper of the medals of the King's chambers; and Father Castel, a Jesuit author of the ocular clavichord.[40] All these recommendations except that of M. Damesin came to me from the Abbé de Mably.[41]

3. M. Damesin provided for my most urgent needs through two acquaintances he procured for me. One, M. de Gasc President *à Mortier* of the Parlement of Bordeaux, who played the violin very well: the other, M. the Abbé de Leon who then lodged in the Sorbonne; a very amiable young Lord, who died in the prime of his life after having shone in the world for several moments under the name of Chevalier de Rohan.[42] Both had a whim for learning composition. I gave them several months of lessons which sustained my shrinking purse a little. The Abbé de Leon acquired a friendship for me and wanted to have me as his secretary: but he was not rich and in all he could offer only eight hundred francs which I refused, very regretfully, but which could not suffice for my lodging, my nourishment, and my upkeep.

4. M. de Bose received me extremely well. He loved learning, he had some, but he was a bit of a pedant. Mme de Bose could have been his daughter; she was brilliant and affected. I dined there sometimes; one could not have a more awkward and foolish manner than I had with regard to her. Her casual bearing intimidated me and rendered mine more laughable. When she offered me a plate, I modestly stuck out my fork to stab a little piece of what she offered me, so that she returned the plate she had intended for me to her lackey while turning away so that I would not see her laugh. She hardly suspected that there was any intelligence in this Bumpkin's head. M. de Bose presented me to his friend M. de Réaumur, who came to dine with him every Friday, the day of the Academy of the Sciences.[43] He spoke to him about my project and of the desire I had to submit it to the Academy's examination. M. de Réaumur took on the proposal which was accepted; on the given day I was introduced and presented by M. de Réaumur, and the same day August 22, 1742, I had the honor of reading to the Academy the Memorandum I had prepared for this.[44] Although this illustrious assembly was assuredly very imposing, I was much less intimidated there than in front of Mme de Bose, and I passably extricated myself from my readings and my answers. The Memorandum succeeded, and attracted compliments to me which surprised me as much as they flattered me, since I found it hard to imagine that an Academy would find that anyone who did not belong to it could have common sense. The Commissioners they gave me were Messieurs de

Mairan, Hellot, and de Fouchy. All three people of merit certainly; but not one of whom knew music, at least enough to be in a position to judge concerning my project.[45]

5. During my conferences with these Gentlemen I became convinced with as much certainty as surprise that if learned people sometimes have fewer prejudices than other men, in return they hold on even more strongly to the ones they do have. However weak, however false the majority of their objections might be, and although I responded to them, timidly, I admit, and in bad terms, but with peremptory arguments, I did not succeed a single time in making myself understood and satisfying them. I was always dumbfounded by the ease with which they refuted me with the aid of some sonorous phrases without having understood me. Somehow or other they dug up the fact that a monk called Father Souhaitti had formerly imagined noting the Scale by numbers.[46] This was enough for them to claim that my System was not new; and so much for that; for although I had never heard of Father Souhaitti, and although his way of writing the seven notes of the Plain Chant without even dreaming about octaves in no way deserved to enter in parallel with my simple and convenient invention for easily noting with numbers any music imaginable, keys, silences, octaves, measures, tempos, and length of the notes; things about which Souhaitti had not even dreamed; nevertheless it was very true to say that as for the elementary expression of the seven notes he was its first inventor. But aside from the fact that they attributed more importance to that primitive invention than it had, they did not stop there, and as soon as they wanted to talk about the basis of the System, they did nothing more than talk nonsense. The biggest advantage of mine was to do away with transpositions and Keys, so that the same piece was noted and transposed at will into whatever pitch one wanted by means of a presumed change of a single initial letter at the front of the tune. These Gentlemen had heard it said among the note scrapers of Paris that the method of executing by transposition was worthless. They departed from this to turn my System's most marked advantage into an invincible objection against it, and they decided that my note was good for the vocal and bad for the instrumental; instead of deciding as they ought to have done that it was good for the vocal and better for the instrumental. Based on their report the Academy granted me a certificate full of very fine compliments, through which one discerned at bottom, that it judged my System to be neither new nor useful. I did not think that I ought to use such a piece to adorn the work entitled *Dissertation on Modern Music* with which I appealed to the public.

6. On that occasion I had cause to remark how much, in order to judge

well about a thing, unique but profound knowledge of it, even along with a limited mind, is preferable to all the enlightenment given by the cultivation of the Sciences, unless one joins this enlightenment to the particular study of the subject at issue. The only solid objection that could be made to my System was made by Rameau. Hardly had I explained it to him when he saw its weak point. "Your signs," he said to me, "are very good, in that they determine the length simply and clearly, in that they represent the intervals plainly and always show the simple in the redoubled, all things not done by the ordinary notation: but they are bad in that they demand an operation of the mind which cannot always follow the rapidity of execution."[47] "The position of our notes," he continued, "depicts itself to the eye without the conjunction of this operation. If two notes, one very high, the other very low, are joined by a passage of intermediary notes, at the first glance I see the progress from one to the other by conjoined degrees;[48] but in order to assure myself of this passage with you, I must necessarily run through all your numbers one after the other; the glance cannot take its place at all." The objection appeared unanswerable to me, and I acknowledged it instantly: although it might be simple and striking, only a great practice of the art could suggest it, and it is not surprising that it did not come from any Academician; but it is the case that all these great learned men who know so many things, know so little that each one ought to judge only about his own profession.

7. My frequent visits to my Commissioners and to other academicians put me in a position to make the acquaintance of all the most distinguished literary people in Paris, and from this I had already made their acquaintance when I suddenly found myself enrolled among them later on. As for the present, having concentrated on my System of music, I persisted in wanting to make a revolution in that art with it, and in that way to arrive at a celebrity which in the fine arts is always joined with fortune at Paris. I shut myself up in my room and worked for two or three months with an inexpressible ardor to recast the memorandum that I had read to the Academy into a work intended for the public. The difficulty was to find a book dealer who wanted to take on my manuscript; since there were some expenses to pay for the new characters, since book dealers do not throw their *écus* at the head of beginners, and since it nevertheless seemed to me very just that my work return to me the bread I had eaten while writing it.

8. Bonneford procured for me Quillau the father who made an agreement of half profit with me, without counting the privilege for which I paid by myself.[49] This Quillau managed things so that I lost the cost of my privilege and never drew a *liard*[50] from this Edition which in all

likelihood had a mediocre sale, although the Abbé Desfontaines[51] promised me that he would make it succeed, and the other Journalists said enough good things about it.

9. The biggest obstacle to a trial of my System was the fear that if it was not accepted, the time put into learning it might be lost. To that I said that the practice of my notation made the ideas so clear that for learning music with ordinary characters one would still gain[52] time by beginning with mine. To give proof of this by experiment, I taught music for free to a young American called Mlle Desroulins, whose acquaintance M. Roguin had procured for me; in three months she was capable of deciphering any music whatsoever by means of my notation, and even of singing at sight better than myself everything that was not[53] burdened with difficulties. This success was striking, but unknown. Someone else would have filled up the journals with it; but with some talent for finding useful things, I have never had it for turning them to account.

10. That is how my Hiero-fountain broke again; but this second time I was thirty years old,[54] and I found myself on the pavement of Paris, where one does not live for nothing. The decision I made in this extremity will surprise only those who have not read my first part well. I had just given myself exertions as great as they were useless; I needed to catch my breath. Instead of surrendering to despair, I calmly abandoned myself to my laziness and to the cares of providence, and so as to give it time to do its work, I began to eat up the several Louis I still had left without hurrying, regulating the expense of my careless pleasures without retrenching it, going to the café only every other day, and to a play only two times a week. With regard to expense for girls I had no reform to make there, not having spent a *sou* in that way in my life, except for a single time, about which I will soon have to speak.[55]

11. The security, the voluptuousness, the confidence with which I abandoned myself to this indolent and solitary life, which I did not have means enough to make last for three months, is one of the singularities of my life and one of the peculiarities of my disposition. The extreme need I had for someone to think about me[56] was precisely what deprived me of the courage to show myself, and the necessity of making visits rendered them unbearable to me to the point that I even ceased seeing the Academicians and other literary people with whom I had already insinuated myself. Marivaux, the Abbé de Mably, Fontenelle were almost[57] the only ones to whose homes I continued to go sometimes. I even showed my Play *Narcissus* to the first. He liked it, and had the kindness to touch it up. Diderot, younger than they, was about my age. He loved music; he knew theory; we talked about it together; he also talked to me about his

projects for works. That soon formed between us more intimate connections which lasted fifteen years, and which probably would still endure if unfortunately and very much through his fault, I had not been thrown into his own profession.[58]

12. One would not imagine how I used this short and precious interval I still had left before being forced to beg for my bread: by learning by heart passages from the Poets, which I had learned a hundred times and forgotten as many. Every morning around ten o'clock I went to take a walk at Luxembourg, a Virgil or a Rousseau in my pocket, and then until time to dine I memorized sometimes a sacred Ode and sometimes a Bucolic, without losing heart at the fact that while I was running through the one for the day I did not fail to forget the one from the day before. I recalled that after the defeat of Nicias at Syracuse, the Athenian captives[59] earned their living by reciting Homer's Poems.[60] The use I made of this stroke of erudition was to exercise my propitious memory to retain all the Poets by heart in order to protect myself against poverty.

13. I had another no less solid expedient in Chess to which I regularly dedicated the afternoons at Maugis[61] on the days I did not go to a play. There I made the acquaintance of M. de Légal, of a M. Husson, of Philidor, of all the great chess players of that time, and did not become more skillful from it. I did not doubt, nevertheless, that in the end I would become stronger than all of them, and in my view that was enough to serve as a resource for me. Whatever foolishness I became infatuated with, I always brought the same manner of reasoning to it. I said to myself, "Whoever excels in something is always sure of being sought after. Be first, then, in anything at all; I will be sought after; opportunities will present themselves, and my merit will do the rest." This childishness was not the sophism of my reason, it was that of my indolence. Frightened of the great and rapid efforts I would have needed to make in order to exert myself, I tried to flatter my laziness, and I veiled its shamefulness from myself by means of arguments worthy of it.

1.[62] I calmly waited for the end of my money this way, and I believe that I would have arrived at the last sou without getting any more alarmed if Father Castel, whom I sometimes went to see on my way to the café, had not roused me from my lethargy. Father Castel was crazy, but a good man on the whole: he was angry at seeing me consumed this way without doing anything. He said to me, "Since the musicians, since the Learned do not sing in unison with you, change strings and see the women. Perhaps you will succeed better on that side. I have spoken about you to Mme de Beuzeval;[63] go see her in my name. She is a good woman who will be pleased to see a countryman of her son and her husband. At her house you will see her daughter Mme de Broglie, who is an intelligent woman. Mme Dupin is another one to whom I have spoken about you also: bring her your work; she wants to see you, and will receive you well. One does nothing in Paris except by means of women. They are like the curves of which wise men are the asymptotes; they ceaselessly approach them, but they never touch them."

2.[64] After having put off this terrible conscripted labor from one day to another,[65] at last I took courage, and I went to see Mme de Beuzenwal. She received me with kindness: when Mme de Broglie entered her room, she said to her, "My daughter, this is M. Rousseau about whom Father Castel has spoken to us." Mme de Broglie paid me a compliment on my work, and leading me to her clavichord, made me see that she had paid attention to it. Seeing from her clock that it was almost one o'clock I wanted to go away. Mme de Beuzenval said to me, "You are far from your neighborhood, stay; you will dine here." I accepted without any urging. A quarter of an hour later, I understood from something that was said that the dinner to which she was inviting me was that of her Servants. Mme de Beuzenwal was a very good woman, but limited, and, too full of her illustrious Polish nobility, she had little idea of the consideration owed to talents. On that occasion she even judged me by my bearing more than by my outfit, which, although very simple was extremely neat, did not at all announce a man made to dine with the Servants. I had forgotten the way there too long ago to want to relearn it. Without letting all my resentment be seen, I said to Mme de Beuzenwal that a little business which I had just remembered called me back to my neighborhood, and I wanted to leave. Mme de Broglie drew near her mother, and said several words in her ear that had an effect. Mme de Beuzenwal stood up to hold me back, and said to me, "I count upon you doing us the honor of dining with us." I believed that playing the proud man would be playing the fool, and I stayed. Besides, Mme de Broglie's kindness had touched me and rendered her interesting to me. I was extremely glad to dine with her, and I hoped that in getting to know me better, she would not regret having procured me that honor. M. the President de Lamoignon, a great friend of the house, was also dining there.[66] Like Mme de Broglie he had that little jargon of Paris, all in small talk, all in little delicate allusions. There was no way for the poor Jean-Jacques to shine in this. I had the good sense to not to wish to play the pleasing man when Minerva was opposed, and I kept quiet. Fortunate! If only I had always been so wise. I would not be in the abyss I am in today.

3.[67] I was devastated by my coarseness, and by not being able to justify in Mme de Broglie's eyes what she had done in my favor. After dinner I took my ordinary resource into my head. In my pocket I had a letter in verse written to Parisot during my stay in Lyon.[68] This piece was not lacking in warmth; I put some into my manner of reciting it, and I made all three of them cry. Whether there was vanity or truth in my interpretation, I believed I saw that Mme de Broglie's glances said to her mother, "Very well, Mamma! Was I wrong to tell you that this man was more fit to dine with you than with your women?" Up to that moment, I had had a bit of a heavy heart, but after having avenged myself this way, I was content. Pushing the favorable judgment she had formed of me a little too far, Mme de Broglie believed that I was going to cause a sensation in Paris, and become a favorite of the ladies. To guide my inexperience she gave me *The Confessions of the Comte de* ***.[69] "This book," she said to me, "is a mentor which you will need in the world: You will do well to consult it sometimes." I have kept that copy for more than twenty years with gratitude for the hand by which it came to me, but often[70] laughing at the opinion which this Lady appeared to have of my gallant merit. From the moment I read this work I desired to obtain its author's friendship. My inclination inspired me very well: he is the only true friend I have had among literary people.*

From then on I dared to depend on the fact that since Mme the Baronne de Beuzenwal and Mme the Marquise de Broglie were taking an interest in me, they would not leave me without means for long, and I was not deceived. Now let us talk about my admittance to Mme Dupin's house, which had longer consequences.

As is known, Mme Dupin was a daughter of Samuel Bernard and of Mme Fontaine. There were three sisters who could be called the three graces. Mme de la Touche, who had an escapade in England with the Duke of Kingston. Mme D'Arty, the mistress, and even more, the friend, the sole and sincere friend of M. the Prince de Conty. An adorable woman, both from the sweetness, from the kindness of her charming character, and from the attractiveness of her mind, and from the unfailing gaiety of her mood. Finally Mme Dupin, the most beautiful of the three and the only one not reproached for a lapse in her behavior. She was the reward for the hospitality of M. Dupin, to whom her mother gave her along with a position as farmer general and an immense fortune, in gratitude for the good welcome he had given her in his province.[72] When I saw her for the first time she was still one of the most beautiful women

---

*I believed this for such a long time and so perfectly that after my return to Paris I entrusted the manuscript of my confessions to him. The distrustful J.-J. has never been able to believe in perfidy and falseness until after he has been their victim.[71]

in Paris. She received me at her dressing table. She had bare arms, dishevelled hair, her dressing gown poorly arranged. This bearing was very new to me; my poor head could not stand it: I got flustered, I lost my bearings; and in short, I was smitten with Mme Dupin.

My confusion did not appear to harm me with her;[73] she took no notice of it whatsoever. She welcomed the book and its author, spoke to me about my project as a well-informed person, sang, accompanied herself on the Clavichord, kept me to dinner, had me put beside her at the table; it did not require that much to make me crazy, I became so. She permitted me to come to see her; I made use of, I abused this permission. I went there almost every day, I dined there two or three times a week. I was dying from the desire to speak; I never dared. Several reasons reinforced my natural timidity. Admittance to an opulent house was an open door to fortune; in my situation I did not wish to risk having it closed to me. Entirely lovable though she was, Mme Dupin was serious and cold; I found nothing provocative enough in her manners to embolden me. Her house,[74] as brilliant at that time as any other in Paris, drew together social circles which needed only to be a little less numerous to be the elite of every sort. She liked to see all the glamourous people: Nobility, literary people, beautiful women. Only Dukes, Ambassadors, knights of the *cordon bleu*[75] were seen at her home. Mme the Princesse de Rohan, Mme the Comtesse de Forcalquier, Mme de Mirepoix, Mme de Brignolé, Lady Hervey could pass for her friends. M. de Fontenelle, the Abbé de St. Pierre, the Abbé Sallier, M. de Fourmont, M. de Bernis, M. de Buffon, M. de Voltaire were in her circle and came to her dinners.[76] If her reserved bearing did not attract young people very much, her social circle—all the better composed—was only more imposing because of it, and there was no way for poor J.-J. to flatter himself for shining very much in the midst of all that. Thus I did not dare to speak, but not being able to keep silent any longer, I dared to write. She kept my letter for two days without speaking to me about it. The third day she returned it to me while verbally addressing several words of exhortation to me in a cold tone that froze me. I wanted to speak, speech expired on my lips: my sudden passion was extinguished along with hope, and after a declaration in due form, I continued to live with her as before, without speaking to her any longer about anything, even with my eyes.

I believed my stupidity had been forgotten; I was mistaken. M. de Francueil, M. Dupin's son and Madame's Stepson, was about her age and mine.[77] He had wit, appearance, he could have pretensions; it was said that he did have them with regard to her, perhaps only because she had given him a very ugly, very sweet wife and she lived perfectly well with both of them. M. de Francueil loved and cultivated talents. Music, which he knew extremely well, was a means of connection between us. I saw a lot of him; I became attached to him: suddenly he had me understand that Mme Dupin found my visits too frequent, and asked me to discontinue them. This compliment might have been in its place when she returned my letter to me; but eight or ten days afterwards, and without any other cause, it seems to me that it came improperly. That brought about a position all the more bizarre, in that I was not regarded less well than before at M. and Mme de Francueil's home. Nevertheless, I went there more rarely, and I would have ceased going there completely, if—from another unforeseen caprice—Mme Dupin had not had me asked to look after her son for eight or ten days, who was staying alone during that interval because he was changing Tutors. I passed those eight days in a torture which only the pleasure of obeying[78] Mme Dupin could make bearable to me: for as far back as then the poor Chenonceau had that unruly head which almost dishonored his family, and which caused him to die on the Isle de Bourbon.[79] While I was with him I kept him from doing any harm to himself or others, and that is all: still this was more than a little trouble, and I would not have been burdened with him for eight more days, even if Mme Dupin had given herself to me as recompense.

M. de Francueil acquired a friendship for me, I worked with him; together we began a Chemistry Course with Rouelle.[80] To be nearer to him I left my hotel St. Quentin and went to lodge at the tennis court on rue Verdelet, which leads to rue Plâtriére where M. Dupin lodged. There, as the consequence of a neglected cold, I caught an inflammation of the chest from which I almost died. In my youth I often had those inflammatory illnesses, pleurisies, and above all quinsies to which I was very subject, the record of which I do not keep here, and which all have made me see death close enough to familiarize me with its image. During my convalescence I had time to reflect on my condition, and to deplore my timidity, my weakness, and my indolence, which, in spite of the fire with which I felt myself set aflame, let me languish in idleness of mind, always at the gate of poverty. The day before I had fallen sick, I had gone to an Opera by Royer that was being given then and whose title I have forgotten.[81] In spite of my bias for the talents of other people which had always made me lack belief in my own, I could not keep myself from finding that music weak, without warmth, without invention. I sometimes dared to say to myself, "It seems to me that I would do better than that." But the terrible idea I had about the composition of an Opera and the importance that I heard given to that undertaking by people of the art immediately discouraged me from it, and made me blush at daring to think [82] about it. Furthermore, where could I find someone who wanted to furnish me with the words, and take the trouble to fashion them to my taste? These ideas of music and opera came back to me during my illness, and in the transport of my fever I composed [83] songs, duos, choruses. I am certain I composed two or three pieces *di prima intenzione* [84] worthy perhaps of the admiration of masters, if they could have heard them executed. Oh if one could keep a record of the dreams of a feverish man, what great and sublime things would sometimes be seen to issue from his delirium.

These subjects of music and Opera still occupied me during my convalescence, but more tranquilly. As a result of thinking about them and even in spite of myself, I wanted to clear the matter up and try to write an Opera by myself, words and music. This was not exactly my first try. At Chambéry I had [85] written an Opera tragedy entitled *Iphis and Anaxaretes*, which I had had the good sense to throw into the fire. I had written another at Lyon entitled, *The Discovery of the New World*, with which, after having read it to M. Bordes, the Abbé de Mably, the Abbé Trublet, [86] and others I had finished by doing the same thing, although I had already written the music of the prologue and first Act, and, upon seeing this music, David had told me that there were some pieces worthy of Buononcini. [87]

This time, before putting my hand to the work, I gave myself time to meditate on my plot. I planned three different subjects in three separate acts in a heroic Ballet, each in a different musical character and taking for each subject the loves of a Poet; I entitled this Opera *The Gallant Muses*. [88] My first Act, in a strong genre of music, was Tasso: the second, in a tender genre of music, was Ovid; and the third, entitled Anacreon, was supposed to breathe the gaiety of the Dithyramb. I tried myself out first on the first Act, and I abandoned myself to it with an ardor that made me taste the delights of zest in composition for the first time. One evening when I was about to go into the Opera, feeling myself tormented, mastered by my ideas, I put my money back into my pocket, I run to close myself up in my room, I put myself to bed after having completely closed all my curtains to keep the light from coming in, and there—abandoning myself to poetic and musical oestrus [89]—I rapidly composed the best part of my act in seven or eight hours. I can say that my loves for the Princesse of Ferrara (for I was Tasso for that time) and my noble and proud feelings in regard to her unjust brother gave me a night that was a hundred times more delightful than I would have found in the arms of the Princess herself. [90] Only a very small part of what I had done remained in my head in the morning: but this little—almost effaced by lassitude and sleep—still did not fail to show the energy of the pieces whose debris it presented.

At that time I did not push this work extremely far, having been diverted from it by other business. While I attached myself to the Dupin household, Mme de Beuzenwal and Mme de Broglie, whom I continued to see sometimes, had not forgotten me. M. the Comte de Montaigu, Captain in the Guards, had just been named Ambassador to Venice.[91] He was an Ambassador of Barjac's making,[92] to whom he[93] assiduously paid his court. His brother the Chevalier de Montaigu,[94] M. the Dauphin's Gentleman of the Sleeve, was acquainted with these two Ladies, and with the Abbé Alary of the French Academy, whom I also saw sometimes. Knowing that the[95] Ambassador was looking for a Secretary, Mme de Broglie proposed me. We entered into negotiations. I asked for an emolument of fifty Louis, which was very little in a place in which one is obliged to keep up an appearance. He wanted to give me only a hundred pistoles and for me to make the trip at my own expense.[96] The proposal was ridiculous. We could not come to an agreement. M. de Francueil, who was making efforts to hold me back, got the better of him. I stayed, and M. de Montaigu left, taking another Secretary called M. Follau, who had been given to him by the office of foreign affairs. They had hardly arrived in Venice when they had a falling out. Seeing that he had a madman to deal with, Follau left him in the lurch. And, having only a young[97] Abbé called de Binis who wrote under the Secretary and was not in a position to fill his place, M. de Montaigu had recourse to me. His brother the Chevalier, an intelligent man, got around me so well, making me understand that there were rights attached to the place of Secretary, that he made me accept the thousand francs. I had twenty Louis for my trip, and I left.

At Lyon I would have very much wanted to take the Mont Cenis road to see my poor mamma in passing.[98] But I went down the Rhône and was to embark at Toulon[99] both because of the war and for reasons of economy, and to acquire a passport from M. de Mirepoix who was commanding in Provence at that time and to whom I was sent. Not being able to get along without me, M. de Montaigu wrote me letter upon letter to hurry my trip: an incident slowed it down.

It was the time of the plague at Messina.[100] The English fleet had anchored there, and searched the felucca I was on.[101] That subjected us to a quarantine of twenty-one days upon arriving at Genoa after a long and troublesome[102] crossing. They gave the passengers the choice of undergoing it on board, or in the lazaretto[103] in which they warned us that we would find only the four walls, because they had not yet had time to furnish it. Everyone chose the felucca. The unbearable heat, the cramped space, the impossibility of walking there, the vermin, made me prefer the lazaretto at any risk. I was led into a big building of two absolutely naked stories, where I found neither window, nor bed, nor table, nor chair, not even a stool to sit down on nor a bundle of hay to sleep on. They brought me my coat, my night bag, my two trunks; they closed some big doors with big locks, and I stayed there, master of walking at my ease from room to room and story to story, finding the same solitude and the same nakedness everywhere.

All that did not make me repent at having chosen the lazaretto rather than the Felucca, and like a new[104] Robinson I began to organize myself for my twenty-one days as I would have done for my whole life.[105] I first had the amusement of hunting for the fleas I had caught in the Felucca. As I finally made myself clean by dint of changing linen and togs, I proceeded to furnishing the Room I had chosen for myself. I made myself a good mattress out of my coats and my shirts, some sheets out of several handkerchiefs that I sewed together, a blanket out of my bathrobe, a pillow out of my rolled up cloak. I made myself a seat out of one chest set flat and a table out of the other set on its side. I pulled out some paper, a writing desk; I arranged a dozen Books I had by way of a library. In short I made myself so‾comfortable that, with the exception of curtains and windows, I lived almost as comfortably in this absolutely naked Lazaretto as in my tennis court of the rue Verdelet. My meals were served with a lot of pomp; two Grenadiers with bayonets at the end of their rifles escorted them; the flight of stairs was my dining room, a landing served as my table, the lower step served as my seat, and when my dinner had been served, they sounded a small bell while withdrawing in order to notify me to put myself at the table. Between my meals, when I was not reading or writing, or when I was not working at my furnishings, I went to take a walk in the Protestant Cemetery which served as my Courtyard, or I went up into a tower that opened on the port, and where I could see the vessels come and go. In that way I passed fourteen days, and I would have passed the entire twenty there without being bored for a moment, if M. de Jonville, Envoy of France, whom I reached with a vinegared, perfumed, and half-burned letter, had not had my time shortened by eight days: I went to pass them at his home, and I found myself better, I admit, from the board at his house than from that of the Lazaretto. He showed me many marks of affection. His Secretary Dupont was a good chap who brought me both to Genoa and the country, into several houses where one had a rather good time, and I struck up an acquaintance and correspondence with him, which we kept up for an extremely long time. I pursued my route pleasantly across Lombardy. I saw Milan, Verona, Bresse, Padua, and at last I arrived at Venice impatiently awaited by M. the Ambassador.

I found heaps of Dispatches both from the Court and from other Ambassadors, the coded ones of which he had not been able to read, although he had all the ciphers necessary for doing so. Never having worked in any Office or seen a Minister's cipher in my life, at first I feared that I might be at a loss, but I found that nothing was more simple and in less than eight days I had deciphered all of them, which certainly was not worth the trouble; for aside from the fact that the Embassy of Venice is always rather idle, one would not have wanted to entrust the slightest negotiation to such a man.[106] Until my arrival he had found himself in a great perplexity, not knowing either how to dictate or to write legibly. I was very useful to him, he felt it and treated me well. An additional motive led him to do so. Since M. Froulay his predecessor,[107] whose head had become deranged, the Consul of France called M. Le Blond had remained as chargé d'affaires of the Embassy, and since M. de Montaigu's arrival, he continued to do it until he had acquainted him with the situation. Jealous that someone else was doing his job, although he was incapable of it himself,[108] M. de Montaigu took a dislike to the Consul, and as soon as I had arrived deprived him of the Secretary of the Embassy's functions in order to give them to me. They were inseparable from the title; he told me to take them over. As long as I stayed with him he sent only me to the Senate and to its Conferent[109] under this title; and at bottom it was extremely natural that he preferred to have his own man as secretary of the Embassy rather than a consul, or a Clerk of the Offices named by the Court.

That made my situation pleasant enough and kept his Gentlemen who were Italians—as were his pages and the majority of his people—from disputing my primacy in his house. I successfully made use of the authority attached to it to maintain his right of ambassadorial privilege—that is to say the immunity of his neighborhood—against the attempts that were made several times to violate it, and which his Venetian Officers had been careful not to resist. But also I never allowed bandits to take refuge there, although this could have returned advantages to me of which his Excellency would not have disdained his share.

He even dared to lay claim to the rights of the Secretariat, which was called the Chancellery. Although a war was going on,[110] there did not fail to be many passports issued. Each of these Passports paid a sequin[111] to the Secretary who drew it up and countersigned it. All my predecessors had had this sequin paid to themselves both by the French and foreigners alike. I found this practice unjust and even though I was not French I repealed it for the French: but I demanded my right so rigorously from all others that when the Marquis Scotti, a brother of the Queen of Spain's favorite, had me asked for a passport without sending the sequin, I had him asked for it; a boldness which the vindictive Italian did not forget. As soon as the reform I had made in the tax on Passports was known, the only people who presented themselves for them were crowds of pretended Frenchmen, who said in abominable gibberish that they were one a Provençal, another a Picard, another a Bourguignon. Since I have a rather subtle ear, I was hardly their dupe, and I doubt that a single Italian tricked me out of my sequin and that a single Frenchman paid it.[112] I had the stupidity to tell M. de Montaigu, who knew nothing about anything, what I had done. This word, sequins, made him open his ears, and without telling me his opinion about the suppression of those of the French, he demanded that I enter into partnership with him on the others, promising me equivalent advantages. More indignant at this baseness than affected by my own interest, I distinctly rejected his proposition, he insisted, I flared up. "No, Sir," I told him in a very lively way, "let Your Excellency keep what is his, and leave me what is mine; I will never cede him a sou." Seeing that he was gaining[113] nothing by this method, he took another one, and was not ashamed to tell me that since I had the profits from his chancellery, it was just that I pay its expenses. I did not want to quibble over this point, and from then on out of my own money I furnished ink, paper, wax, candles, ribbon, down to the Seal[114] which I had remade without him ever reimbursing me a liard for it. That did not keep me from giving a little share of the product of the Passports to the Abbé de Binis, a good chap, and who was very far from claiming anything of the sort. If he was obliging with regard to me, I was not less honest with regard to him, and we always lived well together.

Upon trying my job, I found it less troublesome than I had feared for a man without experience, with an Ambassador who did not have any more, and in addition whose ignorance and obstinacy contradicted, as if for the sake of contradicting, everything good that good sense and some enlightenment inspired me to do for his service and that of the King. The most reasonable thing he did was to link himself with the Marquis Mari the Spanish Ambassador, a skillful and subtle man, who might have led him by the nose if he wanted to, but who—given the union of interest of the two crowns—usually advised him well enough, if the other did not spoil his advice by always stuffing something of his own into its execution. The only thing they had to do in concert was to induce the Venetians to maintain their neutrality. The latter did not fail to protest their fidelity in observing it, even though they were publicly furnishing munitions to the Austrian Troops and even some recruits, under pretext of desertion. In spite of my representations, M. de Montaigu, who I believe wanted to please the Republic, did not fail also to make me certify in all his Dispatches that it would never transgress against its neutrality. At every moment that poor man's obstinacy and stupidity made me write and commit extravagant acts which I was very much forced to be the agent of, because he wanted it, but which sometimes made my profession unbearable to me and even almost impracticable. For example, he absolutely wanted the greatest part of his Dispatch to the King and to the Minister to be in cipher, although both contained absolutely nothing that required this precaution. I pointed out that between Friday, when the Dispatches from the Court arrived, and Saturday, when ours left, there was not enough time to devote both to ciphers and to the heavy correspondence with which I was charged for the same Courier. He found an admirable expedient for that; this was to write as early as Thursday the answer to the Dispatches which should arrive the next day. This idea even appeared to him so happily found, whatever I might tell him about the impossibility, about the absurdity of its execution, that I had to let it pass, and therefore the whole time I remained with him—after having kept note of several words that he told me at random during the week, and of some commonplace news that I skimmed off here and there—supplied with these materials alone, I never failed to bring him on Thursday morning the rough draft of the Dispatches which were supposed to leave on Saturday, aside from some additions or corrections which I hastily made based on the ones that might come on Friday and to which ours served as answers. He had another extremely pleasant quirk which gave his correspondence a ridiculousness that is hard to imagine. This was to send each piece of news back to its source instead of making it follow its course. He pointed out the news from the Court to M. Amelot, that from Paris to M. de Maurepas, that from Sweden to M. d'Havrincourt, that from Petersburg to M. de la Chetardie, and sometimes to each the news which came from himself, and which I dressed up [115] in slightly different terms. [116] Since out of everything I brought him to sign he went through only the Dispatches from the Court, and signed those of the other Ambassadors without reading them, that made me a little more the master of fashioning these latter in my way, and at least I made the news interchange. But it was impossible for me to give a reasonable turn to the essential Dispatches; I was lucky when he did not take it into his head to sprinkle into them impromptu some lines of his own inspiration, which forced me to return hastily to transcribe the whole Dispatch, adorned with that new impertinence, to which I had to give the honor of the cipher without which he would not have signed it. Twenty times I was tempted out of love for his glory to cipher something other than what he had said: but since I felt that nothing could authorize such an unfaithfulness, I let him rave at his own risk; satisfied to speak to him frankly, and to fulfill my duty with regard to him to my own glory.

This is what I always did with an uprightness, a zeal, and a courage that deserved another recompense on his part than the one I received from him in the end. For once it was time for me to be what Heaven (which had endowed me with a happy natural disposition), what the education I had received from the best of women, what the one I had given myself had made me be, and I was. Abandoned to myself alone, without a friend, without advice, without experience in a foreign country, serving a foreign nation, in the midst of a crowd of rascals who stirred me up [117] to imitate them for their own interest and to keep off the scandal of good example; far from doing anything of the kind, I served France (to which I owed nothing) well, and the Ambassador better, as was just, in everything that depended on me. Irreproachable in a post that was sufficiently in view, I deserved, I obtained the esteem of the Republic, that of all the Ambassadors with whom we were in correspondence and the affection of all the French established in Venice, without excepting even the Consul whom I supplanted regretfully in the functions that I knew to be due to him, and which gave me more trouble than pleasure.

Having abandoned himself without reserve to the Marquis Mari, who did not enter into the details of his duties, M. de Montaigu neglected them to such an extent that without me the French who were at Venice would not have noticed that there was an Ambassador from their nation there. Since they were always sent packing without him wanting to listen to them when they needed his protection, they became discouraged, and none of them were seen any more either in his retinue or at his table, to which he never invited them. I often did on my own authority what he should have done: I rendered all the services that were in my power to the French who had recourse to him or to me. In any other country I would have done more; but, since I was not able to see anyone in service because of my place, I was often forced to have recourse to the Consul, and since the Consul had settled in the country where he had his family, he had to maintain discretion, which prevented him from doing what he would have liked. Nevertheless, sometimes when I saw him give way and not dare to speak, I ventured hazardous steps, several of which succeeded. I recall one of them, whose remembrance still makes me laugh. One would hardly suspect that it is to me that the lovers of the theater in Paris owed Coralline and her sister Camille: nevertheless nothing is more true. Their father, Veronese, had committed himself to the Italian troupe along with his children, and after he had received two thousand francs for his trip, instead of leaving he had calmly begun at the theater

San Luca* at Venice where Coralline, though she was still wholly a child, attracted almost everyone. M. the Duc de Gesvres, as first Gentleman of the Bedchamber, wrote to the Ambassador to reclaim the father and the daughter. Giving me the letter, M. de Montaigu said to me as my entire instruction, "*See to this.*" I went to M. Le Blond to ask him to speak to the Patrician to whom the theater of San Luca belonged and who I believe was a Zustiniani, so that he might send back Veronese who was committed to the service of the King. Le Blond, who did not care too much for the commission, did it badly. Zustiniani beat around the bush, and Veronese was not sent back at all. I was irritated; it was the time of the Carnival. Having put on a Domino and mask I had myself brought to the Palazzo Zustiniani. Everyone who saw the entry of my Gondola with the livery of the Ambassador was struck: Venice had never seen such a thing. I enter, I have myself announced under the name of *una Siora Maschera*.[119] As soon as I was introduced, I remove my mask and name myself. The Senator turned white and remained stupefied. "Sir," I said to him in Venetian, "it is with regret that I pester Your Excellency with my visit; but at your theater of San Luca you have a man named Veronese who is committed to the service of the King and for whom you have been asked unsuccessfully: I come to reclaim him in His Majesty's name." My short harangue had the desired effect. Hardly had I left when my man ran to give an account of his adventure to the State Inquisitors who gave him a dressing down. Veronese was dismissed the same day. I had him told that if he did not leave within a week I would have him arrested, and he left.

On another occasion I extricated a captain of a merchant Vessel all by myself, and almost without anyone's assistance. He was called Captain Olivet from Marseille; I have forgotten the name of the Vessel.[120] His crew had picked a quarrel with some Slavonians in the service of the Republic; there had been some assault and battery, and the Vessel had been put under arrest with such severity that no one, except the Captain alone, could board or leave it without permission.[121] He had recourse to the Ambassador, who sent him packing; he went to the Consul, who told him that this was not a commercial affair and that he could not get mixed up in it; no longer knowing what to do, he came back to me. I pointed out to M. de Montaigu that he ought to permit me to give a Memorandum about this affair to the Senate; I do not recall whether he agreed to it and whether I presented the Memorandum, but I recall very well that

---

*I am in doubt about whether it might not have been *San Samuelo*. Proper names absolutely escape me.[118]

my steps came to nothing and, since the embargo was still going on, I made a decision that succeeded. I inserted the relation of this business into a dispatch to M. de Maurepas, and I even had rather a lot of trouble getting M. de Montaigu to consent to let this article through. I knew that our Dispatches were opened at Venice, although they were not really worth the trouble of opening. I had the proof of it in articles that I found word for word in the gazette, an infidelity about which I had futilely tried to bring the Ambassador to complain. My object in speaking about this vexation in the Dispatch was to make use of their curiosity to scare them and to commit them to freeing the Vessel; for if he had had to wait for the answer from the Court, the Captain would have been ruined before it had come. I did more; I proceeded to the Vessel to interrogate the crew. I took with me the Abbé Patizel, Chancellor of the Consulate, who came only reluctantly, so much did all these poor people fear displeasing the Senate! Not being able to climb on board because of the prohibition, I stayed in my Gondola and I drew up my statement from there, interrogating every crew member one after the other in a loud voice, and directing my questions in such a way as to elicit answers that would be advantageous to them. I wanted to engage Patizel to make the interrogations and the statement himself, which was in fact more his profession than mine: he absolutely did not want to consent to it, did not say a single word, and hardly wanted to sign the statement after me.[122] This slightly bold step nevertheless had a fortunate success, and the Vessel was freed a long time before the Minister's answer. The Captain wanted to give me a gift. Without getting angry I told him, while slapping him on the shoulder, "Captain Olivet, do you believe that someone who does not receive from the French the fees for Passports which he finds to be an established right, is a man who would sell them the King's protection?" He wanted at least to give me a dinner on board which I accepted, and to which I brought the Secretary of the Embassy of Spain, named Carrio, an intelligent man [123] and very amiable, who afterwards became Secretary of the Embassy at Paris, with whom I was intimately connected following the example of our Ambassadors.

I would have been happy if, while I was doing all the good I could do with the most perfect disinterestedness, I had known how to put enough order and attention into all the little details not to be their dupe and serve others at my own expense. But in places like the one I occupied in which the slightest faults are not without consequences, I exhausted all my attention in order not to do anything contrary to my service; up to the end I had the greatest order and the greatest exactitude in everything that related to my essential duty. Aside from some errors that a forced haste caused me to make in ciphering, and about which M. Amelot's clerks complained one time, neither the Ambassador nor anyone else ever had a single act of negligence with which to reproach me in any of my functions; that is notable for a man as negligent and as heedless as I am:[124] but I sometimes lacked memory and care in the private business with which I burdened myself, and the love of justice has always caused me to bear the harm from my own action before anyone dreamed of complaining. I will cite only a single instance, which relates to my departure from Venice, and whose after-effect I felt later on at Paris.

Our cook called Rousselot had brought from France an old promissory note for two hundred francs, which a Wigmaker among his friends had from a noble Venetian called Zanetto Nani, for supplying Wigs. Rousselot brought me this note asking me to try to get something as a settlement for it. I knew, he knew also that the constant practice of noble Venetians upon returning to their fatherland is never to pay debts they have contracted in foreign countries: if one wants to compel them, they use up the unfortunate creditor in so many delays and expenses that he becomes discouraged and ends by abandoning everything or settling for almost nothing. I asked M. Le Blond to speak to Zanetto; the latter acknowledged the bill, not the payment. As a result of a battle he finally promised three Sequins. When Le Blond brought him the bill the three sequins were not found to be ready; it was necessary to wait. During that wait my quarrel with the Ambassador took place and my departure from him. I left the papers of the Embassy in the greatest order, but Rousselot's bill was not found. M. Le Blond assured me that he had returned it; I knew him to be too honest a man to doubt it, but it was impossible for me to recall what had become of that bill. Since Zanetto had admitted the debt, I asked M. Le Blond to try to get the three sequins based on a receipt,[125] or to engage him to renew the bill by a Duplicate. When he realized that the bill was lost, Zanetto did not want to do either the one or the other. I offered Rousselot the three sequins from my purse for the discharge of the bill. He refused them and told me to come to terms with the Creditor at Paris, whose address he gave me. Knowing what had happened, the wigmaker wanted his bill or his money in full. In my indignation, what would I not have given to find that cursed bill again! I paid the two hundred francs, and did so in my greatest distress.[126] That is how the loss of the bill was worth the payment of the entire sum to the Creditor, while if—unfortunately for him—this bill had been found, it would have been hard for him to get the ten écus promised by His Excellency Zanetto Nani.

The talent I believed I felt in myself for my employment made me perform it with relish, and aside from the society of my friend de Carrio, that of the virtuous Altuna about whom I will soon have cause to speak, aside from the very innocent recreations of the Piazzo di San Marco, the Theater, and some visits we made almost always together, I made my duties into my only pleasures. Although my work was not extremely troublesome, particularly with the aid of the Abbé de Binis, since the correspondence was very extensive and it was in time of war, I did not fail to be reasonably busy. I worked a good part of the morning every day and sometimes until midnight on the days of the Courier. I dedicated the remainder of the time to the study of the profession I was beginning, and in which, from the success of my beginning, I very much counted on being employed more advantageously afterward. In fact there was only a single voice on my account beginning with that of the Ambassador, who loudly congratulated himself for my service, who never complained about it, and whose entire rage in what followed came only from the fact that I finally wanted my dismissal after having complained futilely. The Ambassadors and Ministers of the King with whom we were in correspondence gave him compliments about the merit of his Secretary which ought to have flattered him, and which produced an entirely contrary effect in his unruly head. Above all he received one on a vital occasion, for which he never pardoned me. This is worth the trouble of explaining.

He could be bothered so little that even on Saturday, the day of almost all the Couriers, he could not wait until the work was finished in order to leave, and ceaselessly pestered me to expedite the Dispatches for the King and Ministers, he signed them hastily, and then ran somewhere or other, leaving the majority of the other letters without signature, which forced me to turn them into bulletins when it was only news; but when it was a question of business that regarded the King's service, it was very necessary that someone sign, and I signed. I acted this way for an important notice that we had just received from M. Vincent, the King's chargé d'affaires at Vienna. It was at the time that the Prince de Lobkowitz was marching to Naples, and that the Comte de Gages made that memorable retreat, the finest war maneuver of the whole century, and about which Europe has spoken too little.[127] The notice stated that a man, whose description M. Vincent was sending us, was leaving Vienna and was supposed to pass through Venice going furtively into Abruzzo, charged with stirring up the People there at the approach of the Austrians. In the absence of M. the Comte de Montaigu who was not interested in anything, I had this notice pass to M. the Marquis de l'Hôpital so opportunely that it is perhaps to this poor Jean-Jacques, who is so scoffed at, that the house of Bourbon owes the preservation of the Kingdom of Naples.

As was just, in thanking his colleague the Marquis de l'Hôpital, spoke to him about his Secretary and about the service he had just rendered to the common cause. Comte de Montaigu, who had to reproach himself for his negligence in this business, believed he glimpsed a reproach in this compliment and spoke to me about it testily. I had been in the position of acting with the Comte de Castellane, Ambassador to Constantinople, as with the Marquis de l'Hôpital, although in less important things. Since there was no post for Constantinople except the couriers which the Senate sends from time to time to its Bayle,[128] notice of the departure of these Couriers was given to the Ambassador of France, so that he could write to his colleague by that means if he judged it appropriate. This notice usually came a day or two in advance: but they thought so little of M. de Montaigu that they were content to send to him as a formality an hour or two before the Courier's departure; several times that put me in the position[129] of writing the Dispatch in his absence. In responding to them M. de Castellane made mention of me in decent terms: M. de Jonville from Genoa did as much; so many new grievances.

I admit that I did not flee from occasions to make myself known, but I did not seek them inappropriately either, and it appeared to me extremely just, while serving well, to aspire to the natural reward from good services, which is the esteem of those who are in a position to judge about them and to recompense them. I will not say whether my exactitude in fulfilling my functions was a legitimate subject of complaint on the part of the Ambassador, but I will very well say that it is the only one that he articulated until the day of our separation.

His house, which he had never put on to a very good footing, was filled with riffraff: the French were mistreated there, the Italians took the ascendancy, and even among them the good servants attached to the Embassy for a long time were all indecently driven out, among others his first Gentleman, who had been the same with the Comte de Froulay, and who I believe was called Comte Peati, or a name very close. The second Gentleman, chosen by M. de Montaigu, was a bandit from Mantua called Dominique Vitali, to whom the Ambassador entrusted the care of his house, and who, by dint of fawning and base haggling, obtained his confidence and became his favorite, to the great prejudice of the few decent people who were still there and of the Secretary who was at their head. The upright eye of a decent man is always unsettling for rascals. No more than that would have been needed for him to acquire a hatred for me; but that hatred had yet another cause which rendered it much more cruel. I must state that cause, so that I can be condemned if I was wrong.

In accordance with the normal practice the Ambassador had a Box at each of the five theaters. Every day at dinner he named the Theater to which he wished to go that day; I chose after him, and the Gentlemen disposed of the other Boxes. Upon leaving I took the key of the Box I had chosen. One day, since Vitali [130] was not there, I directed the footman who served me to bring my key to a house which I indicated to him. Instead of sending my key Vitali said that he had disposed of it. I was all the more indignant, since the footman had reported to me about my errand in front of everyone. That night, Vitali wanted to give me some words of excuse which I did not accept at all. "Tomorrow, Sir," I said to him, "you will come to make them to me at such an hour in the house where I received the affront and before the people who witnessed it, or the day after tomorrow whatever happens, I declare to you that either you or I will leave here." This determined tone made an impression on him. He came to the place and at the time to make me a public apology with a baseness worthy of him: but he took his measures at leisure, and all the while greatly fawning over me, he worked so much in the Italian manner, that, not being able to bring the Ambassador to dismiss me, he made it necessary for me to demand dismissal.

Such a wretch was certainly not made to know me, but he knew enough about me to serve his purposes. He knew that I was good and gentle to excess in bearing involuntary wrongs, proud and quite impatient with premeditated offenses, loving modesty and dignity in suitable things, and not less demanding of the honor due to me than I was attentive about rendering the honor which I owed to others. It is through this that he undertook and achieved the goal of discouraging me. He turned the house upside down, he removed from it what I had tried to maintain of rule, subordination, propriety, order. A house without a woman needs a somewhat severe discipline to make the restraint that is inseparable from dignity reign there. He soon made ours into a place of debauchery and licence, a den of rascals and debauched people. In the place of the one he had had dismissed, he gave as second Gentleman to His Excellency another Pimp like himself, who kept a public Bordello at the Maltese Cross, and these two well-matched scoundrels were of a modesty equal to their insolence. Aside from the Ambassador's room alone, which was not even in excessively proper order, there was not a single corner in the house bearable for a decent man.

Since His Excellency did not sup, in the evening the Gentlemen and I had a private table where the Abbé de Binis and the Pages also ate. In the nastiest slop house one is served in a more cleanly way, in a more modest way, with less dirty linen, and one eats better. We were given a single very black little candle, pewter plates, iron forks. Still let whatever happens in private pass; but I was deprived of my Gondola: alone among all the Ambassadors' Secretaries, I was forced to hire one or to go on foot, and I no longer had His Excellency's livery except when I went to the Senate. Moreover nothing that happened inside was unknown in the city. All the Ambassador's Officers let out loud cries. Dominique, the sole cause of everything, cried the loudest, knowing very well that the immodesty with which we were treated was felt more by me than by all the others. Alone of the household I said nothing outside, but I complained in a lively manner to the Ambassador, both about the rest and [131] about himself, who—secretly excited by his stooge—each day gave me some new affront. Forced to spend a lot to keep myself up on a par with my colleagues and suitably to my post, I could not save a sou from my salary, and when I asked him for money, he spoke to me about his esteem and his confidence, as if that should have filled my purse and provided for everything. [132]

These two bandits [133] ended by completely turning the head of their master who already did not have a very upright [134] one, and ruined him in a continuous buying and selling through fool's bargains that they persuaded him were steals. They had him rent a Palazzo on the Brenta for twice its value, the surplus of which they split with the owner. It apartments were inlaid with mosaics, and adorned with columns and pilasters of very beautiful marble, in the fashion of the country. M. de Montaigu had all that superbly masked with a pine paneling for the sole reason that at Paris apartments are paneled that way. It was from a similar reason that, alone of all the Ambassadors who were at Venice, he took away his Pages' swords and his footmen's canes. That is the sort of man he was who, always from the same motive perhaps, took a dislike to me, solely from the fact that I served him faithfully.

I patiently endured his disdain, his brutality, his bad treatment as long as I did not believe I was seeing hatred in the ill-humor I saw: but as soon as I saw the concerted plan to deprive me of the honor I deserved from my good service, I resolved to renounce it. The first mark I received of his ill will was on the occasion of a dinner that he was supposed to give for M. the Duc of Modena and his family who were then in Venice, and for which he notified me that I would not have a place at his table. I answered him, irritated, but without getting angry, that since I had the honor of dining there daily, if M. the Duc of Modena required me to abstain when he came, it was in accordance with His Excellency's dignity and my duty not to consent to it. "What," said he with fury, "my Secretary who is not even a Gentleman claims to dine with a Sovereign when my Gentlemen do not dine with him?" "Yes, Sir," I answered him, "as long as I fill it, the post with which Your Excellency has honored me ennobles me so much that I even have precedence over your Gentlemen, or so-called Gentlemen, and am admitted where they cannot be. You are not unaware that the day that you make your public entrance I am called by etiquette and by immemorial practice to follow you in Ceremonial dress, and to have the honor of dining with you at the Palazzo San Marco, and I do not see why a man who can and should eat in public with the Doge and the Senate of Venice, would not be able to eat in private with M. the Duc of Modena." Although the argument was unanswerable, the Ambassador did not give way to it at all: but we did not have occasion to renew the dispute since M. the Duc of Modena did not come to dine with him.[135]

From then on he did not stop giving me trouble, giving me unjust slights, exerting himself to deprive me of the little prerogatives attached to my post in order to transmit them to his dear Vitali, and I am sure that if he had dared to send him to the Senate in my place, he would have done so. He usually employed the Abbé de Binis for writing his private letters in his office: he made use of him to write to M. de Maurepas an account of the affair of Captain Olivet in which—far from making any mention to him of me, who alone had gotten involved in it—he deprived me even of the honor of the statement a copy of which he sent him, in order to attribute it to Patizel who had not said a single word. He wanted to mortify me and gratify his favorite, but he did not want to get rid of me. He felt that it would not be as easy for him to find a successor to me as to M. Follau, who had already made him known. He absolutely needed a Secretary who knew Italian, because of answers to the Senate, who made all his Dispatches, all his business without meddling in anything, who joined to the merit of serving him well the baseness of being obliging to Messieurs his knaves of Gentlemen. Thus he wanted to keep me and humble me, by keeping me far from my country and his, without money to return there, and he would have succeeded, perhaps, if he had gone about it[136] moderately: but Vitali, who had other purposes, and who wanted to force me to reach my decision, succeeded completely. As soon as I saw that I was wasting all my efforts, that the Ambassador made my services into crimes instead of being grateful to me for them, that I no longer had anything for which to hope with him but annoyances inside, injustice outside, and that, in the general disparagement into which he had put himself, his bad offices could harm me without the good ones being able to serve me, I made my decision and asked him for my dismissal, leaving him time to provide himself with a Secretary. Without telling me either yes or no, he still went along at his pace. Seeing that nothing was going better for me and that he was not beginning in the duty of looking for anyone, I wrote to his brother, and enumerating my motives to him, I asked him [137] to obtain my dismissal from His Excellency, adding that one way or another it was impossible for me to stay. I waited for a long time, and had no answer at all. I began to be extremely perplexed: but finally the Ambassador received a letter from his brother. It must have been lively; for, although he was subject to very ferocious rages, I never [138] saw him in a similar one. After torrents of abominable insults, no longer knowing what to say, he accused me of having sold his ciphers. I began to laugh, and asked him in a mocking tone whether he believed that there was in all Venice a man foolish enough to give an écu for them? That answer made him foam with rage. He made a show of calling his people, to have me, he said, thrown out the window. Until then I had been extremely calm: but at that threat anger and indignation carried me away in my turn. I threw myself toward the door, and after having pulled a knob that closed it from the inside, "No, Monsieur the Comte," I said to him going back toward him with a serious step; "your people will not meddle in this business: Be good enough to let it pass between us." [139] My action, my manner calmed him at the very instant: surprise and fright were marked in his bearing. When I saw him come back from his fury, I made him my farewell in a few words, then without waiting for his answer I went to open the door again, I went out and passed composedly into the antechamber in the midst of his people who stood up as usual, and who, I believe, would have sooner leant a strong hand against him than for him against me. Without going back up to my room I went down the stairway immediately, and left the Palazzo at once never to return there again. [140]

I went straight to M. Le Blond's to recount the adventure to him. He was not very surprised by it; he knew the man. He kept me to dinner. This dinner, although impromptu, was brilliant. All the French of reputation who were in Venice were there. Not even a cat was at the Ambassador's. The Consul recounted my case to the company. To this recital there was but one cry, which was not in favor of His Excellency. He had not settled my account, had not given me a sou, and being reduced for my sole resource to several Louis that I had on me, I was in a perplexity about my return. All purses were open to me. I took twenty sequins from M. Le Blond's, as much from M. de St. Cyr's with whom I had the most connection after him; I thanked all the others, and while waiting for my departure I went to lodge with the Chancellor of the Consulate, to prove to the public that the nation was not an accomplice to the Ambassador's injustices. The latter, furious at seeing me feted in my misfortune, and himself abandoned, Ambassador though he was, lost his head completely and behaved like a man in a frenzy. He forgot himself to the point of presenting a Memorandum to the Senate to have me arrested. Upon notice being given to me by the Abbé de Binis, I resolved to stay another two weeks, instead of leaving two days later as I had counted on doing. My conduct had been seen and approved; I was universally esteemed. The Seigneury did not even deign to answer the Ambassador's extravagant Memorandum, and had me told by the Consul that I could stay at Venice as long as I pleased without being anxious about the proceedings of a madman. I continued to see my friends: I went to take leave of M. the Ambassador of Spain, who received me very well, and of the Comte de Finochietti, Minister from Naples, whom I did not find at home, but to whom I wrote, and who answered me with the most obliging letter in the world. I left, at last, not leaving—in spite of my difficulties—any debts other than the loans about which I just spoke, and fifty écus with a merchant named Morandi, which Carrio took it upon himself to pay, and which I never gave back to him, although we have often seen each other since that time: but as for the two loans about which I spoke, I repaid them very exactly, as soon as I could.

Let us not leave Venice without saying a word about the famous amusements of that City, or at least about the very small share I took of them during my stay there. It has been seen in the course of my youth how little I chased after the pleasures of that age or at least the things given that name. I did not change my taste at Venice, but my occupations, which moreover would have kept me from them, caused the simple recreations that I did permit myself to be more lively. The first and the sweetest was the society of people of merit, Messieurs Le Blond, de St. Cyr, Carrio, Altuna, and a Friulian gentleman whose name I greatly regret having forgotten, and whose amiable remembrance I do not recall without emotion: of all the men I have known in my life he was the one whose heart resembled mine the most. We were also tied with two or three Englishmen who were full of wit and knowledge, as passionate about music as we were. All these Gentlemen had their wives or their beloveds or their mistresses, these last almost all girls with talents, at whose houses we made music or had balls. We also gambled there but very little since lively tastes, talents, the theater made this amusement insipid for us. Gambling is the resource only of bored people. From Paris I had brought the prejudice they have in that country against Italian music; but from nature I had also received that sensitivity of discrimination against which prejudices do not prevail. Soon I had for that music the passion which it inspires in anyone made to judge it. While listening to the barcaroles[141] I found that I had not heard singing until then, and soon I became so infatuated with the opera that—being bored by the babbling, eating, and gambling in the boxes when I would have liked to listen—I often slipped away from the company to go to another side. There, closed up in my box all alone, I abandoned myself to the pleasure of enjoying the Spectacle at my ease and until the end in spite of its length.[142] One day at the theater of San Chrysostomo I fell asleep and very much more deeply than I would have done in my bed. The noisy and brilliant tunes did not wake me up at all. But who could express the delightful sensation made on me by the sweet harmony and the angelic songs of the tunes that awakened me. What an awakening! What rapture! what ecstasy, when I opened my ears and eyes at the same instant! My first idea was to believe myself in Paradise. This ravishing piece which I still recall and which I will never forget in my life began this way

> *Conservami la bella*
> *Che si m'accende il cor.*[143]

I wanted to have this piece, I had it, and I kept it for a long time; but it was not the same on my paper as it was in my memory. It was certainly the same notes, but it was not the same thing. Never can that divine tune be performed except in my head, as it was in fact performed the day it awakened me.

A music to my taste very superior to that of the Operas and which does not have its like in Italy or in the rest of the world is that of the *Scuole*. The *Scuole* are houses of charity established to give an education to girls without property, and whom the Republic provides with an endowment afterwards, either for marriage or for the cloister. Music is in the first rank of the talents cultivated in these girls. Every Sunday at the Church of each of these four *Scuole* during Vespers there are motets by a large Choir and a large Orchestra, composed and conducted by the greatest masters in Italy, performed in grated Balconies, solely by girls the oldest of whom is not twenty years old. I have no idea of anything as voluptuous, as touching as this music: the richness of the art, the exquisite taste of the songs, the beauty of the voices, the exactness of the performance, everything in these delightful concerts combines to produce an impression which is assuredly not suitable to the dignity of the place, but from which I doubt that any man's heart is safe. Never did either Carrio or I miss these Vespers at the *Mendicanti*, and we were not the only ones. The Church was always full of devotees, even the Actors from the Opera came to improve themselves in truly tasteful singing based upon these excellent models. What grieved me was the cursed grating, which let only the sounds pass through, and hid from me the Angels of beauty worthy of them. I did not talk about anything else. One day when I was speaking about it at M. Le

Blond's, he said to me, "If you are so curious to see these girls, it is easy to satisfy you. I am one of the administrators of the house. I want to give you an afternoon snack there with them." I did not let him rest until he kept his word. Entering into the drawing room that closed up these so coveted beauties, I felt a shuddering of love that I had never experienced before. M. Le Blond introduced to me one after another of these famous singers, whose voice and name were all that I knew. "Come, Sophie," . . . she was horrid looking. "Come, Cattina," . . . she had one eye missing. "Come, Bettina," . . . small pox had disfigured her. Virtually not a single one without some notable flaw. The Tormentor laughed at my cruel surprise. Two or three, nevertheless, appeared passable to me: they sang only in the chorus. I was disconsolate. During the snack they were teased, they became gay. Ugliness[144] does not exclude graces; I found some in them. I said to myself, "One does not sing this way without a soul: they have them." Finally my manner of seeing them changed so well that I left almost in love with all these ugly girls. I hardly dared go back to their vespers. I had the opportunity to reassure myself. I continued to find their songs delightful, and their voices camouflaged their faces so well, that as long as they sang, I persisted in finding them beautiful in spite of my eyes.

In Italy music costs so little that it is not worth the bother of doing without it when one has some taste for it. I rented a Clavichord, and for one little écu I had four or five symphony musicians at my rooms with whom I practiced once a week, performing the pieces that had given me the most pleasure at the Opera. I also had some Instrumental pieces from my *Gallant Muses* tried there. Either because they pleased him or because he wanted to cajole me, the Ballet Master of San Giovanni Crysostomo had me asked for two of them which I had the pleasure of hearing performed by that admirable Orchestra and which were danced by a little Bettina, a pretty and, above all, amiable girl, kept by one of our friends, a Spaniard called Fagoaga, and at whose home we went to pass the evening rather often.[145]

"But with regard to girls, one does not abstain from them in a City like Venice; do you have nothing to confess on that score?" someone might say to me. Yes, in fact I do have something to say, and I am going to proceed to this confession with the same naiveté that I have put into all the others.

I have always been disgusted by[146] prostitutes, and I had nothing else within my reach at Venice, entrance to the majority of the houses of the country[147] being forbidden to me because of my position. M. Le Blond's daughters were very amiable, but hard to approach, and I had too much consideration for the father and mother to even think of coveting them.

I would have had more taste for a young person called Mademoiselle de Cataneo, daughter of the King of Prussia's Agent. But Carrio was in love with her; there was even a question of marriage. He was in easy circumstances and I had nothing; he had a hundred Louis in salary, I had only a hundred pistoles, and aside from the fact that I did not want to poach on a friend's preserve, I knew that everywhere, and above all at Venice, one ought not to get mixed up in playing the gallant with such a poorly furnished purse.[148] I had not lost the fatal[149] habit of leading my needs astray; too occupied to feel ardently those given by the climate, I lived almost a year in that City as moderately as I had done at Paris, and I left it at the end of eighteen months without having drawn near the opposite sex except for only two times, through the singular occasions which I am going to tell.

The first was procured for me by the decent Gentleman Vitali, some time after the apology that I obliged him to ask me for in all the formalities. At table[150] we were talking about the amusements of Venice: these Gentlemen reproached me for my indifference toward the most lively of all, vaunting the engaging manner of the Venetian Courtesans and saying that there were not any in the world worth as much. Dominique said that I had to become acquainted with the most amiable of all, that he wanted to bring me to her, and that I would be satisfied with her. I began to laugh at this obliging offer, and Comte Piati, a man already old and venerable, said with more frankness than I would have expected from an Italian that he believed me to be too wise[151] to let myself be brought to girls by my enemy. In fact I had neither the intention nor the temptation to do so, and in spite of that, from one of those inconsistencies that I can barely understand myself[152] I ended by letting myself be drawn along against my taste, my heart, my reason, my will itself, solely from weakness, from shame at showing suspicion, and, as is said in that country, *per non parer troppo coglione*.[153] La Padoana,[154] to whom we went, had pretty enough appearance,[155] even beautiful, but not of a beauty that pleased me. Dominique left me with her; I had Sorbet brought, I had her sing, and after a half hour I wanted to go away leaving a Ducat[156] on the table; but she had the singular scruple of not wanting what she had not earned, and I had the singular stupidity of removing her scruple. I returned from her to the Palazzo so persuaded that I was infected that the first thing I did upon arriving was to send to have a Surgeon looked for to ask him for infusions. Nothing could equal the discomfort of mind that I suffered during three weeks without any real incommodity, any apparent sign justifying it.[157] I could not conceive that one could leave Padoana's arms with impunity. The surgeon himself had every difficulty imaginable in reassuring me. He could not succeed at it except by persuading me that I was conformed in a peculiar manner, so as to not be capable of being infected easily; and, although I have perhaps exposed myself to that experience less than any other man, the fact that my health never received an attack from that side proves to me that the Surgeon was right. Nevertheless, that opinion has never made me rash and if in fact I possess that advantage from nature, I can say that I have not abused it.

My other adventure, although also with a girl, was of a very different sort as to both its origin and its effects. I have said that Captain Olivet had given me a dinner on board his ship and that I had brought the secretary of Spain. I expected a salute from the cannon. The crew received us in formation, but not a single powder was burnt, which mortified me very much because of Carrio whom I saw was a little irritated by it; and it was true that on merchant vessels the Cannon salute is accorded to people who certainly did not deserve it[158] as much as we did; moreover I believed I deserved some distinction from the Captain. I could not disguise myself because that is always impossible for me, and although the dinner was very good and Olivet did the honors very well, I began it in a bad mood, eating little, and speaking even less. At the first toast I expected at least a salvo: nothing. Carrio who read in my soul laughed at seeing me grumbling like a child. A third of the way through the dinner I saw a gondola approach. "By my faith, Sir," the Captain said to me, "watch out for yourself, here is the enemy." I asked him what he meant by that; he answered by joking. The gondola came alongside, and I saw a dazzling young person leave it who was extremely stylishly done up and extremely nimble, who was in the room in three leaps, and I saw her settled beside me before I had noticed that a place had been set. She was as charming as she was lively, a brunette of at most twenty years old. She spoke only Italian; her accent alone would have been enough to turn my head. While eating, while chatting, she looks at me, stares at me a moment: Then crying out, "Holy Virgin! Ah my dear Brémond how long it has been since I have seen you!" throws herself into my arms, glues her mouth against mine, and squeezes me enough to smother me. Her big black eyes of the oriental type cast bursts of fire into my heart, and although surprise at first made some diversion, voluptuousness overtook me very rapidly, to the point that, in spite of the spectators, it was soon necessary for that beauty to restrain me herself; for I was drunk or rather in a fury. When she saw me at the point at which she wanted me, she put more moderation into her caresses, but not into her vivacity, and when it pleased her to explain to us the true or false cause of all that petulance, she told us that I resembled M. de Brémond, the Customs Director of Tuscany, to the point of deceiving the very man himself, that she had been mad about M. de Brémond, that she was still mad about him; that she had left him because she was a fool; that she was taking me in his place, that she wanted to love me because that suited her, that for the same reason I had to love her as long as that suited her, and that when she jilted me, I would be patient as her dear Brémond had been. What was said was done. She took possession of me as of a man who belonged to her, gave me her gloves to hold, her fan, her belt, her headdress; ordered me to go here or there, to do this or that, and I obeyed. She told me to go send her gondola back because she wanted to use mine, and I went: she told me to give up my place and to ask Carrio to put himself there, because she had something to say to him, and I did it. They chatted together for a very long time and in a whisper; I let them do it. She called me, I came back. "Listen, Zanetto," she said to me, "I do not at all want to be loved in the French way, and it would not do any good. At the first moment of boredom, go away; but do not stay halfway, I warn you." After dinner we went to see the glassworks at Murano. She bought many little trinkets for which she unceremoniously let us pay. But she gave away in all the gratuities much more than we had spent. From the indifference with which she threw her money around and let us throw ours, we saw that it was not of any value for her. When she demanded payment I believe that it was more out of vanity than greed.[159] She was flattered by the value that was put on her favors.

In the evening we took her home. While chatting I saw two pistols on her dressing-table. "Aha!" I said picking one of them up, "here is a beauty-mark box of a new manufacture; is it possible to know what it is used for? I know you have other weapons that fire better than these." After several pleasantries in the same tone, she said to us with a naive pride that made her even more charming, "When I give my favors to people whom I do not love at all, I make them pay for the boredom they give me; nothing is more just: but while putting up with their caresses, I do not wish to endure their insults, and I will not fail to shoot the first one who fails to respect me."

Upon leaving her I made an appointment with her for the next day. I did not keep her waiting. I found her in *vestito di confidenza*,[160] in a more than seductive dishabille which is known only in southern countries, and which I will not amuse myself by describing, although I recall it all too well. I will say only that her ruffles and her bodice were edged with silk thread trimmed with rose-colored tassels. This appeared to me to set off her beautiful skin extremely well. I saw afterwards that this was the fashion at Venice, and its effect is so charming that I am surprised that this fashion has never passed into France. I had no idea whatsoever of the delights awaiting me. I have spoken about Mme de Larnage in the transports that the remembrance of her still gives me sometimes; but how old and ugly and cold she was next to my Zulietta! Do not try to imagine the charms and graces of that girl enchantress; you would remain too far from the truth. The young virgins of the cloisters are less fresh, the beauties of the seraglio are less lively, the Houris of Paradise are less piquant. Never has such sweet enjoyment been offered to the heart and senses of a mortal. Ah at least, if I had known how to taste it fully and completely for a single moment! . . . I tasted it, but without charm. I dulled all its delights, I killed them as if without a cause. No, nature did not make me to enjoy. It put into my unruly head the poison for that ineffable happiness, the appetite for which it put into my heart.

If there is one circumstance in my life that depicts my natural disposition [161] well, it is the one I am about to recount. The strength with which I recall the object of my book at this moment will make me despise the false decorum that would prevent me from fulfilling it here. Whoever you may be who wishes to know a man, dare to read the two or three pages that follow; you are about to know J.-J. Rousseau to the full.

I entered a Courtesan's room as the sanctuary of love and beauty; in it I believed I saw the divinity in her person. I would never have believed that without respect and esteem one could feel anything similar to what she made me experience. Hardly had I known [162] the worth of her charms and her caresses in the first familiarities, when from fear of losing their fruit too early, I wanted to hasten to pluck it. Suddenly instead of the flames which were devouring me, I feel a mortal coldness running through my veins; my legs shake me, and ready to faint, I sit down, and I weep like a child.

Who would be able to guess the cause of my tears, and what passed through my head at that moment? I said to myself, "This object of which I dispose is the masterpiece of nature and love; the mind, the body, everything about it is perfect; she is as good and generous as she is lovable and beautiful. Nobles, Princes ought to be her slaves; scepters ought to be at her feet. Nevertheless, here she is a wretched trollop abandoned to the public; a merchant Ship Captain disposes of her; she has just thrown herself at my head, at me whom she knows has nothing, at me whose merit—which she cannot know—must be nothing in her eyes. There is something inconceivable in this. Either my heart fools me, fascinates my senses, and makes me the dupe of a worthless slut, or some hidden flaw of which I am unaware must destroy the effect of her charms and make her odious to those who ought to contend over her." I began to look for this flaw with a singular application of mind, and it did not even enter my mind that the pox could have any part in it. The freshness of her flesh, the brightness of her coloring, the whiteness of her teeth, the sweetness of her breath, the air of cleanliness spread over her whole person drove this idea away from me so perfectly that—still in doubt about my condition after la Padoana—I rather made a scruple for myself of not being healthy enough for her, and I am very persuaded that my confidence in this was not mistaken.

These reflections, which were so well timed, agitated me to the point of weeping. Zulietta, for whom this certainly made up a completely new spectacle in the circumstances, was bewildered for a moment. But when she made a turn around the room and passed in front of her mirror, she understood, and my eyes confirmed to her, that disgust was not playing any part in this bizarre behavior. It was not hard for her to cure me of it and to erase this little shame. But at the moment that I was ready to swoon upon a breast which seemed to be receiving the mouth and the hand of a man for the first time, I noticed that she had a malformed nipple. I panic, I examine, I believe I see that this nipple is not conformed like the other one. Behold me seeking in my head how someone could have a malformed nipple, and, having persuaded myself that it depended on some notable natural vice, as a result of turning and returning this idea, I saw as clear as day that, in the most charming person I could imagine, I was holding in my arms only a sort of monster, the outcast of nature, men, and love. I pushed stupidity to the point of talking to her about this malformed nipple. At first she took the matter as a joke, and said and did things in her sprightly mood that made me die of love. But since I maintained an undercurrent of uneasiness which I could not hide from her, I finally saw her blush, straighten her clothes, hold herself erect, and go put herself at her window without saying a single word. I wanted to put myself beside her; she went away, sat down on a couch, got up the moment afterward, and walking around the room fanning herself, said to me with a cold and disdainful tone, "*Zanetto, lascia le Donne, e studia la matematica.*"[163]

Before I left her, I asked for another meeting for the next day which she put off until the third day adding, with an ironic smile, that I must need some rest. I passed this time ill at ease, my heart full of her charms and her graces, feeling my extravagance, reproaching myself for it, regretting the moments which I had used so poorly and which it had only depended on me to make the sweetest of my life, waiting with the most lively impatience for the one when I would repair the loss, and nevertheless in spite of everything I could do still anxious to reconcile the perfections of that adorable girl with the unworthiness of her condition. I ran, I flew to her at the stated hour. I do not know if her ardent temperament would have been more satisfied with this visit. At least her pride would have been, and in advance I looked forward to the delightful enjoyment of showing her that I knew how to redress my wrongs in every way. She spared me that test. The Gondolier, whom I sent to her when we touched land, reported to me that she had left for Florence the day before. If I had not felt all my love in possessing her, I felt it very cruelly in losing her. My senseless regret has not left me. Entirely lovable, entirely charming though she was to my eyes, I could console myself for losing her; but I admit that I could not console myself for the fact that she carried off only a contemptuous memory of me.

There are my two stories. The eighteen months [164] I passed in Venice furnished me with nothing further to say except a mere project at most. Carrio was a ladies' man. Bored at always visiting only girls who belonged to other men, he had the whim of having one in his turn, and since we were inseparable, he proposed to me the arrangement—hardly rare at Venice—of having one between the two of us. I agreed to it. It was a question of finding a safe one. He looked around until he unearthed a little girl of eleven or twelve years of age whose worthless mother was looking to sell her. [165] We went to see her together. My innermost emotions were stirred when I saw this child. She was blond and gentle as a lamb: one would never have believed she was Italian. One lives on very little at Venice: we gave some money to the mother and provided for the girl's upkeep. She had a voice; to provide her with a talent as a resort, we gave her a spinet and a singing teacher. All this cost us barely two sequins each a month, and we saved more in other expenses: but since it was necessary to wait until she was mature, this was sowing a lot before reaping. Nevertheless, content with going there to pass evenings, to chat and play with that child very innocently, we were perhaps more pleasantly amused than if we had possessed her. So true is it that what attaches us most to women is less debauchery than a certain pleasantness in living with them. Imperceptibly my heart became attached to the little Anzoletta, but with a paternal attachment, in which the senses had so little share that as it increased I would have been [166] less and less able to make them enter, and I felt that I would have been horrified at approaching that girl when she became nubile, as at an abominable incest. I saw the good Carrio's feelings taking the same turn without him being aware of it. Without thinking about it we were indulging in pleasures no less sweet, but very different from those we had been thinking of at first, and I am certain that however beautiful this poor child might have become, far from ever being the corruptors of her innocence, we would have been its protectors. My catastrophe, which happened a little later, did not allow me to have a share in this good work, and I have only the inclination of my heart to praise myself for in this business. Let us return to my trip.

When I left M. de Montaigu, my first plan was to withdraw to Geneva, while waiting until a better fate might reunite me to my poor mamma by overturning the obstacles; but the stir made by our quarrel and his stupidity in writing about it to the Court made me decide to go there myself to account for my behavior, and complain about that of a wild man.[167] From Venice I notified M. du Theil, who was temporarily in charge of foreign affairs after M. Amelot's death, about my resolution. I left as soon as my letter did: I took my route by way of Bergamo, Como, and Domodossola; I crossed the Simplon. At Sion M. de Chaignon, the chargé d'affaires of France, did me a thousand kindnesses: at Geneva M. de la Closure[168] did me as many. There I renewed my acquaintance with M. de Gauffecourt from whom I had some money to receive. I had gone through Nyon without seeing my father; not that this did not pain me extremely; but I had not been able to resolve to show myself to my step-mother after my disaster, certain that she would judge me without wanting to listen to me. My father's old friend, the book dealer Du Villard, reproached me ardently for this wrong. I told him its cause, and in order to remedy it without exposing myself to seeing my step-mother, I took a carriage, and we went together to Nyon and got off at a tavern. Du Villard went to look for my poor father, who came at a run to embrace me. We ate supper together, and after having passed an evening that was very sweet to my heart, I returned the next morning to Geneva with Du Villard, for whom I have always preserved gratitude for the good he did me on that occasion.

My shortest road was not by way of Lyon, but I wanted to pass through it to verify a very low piece of knavery by M. de Montaigu. I had had a little chest containing a coat embroidered in gold, some pairs of cuffs, and six pairs of white silk stockings come from Paris; nothing more.[169] On the proposal he made about it himself I had this chest or rather this box added to his baggage. In the Apothecary's bill which he wanted to give me as payment for my salary and which he had written in his own hand, he had put that this box, which he called a bale, weighed eleven quintals,[170] and he had me pay carriage on it at an enormous price. Through the efforts of M. Boy de la Tour to whom I had been recommended by his uncle M. Roguin, it was verified on the records of the Customs Houses of Lyon and Marseille that the so-called bale weighed only forty-five pounds, and had paid the carriage only at the rate for this weight. I joined this authentic extract to M. de Montaigu's bill, and armed with these pieces and several others of the same strength, I returned to Paris very impatient to make use of them. During that entire long route I had some small adventures at Como, in Valais, and elsewhere. I saw several things, among others the Borromean Islands which deserved[171] to be described. But time is gaining on me, spies plague me; I am forced to do hastily and poorly a work which requires the leisure and tranquillity which I lack. If providence, casting its eyes on me, ever procures me calmer days at last, I dedicate them to recasting this work if I can, or at least to writing a supplement which I feel it needs very much.*

The rumor of my story had preceded me, and when I arrived I found that in the Offices and the public everyone was scandalized by the Ambassador's follies. In spite of that, in spite of the public outcry in Venice, in spite of the unanswerable proofs I produced, I was not able to obtain any justice. Far from having either satisfaction or reparation I was even left to the Ambassador's discretion for my salary, and that for the sole reason that, since I was not French, I did not have a right to the national protection, and it was a private business between him and me. Everyone[173] agreed with me that I was offended against, injured, unlucky, that the Ambassador was a cruel, iniquitous crank, and that this entire business would dishonor him forever. But he was the Ambassador, I myself was only the Secretary and that was that. Good order, or what was called that, wished me to obtain no justice whatsoever, and I obtained none. I imagined that as a result of making an outcry and treating this madman publicly as he deserved, I would finally be told to be quiet, and that was what I was waiting for, well resolved not to obey until after it was pronounced. But there was no Minister of foreign affairs at that time. They let me chatter, they even encouraged me, they made a *chorus*: but the business always remained there, until tired of always being right and never receiving justice, I finally lost courage and gave up everything.

The only person who received me poorly and from whom I would have least expected that injustice was Mme de Beuzenwal. Full of the prerogatives of rank and nobility, she could never get it into her head that an Ambassador could be in the wrong with his Secretary. The welcome she gave me was in conformity with this prejudice. I was so irritated by it that upon leaving her house I wrote her perhaps one of the strongest and sharpest letters that I have written, and never went back. Father Castel received me better; but through the Jesuitical fawning, I saw him follow faithfully enough one of the great maxims of the society,[174] which

---

* I have renounced this project.[172]

is always to sacrifice the weaker to the more powerful. The lively feeling of the justice of my case and my natural pride did not let me endure this partiality patiently. I stopped seeing Father Castel, and consequently stopped going to the Jesuits where I knew only him. Moreover the tyrannical and intriguing spirit of his colleagues, so different from the geniality of the good Father Hemet,[175] gave me such an aversion for their company that I did not see any of them after that time, aside from Father Berthier whom I saw two or three times at the house of M. Dupin, with whom he was working with all his strength on the refutation of Montesquieu.[176]

Let us finish so as not to return again to what I have left to say about M. de Montaigu. In our quarrels I had told him that he did not need a secretary but a Procurator's Clerk. He followed this advice, and in fact took as a successor to me a true attorney who stole twenty or thirty thousand livres from him in less than a year. He fired him, had him put in prison, expelled his gentlemen with a disturbance and scandal, made quarrels for himself everywhere, received affronts that a valet would not put up with, and as a result of follies ended by having himself recalled and sent to plant his cabbages in retirement. Apparently his affair with me was not forgotten among the reprimands he received from the Court. At least a short time after his return he sent me his steward to settle my account and give me some money. I did not have any at that moment; my debts from Venice, debts of honor if ever there were any, weighed on my heart. I seized the means that presented itself to pay them off, along with Zanetto Nani's bill. I received what they wanted to give me, I paid all my debts, and I remained without a sou as before, but relieved of a weight that had been unbearable for me. Since that time I have not heard M. de Montaigu spoken of except for his death which I learned about from the public press. May God give peace to that poor man. He was as fit for the profession of Ambassador as I had been in my youth for that of pettifogger. Nevertheless, it had been up to him alone to have maintained himself honorably by means of my services, and to make me advance rapidly in the Station for which the Comte de Gouvon had destined me in my youth, and for which I had made myself capable at a more advanced age all by myself.

The justice and uselessness of my complaints left a seed of indignation in my soul against our foolish civil institutions in which the true public good and genuine justice are always sacrificed to some apparent order or other, in fact destructive of all order, and which does nothing but add the sanction of public authority to the oppression of the weak and the iniquity of the strong. Two things kept this seed from developing at that time as it did later on: one that this business pertained to myself, and that private interest, which has never produced anything great and noble, cannot draw from my heart the divine outbursts which can be produced in it only by the purest love of the just and the beautiful. The other was the charm of friendship which tempered and calmed my anger by the ascendancy of a gentler feeling. At Venice I had become acquainted with a Biscayan friend of my friend de Carrio, and worthy of being the same of any good man. This amiable young man, born to have all talents and all virtues, had just made a tour of Italy to acquire a taste for the fine arts, and imagining that he had nothing more to acquire, he wanted to return from it in uprightness to his own fatherland. I told him that the Arts were only the relaxation of a genius like his which was made to cultivate the sciences, and I advised him to make a trip and a six-month stay at Paris in order to acquire the taste for them. He believed me and went to Paris. He was there and was waiting for me when I arrived. His lodging was too big for him; he offered me half of it, I accepted it. I found him in the fervor of high knowledge.[177] Nothing was outside his grasp; he devoured and digested everything with a prodigious rapidity. How he thanked me for having procured this food for his mind which was tormented by the need to know without him even suspecting it! What treasures of enlightenment and virtues did I find in that strong soul! I felt that he was the friend I needed: we became intimate. Our tastes were not the same: we always disputed. Since we were both stubborn, we never agreed about anything. Even so we could not separate, and while we contradicted each other ceaselessly, neither of us would have wanted the other to act differently.

Ignacio Emanuel de Altuna was one of those rare men that Spain alone produces, and of whom she produces too few for her glory. He did not have those violent national passions common in his country. The idea of vengeance could no more enter into his mind than its desire into his heart. He was too proud to be vindictive, and I often heard him say very coolly that a mortal could not offend his soul. He was gallant without being tender. He played with women as with pretty children. He took pleasure with the mistresses of his friends, but I never saw him with one, or with any desire to have one. The flames of virtue with which his heart was devoured never allowed those of the senses to be born. After his travels he got married, he died young, he left children behind, and I am as persuaded as I am of my own existence that his wife is the first and the only one who caused him to know the pleasures of love. On the outside he was as devout as a Spaniard, but on the inside was the piety of an angel. As long as I have existed, I have not seen anyone aside from myself who was tolerant except for him. He never enquired about how any man thought in matters of religion. It mattered little to him whether his friend was a

Jew, Protestant, Turk, bigot,[178] atheist, as long as he was a decent man. Obstinate, stubborn with regard to indifferent opinions, as soon as it was a question of religion, even of morality, he gathered his thoughts, kept silent, or simply said, "I am responsible only for myself." It is unbelievable that one could bring together so much elevation of soul with a mind for details carried to the point of minutia. He divided up and fixed the use of his day in advance by hours, quarter hours, and minutes, and followed this distribution with such scrupulousness that if the hour sounded while he was reading a sentence, he closed the book without finishing it. From all these measures of time broken up this way, he had some for such and such a study, he had some for such another one; he had some for reflection, for conversation, for worship, for Locke, for the rosary, for visits, for music, for painting; and there was neither pleasure nor temptation nor desire to be obliging that could transpose this order. Only a duty to fulfill could have done that. When he made a list of his distributions for me so that I could conform to it, I began by laughing, and I finished by weeping with admiration. He never bothered anyone or put up with bother;[179] he was blunt with people who wanted to bother him through politeness. He was quick-tempered without being sulky. I often saw him angry, but I never saw him cross. Nothing was as gay as his disposition: he put up with raillery, and he loved to engage in it. He even shone in it and he had talent for epigrams. When he was animated he was noisy and boisterous in words; his voice was heard from far away. But while he was shouting one saw him smile, and all through his rages some joking phrase came to him that made everyone burst out. He no more had the Spanish complexion than its stolid disposition. He had white skin, ruddy cheeks, chestnut hair that was almost blond. He was tall and well put together. His body was formed as a residence for his soul.

Wise of heart as well as head, this man knew men and was my friend. This is my entire answer to anyone who is not. We became friends so well that we formed the plan of passing our lives together. I was supposed to go to [180] Azcoitia in several years to live with him on his estate. All the parts of this project were arranged between us on the eve of his departure. The only thing lacking was what does not depend on men in the best laid plans. Subsequent events, my disasters, his marriage, finally his death separated us forever.[181] One would say that only the black plots of the wicked succeed: the innocent plans of the good are almost never fulfilled.

Having felt the inconvenience of dependency, I firmly promised myself not to expose myself to it any longer. Having seen the plans of ambition which occasion had caused me to form reversed from their birth, having been rebuffed from returning into the career I had begun so well, and from which nevertheless I had just been expelled, I resolved no longer to attach myself to anyone, but to remain independent while turning to account my talents whose extent I was beginning to feel at last and which I had thought too modestly about until then. I again took up work on my Opera, which I had interrupted to go to Venice; and, after Altuna's departure, in order to abandon myself to it more tranquilly, I returned to lodge at my former hotel St. Quentin, which was more convenient for working at my ease than the noisy rue St. Honoré because it was in a solitary neighborhood not far from the Luxembourg Gardens. There the only real consolation that Heaven has made me taste in my misery and which alone makes it bearable to me was waiting for me. This is not a passing acquaintance; I ought to enter into some detail about how it was made.

We had a new landlady who was from Orléans. She took on a girl from her country to work on the laundry. She was about twenty-two or twenty-three years old and ate with us as the landlady did. This girl, called Therese le Vasseur,[182] was from a good family. Her father was Officer at the Mint at Orléans, her mother was a tradeswoman. They had many children. When the mint at Orléans ceased to operate, the father found himself unemployed; the mother, having suffered bankruptcy, managed her business badly, left commercial life, and came to Paris with her husband and daughter, who fed all three of them with her labor.

The first time I saw this girl appear at the table, I was struck by her modest bearing, and even more by her lively and sweet expression, which has never had its like for me. Aside from M. de Bonnefond,[183] the table was composed of several Irish Abbés, Gascons, and other people of a similar cut. Our landlady herself had led a dissipated life: I was the only one there who spoke and behaved modestly. They teased the little one; I took up her defense. Immediately the lampoons fell upon me. If I had naturally had no taste for that poor girl, compassion, contrariness would have given it to me. I have always liked decency in manners and in conversation, above all with the opposite sex. I loudly became her champion. I saw that she was grateful for my efforts, and her glances, which were animated by the gratitude which she did not dare to express with her mouth, only became more penetrating because of it.

She was very timid; so was I. The connection that this common inclination seemed to keep off nevertheless was formed very rapidly. The Landlady, who noticed it, became furious, and her brutalities furthered my affair with the little one, who—because she had no support but me alone in the house—saw me go out with pain, and sighed for her protector's return. The relation of our hearts, the agreement of our inclinations soon had its usual effect. In me she believed she saw a decent man; she was not mistaken. In her I believed I saw a sensitive, simple girl without coquetry; I was not mistaken either. I declared to her in advance that I would never either abandon her or marry her. Love, esteem, naive sincerity were the ministers of my triumph, and it was because her heart was tender and decent that I was fortunate even though I was not daring.

Her fear that I might get angry at not finding in her what she believed I was looking for postponed my happiness more than anything else. I saw her bewildered and confused before giving herself, wanting to make herself understood, and not daring to explain herself. Far from imagining the genuine cause of her perplexity, I imagined a very false one for it, and one that was very insulting to her morals, and believing that she was warning me that my health was running some risks, I fell into perplexities which did not hold me back, but which poisoned my happiness for several days. Since we did not understand each other at all, our conversations on this subject were so many enigmas and more than laughable nonsense. She was ready to believe that I was absolutely crazy; I was ready not to know what to think about her any more.[184] Finally we had it out: while weeping she admitted to me a single fault committed upon leaving childhood, the fruit of her ignorance and the skill of a seducer. As soon as I understood her I made a shout of joy.[185] "Virginity!" I shouted; "It is a fine thing to look for it in Paris at twenty years of age! Ah, my Therese! I am only too happy to possess you good and healthy, and not to find what I was not looking for."

At first I had sought only to give myself amusement. I saw that I had done more and that I had given myself a companion. A little experience with that excellent girl, a little reflection about my situation made me feel that, although I had been thinking only about my pleasures, I had done much for my happiness. In place of extinguished ambition I needed a lively feeling that filled my heart. I needed, to say it all, a successor to Mamma; since I must no longer live with her, I needed someone who could live with her student, and in whom I might find the simplicity, the docility of heart that she had found in me. The sweetness of private and domestic life had to compensate me for the brilliant fate I was renouncing. When I was absolutely alone my heart was empty, but only one was needed to fill it up. Fate had deprived me of, at least in part had alienated from me, the one for whom nature had made me. From that time I was alone, for there has never been any intermediate point for me between all and nothing. In Therese I found the supplement I needed; because of her I lived as happily as I could given the course of events.

At first I wanted to form her mind. I wasted my effort, Her mind is what nature has made it; cultivation and effort do not take hold there. I do not blush at all to admit that she has never known[186] how to read very well, although she writes passably. When I went to lodge in the rue Neuve des Petits-Champs, across from my windows at the Hôtel de Pontchartrain there was a sundial upon which I strove for more than a month to get her to know how to tell time. She still barely knows how at present. She has never been able to follow the order of the twelve months of the year, and does not know a single sum, in spite of all the efforts I have made to show her them. She does not know either how to count change or the price of anything. The word that comes to her in speaking is often[187] the opposite of the one she wants to say. In the past I had a dictionary of her sayings made up to amuse Mme de Luxembourg, and her malapropisms have become famous in the social circles in which I have lived. But this person, so limited and if you wish so stupid, gives excellent advice in difficult circumstances. Often in Switzerland, in England, in France, in the catastrophes in which I have found myself, she has seen what I did not see myself, she has given me the best advice to follow, she has extricated me from dangers into which I was blindly rushing, and among Ladies of the highest rank, among Nobles and princes, her feelings, her good sense, her answers and her conduct have drawn universal esteem upon her, and upon me compliments (the sincerity of which I felt) about her merit.

With people one loves, feeling nourishes the mind as well as the heart, and one has little need to seek ideas elsewhere. I lived with my Therese as pleasantly as with the finest genius in the universe. Her mother, proud of having been brought up with the Marquise de Monpipeau long before, played the fine wit, wanted to direct her mind, and spoiled the simplicity of our relations through her wiles. The annoyance of this badgering caused me to rise a little above the stupid shame of not daring to show myself with Therese in public, and we made little country walks tête-à-tête and little afternoon snacks that were delightful to me. I saw that she loved me sincerely, and that redoubled my tenderness. This sweet intimacy took the place of everything for me; the future no longer touched me or touched me only as the present prolonged: I desired nothing but to ensure its endurance.

This attachment made any other dissipation superfluous and insipid to me. I no longer went out except to go to Therese's; her residence almost became mine. This quiet[188] life became so advantageous for my work that in less than three months my opera was entirely done, words and music. Only several accompaniments and some filling in remained to be done. This menial labor bored me extremely. I proposed to Philidor that he take care of it, while giving him a share of the profit. He came two times, and did some filling in for the Ovid act: but he could not absorb himself in this painstaking work for a distant and even uncertain profit. He no longer came, and I finished my work myself.

Now that my Opera was done, it was a question of turning it to account: this was a much more difficult Operation. One does not achieve anything at Paris when one lives isolated there. I thought of making my way through M. de la Popliniére to whom Gauffecourt had introduced me upon returning from Geneva. M. de la Popliniére was Rameau's Patron: Mme de la Popliniére was his very humble student.[189] Rameau caused, as they say, the rain and the sunshine in that house. Judging that he would champion the work of one of his disciples with pleasure, I wanted to show him mine. He refused to look at it, saying that he could not read scores, and that it fatigued him too much. To that La Popliniére said that they could have him listen to it, and offered to assemble musicians for me to perform some portions of it: I did not ask for anything more. Rameau consented while grumbling, and repeating ceaselessly that the composition of a man who was not born into the profession and who had learned music all alone must be a fine thing. I hurried to put five or six choice pieces into parts. They gave me ten symphonists, and for Singers, Albert, Berard, and Mlle Boubonnois.[190] As early as the overture Rameau began to make it understood from his excessive praise that it could not be by me. He did not let a single piece by without giving signs of impatience: but at a Counter-Tenor tune the song of which was manly and sonorous and the accompaniment very brilliant, he could no longer contain himself. He addressed me with a brutality that scandalized everyone, maintaining that a part of what he had just heard was by a man consummate in the art and the rest by an ignoramus who did not even know music; and it is true that my uneven and irregular work was sometimes sublime and sometimes very flat, as must be one by anyone who raises himself up only through some bursts of genius and who is not sustained by Science. Rameau claimed to see in me only a little pilferer without talent and without taste. The audience and above all the master of the house did not think the same way. M. de Richelieu,[191] who at that time saw M. and—as is known—Mme de la Popliniére very much, heard my work spoken of and wanted to hear it completely with the plan of having it given at the court if he was satisfied with it. It was performed with a large Chorus and large Orchestra at the King's expense at the home of M. de Bonneval, the Intendant of Menus Plaisirs.[192] Francoeur[193] directed the performance. Its effect was surprising. M. the Duc did not stop exclaiming and applauding, and at the end of a Chorus in the Tasso act he got up, came to me, and shaking my hand, he said to me, "M. Rousseau, this is harmony that enraptures. I have never heard anything more beautiful: I want to have this work given at Versailles." Mme de la Poplinière, who was there, did not say a word. Rameau, although invited, had not wanted to come. The next day Mme de la Poplinière gave me an extremely harsh welcome at her dressing-table, affected to disparage my piece, and told me that, although a bit of tinsel had at first dazzled M. de Richelieu, he had soon completely recovered from it, and that she did not advise me to count on my opera. M. the Duc arrived a little later and used a completely different language with me, said flattering things to me about my talents, and still appeared disposed to have my piece given before the King. There was, he said, only the Tasso act which could not pass at Court: it was necessary to write another. Based on this word alone I went to shut myself up at home and in three weeks in place of the Tasso I had written another Act, the subject of which was Hesiod inspired by a muse. I found the secret of introducing into this act a part of the history of my talents, and the jealousy with which Rameau wanted to honor them. In this new act there was a less gigantic and better sustained elevation than in the Tasso one. Its music was as noble and much better written, and if the two other acts had been worth that one, the entire piece could have undergone performance favorably: but while I was finishing putting it into condition, another enterprise suspended its execution.

The winter that followed the Battle of Fontenoy, there were many celebrations at Versailles, among others several Operas at the theater of the Petites-Ecuries. Among this number was the Drama by Voltaire entitled *The Princess of Navarre*, for which Rameau had written the music, and which had just been changed and recast under the name of the *Festivals of Ramiro*. This new subject required several changes to the divertissements of the former one, in both the verses and the music. It was a question of finding someone who could fulfill this double object, since both Voltaire, then in Lorraine, and Rameau were occupied at that time on the Opera, *The Temple of Glory*, and could not give any effort to the other. M. de Richelieu thought of me, proposed to me that I take care of it, and sent me the Poem and the Music separately so I could examine better what there was to do. Before anything, I did not want to touch the words except with the Author's assent,[194] and on this subject I wrote him a very decent and even respectful letter, as was suitable. Here is his answer, the original of which is in the bundle A. #I.

December 15, 1745

Sir, you bring together two talents which have always been separate until now. Here are two good reasons for me to esteem and seek to love you already. I am sorry for you that you are using these two talents on a work that is not very worthy of them. Several months ago M. the Duc de Richelieu ordered me absolutely to write in the blink of an eye a little and bad sketch of some insipid and truncated scenes which were supposed to be adjusted to some divertissements that were not written for them at all. I obeyed with the greatest exactness, I wrote very quickly and very badly. I sent this wretched sketch to M. the Duc de Richelieu, count- ing[195] upon him not making use of it, or upon me correcting it. Fortunately it is in your hands, you are its absolute master; I have entirely lost the whole thing from sight. I do not doubt that you have corrected all the mistakes that necessarily slipped through in so rapid a composition of a simple sketch, that you have[196] compensated for everything.

I remember that among other blunders it is not said in the scenes that link the divertissements how Princess Grenadine passes suddenly from a prison into a garden or a Palace. Since it is not a magician who is giving her these celebra- tions, but a Spanish Nobleman, it seems to me that nothing ought to be done by enchantment. I beg you, Sir, to look at this place again about which I have only a confused idea. See whether it is necessary for the prison to be opened and whether our Princess is made to pass from that prison into a beautiful gilt and varnished Palace, prepared for her. I know[197] very well that all this is extremely wretched, and that it is beneath a thinking being to make a serious business out of these bagatelles;[198] but in the end, since it is a question of displeasing as little as one can, it is necessary to put as much reason as one can, even into a bad divertissement of an Opera.

I leave everything to you and to M. Ballod, and I count on having the honor of giving you my thanks soon, and of assuring you, Sir, to what point I have that of being etc.

Do not be surprised at the great politeness of this letter compared to the other half-flippant letters he has written me since that time. He believed I was in great favor with M. de Richelieu, and the courtier's suppleness for which he is known obliged him to more consideration for a newcomer until he knew the extent of his influence better.

Authorized by M. de Voltaire and dispensed from all consideration for Rameau, who sought only to injure me, I began to work, and in two months my task was done. As for the verses it was limited to very little. I tried only not to let the difference in styles be felt, and I had the presump- tion to believe I had succeeded. My work on the music was longer and more troublesome. Aside from the fact that I had to write several stately pieces, the Overture among others, the whole Recitative, with which I had been burdened, was extremely difficult, in that it was necessary to connect—often in a few verses and with very rapid modulations—instru- mental parts and choruses in keys that were very far apart; for, to prevent Rameau from accusing me of having disfigured his tunes, I did not want to change or transpose any of them. I succeeded at this Recitative. It was well accented, full of energy, and above all excellently modulated. The idea of the two superior men with whom they deigned to associate me had raised up my genius, and I can say that in this thankless work that brought no glory, about which the public could not even be informed, I almost always kept myself close to my models.

In the condition into which I had put it, the Piece was rehearsed at the large theater of the Opera. Of the three Authors, I alone was there. Voltaire was absent, and Rameau did not come, or hid himself.

The words of the first monologue were very mournful; here is its beginning.

O mort! viens terminer les malheurs de ma vie.[199]

It had been very necessary to write a matching music. Nevertheless, Mme de la Popliniére founded her blame on this, by very bitterly accusing me of having written funeral music. M. de Richelieu began judiciously by informing himself of who wrote the verses[200] of this monologue. I presented him the manuscript he had sent me, and which was evidence that it was by Voltaire. "In this case," he said, "it is Voltaire alone who is wrong." During the rehearsal everything that was by me was successively censured by Mme de la Popliniére and justified by M. de Richelieu. But in the end I had to yield to the stronger party, and I was informed that several things in my work had to be redone about which it was necessary to consult M. Rameau. Downcast at such a conclusion in place of the praise that I expected, and which certainly was due to me, I returned home with death in my heart. I fell sick there, worn out by fatigue, devoured by grief, and for six weeks I was in no condition to go out.

Rameau, who was entrusted with the changes indicated by Mme de la Popliniére, sent to ask me for the overture of my big Opera, to substitute it for the one I had just done. Fortunately I sensed the trick, and I refused it. Since there were no more than five or six days until the performance,[201] he did not have time to write one, and it was necessary to leave mine in. It was in the Italian manner and of a style very new in France at that time. Nevertheless, it was savored, and I learned through M. de Valmalette, the King's Steward and son-in-law of my relative and friend M. Mussard, that the devotees had been very satisfied with my work, and that the public had not distinguished it from Rameau's: but in concert with Mme de la Popliniére the latter took some measures so that it would not be known that I had even worked on it. On the books that are distributed to the spectators, and where the Authors are always named, only Voltaire was named,[202] and Rameau preferred for his name to be suppressed, rather than to see it associated with mine there.

As soon as I was in a condition to go out I wanted to go to M. de Richelieu: it was too late. He had just left for Dunkirk, where he was supposed to command the landing force intended for Scotland.[203] Upon his return, in order to authorize my laziness I told myself that it was too late. Because I did not see him again after that, I lost the honor my work deserved, the honorarium it should have procured for me; and my time, my labor, my grief, my illness, and the money it cost me, all that was at my expense, without returning me a sou of profit or rather compensation. Nevertheless, it always appeared to me that M. de Richelieu naturally had some inclination for me, and thought advantageously of my talents. But my misfortune and Mme de la Popliniére prevented all the effect of his good will.

I could not understand anything about the aversion of that woman whom I had struggled to please and to whom I paid my Court regularly enough. Gauffecourt explained its causes to me. "First," he told me, "her friendship for Rameau whose titular booster she is, and who does not want to put up with any rival, and further, an original sin that damns you with regard to her and for which she will never pardon you; that is to be a Genevan." Upon that he explained that the Abbé Hubert, who was M. de la Popliniére's sincere friend, had tried to prevent him from marrying that woman whom he knew well, and that after the marriage she had sworn an implacable hatred to him as well as to all Genevans. "Although la Popliniére," he added, "has some friendship for you—and I know he does—do not count on his support. He is in love with his wife; she hates you, she is wicked, she is skillful; you will never do anything in that house." I accepted it as a given.

At about the same time this same Gauffecourt rendered me a service I needed very much. I had just lost my virtuous father who was around sixty years old.[204] I felt this loss less than I would have at other times when the difficulties of my situation might have occupied me less. During his life I had not at all wished to lay claim to what was left of my mother's property and from which he drew the small income. After his death I no longer had any scruple on this matter. But the lack of juridical proof of my brother's death caused a difficulty that Gauffecourt took it upon himself to clear up, and in fact he did clear it up through the good offices of the Lawyer de Lorme. Since I had the greatest need of this small fund, and since the outcome was doubtful I waited for definite news about it with the most lively eagerness. Upon returning home one night, I found the letter that should contain that news, and I picked it up to open it with a trembling of impatience for which I was ashamed inside myself. "What!" I said to myself disdainfully, "will Jean-Jacques let himself be subjected to this point by self-interest and curiosity." On the spot I put the letter back on my mantlepiece. I got undressed, went to bed tranquilly, slept better than usual, and got up rather late the next day without thinking about my letter anymore. While getting dressed I noticed it, I opened it without rushing, I found a bill of exchange in it. I had many pleasures at the same time, but I can swear that the most lively was that of having been able to conquer myself. I would have twenty similar episodes to cite in my life, but I am too rushed to be able to say everything. I sent a small part of this money to my poor mamma, regretting with tears the happy time when I would have put all of it at her feet. All her letters felt the effect of her distress. She sent me heaps of recipes and secrets from which she claimed I would make my fortune and hers. Already the feeling of her misery was contracting her heart and shrinking her mind. The little I sent her was the prey of the rascals who importuned her. She got no profit from anything. That disgusted me with sharing what I needed with these wretches, above all after the useless attempt I made to rescue her from them, as will be told below.[205]

Time flowed away and money with it. We were two, even four, or to state more accurately we were seven or eight. For although Therese was of a disinterestedness which has few rivals, her mother was not like her. As soon as she saw herself a little replenished through my efforts, she had her whole family come to divide up the fruit. Sisters, sons, daughters, grand-daughters, all came, except her oldest daughter who was married to the director of Carriages at Angers. Everything I was doing for Therese was diverted by her mother in favor of these ravenous people. Since I was not dealing with a greedy person and I was not subjected by a mad passion I did not do anything foolish. Satisfied at keeping Therese decently but without luxury, sheltered from pressing needs, I consented that what she earned by her labor be entirely to her mother's profit, and I did not limit myself to that. But, through a fatality that pursued me, while Mamma was a prey to her boors, Therese was a prey to her family, and I could not do anything on any side that profited the one for whom I had intended it. It was peculiar that the youngest of Mme le Vasseur's children, the only one who had not been given a dowry, was the only one who fed her father and her mother and that—after having been beaten for a long time by her brothers, by her sisters, even by her nieces—this poor girl was now plundered by them without being able to defend herself any better from their thefts than from their blows. Only one of her nieces, called Goton Le Duc,[206] was rather amiable and with a rather gentle character although spoiled by the example and lessons of the others. Since I often saw them together I gave them the names they gave each other: I called the niece *my niece* and the aunt *my aunt*. Both called me their Uncle. From that came the name of *Aunt* by which I have continued to call Therese, and which my friends repeated sometimes when joking.

One can feel that I did not have a moment to lose in trying to extricate myself from such a situation. Judging that M. de Richelieu had forgotten me and no longer hoping for anything from the direction of the Court; I made several attempts to get my Opera performed in Paris; but I experienced difficulties that required a lot of time to vanquish, and I was more pressed from day to day. I took it into my head to present my little Play *Narcissus* to the Italian company: it was accepted there and I had free admission, which gave me a great pleasure. But that was all. I could never succeed at getting my play performed, and, bored with paying Court to Actors, I gave them up. Finally I came back to the last expedient I had left, and the only one I should have taken. While frequenting M. de la Popliniére's house I had distanced myself from M. Dupin's. Although they were relatives, the two Ladies did not get along and did not see each other at all. There was no society between the two houses and Thieriot alone was at home in both. He was charged with trying to bring me back to M. Dupin's. M. de Francueil was studying natural history and chemistry at that time and was making a collection. I believe that he aspired to the Academy of Sciences: for that purpose he wanted to write a book, and he judged that I could be useful to him in this labor. Mme Dupin, who on her side was considering another book, had just about the same intentions for me. They would have liked to have me in common as a sort of Secretary, and that was the object of Thieriot's urging. As a preliminary I required M. de Francueil to use his influence along with Jelyotte's[207] to get my work rehearsed at the Opera; he agreed to it. *The Gallant Muses* was rehearsed several times first in the Storeroom, then in the great theater. There were many people at the great rehearsal, and several pieces were very much applauded. Nevertheless, I myself felt during the performance, which was extremely badly conducted by Rebel,[208] that the piece would not pass, and even that it was not in a condition to appear without great corrections. Thus I retracted it without saying a word, and without exposing myself to a refusal: but I saw clearly from several indications that even if the work had been perfect it would not have passed. Francueil had certainly promised me to get it rehearsed, but not to get it accepted. He kept his word to me precisely. I always believed that I saw on that occasion and many others that neither he nor Mme Dupin cared to allow me to acquire a positive reputation in the world, perhaps out of fear that when their books were seen it might be assumed that they had grafted their talents onto mine.[209] Nevertheless, since Mme Dupin always assumed that I had very mediocre ones, and since she never used me except to write under her dictation, or in research of pure erudition,[210] this reproach, above all with regard to her, would have been very unjust.

This final poor success completely discouraged me. I abandoned all plans for advancement and glory, and without thinking any longer about true or vain talents which succeeded so little for me, I dedicated my time and my efforts to procuring my subsistence and that of my Therese, as might please those who were taking it upon themselves to provide for it. Thus I attached myself completely to Mme Dupin and M. de Francueil. That did not throw me into great opulence; for with the eight to nine hundred francs a year that I had the first two years, I barely had enough to provide for my primary needs, since I was forced to lodge in their neighborhood in a furnished room in a rather expensive quarter, and paid another rent at the far end of Paris at the end of the rue St. Jacques where I went to eat supper almost every night whatever the weather might be. I soon acquired the pace and even the taste for my new occupations. I became attached to Chemistry. Along with M. de Francueil I took several courses with M. Rouelle, and for good or ill we began to scribble on paper about that science whose elements we barely possessed.[211] In 1747 we went to pass the autumn in Tourraine at the Chateau of Chenonceaux, the royal house on the Cher, built by Henri II for Diane de Poitiers whose initials one still sees there, and now owned by M. Dupin the farmer general. We amused ourselves very much in that beautiful place; we made very good cheer there; I became fat as a Monk. We made a lot of music. I composed several Trios for singing full of a rather strong harmony and about which I will speak again perhaps in my supplement if I ever write one.[212] We acted Plays there; in two weeks I wrote one in three acts entitled *The Reckless Engagement*,[213] which will be found among my papers, and which has no merit other than much gaiety. I composed other little works there, among others a piece in verse entitled *Sylvie's Lane*,[214] from the name of a lane in the Park that borders the Cher, and all that was done without discontinuing my work on Chemistry and the one I was doing with Mme Dupin.

While I was growing fat at Chenonceaux, my poor Therese was growing fat in another way at Paris, and when I returned there I found the product that I had put into work[215] more advanced than I had thought. Given my situation, that might have thrown me into an extreme perplexity, if some dinner companions had not furnished me with the only resource that could extricate me from it. This is one of those essential

stories that I cannot write with too much simplicity, because in commenting on them I would have to excuse myself or charge myself, and I ought
not to do either here.

During Altuna's stay at Paris, instead of going to eat at a restaurant,
he and I usually ate in our neighborhood, almost across from the cul-de-
sac of the Opera, at a Mme la Selle's, a tailor's wife, who served rather
poor meals, but whose table did not fail to be sought after, because of
the good and reliable company found there; for they did not accept anyone unknown, and one had to be introduced by someone who usually
ate there. Commander de Graville, an old rake full of politeness and wit,
but lewd, lodged there, and attracted a mad and brilliant young group of
Officers in the Guards and Musketeers. Commander de Nonant, Knight
of all the Opera girls, daily brought all the news[216] from that bawdy
house. M. Du Plessis, a retired Lieutenant Colonel, a good and wise old
man, and Ancelet* Officer of the Musketeers, maintained a certain order
among these young people. Merchants, financiers, tradesmen, but polite,
decent ones and among those who were distinguished in their profession came there; M. de Besse, M. de Forcade, and others whose names
I have forgotten. In sum, one saw presentable people there from all stations, except Abbés and lawyers whom I never saw there and there was an
understanding not to introduce any of them. This rather numerous table
was very gay without being noisy, and they were lewd without grossness.
The old Commander with all his tales—coarse as to their substance—
never lost his politeness from the old Court, and never did a filthy word
leave his mouth without it being so amusing that women would have pardoned it. His tone served as the rule for the whole table: all these young
people related their gallant adventures with as much licence as grace, and
there was no shortage of tales about girls since the storehouse was at the
door: for the lane through which one went to Mme la Selle's also ran
by the shop of la Duchapt the famous milliner which at that time had
very pretty girls with whom our Gentlemen went to chat before or after
dinner. I would have amused myself there like the others if I had been
more bold. I only needed to enter as they did; I never dared. As for Mme

---

*It was to this M. Ancelet that I gave a little Play of mine entitled *The Prisoners of War*
that I had written after the disasters of the French in Bavaria and Bohemia, and which I
never dared acknowledge or show, and that for the singular reason that perhaps never have
the King or France or the French been better or more wholeheartedly praised than in this
Piece, and that as titular Republican and rebel, I did not dare to admit that I was the pane-
gyrist of a nation whose maxims were all opposed to mine. More grieved about France's
misfortunes than the French themselves, I was afraid that the marks of a sincere attachment,
the epoch and cause of which I have told in my first part and which I was ashamed to show,
might be accused of being flattery and cowardice.[217]

la Selle, I continued to go to eat there rather often after Altuna's departure. There I learned crowds of very amusing anecdotes, and also little by little I acquired, thanks to Heaven not the morals but the maxims I saw established there. Decent persons harmed, husbands deceived, women seduced, clandestine births were the most common texts there, and the one who best peopled the foundling hospital was always the most applauded. That won me over; I formed my way of thinking upon the one I saw reigning among very amiable, and at bottom very decent people, and I said to myself: since it is the practice of the country, when one lives there one can follow it, here is the expedient I was looking for.[218] I decided wantonly, without the slightest scruple, and the only one I had to overcome was Therese's whom I might have had all the trouble in the world in making adopt this only means of saving her honor. Since her mother— who furthermore, feared a new bother of a brat—came to my aid, she let herself be overcome. A prudent and reliable midwife, called Mlle Gouin, who resided at the Pointe St. Eustache was chosen, to entrust with this deposit, and when the time came Therese was led by her mother to la Gouin's[219] to have her delivery there. I went to see her there several times, and I carried a cipher to her which I had made doubly on two cards, one of which was placed in the child's swaddling clothes, and it was left by the midwife at the office of the foundling hospital following the usual procedure. The following year the same inconvenience and the same expedient, aside from the cipher which was neglected. No more reflection on my part, no more approbation on mother's; she obeyed groaning. One will see in succession all the vicissitudes that this fatal conduct has produced in my manner of thinking as well as in my destiny. As for now let us keep to this first period. Its consequences as cruel as they were unforeseen will force me to return to it only too often.

I note here the period of my first acquaintance with Mme d'Epinay, whose name will return often in these memoirs. She was called Mademoiselle Des Clavelles, and had just married M. d'Epinay the son of M. De Lalive de Bellegarde the farmer general. Her husband was fond of music, as was M. de Francueil. She was fond of music also, and the passion for this art formed a great intimacy among these three people. M. de Francueil introduced me into Mme d'Epinay's house; I ate supper there with him sometimes. She was amiable, had wit, talents, it was certainly a good acquaintance to make. But she had a friend called Mlle d'Ette who passed as wicked, and who lived with the Chevalier de Valory, who did not pass as good. I believe that the company of these two persons did a wrong to Mme d'Epinay, to whom nature had given, along with a very demanding temperament, excellent qualities to govern it or redeem her lapses.

M. de Francueil imparted to her a portion of the friendship he had for me, and admitted his connections with her to me, about which for that reason, I would not speak here, if they had not become public, even to the point of not being hidden from M. d'Epinay. M. de Francueil even told me very peculiar secrets about this Lady which she never told me herself and about which she never thought I was informed; for I did not open nor will I open my mouth about them in my life, either to her, or to anyone whatsoever.[220] All this confidence from both sides made my situation very perplexing, above all with Mme de Francueil, who knew me well enough not to distrust me, although I had relations with her rival. As best I could, I consoled this poor woman, to whom her husband certainly did not return the love she had for him. I listened to these three persons separately. I kept their secrets with the greatest faithfulness, without any of the three ever extracting any of the secrets of the other two, and without dissimulating to either of the two women my attachment for her rival. Mme de Francueil, who wanted to make use of me for many things, suffered explicit refusals, and once when Mme d'Epinay wanted to burden me with a letter for Francueil, not only did she receive a similar one, but also a very clear declaration that if she wanted to dismiss me from her house forever, she had only to make me a similar proposition a second time. I must do justice to Mme d'Epinay. Far from appearing to be displeased by this action, she spoke about it to Francueil with praise, and did not receive me any less well. This is how, in the stormy relations among three people whom I had to treat considerately, upon whom I depended to some extent, and for whom I had attachment, I preserved their friendship, their esteem, their confidence up to the end, by behaving with gentleness and the desire to be obliging but always uprightly and firmly. In spite of my stupidity and awkwardness Mme d'Epinay wanted to put me into the entertainments at la Chevrette, a Chateau near St. Denis belonging to M. de Bellegarde. There was a theater there in which they often performed plays. They burdened me with a role which I studied uninterruptedly for six months, and in which it was necessary to give me prompting from one end of the performance to the other. After this test no more roles were proposed to me.

In making Mme d'Epinay's acquaintance, I also made that of her sister-in-law Mademoiselle de Bellegarde, who soon became the Comtesse de Houdetot.[221] The first time I saw her she was on the eve of her marriage;[222] and she chatted with me for a long time with that charming familiarity that is so natural to her. I found her very amiable, but I was very far from foreseeing that this young person would one day bring about my life's destiny, and would sweep me away, although very innocently, into the abyss where I am today.[223]

Although I have not spoken about Diderot since my return from Venice, nor about my friend M. Roguin either, I nevertheless had not neglected either of them, and above all I was tied more intimately day by day with the former. He had a Nannette just as I had a Therese; this was one additional conformity between us. But the difference was that my Therese,[224] as good-looking as his Nannette, had a sweet disposition and a lovable character, fit to attach a decent man, instead of which his Nanette, a shrew and fishwife, showed nothing to the eyes of other people that could redeem her bad education. Still he married her: this was extremely well done if he had promised it. As for me who had promised nothing like it, I did not rush to imitate him.

I was also connected with the Abbé de Condillac, who, like myself, was a nobody in literature, but who was made to become what he is today. I am perhaps the first who saw his scope and who esteemed him at his true value. He also appeared to be pleased with me, and while I was writing my *Hesiod* act, shut up in my Room on rue Jean St. Denis near the Opera, he sometimes came to dine with me tête-à-tête Dutch treat. At that time he was working on the *Essay on the Origin of Human Knowledge*, which is his first work. When it was finished the difficulty was to find a book dealer who wanted to take it on. The book dealers of Paris are arrogant and harsh for any man who is beginning, and metaphysics—at that time very little in fashion—did not offer a very attractive subject. I spoke to Diderot about Condillac and his work; I had them become acquainted. They were made to get along with each other, they did get along. Diderot engaged the book dealer Durand to take the Abbé's manuscript, and from his first book this great metaphysician had, and almost as a favor, a hundred écus that he perhaps would not have found without me.[225] Since we resided in neighborhoods extremely far away from each other, all three of us gathered once a week at the Palais-royal, and we went to dine together at the Hôtel du Panier Fleuri. These little weekly dinners must have pleased Diderot extremely; for he, who missed almost all of his appointments,[226] never missed one of these. There I formed the project of a periodic pamphlet entitled *The Banterer*, that Diderot and I were supposed to write alternately.[227] I sketched the first pamphlet, and that caused me to make the acquaintance of d'Alembert to whom Diderot had spoken about it. Unforeseen events obstructed us, and the project remained there.

These two Authors had just undertaken the *Encyclopedic Dictionary*, which at first was only supposed to be a sort of translation of Chambers, more or less similar to that of the *Dictionary of Medicine* by James,[228] which Diderot had just finished. He wanted to have me participate somehow in this second undertaking, and proposed to me the part on music which I accepted and which I executed very hastily and very badly in the three months he had given to me as he had to all the Authors who were supposed to cooperate in this undertaking: but I was the only one who was ready in the prescribed term. I sent him my manuscript which I had had put into a fair copy by one of M. de Francueil's lackeys called Dupont who wrote very well, and to whom I paid ten écus taken from my pocket which were never reimbursed to me. On behalf of the Book dealers, Diderot had promised me a payment about which he never spoke to me again, nor I to him.[229]

This undertaking of the Encyclopedia was interrupted by his detention. The *Philosophical Thoughts* had attracted some troubles onto him which had no consequences at all. It was not the same with the *Letter on the Blind* which had nothing reprehensible but some personal barbs with which Mme du Pré de St. Maur and M. de Réaumur were shocked, and for which he was put into the Keep of Vincennes.[230] Nothing will ever depict the anguish that the misfortune of my friend made me feel. My fatal imagination which always makes the bad into the worse got frightened. I believed he was there for the rest of his life. My head almost turned. I wrote to Mme de Pompadour to beseech her to have him released or to receive permission to have me locked up with him. I had no answer to my letter: it was too unreasonable to be effective, and I do not flatter myself that it contributed to the softening they gave some time afterwards to the poor Diderot's captivity. But if it had lasted some time still with the same rigor I believe that I would have died out of despair at the foot of the unhappy Keep. Besides if my letter produced little effect I did not make much of it either; for I talked about it only to very few people, and never to Diderot himself.[231]

Book VIII[1]

I was obliged to make a pause at the end of the preceding Book. With this one begins the long chain of my misfortunes in its first origin.

Having lived in two of the most brilliant houses of Paris, I had not failed to make some acquaintances in spite of my lack of aplomb. Among others, at Mme Dupin's I had made that of the young crown prince of Saxe-Gotha and of his Tutor the Baron de Thun.[2] At M. de la Popliniére's I had made that of M. Segui, a friend of the Baron de Thun, and known in the literary world through his fine edition of Rousseau.[3] The Baron invited M. Seguy and me to go to pass a day or two at Fontenay-sous-Bois,[4] where the Prince had a house. We went there. While passing in front of Vincennes, at the sight of the Keep I felt a rending of the heart the effect of which the Baron noticed on my face. At supper the Prince spoke about Diderot's detention. In order to make me speak the Baron accused the prisoner of imprudence: some of which I put into the impetuous manner I defended him. They pardoned that excess of zeal in someone inspired by an unfortunate friend and changed the subject. Two Germans attached to the Prince were there. One called M. Klupffell,[5] a very witty man, was his Chaplain, and later on became his Tutor after having supplanted the Baron. The other was a young man called M. Grimm, who served him as a reader while waiting to find some position, and whose very sparing outfit announced his pressing need to find one.[6] From that very night Klupffell and I began a connection that soon became friendship. The connection with the Said Grimm did not exactly proceed so fast. He hardly put himself forward, being very far from that supercilious tone that prosperity gave him afterward. The next day at dinner we spoke about music; he spoke well about it. I was carried away with joy when I learned that he accompanied on the Clavichord. After dinner some[7] music was brought in. We made music all day at the Prince's Clavichord, and thus began that friendship which at first was so sweet for me, finally so fatal, and about which I will have so much to say from now on.

Upon returning to Paris I learned the agreeable news that Diderot had left the Keep, and he had been given the Chateau and park of Vincennes as prison on his parole with permission to see his friends.[8] How hard it was for me not to be able to run there that very instant! But being held back for two or three days at Mme Dupin's by essential concerns, after three or four centuries of impatience I flew into my friend's arms. Inexpressible moment! He was not alone. D'Alembert[9] and the Treasurer of the Ste. Chapelle were with him. Upon entering I saw only him, I only made a leap, a shout, I pressed my face onto his, I clasped him closely without speaking to him except with my tears and my sobs; I choked with tenderness and joy. His first movement after leaving my arms[10] was to turn toward the Ecclesiastic and say to him, "You see, Sir, how my friends love me." Having abandoned myself entirely to my emotion, I did not reflect on that way of drawing an advantage from it at the time. But when I have thought about it sometimes since then, I have always judged that in Diderot's place, that would not have been the first idea that would have come to me.

I found him very much affected by his imprisonment. The Keep had made a terrible impression on him and, although he was extremely pleasantly situated at the Chateau and master of his walks in a park that is not even closed in by walls, he needed the society of his friends so as not to surrender to his dark mood. Since I was certainly the one who commiserated the most with his pain, I believed I was also the one whose sight would be most consoling to him, and, in spite of very demanding occupations, at least every second day, I went either alone or with his wife to pass the afternoon with him.

That year 1749 the Summer was excessively hot. From Paris to Vincennes adds up to two leagues. Hardly in a condition to pay for cabs, at two o'clock in the afternoon I went on foot when I was alone, and I went quickly so as to arrive earlier. The trees on the road, always pruned in the fashion of the country, gave almost no shade, and often exhausted from the heat and fatigue, I spread out on the ground when I was not able to go any farther. I took it into my head to take some book along to moderate my pace. One day I took the *Mercury of France* and while walking and glancing over it I fell upon this question proposed by the Academy of Dijon for the prize for the following year: *Has the progress of the sciences and arts tended to corrupt or purify morals?*[11]

At the moment of that reading I saw another universe and I became another man. Although I have a lively remembrance of the impression I received from it, its details have escaped me since I set them down[12] in one of my four letters to M. de Malesherbes.[13] This is one of the peculiarities of my memory that deserves to be told. If it serves me, it does so only as long as I have relied on it, as soon as I entrust the deposit to paper it abandons me, and as soon as I have written a thing one time I no longer remember it at all. This peculiarity follows me even into music. Before I learned it, I knew multitudes of songs by heart: since I have known how to sing tunes that were noted down, I have been unable to retain any of them, and today I doubt that I can repeat a single one of those I have loved most fully.

What I do recall very distinctly on this occasion is that, when I arrived at Vincennes, I was in an agitation that bordered on delirium. Diderot noticed it; I told him its cause, and I read him the prosopopeia of Fabricius [14] written in pencil under an Oak. [15] He exhorted me to give vent to my ideas and to compete for the prize. [16] I did so, and from that instant I was lost. All the rest of my life and misfortunes was the inevitable effect [17] of that instant of aberration.

With the most inconceivable rapidity my feelings raised themselves to the tone of my ideas. All my little passions were stifled by enthusiasm for truth, for freedom, for virtue, and what is most surprising is that this effervescence maintained itself in my heart during more than four or five years to as high a degree perhaps as it has ever been in the heart of any other man. [18]

I worked on this discourse in a very peculiar manner and one which I have almost always followed in my other works. I dedicated the insomnias of my nights to it. I meditated in my bed with my eyes closed, and I shaped and reshaped my passages in my head with unbelievable difficulty; then when I had succeeded in being satisfied with them, I deposited them in my memory until I could put them on paper: but the time it took to get up and get dressed made me lose everything, and when I had applied myself to my paper, almost nothing of what I had composed came to me any more. I took it into my head to take Mme le Vasseur as Secretary. I had her lodged closer to me, along with her daughter and her husband, and in order to spare me a servant it was she who came every morning to light my fire and perform my little service. Upon her arrival I dictated my work from the night to her from my bed, and this practice—which I followed for a long time—has saved me from forgetting many things.

When this Discourse was done I showed it to Diderot who was satisfied with it, and who indicated some corrections for me. Nevertheless this work, full of warmth and strength, is absolutely lacking in logic and order; of all the ones that have come from my pen it is the weakest in reasoning and the poorest in unity and harmony; but whatever talent one might have been born with, the art of writing is not learned all at once.

I sent this Piece off without speaking about it to anyone else, except I think to Grimm, with whom I began to live in the greatest intimacy after his entrance into the Comte de Friese's [19] household. He had a Clavichord which served as a meeting point for us, and around which I passed with him all the moments I had free, singing Italian songs and barcaroles without respite and without rest from morning to night or rather from night to morning, and whenever I was not found at Mme Dupin's I was sure to be found at M. Grimm's, or at least with him, either taking a walk or at the theater. I stopped going to the Comédie Italienne where I had my free admission but which he did not like, in order to go with him—and pay—to the Comédie Française with which he was impassioned. In sum, such a powerful attraction linked me to that young man and I became so inseparable from him that the poor aunt herself was neglected for him; that is to say I saw her less, for my attachment for her has never weakened for a moment of my life.

This impossibility of dividing the little time I had free among those I loved renewed more keenly than ever the desire I had had for a long time of making a single household with Therese: but the encumbrance of her numerous family and above all the lack of money to buy furnishings had kept me back until then. The occasion for making an effort presented itself, and I took advantage of it. Feeling very well that eight to nine hundred francs a year could not be enough for me, M. de Francueil and Mme Dupin raised my annual fee to fifty louis[20] at their own initiative, and moreover, learning that I was seeking to set myself up with furnishings, Mme Dupin gave me some help; with the furnishings Thérese already had, we put everything in common, and having rented a little apartment at the Hôtel de Languedoc, rue de Grenelle St. Honoré with some very good people, we settled ourselves in there as best we could, and we resided there peacefully and pleasantly for seven years up until my moving away for the Hermitage.

Thérése's father was a very gentle good old man who was extremely afraid of his wife, and who, because of that, had given her the nickname of the Lieutenant-Criminel,[21] which Grimm afterwards transferred to the daughter as a joke. Mme le Vasseur was not lacking in intelligence that is to say craftiness,[22] she prided herself even for politeness and the airs of high society; but she had a mysterious wheedling that was unbearable to me; she gave her daughter rather bad advice, tried to make her dissemble with me, and cajoled my friends separately each at the other's expense and at mine: otherwise she was a good enough mother because she found it to her advantage to be so, by covering over her daughter's faults because she took advantage of them. This woman, whom I heaped with attentions, efforts, little presents, and whom I took it very much to heart to make love me, was—as a result of the impossibility of succeeding that I experienced—the sole cause of pain that I had in my little household, and otherwise, I can say that during those six or seven years I tasted the most perfect domestic happiness that human weakness can allow. My Therese's heart was that of an angel: our attachment increased with our intimacy, and each day we felt more how much we were made for each other. If our pleasures could be described, their simplicity would make one laugh. Our walks tête-à-tête outside the city where I magnificently dispensed eight or ten sous at some roadside inn. Our little suppers at the casement of my window, sitting across from each other on two little chairs posed on a trunk which filled the breadth of the embrasure. In this situation the window served us as a table, we breathed the air, we could see the surroundings, the passersby, and—although we were in the fourth story—dive into the street eating all the while. Who will describe, who will feel the charms of these meals, consisting only of a quarter loaf of coarse bread, some cherries, a little piece of cheese, and a quarter-pint of wine which we drank together. Friendship, trust, intimacy, sweetness of soul, how delightful our seasonings were. Sometimes we stayed there until midnight without thinking about it and without suspecting the time, unless the old Mamma had informed us of it. But let us leave these details which will appear insipid or laughable. I have always said and felt it: genuine enjoyment cannot be described at all.

At about the same time I had a coarser enjoyment, the last of that sort with which I have to reproach myself. I have said that the Minister Klupf-fell was likable; my connections with him were hardly less close than with Grimm, and became as familiar; they sometimes ate at my home. These meals, a little more than simple, were enlivened by Klupffell's subtle and foolish dirty remarks and by the amusing Germanisms of Grimm, who had not yet become a purist. Sensuality did not preside at our little orgies, but joy took its place, and we found that we got along so well together that we could no longer leave each other. Klupffell had furnished a room for a little girl who[23] did not fail to belong to everyone, because he could not maintain her by himself. One night, while we were entering a coffee-house, we found him leaving it to go eat supper with her. We bantered with him; he avenged himself for it gallantly by taking us to the supper, and then bantering at us in our turn. This poor creature appeared to me to be of a rather good natural disposition, very gentle, and hardly made for her profession, for which a hag whom she had with her trained her the best she could. The conversation and the wine enlivened us to the point of forgetting ourselves. The good Klupffell did not want to do his honors half-way and one after the other all three of us went into the neighboring room with the poor little one, who did not know whether she should laugh or cry. Grimm has always affirmed that he did not touch her: then he stayed with her for so long to amuse himself by making us impatient, and if he did abstain, it is hardly probable that it was out of a scruple, because he lodged with girls in the same St. Roch neighborhood before he entered the household of the Comte de Friese.

I left the rue des Moineaux where this girl lodged just as ashamed as St. Preux was when he left the house where they got him drunk, and I recalled my story well while I was writing his.[24] From some sign and above all from my confused manner Therese noticed that I had some reproach to make to myself; I lessened its weight by my frank and prompt confession. I acted well; for as early as the next day Grimm came in triumph to tell her my crime while aggravating it, and since then he has never missed reminding her of it malignantly; he is all the more culpable in this because, since I had freely and willingly[25] put him into my confidence, I had a right to expect that he would not make me regret it. Never have I felt my Therese's kindness of heart better than on that occasion: for she was more shocked at Grimm's action than offended at my infidelity, and from her side I experienced only some touching and tender reproaches in which I never noticed the slightest trace of resentment.

That excellent girl's simplicity of mind equaled her kindness of heart, that says everything; but an example that presents itself nevertheless deserves to be added. I had told her that Klupffell was a Minister and Chaplain of the Prince of Saxe-Gotha. For her a Minister was such a singular man,[26] that, comically confusing the most disparate ideas, she took it into her head to take Klupffell for the Pope; I believed she was crazy the first time she told me, as I returned, that the Pope had come to see me. I had her explain and I did not lose a moment in going to tell this story to Grimm and Klupffell, to whom the name of Pope remained among us. We gave the girl of the rue des Moineaux the name Pope Joan.[27] Our laughter was inextinguishable; we choked from it. Those who have made me say in a letter which they were pleased to attribute to me, that I had laughed only twice in my life, did not know me at that time nor in my youth: for assuredly that idea could never have come to them.

The following year 1750, when I was no longer thinking about my discourse, I learned that it had won the prize at Dijon.[28] This news reawoke all the ideas that had dictated it to me, animated them with a new strength, and finished setting into fermentation in my heart that first leaven of heroism and virtue which my Father and my fatherland and Plutarch had put there in my childhood. I no longer found anything great and beautiful but to be free and virtuous, above fortune and opinion, and to suffice to oneself. Although false shame and the fear of hisses kept me from behaving upon these principles at first and from brusquely quarreling openly with the maxims of my century, from then on I had the decided will to do so, and I delayed executing this only for the amount of time it took for the contradictions to irritate it and render it triumphant.

While I was philosophizing about the duties of man, an event happened to make me reflect better about my own. Therese became pregnant for the third time. Being too sincere with myself, too proud inside to want to make my actions give the lie to my principles, I began to examine the destination of my children and my connection with their mother according to the laws of nature, justice, and reason, and according to those of that pure, holy religion eternal as its Author, which men have soiled while feigning to want to purify it, and which by means of their formulas they have made into merely a religion of words, seeing that it costs little to prescribe the impossible, when one dispenses oneself from practicing it.

If I was mistaken in my results, nothing is more surprising than the security of soul with which I abandoned myself to them. If I was one of those low-born men, deaf to the gentle voice of nature, inside of whom no true feeling of justice and humanity ever sprouts, this hardening would be very simple to explain. But that warmth of heart; that very lively sensitivity; that facility at forming attachments; that strength with which they subject me; those cruel wrenchings when it is necessary to sever them; that innate good will for my fellows,[29] that ardent love of the great, the true, the beautiful, the just; that horror of evil of every sort; that impossibility of hating, of doing harm, and even of wanting to; that pity, that lively and sweet emotion that I feel at the sight of all that is virtuous, generous, lovable; can all this ever be reconciled in the same soul with the depravity which caused the sweetest of duties to be trampled underfoot without scruple? No, I feel it and say it loudly; that is not possible. Never for a single instant of his life could J.-J. have been a man without feeling, without innermost emotions,[30] a denatured father. I might have deceived myself, but not hardened myself. If I stated my reasons, I would be saying too much about them. Since they were able to seduce me they would seduce many others: I do not want to expose the young people who might read me to allowing themselves to be deceived by the same error. I will content myself with saying that my reason was such[31] that by abandoning my children to public education for lack of power to bring them up myself; by destining them to become workers and peasants rather than adventurers and fortune hunters, I believed I was performing an action of a Citizen and father, and I looked at myself as a member of Plato's Republic. More than once since then, the regrets of my heart have taught me that I had deceived myself, but my reason has been far from giving me the same admonition; I have often thanked Heaven for having protected them from their father's fate that way, and from the one that threatened them when I would have been forced to abandon them. If I had left them with Mme d'Epinay or Mme de Luxembourg, who, either from friendship, or from generosity, or from some other motive, wanted to take care of them afterward, would they have been happier, would they at least have been raised as decent people? I do not know; but I am sure that they would have been brought to hate, perhaps to betray their parents: it was a hundred times better that they never knew them.

Thus my third child was put in the foundling hospital just like the earlier ones, and it was the same for the two following ones; for I had five of them in all. That arrangement appeared so good, so sensible, so legitimate to me that if I did not openly boast about it this was solely out of regard for the mother, but I did tell it to everyone to whom I had declared our relations;[32] I told it to Diderot, to Grimm, I informed Mme d'Epinay of it later, and even later Mme de Luxembourg, and did so freely, frankly, without any sort of necessity, and being able to hide it easily from everyone; for la Gouin was an honest woman, very discreet, and upon whom I counted perfectly. The only one of my friends to whom I had some interest in confiding was Thyerri[33] the doctor who took care of my poor aunt in one of her confinements during which she was very ill. In a word, I made no mystery of my conduct, not only because I have never been able to hide anything from my friends, but because in fact I saw nothing evil in it. Everything weighed, I chose the best for my children or what I believed to be so. I would have wished, I would still wish to have been brought up and nurtured as they have been.

While I was confiding my secrets this way, Mme le Vasseur confided hers also on her side, but with less disinterested intentions. I had introduced her and her daughter to Mme Dupin, who out of friendship for me had a thousand kindnesses for them. The mother put her into her daughter's secret. Mme Dupin, who is good and generous, and whom she did not tell how attentive I was to provide for everything in spite of the scantiness of my resources, provided for it on her side with a liberality which—by the mother's order—the daughter always hid from me during my stay at Paris, and which she admitted to me only at the Hermitage, following several other outpourings of the heart. I did not know that Mme Dupin, who never gave me the slightest semblance of it, was so well informed: I still do not know whether her daughter-in-law Mme de Chenonceaux was also: but her step-daughter-in-law Mme de Francueil was and could not keep quiet about it. She spoke to me about it the following year when I had already left their house. That induced me to write a letter to her on this subject which will be found in my collection, and in which I expose those among my reasons that I could tell without compromising Mme le Vasseur and her family; for the most determinant ones came from there, and I was silent about them.[34]

I am certain about Mme Dupin's discretion and about Mme de Chenonceaux's friendship; I was the same about Mme de Francueil's, who moreover died a long time before my secret was noised abroad. It could never have been done except by the very people to whom I had confided it, and in fact was not done until my rupture with them. From this fact alone they are judged: without wishing to exculpate myself from the blame I deserve, [I would rather be burdened with it][35] than with the blame their wickedness deserves. My fault is great, but it is an error: I neglected my duties, but the desire to harm did not enter my heart, and the innermost emotions of a father could not speak very powerfully for children one has never seen: but to betray the confidence of friendship, to violate the most holy of all compacts, to publish secrets poured into our bosom, wantonly to dishonor the friend one has deceived, and who still respects us when he leaves us, those are not faults;[36] they are acts of baseness of soul and of heinousness.

I have promised my confession, not my justification: thus I stop here at this point. It is up to me to be truthful, it is up to the reader to be just. I will never ask anything more of him.

M. de Chenonceaux's marriage made his mother's house even more pleasant for me because of the merit and intelligence of the new bride, a very amiable young person, and one who appeared to single me out among M. Dupin's scribes. She was the only daughter of Mme the Vicomtesse de Rochechouart,[37] a great friend of the Comte de Friese, and as a consequence of Grimm who clung to him. Nevertheless, I was the one who introduced him to her daughter's house; but their dispositions did not fit each other, that connection had no consequences at all, and Grimm—who from that time on was taking aim at the solid—preferred the mother, a woman of high society, to the daughter, who wanted reliable friends who got along with her, without getting mixed up in any intrigue, or seeking influence among the Great. Since she did not find in Mme de Chenonceaux all the docility she expected from her, Mme Dupin made her house very sad for her, and Mme de Chenonceaux, who was proud of her merit and perhaps of her birth, preferred to renounce the pleasures of society and to remain almost alone in her apartment than to bear a yoke for which she did not feel herself made. This sort of exile increased my attachment for her by means of that natural inclination that attracts me to the unfortunate. In her I found a metaphysical and thinking mind, although every so often a little sophistic. Her conversation, which was not at all that of a young woman who is leaving the convent, was very attractive to me. Nevertheless, she was not twenty-years old. Her complexion was of a dazzling whiteness; her stature would have been tall and beautiful if she had held herself up better. Her uncommonly beautiful ash blonde hair reminded me of that of my poor Mamma in her beautiful age, and made my heart flutter in a lively way. But the severe principles I had just made for myself, and which I was resolved to follow at all cost, protected me from her and her charms. For a whole summer I passed three or four hours a day with her in tête-à-tête, gravely showing her arithmetic and boring her with my eternal numbers, without saying a single gallant word to her or ogling her. Five or six years later I would not have been so wise or so foolish; but it was written that I was to love with love only once in my life, and that someone other than she would have the first and last sighs of my heart.

Since I had been at Mme Dupin's I was always satisfied with my lot without showing any desire to see it improved. The increase she had made in my pay jointly with M. de Francueil had come solely from their own initiative. That year, M. de Francueil, who was acquiring more friendship for me day by day, thought of setting me up a little more liberally and in a less precarious situation. He was a Receiver General of finances. M. Dudoyer his Cashier was old, rich, and wanted to retire. M. de Francueil offered me that place, and, in order to put myself in a position to fulfill it I went to M. Dudoyer for several weeks to acquire the necessary instructions. But, either because I had little talent for that employment, or because Dudoyer—who appeared to me to want to give himself another successor—did not instruct me in good faith, I acquired the knowledge I needed slowly and poorly, and I could never get all that deliberately confused order of accounts into my head very well. Nevertheless, without having grasped the fine points of the profession, I did not fail to acquire its ordinary workings well enough to be able to carry it on briskly.[38] I even began its functions; I kept the Registers and the Money box; I gave and received money, receipts, and, although I had as little taste as I had talent for this profession, since maturity of years was beginning to make me wise, I was determined to overcome my repugnance in order to abandon myself entirely to my employment. Unfortunately, as I was beginning to put myself under way, M. de Francueil made a small trip during which I remained in charge of his money box which nevertheless had only twenty-five to thirty thousand francs in it at the time. The cares, the anxiety of mind which this deposit gave me, made me feel that I was not at all fit to be a Cashier, and I do not doubt that the undue worry I had during this absence contributed to the illness into which I fell after his return.

I said in my first part that I was born dying. A vice of conformation in the Bladder made me suffer an almost continual retention of urine during my earliest years, and my aunt Suson who took care of me had unbelievable difficulties keeping me alive. Nevertheless she succeeded; my robust constitution finally got over it, and my health asserted itself so much during my youth that except for the malady of languor whose story I have recounted, and a frequent need to urinate which the slightest overexcitement always made inconvenient for me, I arrived at the age of thirty almost without feeling the effect of my first infirmity. The first new feeling I had of it was upon my arrival at Venice. The fatigue from the trip and the terrible heat I had suffered gave me a burning in the urine and illness in the kidneys that I kept until the beginning of winter. After having seen la Padoana I believed myself dead and did not have the slightest discomfort. After having exhausted myself more by imagination than by body for my Zulietta, I was healthier than ever. It was only after Diderot's imprisonment that an overexcitement contracted on my trips to Vincennes during the terrible heat we had at the time gave me a violent pain in the kidneys, since which I have never recovered my earliest health.

At the moment about which I am speaking, perhaps because I was a little fatigued from the depressing work with that cursed Money box, I fell back lower than hitherto, and I remained in my bed for five or six weeks[39] in the saddest condition that one can imagine. Mme Dupin sent me the famous Morand[40] who, in spite of his skillfulness and the delicacy of his touch, made me suffer unbelievable pain and could never succeed in probing me. He advised me to have recourse to Daran,[41] whose more flexible catheters in fact succeed in being inserted;[42] but when he gave an account of my condition to Mme Dupin, Morand declared to her that I would not be alive in six months. This speech, which reached me, made me make some serious reflections about my position and about the stupidity of sacrificing the peace and pleasantness of the few days I had left to live to the subjugation of an employment for which I felt only distaste. Moreover, how could the severe principles I had just adopted be harmonized with a station which had so little relation to them, and would not I, a Cashier of a Receiver General of finances, be preaching disinterestedness and poverty in good grace? These ideas fermented so much in my head along with the fever, they became combined with such strength, that nothing since then has been able to extract them, and during my convalescence, I confirmed in coolness the resolutions I made in my delirium. I renounced forever every project of fortune and advancement. Determined to pass the little time I had left to live in independence and poverty, I applied all the strength of my soul to breaking the irons of opinion, and to doing courageously everything that appeared good to me, without bothering myself in any way about the judgment of men. The obstacles I had to combat and the efforts I made to triumph over them are unbelievable. I succeeded as much as possible, and more than I myself had hoped. If I had also shaken off the yoke of friendship as well as that of opinion I would have attained the goal of my plan, perhaps the greatest or at least the most useful to virtue that a mortal might ever have conceived: but while I trampled underfoot the senseless judgments of the vulgar mob of self-proclaimed grandees and self-proclaimed wise men, I let myself be subjugated and led about like a child by some self-proclaimed friends, who—jealous at seeing me walk[43] alone in a new route and all the while appearing to be very much occupied with making me happy—in fact occupied themselves only with making me ridiculous, and began by working to degrade me so as to succeed afterwards in defaming me. It was less my literary celebrity than my personal reform, whose period I mark here, that attracted their jealousy to me: perhaps they would have pardoned me for shining in the art of writing; but they could not pardon me for using my behavior to give an example[44] which seemed to be troublesome to them. I was born for friendship, my easygoing and gentle disposition nourished it without effort. As long as I lived unknown to the public I was loved by everyone who knew me, and I did not have a single enemy. But as soon as I had a name I no longer had any friends. This was a very great misfortune, an even greater one was to be surrounded by people who took that name, and who made use of the rights it gave them only to drag me to my ruin. The sequel of these Memoirs will develop this odious scheme; here I show only its origin: one will soon see its first knot formed.

Even in the independence in which I wished to live, I needed to exist. I imagined a very simple means for doing so: it was to copy music at so much a page. If some more solid occupation could have fulfilled the same goal, I would have taken it; but since this talent was to my taste and the only one that could give me bread from day to day without personal subjugation, I kept to it. Believing I no longer needed foresight, and making vanity keep silent, out of a Cashier of a Financier I made myself a music copyist. I believed I had gained very much from this choice, and I have repented it so little that I have left this profession only from force only to take it up again as soon as I could.[45] The success of my first discourse made the execution of this resolution easier for me. When it had won the prize,[46] Diderot took it upon himself to get it published. While I was in my bed he wrote me a note to announce its publication and effect to me.[47] "*It is succeeding,*" he notified me, "*beyond the skies; there is no precedent for such a success.*" This favor of the public, in no way courted and for an unknown Author, gave me the first genuine assurance of my talent which I had always doubted until then in spite of the internal feeling.[48] I understood all the advantage I could take from it for the decision I was ready to reach, and I judged that a copyist of some celebrity in letters would not be likely to lack work.

As soon as my resolution was completely formed and completely confirmed I wrote a note to M. de Francueil to announce it to him, to thank him, as well as Mme Dupin for all their kindnesses, and to ask for their custom. Because he did not understand a thing in this note and believed I was still in the transport of fever, Francueil hastened to me; but he found my resolution so completely formed that he could not succeed in shaking it. He went to tell Mme Dupin and everyone that I had gone mad; I allowed it to be said and went on my way. I began my reform with my adornment; I gave up gilt and white gloves, I put on a round wig, I took off my sword, I sold my watch, saying to myself with an unbelievable joy, "Thank Heaven, I will no longer need to know what time it is." M. de Francueil had the decency to wait a rather long time before disposing of his money box. Finally seeing my decision very much made, he gave it to M. d'Alibard, formerly Tutor of the young Chenonceaux, and known in botany from his *Flora parisiensis.**

However austere my sumptuary reform might have been, at first I did not extend it to my linen, which was fine and plentiful, the remnant of my outfit from Venice, and for which I had a particular attachment. As a result of making it into an object of cleanliness, I had made it into an object of luxury which did not fail to be costly. Someone performed me the good service of freeing me from this servitude. On Christmas Eve, while the Governesses[49] were at Vespers and I was at the Sacred Concert, someone forced the door of an attic where all our laundry was spread out after a washing that had just been done. Everything was stolen including forty-two Shirts of mine of very fine cloth, and which made up the basis[50] of my wardrobe in linen. From the way the neighbors described a man they had seen leaving the house carrying some packages at the same time, Therese and I suspected her brother who was known to be a very bad sort. The mother denied this suspicion in a lively way, but so many indications confirmed it that it remained with us in spite of everything she could do. I did not dare to make exact inquiries from fear of finding more than I would have liked. This brother no longer showed himself in

---

*I do not doubt that all this is now recounted very differently by Francueil and his confederates: but I refer to what he said about it then and for a long time afterwards to everyone until the formation of the plot, and the remembrance of which must have been preserved by people of good sense and good faith.

my home, and finally disappeared completely.[51] I deplored Therese's lot and mine of belonging to such a mixed family, and I exhorted her more than ever to shake off such a dangerous yoke. This adventure cured me of the passion for fine linen, and since then I have had only very common material, more suited to the rest of my outfit.

Having completed my reform this way, I no longer dreamed about anything but making it solid and durable, by working to uproot from my heart everything that still depended on the judgment of men, everything that could turn me away from what was good and reasonable in itself out of fear of blame. With the aid of the commotion my work made, my resolution made a commotion also and attracted some custom to me; so that I began my profession rather successfully. Nevertheless, several causes kept me from succeeding in it as I could have done in other circumstances. First, my ill health. The attack I had just suffered had consequences which never left me as healthy as before, and I believe that the Doctors to whom I abandoned myself did me as much harm as the illness. I saw successively Morand, Daran, Helvetius,[52] Malouin,[53] Thyerri, all very learned, all my friends, who each treated me in his fashion, did not relieve me at all, and weakened me considerably. The more I submitted to their direction, the more I became jaundiced, thin, weak. Because it measured my condition by the effect of their drugs, my imagination, which they alarmed, showed me only a succession of sufferings, retentions, gravel, kidney stones up to my death. Everything that relieved other people—infusions, baths, blood-letting—made my ills worse. Having noticed that Daran's probes, which alone had some effect on me and without which I did not believe I could live anymore,[54] nevertheless gave me only a momentary relief, at great expense I began to make an immense store of probes to be able to use them my whole life, even in case Daran was not available.[55] For the eight or ten years during which I used them so often, I must have spent fifty Louis on them considering how many I have left.[56] One feels that such a costly, such a painful, such a bothersome treatment did not let me work without distraction, and that a dying man does not put a very lively ardor into earning his daily bread.

Literary occupations made another distraction that was no less prejudicial to my daily work. Hardly had my *Discourse* appeared when the defenders of letters pounced on me as if by agreement. Indignant at seeing so many little Messieurs Josses[57] who did not even understand the question wish to decide it as masters, I took up the pen and I treated some of them in a manner that did not leave the laughers on their side. A certain M. Gautier from Nancy, the first who fell under my pen,[58] was roughly handled in a letter to M. Grimm. The second was King Stanislaus himself who did not disdain entering the lists with me. The honor he did me forced me to change my tone in order to answer him; I took on a more serious one, but not less strong, and without failing in respect to the Author, I wholly refuted the work. I knew that a Jesuit called Father de Menou had put his hand into it; I relied on my sense of discrimination to disentangle what was by the Prince and what was by the Monk, and falling roughly on all the Jesuitical sentences, as I proceeded I pointed out an anachronism that I believed could have come only from the Reverend.[59] Up to the present, this piece, which somehow or other has made less commotion than my other writings, is a unique work in its type. In it I seized the occasion I was offered to teach the public how a private man could defend the cause of truth even against a sovereign. It is difficult to take a more proud and at the same time more respectful tone than the one I took to answer him. I had the good fortune to be dealing with an adversary for whom my heart was full of esteem and therefore could bear witness of it to him without adulation; that is what I did successfully enough, but always with dignity. Being frightened for me, my friends already believed they saw me in the Bastille. I did not fear that for a single moment, and I was right. After having seen my answer this good Prince said, "That is enough for me, I will not have anything more to do with it." Since then I have received several marks of esteem and benevolence from him some of which I will be citing,[60] and my writing circulated tranquilly around France and Europe without anyone finding anything to blame in it.

A little time afterward I had another adversary whom I had not expected: the same M. Bordes of Lyon who ten years before had performed so many acts of friendship for me and rendered several services. I had not forgotten him, but I had neglected him out of laziness, and I had not sent him my writings from lack of an occasion ready to hand to get them to him. Thus I was wrong, and he attacked me, honestly however, and I responded the same way. He replied in a more decided tone. That gave occasion to my final reply, after which he said nothing more;[61] but he became my most ardent enemy, seized the time of my misfortunes to make horrid libels against me,[62] and made a trip to London expressly to harm me there.[63]

All these polemics occupied me very much, with much loss of time for my copying, little progress for the truth, and little profit for my purse; Pissot, who was my publisher at that time, always gave me very little for my pamphlets, often nothing at all, and for example, I did not have a liard from my first *Discourse*, Diderot gave it to him for free. I had to wait for a long time and to extract the little he gave me sou by sou; nevertheless, the copying did not go along at all. I performed two Professions, that is how to do both of them badly.

They were in contradiction in yet another way: from the divergent ways of life to which they subjected me. The success of my first Writings had put me in fashion. The station I had taken up stirred up curiosity: They wanted to know this bizarre man who sought out no one and cared about nothing except living freely and happily[64] in his way: that was enough for him to be unable to do so. My room was never empty of people who came to take possession of my time under diverse pretexts. Women used a thousand ruses to get me to dine with them. The more blunt I was with people, the more they persisted. I could not refuse everyone. While making myself a thousand enemies by my refusals, I was incessantly subjugated by my compliance, and however I set about it, I did not have an hour a day to myself.

I felt then that it is not always as easy as one imagines to be poor and independent. I wanted to live from my profession; the public did not want me to do so. A thousand little ways were imagined to compensate me for the time they made me lose.[65] Soon I would have had to show myself like Punch at so much per person. I do not know a more debasing and more cruel subjugation than that one. I saw no remedy for it except to refuse the big and small gifts and not to make an exception for anyone whatsoever. All that only attracted givers who wanted to have the glory of overcoming my resistance and of forcing me to be obliged to them in spite of myself. The sort that would not have given me an écu if I had asked for it did not cease importuning me with their offers and, in order to avenge themselves for seeing them rejected, accused my refusals of being arrogance and ostentation.

It will be very much suspected that the decision I had made and the system I wanted to follow were not to Mme le Vasseur's taste. All the daughter's disinterestedness did not keep her from following her mother's directions, and the Governesses, as Gauffecourt called them, were not always as firm as I was in their refusals. Although many things were hidden from me, I saw enough of them to judge that I was not seeing everything, and that tormented me, less from the accusation of connivance which it was easy for me to foresee, than from the cruel idea of never being able to be master in my home or of myself. I begged, I entreated, I got angry, all without success; the Mamma made me pass for an eternal scold, for a curmudgeon. There were continuous whisperings with my friends, everything was a mystery and a secret for me in my household, and—in order not to expose myself ceaselessly to storms—I no longer dared to inform myself about what was going on there. To extricate myself from all these worries I would have needed a firmness of which I was not capable. I could shout and not act; they let me talk and went on their way.

This continual friction and the daily badgering to which I was subjected finally made my residence and stay in Paris unpleasant for me. When my discomforts allowed me to go out, and I did not let myself be dragged here or there by my acquaintances, I went to take a walk by myself, I dreamed about my great system,[66] I threw some of it onto paper with the aid of a blank booklet and a pencil which I always had in my pocket. This is how the unforeseen unpleasantness of a condition of my choosing threw me completely into literature as a diversion, and this is how I introduced into all my earliest works the bile and ill-humor that made me occupy myself with them.

Another thing contributed further to this. Thrown into the world in spite of myself, without having its tone, without being in a position to acquire it and to be able to subject myself to it,[67] I took it into my head to acquire one of my own which might dispense me from it. Since my stupid and sullen timidity which I could not overcome had as its principle the fear of failing in decorum, in order to embolden myself[68] I made the decision to trample it underfoot. I made myself cynical and caustic out of shame; I pretended to despise the politeness which I did not know how to practice. It is true that since this harshness was in agreement with my new principles it was ennobled in my soul, and acquired the intrepidity of virtue there, and it is, I dare to say, on this august basis that it maintained itself better and for a longer time than one ought to have expected from an effort so contrary to my natural disposition. Nevertheless, in spite of the reputation for misanthropy which my outward appearance and several happy remarks gave me in the world, it is certain that in private I always kept up my persona poorly, that my friends and my acquaintances led this very fierce Bear[69] like a lamb, and that, limiting my sarcasms to harsh but general truths, I was never able to say a[70] disagreeable word to anyone whatsoever.

The Village Soothsayer put me completely in fashion, and soon there might not have been a man in Paris more sought after than I was. The story of this Piece, which is epoch-making, depends on that of the relations I had at that time. It is a detail into which I ought to enter for the intelligibility[71] of what follows.

I had a rather large number of acquaintances, but only two friends of choice, Diderot and Grimm. From an effect of my desire to bring together everything that is dear to me, I was too much the friend of both of them for them not to be the same with each other soon. I brought

them together; they got along, and became even more closely united between themselves than with me. Diderot had numberless acquaintances,
but Grimm—a foreigner and a newcomer—needed to make some. I did
not ask for anything better than to procure some for him. I had given
him Diderot; I gave him Gauffecourt. I brought him to Mme de Chenonceaux's, to Mme d'Epinay's, to the Baron d'Holback's, with whom I found
myself tied almost in spite of myself.[72] All my friends became his, that
was entirely simple: but none of his ever became mine; that is what was[73]
less simple. While he was lodging at the Comte de Friese's, he often had
us to dine at his house; but never did I receive any testimony of friendship or benevolence from the Comte de Friese, nor from his relative the
Comte de Schomberg,[74] who was very familiar with Grimm, nor from
any of the people either men or women with whom Grimm had connections through them. I except only the Abbé Raynal,[75] who, although he
was his friend, showed himself to be one of mine, and when the occasion
presented itself offered me his purse with an uncommon generosity. But
I had known the Abbé Raynal for a long time before Grimm knew him,
and I had always been attached to him ever since he had performed an
action full of delicacy and decency for me upon a very slight occasion, but
which I have never forgotten.

This Abbé Raynal is certainly a warm friend. I had the proof of it at
about the time I am speaking of, with regard to the same Grimm with
whom he was very closely tied. After having been on friendly terms with
Mlle Fel[76] for some time, Grimm suddenly took it into his head to become
desperately in love and to want to supplant Cahusac.[77] Priding herself on
constancy, the beauty rejected this new pretender. The latter took the affair in the tragic manner and took it into his head to want to die from
it. He suddenly fell into the strangest illness that has perhaps ever been
heard of. He passed days and nights in a continuous lethargy, his eyes
very open, his pulse beating well, but without speaking, without eating,
without moving, sometimes appearing to hear, but never answering, not
even by a sign, and otherwise without agitation, without pain, without
fever, and staying that way as if he had died. The Abbé Raynal and I
took turns caring for him: being more robust and in better health, the
Abbé spent the nights there, I the days, without either of us ever leaving
him until the other had arrived. Alarmed, the Comte de Friese brought
him Senac[78] who, after he had examined him thoroughly, said that it
would be nothing and ordered nothing. My fright for my friend made
me observe the doctor's countenance carefully, and I saw him smile as he
was leaving. Nevertheless, the sick man stayed immobile for several days,
without taking either broth or anything at all except preserved cherries,

which I put on his tongue from time to time, and which he swallowed extremely well. One fine morning he got up, got dressed, and took up his normal course of life again, without ever speaking to me again, nor to the Abbé Raynal that I know of, nor to anyone about this peculiar lethargy, nor about the care we had given him while it lasted.[79]

This adventure did not fail to make a commotion, and it might really have been a marvelous anecdote if the cruelty of an Opera girl had caused a man to die of despair. This beautiful passion put Grimm into fashion; soon he passed for a prodigy of love, friendship, attachment of every sort. This opinion made him sought after and celebrated in high society, and thereby distanced him from me who had never been anything but a last resort for him. I saw him ready to slip away from me completely;[80] for all the lively feelings he was showing off were the same ones I had for him with less commotion. I was very glad that he was succeeding in the world, but I would not have wanted it to be while forgetting his friend. One day I said to him, "Grimm, you neglect me, I pardon you for it. When the first intoxication of noisy successes[81] has had its effect and you feel its emptiness, I hope you will come back to me, and you will always find me here. As for now do not bother yourself at all; I leave you free and I am waiting for you." He told me that I was right, made his arrangements accordingly, and put himself so much at ease that I no longer saw him except with our common friends.

Our principal meeting point, before he was as linked with Mme d'Epinay as he was later on, was the Baron d'Holback's house. The said Baron was a son of a parvenu, who enjoyed a rather large fortune which he used nobly, receiving literary people and people of merit[82] in his home, and by means of his learning and enlightenment[83] held up his place well in their midst. Linked for a long time with Diderot, he had sought me out by his intervention, even before my name was known. A natural repugnance kept me from responding to his advances for a long time. One day he asked me the reason for it, I said to him,[84] "You are too rich." He persisted and finally overcame. My greatest misfortune was always to be incapable of resisting cajolery: I have never done well in having yielded to it.

Another acquaintance which became friendship as soon as I had a title to claim it was that of M. Duclos.[85] It had been several years since I had seen him for the first time at la Chevrette with Mme d'Epinay with whom he was on very good terms. We only dined together, he left the same day. But we chatted for several moments after dinner. Mme d'Epinay had spoken to him about me and about my Opera *The Gallant Muses*. Duclos, endowed with too great talents not to love those who had some, was predisposed toward me and had invited me to go to see him. In spite of my former inclination reinforced by acquaintance, my timidity, my laziness held me back in so far as I had no passport with regard to him except his desire to be obliging:[86] but, encouraged by my first success and by his praises which came to me, I went to see him, he came to see me, and in this way there began relations between us that will always make him dear to me, and from which I owe the knowledge, aside from the testimony of my own heart, that uprightness and probity can sometimes go together with the cultivation of letters.[87]

Several other less solid[88] relations which I do not mention here were the effect of my first successes and lasted until curiosity was satisfied. I was a man with whom, as soon as he was seen, there was nothing new to see as early as the next day. Nevertheless, a woman who sought me out at that time held on more solidly than all the others: this was Mme the Marquise de Créqui,[89] niece of M. the Bailli de Froulay, Ambassador to Malta, whose brother had preceded M. de Montaigu in the Embassy at Venice,[90] and whom I had been to see upon my return from that country.[91] Mme de Créqui wrote to me; I went to her: she acquired a friendship for me. I dined there sometimes; I saw several literary people there, and among others M. Saurin, the Author of *Spartacus*, of *Barnevelt* etc., who has become my cruelest enemy since then, without me being able to imagine any other cause of it, except that I bear the name of a man whom his father very basely persecuted.[92]

One sees that for a copyist who ought to be busy with his profession from morning to night, I had very many distractions which did not make my day extremely lucrative, and which kept me from being attentive enough to what I was doing to do it well; also I lost more than half the time that I was allowed in erasing or scratching out my mistakes or beginning my sheet over again. This badgering made Paris more unbearable to me each day, and made me seek out the country with ardor. Several times I went to pass a few days at Marcoussis the Vicar of which Mme le Vasseur knew, at whose house we all settled down, in such a manner as not to make him worse off because of it. Grimm came there with us once.*

The Vicar had a good voice, sang well, and, although he did not know music, he learned his part with much ease and precision. We passed the time there singing my trios from Chenonceaux. I wrote two or three

---

* Since I have neglected to recount here a small but memorable adventure which I had there with the said M. Grimm one morning when we were supposed to go dine at the fountain of St. Vandrille, I will not come back to it; but in thinking about it again later on I concluded that as far back as then he was brooding in the bottom of his heart over the plot that he has executed since with such a prodigious success.

new ones on words that Grimm and the Vicar put together for better or worse. I cannot keep myself from regretting these trios written and sung in moments of very pure joy, and which I have left at Wootton with all my music. Mlle Davenport has perhaps already made curling papers out of them; but they deserved to be preserved and are for the most part of a very good counterpoint.[93] It was after one of these little trips when I had the pleasure of seeing the Aunt, at her ease, very cheerful, and during which I was extremely cheered up also, that I wrote to the Vicar extremely rapidly and extremely poorly a letter in verse that will be found among my papers.[94]

Closer to Paris I had another resort[95] extremely to my taste with my compatriot, my relative, and my friend M. Mussard,[96] who had made a charming refuge at Passy where I passed some very peaceful moments. M. Mussard was a jeweler, a man of good sense, who, after having acquired an honest fortune in his business dealings and after having married his only daughter to M. de Valmalette the son of an Exchange agent and the King's steward, made the wise decision to leave the trade and business in his elderly years, and to put an interval of rest and enjoyment between the bustle of life and death. The good man Mussard, a true practical philosopher, lived without a care in a very pleasant[97] house which he had built himself and with a very pretty garden which he had planted with his own hands. While excavating deeply the terraces of this garden, he found fossil shells, and he found them in such great quantity that his overstrung imagination saw nothing but shells in nature, and in the end he seriously believed that the[98] universe was nothing but shells, the remains of shells, and that the whole earth was nothing but Powdered Shells. Always occupied with this object and with his peculiar discoveries, he got so warmed up over these ideas that they would have finally turned into a system in his head, that is to say, into madness, if very fortunately for his reason but very unfortunately for his friends to whom he was dear and[99] who found the most pleasant refuge with him, death had not come to remove him from them by the strangest and cruelest illness. This was a constantly growing tumor in the stomach which kept him from eating, without its cause being found for a very long time, and which ended by making him die of hunger after several years of suffering. I cannot recall without heartache the last days of that poor and worthy man, who—still receiving with so much pleasure Lenieps[100] and me, the only friends whom the spectacle of the ills he suffered did not keep away from him until his final hour—who, I say, was reduced to devouring with his eyes the meal he had served to us, almost unable to sip several tastes of a very light tea which he had to vomit up a moment afterwards. But before these times of suffering how many pleasant ones did I pass with him with the select friends he had made for himself. At their head I put the Abbé Prêvot,[101] a very amiable man and very simple, whose heart enlivened his writings, worthy of immortality, and who had nothing in his disposition or in his society of the somber coloring that he gave to his Works; Doctor Procope,[102] a little Aesop of a ladies' man; Boulanger the famous posthumous Author of *Oriental Despotism*, and who I believe extended Mussard's systems on the age of the world.[103] Among the women, Voltaire's niece Mme Denis, who being only a good woman then, did not yet play the fine wit;[104] Mme Vanloo, not beautiful, certainly, but charming, who sang like an angel;[105] Mme de Valmalette herself, who sang also, and who, although extremely thin, might have been very lovable, if she had had less pretension of being so. Such was just about M. de Mussard's whole social circle, which would have pleased me enough, if his tête-à-tête with his conchyliomania had not pleased me even more, and I can say that for more than six months I worked in his study with as much pleasure as he did himself.

For a long time he claimed that the waters of Passy would be salutary for my condition and he exhorted me to come take them at his home. To get out of the urban throng a little, I finally yielded, and I went to pass eight or ten days at Passy, which did me more good because I was in the country than because I took the waters there. Mussard played the Violoncello, and loved Italian music passionately. One night we talked about it very much before going to bed, and above all about the *Opera Buffa*[106] which we had both seen in Italy, and with which we were both enraptured. Not sleeping during the night, I began to dream about how one could write songs to give the idea of a Drama of this type in France; for *The Loves of Ragonde* did not resemble it in the least.[107] While walking and taking the waters in the morning I made some sorts of verses very hastily, and to them I adapted the songs that came to me while I made them. I scribbled out the whole in a sort of vaulted room which was at the end of the garden, and at tea I could not keep myself from showing these tunes to Mussard and to Mlle Du Vernois his housekeeper, who was in truth a very good and amiable girl. The three pieces I had sketched were, the first Monologue: *j'ai perdu mon Serviteur*, the Soothsayer's aria: *l'amour croit s'il s'inquiet*, and the last Duet: *à jamais Colin, je t'engage*, etc.[108] I so little imagined that this was worth the trouble of being continued, that, without the applause and the encouragement of both of them, I was going to throw my scraps in the fire and not think about them anymore, as I had done so many times for things at least as good: but they got me so excited that in six days my Drama was within several verses of being written and all my music sketched out: so much so that I had no more to do at Paris than a little recitative and all the filling-in,[109] and I finished it all with such rapidity that in three weeks my scenes were put in a fair copy and in condition to be performed. Only the divertissement was lacking, which was not written until a long time afterward.[110]

Being excited by the composition of this work, I had a great passion to hear it, and I would have given the whole world to see it performed at my whim, behind closed doors, as it is said Lully had *Armide* played one time for himself alone.[111] Since I could not have this pleasure except along with the public, in order to enjoy my Piece I necessarily had to get it accepted by the Opera. Unfortunately it was in an absolutely new genre to which ears were not at all accustomed, and moreover the poor success of *The Gallant Muses* made me foresee that of[112] the *Soothsayer* if I presented it under my name. Duclos extricated me from the difficulty and took it upon himself to get the work tried while leaving the Author unknown. So as not to reveal myself I was not present at that rehearsal, and the *little Violins** who directed it themselves did not know who its Author was until after a general acclamation had attested the goodness of the work. Everyone who heard it was so enchanted by it that, as early as the next day, nothing else was spoken of in all social circles. M. de Cury the Intendant of the Menus,[114] who had been present at the rehearsal, asked for the Work to be given at Court. Judging that I would be less the master of my Piece at Court than at Paris, Duclos, who knew my intentions, refused it. Cury laid claim to it by authority, Duclos held firm, and the debate between them became so lively that one day at the Opera they were going to step outside together if they had not been separated. They wanted to address themselves to me; I sent the decision of the matter back to M. Duclos. They had to go back to him. M. the Duc d'Aumont got mixed up in it.[115] Finally Duclos believed he ought to give way to authority, and the Piece was given to be played at Fontainebleau.

The part to which I was the most attached and where I departed most from the common route was the Recitative.[116] Mine was accentuated in an entirely new manner and went with the flow of the words. They did not dare to leave this horrible innovation, they feared it might revolt sheeplike ears. I consented to Francueil and Jelyotte[117] writing another Recitative, but I did not want to get mixed up in it.

When everything was ready and the day fixed for the performance, they proposed the trip to Fontainebleau to me at least to see the last Rehearsal. I went with Mlle Fel, Grimm, and I believe the Abbé Raynal, in a

---

*This is how they referred to Rebel and Francoeur, who had made themselves known in their youth by always going together to play the violin in homes.[113]

carriage from the Court. The Rehearsal was passable; I was more satisfied with it than I had expected. The Orchestra was numerous, composed of musicians from the Opera and the King's Music. Jelyotte played Colin, Mlle Fel Colette, Cuvillier the Soothsayer; the Choruses were those of the Opera. I said little; Jelyotte had directed everything; I did not want to inspect what he had done, and in spite of my Roman tone, I was as bashful as a schoolboy in the midst of all these people.

The next day, the day of the performance,[118] I went to breakfast at the Café du Grand Commun. Many people were there. They were talking about the rehearsal of the day before, and how hard it had been to get into it. An Officer who was there said that he had gotten in without difficulty, recounted at length what had happened, depicted the Author, reported what he had done, what he had said; but what amazed me about this rather long narrative, made with both assurance and simplicity, was that there was not a single word of truth to be found in it. It was very clear to me that the one who was speaking so knowledgeably about this rehearsal had not been there at all, since that Author whom he said he had seen so much was before his very eyes without him knowing it. What was most peculiar in this scene was the effect it had on me. This man was elderly; he did not have a foppish and conceited manner or tone at all; his physiognomy indicated a man of merit, his cross of St. Louis indicated a former officer. He appealed to me in spite of his impudence and in spite of me: while he was retailing his lies, I blushed, I lowered my eyes, I was on thorns; several times I sought within myself for some way to believe he was in error and in good faith. Finally trembling that someone might recognize me and insult him with it, I hastened to finish my chocolate without saying anything, and lowering my head while passing in front of him, I left as early as I could, while the people present perorated about his report. In the street I noticed that I was in a sweat, and I am sure that if someone had recognized and named me before my exit, they would have seen the shame and embarrassment of a guilty man, from the sole feeling of the pain that this poor man would have to suffer if his lie was recognized.[119]

Here I am at one of the critical moments of my life in which it is difficult to do nothing but narrate, because it is almost impossible for the narration itself not to bear the imprint of censure or defense. Nevertheless, I will try to report how and on what motives I behaved, without adding either praise or blame.

That day I was in the same careless outfit that was usual for me; unshaven and a rather poorly combed wig. Taking this lack of propriety for an act of courage, in this manner I entered the same room into which the King, the Queen, the royal family, and all the Court were to arrive shortly[120] afterward. I went to take up my position in the box to which M. de Cury led me, and which was his. It was a large stage-box across from a more elevated little box where the King was placed with Mme de Pompadour. Surrounded by Ladies and the only man in the front of the Box, I could not doubt that I had been put there precisely to be within sight. When it was lit up, I began to be ill at ease seeing myself in this outfit in the midst of people who were all excessively adorned: I asked myself whether I was in my place, whether I was suitably dressed? and after several minutes of anxiety, I answered myself, yes, with an intrepidity that perhaps came more from the impossibility of withdrawing than from the strength of my reasons. I told myself, "I am in my place, since I am seeing my piece played, since I was invited, since that is the only reason I composed it, and since after all no one has more right than myself to enjoy the fruit of my labor and my talents. I am dressed in my ordinary way, neither better nor worse. If I begin to be enslaved to opinion in something, I will soon be enslaved to it in everything all over again. To be always myself wherever I am I must not blush at being dressed in accordance with the station I have chosen; my exterior is simple and untidy, but not dirty or improper; in itself a beard is not at all improper because it is nature that gives it to us and because according to times and fashions it is sometimes an ornament. I will be found ridiculous, impertinent; ah what does it matter to me: I ought to be able to endure ridicule[121] and blame as long as they are not deserved." After this little soliloquy I became so well steadied that I would have been intrepid if I had needed to be so. But from either the effect of the presence of the master, or the natural inclination of hearts, I noticed nothing except what was obliging and decent in the curiosity of which I was the object. I was touched by it to the point of beginning to be anxious about myself again and about the fate of my piece, fearing to efface such favorable prejudices which seemed to seek only to applaud me. I was armed against their raillery; but their caressing air, which I had not expected, subjugated me so much that I was trembling like a child when the performance began.

I soon had reason enough to be reassured. The Piece was very poorly performed with regard to the Actors, but well sung and well executed with regard to the music. From the first scene, which is genuinely of a touching naiveté, I heard rise up in the boxes a murmur of surprise and applause unheard of until then in this sort of piece. The growing fermentation soon grew so much that it could be felt in the whole assembly, and to speak in Montesquieu's way, to increase its effect by its very effect. At the Scene of the two good little people this effect was at its height.[122]

One does not clap in front of the King; this made it so that everything was heard; the piece and the author gained from it. Around me I heard a whispering of women who seemed as beautiful as angels to me, and who said to each other in a whisper, "That is charming, that is ravishing; there is not a sound in it that does not speak to the heart."[123] The pleasure of giving some emotion to so many lovable persons moved me to the point of tears, and I could not hold them back at the first duo, while noticing that I was not alone in crying. I had a moment of return to myself in recalling M. de Treitorens's concert. This reminiscence had the effect of the slave who held the crown on the head of the triumphant generals, but it was short, and I soon abandoned myself fully and without distraction to the pleasure of savoring my glory.[124] Nevertheless, I am sure that at this moment the pleasure of sex entered into it much more than an author's vanity, and surely if there had only been men there, I would not have been devoured, as I was ceaselessly, with the desire to collect with my lips the delicious tears I was causing to flow. I have seen Pieces excite more lively outbursts of admiration, but never as full, as sweet, as touching an intoxication reign during a whole spectacle, and above all at the court on the day of the first performance. Those who saw this one ought to remember it; for the effect was unique.

The same evening M. the Duc d'Aumont had me told to be at the Chateau the next day at eleven o'clock, and that he would present me to the King. M. de Cury, who gave me this message, added that it was believed that it was a question of a pension, and that the King wanted to announce it to me himself.

Will it be believed that the night that followed such a brilliant day was a night of anguish and perplexity for me. My first idea—after the one of this presentation—proceeded to a frequent need to leave which had made me suffer very much the very night of the spectacle, and which might torment me the next day when I would be in the Gallery or in the King's apartments among all those Nobles, waiting for His Majesty's passage. This infirmity was the principal cause that kept me isolated from the social circles, and which prevented me from shutting myself up in a room with women. The mere idea of the situation into which this need might put me was able to give it to me to the point of making me ready to faint or cause a scandal to which I would have preferred death. Only people who know this condition can judge the fright of running its risk.

Next I imagined myself in front of the King, having been presented to His Majesty who deigned to stop and address a word to me. There exactness and presence of mind were necessary in order to answer. Would my cursed timidity which troubled me before the slightest unknown person permit me to choose what needed to be said on the spur of the moment? Without departing from the severe manner and tone that I had acquired, I wanted to show myself grateful for the honor done to me by such a great Monarch. It was necessary to wrap up some great and useful truth in a fine and deserved praise. To prepare a happy answer in advance it would have been necessary to foresee exactly what he might say to me, and even after that in his presence I was sure that I would not find a word of what I had meditated. What would become of me at that moment and under the eyes of the whole Court, if one of my usual blunders escaped me in my perplexity? This danger alarmed me, frightened me, made me shudder to the point of making me decide not to expose myself to it at any risk.

It is true that I was losing the pension that in some manner was being offered to me; but I was also exempting myself from the yoke it might have imposed on me. Farewell truth, freedom, courage. After that how could I dare to speak of independence and disinterestedness? Upon receiving this pension I would have to do nothing any longer but flatter or be silent: still who was assuring me that it would have been paid to me? How many steps to take, how many people to solicit! It would cost me more efforts and much more unpleasant ones to preserve it than to do without it. Thus in renouncing it I believed I was making a decision quite consistent with my principles and sacrificing appearance to reality. I told my resolution to Grimm who said nothing to oppose me. To the others I alleged my health and I left the same morning.

My departure made a commotion and was generally blamed. My reasons could not be felt by everyone. To accuse me of a foolish pride was much easier, and better satisfied the jealousy of anyone who felt within himself that he would not have behaved that way. The next day Jelyotte wrote me a note in which he detailed the success of my piece and how infatuated the King himself was. "All day long," he notified me, "His Majesty does not stop singing with the most out-of-tune voice in his Kingdom: 'j'ai perdu mon serviteur; j'ai perdu tout mon bonheur.'"[125] He added that in two weeks they were to give a second performance of the *Soothsayer*, which verified the complete success of the first in the eyes of the whole public.

Two days later about nine in the evening, just as I was going into Mme d'Epinay's where I was going to sup, I was met at the door by a cab. Someone who was in this cab signaled me to get in; I got in: it was Diderot. He spoke to me about the pension with a warmth that I would not have expected from a philosopher on such a subject.[126] He made no crime of my not having wished to be presented to the King, but he made a terrible one out of my indifference toward the pension. He told me that if

I was disinterested on my own account, I was not allowed to be so on Mme le Vasseur's and her daughter's; that I owed it to them to omit no possible and decent means of giving them bread, and that since it could not be said, after all, that I had refused that pension, he maintained that since they had appeared disposed to grant it to me, I ought to solicit it and obtain it at any cost whatsoever. Although I was touched by his zeal, I could not relish his maxims, and we had a very lively dispute on this subject, the first that I had had with him, and we have never had any except of this sort, him prescribing to me what he claimed I ought to do, and me defending myself, because I believed I ought not to do it.

It was late when we left each other. I wanted to bring him to sup at Mme d'Epinay's; he did not want to, and whatever efforts I made at different times to induce him to see her, out of the desire to bring together all the people I love, even to the point of bringing her to his door, which he kept closed to us, he always stood his ground, speaking about her only in very contemptuous terms. It was only after my falling out with her and with him that they joined together, and he began to speak about her honorably.

From that time Diderot and Grimm seemed to take up the task of alienating the Governesses from me, making them understand that if they were not better off it was out of bad will on my part, and that they would never do anything with me. They tried to incite them to leave me by promising them a salt franchise, a tobacco store, and I know not what else through Mme d'Epinay's influence. They even wanted to carry along Duclos as well as d'Holback in their conspiracy, but the former always refused. At the time I had some wind of all these tricks; but I did not learn about them very distinctly until a long time afterwards, and I often had to deplore the blind and indiscreet zeal of my friends who, seeking to reduce me—indisposed as I was—to the saddest solitude, labored in their idea of making me happy, by the means most fit in fact for making me miserable.

The following Carnival, in 1753, *The Soothsayer* was played at Paris and in the interval I had the time to write its overture and divertissement. As it is printed this divertissement ought to be in action from beginning to end, and on a coherent subject, which in my view, provided some very pleasant tableaux. But when I proposed this idea to the Opera they did not even listen to me, and it was necessary to stitch on songs and dances in the ordinary way; which made it happen that this divertissement had a very mediocre success even though it was full of charming ideas which did not spoil the effect of the scenes at all. I removed Jelyotte's recitative and put mine back in, as I had written it at first and as it is printed; and, far from shocking anyone, this recitative, a little Frenchified I admit, that is to say drawled by the Actors, had no less success than the tunes, and appeared at least as well composed even to the public. I dedicated my Piece to M. Duclos who had protected it and I declared that this would be my only dedication. Nevertheless, with his consent, I did make a second one; but he must have held himself even more honored by this exception than if I had not made any.[127]

I have many anecdotes about this Piece, but things that are more important to say do not leave me the leisure to expand upon them here. Perhaps I will come back to them some day in the supplement. Nevertheless I cannot omit one that might have a bearing on everything that follows. One day in the Baron d'Holback's study I was looking over his music; after having skimmed over many examples of it, he said to me while showing me a collection of Pieces for Clavichord, "Here are some Pieces which have been composed for me; they are full of taste, very melodious, no one knows them nor will see them but me alone. You ought to choose one of them to insert in your divertissement." Having in my head subjects for many more Tunes and Symphonies than I could use, I wanted his very little. Nevertheless, he pressed me so much, that out of a desire to be obliging I chose a Pastoral which I abridged, and put into a trio for the entrance of Collette's companions. Upon entering Grimm's one day several months afterwards and while *The Soothsayer* was being performed, I found everyone around his clavichord, from which he got up brusquely at my arrival. Looking unconsciously on his music stand, I saw this same collection of the Baron d'Holback open precisely to that same Piece which he had pressed me to take, while assuring me that it would never leave his hands. Some time afterwards I again saw this same collection open[128] on M. d'Epinay's Clavichord, one day when he was having music at his home. Neither Grimm nor anyone else ever spoke to me about that tune, and I speak about it here myself only because a rumor was spread around some time afterwards that I was not the Author of the *Village Soothsayer*.[129] Since I was never a great note-scraper, I am persuaded that without my Dictionary of Music, in the end they would have said that I did not know it.*[130]

Sometime before *The Village Soothsayer* was given, the Italian Buffons arrived in Paris and were made to play in the Opera theater, without anyone foreseeing the effect they were going to have there.[131] Although they were detestable and the Orchestra, which was very ignorant at that time, mangled at pleasure the pieces they gave, they did not fail to inflict an

---

* I hardly foresaw that they would say it in the end in spite of the Dictionary.

injury on French Opera which it has never put right. The comparison of these two types of music, heard the same day at the same theater, unblocked French ears; none of them could endure the dragging of their music after the lively and marked accent of the Italian. As soon as the Bouffons had finished everyone left. The order had to be changed and the Bouffons put at the end. *Eglé, Pygmalion, The Sylph* were presented; nothing held up.[132] Only the *Village Soothsayer* bore the comparison and was pleasing even after the *Serva Padrona*.[133] When I composed my Interlude my mind was full of those works; they gave me the idea for it, and I was very far from foreseeing that they would be passed in review beside it. If I had been a pilferer how many thefts would then have become manifest, and how much care would have been taken to make them felt. But nothing of the kind: try as they might; they had not found in my music the slightest reminiscence of any other, and compared to the alleged originals, all my songs were found to be as new as the musical characters I had created. If one had put Mondonville[134] or Rameau to a similar test, they would have emerged from it only in tatters.

The Bouffons won very ardent members of the sect for Italian music. All of Paris was divided into two parties that were more excited than if it had been a question of an affair of State or of Religion. The more powerful, more numerous one, composed of the Nobles, the rich, and the women, supported French music; the other more lively, more proud, more enthusiastic, was composed of true connoisseurs, people with talents, men of genius. Its little cluster assembled at the Opera under the Queen's Box. The other party filled up all the rest of the pit and the room; but its principal focus was under the King's Box. This is where those party names famous at that time of *King's Corner* and *Queen's Corner* came from. As it became animated, the dispute produced some pamphlets. The King's Corner wanted to joke; it was mocked by *The Little Prophet*;[135] it wanted to get mixed up in reasoning; it was crushed by the *Letter on French Music*.[136] These two little Writings, one by Grimm and the other by me, are the only ones that survived that quarrel; all the others are already dead.

But *The Little Prophet*, which people persisted for a long time in attributing to me in spite of denials, was taken as a joke and did not do the slightest harm to its author; instead of which the letter on music was taken seriously, and raised against me the whole Nation, which believed itself offended in its music. The description of the unbelievable effect of this pamphlet would be worthy of the pen of Tacitus. It was the time of the great quarrel of the Parlement and the Clergy. The Parlement had just been exiled; the fermentation was at its peak; everything threatened an approaching uprising. The Pamphlet appeared; instantly all the other quarrels were forgotten; only the peril of French music was thought of, and there was no longer any uprising except against me. It was so strong that the Nation has never entirely recovered from it. At the Court they wavered only between the Bastille and exile, and the *lettre de cachet*[137] was going to be expedited, if M. de Voyer[138] had not made them feel how ridiculous it was. When you read that this pamphlet perhaps prevented a revolution in the State, you will believe you are dreaming. Nevertheless, it is a very real truth which all of Paris can still attest, since today is only fifteen years since this peculiar anecdote.[139]

Although no attempt was made on my freedom, I was not spared insults at least; even my life was in danger. The Orchestra of the Opera formed the decent plot of assassinating me when I left it. I was told about it: because of it I only attended the Opera more assiduously, and only a long time afterward I learned that M. Ancelet, an Officer of the Musketeers, who felt friendship for me, had turned aside the effect of the plot by having me escorted at my departure from the show without me knowing it. The City had just been given the direction of the Opera. The first exploit of the Dean of the Guild was to have my free admission taken away, and that in the most indecent manner possible;[140] that is to say, by having me rejected publicly at my entrance; in such a way that I was obliged to take a ticket for the amphitheater so as not to receive the affront of being turned away from it that day. The injustice was all the more flagrant, since the only price that I had put on my piece in granting it to them was my free admission in perpetuity: for even though this was a right for all Authors, and though I had this right by a double title,[141] I did not fail to stipulate for it expressly in M. Duclos's presence. It is true that the Cashier of the Opera sent me fifteen Louis for my honorarium for which I had not asked; but aside from the fact that these fifteen Louis did not make up even the sum that was due to me according to the rules, this payment had nothing in common with the formally stipulated right of admission, which was entirely independent of it. In this proceeding there was such a combination of iniquity and brutality, that the public—at that time in its greatest animosity against me—did not fail to be unanimously shocked by it, and the next day those who had insulted me the day before shouted loudly in the room that it was shameful to deprive an Author of his free admission in this way when he had deserved it so much and could even lay claim to two of them. So accurate is the Italian proverb that *ogn'un ama la giustizia in casa d'altrui*.[142]

With regard to this I had only one decision to make; it was to lay claim to my work, since I had had the agreed upon[143] price taken away from me. I wrote to that effect to M. d'Argenson who had the department of the Opera, and to my letter I joined a Memorandum which was unanswerable, and which remained without answer and without effect just as my letter did. The silence of that unjust man remained in my heart, and did not contribute to increasing the very mediocre esteem that I always had for his character and for his talents. This is how they kept my piece at the Opera while depriving me of the price for which I had granted it. From the weak to the strong this would be stealing, from the strong to the weak it is only appropriating someone else's goods.

As for the pecuniary product of that work, although it did not bring me a quarter of what it would have brought into someone else's hands, it did not fail to be large enough to put me in a condition to exist for several years, and supplement the copying, which was still going rather poorly. I had a hundred Louis from the King, fifty from Madame de Pompadour for the performance at Bellevue, where she herself performed the role of Colin, fifty from the Opera, and five hundred francs from Pissot for the printing; so that, in spite of my bad luck and my awkwardness, this Interlude, which never cost me anything but five or six weeks of labor, brought me almost as much money as *Emile*, which cost me twenty years of meditation and three years of labor, has brought me since: but I paid very much for the easy pecuniary circumstances into which this piece put me by the infinite afflictions it attracted to me. It was the germ of the secret jealousies that burst out only a long time afterward. From its success I no longer remarked either in Grimm or in Diderot or in almost any of the literary people of my acquaintance that cordiality, that frankness, that pleasure at seeing me which I had believed I found in them until then. As soon as I appeared at the Baron's the conversation ceased to be general. They assembled in little clusters, they whispered in each others' ears, and I remained alone without knowing with whom to speak. I endured this shocking neglect for a long time, and seeing that Mme d'Holback, who was sweet and amiable, always received me well, I bore her husband's rudeness as long as possible. But one day he tackled me without a subject, without a pretext, and with such a brutality in front of Diderot who did not say a word, and in front of Margency,[144] who has told me often since then that he admired the gentleness and moderation of my answers, that finally having been driven out of his house by this unworthy treatment, I left it resolved not to return there again.[145] That did not keep me from always speaking honorably about him and his house; whereas he never expressed himself on my account in anything but insulting, disdainful terms, without designating me otherwise than by "*that little prig*," and nevertheless without being able to articulate any wrong of any sort

I had ever done him or anyone in whom he took an interest. This is how
he ended by verifying my predictions and my fears. As for me, I believe
that my so-called friends would have pardoned me for writing Books,
and excellent books, because that glory was not foreign to them; but that
they could not forgive me for having written an Opera nor for the brilliant success that work had, because none of them was in a condition to
forge ahead in the same career nor to aspire to the same honors.[146] Duclos
alone, being above such jealousy, even appeared to increase his friendship
for me and introduced me at Mlle Quinault's[147] where I found as many
attentions, decencies, caresses, as I had found wanting at M. d'Holback's.

While the *Village Soothsayer* was playing at the Opera, its Author was
also involved at the Comédie Française, but a little less fortunately. Since
I had not been able to get my *Narcissus* played at the Italians in seven or
eight years, I was disgusted with this theater because of the bad acting
of the actors in French, and I would have liked very much to have gotten
my piece passed to the French Theatre rather than with them. I spoke
about this desire to the Actor La Noue, whose acquaintance I had made
and who, as is known, was a man of merit and an Author.[148] *Narcissus*
pleased him, he took it upon himself to have it performed anonymously,
and while waiting, he procured me free admission, which gave me a great
pleasure; for I have always preferred the French theater to the two others.
The Piece was received with applause, and performed without the author
being named, but I have reason to believe that the Actors and many
others were not ignorant of it. The Young Ladies Gaussin and Grandval[149] played the roles of the women in love, and although in my opinion
an understanding of the whole was lacking, one could not call it an absolutely poorly played Piece. Nevertheless, I was surprised and touched by
the indulgence of the public which had the patience to listen tranquilly
from one end to the other, and even to put up with a second performance
of it, without giving the slightest sign of impatience. As for me, I got so
bored at the first that I could not hold still until the end, and leaving the
theater,[150] I went into the Café de Procope where I found Boissy[151] and
several others, who probably had gotten bored as I had. There I loudly
said my *peccavi*,[152] humbly or proudly[153] admitting myself to be the author
of the Piece, and talking about it in the way everyone thought about it.
That public admission of the Author of a bad Piece that failed was extremely admired and hardly appeared very difficult to me. I even found
in it a compensation of amour-propre in the courage with which it was
done, and I believe that on this occasion there was more pride in speaking
than there would have been foolish shame in keeping quiet. Nevertheless,
since it was certain that the piece would bear reading even though it was

stiff in performance, I had it printed, and in the Preface—which is one of my good writings—I began to put my principles in open view a little more than I had done until then.[154]

I soon had an occasion to develop them completely in a work of the greatest importance; for it was, I think, in that year 1753 that the Program of the Academy of Dijon appeared on the origin of inequality among men.[155] Struck by this great question, I was surprised that this Academy dared to propose it; but since it had had this courage, I could certainly have the courage to tackle it, and I undertook to do so.

In order to meditate on this great subject at my ease I made a trip of seven or eight days to St. Germain with Therese, our landlady, who was a good woman, and one of her friends. I count this excursion as one of the most pleasant ones of my life. The weather was very fine; these good women took over the efforts and the expense; Therese amused herself with them, and I, without a care in the world, came in at meal times to be cheerful without restraint. All the rest of the day, deep in the forest, I sought, I found the image of the first times whose history I proudly traced; I made a clean sweep of the petty falsehoods of men, I dared to strip naked their nature, to follow the progress of time and things that have disfigured it, and comparing the man of man with the natural man, to show them the genuine source of his miseries in his pretended perfection. Exalted by these sublime contemplations, my soul raised[156] itself close to the divinity, and from there seeing my fellows follow in the blind route of their prejudices, errors, misfortunes, crimes, I cried out to them in a feeble voice which they could not hear, "Madmen, who moan ceaselessly about nature, learn that all your ills come to you from yourselves."

From these meditations resulted the *Discourse on Inequality*, a work that was more to Diderot's taste than all my other Writings, and for which his advice was most useful to me,* but which found only a few readers who understood it in all of Europe, and none of these wanted to talk about it. It had been written to compete for the prize, thus I sent it, but I was certain in advance that it would not get it, knowing well that the prizes of Academies are not established for pieces of that stuff.

This excursion and this occupation did some good for my mood and

---

*At the time I wrote this I did not yet have any suspicion about Diderot's and Grimm's great plot, without which I would have easily recognized how much the former abused my trust in order to give my writings that harsh tone and dark air which they no longer had when he ceased to direct me. The piece about the philosopher who reasons with himself while blocking his ears in order to harden himself to the moans of an unfortunate man is of his making, and he had provided me with others still stronger that I could not resolve to use. But attributing this dark mood to the one given to him by the Keep of Vincennes— a rather strong dose of which is also found in his Clairval—it never entered my mind to suspect the slightest wickedness in him.[157]

my health. Several years before, being tormented by my retention, I had abandoned myself completely to the Doctors, who had exhausted my strength and destroyed my temperament without alleviating my illness. Upon returning from St. Germain I found myself stronger and felt much better. I followed this indication and resolved to be cured or die without doctors and without remedies, I bade them farewell forever, and I began to live from day to day, staying quiet when I could not move, and walking as soon as I was strong enough to do so. The pace of Paris among people of pretensions was so little to my taste; the cabals of literary people, their shameful quarrels, the lack of good faith in their books, their cutting manner in society were all so odious to me, so antipathetic, I found so little sweetness, openness of heart, frankness even in the company of my friends, that—weary of this tumultuous life—I began to sigh ardently after the stay in the country, and because I did not believe that my profession would allow me to settle there, I ran there at least to pass the free hours I had. For several months, right after my dinner, I went to take a walk in the Bois de Boulogne, meditating on subjects for works, and I did not come back until night.

Since Gauffecourt—with whom I was extremely closely tied at that time—found himself obliged to go to Geneva for his work, he proposed this trip to me; I agreed. I was not well enough to do without the efforts of the Governess: it was decided that she would come on the trip, that her mother would watch over the house, and when all our arrangements were made, all three of us left together the first of June 1754.

I must mark this trip as the epoch of the first experience which, up to the age of forty-two which I was at that time, damaged the fully trusting natural disposition with which I was born, and to which I had always abandoned myself without reserve and without disadvantage. We shared a carriage that carried us with the same horses by very small stages. I often got out and walked on foot. We were hardly half-way on our route when Therese showed the greatest repugnance at staying alone in the carriage with Gauffecourt, and when I wanted to get out in spite of her entreaties, she got out and walked also. I scolded her for a long time for this caprice and even was completely opposed to it, to the point that she finally saw herself forced to declare its cause to me. I believed I was dreaming, I fell from the clouds when I learned that since our departure my friend M. de Gauffecourt, more than sixty years old, gouty, impotent, worn out from pleasures and enjoyments, was laboring[158] to corrupt a person who was no longer either beautiful or young, who belonged to his friend, and that he did so by the basest, most shameful means to the point of presenting her his purse, to the point of trying to excite her through reading from an abominable book, and through the sight of the filthy pictures with which it was full. Once Therese indignantly threw his nasty book out the door, and I learned that on the first day, when a violent migraine had made me go to bed without supper, he had used all the time of this tête-à-tête in attempts and maneuvers more worthy of a satyr and a billy goat than of a decent man to whom I had entrusted my companion and myself. What a surprise! what a completely new heartache for me! For the first time in my life I, who until then had believed friendship to be inseparable from all the lovable and noble feelings that make all its charm, saw myself forced to join it with disdain, and to remove my trust and my esteem from a man I love and by whom I believe myself loved! The wretch hid his base deed from me; in order not to expose Therese I saw myself forced to hide my contempt, and to harbor at the bottom of my heart feelings which he [159] should not know. Sweet and holy illusion of friendship, Gauffecourt first raised your veil from my eyes. How many cruel hands have kept it from falling back since then!

At Lyon I left Gauffecourt in order to take my route for Savoy, not being able to resolve once again to pass so close to mamma without seeing her again. I saw her again . . . in what a condition, my God! what degradation! what was left of her first virtue? Was this the same Mme de Warens, formerly so brilliant, to whom the Curate Pontverre had sent me? How my heart was broken! I no longer saw any other resource for her than to move out of her country. Vividly and vainly I repeated to her the entreaties I had made her several times in my letters to come to live peacefully with me, who wanted to dedicate my days and those of Therese to make hers happy. Attached to her pension, from which nevertheless she had no longer drawn anything for a long time even though it was paid punctually,[160] she did not listen to me. I again gave her some slight part of my purse, much less than I should have done, much less than I would have done if I had not been perfectly sure that she would not profit from it by a sou.[161] During my stay at Geneva, she made a trip to Chablais and came to see me at Grange-Canal. She lacked money to finish her trip; I did not have what she needed on me; I sent it to her an hour later by means of Therese. Poor Mamma! Once more let me tell this feature of her heart. She had only a little ring left as her last jewel. She took it off her finger to put it on Therese's, who instantly put it back on hers while kissing that noble hand which she watered with her tears. Ah! that was the moment to pay my debt! I should have left everything to follow her, to attach myself to her until her last hour, and share her fate whatever it might be. I did nothing of the kind. Distracted by another attachment, I felt mine for her relax from lack of hope of being able to make it useful to her. I groaned over her and did not follow her. Of all the instances of remorse that I have felt in my life this is the most lively and the most permanent. Because of that I deserved the terrible chastisements that have not ceased to weigh me down since then; may they atone for my ingratitude. It was in my behavior, but it has rent my heart too much for this ever to have been the heart of an ingrate.

Before my departure from Paris I had sketched out the dedication of my *Discourse on Inequality*. I finished it at Chambéry and dated it from the same place, judging that it was better not to date it either from France or from Geneva in order to avoid all quibbling.[162] Having arrived in that city I abandoned myself to the republican enthusiasm which had brought me there. This enthusiasm increased as a result of the welcome I received. Feted, fawned upon by all stations, I abandoned myself entirely to patriotic zeal, and ashamed at being excluded from my rights as a Citizen by the profession of a worship other than that of my forefathers, I resolved to take this latter[163] back openly. I thought that since the[164] Gospel was the same for all Christians, and the basis of dogma was different only in the things one got mixed up in explaining that one did not understand, in each country it was up to the Sovereign alone to settle both the worship and this unintelligible dogma, and that consequently it was part of the Citizen's duty to accept the dogma and to follow the worship prescribed by the law. Far from shaking my faith, frequentation of the Encyclopedists had strengthened it as a result of my natural aversion for disputation and for factions. The study of man and of the universe had shown me everywhere final causes and the intelligence that directs them. The reading of the Bible and above all of the Gospel to which I had applied myself for several years had made me despise the base and foolish interpretations given to Jesus Christ by the people least worthy of understanding him. In a word, while attaching me to what is essential in Religion, philosophy had detached me from that farrago of little formulas with which men have obfuscated it. Judging that for a reasonable man there were not two ways of being Christian, I also judged that everything that is form and discipline in each country fell within the competence of the laws. From this principle—which is so sensible, so social, so pacific, and which has drawn such cruel persecutions on me—it followed that, wanting to be a Citizen, I ought to be a Protestant and return into the worship established in my country.[165] I decided to do so; I even submitted to the instructions of the Pastor of the parish in which I was lodged, which was outside of the City.[166] I desired only not to be obliged to appear in the Consistory. The Ecclesiastic Edict, nevertheless, was explicit on this; they very much wanted to diverge from it in my favor, and they named a commission of five or six members to received my profession of faith in private. Unfortunately, the Minister Perdriau,[167] an amiable and gentle man, with whom I was intimate, took it into his head to tell me that they were delighted to hear me speak in this little assembly. This expectation frightened me so extremely that, when I needed to recite a little speech that I had prepared day and night for three weeks, I became confused to the point of not being able to say a single word of it, and I played the role of the most foolish schoolboy in this meeting. The Commissioners spoke for me, I dumbly answered *"yes"* and *"no"*: subsequently I was admitted to the communion and reintegrated into my rights as a Citizen: I was inscribed as such in the roll of the Guards who are paid only by Citizens and Bourgeois, and I attended an extraordinary General Council to receive the Oath from the Syndic Mussard.[168] I was so touched by the kindnesses which the Council and the Consistory witnessed to me on this occasion, and the obliging and decent dealings of all the Magistrates, Ministers, and Citizens that, pressed by the good man De Luc[169] who importuned me ceaselessly and even more by my own inclination, I thought of returning to Paris only to dissolve my household, put my little affairs in proper order, place Mme le Vasseur and her husband or provide for their subsistence, and come back with Therese to establish myself at Geneva for the remainder of my days.

Having made this resolution, I took a respite from serious matters to amuse myself with my friends until time for my departure. Of all these amusements the one that pleased me the most was an excursion around the Lake that I made in a boat with Deluc the father, his daughter-in-law, his two sons, and my Therese. We put seven days into this tour in the most beautiful weather in the world. I kept the lively remembrance of the sites that had struck me at the other extremity of the lake, and whose description I made several years later in the *Nouvelle Héloïse*.

The principal connections I made at Geneva, other than the De Lucs about whom I have spoken, were: the young Minister Vernes, whom I had already known at Paris and about whom I would have predicted better than he turned out to be worth;[170] M. Perdriau, at that time a country pastor, today professor of belles lettres, whose society—full of gentleness and civility—I will always miss, although he has believed it would look better for him to detach himself from me; M. Jalabert,[171] at that time professor of physics, since Counsellor and Syndic, to whom I read my discourse on inequality (but not the dedication) and who appeared enraptured by it; Professor Lullin,[172] with whom I remained in correspondence until his death, and who had even charged me with purchases of Books for the Library; Professor Vernet,[173] who turned his back on me like everyone, after I gave him proofs of attachment and trust that would have touched him if a theologian could be touched by something; Chappuis,[174] the clerk and successor of Gauffecourt whom he wished to supplant,[175] and who soon was supplanted himself; Marcet de Méziéres,[176] an old friend of my father and who had also shown himself to be mine, but who, after having formerly deserved well from the fatherland having made himself a dramatic Author and claimant to the Two Hundred,[177] changed his maxims and became ridiculous before his death. But the one from whom I expected the most was Moultou:[178] a young man of the greatest promise from his talents, from his mind which was full of fire, whom I have always loved, although his conduct with regard to me has often been equivocal, and although he had connections with my cruelest enemies, but even with all this whom I still cannot keep myself from regarding as called to be the defender of my memory and the avenger of his friend some day.[179]

In the midst of these dissipations I did not lose either the taste for or the habit of my solitary walks and I often made rather long ones on the banks of the lake, during which my head did not remain idle since it was accustomed to work: I digested the already formed plan of my Political Institutions about which I will soon have to speak;[180] I meditated a history of the Valais, a plan for a Tragedy in prose, whose subject which was nothing less than Lucretia did not deprive me of the hope of[181] astounding the laughers, although I would be daring to allow this unfortunate person appear again, when she could no longer do so in any French Theater.[182] At the same time I made an attempt on Tacitus, and I translated the first Book of his history which will be found among my papers.

After a stay of four months at Geneva I returned to Paris in the month of October, and I avoided passing by way of Lyon so as not to find myself on the road with Gauffecourt again. Since my arrangements did not involve returning to Geneva until the next Spring, during the winter I reacquired my habits and my occupations, the principal of which was to see the proofs of my discourse on inequality, which I was having printed in Holland by the publisher Rey whose acquaintance I had just made at Geneva. Since this Work was dedicated to the Republic, and since this Dedication might not please the Council, I wanted to wait for the effect it would make at Geneva before returning there. This effect was not favorable to me, and this dedication—dictated to me by the purest patriotism—only attracted me enemies in the Council and jealous people in the bourgeoisie. M. Chouet, then first Syndic, wrote me a decent but cold letter which will be found in my collections, Bundle A #3.[183] I received some compliments from private people, among others from De Luc and Jalabert, and that was all: I did not see that any Genevan was truly grateful to me for the zeal of heart that is felt in that work. This indifference scandalized everyone who noticed it. I remember that, one day when I was dining at Clichy at Mme Dupin's along with Crommelin, Resident of the Republic,[184] and with M. de Mairan,[185] the latter said at the full table that the Council owed me a presentation and public honors for that work, and that it would dishonor itself if it failed to do this.[186] Crommelin, who was a dark little man and basely wicked, did not dare to answer anything in my presence, but he made a frightful grimace, which made Mme Dupin laugh. The only advantage this work procured me— aside from the one of having satisfied my heart—was the title of Citizen which was given to me by my friends, then by the public after their example, and which I later on lost for having deserved it too well.[187]

This poor success nevertheless would not have diverted me from executing my retirement to Geneva, if motives that were more powerful over my heart had not cooperated with it. M. d'Epinay, wishing to add a wing that was lacking to the Chateau de la Chevrette, went to an immense expense to finish it. One day, when I had gone to these works[188] with Mme d'Epinay, we pushed our walk a quarter of a league farther up to the Reservoir of the waters of the Park which touched the forest of Montmorency, and where there was a pretty kitchen garden with an extremely dilapidated little[189] cabin that was called the Hermitage. This solitary and very pleasant spot had struck me when I saw it for the first time before my trip to Geneva. It had slipped out of me to say in my rapture, "Ah, Madame, what a delightful dwelling place! here is a refuge made exactly for me." Mme d'Epinay did not take up my speech very much; but on this second trip I was entirely surprised to find, in place of the old hovel, a little house almost entirely new, extremely well arranged, and very livable for a little household of three persons. Mme d'Epinay had had this work done in silence and at very little expense, by separating some material and some workmen from those on the Chateau. On the second trip, when she saw my surprise she said to me, "My Bear, here is your refuge; it is you who have chosen it; it is friendship that offers it to you; I hope it will take away from you the cruel idea of distancing yourself from me." I do not believe I have been more keenly, more delightfully moved in my life; I moistened my friend's beneficent hand with tears, and if I was not overcome from that very instant, I was extremely shaken. Mme d'Epinay, who did not want to be contradicted, became so pressing, used so many means, so many people to get around me, up to the point of winning over Mme le Vasseur and her daughter, that she finally triumphed over my resolutions. Renouncing the stay in my fatherland I resolved, I promised to live in the Hermitage, and, while waiting for the building to dry out, she took care to prepare its furnishings, so that everything was ready to enter it the next spring.

One thing that helped very much to decide me was Voltaire's settling near Geneva:[190] I understood that that man would cause a revolution there, that I would find again in my fatherland the tone, the appearance, the morals that were driving me away from Paris; that I would have to battle ceaselessly, and that I would not have any choice in my behavior but that of being an unbearable pedant, or a lax and bad citizen. The letter that Voltaire wrote me about my last work gave me reason to insinuate my fears into my response; the effect it produced confirmed them.[191] From then on I considered Geneva to be ruined and I was not mistaken. Perhaps I should have gone to face the storm if I felt myself to have the talent to do so. But what could I have done alone, timid and speaking very poorly, against an arrogant, opulent man backed up by the influence of the Great, with a brilliant ostentatious eloquence, and already the idol of the women and young people? I feared to expose my courage to the peril uselessly; I did not listen to anything but my peaceful natural character, my love of repose, which, if it fooled me, still fools me today on the same matter. By withdrawing to Geneva I might have spared myself some great misfortunes; but I doubt that I could have done anything great and useful for my country, even with all my ardent and patriotic zeal.

Tronchin, who went to Geneva to settle at about the same time, came to Paris some time afterward to play the quack and carried off some treasures. Upon his arrival he came to see me with the Chevalier de Jaucourt.[192] Mme d'Epinay wanted very much to consult him in private, but it was not easy to penetrate the crowd. She had recourse to me. I engaged Tronchin to go see her. In this way they began relations under my auspices which they drew tighter afterwards at my expense. Such has always been my destiny: as soon as I have brought together two friends I had separately, they have never failed to become united against me. Although in the plot which the Tronchins formed from that time to enslave their fatherland they all must have hated me mortally, nevertheless for a long time the Doctor continued to bear witness to me of his benevolence.[193] Even after his return to Geneva he wrote to me to propose the honorary position of Librarian for me. But my decision had been made, and this offer did not weaken me.

During this time I returned to M. d'Holback's house. The occasion for it had been the death of his wife, which had occurred, along with that of Mme de Francueil, during my stay in Geneva. When he notified me of it, Diderot spoke to me about the husband's profound affliction. His suffering moved my heart. I myself keenly missed that amiable woman. I wrote to M. d'Holback on this subject.[194] This sad event made me forget all his wrongs, and when I had come back from Geneva and he himself had come back from a tour of France which he had made along with Grimm and other friends in order to distract himself, I went to see him, and I continued to do so until my departure for the Hermitage. When it became known in his coterie that Mme d'Epinay, whom he did not yet see at all, was preparing a lodging for me, sarcasms fell on me like hail, founded on the fact that since I needed the incense and amusements of the city, I would not put up with solitude for even two weeks. Feeling what was in myself, I let them talk and I went on my way. M. d'Holback did not fail to be useful* to me for placing the good old man le Vasseur who was more than eighty years old, and whose wife—who felt herself overburdened with him—did not stop begging me to relieve her of him. He was put in a house of charity where age and regret at seeing himself far from his family sent him to the grave almost as soon as he arrived. His wife and his other children regretted him little. But Therese, who loved him tenderly, has never been able to console herself for his loss, and for having allowed it to happen that so near his end he went far from her to finish his days.

About the same time I had a visit which I hardly expected, although it was from a very old acquaintance. I am speaking of my friend Venture, who came to surprise me one fine morning, when he was the last person I was thinking about. Another man was with him. How changed he appeared to me! Instead of his former graces I no longer found in him anything but a crapulous air, which kept me[196] from opening up with him. Either my eyes were no longer the same, or debauchery had besotted his mind, or all his first brightness depended on the youth that he no longer had. I saw him almost with indifference, and we separated rather coldly. But when he was gone the remembrance of our former relations recalled to me so vividly that of my youthful years, so sweetly, so wisely[197] dedicated to that angelic woman who now was hardly less changed than he, the little anecdotes of that happy time, the romantic day at Toune passed with so much innocence and enjoyment between those two charming girls from whom a kissed hand had been the sole favor, and who in spite of that had left me with such lively, such touching, such durable regrets, all those ravishing deliriums of a young heart, which I had felt then in all their strength, and whose time I believed was gone

*Here is an example of the tricks my memory plays on me. A long time after having written this I just learned while chatting with my wife about her old good man of a father, that it was not at all M. d'Holback but M. de Chenonceaux, who at that time was one of the Administrators of the Hôtel Dieu, who had him placed. I had so totally lost the idea of him and I had that of M. d'Holback so present that I would have sworn for this latter.[195]

forever: all these tender reminiscences caused me to shed tears over my vanished youth and over those raptures henceforth lost for me. Ah! how many of them would I have shed over their belated and fatal return, if I had foreseen the evils that it was going to cost me.

Before leaving Paris, during the winter that preceded my withdrawal, I had a pleasure very much in accordance with my heart, and which I tasted in all its purity. Palissot,[198] an academician from Nancy who was known because of some Dramas, had just presented one of them at Luneville before the King of Poland. He apparently believed he could pay his court by introducing in this Drama a man who had dared to pit himself against the King pen in hand. Stanislas, who was generous, and who did not like satire, was indignant that someone dared to make personal attacks in his presence this way. M. the Comte de Tressan[199] wrote to d'Alembert and me by the order of this Prince to inform me that His Majesty's intention was that the said Palissot be expelled from his Academy. My answer was a lively prayer to M. de Tressan to intercede with the King of Poland to obtain clemency for the Said Palissot. The clemency was granted,[200] and when he notified me of it in the King's name, M. de Tressan added that this fact would be inscribed in the records of the Academy. I replied that this was less granting clemency than perpetuating a punishment. At last as a result of solicitations I obtained the promise that there would be no mention of anything in the records and that there would remain no public trace of this affair. All this was accompanied by testimonies of esteem and consideration as much on the part of the King as on that of M. de Tressan with which I was extremely flattered, and I felt on this occasion that the esteem of men who are so worthy of it themselves produces a very much sweeter and more noble feeling in the soul than that of vanity. In my collection I have transcribed M. de Tressan's letters with my answers, and the originals of them will be found in bundle A. #9, 10, and 11.[201]

I feel very well that if these Memoirs ever succeed in seeing the light I myself am perpetuating the remembrance of a fact the trace of which I wanted to efface; but I am transmitting many others in spite of myself. Since the great object of my enterprise is always present to my eyes, the indispensable duty of fulfilling it in all its extent, will not let me be diverted through very weak considerations that would turn me away from my goal. In the strange, in the unique situation in which I find myself I owe myself the truth too much to owe anything more to anyone else. To know me well it is necessary to know me in all my good and bad relations. My confessions are necessarily tied with those of many people: I make both with the same frankness in everything that relates to me, not believing that I owe to anyone whatsoever more discretion than I have for myself and wanting always to have much more. I want always to be just and truthful, to say about someone else as much good as I can, never to say anything but the evil that regards me and only as much as I am forced to. Who has the right to demand more of me in the position into which I have been put? My confessions are not at all made to appear during my life nor that of interested persons. If I was the master of my destiny and of that of this writing it would see the light only a long time after my death and theirs. But the efforts that the terror of the truth is causing my powerful oppressors to make in order to efface its traces force me to do everything that right and the most exact and most severe justice allow me to do in order to preserve them. If my memory should be extinguished along with me, I would endure an unjust and transitory opprobrium without a murmur rather than compromise anyone: but since in the end my name must live,[202] I ought to try to transmit along with it the remembrance of the unfortunate man who bore it, as it was really, and not as unjust[203] enemies work without respite to depict it.[204]

Book IX[1]

[1.]ɪ.[2] My impatience to begin living in the hermitage[3] did not allow me to wait for the return of the fine weather, and as soon as my lodging was ready, I hastened to make my way there, to the great hoots of the Holbachic coterie, who loudly predicted that I would not bear three months of solitude, and that in a little while they would see me return with my tail between my legs to live like them in Paris. As for myself who, after having been out of my element for fifteen years, saw myself about to return to it, I did not even pay attention to their jokes. Since I had been thrown into the world in spite of myself I had not ceased to regret my dear Charmettes and the sweet life I had led there. I felt myself made for retirement and the country; it was impossible for me to live happily anywhere else. At Venice in the course of public affairs, in the dignity of a position as a sort of representative, in the pride of projects for advancement; at Paris in the whirlwind of high society, in the sensuality of suppers, in the brilliance of spectacles, in the fumes of vainglory; always the remembrance of my groves, my streams, my solitary walks, came to distract me, to sadden me, to wring sighs and desires from me. All the labors to which I had been able to subject myself, all the projects of ambition which had animated my zeal by fits and starts, had no goal other than someday to attain the blessed rustic leisure that I was congratulating myself upon reaching at this moment. Although I had not put myself into the decent easy circumstances which I had believed were the only thing that could lead me there, I judged that I was in a position to do without them because of my peculiar situation, and that I could reach the same goal by an entirely opposite road. I did not have a sou of income, but I had a name, some talents, I was sober, and I had gotten away from the most expensive needs, all those of opinion. Aside from that, even though I was lazy, I was industrious when I wanted to be, and my laziness was less that of a sluggard than that of an independent man who likes to work[4] only on his own schedule. My profession of music copyist was neither brilliant nor lucrative, but it was reliable. In high society they approved of me for having had the courage to choose it. I could count on work not being lacking and it could be enough for me to live on if I worked well. Two thousand francs that I had left from the yield from the *Village Soothsayer* and my other Writings gave me an advance so I would not be in financial straits, and, even without fleecing the publishers, several works that I had on the loom promised me sufficient supplements for me to be able to work at my ease without wearing myself out, and even while turning my leisure walks to advantage. My little household, composed of three persons who were all occupied usefully, was not very costly to keep up. In sum, my resources, proportioned to my needs and my desires, could reasonably promise me a happy and durable life in the one my inclination had made me choose.

2. I could have thrown myself completely toward the most lucrative direction, and, instead of enslaving my pen to copying, devoted it entirely to Writings, which, from the flight I had taken and which I felt myself in a condition to sustain, could make me live in abundance and even in opulence if only I wanted to join the maneuvers of an author to the effort of publishing good books. But[5] I felt that writing in order to have bread might soon stifle my genius and kill my talent which was less in my pen than in my heart, and had been born solely out of an elevated and proud way of thinking which alone could nourish it. Nothing vigorous, nothing great can come from an entirely venal pen. Necessity, greediness perhaps, might have made me write more quickly than well. If the need for success had not plunged[6] me into cabals it might have made me seek to say fewer things that were useful and true than things that might please the multitude, and from a distinguished author[7] which I could be, I would have become only a pen-pusher. No no, I have always felt that the station of Author was not, could not be illustrious and respectable except to the extent that it was not a profession. It is too difficult to think nobly when one thinks only in order to live. In order to be able, in order to dare to say great truths one must not be dependent on success. I cast my books into the public with the certainty of having spoken for the common good, without any concern for the rest. If the work was rejected, so much the worse for those who did not want to profit from it. As for me I did not need their approval in order to live. My profession could nourish me if my books did not sell, and that is precisely what made them sell.

3. It was on April 9, 1756, that I left the City never to live there again; for I do not count as living there some short stays I have made since both at Paris and London and in other cities, but always passing through or always in spite of myself.[8] Mme d'Epinay came to take all three of us in her coach; her farmer came to take charge of my little luggage, and I was installed as early as the same day. I found my little retreat arranged and furnished simply, but cleanly and even with taste. The hand that had given its efforts to this furnishing gave it an inestimable worth in my eyes, and I found it delightful to be my friend's guest in a house of my choice which she had built expressly for me.

4. Although it was cold and there was even still some snow, the earth was beginning to vegetate; one saw violets and Primroses, the buds of the trees were beginning to sprout, and the very night of my arrival was marked by the first song of the nightingale, which made itself heard almost at my window in a grove of trees that touched the house. Since I had forgotten my transplantation, upon awakening after a light sleep I still believed myself to be in rue de Grenelle, when this warbling suddenly made me shiver, and I cried out in my rapture, "At last all my wishes have been accomplished." My first concern was to abandon myself to the[9] impression of the rustic objects with which I was surrounded. Instead of beginning by organizing myself in my lodging I began by organizing myself for my walks, and there was not a footpath, not a copse, not a grove, not a nook around my residence that I had not looked over as early as the next day. The more I examined this charming retreat, the more I felt it was made for me. In the mind's eye this solitary, rather than wild, place transported me to the end of the world. It had some of those touching beauties that one hardly ever finds near cities, and finding oneself transported there suddenly, one would never be able to believe that one was four leagues from Paris.

5. After several days abandoned to my rustic delirium I thought of arranging my old papers and putting my occupations in order. As I had always done, I destined my mornings to copying and my after-dinners to taking a walk, provided with my little white booklet and my pencil: for since I have never been able to write and think at my ease except *sub dio*[10] I was not tempted to change my method, and I very much counted upon having the forest of Montmorency—which was almost at my door—as my study for working from then on. I had begun several Writings; I reviewed them. I was magnificent enough in projects; but in the bustle of the city the execution had proceeded slowly until then. I was counting on putting a little more diligence into them when I had less distraction. I believe I fulfilled that expectation rather well, and for a man who was often sick, was often at la Chevrette, at Eaubonne, at the Chateau of Montmorency,[11] was often badgered in his own home by curious idlers, and was always occupied with copying for half the day, if one counts and measures the writings I did in the six years I spent at the Hermitage and Montmorency, one will find, I am sure, that if I wasted my time during that interval, at least it was not by being idle.

[2.]1. Of the various writings I had in progress, the one which I meditated about for the longest time, which I attended to with the most relish, which I wanted to work on for my whole life, and which in my opinion ought to put the seal on my reputation was my *Political Institutions*. I had conceived its first idea thirteen or fourteen years before, when—being at Venice—I had had some occasion to notice the flaws of that so vaunted Government. Since then, my views had been much more extended by means of historical study of morality. I had seen that everything depends radically on politics, and that, from whatever aspect one considers it, no people ever would be anything other than what it was made into by the nature of its Government; thus this great question of the best possible Government appeared to me to be reduced to this one. What is the nature of Government suited to forming a people that was the most virtuous, most enlightened, most wise, in sum, the best, taking this word in its most extended sense. I had believed I had seen that this question depended very closely on this other one, if it even differs from it. What is the Government which by its nature keeps itself closest to the law? From that, what is law? and a chain of questions of that importance. I saw that all this was leading me to great truths, useful to the happiness of the human race, but above all to that of my fatherland, where on the trip I had just made I had not found them forming what I thought to be sufficiently precise and clear concepts about the laws and freedom and I had believed that this indirect way of giving them these concepts was the one most suited for sparing the amour-propre of its members, and for getting myself pardoned for having been able to see a little farther than they could.[12]

2. Although I had been laboring on that work for five or six years already, it was still barely advanced. Books of this sort require meditation, leisure, tranquillity. Furthermore, I was writing this one in secret[13] and I had not wanted to communicate my project to anyone, not even to Diderot. I feared that it might appear too bold for the century and the country in which I was writing, and that my friends'* fright might bother me in the execution. I did not yet know whether it would be done in time and in a manner capable of appearing in my lifetime. I wanted to be able to give my subject everything it required of me without constraint; very certain that, since I did not have a satirical disposition at all, and never wanted to seek out personal applications, I would always be irreproachable in all equity. Doubtless, I wanted to make full use of the right of thinking which I had by my birth; but while always respecting the Government under which I had to live, without ever disobeying its

---

*It was above all Duclos's wise severity that inspired this fear in me: as for Diderot, somehow or other all my conferences with him always tended to make me more satirical and mordant than my natural disposition brought me to be. It was this very thing that diverted me from consulting him on an enterprise in which I wanted to put only all the force of reasoning, without any vestige of ill-humor and partiality. The tone I had taken in that work can be judged from that of the *Social Contract*, which is extracted from it.

laws, and, being very attentive to not violating the right of nations, I did not want[14] to renounce its advantages out of fear either.

3. I even admit that as a foreigner and living in France, I found my position very favorable for daring to speak the truth; knowing well that continuing—as I wanted to do—not[15] to print anything in the State without permission, in this way I did not owe to any one an account of my maxims and their publication anywhere else. I would have been much less free at Geneva itself, where, wherever my books might be printed, the magistrate had the right of caviling over their contents.[16] This consideration had very much contributed to making me give way to Mme d'Epinay's entreaties and renounce the project of going to settle in Geneva.[17] I felt, as I have said in *Emile*, that unless one is a man of intrigues, if one wants to dedicate books to the true good of the fatherland, one must not compose them in its bosom.[18]

4. What made me find my position more fortunate was the persuasion I had that, although perhaps the government of France did not look at me in an extremely favorable way, it would make it an honor for itself, if not to protect me, at least to leave me in peace. It seemed to me that it was a very simple and nevertheless very skillful stroke of policy to make it into a merit for oneself to tolerate what one could not prevent; since if I had been driven out of France, which was all they had the right to do, my books would have been written anyway, and perhaps with less restraint; instead of which, by leaving me in peace, they kept the author as security for his works, and moreover, they erased some very deeply rooted prejudices in the rest of Europe, by giving themselves the reputation for having an enlightened respect for the right of nations.

5. Those who judge based on the outcome that my trust deceived me might be very much deceived themselves. In the storm that has submerged me, my books have served as a pretext, but it was my person they were after. They cared very little about the author, but they wanted to ruin Jean-Jacques, and the greatest harm they found in my Writings was the honor they could do me. Let us not run on about the future; I do not know whether this mystery, which is still one for me, will be clarified for the readers' eyes by what follows.[19] I know only that if my demonstrated principles should have drawn upon me the treatment I have suffered, I would have been their victim much sooner, since of all my writings the one in which these principles are demonstrated with the greatest boldness not to say audacity, had appeared, had had its effect, even before my retirement to the hermitage, without anyone dreaming, I do not say, of picking a quarrel with me, but of even preventing the publication of the work in France, where it was sold as publicly as in Holland.[20] Since then

La Nouvelle Héloïse appeared also with the same ease, I dare to say with the same applause, and, what seems almost unbelievable,[21] the profession of faith of that very Héloïse dying is exactly the same as that of the Savoyard Vicar.[22] Everything that is bold in *The Social Contract* was previously in the *Discourse on Inequality*; everything that was bold in *Emile* was previously in Julie. Now these bold things excited no clamor against the two former works; thus they were not the things that excited it against the latter.

6. Another undertaking of about the same type, but the plan for which was more recent, occupied me more at this moment: it was the abridgment of the Abbé de St. Pierre's works, which I have not been able to speak about until now because I have been carried along by the thread of my narration. After my return from Geneva, the idea had been suggested to me by the Abbé de Mably, not directly, but through the intervention of Mme Dupin, who had a sort of interest in getting me to adopt it. She was one of the three or four pretty women of Paris, whose spoiled child the old Abbé de St. Pierre had been, and if she had not definitely had his preference, she had at least shared it with Mme d'Aiguillon.[23] She preserved a respect and affection for the memory of the good man that did honor to them both, and her amour-propre might have been flattered at seeing the still-born works of her friend resuscitated by her secretary. These same works did not fail to contain some things that were excellent but so poorly stated that reading them was hard to endure,[24] and it is surprising that the Abbé de St. Pierre, who looked at his readers as big children, nevertheless spoke to them as if they were men from the little effort he took to make himself listened to.[25] For this purpose they had proposed this labor to me as useful in itself, and as very suitable to a man who was laborious in unskilled work, but lazy as an author, who— finding the effort of thinking very tiring—preferred to clarify and push someone else's ideas in things to his taste over creating them himself. Besides, by not being limited to the function of translator, I was not forbidden to think for myself sometimes, and I could give such a form to my work that very important truths would pass in it under the Abbé de St. Pierre's cloak even more happily than under my own. Furthermore, the undertaking was not light: it was a question of nothing less than reading, meditating, abridging twenty-three[26] volumes that were diffuse, confused, full of tedious passages, unnecessary repetitions, little short-sighted[27] or false ideas, among which it was necessary to fish for some great, fine ones which gave one the courage to bear this painful labor. I would have often abandoned it myself if I could have decently backed out of it; but, by receiving the Abbé's manuscripts that were given to me by

his nephew the Comte de St. Pierre through St. Lambert's solicitation, I had in a way committed myself to make use of them, and it was necessary either to return them or try to turn them to account. It was in this latter intention that I had brought these manuscripts to the Hermitage, and it was the first work to which I counted on giving my leisure there.

[7.] [28] I was meditating a third work whose idea I owed to some observations made on myself, and I felt all the more encouraged to undertake it since I had reason to hope that I would write a book that was truly useful to men, and even one of the most useful that could be offered to them, if the execution corresponded worthily to the plan I had traced for myself. It has been noticed that in the course of their life the majority of men are often unlike themselves and seem to be transformed into entirely different men. I did not want to write a book in order to establish such a well-known thing: I had a newer and even more important object. It was to look for [29] the causes of these variations and to pay particular attention to the ones that depend on us to show how we could direct them ourselves so as to make ourselves better and more certain of ourselves. [30] For it is indisputably more difficult for a decent man to resist already completely formed [31] desires which he ought to overcome, than to forestall, change, or modify these same desires in their source if he were in a position to go back to it. A tempted man resists one time because he is strong, and succumbs another time because he is weak; if he had been the same as before, he would not have succumbed.

[8.] By probing myself and by seeking in others what these different manners of being depended on, I found that in large part they depended on the prior impression of external objects, and that—since we are continuously modified by our senses and our organs—in our ideas, in our feelings, in our very actions we carried the effect of these modifications without being aware of it. The striking and numerous observations I had collected were beyond all dispute, and by means of their physical principles, they appeared to me suitable for providing an external regimen which—varied according to circumstances—could put or maintain the soul in the condition most favorable to virtue. From how many errors would reason be saved, how many vices would be kept from being born if one knew how to force the animal economy to favor the moral order it so often troubles! Climates, seasons, sounds, colors, darkness, light, the elements, food, noise, silence, motion, rest, all act on our machine and consequently on our soul; all offer us a thousand almost guaranteed holds for governing in their origin the feelings by which we let ourselves be dominated. Such was the fundamental idea the outline for which I already had on paper, and from which I hoped for an all the more certain effect on well-disposed people who, while they sincerely love virtue, mistrust their weakness, since it appeared easy to me to write a book out of it that would be as pleasant to read as it was to compose. Nevertheless, I worked very little on this work whose title was *sensitive morality*, or *the Wise Man's materialism*. Distractions whose cause will soon be learned kept me from occupying myself with it, and the fate of my outline, which was more closely related to my own fate than it might seem, will also be known.[32]

[9.] Aside from all that, for some time I had been meditating about a system of education to which Mme de Chenonceaux—who had been alarmed for the sake of her son because of her husband's system—had asked me to turn my attention. The authority of friendship caused this object to occupy my heart more than all the others, although in itself it was less to my taste. Also, out of all the subjects I have just been speaking about, this is the only one that I have conducted to its end. The goal which I had proposed for myself in working on it seems to have entitled its author to another destiny. But let us not anticipate this sad subject here. I will be forced to speak about it only too much in the continuation of this writing.

[10.] All these different projects offered me subjects of meditations for my walks: for as I believe I have said, I cannot meditate[33] except while I am walking; as soon as I stop I do not think any more, and my head does not go except with my feet. Nevertheless, I had the foresight also to provide for a work inside a study for rainy days. This was my *Dictionary of Music* whose scattered, mutilated, shapeless materials made it necessary to begin the work again almost anew. I brought some books which I needed for doing it; I had passed two months making extracts from many others which had been loaned to me from the King's Library and some of which I was even permitted to take to the hermitage. These were my provisions for compiling at home when the weather did not allow me to go out and I was bored with my copying. This arrangement suited me so well that I took advantage of it both at the Hermitage and at Montmorency and even later on at Môtiers, where I finished this labor doing others all the while, and always finding that a change of work is a genuine relaxation.

[**3.**]1. For some time I followed the distribution I had prescribed[34] for myself precisely enough, and I found it very satisfying; but when the fine weather brought Mme d'Epinay back more frequently to Epinay or to la Chevrette, I found that the attention which at first did not pain me, but which I had not taken into account, upset my other projects very much. I have already said that Mme d'Epinay had some very lovable qualities: she loved her friends very much, she served them with much zeal, and spared neither her time nor her efforts for them, she certainly very much deserved for them to give her some attention in return. Until then I had fulfilled this duty without thinking it was one; but finally I understood that I had burdened myself with a chain whose weight friendship alone kept me from feeling: I had aggravated this weight through my repugnance for large social circles. Mme d'Epinay availed herself of this to make a proposal that appeared to accommodate me, and which accommodated her more. It was to inform me every time she was alone or almost so. I agreed to it without seeing what I was engaging myself to. It followed from this that I no longer paid her visits at my convenience but at hers, and that I was never sure of being able to dispose of myself a single day. This bother very much impaired the pleasure I had taken in going to see her until then. I found that I was being given this freedom which she had promised me so much only on the condition of never availing myself of it, and when I wanted to try it once or twice, there were so many messages, so many notes, so many alarms about my health, that I saw very well that only the excuse of being flat in bed could dispense me from running at her first word. I had to submit to this yoke; I did so, and even willingly enough for such a great enemy of dependence, because the sincere attachment I had for her in large part kept me from feeling the bond that was linked with it. In this way she filled up, for well or ill, the voids which the absence of her ordinary court left in her amusements. It was a very slender supplement for her, but one that was still worth more than an absolute solitude which she could not bear. Nevertheless, she had a means for filling it up much more easily since she had wanted to try her hand at literature, and since she had stuck it into her head to write— whether one liked it or not—novels, letter, comedies, stories, and other twaddle like that. But what amused her was not so much writing them as reading them, and if she happened to scribble two or three consecutive pages, she had to be sure of at least two or three benevolent listeners at the end of this immense labor. I hardly had the honor of being in the number of the elect except in someone else's place. By myself I counted for almost nothing in everything, and did so not only in Mme d'Epinay's society, but in M. d'Holback's, and everywhere where M. Grimm set the tone. That nullity suited me extremely well everywhere else but in tête-à-tête, where I did not know what countenance to keep up, not daring to speak about literature about which it did not behoove me to judge, nor about gallantry since I was too timid and feared being ridiculed as an aged lady's man more than death; aside from the fact that this idea never came to me around Mme d'Epinay, and perhaps never would have come to me a single time in my life, if I had passed it entirely with her:

not that I had any repugnance for her person; on the contrary; perhaps I liked her too much as a friend to be capable of loving her as a lover. I felt pleasure at seeing her, at chatting with her. Her conversation, although pleasant enough in a social circle, was arid in private; mine, which was no more florid, was not a great help for her. Ashamed of too long a silence, I exerted myself to enhance the conversation, and, although it might often have fatigued me, it never bored me. I was extremely glad to give her some little attentions, to give her very fraternal little kisses, which did not appear to be any more sensual for her, that was all. She was extremely thin, extremely white, with a chest like the back of my hand. This flaw alone would have sufficed to chill me: never have my heart or my senses been able to see a woman in someone who did not have breasts, and other causes useless to mention have always made me forget her sex around her.[35]

2. Having made up my mind this way about a necessary subjugation, I abandoned myself to it without resistance, and at least the first year found it less onerous than I would have expected. Mme d'Epinay, who ordinarily passed almost the entire summer in the country, passed only a part of this one there; either because business kept her more at Paris, or because Grimm's absence made the stay at la Chevrette less pleasant for her. I took advantage of the intervals she did not spend there, or during those when she had many people there, to enjoy my solitude with my good Therese and her mother, in a manner that made me feel its value very well. Although for several years I had been going to the country rather frequently, I had done so almost without tasting it, and these trips, which were always made with pretentious people and were always spoiled by the bother, did nothing but sharpen my taste for the rustic pleasures whose image I glimpsed from close up only in order to feel their privation better. I was so bored with salons, with fountains, arbors, flower-beds, and with the most boring people showing off all these things: I was so worn out by pamphlets, clavichords, games of Trio,[36] knotting silk, foolish witticisms, insipid simpering, little story-tellers, and big suppers, that when I looked out of the corner of my eye at a simple poor thorn bush, a hedge, a barn, a field, when I breathed in the fumes of a good chervil omelette while going through a hamlet, when I heard from afar the rustic refrain of the laceworkers' song, I sent the rouge and flounces and ambergris to the devil, and—regretting the housewife's dinner and the local wine— I would have wholeheartedly slapped the face of Monsieur the Chef and Monsieur the Steward, who made me dine at the hour when I sup, sup at the hour when I sleep, but above all Messieurs the lackeys who devoured my portion with their eyes, and under penalty of dying of thirst sold me

their master's doctored wine ten times more expensively than I would have paid for the best at the tavern.

[3.][37] There I was then at last at home in a pleasant and solitary refuge, master of making my days flow by in that independent, equitable, and peaceful life for which I felt myself born. Before saying what effect this position, which was so new for me, had on my heart, it is fitting for me to recapitulate its hidden affections, so that the progress of these new modifications might be followed better in its causes.

[4.]1. I have always regarded the day that united me with my Therese as the one that settled my moral being. I needed an attachment, because, in sum, the one that should have sufficed for me had been broken so cruelly. The thirst for happiness is never extinguished in the heart of man. Mamma was growing old and was demeaning herself. It had been proven to me that she could no longer be happy here below. It remained for me to seek a happiness that would suit me, now that I had lost all hope of ever sharing hers. For some time I floated from idea to idea and from project to project. My trip to Venice might have thrown me into public affairs if the man with whom I was going to be stuck had had common sense. I am easy to discourage, above all in difficult and long-term undertakings. The ill success of this one disgusted me with all others, and in accordance with my old maxim, since I regarded distant objects as bait for dupes,[38] I decided to live from day to day from then on, because I no longer saw anything in life that could tempt me to exert myself.

2. It was precisely at that time that our acquaintance was made. That good girl's sweet character appeared to me to agree so well with mine that I united myself to her with an attachment proof against time and wrongs, and which was always only increased by everything that should have broken it. The strength of this attachment will be known in what follows when I uncover the wounds, the wounds with which she rent my heart at the height of my miseries, without a single word of complaint about it having escaped me to anyone up until the moment I write this.

3. When one learns that, after having done everything, braved everything not to be separated from her, that after twenty-five years passed with her in spite of fate and men, I have ended by marrying her[39] in my old age without expectation and without solicitation on her part, without engagement or promise on mine, one will believe that a desperate love, which turned my head from the first day, has only led me by degrees to the final extravagance, and one will believe this even more when one learns the particular and strong reasons that ought to have prevented me from ever reaching that point. What will the reader think then, when I

tell him[40] in all the truthfulness he must be acquainted with from me by now, that from the first moment I saw her up to this day I have never felt the slightest spark of love for her, that I no more desired to possess her than Mme de Warens, and that the needs of the senses which I satisfied with her have been solely sexual, without being at all connected with the individual?[41] He will believe that I am constituted differently from any other man and am incapable of feeling love, because it did not enter at all into the feelings which attached me to the women who have been the dearest to me. Patience, oh my reader! the fatal moment approaches when you will be only too well disabused.

4. I am repeating myself, I know it; it is necessary. The first of my needs, the greatest, the strongest, the most inextinguishable, was entirely in my heart: it was the need for an intimate society and as intimate as it could be; it was above all for this that I needed a woman rather than a man, a lover rather than a friend. This peculiar need was such that the closest union of bodies could not even be enough for it: I would have needed two souls in the same body; since I did not have that, I always felt some void. At the moment I believed I no longer felt it. This young person, lovable because of a thousand excellent qualities, and even because of looks at that time, without a shadow of artifice or coquetry, might have limited my existence to her alone, if I had been able to limit hers to me as I had hoped. I had nothing to fear on the part of men; I am sure of being the only one she has genuinely loved, and her tranquil senses hardly required others, even when I ceased to be one for her in that regard.[42] I had no family at all; she had one; and that family, all of whose natural dispositions differed too much from hers, was not the sort that I could make into my own. That was the first cause of my misfortune. What would I not have given to make myself her mother's child! I did everything to succeed in this and could not reach the goal. I might very well have wanted to unite all our interests; that was impossible. She always made one for herself different from mine, contrary to mine, and even to her daughter's, which already was no longer separate from mine. She and her other children and grandchildren became so many bloodsuckers, and the smallest evil they did to Therese was to steal from her. Accustomed to giving way even to her nieces, the poor girl let herself be stripped and governed without saying a word; and I saw with pain that while I was exhausting my purse and my lessons, I was not doing anything for her that she could take advantage of. I tried to detach her from her mother; she always resisted it. I respected her resistance and esteemed her more for it: but her refusal did not turn any less to her disadvantage and mine. Having abandoned herself to her mother and her relatives, she belonged

to them more than to me, more than to herself. Their greed was less ruinous to her than their advice was pernicious; finally if, thanks to her love for me, thanks to her good natural disposition, she was not completely subjugated; she was enough so, at least, to hinder in great part the effect of the good maxims I made efforts to inspire in her; she was subjugated enough that, whatever method I might use, we have always continued to be two.

5. That is how the void in my heart was never very well filled, even in a sincere and reciprocal attachment into which I had put all the tenderness of this heart. The children, through whom it might have been, came; this was still worse. I shuddered at giving them over to that poorly brought up family to be brought up even worse by them. The risks from the education of the foundling hospital were much less.[43] This reason for the decision I made, stronger than all those I enunciated in my letter to Mme de Francueil, was nevertheless the only one I did not dare to tell her. I preferred to be less cleared of so serious a blame,[44] and to spare the family of a person I loved. But one can judge from the morals of her unfortunate brother, if ever I ought to expose my children to receiving an education similar to his, whatever people might say about it.

6. Since I was not able to taste in its fullness that intimate society the need for which I felt, I sought supplements for it which did not fill the void but which allowed me to feel it less. For lack of a friend who was entirely mine, I needed friends whose impulse overcame my inertia: that is how I cultivated, I tightened my relations with Diderot, with the Abbé de Condillac, how I made a new, even closer one with Grimm, and finally how, without thinking about it, I found myself thrown back without thinking about it into literature, from which I believed I had departed forever, through that unfortunate discourse whose story I have recounted.

7. My debut led me by means of a new route[45] into another intellectual world whose simple and proud economy I was unable to envisage without enthusiasm. Soon as a result of occupying myself with it I no longer saw anything but error and folly in the doctrine of our wise men, anything but oppression and misery in our social order. In the illusion of my foolish pride I believed I was made to dissipate all these illusions; and, judging that I needed to put my conduct into accord with my principles in order to get a hearing, I took on the singular course which I have not been allowed to follow, and my pretended friends have not been able to pardon me for setting an example which first made me ridiculous, and which might finally have made me respectable, if I could have persevered in it.

[8.] [46] Until then I had been good; from then on I became virtuous, or at least intoxicated with virtue. This intoxication had begun in my head, but it had passed into my heart. The noblest pride sprang up on the ruins of uprooted vanity. I play acted nothing; I in fact became what I appeared to be, and during the period of at least four years that this effervescence lasted in all its force, between Heaven and myself there was nothing great and beautiful that could enter into the heart of a man of which I was not capable. That is the source of my sudden eloquence; that is the source from which that truly celestial fire that was setting me ablaze spread out in my first books, and the slightest spark of which had not escaped for forty years because it had not yet been kindled.

9. I was truly transformed; my friends, my acquaintances no longer recognized me. I was no longer that timid and bashful—rather than modest—man, who did not dare either to introduce himself or speak; who was disconcerted by a playful word, who was made to blush by a look from a woman. Audacious, proud, intrepid, everywhere I carried an assurance that was all the more firm since it was simple and resided in my soul more than in my bearing. The scorn that my deep meditations had inspired me for the morals, the maxims, and the prejudices of my century made me insensitive to the banter of the people who had them, and I crushed their little witty phrases with my apophthegms, as I would crush an insect between my fingers. What a change! [47] All Paris repeated the bitter and mordant sarcasms of this same man who two years before and ten years afterward could never find what he wanted to say, or the word he ought to use. Look for the condition in the world most contrary to my natural disposition; this one will be found. Recall those short moments of my life in which I became someone else, and ceased to be me; the time about which I am speaking is one of them; but instead of lasting six days, six weeks, it lasted almost six years, and would perhaps still be lasting, if it were not for the particular circumstances that made it cease, and returned me to nature above which I had wanted to raise myself.

10. This change began as soon as I had left Paris, and the spectacle of that big City's vices ceased to nourish the indignation it had inspired in me. When I no longer saw men, I ceased to despise them: when I no longer saw the wicked I ceased to hate them. My heart, which is hardly formed for hatred, could no longer do anything but deplore their misery and not distinguish their wickedness from it. This sweeter but much less sublime condition soon subdued the ardent enthusiasm that had carried me away for such a long time; and, without anyone noticing it, almost without noticing it myself, I again became fearful, accommodating, [48] timid, in a word the same Jean-Jacques I had been before.

ii. If the revolution had done nothing but return me to myself and stop there, all would have been well; but unfortunately it went farther and carried me away rapidly to the other extreme. From that time my soul has been in motion and has no longer done anything but pass through the line of rest and its ever renewed oscillations have never allowed it to stay there. Let us enter into the details of this second revolution: a terrible and fatal epoch of a fate which has no precedent among mortals.

[5.]1. Since there were only three of us in our retreat, leisure and solitude should naturally have tightened our intimacy. That is what it did between Therese and me. Tête-à-tête under the shade we passed charming hours whose sweetness I had never felt so well. She appeared to me to relish it herself even more than she had done until then. She opened her heart to me without reserve, and informed me of things about her mother and her family about which she had had the strength to keep silent to me about for a long time. From Mme Dupin both of them had received multitudes of presents intended for me, but which the old sly one had appropriated for herself and for her other children, without leaving any of them for Therese, and with very severe prohibitions against speaking to me about it so that I would not get angry; an order which the poor girl had followed with an unbelievable obedience.

2. But a thing that surprised me much more was to learn that—aside from the private conversations which Diderot and Grimm had often had with both of them in order to detach them from me, and which had not succeeded because of Therese's resistance—since then both had had frequent and secret colloquies with her mother, without Therese having been able to find out what was being brewed up among them. She knew only that little presents were mixed up in it, and that there were little comings and goings about which they tried to make a mystery to her, and about whose motive she was absolutely ignorant. When we left Paris Mme Le Vasseur had already been in the habit for a long time of going to see M. Grimm two or three times a month, and of passing several hours there in conversations so secret that Grimm's lackey was always dismissed.

3. I judged that motive for this was nothing other than the same project into which they had attempted to make the daughter enter by promising to procure for them a salt concession, or a Tobacco franchise through Mme d'Epinay, and in a word tempting them with the lure of gain. They had represented to them that since I was not in a position to do anything for them, I could not even succeed in doing anything for myself because of them. Since I did not see anything in all this but a good intention, I was not absolutely annoyed with them about it. It was only the mystery

that revolted me, above all on the part of the old woman, who, further-more, from day to day became more toadying and more wheedling with me;[49] which did not keep her from ceaselessly reproaching her daughter in secret for loving me too much, for telling me everything, for being only a stupid girl, and from telling her that she would be a dupe because of it.

4. This woman possessed the art of drawing the payment for ten millings from one sack[50] to a supreme degree, of hiding from one what she received from the other, and from me what she received from every-one. I could have pardoned her for her greed, but I could not pardon her for her dissimulation. What could she have to hide from me, from me who she knew very well made her daughter's and her happiness almost into my only happiness? What I had done for her daughter I had done for myself, but what I had done for her deserved some gratitude on her part; she ought to have been grateful for it, at least to her daughter, and to love me for the love of the one who loved me. I had taken her out of the most complete poverty, she derived her subsistence from me, she owed all these acquaintances she turned to such good account to me. For a long time Therese had nourished her with her labor and now she nourished her with my bread. She derived everything from that daughter for whom she had done nothing, and her other children—to whom she had given dowries and for whom she had ruined herself—far from helping her to subsist, devoured both her subsistence and mine. In such a situation I thought that she ought to look upon me as her sole friend, her most reli-able protector, and far from keeping my own business a secret from me, far from plotting against me in my own house, to warn me faithfully of everything that might interest me, if she learned it before I did. In what light then could I see her false and mysterious[51] behavior? What should I think, above all, about the feelings she was endeavoring to give her daughter?[52] What monstrous ingratitude must hers be when she sought to inspire it in her daughter.

5. In the end all these reflections alienated my heart from this woman, to the point that I could no longer see her without disdain. Nevertheless, I never ceased to treat my companion's mother with respect, and to show her almost the respect and consideration of a son in everything; but it is true that I did not like to stay with her for very long, and I hardly have it in me to be able to constrain myself.

6. Here again is one of those short moments of my life in which I have seen happiness from very close up without being able to reach it, and without it having been my fault that I missed it. If that woman had been of a good character all three of us would have been happy up to

the end of our days; only the last one living would be left to be pitied. Instead of that, you are going to see the progress of things, and you will judge whether I could have changed it.

7. Mme le Vasseur, who saw that I had gained some ground in her daughter's heart and that she had lost it, endeavored to take it back, and instead of returning to me through her, attempted to alienate her from me completely. One of the means she employed was to call her family to her aid. I had begged Therese not to have any of them come to the hermitage, she promised me this. They had them come in my absence without consulting her, and then they made her promise to say nothing to me about it. Once the first step was made, all the rest was easy; once one has made a secret of something from someone one loves, one soon no longer has any scruple about making secrets about everything. As soon as I was at la Chevrette, the Hermitage was filled with a crowd of people who enjoyed themselves rather well there. A mother always has very strong influence over a daughter who has a good natural disposition. Nevertheless, whatever method the old woman used, she could never get Therese to enter into her aims and to engage her to conspire against me. As for herself, she made an irreversible decision, and seeing on one side her daughter and me, with whom she could live; and that was all; on the other, Diderot, Grimm, d'Holback, Mme d'Epinay, who promised much and gave something, she estimated that one could never be in the wrong in the party of a Farmer General and a Baron. If I had had better eyes, from then on I would have seen that I was nourishing a serpent in my bosom: but my blind confidence that nothing had yet altered was such, that I did not even imagine that anyone could want to harm someone he ought to love; when I saw a thousand schemes being hatched around me, I could only complain about the tyranny of the people I called my friends, and who, in my view, wanted to force me to be happy in their way rather than in my own.

8. Although Therese refused to enter into the conspiracy with her mother, she kept her secret once again: her motive was praiseworthy; I will not say whether she did well or ill. Two women who have secrets love to prattle together: that brought them together, and by dividing herself Therese sometimes allowed me to feel that I was alone; for I could no longer count as a society the one that the three of us had together. It was then that I keenly felt the wrong I had committed during our first relations of not taking advantage of the docility her love gave her in order to adorn her with talents and knowledge, which, by keeping us closer in our retreat, would have filled up her time and mine pleasantly without ever letting us feel the tediousness of tête-à-tête. It was not that conver-

sation dried up between us and that she appeared to be bored on our walks; but in the end we did not have enough common ideas to make up a big storehouse: we could no longer speak ceaselessly about our plans which from then on were limited to enjoying. The objects that presented themselves inspired me with reflections that were not in her grasp. An attachment of twelve[53] years no longer needed words; we knew each other too well to have anything to teach each other any longer. There remained the resource of babblers, backbiting, and gibes. It is above all in solitude that one feels the advantage of living with someone who knows how to think. I did not need this resource in order to take pleasure in being with her; but she would have needed it always to take pleasure in being with me. The worst thing was that along with that we had to take our tête-à-têtes in secret: her mother, who had become tiresome to me, forced me to watch out for them. I was bothered in my own home; that says it all; the appearance of love spoiled the good friendship. We had an intimate relationship without living in intimacy.

9. As soon as I believed I saw that Therese sometimes looked for pretexts to avoid the walks I proposed to her, I ceased proposing them, without being annoyed with her for not taking as much pleasure in them as I did. Pleasure is not a thing that depends on the will. I was sure of her heart, that was enough for me. As long as my pleasures were hers, I relished them with her:[54] when they were not, I preferred her contentment to my own.

10. This is how, half frustrated in my expectation, leading a life according to my taste, in an abode of my choice, with a person who was dear to me, I nevertheless came to feel myself almost isolated. What I was missing kept me from tasting what I had. In the matter of happiness and enjoyment, I needed everything or nothing. It will be seen why such detail has appeared necessary to me. Now I take up the thread of my narrative again.

[6.]1. I believed I had some treasures in the[55] manuscripts that the Comte de St. Pierre had given me. When I examined them I saw that this was little more than the collection of his Uncle's printed works, annotated and corrected in his hand with some[56] other little pieces which had not seen the light of day. His writings on morality confirmed me in the idea I had been given by some letters from him which Mme de Crequi had shown me, that he had more intelligence than I had believed; but the thorough examination of his political works showed me only superficial views, projects that were useful but impracticable because of the idea[57] from which the author was never able to depart that men were led by their enlightenment rather than by their passions. The high opinion he had of modern knowledge had made him adopt that false principle of perfected reason, the basis of all the establishments he proposed, and the source of all his political sophisms. This rare man, the honor of his century and his species, and perhaps the only one since the human race has existed who had no other passion than that of reason, nevertheless did nothing but proceed from error to error in all his systems, out of having wished to make men similar to him, instead of taking them as they are and they will continue to be. He worked only for imaginary beings while thinking that he was working for his contemporaries.[58]

2. Having seen all that, I found myself in some perplexity about the form to give my work. To let the author's visions pass was not to do anything useful: to refute them rigorously was to do something dishonorable, since the custody of his manuscripts, which I had accepted and even asked for, imposed on me the obligation of treating their author honorably. Finally I made the decision that appeared to me most modest, most judicious, and most useful.[59] It was to present the author's ideas and mine separately, and to do so, to enter into his intentions, to clarify them, to extend them, and to spare nothing to make them valued at their full worth.

3. My work then should be made up of two absolutely separate parts; the one designed to exposing the author's several projects in the way I have just said. In the other, which ought not to appear until after the first had had its effect, I would have brought my judgment to bear about these same projects, which, I admit, might have sometimes exposed them to the fate of the sonnet of the *Misanthrope*.[60] At the front of the whole work was to be a life of the Author for which I had gathered some rather good materials which I flattered myself I would not spoil while using them. I had seen the Abbé de St. Pierre a little in his old age, and the veneration I had for his memory was security for me that, all things considered, M. the Comte would not be dissatisfied with the manner in which I treated his relative.

[4.][61] I made my attempt on the perpetual peace, the most substantial and the most polished of all the works that made up this collection, and before abandoning myself to my reflections, I had the courage to read absolutely everything the Abbé had written on this fine subject, without ever becoming discouraged by his tedious passages and unnecessary repetitions. The public has seen this abridgment, thus I have nothing to say about it.[62] As for the judgment I brought to bear on it, it has not been printed and I do not know whether it ever will be: but it was written at the same time as the abridgment. I passed from that to the polysynody or plurality of Counsels; a work done under the Regent in order to favor the administration he had chosen, and which got the Abbé de St. Pierre dismissed from the French Academy because of several barbs against the preceding administration about which the Duchesse du Maine and Cardinal de Polignac were angry.[63] I finished this work like the previous one, the judgment as well as the abridgment: but stopped there, without wanting to continue this enterprise, which I should not have begun.

[5.] The reflection that made me renounce it presented itself by its own accord, and it was surprising that it did not come to me sooner. The majority of the Abbé de St. Pierre's writings were or contained critical observations on some parts of the government of France, and some were even so free that he was lucky to have made them with impunity. But in the Offices of the Ministers they had always looked upon the Abbé de St. Pierre as a sort of[64] preacher rather than as a true political thinker, and they let him say everything at his ease, because they saw very well that no one was listening to him. If I had succeeded in getting him heard the case would have been[65] different. He was French, I was not; and by taking it into my head to repeat his censures, even though under his name, I exposed myself to having myself asked, a little rudely, but without injustice, what I was meddling with. Fortunately before going farther, I saw the hold I was going to give against myself, and I withdrew very quickly. I knew that living alone in the midst of men, and men all more powerful than I was, there was no way whatsoever by which I could ever tackle it and shelter myself from the harm they might want to do me. There was only one thing in this that depended on me: it was to act in such a way that at least if they wanted to harm me, they could do it only unjustly. This maxim which made me abandon the Abbé de St. Pierre has often made me renounce much dearer projects. Always prompt to make a crime out of adversity, those people[66] would be very surprised if they knew all the efforts I have taken in my life, so that in my misfortunes it could never be said to me with truth,[67] *"You have deserved them very much."*

[7.1.] Having abandoned this work, I was left uncertain for some time about what I would do to follow it, and this interval of inaction was my ruin since it let me turn my reflections toward myself, for lack of a foreign object which might occupy me. I no longer had any plan for the future that could amuse my imagination. It was not even possible to make one up, because my present situation was precisely the one in which all my desires were brought together: I had no more of them to form, and I still had an empty heart. This state was all the more cruel because I saw none whatsoever to prefer to it. I had gathered my most tender affections in accord with my heart in a person who returned them to me. I was living with her without restraint, and so to speak, at my discretion. Nevertheless a secret heartache did not leave me either when I was with her or far away. While possessing her I felt that I still lacked her, and the mere idea that I was not everything to her made it so that she was almost nothing to me.

I had friends of both sexes to whom I was attached by the purest friendship, by the most perfect esteem; I counted on the truest return on their part, and it did not even enter my mind to doubt their sincerity a single time. Nevertheless this friendship was more tormenting than sweet to me, because of their obstinacy, even their affectation in contradicting all my tastes, my inclinations, my way of living, so much that it was enough for me to appear to desire a thing that concerned only myself, and which did not depend on them, to see them all instantly conspire to force me to renounce it. This obstinacy to control me in everything within my whims—which was all the more unjust because far from controlling theirs I did not even inquire about them—became so cruelly burdensome to me that finally I did not receive one of their letters without feeling a certain fright while I was opening it which was only too justified when I read it. I found this to be treating me too much like a child for people all of whom were younger than I was, and all of whom themselves very much needed the lessons they were lavishing on me. "Love me," I told them "as I love you, and otherwise, do not meddle in my business any more than I meddle in yours; this is all I ask of you." If they granted me one of these two things, at least it was not the latter.

I had an isolated residence in a charming solitude; as master of my home, I could live there in my way without there being anyone to control me: but this habitation imposed duties on me, sweet to fulfill, but indispensable. All my freedom was only precarious; more enslaved than if I were under orders, I was supposed to be so by own my will: I did not have a single day in which I could say when I got up, "I will use this day as I please." Much more; aside from my dependence on Mme d'Epinay's arrangements, I had another much more intrusive dependence on the public and unexpected arrivals. The distance I was from Paris did not prevent heaps of idlers from coming to me daily who, not knowing what to do with their own time, squandered mine without any scruple. When I least expected it I was pitilessly beset, and I rarely made a fine plan for my day without seeing it upset by someone arriving.

In short; not finding any pure enjoyment whatsoever in the midst of the good things I had coveted the most, I returned by fits and starts to the unclouded days of my youth, and sometimes while sighing I cried out to myself, "Ah this is not les Charmettes."

Remembrances of the various times of my life led me to reflect on the point to which I had come, and I already saw myself on the downward slope of age, prey to painful ills and believing the end of my career was approaching, without me having tasted in their fullness almost any of the pleasures for which my heart was greedy, without having given vent to the lively feelings which I felt in reserve there, without having savored, without having at least skimmed that intoxicating voluptuousness which I felt in all its force in my soul, and which, for lack of an object, found itself always under restraint without being able to find a vent other than through my sighs.

How could it be that up to then, even though I had a naturally expansive soul for which to live was to love, I had not found a friend entirely my own, a genuine friend, I who felt myself so well made to be one? How could it be that with such inflammable senses, with a heart entirely full of love I had not at least one[68] time burned with its flame for a specific object? Devoured with the need to love without ever having been able to satisfy it very well, I saw myself reaching the gateway of old age, and dying without having lived.

These sad but touching reflections made me withdraw into myself with a regret that was not without sweetness. It seemed to me that destiny owed me something it had not given me. What good was it to have caused me to be born with exquisite faculties only to leave them unused until the end? While giving me the feeling of this injustice, that of my internal worth compensated me in some measure and made me shed tears which I loved to let flow.

I made these meditations in the finest season of the year, in the month of June, under fresh groves, to the song of the nightingale, to the murmuring of streams. Everything cooperated in plunging me back into that too seductive slackness for which I was born but from which I should have been freed forever by the harsh and severe tone to which a long effervescence had just raised me. Unfortunately I went on to recall the dinner at the Chateau of Toune and my encounter with those two charming girls in the same season and in places very much like the ones I was in at that moment.[69] This remembrance, which was made even sweeter by the innocence that was joined with it, recalled others of the same sort to me. Soon I saw all the objects that had given me emotion in my youth assembled around me, Mlle Galley, Mlle de Graffenried, Mlle de Breil, Mme Basile, Mme de Larnage, my pretty students, and all the way to the piquant Zulietta, whom my heart could not forget. I saw myself surrounded by a seraglio of Houris from my old acquaintances, the most lively taste for whom was not a new feeling for me. My blood catches fire and sparkles, my head turns in spite of my already greying hair, and behold the grave Citizen of Geneva, behold the austere Jean-Jacques nearly forty-five years old suddenly becoming the extravagant shepherd again. The intoxication by which I was seized, although so sudden and so mad, was so durable and so strong that my cure required nothing less than the unforeseen and terrible crisis of misfortunes into which it precipitated me.

This intoxication, however far it might have gone, nevertheless did not reach the point of making me forget my age and my situation, of flattering myself at still being able to inspire love, of attempting to communicate at last that devouring but sterile fire by which I had felt my heart consumed in vain ever since my childhood. I did not hope for it at all, I did not even desire it. I knew that the time for loving had passed, I felt the ridiculousness of those superannuated ladies' men too much to fall into it, and I was not the man to become conceited and self-confident upon my decline after having been so little so during the prime of my life. Moreover, as a friend of peace, I would have feared domestic storms, and I loved my Therese too sincerely to expose her to the grief of seeing me bring to other people more lively feelings than the ones she inspired in me.

What did I do on that occasion? Already my Reader has guessed it, if only he has followed me up to this point. The impossibility of reaching real beings threw me into the country of chimeras, and seeing nothing existing that was worthy of my delirium, I nourished it in an ideal world which my creative imagination soon peopled with beings in accordance with my heart. Never did this resource come more opportunely and never was it found to be so fecund. In my continuous ecstasies I intoxicated myself with torrents of the most delightful feelings that have ever entered into the heart of a man. Completely forgetting the human race, I made for myself societies of perfect creatures as celestial by their virtues as by their beauties, reliable, tender, faithful friends such as I never found here below. I acquired such a taste for soaring into the empyrean this way in the midst of the charming objects with which I had surrounded myself, that I passed hours, days there, without counting, and losing the remembrance of all other things; hardly had I eaten a bite in haste than I burned to escape to run to find my groves again. When, being ready to depart for the enchanted world, I saw some wretched mortals arrive who came to hold me back on the earth, I could neither moderate nor hide my disdain, and no longer being master of myself, I gave them such a brusque welcome, that it could bear the name of brutal. That only increased my reputation for misanthropy, from everything that would have acquired me a very contrary one, if they had read better within my heart.

[**8**.1.] At the height of my greatest exaltation I was suddenly pulled back by the cord like a Kite and put back in my place by nature with the aid of a rather lively attack of my illness. I used the only remedy that might have relieved me, namely the catheters, and that brought about a respite from my angelic loves: for aside from the fact that one is hardly amorous when one is suffering, my imagination, which is enlivened in the country and under the trees, languishes and dies in a room and under the beams of a ceiling. I have often regretted[70] that Dryads do not exist; I would have infallibly fixed my attachment among them.

Other domestic worries came to increase my afflictions at the same time. While paying me the finest compliments in the world, Mme le Vasseur alienated her daughter from me as much as she could. I received letters from my former neighbors that informed me that without my knowledge the good old woman had incurred several debts in the name of Therese, who knew it and who had not told me anything about it. Debts to pay angered me much less than the secret that had been kept from me about it. Ah! how could she from whom I had never kept any secret keep one from me? Can one dissimulate with people one loves? The Holbachic coterie, who did not see me making any trips to Paris, began to fear in earnest that I might like being in the country, and that I might be mad enough to remain there. With that began the pestering by which they sought indirectly to call me back to the city. Diderot, who did not want to show himself so soon, began by dispatching to me Deleyre[71] for whom I had procured his acquaintance, who received and passed on to me the impressions Diderot wanted to give him, without Deleyre seeing[72] their true aim.

Everything seemed to cooperate in drawing me out of my sweet and foolish reverie. I was not cured of my attack when I received a copy of the *Poem on the Ruin of Lisbon* which I assumed had been sent to me by the author.[73] That gave me the obligation to write to him and to speak to him about his piece. I did so by means of a letter that was printed a long time afterwards without my assent, as will be said below.[74]

Struck at seeing this poor man burdened down, so to speak, with prosperity and glory nevertheless declaiming bitterly against the miseries of this life and always finding all to be evil, I formed the senseless project of making him return into himself and of proving to him that all was good.[75] While always appearing to believe in God, Voltaire really never believed in anything but the Devil; since his so-called God is nothing but a maleficent being who according to him takes pleasure only in harming. The absurdity of this doctrine, which leaps to the eyes, is revolting above all in a man loaded with good things of every sort who, from the bosom of happiness, seeks to make his fellows despair by means of the horrible and cruel image of all the calamities from which he is exempt. Being more authorized than he was to count and weigh the evils of human life, I made an equitable examination of them, and I proved to him that out of all these evils, there was not one from which providence was not exculpated, and which did not have its source more in the abuse that man has made of his faculties than in nature itself. In this letter I treated him with all the regard, all the consideration, all the care, and I can say with all the respect possible. Nevertheless, since I knew he had an extremely irritable amour-propre, I did not send this letter to him, but to Doctor Tronchin his doctor and his friend, with full power to give or suppress it, in accordance with what he found most suitable. Tronchin gave the letter. Voltaire answered me in a few lines that being sick and himself a nurse he was putting off his answer to another time, and did not say a word on the question. When he sent me this letter, Tronchin joined to it one in which he showed little esteem for the person who had given it to him. Since I do not at all like to make a display of these sorts of little triumphs, I never published or even showed these two letters; but the originals are in my collections, bundle A. #20 and 21.[76] Since then Voltaire has published that answer he had promised me, but which he did not send to me. It is nothing other than the Novel, *Candide*, about which I cannot speak, because I have not read it.[77]

All these distractions should have radically cured me of my fantastic loves, and perhaps this was a way that Heaven offered me to forestall their fatal consequences: but my bad star was the stronger one, and hardly had I begun to go out again, when my heart, my head, and my feet took the same paths. I say, the same, in certain respects; for since my ideas were a little less exalted, they stayed on earth this time, but with such an exquisite selection of everything lovable that could be found of every kind, that this elite was hardly less chimerical than the imaginary world I had abandoned.

1. I drew for myself the most ravishing images of love, friendship, the two idols of my heart. I liked to adorn them with all the charms of the sex which I had always adored. I imagined two female friends rather than two male friends, because if the example is more rare,[78] it is also more lovable. I endowed them with two analogous but different characters, with two appearances, not perfect but to my taste, which enlivened benevolence and sensitivity. I made one a brunette and the other blonde, one lively and the other gentle, one wise and the other weak, but with such a touching weakness that virtue seemed to gain from it. I gave to one of the two a lover for whom the other was his tender friend and even something more, but I admitted neither rivalry nor quarrels nor jealousy, because it hurts me to imagine every painful feeling, and because I did not want to tarnish this cheerful picture with anything that might have degraded nature. In-

fatuated with my two charming models, I identified myself with the lover and friend as much as I could; but I made him lovable and young, into the bargain giving him the virtues and flaws I felt in myself.

To place my characters in an abode that suited them, I passed successively in review the most beautiful places I had seen in my travels, but I did not find a grove fresh enough, a countryside touching enough to my taste. The Valleys of Thessaly might have satisfied me if I had seen them; but, being fatigued with inventing, my imagination wanted some real place that could serve it as a fulcrum, and give me an illusion about the reality of the inhabitants I wanted to put there. For a long time I thought about the Borromean islands whose delightful appearance had enraptured me, but I found too much ornament and art there for my characters. Nevertheless I[79] needed a lake, and I ended by choosing the one around which my heart has never ceased to wander. I settled on the part of the shores of this lake upon which my wishes have placed my residence for a long time in the imaginary happiness to which fate limited me.[80] My poor mamma's native place still had an attraction of predilection for me. The contrast of positions, the richness and variety of sites, the magnificence, the majesty of the whole[81] which ravished the senses, moved the heart, raised up the soul, finally decided me, and I established my young wards at Vevey. That is all that I imagined at the first leap; the remainder was added only later on.

For a long time I limited myself to such a vague plan, because it was enough to fill my imagination with agreeable objects, and my heart with the feelings with which it loves to nourish itself. As a result of returning, these fictions finally took on more consistency and were fixed in my brain under a determined form. It was then that the whim took me of expressing some of the situations they offered to me on paper, and recalling everything I had felt in my youth, of giving vent this way in some measure to the desire to love which I had not[82] been able to satisfy, and with which I felt myself devoured.

At first I threw down on the paper some scattered letters without sequence and without connection, and when I took it into my head to want to stitch them together I was often extremely perplexed to do so. What is hardly believable and very true is that the two first Parts were written almost entirely in this manner; without me having any well-formed plan, and even without foreseeing that one day, I would be tempted to make a work in proper order out of it. Thus one can see that these two Parts, formed after the event out of materials that had not been hewn for the place they occupy, are full of verbal padding that one does not find in the others.

At the height of my sweet reveries I had a visit from Mme d'Houdetot, the first she had made me in her life, but which unfortunately was not the last, as will be seen below. The Comtesse de Houdetot was the daughter of the late M. de Bellegarde the Farmer General, sister of M. d'Epinay and of Messieurs de la Live and de la Briche, who both have been Introducers of Ambassadors since then. I have spoken about making her acquaintance when she was a girl.[83] Since her marriage I saw her only at holidays at la Chevrette at her sister-in-law Mme d'Epinay's home. Having often passed several days with her both at la Chevrette and at Epinay, not only did I always find her very amiable, but I believed I also saw benevolence for me in her: she rather liked to go for walks with me; we were both walkers, and conversation did not run dry between us. Nevertheless, I never went to see her at Paris, although she had requested me to do so and even entreated me several times. Her relations with M. de St. Lambert, with whom I was beginning to have some, made her even more interesting to me, and it was to bring me news about that friend, who I believe was at Mahon at that time, that she came to see me at the Hermitage.[84]

This visit had a little of the air of the beginning of a novel. She went astray on the road. Her coachman, leaving the path that turned, wanted to cross in a straight line from the Clairveaux mill to the Hermitage: her carriage got bogged down at the bottom of the small valley; she wanted to get out and make the rest of the journey on foot. Her dainty shoe was soon soaked through; she sank in the mud, her people had all the trouble in the world in pulling her out, and finally she arrived at the Hermitage in boots, and piercing the air with bursts of laughter, in which I mixed my own when I saw her arrive: she had to change everything; Therese provided for it, and I urged her to forget dignity to make a rustic collation which she very much enjoyed. It was late, she stayed for a very short time; but the interview was so gay that she acquired a taste for it, and appeared disposed to come again. Nevertheless, she did not execute this project until the following year; but alas! this delay did not protect me from anything.

I passed the autumn in an occupation which you would not expect, in guarding M. d'Epinay's fruit. The Hermitage was the reservoir for the water of the Park of la Chevrette. There was a garden walled in and furnished with espaliers and other trees, which gave more fruit to M. d'Epinay than his kitchen-garden at la Chevrette, although three-quarters of it was stolen from him.[85] So as not to be an absolutely useless guest, I took upon myself the direction of the garden and the inspection of the gardener. All went well up to the fruit season, but to the extent that it ripened I saw it disappear, without knowing what was becoming of it. The gardener assured me that it was the Dormice that were eating everything. I waged war on the Dormice, I destroyed many of them, and the fruit did not disappear any less. I watched so well that finally I found out that the gardener himself was the big Dormouse. He lodged at Montmorency, from where he came during the night with his wife and his children to carry away the deposits of fruit he had made during the day, and which he had sold at the covered market at Paris as publicly as if he had had his own garden. This wretch whom I heaped with benefits, whose children were dressed by Therese and whose father was a beggar whom I almost supported, robbed us as easily as he did impudently, since none of the three of us was vigilant enough to prevent him, and in one night alone he succeeded in emptying my cellar, in which I found nothing the next day. As long as this appeared to apply only to me, I put up with everything; but when I wanted to give an account of the fruit, I was obliged to denounce its thief. Mme d'Epinay asked me to pay him, to turn him out, and to look for someone else; which I did. Since this big rascal prowled around the Hermitage every night, armed with a big nailed cudgel which had the appearance of a bludgeon, and followed by other good-for-nothings of his sort, I had[86] his successor sleep at the Hermitage every night in order to reassure the Governesses whom this man frightened terribly, and since even that did not calm them, I had Mme d'Epinay asked for a gun which I kept in the Gardener's room, along with the order for him not to use it unless it was necessary, if they tried to force the door or to scale the garden, and to shoot only powder, solely to frighten the robbers. This was assuredly the least precaution that could be taken for the common safety by an indisposed man, who had to pass the winter in the middle of the woods, alone with two timid women. In the end I made the acquisition of a little dog to serve as sentinel. When De Leyre came to see me at that time, I told him my circumstances, and laughed with him about my military apparatus.

Upon returning to Paris he wanted to amuse Diderot with it in his turn, and that is how the Holbachic coterie learned that I seriously wanted to pass the winter at the hermitage. This constancy which they had not been able to imagine disoriented them, and while waiting to imagine some other scolding to make my stay unpleasant for me,[87] by means of Diderot they dispatched to me the same De Leyre, who—even though at first he had found my precautions very straightforward—ended by finding them inconsistent with my principles and worse than ridiculous, in some letters in which he loaded me with bitter pleasantries sharp enough to offend me if my mood had been turned in that direction. But, since at that time I was saturated with affectionate and tender feelings, and was not susceptible to any others, I saw only matter for laughing in his sharp sarcasms, and did not find him anything but playful, where anyone else would have found him extravagant.[88]

By dint of vigilance and efforts, I succeeded in guarding the garden so well that, although the harvest of the fruit had almost failed that year, the product was triple that of the preceding years, and it is true that I did not spare myself at all to preserve it, up to the point of escorting the shipments I made to la Chevrette and to Epinay, up to the point of carrying some baskets myself, and I remember that the Aunt and I carried one so heavy that, being ready to succumb under the burden, we were constrained to rest every ten steps and arrived only completely bathed in perspiration.

When the bad weather began to close me up in the dwelling, I wanted to take up my housebound occupations again; I could not do so. Everywhere I saw only the two charming friends, their friend, the people close to them, the country they inhabited, the objects created or embellished for them by my imagination. I no longer belonged to myself for a moment, the delirium no longer left me. After many useless efforts to ward off all these fictions, I was finally completely seduced by them, and I no longer occupied myself with anything but trying to put some order and some sequence in them in order to make a sort of Novel out of them.

My great perplexity was the shame of giving myself the lie so clearly and so loudly in this way. After the severe principles I had just established with so much uproar, after the austere maxims I had so strongly preached, after so many mordant invectives against effeminate books that breathed love and softness, could anything more unexpected, more shocking be imagined, than to see myself suddenly inscribed by my own hand among the authors of those books I had censured so harshly? I felt this inconsistency with all its force, I reproached myself for it, I blushed about it, I was vexed about it: but all that was not enough to bring me back to reason. Being completely subjugated, I had to submit at all costs, and resolve to brave the "what will people say"; aside from deliberating afterwards about whether I would resolve to show my work or not: for I did not yet assume that I would publish it.

This decision being made, I throw myself into my reveries up to my neck, and as a result of turning and returning them in my head, I finally form the sort of plan whose execution has been seen. It was certainly the best use that could be made of my follies: love of the good, which has never left my heart,[89] turned them to some useful objects which morality could take advantage of. My voluptuous pictures would have lost all their graces if the sweet coloring of innocence had been missing from them.

A weak girl is an object of pity, whom love could make interesting and who often is not less lovable: but who could bear the spectacle of fashionable morals without indignation and what is more revolting than the pride of an unfaithful woman who openly tramples all her duties underfoot and demands that her husband be penetrated with gratitude for the favor she grants him of trying very hard not to let herself to be caught in the act? Perfect beings do not exist in nature and their lessons are not close enough to us. But let a young person born with a heart as tender as it is decent allow herself be overcome by love as a girl, and as a woman to find again the strength to overcome it in her turn and become virtuous again:[90] whoever tells you that this picture is scandalous in its totality and is not useful, is a liar and a hypocrite; do not listen to him.

Aside from this object of morals and conjugal decency, which is radically connected to the whole social order, I made myself a more secret one of concord and public peace, which is perhaps a greater and more important object in itself, and was so at least at that moment. Far from being calmed, the storm excited by the Encyclopedia was then at its greatest strength.[91] Having exploded against each other with the highest degree of rage, the two parties resembled rabid Wolves, desperate to tear each other to pieces rather than Christians and philosophers who reciprocally wish to enlighten, convince, and restore each other to the path of truth. Perhaps only turbulent Leaders who had some influence on each side were lacking for it to degenerate into a civil war, and God knows what a civil war of religion might bring about, in which the cruelest intolerance was at bottom the same on both sides. A born enemy of all partisan spirit I had frankly told both sides some harsh truths, which they had not listened to. I took another expedient into my head which, in my simplicity,[92] appeared admirable to me: it was to soften their reciprocal hatred by destroying their prejudices, and to show to each party merit and virtue in the other one, worthy of public esteem and of the respect of all mortals.[93] This hardly sensible project, which assumed good faith in men, and through which I fell into the flaw that I reproached in the Abbé de St. Pierre, had the success it ought to have; it did not reconcile the parties at all, and it brought them together only to curse me. While waiting for experience to make me feel my madness, I abandoned myself to it, I dare say, with a zeal[94] worthy of the motive that inspired me with it, and I drew the two characters of Wolmar and Julie in a rapture that made me hope[95] to succeed in making both of them lovable and, what is more, the one by means of the other.[96]

Content with having roughly sketched out my plan, I came back to detailed situations which I had traced, and from the arrangement I gave them there resulted the first two Parts of Julie, which I wrote and made a fair copy of during that winter with an inexpressible pleasure, using the finest gilt paper for it, azure and silver powder for drying the writing, slender blue ribbon for sewing my notebooks,[97] in sum not finding anything gallant enough, anything dainty enough for the charming girls whom I was mad about[98] like another Pygmalion.[99] Every evening at my fireside I read and reread these two Parts to the Governesses. Without saying anything the daughter sobbed along with me from emotion; the mother, who did not understand anything of it because she did not find any compliment in it, stayed quiet, and was satisfied always to repeat to me in the moments of silence, "*Sir, that is very fine.*"

Mme d'Epinay, who was anxious at knowing me to be alone in the winter in the middle of the woods in an isolated house, sent to learn news about me very often. Never did I have such entrancing testimonies of her friendship for me and never did mine respond in a more lively way. I would be wrong not to specify that among these testimonies she sent me her portrait, and that she asked me for instructions to have the one of me painted by La Tour,[100] and which had been exhibited at the Salon. I ought not to omit another of her attentions either, which will appear laughable, but which forms a [feature][101] in the history of my character by means of the impression it made on me. One day when it was freezing very hard, when I opened a package she sent me of several commissions with which she had been burdened, I found an English flannel petticoat which she noted that she had worn and out of which she wanted me to have a waistcoat made. The wording of her note was charming, full of endearment and naiveté. This more than friendly concern appeared so tender to me, as if she had stripped herself to clothe me, that in my emotion I kissed the note and the petticoat twenty times while weeping; Therese thought I had gone mad. It is peculiar that out of all the marks of friendship that Mme d'Epinay lavished on me, none ever touched me the way that one did, and that even after our rupture I have never thought about it again without emotion. For a long time I preserved her little note, and I would still have it, if it had not had the fate of my other letters from the same time.[102]

Although at that time my retentions did not allow me much of a respite in the winter, and for a part of that one I was reduced to the use of probes, everything considered it was nevertheless, the most pleasant and tranquil season I had passed since my arrival in France. For the four or five months that the bad weather additionally[103] kept me safe from unexpected arrivals, I savored more than I have done before or since, that independent, equitable, and simple life the enjoyment of which only in-

creased its value for me, without any other company than that of the two
Governesses in reality, and that of the two Cousins in idea. Moreover that
is time above all during which I congratulated myself every day for the
decision I had had the good sense to make, without regard for the clamors of my friends, who were angry at seeing me emancipated from their
tyranny; and when I learned about the [104] attempt of a wild man, when De
Leyre and Mme d'Epinay spoke to me in their letters about the trouble
and agitation that reigned in Paris,[105] how much did I thank Heaven for
having kept me away from these spectacles of horrors and crimes which
would have done nothing but nourish, but sharpen, the bilious mood
which the sight of public disorders had given me; whereas, since I no
longer saw anything around my retreat except cheerful and gentle objects, my heart abandoned itself only to lovable feelings. I note here with
satisfaction the course of the last peaceful moments I have been allowed.
Following this winter that was so calm, the spring saw burst open the
seed of the misfortunes that remain for me to describe and in whose web
there will no longer be seen any similar interval in which I had the leisure
to breathe.

Nevertheless, I believe I recall that during that interval of peace and
even in the depth of my solitude I was not left entirely tranquil by the
Holbachians. Diderot stirred up some worries for me, and I am extremely
mistaken if it is not during that winter that *The Natural Son* appeared,
about which I will soon have to speak.[106] Aside from the fact that as a
result of causes that will be learned from what follows I have few reliable monuments remaining from that epoch, those that have been left to
me are very imprecise as to dates. Diderot never dated his letters. Mme
d'Epinay, Mme d'Houdetot hardly dated theirs except with the day of
the week, and Deleyre did as they did most often. When I wanted to
arrange these letters in their order it was necessary to feel my way in
order to supply some uncertain dates upon which I cannot count. Thus,
because I cannot fix the beginning of these fallings-out with certainty,
I prefer to relate everything I can recall about them below in a single
section.

The return of Spring had redoubled my tender delirium, and in my
amorous transports I had composed several letters for the last Parts of
Julie which [107] feel the effect of the rapture in which I wrote them. Among
others, I can cite those from Elyseum and the outing on the lake, which
if I remember them well are at the end of the fourth part.[108] Anyone who
reads these two letters and does not feel his heart soften and melt in the
emotion that dictated them to me, ought to close the book; he is not fit
to judge about matters of feeling.

At precisely the same time I had a second unforeseen visit from Mme d'Houdetot. In the absence of her husband, who was a Captain in the Gendarmerie and of her lover who was also in the service, she had come to Eaubonne in the middle of the valley of Montmorency where she had rented a rather pretty house. It was from there that she came to make a new excursion to the Hermitage.[109] On this trip she was on horseback and dressed like a man. Although I hardly like these sorts of masquerades,[110] I was smitten by the romantic air of this one, and this time it was love. Since it was the first and only one in my whole life and since its consequences will forever make it memorable and terrible to my remembrance, allow me to enter into some detail on this point.

Mme the Comtesse de Houdetot was approaching thirty[111] and was not beautiful. Her face was marked with smallpox, her complexion lacked delicacy, she was nearsighted, and her eyes were slightly round: but with all that she had a youthful air, and her physiognomy, lively and sweet at the same time, was affectionate. She had a forest of thick black naturally curly hair which fell to her knees: her waist was dainty, and she put into all her movements both gaucheness and grace at the same time. She had a very natural and very pleasant wit; gaiety, giddiness, and naiveté were happily blended in it: she was well stocked with charming witticisms which she never strove after, and which sometimes came out in spite of her. She had several agreeable talents, played the Clavichord, danced well, wrote rather pretty verses. As for her character it was angelic; sweetness of soul formed its basis, but except for prudence and strength it brought together all the virtues. She was above all of such reliability in dealings, of such faithfulness in society that even her enemies did not need to hide themselves from her. I understand by her enemies those men, or rather those women who hated her, for as for her she did not have a heart that could hate, and I believe that this conformity[112] contributed much to rouse my passion for her. In the confidences of the most intimate friendship I never heard her speak ill of absent people, not even of her sister-in-law. She could neither disguise what she was thinking from anyone nor even repress any of her feelings, and I am persuaded that she spoke about her lover even to her husband, as she spoke about him to her friends, to her acquaintances, and to everyone indiscriminately. Finally what irrefutably proves the purity, the sincerity of her excellent natural disposition, is that, since she was subject to the most enormous distractions and to the most laughable giddiness, things that were very imprudent for herself often escaped her, but never any that were offensive for anyone whatsoever.

When she was very young she had been married against her inclination to the Comte d'Houdetot, a man of Rank, a good soldier, but a gambler, argumentative, hardly lovable at all, and whom she never loved. In M. de St. Lambert she found all her husband's merits with more agreeable qualities, intelligence, virtues,[113] talents. If one must make allowance for something in the morals of the age, it is doubtless for an [114] attachment purified by its duration, honored by its effects, and cemented only by a reciprocal esteem.[115]

From what I have been able to believe it was a little out of taste, but much more to gratify St. Lambert that she came to see me. He had exhorted her to do so, and he was right to believe that the friendship that was beginning to be established between us would make this society agreeable to all three. She knew that I was informed about their relations, and since she could speak to me about him without constraint, it was natural that she was pleased with me. She came, I saw her, I was intoxicated with love without an object, that intoxication fascinated my eyes, that object became fixed on her, I saw my Julie in Mme d'Houdetot, and soon I no longer saw anything but Mme d'Houdetot, but invested with all the perfections with which I had just adorned the idol of my heart. To finish me off, she spoke to me about St. Lambert as a passionate lover. Contagious strength of love! while listening to her, while feeling myself near her, I was seized by a delightful[116] shivering which I had never experienced with anyone. She spoke and I felt myself moved; I believed I was doing nothing but taking an interest in her feelings while I was acquiring similar ones; in deep draughts I swallowed the poisoned cup whose sweetness alone I felt as yet. At last, without me noticing it and without her noticing it she inspired me for herself with everything she expressed for her lover. Alas! it was very late, it was very cruel, to burn with a passion no less keen than unhappy, for a woman whose heart was full of another love!

In spite of the extraordinary movements I had experienced near her, at first I did not notice what had happened to me: it was only after her departure that, when I wanted to think about Julie, I was struck at no longer being able to think about anything but Mme d'Houdetot. Then the scales fell from my eyes; I felt my misfortune, I shuddered at it, but I could not foresee its consequences.

For a long time I hesitated about how I should behave with her, as if genuine love leaves enough reason for following deliberations. I had not decided when she came back to take me unawares. Then I learned. Shame, the companion of evil, rendered me mute while I trembled before her; I did not dare to open my mouth or raise my eyes; I was in an inexpressible turmoil that it was impossible for her not to see. I decided to admit it to her, and to let her guess the cause: that was telling it to her clearly enough.

If I had been young and lovable and in what followed Mme d'Houdetot had been weak, I would blame her behavior here; but since none of that was true, I can only applaud and admire it. The decision she made was equally that of generosity and prudence. She could not remove herself from me brusquely without telling the cause of it to St. Lambert, who had himself urged her to see me; that was to expose two friends to a rupture and perhaps to an outburst that she wished to avoid.[117] She had esteem and benevolence for me. She pitied my folly; without flattering it she was sorry for it and tried to cure me of it. She was very glad to preserve a friend she valued for her lover and herself: she spoke to me about nothing with more pleasure than the intimate and sweet society we could form among the three of us when I became reasonable; she did not always limit herself to these amicable exhortations, and when necessary did not spare me the harsher reproaches I had very much deserved.

I spared them to myself even less. As soon as I was alone I returned to myself; I was calmer after I had spoken: love known by the one who inspires it becomes more bearable because of this. The strength with which I reproached myself for mine would have cured me of it if that had been possible. What powerful motives did I not call to my aid to stifle it? My morals, my feelings, my principles, shame, the infidelity, the crime, the abuse of a deposit entrusted by friendship: finally the ridiculousness of burning from the most extravagant passion at my age, for an object whose preoccupied heart could neither give me any return nor leave me any hope: a passion furthermore that, far from having anything to gain from constancy, became less tolerable from day to day.

Who would believe that this last consideration which ought to add weight to all the others was the one that eluded them? "What scruple," I thought, "can I have over a folly harmful to myself alone? Am I then a young Cavalier of whom Mme d'Houdetot should be extremely afraid? Would someone not say from my presumptuous remorse that[118] my gallantry, my manner, my appearance is going to seduce her? Ah poor Jean-Jacques love at your ease in security of conscience, and do not fear that your sighs might injure St. Lambert."

It has been seen that I have never been conceited, even in my youth. This manner of thinking was in my turn of mind, it favored my passion: it was enough for me to abandon myself to it without reserve, and even to laugh at the impertinent scruple that I believed I had more out of vanity than out of reason. A great lesson for decent souls, that vice never attacks openly, but it finds the means of surprising, by always masking itself with some sophism, and often with some virtue.

Guilty without remorse, I soon was so without measure, and willingly, see how my passion followed the track of my natural disposition so as to sweep me away into the abyss at last. At first, to reassure me it took on a humble manner, and to make me enterprising it pushed this humility to the point of defiance. Without ceasing to recall me to my duty, to reason, without ever favoring my madness for a moment, Mme d'Houdetot treated me moreover with the greatest sweetness, and took the tone of the most tender friendship with me. This friendship might have been enough for me, I protest, if I had believed it sincere; but finding it too lively to be true, was I not going to put it into my head that the love which was already so little suitable to my age, to my bearing,[119] had debased me in Mme d'Houdetot's eyes, that this young madwoman wanted only to divert herself with me and my superannuated sweet nothings, that she had confided them to St. Lambert, and that—since indignation at my infidelity had made her lover enter into her intentions—the two of them were entering an understanding to make my head turn completely and to banter with me. This stupidity, which had made me behave extravagantly at twenty-six years of age with Mme de Larnage whom I did not know, might have been pardonable at forty-five with Mme d'Houdetot, if I had not known that both she and her lover were people who were too decent to make such a barbarous amusement for themselves.

Mme d'Houdetot continued to pay me visits which I did not delay in returning to her. She loved to walk as much as I did: we made long walks in an enchanted country. Content to love, to dare to say it, I would have been in the sweetest situation if my extravagance had not destroyed all its charm for me. At first she did not understand anything from the foolish mood with which I received her blandishments: but my heart, incapable of ever being able to hide anything that was going on in it, did not allow her to remain ignorant about my suspicions for long; she wanted to laugh at them; that expedient did not succeed; an outburst of rage would have been its effect: she changed her tone. Her compassionate sweetness was invincible; she made me reproaches that pierced me; over my unjust fears she bore witness to me of anxieties of which I took advantage. I demanded proofs that she was not making fun of me. She saw that there was no other means of reassuring me. I became pressing, the step was delicate. It is surprising, it is perhaps unique, that a woman who could have arrived at the point of bargaining could have extricated herself at such a small cost. She refused me nothing that could be granted by the most tender friendship. She granted me nothing that could make her unfaithful, and I had the humiliation of seeing that the blazing up with which her slightest favors set my senses aflame did not ever carry the slightest spark to hers.

I have said somewhere that one must grant nothing to the senses when one wants to refuse them anything.[120] To know how false I found this maxim to be with Mme d'Houdetot, and how right she was to count on herself, I would have to enter into the details of our long and frequent tête-à-têtes and to follow them in all their liveliness during the four months that we passed together, in an intimacy almost without precedent among two friends of different sexes, which were restricted within limits from which we never departed. Ah! if I had delayed such a long time in feeling genuine love, how much did my heart and my senses pay the arrears then, and what raptures must one experience with a loved object who loves us, if even a love not shared could inspire ones such as I experienced?

But I am wrong to say a love not shared; in a way mine was; it was equal on the two sides, although it was not reciprocal. We were both intoxicated with love; she for her lover, me for her; our sighs, our delightful tears merged. Tender confidants of each other, our feelings were so much related to each other, that it was impossible for them not to mingle in something; and yet in the middle of this dangerous intoxication, never did she forget herself for a moment, and I protest, I swear,[121] that if I attempted to made her unfaithful sometimes when I was led astray by my senses, I never genuinely desired it. The vehemence of my passion kept it contained all by itself. The duty of privations had exalted my soul. In my eyes the gleam of all the virtues adorned the idol of my heart; to soil its divine image would have annihilated it. I could have committed the crime, it was committed in my heart a hundred times: but to debase my Sophie! ah that could never be! No no I told her directly a hundred times; had I been the master of satisfying myself, had her own will put itself at my discretion, aside from several short moments of delirium, I would have refused to be happy at this price. I loved her too much to want to possess her.

It is almost a league from the Hermitage to Eaubonne; in my frequent trips it sometimes happened that I slept there; one night after having supped tête-à-tête, we went to take a walk in the garden in a very beautiful moonlight. At the end of the garden was a rather large copse from where we made our way to a pretty grove adorned with a waterfall for which I had given her the idea and which she had had executed. Immortal remembrance of innocence and enjoyment! It was in this grove, sitting with her on a grassy bank under an Acacia completely burdened with flowers, that, in order to render the movements of my heart, I found a language truly worthy of them. This was the first and the only time in my life; but I was sublime, if one can give this name to everything lovable and seductive that the most tender and most ardent love can carry into a man's heart. What intoxicating tears I shed on her knees! how I made her shed them in spite of herself! Finally in an involuntary outburst she cried, "No, never has a man been so lovable, and never has a lover loved as you have! but your friend St. Lambert is listening to you, and my heart cannot love twice." I broke off, sighing; I embraced her: what an embrace! But that was all. She lived alone for six months, that is to say far from her lover and her husband; I saw her almost every day for almost three of them, and love was always a third between her and me. We had supped tête-à-tête, we were alone, in a grove, by moonlight, and after two hours of the most lively and most tender conversation, she left this grove and the arms of her friend in the middle of the night as unsullied, as pure in body and heart as she had entered it. Reader, weigh all these circumstances; I will add nothing more.

And do not go on to imagine that my senses left me calm on this occasion, as they did with Therese and with Mamma. I have already said it, it was love this time, and love in all its energy and in all its furies. I will describe neither the agitations, nor the quiverings, nor the palpitations, nor the convulsive movements, nor the swoons of the heart that I experienced continuously; one can judge about them from the effect that her image alone caused upon me. I have said that it was a long way from the Hermitage to Eaubonne: I passed through the hills of Andilly, which are charming: while walking I dreamed about the one whom I was going to see, about the affectionate welcome she would give me, about the kiss that was waiting for me at my arrival. Before I even received it this single kiss, this fatal kiss set my blood on fire to such a point that my head became cloudy, a dizziness blinded me, my trembling knees could not hold me up, I was forced to stop, to sit down; my whole machine was in an inconceivable disorder, I was ready to faint. Having learned of the danger, upon leaving I sought to distract myself and think about something else. I had not made twenty steps when the same remembrances and all the accidents that were its consequence came back to assail me without me being able to free myself from them, and whatever measure I might have taken to do so, I do not believe that I ever happened to make this journey with impunity by myself. I arrived at Eaubonne weak, exhausted, dead tired, holding myself up with difficulty. At the instant I saw her everything was restored: near her I no longer felt anything but the importunity of an inexhaustible and always useless vigor. On my route, in sight of Eaubonne, there was a pleasant terrace called Mount Olympe, where we sometimes made our way each from his own side. I arrived first, I had to wait for her; but how dearly did this waiting cost me! To distract myself I tried to write notes with my pencil which I could have traced with my purest blood: I was never able to finish one of them that was readable. When she found one in a niche we had agreed upon, she could see nothing else in it but the truly deplorable state I was in when I wrote it. This state and above all its duration during three months of continuous irritation and privation threw me into an exhaustion from which I could not extricate myself for several years and ended by giving me a hernia which I will carry or which will carry me to the tomb. Such has been the only amorous enjoyment of the man with the most combustible, but simultaneously most timid temperament that perhaps nature has ever produced. Such have been the last fine days that were counted out to me on the earth: here begins the long web of the misfortunes of my life, in which one will see little interruption.

In the whole course of my life one has seen that my heart, transparent as crystal, has never been able to hide for an entire minute a slightly lively feeling that has taken refuge in it. Judge whether I was capable of hiding my love for Mme d'Houdetot for very long. Our intimacy struck every eye, we put neither secret nor mystery in it. It was not of a nature to have any need of them, and since Mme d'Houdetot had the most tender friendship for me for which she did not reproach herself at all, since I had an esteem for her all the justice of which no one knew better than I; she being frank, heedless, giddy, I being true, clumsy, proud, impatient, touchy; in our deceptive security we exposed ourselves much more than we would have if we had been guilty. Both of us went to la Chevrette; we often found ourselves together there, sometimes even by appointment. We lived there in our ordinary way; taking walks together every day tête-à-tête speaking about our loves, our duties, our friend, our innocent projects, in the Park, across from Mme d'Epinay's suite, under her windows, from where she ceaselessly examined us, and, since she believed she was affronted, by means of her eyes she sated her heart with rage and indignation.

Women all have the art of hiding their fury, above all when it is sharp. Mme d'Epinay, violent but deliberate, especially possessed this art to an eminent degree. She pretended that she did not see anything, did not suspect anything, and at the same time that she redoubled attentions, cares, and almost flirting with me, she affected to harass her sister-in-law with dishonest dealings, and marks of a disdain that she seemed to want to impart to me. One can judge very well that she did not succeed; but I was on the rack. Torn apart by contradictory feelings, at the same time that I was touched by her blandishments, I could hardly contain my anger when I saw her fail to respect Mme d'Houdetot. The angelic sweetness of the latter made her put up with everything without complaining, and even without being annoyed with her about it. Besides she was often so heedless, and always so little sensitive to such things, that half the time she did not notice them.

I was so preoccupied with my passion, that, since I saw nothing but Sophie (that was one of Mme d'Houdetot's names) I did not even notice that I had become the laughingstock of the whole house and of the chance arrivals. Baron d'Holback, who as far as I know had never come to la Chevrette, was among these latter. If I had been as diffident as I became later, I would have very much suspected Mme d'Epinay of having arranged this trip in order to give him the amusing gift of seeing the Citizen in love. But at that time I was so stupid that I did not even see what was glaringly obvious to everyone. Nevertheless, all my stupidity did not keep me from finding a more content, more jovial air than usual in the Baron. Instead of looking blackly at me in accordance with his custom, he let fly a hundred bantering remarks of which I understood nothing. I opened my eyes wide without answering anything; Mme d'Epinay held her sides from laughing; I did not know what possessed them. Since nothing yet went beyond the limits of joking, the best thing I could have done if I had realized it would have been to join in with it. But it is true that, through the Baron's joking gaiety, a malignant joy could be seen shining in his eyes, which perhaps would have made me anxious, if I had noticed it as much at the time as I recalled it later.

One day when I went to see Mme d'Houdetot at Eaubonne on her return from one of her trips to Paris, I found her sad, and I saw that she had been weeping. I was obliged to constrain myself, because her husband's sister, Mme de Blainville,[122] was there: but as soon as I could find a moment, I showed her my anxiety. "Ah!" she said to me while sighing, "I fear very much that your follies might cost me the repose of my life. St. Lambert is informed and poorly informed. He does justice to me; but he is in a bad temper, and what is worse, he is hiding part of it from me. Fortunately I have held back nothing from him about our relations, which were formed under his auspices. My letters were as full of you as my heart was: I have hidden from him only your insane love of which I hoped to cure you and which I see that he is making into a crime of me without speaking to me about it. Someone has served us badly; someone has wronged me, but what does it matter. Let us either break off completely, or be what you should be. I do not want to have anything to hide from my lover any longer."

That was the first moment when I was sensitive to the shame of seeing myself humiliated by the feeling of my fault in front of a young woman whose just reproaches I was suffering,[123] and whose Mentor I should have been. The indignation I felt against myself from this perhaps would have been enough to overcome my weakness, if the tender compassion which its victim inspired in me had not softened my heart again. Alas! was that the moment to be able to harden it, while it was inundated by tears that pierced it from all sides. That softening was soon changed into anger against the vile denouncers who had seen only the evil of a criminal but involuntary feeling, without believing, without even imagining the sincere decency of heart that redeemed it. We did not remain in doubt for long about whose hand the blow came from.

We both knew that Mme d'Epinay was exchanging letters with St. Lambert. This was not the first storm she had stirred up for Mme d'Houdetot, from whom she had made a thousand efforts to detach him, and the [124] success of some of these efforts made Mme d'Houdetot tremble over the consequences. Moreover Grimm, who it seems to me had followed M. de Castries into the army,[125] was in Westphalia as well as St. Lambert; they saw each other sometimes. Grimm had made some attempts with Mme d'Houdetot which had not succeeded. Becoming very irritated, Grimm completely stopped seeing her. Judge the coolness with which, modest as he is known to be, he supposed her to prefer a man older than he, and about whom Grimm, since he had been frequenting the Great, spoke only as his protégé.

My suspicions about Mme d'Epinay changed into certainty, when I learned what had passed in my home. When I was at la Chevrette Therese often came there, either to bring me my letters, or to give me attentions necessary for my bad health. Mme d'Epinay had asked her whether Mme d'Houdetot and I did not write to each other. Upon her admission, Mme d'Epinay pressed her to deliver Mme d'Houdetot's letters to her, assuring her that she would seal them up again so well that it would not be apparent. Without showing how much this proposal scandalized her, and even without warning me, Therese was content to hide better the letters she brought me: a very fortunate precaution; for Mme d'Epinay had her arrival watched for, and waiting for her in the passage, several times pushed audacity to the point of searching in her apron. She did more: one day when she had invited herself to come with M. de Margency to dine at the Hermitage for the first time since I had resided there, she took the time while I was taking a walk with Margency to enter into my study with the mother and the daughter, and to press them to show her Mme d'Houdetot's letters. If the mother had known where they were, the letters would have been given up; but fortunately only the daughter knew it and denied that I had saved any of them. A lie assuredly full of honesty, fidelity, generosity, when the truth would only have been a perfidious act. Seeing that she could not seduce her, Mme d'Epinay strove to irritate her out of jealousy, by reproaching her for her pliancy and her blindness. "How can you," she said to her, "not see that they have a criminal relationship between them? If in spite of everything that strikes your eyes you need other proofs, join in doing what is necessary to get them. You say that he tears up Mme d'Houdetot's letters as soon as he has read them. Very well, carefully collect the pieces and give them to me; I take it upon myself to put them back together again." Such were the lessons that my friend gave my companion.

Therese had the discretion to keep silent to me about all these attempts for a rather long time; but seeing my perplexities, she believed she was obliged to tell me everything, so that, now that I knew who I was dealing with, I could take measures to protect myself against the treacheries that were being prepared for me. My indignation, my rage cannot be described. Instead of dissimulating with Mme d'Epinay, following her own example and making use of counterruses, I abandoned myself to the impetuosity of my natural disposition without restraint, and with my ordinary heedlessness I made a completely open outburst. One can judge my imprudence from the following letters, which adequately show how both of us proceeded on this occasion.[126]

Note from Mme d'Epinay (Bundle A. #44)

Why do I not see you then, my dear friend? I am anxious about you. You had promised me so much that you would do nothing but come and go from the Hermitage to here. With regard to that, I have left you free; and nothing at all, you let eight days pass. If I had not been told that you were in good health, I would believe you were ill. I expected you the day before yesterday or yesterday, and I do not see you arrive at all. My God, what is the matter with you? You have no business at all: you do not have any troubles either; for I flatter myself that you would have come on the spot to confide them to me. You are ill then? Relieve me from anxiety very quickly, I beg it of you. Farewell, my dear friend: let this farewell give me a hello from you.

Answer

This Wednesday morning

I cannot tell you anything yet. I am waiting to be better informed, and I will be sooner or later. While waiting, be assured that accused innocence will find a defender ardent enough to made the calumniators repent, whoever they might be.

Second Note from the same (Bundle A. #45)

Do you know that your letter frightens me? What does it mean to say then? I have reread it more than twenty-five times. In truth, I do not understand anything in it. I see only that you are anxious and tormented, and that you are waiting until you are so no longer to speak to me about it. My dear friend, is that what we agreed on? What then has become of that friendship, that confidence, and how have I lost it? Is it with me or for me that you are angry? Whatever might be the case, come immediately this evening, I beseech you to do so. Remember that not eight days ago you promised me to keep nothing in your heart, and to speak to me on the spot. My dear friend, I live in this trust. . . . Stop, I have just read your letter again; I do not conceive any more of it, but it makes me tremble. It seems to me that you are cruelly agitated. I would like to calm you, but since I do not know the subject of your anxieties, until I have seen you, I do not know what to say to you, except that I am entirely as unhappy as you are. If you are not here tonight at six o'clock, I leave tomorrow for the Hermitage, whatever the weather might be and in whatever condition I might be; for I cannot bear this anxiety. Good day, my dear good friend. At all hazards I risk telling you, without knowing whether you need it or not, to try to watch out and stop the progress that anxiety makes in solitude. A fly becomes a monster. I have often experienced it.

Answer

This Wednesday evening

I can neither go to see you nor receive your visit as long as the anxiety I am in lasts. The trust about which you speak no longer exists, and it will not be easy for you to recover it. At present in your eagerness I see only the desire to draw from someone else's admission some advantage that suits your purpose, and my heart, which is so prompt to unbosom itself to a heart that opens to receive it, closes itself to ruse and wiles. I recognize your usual skill in the difficulty you find in understanding my note. Do you believe me enough of a dupe to think that you have not understood it? No, but I cannot defeat your subtleties by means of frankness. I am going to explain myself more clearly, so that you can understand me even less.

Two lovers very closely united and worthy of loving each other are dear to me; I very much expect that you will not know whom I mean, unless I name them to you. I presume that someone has tried to estrange them, and that I have been used to make one of the two jealous. The choice is not extremely clever, but it appeared convenient to wickedness, and it is you whom I suspect of this wickedness. I hope that this is becoming clearer.

In this way then the woman whom I esteem most would, with my knowledge, have the infamy to divide her heart and her person between two lovers, and I would have the infamy of being one of these two craven men? If I knew that you could have thought this way about her and about me for a single moment of your life, I would hate you until my death. But I accuse you of having said it and not of having believed it. I do not understand which of the three you wanted to hurt in such a case; but if you love peace, fear being unlucky enough to succeed. I have not hidden all the ill that I think about certain relations either from you or from her, but I want them to end through a means as decent as its cause, and for an illegitimate love to be changed into an eternal friendship. Would I, who have never done harm to anyone, be the innocent means of doing it to my friends? No, I would never pardon you, I would become your irreconcilable enemy. Only your secrets would [127] be respected; for I will never be a faithless man.

I do not imagine that my present perplexities can last very long. I will soon learn whether I am mistaken. Perhaps then I will have great wrongs to redress, and there is nothing in my life that I will have done so wholeheartedly. But do you know how I will redeem my faults during the little time I have left to pass with you? By doing what no one else but I will do; by telling you frankly what is thought of you in the world, and the gaps you have to repair in your reputation. In spite of all the so-called friends who surround you, when you have seen me leave, you will be able to say farewell to the truth; you will no longer find anyone who tells it to you.

Third Note from the same (Bundle A. #46)

I did not understand your letter of this morning: I told you so, because it was true. I do understand the one from this evening: do not fear that I will ever respond to it; I am too-hard pressed to forget it, and although you might pity me, I cannot defend myself from the bitterness with which it fills my soul. I? employ ruses, wiles with you! I, accused of the blackest of infamies! Farewell, I regret that you have the. . . . Farewell, I do not know what to say. . . . Farewell: I will be very hard-pressed to forgive you. You will come when you wish; you will be received better than your suspicions deserve. Only spare putting yourself to any trouble for the sake of my reputation. The one people give me matters little to me. My behavior is good, and that is enough for me. What is more, I absolutely do not know what has happened to the two people who are as dear to me as to you.

This last letter extricated me from a terrible perplexity and plunged me back into another that was hardly smaller. Although all these letters and answers had come and gone in the space of one day with an extreme rapidity, this period had been enough to put some space between my outbursts of rage, and to allow me to reflect on the enormity of my imprudence. Mme d'Houdetot had recommended nothing to me more than to remain calm, than to leave her the care of extricating herself from this business by herself, and to avoid, above all at this very moment, every rupture and every scandal; and I, by means of the most open and most atrocious insults, I was going to bring rage completely into the heart of a woman who was already only too well-disposed to it. On her part, I should have naturally expected only an answer so proud, so disdainful, so scornful, that without the most unworthy cowardice I would not be able to abstain from leaving her house on the spot. Fortunately, since she was even more skillful than I was quick-tempered, with the turn of her answer she avoided reducing me to that extremity. But it was necessary, either to leave, or to go see her on the spot; the alternative was unavoidable: I made the latter decision, extremely perplexed about what my countenance should be in the explanation I foresaw. For how could I extricate myself without compromising either Mme d'Houdetot or Therese, and bad luck to the one I named! There was nothing that the vengeance of an implacable and intriguing woman did not make me fear for the one who might be its object. It was to prevent this misfortune that I had spoken only about suspicions in my letters so as to be dispensed from stating my proofs. It is true that this made my outbursts more inexcusable, because no simple suspicions could authorize me to treat a woman and especially a friend as I had just treated Mme d'Epinay. But here begins the great and noble task which I have worthily fulfilled, of expiating my faults and my hidden weaknesses, by burdening myself with [128] graver faults of which I was incapable, and which I never committed.

I did not have to endure the dispute I had dreaded, and I got off with a fright. At my approach, Mme d'Epinay leapt to my breast while melting in tears. This unexpected welcome, and on the part of an old friend, moved me extremely;[129] I wept very much also. I said some words to her that did not have much sense; she said some to me that had even less, and everything ended there. The meal was served, we went to table, where—in the expectation of the explanation which I believed had been put off until after the supper—I cut a bad figure; for I am so mastered by the slightest anxiety that occupies me, that I cannot hide it from the least clear-sighted person. My perplexed air ought to have given her some courage; nevertheless, she did not risk the venture at all: there was no more of an explanation after the supper than before. There was no more of one the next day, and our silent tête-à-têtes were filled only with indifferent things, or with some polite remarks on my part, by which I bore witness to her that I still could not pronounce anything about the foundation of my suspicions; I protested to her with very much truth, that if I discovered them to be ill-founded, my entire life would be employed in redressing their injustice. She did not show the slightest curiosity to know precisely what these suspicions were or how they had come to me, and our whole reconciliation, both on her part and mine, consisted in the embrace of the first approach. Since she alone was offended, at least according to the formalities, it appeared to me that it was not up to me to look for a clarification that she was not looking for herself, and I returned as I had come. Moreover, continuing to live with her as before, I soon forgot this quarrel almost entirely, and I stupidly believed that she forgot it herself, because she did not appear to remember it.

As will soon be seen, that was not the only affliction that my weakness brought down on me; but I had others, not less tangible, that I had not brought down on myself, and which had as their cause only the desire to uproot me from my solitude* as a result of tormenting me. These came to me from Diderot and the Holbachians. Since my establishment at the Hermitage, Diderot had not ceased to badger me, either by himself or by means of De Leyre, and from the latter's pleasantries over my wanderings in the grove I soon saw with what pleasure they had travestied the Hermit as a gallant shepherd. But that was not the issue in my disputes with Diderot; they had more serious causes. After the publication of the *Natural Son*, he had sent me a copy of it, which I had read with the interest and attention one gives to the works of a friend. While reading the sort of Poetics in dialogue he had joined with it, I was surprised and even a little saddened to find among several disagreeable but tolerable things against solitaries this scathing and harsh sentence without any qualification.[130] *Only the wicked man is alone*. This sentence is equivocal, and presents two meanings, it seems to me; the one very true, the other very false; since it is even impossible for a man who is and wants to be alone to be able to and to want to harm anyone, and consequently for him to be a wicked man. Thus the sentence in itself required an interpretation. It required one all the more,[131] on the part of an Author who, at the time he had that sentence printed, had a friend who had withdrawn[132] into solitude. It appeared shocking and indecent either to have forgotten that solitary friend when publishing it, or if he had remembered him not to have made—at least in a general maxim—the honorable and just exception that he owed, not only to that friend, but to so many respected wise men who at all times have sought calm and peace in retirement, and of whom, for the first time in the existence of the world, a writer takes it into his head to make into so many scoundrels with a single stroke of the pen.

I loved Diderot tenderly, and I esteemed him sincerely, and I counted on the same feelings on his part with a complete confidence. But exasperated by his indefatigable obstinacy in eternally contradicting me over my tastes, my inclinations, my manner of living, over everything that interested[133] only myself alone; revolted at seeing a man younger than myself wanting to govern me like a child by any means;[134] weary with his ease at promising and his negligence at keeping his promises; annoyed at so many appointments made and missed on his part, and at his whim of always making them anew only to miss them once again; bothered at

---

*That is to say uproot the old woman, whom they needed in order to hatch the plot. It is surprising that during all this long storm my stupid confidence had kept me from understanding that it was not me, but her they wanted to get back to Paris.

waiting for him uselessly three or four times a month on the days chosen by himself and at dining alone in the evening, after having gone before him all the way to St. Denis and having waited for him all day, my heart was already full of his multiplied wrongs. This last appeared more serious to me and afflicted me more. I wrote to him to complain about it, but with a gentleness and an emotion that made me soak my paper with my tears, and my letter was so touching that it should have drawn some from him. One would never be guess what his answer was on this article; here it is word for word. (*Bundle A. #33*).[135]

I am very glad that my work has pleased you, that it has touched you. You do not share my opinion about Hermits. Say as much good about them as you please, you will be the only one in the world about whom I will think it: still there would be a lot to say about this if one could talk to you without getting you angry. An eighty-year-old woman etc. Someone told me about a phrase from a letter from Mme d'Epinay's son which must have distressed you very much, or I know the bottom of your soul poorly.

The last two sentences of this letter need to be explained.[136]

At the beginning of my stay at the Hermitage, Mme le Vasseur appeared to be unhappy there and to find the dwelling-place too lonely. When her remarks about this came back to me, I offered to send her back to Paris if she was happier there, to pay her rent, and to take the same care of her there as if she were still with me. She rejected my offer, protested to me that she was extremely happy at the Hermitage, that the country air did her some good; and that was seen to be true; for she was growing young again, so to speak, and was much healthier than at Paris. Her daughter even assured me that at bottom she would have been very upset if we left the Hermitage, which really was a charming place; that she liked very much the little pottering about the garden and fruits whose handling she had, but that she had said what she had been made to say, in order to attempt to induce me to return to Paris.

When this attempt did not succeed, they attempted to obtain by means of my scruples the effect which my accommodativeness had not produced, and made it a crime of me to keep that old woman there, far from the help she might need at her age, without thinking that she and many other old people whose life is prolonged by the excellent country air could get help from Montmorency which I had at my door, and as if there were elderly people only in Paris, and that everywhere else they were in no condition to live. Mme le Vasseur, who ate a lot and with an extreme voracity, was subject to outbreaks of bile and extreme diarrheas, which lasted several days and served her as a remedy. At Paris she never did anything for it, and let nature act. She behaved the same way at the Hermitage, knowing well that there was nothing better to do. No matter; because there were no Doctors and Apothecaries in the country, to leave her there was to wish for her death, even though she was very healthy there.[137] Diderot should have decided at what age one is no longer allowed to let elderly people live outside [138] of Paris under penalty of homicide.

That was one of the two atrocious accusations based on which he did not except me from his sentence that only the wicked man was alone, and that is what was meant by his pathetic exclamation and the *et cetera* which he had benignly added, "a woman of eighty years! etc."

I believed that I could not respond to this reproach any better than by referring it to Mme le Vasseur herself. I asked her to write her feeling naturally to Mme d'Epinay. To put her more at her ease I did not want to see her letter at all and I showed her the one I am going to transcribe and which I wrote to Mme d'Epinay on the subject of an answer that I had wanted to make to another even harsher letter from Diderot, and which she had kept me from sending.

This Thursday [139]

Mme le Vasseur should be writing to you my good friend; I have asked her to tell you sincerely what she thinks. To put her very much at her ease, I have told her that I do not want to see her letter at all, and I ask you to say nothing to me about what it contains.

I will not send my letter because you are opposed to it, but, since I feel that I am very grievously offended, to acknowledge that I am in the wrong would be a baseness and a falseness that I could not allow myself. The Gospel very well orders the one who receives a slap to offer the other cheek, but not to ask for forgiveness. Do you remember that man in the Comedy who cries out while giving blows with a stick? That is the role of the philosopher.[140]

Do not flatter yourself that the present bad weather will keep him from coming. His anger will give him the time and the strength that friendship refuses him and it will be the first time in his life that he will have come on the day he had promised. He will wear himself out in order to come to repeat to me with his mouth the insults he says to me in his letters; I will endure them with complete patience. He will return to be sick at Paris, and, as usual, I will be an extremely odious man. What is to be done? One must put up with it.

But do you not admire the wisdom of this man who wants to come to take me to St. Denis in a Coach, to dine there, to send me back in a Coach (Bundle A. #33) and whose fortune a week later (Bundle A. #34) [141] no longer permits him to go to the Hermitage any other way than on foot? It is not absolutely impossible—to speak his language—that this is the tone of good faith; but in this case strange changes must have occurred in his fortune in a week.

I share the sorrow given to you by Madame your mother's illness; but you see that your suffering does not approach mine. One suffers less at seeing the people one loves sick than at seeing them unjust and cruel.

Farewell, my good friend, this is the last time I will speak to you about this unfortunate business. You speak to me of going to Paris with a coolness that would delight me at another time.

At Mme d'Epinay's own proposal, I wrote to Diderot what I had done on the subject of Mme le Vasseur, and since Mme le Vasseur had chosen, as one can well believe, to stay at the Hermitage, where she was very healthy, where she always had company, and where she lived very agreeably;[142] since Diderot no longer knew what crime to charge me with, he made this precaution on my part into one, and did not fail to make another one out of the continuation of Mme le Vasseur's stay at the Hermitage, although this continuation was by her[143] choice, and it was, and always was, up to her alone to return to live at Paris, with the same assistance on my part as she had with me.

This is the explanation of the first reproach in Diderot's letter #33. That of the second is in his letter #34. "The Scholar" (that was a joking name given by Grimm to Mme d'Epinay's son) "the scholar ought to have written to you that on the rampart[144] there were twenty poor people who were dying of hunger and cold, and who were waiting for the liard that you used to give them. That is a sample of our little babble and if you heard the rest, it would amuse[145] you the same way."

Here is my answer to this astounding argument which Diderot appeared so proud of.

I believe I answered the *scholar*, that is to say the son of a Farmer General, that I was not sorry for the poor people he had noticed waiting for my liard on the rampart since apparently he had amply compensated them for it; that I appointed him as my substitute; that the poor people of Paris would not have any reason to complain about this exchange; that I would not easily find as good a one[146] for those of Montmorency who needed one much more. There is a good respectable old man here who, after having passed his life working, is dying of hunger in his old age because he is no longer able to work. My conscience is more satisfied with the two sous that I give him every Monday than with the hundred liards I would have distributed to all those beggars on the rampart. You are amusing, you philosophers, when you regard all the inhabitants of the cities as the only men to whom your duties connect you. It is in the country that one learns to love and serve humanity; one learns only to despise it in the cities.[147]

Such were the peculiar scruples upon which an intelligent man seriously had the imbecility to make it into a crime of me to have withdrawn from Paris, and claimed to prove to me by my own example that one could not live out of the capital without being a wicked man. I do not understand today how I was stupid enough to answer him and to get myself angry, instead of laughing in his face as my only answer. Nevertheless

Mme d'Epinay's decisions and the clamors of the Holbachic coterie had so fascinated minds in his favor that I generally passed as being in the wrong in this business, and Mme d'Houdetot, herself a great enthusiast of Diderot, wanted me to go see him at Paris and for me to make all the advances for a reconciliation, which nevertheless did not last very long even though it was wholly sincere and complete on my part. The argument which she used that was victorious over my heart was that, at this moment, Diderot was in misfortune. Aside from the storm excited against the Encyclopedia, he was weathering a very violent one at that time on the subject of his play which, in spite of the little history he had put at its head, he was being accused of having taken entirely from Goldoni.[148] Being even more sensitive to criticism than Voltaire was, Diderot was overpowered by it at that time. Mme de Grafigny[149] had even been wicked enough to cause the rumor to circulate that I had broken with him on this occasion. I concluded that there was justice and generosity in publicly proving the contrary, and I went to pass two days, not only with him, but in his home. This was my second trip to Paris since my establishment at the Hermitage. I had made the first to run to poor Gauffecourt who had an attack of apoplexy from which he never recovered very well, and during which I never left his bedside until he was out of danger.[150]

Diderot received me well. How a friend's embrace can erase wrongs! What resentment can be left in the heart after that? We had few explanations. There was no need for them in the case of reciprocal invectives. There was only one thing to do, namely to forget them. There had not been any underhanded dealings, at least that I knew of: it was not the same as with Mme d'Epinay. He showed me the plan for the *Father of the Family*. "There," I told him, "is the best defense for the *Natural Son*. Keep quiet, work on this piece carefully, and then suddenly throw it in the faces of your enemies as your only answer." He did so and it turned out well.[151] It had been nearly six months since I had sent him the first two parts of Julie so that he could give me his opinion of it. He had not yet read them. We read a notebook together. He found all that "leafy,"[152] that was his term; that is to say loaded down with words and redundant. I had already felt that very well myself: but it was the chattering of a fever; I have never been able to correct it. The last Parts are not like that. The fourth, above all, and the sixth are masterpieces of elocution.

The second day of my stay, he absolutely wanted to bring me to sup at M. d'Holback's. We were far apart; for I even wanted to break the agreement about the manuscript of Chemistry[153] because I was indignant at having an obligation to that man; Diderot prevailed over everything. He swore to me that M. d'Holback loved me with all his heart, that I had to forgive him for a tone that he took with everyone, and from which his friends had to suffer more than anyone. He pointed out to me that to refuse the profit from this manuscript after having accepted it two years before was an affront to the donor which he had not deserved, and that this refusal could even be misinterpreted, as a secret reproach for having waited for so long to conclude the bargain. "I see d'Holback every day," he added; "I know the condition of his soul better than you do. If you do not have cause to be content with it, do you believe your friend capable of advising a base action to you?" In short, with my usual weakness I let myself be subjugated, and we went to sup with the Baron who greeted me in his usual way. But his wife greeted me coldly and almost indecently. I no longer recognized that lovable Caroline who showed that she had so much benevolence for me when she was a girl. I believed I had felt for a long time previously that, since Grimm had been frequenting the house of Aine, I was no longer regarded as well there.[154]

While I was in Paris St. Lambert arrived there from the army. Since I knew nothing about it, I did not see him until after my return to the country, first at la Chevrette, and afterward at the Hermitage where he came with Mme d'Houdetot to ask me to invite him to dine.[155] You can judge whether I greeted them with pleasure! But I took very much more still in seeing their good understanding. Satisfied at not having troubled their happiness, I was happy because of it myself, and I can swear that during all my mad passion, but above all at that moment, if I could have taken Mme d'Houdetot away from him, I would not have wanted to do so, and I would not even have been tempted to do so. I found her so lovable while loving St. Lambert, that I hardly imagined that she could be as much so while loving me, and without wanting to trouble their union, all I most genuinely desired from her in my delirium was that she let herself be loved. In sum, however violent was the passion with which I burned for her, I found it as sweet to be the confidant as the object of her loves, and I never for a moment looked at her lover as my rival, but always as my friend. It will be said that that was not still[156] love: so be it, but then it was more.

As for St. Lambert, he behaved like a decent and judicious man: since I was the only guilty one, I was also the only one punished and that even with indulgence. He treated me harshly but in a friendly way, and I saw that I had lost something in his esteem but nothing in his friendship. I consoled myself for this, knowing that the one would be very much easier to recover than the other, and that he was too sensible to confuse an involuntary and temporary weakness with a vice of character. If I was at fault in everything that had passed, I was very little so. Was I the one who had sought out his mistress, was he not the one who had sent her to me? Was she not the one who had sought me out? could I have avoided receiving her? What could I have done? They alone had done the harm, and it was I who had suffered it. In my place he might have done as much as I had, perhaps worse: for in the end, however faithful, however estimable Mme d'Houdetot might be, she was a woman; he was absent; the occasions were frequent, the temptations were lively, and it might have been very difficult for her always to defend herself with the same success against a more enterprising man. In such a situation it was certainly a lot for her and for me to have been able to impose limits that we never allowed ourselves to pass.

Although at the bottom of my heart I might give myself an honorable enough testimony, appearances were so much against me that the invincible shame that always dominated me gave me the air of a guilty man in front of him, and he[157] took advantage of it in order to humiliate me. A single feature will depict this reciprocal position. After dinner I read him the letter I had written to Voltaire the preceding year, and about which St. Lambert had heard him speak. He fell asleep during the reading, and I— formerly so proud, today so foolish—I never dared to interrupt my reading, and continued to read while he continued to snore. Such were my indignities, and such were his acts of vengeance; but his generosity never allowed him to give vent to them except among the three of us.

When he had gone away again, I found Mme d'Houdetot very much changed with regard to me. I was surprised by it as if I should not have expected it; I was touched by it more than I should have been, and that did me a lot of harm. It seemed that everything from which I expected my cure only drove farther into my heart the arrow which in the end I broke off rather than removed.

I was determined to vanquish myself completely, and to spare nothing to change my mad passion into a pure and lasting friendship. For that purpose, I had made the finest plans in the world, for whose execution I needed Mme d'Houdetot's cooperation. When I wanted to talk to her, I found her listless, perplexed, I felt that she had ceased to be pleased with me, and I saw clearly that something had happened that she did not want to tell me, and that I have never learned. This change, for which I could not obtain an explanation, cut me to the quick. She asked me to give back her letters; I returned all of them to her with a fidelity which she insulted me by doubting for a moment. This doubt was yet another unexpected wrench for my heart which she ought to know so well. She did me justice but not on the spot; I understood that the examination of the package I had returned to her had made her feel her wrong: I even saw that she reproached herself for it, and that made me regain something. She could not take back her letters without returning mine to me. She told me that she had burned them; I dared to doubt it in my turn, and I admit that I still doubt it.[158] No, one does not put such letters in the fire. People have found the ones in Julie to be burning. Ah God! what would they say about these then? No, no, the one who can inspire such a passion will never have the courage to burn the proofs of it.[159] But I am not afraid that she might abuse them either: I do not believe that she is capable of it, and moreover,[160] I had taken precautions in them. The foolish but lively fear of being jeered at had made me begin this correspondence upon a tone that made my letters safe from being circulated. In my intoxication I carried the familiarity I took in them to the point of using the second person familiar: but what a use of familiarity! she surely must not have been offended by it. Nevertheless, she complained about it[161] several times, but unsuccessfully: her complaints only made my fears[162] reawaken, and besides I could not decide to give any ground. If these letters still exist, and they are seen one day, people will know how I have loved.

The suffering that Mme d'Houdetot's cooling off caused me and the certainty of not having deserved it made me make the peculiar decision of complaining about it to St. Lambert himself. While waiting for the effect of the letter I wrote to him on this subject,[163] I threw myself into distractions which I should have sought earlier. There were holidays at la Chevrette for which I wrote the music. The pleasure of doing myself honor in front of Mme d'Houdetot with a talent she loved excited my verve, and yet another object contributed to enlivening it; namely the desire to show that the Author of the *Village Soothsayer* knew music; for I had noticed for a long time that someone was working in secret to render that doubtful, at least as far as composition was concerned. My debut at Paris, the tests to which I had been put at diverse times both at M. Dupin's and at M. de la Poplinière's; the quantity of Music I had composed there during fourteen years in the midst of the most famous artists and under their eyes, finally the opera of *The Gallant Muses*, even that of the *Soothsayer*, a motet I had written for Mlle Fel and which she had sung at the Spiritual Concert; so many meetings I had had on this fine art with the greatest masters, everything seemed as if it should prevent or dissipate such a doubt. Nevertheless, it existed, even at la Chevrette, and I saw that M. d'Epinay was not exempt from it. Without appearing to notice anything, I took it upon myself to compose a Motet for him for the dedication of the Chapel of la Chevrette,[164] and I asked him to furnish me words of his choice. He charged his son's Tutor, De Linant,[165] to write them. De Linant arranged some words suitable to the subject, and eight days after they had been given to me the Motet was finished. This time spite was my Apollo, and never did music that was more full of substance leave my hands. The words began with these words. *Ecce sedes*[166] *hic tonantis.** The pomp of the beginning was in keeping with the words, and everything that followed in the Motet is of a beauty of song that strikes everyone. I had written for a full Orchestra. D'Epinay assembled the best symphony musicians. The Italian singer Mme Bruna sang the motet, and was well accompanied. The motet had such a great success that it was given afterward at the spiritual concert, where, in spite of secret cabals and worthless performance, it had the same applause two times. For M. d'Epinay's birthday I gave the idea of a sort of piece, half Drama, half Pantomime, which Mme D'Epinay composed and for which I again wrote the music. Upon arriving Grimm heard my harmonic success talked about. An hour later it was not talked about any more: but at least as far as I know they did not call into question whether I knew composition.

No sooner was Grimm at la Chevrette, where I was already not very happy, than he finished making my stay unbearable by airs that[168] I have never seen from anyone, and the idea of which I did not even have. On the eve of his arrival I was moved out of the room of favor that I was occupying, next to Mme d'Epinay's; it was prepared for M. Grimm, and I was given another one more distant. "See," I said to Mme d'Epinay while laughing, "how the newcomers dislodge the old ones." She appeared embarrassed. I understood the reason better the same night when I learned that there was a concealed door of communication between her room and the one I was leaving, which she had judged useless to show me. Her relationship with Grimm was known to everyone, both in her home and in the public, even to her husband: nevertheless, far from acknowledging it to me, the confidant of secrets that were much more important to her and whom she was very sure of, she always denied it very strongly. I understood that this reserve came from Grimm, who, while he was the depositary of all my secrets, did not want me to be the same for any of his.

Whatever bias my former feelings—which were not dead—and the real merit of that man might give me in his favor, it could not hold up against the efforts he made to destroy it. His bearing was that of the Comte de Tuffiére;[169] he scarcely deigned to greet me; he did not address a word to me once, and soon broke me of addressing any to him by

*I have learned since that these words were by Santeuil, and that M. de Linant had quietly appropriated them.[167]

not answering me at all. Everywhere he passed as foremost, everywhere took the first place, without ever paying any attention to me. I would let that pass if he had not put a shocking affectation into it: but one will judge about it from a single incident taken out of a thousand. One evening when Mme d'Epinay found herself a little ill, she said that they were bringing her a bite in her room and went up to sup by her fireside. She proposed that I go up with her; I did so. Grimm came afterward. The little table was already set; there were only two place-settings. They serve: Mme d'Epinay takes her place at one side of the fire. M. Grimm takes an armchair, establishes himself on the other side, pulls the little table between the two of them, unfolds his napkin, and prepares to eat without saying a single word to me. Mme d'Epinay blushes, and offers me her own place in order to induce him to make up for his coarseness. He says nothing, did not look at me. Not being able to draw near the fire, I decided to walk around the room while I waited for them to bring me a place-setting.[170] He let me sup at the end of the table, far from the fire, without performing the slightest act of politeness for me, who was ill, his elder, his senior in the house, who had introduced him to it, and for whom he, as the Lady's favorite, should have done the honors. All his manners with me corresponded extremely well to this pattern. He did not treat me precisely as his inferior; he looked at me as nothing. I had difficulty recognizing the former[171] prig who considered himself honored by my glances at the Prince of Saxe-Gotha's house. I had still more reconciling this profound silence and this insulting arrogance with the tender friendship that he boasted about having for me around everyone he knew did have one. It is true that he hardly gave testimony of it except to feel sorry for my fortune about which I did not complain at all, to take pity on my sad lot with which I was content, and to lament[172] at seeing me harshly refuse the beneficent efforts that he said he wanted to make for me. It was with this art that he made his tender generosity admired, my ungrateful misanthropy blamed, and that he insensibly accustomed everyone to imagining only relations of benefits on one side and obligations on the other between a protector such as him and a wretch such as me, without even supposing a friendship of equal to equal as being within the realm of possibilities. As for me I tried in vain to discern what I might be obliged to this new patron for. I had loaned him money; he never loaned me any; I had watched over him in his illness, he scarcely came to see me in mine; I had given him all my friends, he never gave me any of his; I had extolled him with all my power. He . . . if he extolled me he did so less publicly, and did so in another way. Never did he render or even offer

me any service of any type. How was he my Maecenas then? [173] How was
I his protégé? That was beyond me, and still is beyond me.

It is true that he was more or less arrogant with everyone, but with no
one as brutally as with me. I remember that one time St. Lambert almost
threw his plate at Grimm's head after Grimm in a way gave [174] him the
lie publicly at table, by saying to him coarsely, *"That is not true."* To his
naturally cutting tone, he added the presumption of a parvenu, and even
became ridiculous as a result of being impertinent. The company of the
Nobility had seduced him to the point of giving himself airs that one sees
only in the least sensible among them. He never called his lackey except by
"Eh!" as if, from the number of his people, My Lord did not know which
one was on duty, When he gave him commissions he threw the money on
the ground instead of giving it into his hand. Then, completely forgetting that he was a man, he treated him with such a shocking contempt,
with such a harsh disdain in everything, that this poor boy, who was an
extremely good dependable person whom Mme d'Epinay had given him,
left his service without any other ground for complaint than the impossibility of putting up with such treatment: he was the La Fleur of this new
Conceited Man.

As foppish as he was vain, with his large dull eyes and his ungainly
form he had pretensions with women, and since his farce [175] with Mlle
Fel, he passed among several of them for a man of great feelings. That had
put him in fashion and had given him the taste for a feminine cleanliness;
he began to play the dandy, his dressing table became a great business;
everyone knew that he used powder, and I, who believed nothing of the
sort, began to believe it, not only from the improvement in his complexion, and from having found cups of powder on his dressing table, but
from the fact that upon entering his room one morning, I found him
brushing his nails with a little brush made especially for the purpose, a
work which he continued proudly in front of me. I judged that a man
who passes two hours every morning brushing his nails is very capable of
passing several moments filling the hollows of his skin with powder. The
good man Gauffecourt, who was not a very malicious fellow, had rather
jokingly nicknamed him *Tyrant-the-White*.[176]

All these things were only ridiculous, but they were very antipatheti-
cal to my character. They ended by making his character suspect to me.
I found it hard to believe that a man whose head was turned this way
could preserve his heart in the right place. He prided himself on nothing
so much as sensitivity of soul and energy of feeling. How did that accord
with faults that are suited to small souls? How could the lively and continuous outbursts which put a sensitive heart outside of itself allow him

to be ceaselessly occupied with so many little cares for his little person? Oh my God! someone who feels his heart set aflame with this celestial fire seeks to exhale it and wants to show what is inside him. He would like to put his heart on his face; he will never imagine any other makeup.

I recalled the summary of his morality, which Mme d'Epinay had told me, and which she had adopted. This summary consisted in a single article; namely that the sole duty of man is to follow the inclinations of his heart in everything. When I learned about it this morality gave me terrible matter for thought, although at that time I only took it for a witticism. But I soon saw that this principle was really the rule of his conduct, and I had only too much proof of it at my expense later on. It is the esoteric doctrine about which Diderot talked to me so much, but which he never explained to me.[177]

I recalled the frequent warnings that had been given to me several years before that this man was false, that he play acted at feeling, and above all that he did not love me. I remembered several little anecdotes about this recounted to me by M. de Francueil and Mme de Chenonceaux neither of whom esteemed him, and who ought to have known him, because Mme de Chenonceaux was the daughter of Mme de Rochechouart the intimate friend of the late Comte de Friese, and M. de Francueil, who was very closely connected with the Vicomte de Polignac[178] at that time, had lived a lot at the Palais Royal precisely at the time Grimm began to make his way there.[179] All Paris was informed about his despair after the death of the Comte de Friese. It was a question of maintaining the reputation he had given himself[180] after Mlle Fel's cruelty,[181] the charlatanery in which I would have seen better than anyone if I had been less blind at that time. He had to be dragged to the Hôtel de Castries[182] where he worthily played his role of being abandoned to the most mortal affliction. There, every morning he went into the garden to weep at his ease holding his handkerchief bathed in tears over his eyes as long as he was in sight of the Hôtel; but at the turning of a certain lane some people he was not thinking about saw him instantly put the handkerchief into his pocket and take out a book. This observation that was repeated was soon made public all over Paris and was forgotten almost as soon. I had forgotten it myself; an action that involved me served to recall it to me. I was at my last gasp in my bed in the rue de Grenelle: he was in the country, one morning he came to see me completely out of breath, saying that he had just arrived at the very instant; I learned a moment afterward that he had arrived the day before, and that he had been seen at the theater the same day.

A thousand facts of this sort came back to me; but one observation that I was surprised to make so late struck me more than all that. I had given Grimm all my friends without exception; they had all become his. I could separate myself from him so little that I would scarcely have wanted to maintain admittance to a house where he did not have had it. Only Mme de Créqui refused to admit him, and I also almost stopped seeing her from then on. On his side Grimm made other[183] friends for himself, both at his own initiative and at that of the Comte de Friese. Out of all these friends, never did a single one become mine: never did he say a word to me to incite me at least to make their acquaintance, and of all the people I met sometimes in his home, never did a single one show me the slightest benevolence; not even the Comte de Friese at whose home he resided, and consequently with whom it would have been very agreeable for me to form some connection, nor the Comte de Schomberg his relative with whom Grimm was even more familiar.

Here is more; my own friends whom I made his, and who were all tenderly attached to me before this acquaintance, perceptibly changed toward me once it was made. He never gave me any of his, I gave him all of mine, and he finished by depriving me of them. If these are the effects of friendship, what will those of hatred be?

At the beginning even Diderot warned me several times that Grimm, to whom I was giving so much trust, was not my friend. Later on he changed his language,[184] when he himself had ceased to be my friend.

The way I had disposed of my children did not need anyone's concurrence. Nevertheless, I informed my friends about it, solely to inform them of it, so as not to appear better in their eyes than I was. These friends were three in number: Diderot, Grimm, Mme d'Epinay. Duclos, the most worthy of my trust, was the only one to whom I did not give it. He knew it nevertheless; from whom? I do not know. It is hardly probable that this unfaithfulness came from Mme d'Epinay who knew that I had the means of avenging myself cruelly for it by imitating it, if I were capable of doing so. There remain Grimm and Diderot, at that time so united in so many things, above all against me, that it is more than probable that this crime was common to them. I would wager that Duclos, to whom I did not tell my secret and who consequently was the master of it, is the only one who kept it.

In their project of depriving me of the Governesses, Grimm and Diderot had made an effort to get him to join with their intentions: he always disdainfully refused to do so. It was only later on that I learned from him everything that had passed among them in this regard; but I learned enough about it at that time from Therese to see that there was some secret plan in all this, and that they wanted to dispose of me, if not against my will, at least without my knowledge, or that they certainly wanted to make these two persons serve as an instrument in some hidden plan.[185] All this was certainly not upright behavior. Duclos's opposition proves it unanswerably. Whoever wants to do so can believe[186] that this was friendship.

This so-called friendship was as fatal to me inside as outside. The long and frequent conversations with Mme le Vasseur for several years had perceptibly changed that woman with regard to me, and this change was assuredly not favorable to me. About what did they deal in these peculiar tête-à-têtes? Why this profound mystery? Was the conversation of that old woman pleasant enough to take her in secret[187] this way then, and important enough to make such a great secret of it? For the three or four years that these colloquies lasted, they had appeared laughable to me: when I thought about them again at that time I began to be astonished at them. This astonishment would have reached the point of anxiety, if I had known then what that woman was preparing for me.

In spite of the pretended zeal for me upon which Grimm plumed himself outside, and which was difficult to reconcile with the tone he took face to face with me, nothing came back to me from him from any direction that was to my advantage, and the commiseration that he feigned[188] having for me tended very much less to serve me than to debase me. He even deprived me of the resource of the profession I had chosen as much as he could, by disparaging me as a bad copyist, and I acknowledge that he was telling the truth in this, but it was not his place to say it. He proved that he was not joking by making use of another copyist and by leaving me none of the business of which he could deprive me. One might have said that his project was to make me depend on him and his influence for my subsistence, and to dry up its source until I was reduced to that.

To sum it all up; my reason finally stilled my former bias[189] which was still speaking. I judged his character to be at least very suspect and, as to his friendship, I decided it was false. Then, having resolved not to see him any more, I notified Mme d'Epinay of this, supporting my resolution with several unanswerable facts, which I have now forgotten.

She strongly combatted this resolution without knowing too well what to say[190] to the reasons upon which it was founded. She was not yet conniving with him. But the next day instead of explaining herself verbally with me, she delivered a very skillful letter, which they had reworked together, and by means of which she justified him by means of his[191] uncommunicative character without entering into any detail about the facts, and—making a crime out of my having suspected him of perfidy with regard to his friends—exhorted me to be reconciled with him. This letter (which will be found in bundle A. #48)[192] unsettled me. In a conversation which we had afterwards, and in which I found her better prepared than she was the first time, I ended by letting myself be overcome, I came to believe that I might have judged badly, that in that case I really had committed grave wrongs with regard to a friend which I ought to redress. In short, as I had already done several times with Diderot, with the Baron d'Holback, half willingly half out of weakness, I made all the advances that I had a right to demand, I went to M. Grimm's like another George Dandin to make excuses to him for the offenses he had done to me;[193] I still had that false persuasion, which has made me perform a thousand base actions in my life with my sham friends, that there is no hatred whatsoever that cannot be disarmed by means of gentleness and fair dealings; instead of which, on the contrary, the hatred of the wicked does nothing but become further enlivened by the impossibility of finding anything to base it on, and the feeling of their own injustice is only an additional grievance against the person who is its object. Without departing from my own story I have a very strong proof of this maxim in Grimm and in Tronchin who became my two most implacable enemies out of taste, pleasure, whim, without being able to allege any wrong of any sort that I might ever have committed with either of the two,* and whose rage increases from day to day like that of Tigers from the ease they find in slaking it.

I expected that, being mortified by my condescension and my advances, Grimm would receive me with open arms and the most tender friendship. He received me like a Roman Emperor with an arrogance that I had never seen from anyone. I was not at all prepared for this welcome. After I had fulfilled the object that brought me to him in a few words and a timid manner since I was perplexed over a role so little made for me, before he received me in forgiveness, he pronounced with much majesty a long harangue which he had prepared, and which contained the long enumeration of his rare virtues, and above all in friendship. For a long time he stressed a thing that at first struck me very much; that is that he was always seen to preserve the same friends. While he was speaking I said to myself under my breath that it would be very cruel for me to make the only exception to this rule. He returned to it so often and with so much affectation that he made me think that he would be less struck by this maxim if he was only following the feelings of his heart in this,[195] and that

---

* Later on I gave the latter the nickname of Quack only a long time after his declared enmity, and the bloody persecutions that he instigated for me at Geneva and elsewhere. I even soon suppressed this name when I saw myself completely his victim. Base acts of vengeance are unworthy of my heart and hatred never takes hold there.[194]

he was making use of it as an artifice that was useful for his intentions as a means for succeeding. Until then I had been in the same circumstance, I had always preserved all my friends, since my most tender childhood I had not lost a single one of them except by death, and nevertheless I had not made a reflection about it until then; it was not a maxim that I would have prescribed for myself. Thus, since this was an advantage common to both of us, why did he plume himself on it then by preference, unless he was thinking in advance of depriving me of it.[196] Afterward he applied himself to humiliating me by means of proofs of the preference that our common friends gave him over me. I was as well acquainted with this preference as he was; the question was by what title he had obtained it;[197] whether it was by strength of merit or skill; by raising himself or by seeking to lower me. Finally when, as he pleased, he had put between him and me all the distance that could give value to the forgiveness he was going to give me, he granted me the kiss of peace in a light embrace that resembled the accolade that the King gives to new Knights. I fell from the clouds, I was dumbfounded, I did not know what to say, I did not find a word. This whole scene had the air of the reprimand that a Preceptor makes to his disciple when he grants him forgiveness from the rod. I never think about it without feeling how deceptive are judgments founded on appearance to which the vulgar give so much weight, and how often audacity and pride are on the side of the guilty, shame and embarrassment on the side of the innocent.

We were reconciled; in my case that was a relief for my heart which is thrown into mortal anguish by any quarrel. One will suspect very much that such a reconciliation did not change his manners, it only deprived me of the right to complain about them. Also I decided to put up with everything and no longer to say anything.

So many griefs blow after blow threw me into a depression that hardly left me the strength to regain ascendancy over myself. Without an answer from St. Lambert, neglected by Mme d'Houdetot, no longer daring to open myself up to anyone, I began to fear that by making friendship into the idol of my heart I might have used up my life in sacrificing to chimeras. Now that the trial had been made, out of all my connections there remained only two men who had preserved all my esteem and to whom my heart could give its trust: Duclos, whom I had lost sight of since my retirement to the Hermitage, and St. Lambert. I believed I could not very well redress my wrongs with regard to this latter except by unburdening my heart to him without reserve, and I resolved to make my full confessions to him in everything that did not compromise his mistress. I do not doubt that this choice was another trap from my passion to keep me nearer her; but it is certain that I would have thrown myself into the arms of her lover without reserve, that I would have put myself entirely under his guidance, and that I would have pushed frankness as far as it could go. I was ready to write him a second letter to which I was sure he would have responded, when I learned the sad cause of his silence over the first. He had not been able to sustain the fatigues of that campaign up to the end. Mme d'Epinay informed me that he had just had an attack of paralysis, and Mme d'Houdetot, who had ended by being made sick herself because of his affliction, and who was in no condition to write to me on the spot, notified me two or three days afterward from Paris where she was at that time that he had been brought to Aix-la-Chapelle to take the baths there. I do not say that this sad news afflicted me as it did her; but I doubt that the heartache it gave me was less painful than her suffering and her tears. The sorrow of knowing him to be in that condition, increased by the fear that anxiety might have contributed to putting him in it, touched me more than everything that had happened to me until then, and I felt cruelly that in my self-esteem I was lacking the strength I needed to bear so much misfortune. Fortunately this generous friend did not leave me in this depression for very long; he did not forget me in spite of his attack, and it was not long before I learned directly from him that I had very badly judged his feelings and his condition.[198] But it is time to come to the great revolution of my destiny, to the catastrophe that has divided my life into two such different parts, and which has drawn such terrible effects from a very slight cause.

One day when I least expected it, Mme d'Epinay sent for me. Upon entering I noticed in her eyes and in all her countenance a troubled air with which I was all the more struck since that air was not at all ordinary for her, because no one in the world knew better than she did how to govern her face and movements. "My friend," she said to me, "I am leaving for Geneva; my chest is in a bad condition, my health is impaired to the point that I must immediately go to see and consult Tronchin." This resolution, so brusquely made and at the beginning of the bad season of the year, surprised me all the more since I had left her thirty-six hours earlier without there being any question of it. I asked whom she would take along with her. She told me that she would take along her son along with M. de Linant; and then she added casually; "And you, my Bear,[199] won't you come too?" Since I did not believe that she was speaking seriously, because she knew that in the season we were entering I was barely in a condition to leave my room, I made a joke about the usefulness of a retinue of a sick person for another sick person, she herself did not appear to have made the proposal seriously, and there was no longer any question of it. We no longer spoke about anything but the preparations for her trip with which she occupied herself quickly, since she was resolved to leave in two weeks.

I did not need much penetration to understand that there was a secret motive for this trip that was being kept from me. This secret, which was one from me alone in the whole house, was uncovered the very next day by Therese to whom it was revealed by Teissier the steward who learned it from the chambermaid. Although I do not owe this secret to Mme d'Epinay, since I do not possess it from her, it is too much linked with the ones I do possess from her for me to be able to separate it from them: thus I will be silent on this article: but these secrets which have never left nor ever will leave my mouth or my pen have become known by too many people for it to be possible for them to be unknown to anyone close to Mme d'Epinay.[200]

Having been informed of the true motive for this trip, I would have recognized the secret impulsion of an enemy hand in the attempt to make me Mme d'Epinay's chaperon; but she had insisted so little that I persisted in not regarding this attempt as at all serious, and I only laughed at the fine figure I would have cut in it if I had had the stupidity to take it upon myself. Moreover she gained a lot from my refusal, for she succeeded in engaging her husband himself to accompany her.

Some days afterward I received the note from Diderot which I am going to transcribe. This note, merely folded in half, in a manner so that all the contents could be read without difficulty, was addressed to me at Madame d'Epinay's house, and entrusted to M. de Linant, the son's Tutor and the mother's confidant.[201]

Note from Diderot (Bundle A. #52)[202]

I am made to love you, and to give you sorrow. I learn that Mme d'Epinay is going to Geneva, and I do not hear it said that you are accompanying her. My friend, if you are content with Mme d'Epinay, you must leave with her: if discontent you must leave much more rapidly. Are you overburdened by the weight of the obligations you have to her; here is an occasion to acquit yourself in part and to relieve yourself. Will you find another occasion in your life to bear witness to her of your gratitude? She is going into a country where it will be as if she had fallen from the clouds. She is sick: she will need amusement and distraction. Winter! see, my friend. The objection of your health might be stronger than I believe it. But are you more ill today than you were a month ago, and than you will be at the beginning of Spring? Three months from now will you make the trip more comfortably than today? As for me I admit to you that if I could not bear the coach I would take a stick and I would follow her. And then do you not fear that your behavior be misinterpreted? You will be suspected either of ingratitude or of another secret motive. I know very well that whatever you might do, you will always have the testimony of your conscience for you: but is this testimony enough by itself, and is it permissible to neglect, up to a certain point, that of other men. Besides, my friend, it is to acquit myself with you and with me that I write you this note. If it displeases you, throw it in the fire, and let there be no more a question of it than if it had never been written. I salute you, love you, and embrace you.

The trembling of anger, the dizziness that overtook me while I was reading this note, and which barely allowed me to finish it, did not prevent me from noticing the skill with which Diderot affected a gentler, more affectionate, more decent tone in it than in all his other letters, in which he addressed me at the most as my dear fellow without[203] deigning to give me the name of friend in them. I easily saw the roundabout way this note came to me, since its address, form, and course revealed the indirect manner clumsily enough: for we usually wrote to each other by means of the post or the Montmorency messenger, and this was the first and sole time that he made use of this way.

When the first outburst of my indignation allowed me to write, I hastily sketched the following response to him, which I carried on the spot from the Hermitage where I was at that time to la Chevrette, in order to show it to Mme d'Epinay, to whom in my blind rage I wanted to read it, as well as Diderot's note.

My dear friend, you can know neither the strength of the obligations I might have to Mme d'Epinay nor to what point they bind me, nor whether she really needs me in her trip, nor whether she desires me to accompany her, nor whether it is possible for me to do it, nor the reasons that I can have for abstaining. I do not refuse to discuss all these points with you; but while waiting, agree that to prescribe to me so affirmatively what I ought to do without putting yourself in a position to judge about it, is, my dear philosopher, clearly to offer an opinion thoughtlessly. What I see worse than that is that your advice does not come from you. Aside from the fact that I am hardly in the mood to let myself be led by third or fourth hand under your name, in these roundabout turns I find a certain indirectness that does not go[204] with your frankness, and from which you will do well, for yourself and for me, to abstain from now on.

You fear that my behavior is being badly interpreted; but I defy a heart like yours to dare to think badly of mine. Others perhaps would speak better of me if I resembled them more. God preserve me from making myself approved of by them. Let the wicked spy on me and interpret me; Rousseau is not made to fear them nor Diderot to listen to them.

If your note has displeased me, you want me to throw it in the fire so that there might be no more question of it! Do you think that what comes from you can be forgotten this way. My dear fellow, in the pain you give me you hold my tears as cheaply as you hold my life and my health in the efforts you exhort me to make.

If you could correct yourself of this, your friendship would be sweeter to me for it and I would become less pitiable.

Upon entering Mme d'Epinay's room, I found Grimm with her and I was delighted by it. I read them my two letters loudly and in a clear voice with an intrepidity of which I would not[205] have believed myself capable, and upon finishing I added some remarks that did not contradict it. From this unexpected audacity in a man who was ordinarily so fearful, I saw both of them bowled over, dumbfounded, not responding a word; above all I saw that arrogant man lower his eyes to the ground and not dare to sustain the sparks of my gaze; but at the same instant he swore my ruin at the bottom of his heart, and I am sure that they connived it before separating.

It was at about this time that I finally received from Mme d'Houdetot St. Lambert's answer (Bundle A. #57.)[206] dated still from Wolfenbutel a few days after his accident, to my letter which had been delayed for a long time en route. This answer brought me consolations which I needed very much at that moment, by means of the testimonies of esteem and friendship with which it was full, and which gave me the courage and strength to deserve them. From that moment I did my duty; but it is certain that if St. Lambert had been found to be less sensible, less generous, a less decent man, I would have been lost without return.

The weather became bad and people began to leave the country. Mme d'Houdetot notified me of the day on which she was counting on coming to make her farewells in the valley and gave me an appointment at Eaubonne. By chance this was the same day on which Mme d'Epinay was leaving la Chevrette to go to Paris to finish the preparations for her trip. Fortunately she left in the morning and upon leaving her I still had the time to go to dine with her sister-in-law. I had St. Lambert's letter in my pocket; I reread it several times while I walked. This letter served me as an aegis against my weakness. I made and kept the resolution no longer to see in Mme d'Houdetot anything but my friend and my friend's mistress; and I passed four or five hours in tête-à-tête with her in a delightful calm, infinitely preferable, even as to enjoyment, to those onsets of ardent fever which I had had with her until then. Since she knew too well that my heart was not changed, she was sensitive to the efforts I had made to conquer myself; she esteemed me the more for it, and I had the pleasure of seeing that her friendship for me was not at all dead. She informed me of the impending return of St. Lambert, who, although he had recovered well enough from his attack, was no longer in a condition to bear the fatigues of war, and was leaving the service to come to live peacefully close to her. We formed the charming project of a close society among the three of us, and we were able to hope the execution of this project would be durable, given that all the feelings that can unite sensitive and upright hearts made up its basis, and that we gathered together enough talents and knowledge in the three of us for us to suffice to ourselves and not to need of any foreign supplement. Alas! while abandoning myself to the hope of such a sweet life I hardly dreamed of the one that was waiting for me.

Afterward we spoke about my present situation with Mme d'Epinay. I showed her Diderot's letter with my answer, I related to her everything that had passed on this subject, and I declared to her my resolution to leave the Hermitage. She opposed it in a lively way, and by means of reasons that were all powerful over my heart. She indicated to me how much she would have desired me to have made the trip to Geneva, foreseeing that she would not fail to be compromised in my refusal, which Diderot's letter seemed to announce in advance. Nevertheless, since she knew my reasons as well as I did myself, she did not insist on that article; but she entreated me to avoid any outburst at any price whatsoever, and to extenuate my refusal with reasons plausible enough to remove the unjust suspicion that she might have taken part in it. I told her that she was not imposing an easy task on me; but that—resolved to expiate my wrongs even at the price of my reputation—I wanted to give preference to her reputation in everything that honor allowed me to endure. It will soon be known whether I was able to fulfill that engagement.

I can swear that, since my unfortunate passion was far from having lost any of its strength, I never loved my Sophie in as lively a way, as tenderly as I did that day. But such was the impression made on me by St. Lambert's letter, the feeling of duty, and the horror of perfidy, that during that entire interview my senses left me completely in peace with her, and I was not even tempted to kiss her hand. Upon leaving she embraced me in front of her people. This kiss, so different from the ones I had stolen from her sometimes under the foliage, was a proof to me that I had reacquired ascendancy over myself: I am almost assured that if my heart had had time to steady itself in calm, I would not have needed three months to be cured radically.

Here ended my personal relations with Mme d'Houdetot. Relations about which, based on the appearances, each person can judge according to the inclinations of his own heart, but in which the passion this lovable woman inspired in me, perhaps the most lively passion that any man has ever felt, will always be honored between Heaven and us by the rare and painful sacrifices made by both of us to duty, to honor, to love, and to friendship. We were raised up too high[207] in each other's eyes to be able to debase ourselves easily. One would have to be unworthy of every esteem to resolve to lose one of such a high value, and even the energy of the feelings that might have made us guilty kept us from becoming so.

It is thus that after such a long friendship for one of these two women and such strong love for the other, I separately bade them farewell on the same day,[208] to one never to see her again in my life, to the other to see her again only two times on the occasions that I will tell below.

After their departure I found myself in a great perplexity in order to fulfill so many pressing and contradictory duties, the consequences of my imprudent acts. If I had been in my natural state, after the proposal and the refusal of this trip to Geneva, I would have only had to stay calm and there was nothing more to say. But I stupidly made it into a business that could not remain in the condition it was in, and I could not exempt myself from all subsequent explanation except by leaving the Hermitage, which I had just promised Mme d'Houdetot not to do, at least for the present moment. Moreover, she had required that I make an excuse to my so-called friends for the refusal of this trip, so that this refusal might not be imputed to her. Nevertheless, I could not allege its genuine cause, without insulting Mme d'Epinay to whom I certainly owed some gratitude after all she had done for me. Everything well considered, I found myself in the harsh but indispensable alternative of failing in respect toward Mme d'Epinay, Mme d'Houdetot, or myself, and I took the last course. I took it openly, fully, without equivocating, and with a generosity that assuredly was worthy of washing away the faults that had reduced me to this extremity. This sacrifice, which my enemies have been able to put to use, and which perhaps they expected, has caused the ruin of my reputation and, with their efforts, has deprived me of public esteem; but it has given me back my own and has consoled me in my misfortunes. As will be seen, this is neither the last time that I have made such sacrifices, nor also the last one that has been used to crush me.

Grimm was the only one who appeared not to have taken any part in this business; it was to him that I resolved to address myself. I wrote him a long letter in which I exposed the ridiculousness of wanting to make this trip to Geneva into a duty for me, the uselessness, even the trouble I would have been to Mme d'Epinay on it, and the inconveniences that would have resulted from it for myself. In this letter I did not resist the temptation of letting him see that I was informed, and that it appeared peculiar to me that anyone would claim that it was up to me to make this trip, while he himself was dispensed from it and he was not mentioned. To the public, this letter—in which I was forced often to beat around the bush for lack of being able to state my reasons clearly—would have given me the appearance of many wrongs; but it was a model of reserve and discretion for people like Grimm who knew all about the things I did not say and which fully justified my behavior. I did not even fear putting an additional prejudice against me by attributing Diderot's opinion to my other friends, in order to insinuate that Mme d'Houdetot had thought the same, as was true, and keeping silent about the fact that, based on my reasons, she had changed her opinion. I could not better exculpate her of the suspicion of conniving with me, than by appearing to be dissatisfied with her on this point.

This letter ended with an act of trust by which any other man would have been touched; for by exhorting Grimm to weigh my reasons and to notify me of his opinion afterward, I notified him that I would follow this opinion, whatever it might be, and such was my intention, even if he had opined for my departure: for, since M. d'Epinay had made himself his wife's conductor in this trip, my going then took a completely different aspect: whereas at first it was I whom they wanted to burden with this job, and it was a question of him only after my refusal.

Grimm's answer was slow in coming; it was peculiar, I am going to transcribe it here. (See Bundle A. #59.)

"Mme d'Epinay's departure is postponed; her son is ill, she must wait until he recovers. I will muse about your letter. Keep yourself calm at your hermitage. I will have my advice passed to you in time. Since she will surely not leave for several days, there is no rush. While waiting, you can make her your offers if you judge it to be appropriate, although it still appears all the same to me. For, since I know your position as well as you do yourself, I have no doubt whatsoever that she will respond to your offers as she ought to, and the only thing I see to be gained by that is that you will be able to say to those who are pressing you that if you have not gone, it is not for lack of having offered. Besides I do not see why you insist upon the philosopher being the whole world's spokesman, and because his advice is that you leave, why you imagine that all your friends claim the same thing. If you write to Mme d'Epinay her answer can serve you as an answer to all these friends, since you have it so much at heart to reply to them. Farewell, I salute Mme Le Vasseur and the Criminal.*

Being struck with astonishment while I read this letter, I anxiously sought what it could mean, and I found nothing. What? instead of giving me an answer about mine with simplicity, he takes some time to muse about it as if he had not already taken enough. He even warned me about the suspense in which he wants to keep me, as if it was a question of a

---

* M. le Vasseur, whose wife led him a little roughly, called her the *Lieutenant Criminel*. As a pleasantry M. Grimm gave the same to the daughter and it pleased him to cut out the first word in order to shorten it.

deep problem to resolve, or as if it mattered to his intentions to deprive me of all means of penetrating his feeling up to the moment he would like to declare it to me. What do these precautions, these delays, these mysteries mean then? Is it thus that one responds to confidences? Is this the aspect of uprightness and good faith? I sought in vain for some favorable interpretation for this conduct; I did not find any whatsoever. Whatever his plan was, if it was against me, his position made its execution easy, without me being able to put any obstacle in its way from my own. In favor in the house of a great Prince, widely known in the world, giving the tone to our common social circles whose oracle he was, he could dispose of all his mechanisms at his ease with his ordinary skill, and I, alone in my hermitage, far from everything, without anyone's advice, without any communication, I had no other choice but to wait and remain in peace.[209] Only I wrote to Mme d'Epinay a letter as polite as could be about her son's sickness, but in which I did not fall into the[210] trap of offering to leave with her.

After centuries of waiting in the cruel uncertainty in which this barbarous man had plunged me, at the end of eight or ten days I learned that Mme d'Epinay had left and I received a second letter from him. It was only seven or eight lines which I did not finish reading . . . it was a rupture, but in terms such as can be dictated only by the most infernal hatred, and which even became stupid as a result of wanting to be offensive. He forbade me his presence as he would have forbidden me his States. His letter only needed to be read more coolly in order to be laughable. Without transcribing it, without even reading it completely, I sent it back to him on the spot along with this one.

I resisted my just suspicion; I come to know you too late.

Here then is the letter about which you gave yourself leisure to meditate! I send it back to you, it is not for me. You can show mine to the whole earth and hate me openly; it will be one falsehood less on your part.

My saying to him that he could show my preceding letter related to an article in his based on which one will be able to judge the profound skill he put into this whole business.

I have said that for people who did not know all about it, my letter could give many holds on me. He saw this with joy; but how to avail himself of this advantage without compromising himself? By showing this letter he exposed himself to the reproach of abusing his friend's trust.

To get out of this difficulty he conceived of breaking with me in the sharpest manner possible and, in his letter, to exploit the favor he did me of not showing mine. He was very sure that in the indignation of my rage

I would decline his sham discretion and permit him to show my letter to everyone: that was precisely what he wanted, and everything happened as he had arranged it. He had my letter circulate in all Paris with commentaries of his making, which nevertheless did not have all the success that he had promised himself from it. The permission to show my letter which he had been able to extort from me was not found to exempt him from the blame of having so lightly taken me at my word in order to harm me. People always asked what personal wrongs I had done him to authorize such a violent hatred. In sum, it was found that, even if I had committed wrongs that would have obliged him to break, even dead friendship still had rights which he should have respected. But unfortunately Paris is frivolous, these remarks of the moment are forgotten; the absent unfortunate person is neglected, the man who prospers imposes on it by his presence, the game of intrigue and wickedness is maintained, renews itself, and soon its ceaselessly renascent effect effaces everything that preceded it.

This is how, after having deceived me for so long, this man finally laid aside his mask for me, now that he was persuaded that he ceased to need it in the condition to which he had brought things. Being relieved of the fear of being unjust with regard to this wretch, I abandoned him to his own heart and ceased to think about him. A week after I received this letter, I received—dated from Geneva—from Mme d'Epinay her answer to my preceding one. (Bundle B. #10).[211] From the tone she took in it[212] for the first time in her life, I understood that, counting on the success of their measures, both of them were acting in concert, and that, since they regarded me as a ruined man without resource, from then on they were abandoning themselves to the pleasure of completely crushing me without risk.

In fact my position was among the most deplorable. I saw all my friends withdrawing from me, without my being able to know either how or why. Diderot, who was boasting about staying with me all by himself, and who for three months had been promising me a visit, did not come at all. Winter began to make itself felt and with it the attacks of my habitual illnesses. My temperament, although vigorous, was not able to sustain the combats of so many contradictory passions. I was in an exhaustion that left me neither strength nor courage to resist anything; if my commitments, if the continuous remonstrances of Diderot and Mme d'Houdetot had allowed me to leave the Hermitage at that moment, I did not know either where to go or how to drag myself. I remained immobile and stupid, without being able to act or think. The mere idea of a step to make, a letter to write, a word to say, made me shudder. Nevertheless, I could not leave Mme d'Epinay's letter without an answer, without admitting that I deserved the treatment with which she and her friend weighed me down. I decided to notify her of my feelings and my resolutions, not doubting for a moment that out of humanity, out of generosity, out of decorum, out of the good feelings that I had believed to be in her in spite of the bad, that she would not be eager to agree to it. Here is my letter.

From the Hermitage November 23, 1757

If one could die of pain I would not be alive. But I have finally made my decision. Friendship is dead between us, Madame; but that which is no more still keeps rights that I know how to respect. I have not at all forgotten your kindnesses for me, and you can count on all the gratitude from me that one can have for someone whom one must not love any longer. All other explanation would be useless: I have my conscience for me and send you back to your own.

I wished to leave the Hermitage, and I ought to have done so. But it is claimed that I must stay here until spring, and since my friends wish it, I will stay here until spring, if you consent.

When this letter was written and gone, I no longer thought of anything but making myself calm at the Hermitage, by taking care of my health there, seeking to recover strength and to take measures for leaving it in the spring without a commotion and without parading a rupture. But that was not M. Grimm's and Mme d'Epinay's reckoning; as will be seen in a moment.

Several days afterward I finally had the pleasure of receiving from Diderot that visit so often promised and missed.[213] It could not come more opportunely; he was my oldest friend; he was almost the only one I had left: one can judge what pleasure I had seeing him in these circumstances. My heart was full, I poured it out to his. I enlightened him about many facts which they had kept secret from him, disguised or falsely alleged. I informed him about everything that I was allowed to tell him about what had passed. I did not pretend at all to keep secret from him what he knew only too well, that a love as unfortunate as it was senseless had been the instrument of my ruin; but I never acknowledged that Mme d'Houdetot was informed of it, or at least that I had declared it to her. I spoke to him about Mme d'Epinay's unworthy maneuvers to intercept the very innocent letters that her sister-in-law wrote to me. I wanted him to learn these details from the very mouth of the people she[214] had attempted to seduce. Therese did so for him with exactness: but what became of me when it was the mother's turn and I heard her declare and maintain that she knew nothing about it. Those were her terms, and she never departed from them. This was not four days since she had repeated the narrative to me, and she gave me the lie to my face in front of my friend. This stroke appeared decisive to me, and I then keenly felt my imprudence at having kept such a woman near me for so long. I did not extend myself in invectives against her; I hardly deigned to speak several words of disdain to her. I felt what I owed to the daughter whose unshakable uprightness contrasted with the mother's unworthy cowardice. But from then my decision was made on the old woman's account, and I only waited for the moment to execute it.

This moment came sooner than I had expected. On December 10 I received from Mme d'Epinay a response to my preceding letter. Here are its contents.

From Geneva December 1, 1757 (Bundle B. #11)

After having given you all possible marks of friendship and interest for several years, it remains only for me to pity you. You are very unfortunate. I desire your conscience to be as calm as mine. That would be necessary for the repose of your life.

Since you wished to leave the Hermitage and you ought to, I am surprised that your friends have held you back. As for me I do not consult mine about my duties, and I have nothing more to say to you about yours.

A dismissal so unforeseen, but so clearly pronounced did not leave me an instant to hesitate. I needed to leave on the spot whatever the weather might be, in whatever condition I might be, even if I had to sleep in the woods and on the snow with which the earth was covered at that time, and whatever Mme d'Houdetot might say and do; for I wanted very much to gratify her in everything, but not to the point of infamy.

I found myself in the most terrible perplexity in which I have been in my life; but my resolution was made, I swore not to sleep in the Hermitage eight days from then come what may. I set about moving my effects out, determined to leave them in the open field rather than not to return the keys on the eighth day: for above all I wanted to have done everything before it was possible to write to Geneva and receive an answer. I had a courage that I had never felt in myself: my strength had returned. Honor and indignation, upon which Mme d'Epinay had not counted, returned it to me. Fortune aided my audacity. M. Mathas,[215] the fiscal procurator of M. the Prince de Condé, heard someone speak about my perplexity. He had me offered a little house he had in his garden of Mont Louis at Montmorency. I accepted promptly and with gratitude. The bargain was soon made; I hastily had some furniture bought, along with what I already had,[216] to lodge Therese and myself. I had my effects carried with great difficulty and with great expense: in spite of the ice and snow, my move was done in two days and the fifteenth of December I returned the keys of the Hermitage, after I had paid the gardener's wages, since I was not able to pay my rent.

As for Mme le Vasseur, I declared to her that we had to separate: her daughter wanted to weaken me, I was inflexible. I had her leave for Paris in the Messenger's carriage with all the effects and furniture that her daughter and she had in common. I gave her some money, and I promised to pay her rent in her children's home or elsewhere, to provide for her subsistence as much as I could, and never to let her lack bread, as long as I had it myself.

Finally, two days after my arrival at Mont Louis, I wrote the following letter to Mme d'Epinay.

From Montmorency December 17, 1757

Nothing is so simple and so necessary, Madame, as to move out of your house when you do not approve of me staying there. Thus, upon your refusal of consent for me to pass the remainder of the winter at the Hermitage, I left it on the fifteenth of December. My destiny was to enter it in spite of myself and to leave it the same way. I thank you for the stay that you induced me to make there, and I would thank you more if I had paid less dearly for it. Moreover, you are right to believe[217] that I am unfortunate, no one in the world knows better than you how much so I must be. If it is a misfortune to be deceived in the choice of one's friends, it is another one no less cruel to recover from such a sweet error.

Such is the faithful narration of my residence at the Hermitage and of the reasons that made me leave it. I have not been able to cut this narrative, and it is important to follow it with the greatest exactitude; since this epoch of my life has had an influence on the sequel that will extend until my last day.[218]

The extraordinary strength which a momentary effervescence had given me in order to leave the Hermitage abandoned me as soon as I was out of it. I had hardly settled in my new residence when sharp and frequent attacks of my retentions became compounded with the new discomfort of a hernia that tormented me for some time, without my knowing that it was one. I soon fell into the cruelest setbacks. My old friend Doctor Thyeri came to see me and inform me about my old condition. The probes, the catheters, the bandages, all the apparatus of the infirmities of age assembled around me made me feel harshly that one's heart is no longer young with impunity when the body has ceased to be so. The fine weather did not restore my strength at all and I passed the whole year of 1758 in a condition of languor that made me believe that I was reaching the end of my career. I saw its limit approach with a sort of eagerness. Having returned from the chimeras of friendship, detached from everything that had made me love life, I no longer saw anything in it that could make it pleasant for me: I no longer saw anything in it but evils and miseries that prevented me from enjoying myself. I aspired to the moment of being free and escaping my enemies. But let us take up the thread of events again.[2]

It appears that my retirement to Montmorency disconcerted Mme d'Epinay: probably she had not expected it. My sad condition, the rigor of the season, the general neglect in which I found myself, everything made Grimm and her believe that by pushing me to the ultimate extremity, they would reduce me to crying for mercy, and to lowering myself to the ultimate base actions in order to be left in the refuge which honor commanded me to leave. I moved out so abruptly that they did not have time to forestall the blow and nothing was left for them any longer but the choice[3] of playing for double or nothing and ruining me completely or trying to bring me back. Grimm came to the former decision, but I believe that Mme d'Epinay would have preferred the other, and I judge this from her answer to my last letter, in which she very much softened the tone she had taken in the preceding ones and in which she seemed to open the door to a reconciliation. The long delay of this answer, for which she made me wait a whole month, indicates well enough the perplexity in which she found herself for giving it a suitable turn and the deliberations by which it was preceded. She could not advance any farther without compromising[4] herself: but after her preceding letters and after my abrupt departure from her house, one could only be struck by the care she took in this letter not to let a single disagreeable word slip into it. I am going to transcribe it entirely so that one can judge about this.

From Geneva January 17, 1758 (Bundle B. #23)

Sir, I did not receive your letter of December 17 until yesterday. It was sent to me in a chest filled with different things which has been on the road all this time. I will respond only to the postscript; as for the letter, I do not understand it very well, and if we were in the position to explain ourselves, I would very much like to attribute everything that has happened to a misunderstanding. I return to the postscript. You can recall, Monsieur, that we had agreed that the wages of the gardener of the Hermitage would pass through your hands, to make him feel better that he was dependent on you, and for you to avoid scenes as ridiculous and immodest as the ones made by his predecessor. The proof of it is that the first quarter of his wages were returned to you, and that I had agreed with you a few days before my departure to have you reimbursed for your advances. I know that at first you made a difficulty about it: but I had asked you to make these advances; it was a simple thing for me to repay them and we agreed on it. Cahouet[5] notified me that you did not agree to receive this money. There is assuredly some mistake in that. I am giving the order that it be brought back to you, and I do not see why you would want to pay my gardener in spite of our agreements and even beyond the term that you lived in the Hermitage. I thus depend, Sir, that upon recalling everything I had the honor of saying to you, you will not refuse to be reimbursed for the advance that you have been pleased to make for me.

Since I could not have any confidence in Mme d'Epinay after everything that had passed, I did not want to take up with her again at all; I did not respond to this letter and our correspondence ended there.[6] Seeing my decision made, she made hers, and then, entering into all the intentions of Grimm and the Holbachic coterie, she joined her efforts to theirs in order to sink me to the bottom. While they were working at Paris she was working at Geneva. Grimm, who afterward went there to join her, finished what she had begun. Tronchin, whom they did not have any trouble winning over, seconded them powerfully and became the most furious of my persecutors, without having had the slightest subject for complaint from me, any more than Grimm did. In accord, all three underhandedly sowed the seed in Geneva that was seen to bloom there four years afterward.[7]

They had more trouble in Paris where I was better known, and where hearts, less disposed to hatred, did not so easily receive its impressions.

To strike their blows more skillfully they began by spreading it around that it was I who had left them. See the letter from De Leyre (Bundle B. #30).[8] From that, while still pretending to be my friends, they skillfully sowed their malign accusations as complaints about their friend's injustice. That made it so that, being less on guard, people were brought to listen to them more and to blame me. The underhanded accusations of perfidy and ingratitude were spread around more cautiously, and by that very fact had more effect. I knew that they imputed atrocious heinous deeds to me, without ever being able to learn what they made them consist of. All I could deduce from the public clamor was that it came down to these four capital crimes. 1. My retirement to the Country. 2. My love for Mme d'Houdetot. 3. The refusal to accompany Mme d'Epinay to Geneva. 4. The departure from the Hermitage. If they added other grievances to them, they took their measures so precisely that it was perfectly impossible for me ever to learn what their subject was.

Thus it is here that I believe I can fix the establishment of a system adopted since by those who dispose of me, with such a rapid progress and success that it would be held to be a prodigy by anyone who did not know how easily everything that favors the malignity of men establishes itself. I must attempt to explain[9] in a few words what is visible to my eyes in this obscure and profound system.

With a name already famous and known throughout Europe, I had preserved the simplicity of my first tastes. My mortal aversion for everything called party, faction, cabal, had kept me free, independent, without any chain other than my heart's attachments. Alone, a foreigner, isolated, without support, without family, depending only on my principles and my duties, I intrepidly followed routes of uprightness, never flattering or sparing anyone at the expense of justice and truth. Moreover, withdrawn into solitude for two years, without correspondence about news, without an account of the business of the world, without being informed or curious about anything, I lived four leagues from Paris, as separated from that capital by my negligence, as I would have been by the seas in the Isle of Tinian.[10]

On the contrary, Grimm, Diderot, d'Holback, at the center of the whirlwind, moved about in the largest society and almost divided up all of its spheres among themselves. The great, fine wits, literary people, people of the robe, women, in concert they could make themselves heard by all. One must already see the advantage that this position gives to three well-united men against a fourth in the position in which I found myself. It is true that Diderot and d'Holback were not, at least I cannot believe it, people to scheme very black plots;[11] the one was not wicked[12] enough to do it nor the other skillful enough: but by this very fact the party was bound together better. Grimm alone formed his plan in his head, and showed the two others only what they needed to see to cooperate in its execution. The ascendancy that he had acquired over them made this cooperation easy, and the effect of the whole answered to the superiority of his talent.

It was with this superior talent that, feeling the advantage he could draw from our respective positions, he formed the project of reversing my reputation from top to bottom, and making an entirely opposite one for me without compromising himself, by beginning to raise around me an edifice of shadows that it was impossible for me to pierce in order to shed light on his maneuvers and unmask him.

This enterprise was difficult in that its iniquity had to be palliated in the eyes of those who had to cooperate in it. It was necessary to deceive decent people; it was necessary to divert the whole world away from me, not to leave me a single friend, either small nor great. What do I say? it was necessary not to let a single word of truth pierce through to me. If a single generous man came to say to me, "You are playing the virtuous man, nevertheless this is what they are saying about you; what do you have to say?" truth triumphed,[13] and Grimm was lost. He knew it; but he plumbed his own heart and esteemed men only for what they are worth. For the honor of humanity I am sorry that he calculated so accurately.

While walking in these subterranean places his steps were obliged to be slow in order to be sure. He has followed his plan for twelve[14] years and the most difficult thing still remains to do; that is to abuse the entire public. There are still some eyes which have followed him more closely than he thinks. He fears[15] it, and does not yet expose his scheme to the full light of day.* But he has found the hardly difficult way to make power enter into it, and this power disposes of me.[16] Being sustained by this support, he advances with less risk. The satellites of power usually pride themselves very little on uprightness and much less on frankness; the indiscretion of some good man is hardly to be feared any longer. Above all he needs for me to be surrounded by impenetrable shadows, and for his plot to be always hidden from me, knowing well that with whatever art he has hatched the scheme, it would never bear up under my glances. His great skill is to appear to treat me considerately while defaming me, and still to give his perfidy the air of generosity.[17]

I felt the first effects of this system from the underhanded accusations

---

* Since this was written he has overstepped the limits with the fullest and most inconceivable success. I believe that it is Tronchin who gave him the courage and the means to do it.

of the Holbachic coterie, without being able either to know or even conjecture what these accusations consisted of. De Leyre told me in his letters
that heinous deeds were imputed to me. Diderot told me the same thing
more mysteriously,[18] and when I entered into an explanation with either
of them everything was reduced to the chief accusations noted above. I
felt a gradual cooling off in Mme d'Houdetot's letters. I could not attribute this cooling off to St. Lambert, who continued to write to me
with the same friendship and who even came to see me after his return.
I could not impute the fault for it to myself either, because we had separated very satisfied with each other, and because nothing had passed on
my part since that time except my departure from the Hermitage, the necessity of which she herself had felt. Because I did not know on what to
blame this cooling off, which she did not acknowledge, but about which
my heart was not led astray, I was anxious about everything. I knew that
she was treating her sister-in-law and Grimm extremely gingerly, because
of their connections with St. Lambert; I feared their activities. This agitation reopened my sores and made my correspondence stormy to the point
of disgusting her with it completely. I glimpsed a thousand cruel things,
without seeing anything distinctly. I was in the most unbearable position
for a man whose imagination catches fire easily. If I had been completely
isolated, if I had known nothing at all I would have become more tranquil; but my heart still held to some attachments by means of which my
enemies had a thousand holds on me, and the weak rays that pierced into
my refuge served only to let me see the blackness of the mysteries that
were being hidden from me.

I would have succumbed, I do not doubt it at all, to this torment that
was too cruel, too unbearable for my open and frank natural character,
which—because of the impossibility of hiding my feelings—made me
fear everything from what was being hidden from me; but very fortunately, objects sufficiently engaging to my heart presented themselves to
make a salutary diversion from the ones that were occupying me in spite
of myself. In the last visit Diderot had paid me at the Hermitage, he had
spoken to me about the article *Geneva* which d'Alembert had put in the
Encyclopedia;[19] he had informed me that this article, written in concert
with some Genevans of high rank, had the establishment of the Theater at
Geneva as its goal, that consequently measures were being taken, and that
it would not be long before this establishment took place. Since Diderot
appeared to find all this extremely good, since he had no doubt about
its success, and since I had too many other disputes with him to debate
again on this article, I said nothing to him; but being indignant at all this

stratagem of seduction in my fatherland, I impatiently waited for the volume of the Encyclopedia in which this article was, to see whether there might not be a way to make some response to it that could parry this unfortunate blow. I received the volume a little after my establishment at Montlouis, and I found the article to be written with much skill and art, and worthy of the pen from which it had come. Nevertheless, that did not divert me from wanting to respond to it, and in spite of the dejection I was in, in spite of my distress and my illnesses, the rigor of the season, and the inconvenience of my new residence, in which I had not yet had time to settle myself, I began the work with a zeal that surmounted everything.

During a rather severe winter, in the month of February, and in the condition that I have described above, every day I went to pass two hours in the morning, and as much after dinner in a completely open Turret I had at the end of the garden where my habitation was. This Turret, which ended a terraced path, opened onto the valley and pond of Montmorency, and, as the end point of the prospect, offered me the simple but respectable Chateau of St. Gratien the retreat of the virtuous Catinat.[20] It was in this place—at that time iced and without shelter against the wind and snow, and without any other fire than the one in my heart—that I composed my *Letter to d'Alembert on the Theater* in the space of three weeks. Since Julie was not half done, this is the first of my writings in which I found charms in the labor. Until then the indignation of virtue had taken the place of Apollo for me; this time tenderness and gentleness of soul took his place. The injustices of which I had been only the spectator had irritated me; those of which I had become the object saddened me, and this was only the sadness without bile of a too loving, too tender heart, which, having been fooled by those it had believed to be of its own caliber, was forced to retire into itself. Full of everything that had just happened to me, still alarmed by so many violent movements, my heart mixed the feeling of its pains to the ideas that the meditation of my subject had caused to be born in me; my labor felt the effect of this mixture. Without me noticing it, I described my present situation; in it I depicted Grimm, Mme d'Epinay, Mme d'Houdetot, St. Lambert, myself.[21] How many delightful tears did I shed while writing it! Alas! in it one feels only too much that the love, that fatal love which I was exerting myself to cure, had not yet departed from my heart. Along with all this was mixed a certain emotion toward myself; I felt myself to be dying, and believed I was bidding my last farewell to the public. Far from fearing death, I saw it drawing near with joy; but I regretted leaving my fellows without them feeling everything I was worth, without them knowing how much

I would have deserved to be loved by them, if they had known me better. Here are the secret causes of the peculiar tone that reigns in this work, and which contrasts so prodigiously with that of the preceding one.*

I retouched and made a fair copy of this letter and I was getting ready to have it printed,[22] when, after a long silence, I received one from Mme d'Houdetot which plunged me into a new affliction, the most tangible that I had yet experienced. In this letter (Bundle B. #34)[23] she informed me that my passion for her was known throughout Paris, that I had spoken about it to people who had made it public, that when these rumors reached her lover they had almost cost her her life, that in the end he did justice to her, and that their peace was made; but that she owed it to him, as well as to herself and to concern for her reputation, to break off all dealings with me; assuring me, otherwise, that neither of them would ever cease to be concerned about me, that they would defend me in public, and that she would send from time to time to receive news about me.

"And you too, Diderot?" I cried to myself, "Unworthy friend! . . ." Nevertheless I still could not resolve to judge him. My weakness was known to other people who might have caused it to be talked about. I wanted to doubt . . . but soon I no longer could. A little later St. Lambert performed an action worthy of his generosity. Being well enough acquainted with my soul, he judged what condition I must be in; having been betrayed by one part of my friends and forsaken by the others. He came to see me. The first time he had little time to give to me. He came back. Unfortunately, since I was not expecting him I was not at home. Therese, who was there, had a conversation of more than two hours with him in which they told each other mutually many facts about which it was very important to me that we both be informed. The surprise with which I learned from him that no one in the world doubted that I had lived with Mme d'Epinay as Grimm was living now, could be equaled only by the one he himself might have had when he learned how false this rumor was. To the great displeasure of the Lady, St. Lambert was in the same position I was, and all the clarifications that resulted from this conversation completely extinguished all my regret at having broken with her irreversibly. With regard to Mme d'Houdetot, he detailed to Therese several circumstances which were not known either to her, nor even to Mme d'Houdetot; which I alone knew, which I had told only to Diderot alone under the seal of friendship, and it was precisely St. Lambert to whom he had chosen to confide them.[24] This last stroke made up my mind, and having resolved to break with Diderot for ever, I no longer

* The *Discourse on Inequality*.

deliberated about anything but the manner of doing so: for I had noticed that secret ruptures turned to my prejudice, in that they left my cruelest enemies with the mask of friendship.[25]

The rules of decorum established in the world on this article seem to be dictated by the spirit of lying and treachery. Still to appear to be a man's friend when one has ceased to be so is to reserve for oneself means of injuring him by deceiving decent people. I recalled that when the illustrious Montesquieu broke with Father de Tournemine,[26] he hastened to declare it loudly by saying to everyone, "Do not listen to either Father de Tournemine or me when we talk about each other; for we have ceased to be friends." This conduct was very much applauded, and everyone praised its frankness and generosity. I resolved to follow the same example with Diderot: but how could I publish this rupture authentically from my retirement, and nevertheless do so without scandal? I took it into my head to insert in my work in the form of a note a passage from the Book of Ecclesiasticus which declared this rupture and even the subject clearly enough for anyone who was well informed, and signified nothing for the rest of the world. Moreover I made a point in the work of not designating the friend whom I was renouncing except with the honor that one ought always to render even to dead friendship. All this can be seen in the work itself.[27]

Everything in this world depends on luck, and it seems that in adversity every act of courage is a crime. The same stroke that had been admired in Montesquieu drew upon me only blame and reproach. As soon as my work was printed[28] and I had some copies of it, I sent one to St. Lambert who, on the very eve, had written me a note full of the most tender friendship in Mme d'Houdetot's name and his own (Bundle B. #37).[29] Here is the letter he wrote me when he sent me back my copy.

Eaubonne October 10, 1758 (Bundle B. #38)

In truth, Sir, I cannot accept the present you have just made me. At the place in your preface in which, relative to Diderot, you cite a passage from Ecclesiastes [He was wrong, it is from Ecclesiasticus] the book fell from my hands. After our conversations of this summer, you appeared to me convinced that Diderot was innocent of the so-called indiscretions you imputed to him. I do not know whether he may have committed some wrongs toward you; but I do know very well that they do not give you the right to give him a public insult. You are not ignorant of the persecutions he is meeting with,[30] and you are going to mix the voice of an old friend to the cries of envy. I cannot dissimulate to you, Sir,[31] how much this atrocity revolts me. I have no relations with Diderot, but I honor him, and I keenly feel the distress you are giving to a man to whom—at least with me— you have never reproached except for a little weakness. Sir, we differ too much in principles for us ever to agree. Forget my existence; that should not be difficult. I have never done men either the sort of good or harm which they remember for very long. I promise you, Sir, to forget your person, and to remember only your talents.

I felt no less torn apart than indignant at this letter, and when I finally found my pride again in the excess of my misery, I answered him with the following note.

From Montmorency October 11, 1758

Sir, while reading your letter, I have done you the honor of being surprised by it, and I was stupid enough to be upset by it; but I found it unworthy of an answer.

I have no wish whatsoever to continue Mme d'Houdetot's copies.[32] If it does not suit her to keep what she has, she can send it back to me, I will return her money to her. If she does keep it, she must still send for the rest of her paper and her money. At the same time I ask her to return to me the prospectus which was entrusted to her. Farewell, Sir.

Courage in misfortune irritates cowardly hearts but it pleases generous hearts. It appeared that this note made St. Lambert return to himself and that he regretted what he had done; but being too proud in his turn to make up openly, he seized, he perhaps prepared the means of assuaging the blow he had struck me. Two weeks later I received the following letter from M. d'Epinay.[33]

This Thursday the 26th (Bundle B. #10)

I have received, Sir, the book you had the kindness to send me; I am reading it with the greatest pleasure. This is the feeling I have always experienced in reading all the works that have issued from your pen. Receive all my thanks for it. I would have come to give them to you myself if my business had permitted me to stay in your neighborhood for any time; but I have lived at la Chevrette very little this year. M. and Mme Dupin have just asked to dine with me next Sunday. I count upon Messieurs St. Lambert, de Francueil, and Mme d'Houdetot being among the party; you will give me a true pleasure, Sir, if you would be among us. All the persons I will have as guests want you to come and will be charmed to share with me the pleasure of passing a part of the day with you.

I have the honor of being with the most perfect consideration etc.

This letter made my heart beat horribly. After having been the talk of Paris for a year, the idea of going to exhibit myself as a spectacle in Mme d'Houdetot's presence made me tremble, and I had trouble finding enough courage to bear this trial. Nevertheless, since she and St. Lambert wanted it very much, since d'Epinay was speaking in the name of all those invited, and since he named no one whom I would not be very glad to see, I did not believe, all things considered, that I was compromising myself by accepting a dinner to which I had been invited by everyone as it were. Thus I promised. On Sunday the weather was bad. M. d'Epinay sent me his carriage, and I went.

My arrival caused a sensation. I have never received a more affectionate welcome. One would have said that the whole company felt how much I needed to be reassured. Only French hearts know this sort of delicacy. Nevertheless, I found more people than I had expected. Among others the Comte d'Houdetot, whom I did not know at all, and his sister, Mme de Blainville, whom I could have done without. She had come to Eaubonne several times the previous year, and in our solitary walks her sister-in-law had often left her the boredom of waiting impatiently.[34] As a result of this she had nourished a resentment against me which she satisfied during this dinner entirely at her ease; for one feels[35] that the presence of the Comte d'Houdetot and of St. Lambert did not put the laughers on my side, and that a man who is perplexed in the easiest conversations was not extremely brilliant in that one. I have never suffered so much, nor born a worse countenance, nor received more unexpected attacks. Finally, when we had left the table, I distanced myself from that Megaera;[36] I had the pleasure of seeing St. Lambert and Mme d'Houdetot drawing near me, and we chatted together a part of the afternoon, about indifferent things in truth, but with the same familiarity as before my going astray. This action was not lost on my heart, and if St. Lambert could have read in it he would surely have been satisfied. I can swear that, although the sight of Mme d'Houdetot had given me palpitations to the point of swooning when I arrived, I almost did not think about her at all when I was going home; I was occupied only with St. Lambert.

In spite of Mme de Blainville's malicious sarcasms, this dinner did me a lot of good, and I congratulated myself extremely for not having refused it. I recognized, not only that the intrigues of Grimm and the Holbackians had not detached my old acquaintances from me,* but—what gratified me even more—that the feelings of Mme d'Houdetot and of St. Lambert were less changed than I had believed, and I finally understood that there was more jealousy than low esteem in his keeping her separated from me. That consoled me and calmed me. Now that I was certain of not being

---

*That is what I still believed in the simplicity of my heart when I was writing my confessions.

an object of disdain to those who were the object of my esteem, I worked on my own heart with more courage and success. If I did not succeed entirely in extinguishing a guilty and unfortunate passion in it, at least I ruled what was left of it so well that it has not made me commit a single fault since that time. Mme d'Houdetot's copies, which she engaged me to take up again, my works, which I continued to send her when they appeared, still drew me some inconsequential but obliging messages and notes from her direction now and then. She even did more, as will be seen in what follows, and the reciprocal behavior of all three of us, when our dealings had ceased, can serve as a model of the way decent people separate when it no longer suits them to see each other.

Another advantage this dinner procured me was that it was spoken about in Paris, and served as an unanswerable refutation to the rumor my enemies spread everywhere that I had become mortally estranged from everyone who was at it, and above all from M. d'Epinay. Upon leaving the Hermitage I had written him a very decent letter of thanks to which he responded no less decently, and mutual attentions did not cease both with him and with his brother M. de la Live,[37] who even came to see me at Montmorency and sent me his engravings. Aside from Mme d'Houdetot's two sisters-in-law I have never been on bad terms with anyone in her family.

My letter to d'Alembert had a great success. All my works had done so; but this one was more favorable to me. It taught the public to distrust the insinuations of the Holbachic coterie. When I went to the Hermitage it predicted with its ordinary conceitedness that I would not remain there for three months. When it saw that I had remained there for twenty, and that I still settled my residence in the country when I was forced to leave, it maintained that this was pure obstinacy, that I was bored to death in my retirement; but that gnawed by pride, I preferred to perish there as the victim of my stubbornness than to retract what I said and come back to Paris. The letter to d'Alembert breathed a gentleness of soul that was not felt to be at all pretended. If I had been gnawed by ill humor in my retirement it would have been felt in my tone. Ill humor did prevail in all the writings I had done at Paris: it no longer reigned in the first one I had done in the country. That remark was decisive for those who know how to observe. They saw that I had returned into my element.

Nevertheless, this same work, entirely full of gentleness as it was, still made me a new enemy among literary people through my doltishness and usual bad luck. I had made the acquaintance of Marmontel at M. de la Popliniére's, and we had kept up our acquaintance at the Baron's.[38] At that time Marmontel was editing *The Mercury of France*. Since out of pride I did not send my works to the authors of periodicals, and since I nevertheless wanted to send him this one without him believing that it was based on this title nor to get him to speak about it in *The Mercury*, I wrote on his copy that it was not for the author of the *Mercury* but for M. Marmontel. I believed I was paying him a very fine compliment; he believed he saw a cruel offense in it and became my irreconcilable enemy. He wrote against this same letter with politeness but with a bile that is easily felt, and since then he has not missed any occasion to injure me in society, and to abuse me indirectly in his works: it is so difficult to handle the very irritable amour-propre of literary people, and one must be so careful not to leave anything that can have even the slightest equivocal appearance in the compliments one pays them.

Having become tranquil on all sides, I took advantage of the leisure and independence in which I found myself to take up my works again with more consistency. That winter I finished Julie and I sent it to Rey, who had it printed the following year. This labor was nevertheless interrupted again by a little, and even rather disagreeable, diversion. I learned that the Opera was preparing a new performance of the *Village Soothsayer*. Being outraged at seeing those people arrogantly disposing of my property, I again took up the Memorandum that I had sent to M. d'Argenson and which had remained without an answer,[39] and once I had touched it up I had the Resident from Geneva, M. Sellon,[40] send it back along with a letter to M. the Comte de St. Florentin[41]—who had replaced M. d'Argenson in the department of the Opera—which he was kind enough to take it upon himself to do. M. de St. Florentin promised an answer and did not make any. Duclos, to whom I wrote what I had done, spoke about it to the little violins,[42] who offered to return to me, not my Opera, but my free admission which I could no longer take advantage of. Seeing that I could not hope for any justice from any side, I abandoned this business, and, without responding to any of my arguments or listening to them, the direction of the Opera has continued to dispose of as its own property and to draw its profit from *The Village Soothsayer*, which very incontestably belongs only to me alone.*

Since I had shaken off the yoke of my tyrants, I was leading an even and peaceable enough life; having been deprived of the charm of excessively lively attachments I was also free of the weight of their chains. Disgusted with the protector friends who wanted to dispose of my destiny absolutely, and to subjugate me to their so-called benefits in spite of myself,

---

*Since then it belongs to them through a new agreement they made with me very recently.[43]

I was resolved to restrict myself henceforward to relations of simple benevolence which make up life's pleasantness without troubling freedom and whose foundation is made by a footing of equality. I had as many relations of this sort as I needed in order to taste the sweetness of freedom[44] without suffering dependency from them, and as soon as I had tried this type of life, I felt that this was the one that suited me at my age in order to finish my days in calm far from the storm, the fallings out and the worries in which I had just been half submerged.

During my stay at the Hermitage and since my establishment at Montmorency I had made several acquaintances in my neighborhood which were pleasant for me and who did not subject me to anything. At their head was the young Loyseau de Mauleon[45] who, beginning at the Bar at that time, did not[46] know what his place would be there. I did not have the doubts he did. I soon showed him the illustrious career he is seen to be fulfilling today. I predicted to him that if he made himself severe in the selection of cases, and if he was never anything but the defender of justice and virtue, his genius—being raised up by this sublime feeling—would equal that of the greatest orators. He followed my advice and he has felt its effect. His defense of M. de Portes is worthy of Demosthenes.[47] Every year he came to a quarter of a league from the Hermitage to pass his vacation at St. Brice in the fief of Mauleon belonging to his mother and where formerly the great Bossuet had lodged. Such a series of masters would make it hard to maintain the same level of nobility in this fief.

From the same village of St. Brice I had the book dealer Guérin,[48] an intelligent man, lettered, amiable, and of the first rank in his station. He also gave me the acquaintance of his correspondent and friend, Jean Neaulme,[49] a Book dealer from Amsterdam, who published *Emile* later on.

Even closer than St. Brice I had M. Maltor,[50] the Curate of Groslay, better made to be a Statesman and Minister than a Village Curate, and to whom they would have given at least a Diocese to govern if talents decided places. He had been the Comte du Luc's Secretary, and had known Jean Baptiste Rousseau intimately. As full of esteem for the memory of that illustrious exile as of horror for that of the sly Saurin,[51] he knew many curious anecdotes about both of them which Seguy[52] had not put into the life of the former which was still in manuscript, and he assured me that, far from having ever had anything to complain about from him, the Comte du Luc had conserved the most ardent[53] friendship for him until the end of his life. M. Maltor, to whom M. de Vintimille[54] had given that rather good retirement after his patron's death, had formerly been employed in many affairs, which he still remembered even though he was old and about which he reasoned very well. His conversation, no less instructive than amusing, did not feel the effects of his village curacy at all: he united the tone of a man of the world with the knowledge of a scholarly man. Of all my permanent neighbors he was the one whose society was the most pleasant to me and whom I had the most regret at leaving.

At Montmorency I had the Oratorians and among others Father Bertier,[55] a physics professor, to whom I was attached by means of a certain air of geniality that I found in him in spite of some light varnish of pedantry. Nevertheless, I had difficulty reconciling this great simplicity with the desire and the art he had of intruding everywhere, among the great, among the women, among the pious, among the philosophers; he knew how to be all things to all people. I enjoyed myself extremely with him, I spoke about him to everyone. Apparently what I said about him got back to him. One day, while sneering, he thanked me for having found him to be a good fellow. In his smile I found something indefinably sardonic which totally changed his physiognomy in my eyes, and which has often come back to me in memory since then. I cannot compare this smile any better than to Panurge's when he bought Dindenaut's sheep.[56] Our acquaintance had begun a little time after my arrival at the Hermitage, where he came to see me very often. I was already established at Montmorency when he left it to return to reside in Paris. There he often saw Mme Le Vasseur. One day when I least expected it, he wrote to me on behalf of that woman to inform me that M. Grimm was offering to take her upkeep upon himself and to ask for my permission to accept that offer.[57] I learned that it consisted in a pension of three hundred Livres, and that Mme Le Vasseur was to come to reside at Deuil between la Chevrette and Montmorency. I will not say what impression this news made on me, which would have been less surprising if Grimm had had ten thousand livres of income, or some relation with that woman that was easier to understand, and if it had not been made into such a great crime for me to have brought her into the country, where nevertheless he was now pleased to bring her back, as if she had become younger since that time. I understood that the good old woman was asking me for this permission, which she could have very well done without if I had refused it, only so that she would not expose herself to losing what I was giving her from my side. Although this charity appeared very extraordinary to me, it did not strike me then as much as it did later on. But if I had known everything that I have penetrated since, I would have given my consent just as much as I did, and as I was obliged to do, unless I were to raise the bid on M. Grimm's offer. From that time Father Bertier cured me a little of the imputation of good fellow which had appeared so funny to him, and of which I had so thoughtlessly accused him.

This same Father Bertier knew two men who also sought out my acquaintance, I do not know why: for there was assuredly little relation between their tastes and mine. They were children of Melchisedec,[58] whose country or family or probably whose real name was not known. They were Jansenists and passed for disguised Priests, perhaps because of their ridiculous fashion of wearing rapiers to which they were attached. The prodigious mystery they put into all their behavior gave them an air of leaders of a faction, and I never doubted that they wrote the *Ecclesiastic Gazette*.[59] One, tall, benign, fawning, was called M. Ferrand; the other short, thickset, a touchy sneerer was called M. Minard. They referred to each other as cousins. They lodged in Paris with d'Alembert in the home of his nurse called Mme Rousseau, and they had taken a little apartment at Montmorency to pass the summers there. They did their housekeeping themselves without a maid and without an errand-boy. Each alternately had his week to go shopping, do the cooking, and sweep the house. Otherwise they kept themselves up well enough; sometimes we ate at each others' homes. I do not know why they cared about me, as for me I cared about them only because they played chess, and I endured four hours of boredom in order to obtain a poor little game. Since they intruded everywhere and wanted to get mixed up in everything, Therese called them *the Godmothers*,[60] and this name stayed with them at Montmorency.

Along with my landlord M. Mathas, who was a good man, such were my principal acquaintances in the country. There were enough left at Paris for me to live there with pleasure when I wished, outside of the sphere of literary people, in which I counted only Duclos alone as a friend: for De Leyre was still too young, and although he had completely detached himself from the philosophic clique after he had seen its maneuvers with regard to me close up, at least I believed he had,[61] I still could not forget how ready he had been to make himself the spokesman for all those people with me.

Foremost, I had my old and respectable friend M. Roguin. He was a friend from the good times whom I did not owe at all to my writings, but to myself, and whom I have always preserved for that reason. I had the good Lenieps my compatriot, and his daughter Mme Lambert, who was still alive at that time. I had a young Genevan called Coindet,[62] a good boy it seemed to me, painstaking, officious, zealous; but ignorant, credulous, a glutton, supercilious, who had come to see me at the beginning of my residence at the Hermitage, and without any other introducer than himself, had soon established himself in my home in spite of me. He had some taste for drawing and knew artists. He was useful for me for the Engravings of Julie; he took the direction of the drawings and plates upon himself, and discharged this commission well.

I had M. Dupin's house which, while less brilliant than during Mme Dupin's fine days, still did not fail to be one of the best houses in Paris because of its masters' merit, and because of the select society[63] who gathered together there. Since I had preferred no one to them, since I had left them only to live freely, they had not ceased seeing me with friendship, and I was sure of being well received by Mme Dupin at all times. I could even count her as one of my country neighbors, since they had made an establishment at Clichy where I sometimes went to pass a day or two and I would have gone more if Mme Dupin and Mme de Chenonceaux had lived on better terms. But the difficulty of being divided in the same house between two women who did not have an affinity for each other made Clichy too bothersome for me. Since I was attached to Mme de Chenonceaux with a more equal and more familiar friendship, I had the pleasure of seeing her more at my ease at Deuil, almost at my door, where she had rented a little house, and even at my home, where she came to see me rather often.

I had Mme de Crequi, who had thrown herself into high piety and had stopped seeing d'Alembert, Marmontel, and the majority of the literary people, except, I believe, the Abbé Trublet,[64] at that time a sort of half sanctimonious fellow, with whom even she was rather bored. As for me, whom she had sought out, I lost neither her benevolence nor her correspondence. She sent me some Poultry from Le Mans for a New Years gift, and she planned to come to see me the following year, when one of Mme de Luxembourg's trips interfered with hers. I owe her a place apart here; she will always have a distinguished one in my remembrances.[65]

I had one man who, aside from Roguin, I should have put first in the list: my old colleague and friend de Carrio, formerly titular secretary of the Spanish Embassy at Venice, then in Sweden, where he was made chargé d'affaires by his Court, and finally at present appointed Secretary to the Embassy at Paris. He came to surprise me at Montmorency when I least expected him there. He was decorated with an order of Spain whose name I have forgotten, with a fine cross in precious stones. In his proofs of nobility he had been obliged to add a letter to his name of Carrio, and bore that of the Chevalier de Carrion. I found him still the same, the same excellent heart,[66] a mind daily more lovable. I would have taken up the same intimacy with him as before if Coindet, interposing himself between us in his usual way, had not taken advantage of my remoteness to insinuate himself into my place and into his confidence in my name, and to supplant me as a result of zeal for serving me.

The memory of Carrion recalls to me that of one of my country neighbors about whom I would be all the more wrong not to speak, since I have to confess a very inexcusable[67] wrong with regard to him. This was the decent M. Le Blond, who had done me a service at Venice, and who had just made a trip to France with his family and had rented a country house at la Briche not far from Montmorency.* As soon as I learned that he was my neighbor my heart was overjoyed and I made it even more of a festival than a duty to go to pay a visit to him. I left as early as the very next day to do so. I was met by some people who were coming to see me and with whom I had to return. Two days after I leave again; he had dined at Paris with his whole family. A third time he was home: I heard some women's voices, at the door I saw a carriage that scared me. At least the first time, I wanted to see him at my ease and chat with him about our former connections. Finally I put off my visit so much from one day to the other that shame of fulfilling such a duty so late made me not fulfill it at all: after having dared to wait so long I no longer dared to show myself. This negligence, with which M. Le Blond could only be justly indignant, gave my laziness with regard to him the appearance of ingratitude, and nevertheless I felt my heart so little guilty, that if I had been able to give M. Le Blond some true pleasure, even unknown to him, I am very sure that he would not have found me lazy. But indolence, negligence, and delays in little duties to fulfill have always done me more wrong than great[68] vices. My worst faults have been of omission: I have rarely done what should not be done, and unfortunately even more rarely have I done what should.

Since I have returned to my acquaintances from Venice here, I ought not to forget one that is connected to it and which I had interrupted in the same way as the others except for a much shorter time. That is M. de Jonville,[69] who had continued to do many friendly things for me since his return from Genoa. He liked to see me very much and to chat with me about affairs from Italy and M. de Montaigu's follies, about which on his side he knew many features from the offices of foreign affairs in which he had many connections. I also had the pleasure of seeing again in his home my former comrade Dupont, who had purchased a commission in his province and whose business sometimes brought him back to Paris. Little by little M. de Jonville became so eager to have me that he even became bothersome because of it, and although we were lodged in neighborhoods extremely far apart, there was an uproar between us if I passed an entire week without going to dine at his home. When he was at Jonville he always wanted to bring me there; but after having gone once to pass a week which appeared extremely long to me, I no longer wanted

---

* Since I was full of my old and blind confidence when I wrote this, I was very far from suspecting the true motive and effect of this trip to Paris.

to go back. M. de Jonville was certainly a decent and gallant man; even amiable in certain respects; but he had little wit, he was handsome, a bit of a narcissist, and fairly boring. He had a peculiar collection, perhaps unique in the world, with which he was very much occupied, with which he also occupied his guests who were sometimes less amused by it than he was. It was a very complete collection of all the farces of the Court of Paris from more than fifty years ago, where one found many anecdotes which it would have been useless to look for anywhere else. Here are some memoranda for the history of France, which one would hardly take into one's head with any other nation.

One day, at the height of our best terms he gave me such a cold, such an icy welcome, so little in his ordinary tone that, after having given him the chance to explain himself, and even having asked him to, I left his house with the resolution which I have kept of not setting foot in it again; for I rarely go where I have been badly received once, and there was no Diderot here who pleaded on behalf of M. de Jonville. I sought vainly in my head what wrong I could have committed toward him: I found nothing. I was certain that I had never spoken about him or his family except in the most honorable way; for I was sincerely attached to him, and aside from the fact that I had only good to say about him, my most inviolable maxim has always been not [70] to speak any way but honorably about the houses I frequented.

Finally as a result of ruminating, here is what I conjectured. The last time we had seen each other he had given me supper in the home of some girls of his acquaintance with two or three clerks of foreign affairs, very amiable people, and who did not have either a libertine air or tone at all; and I can swear that on my side the evening was passed by meditating rather sadly about the unfortunate fate of these creatures. I did not pay my share because M. de Jonville gave us the supper, and I gave nothing to these girls because I did not make them earn the payment I could have offered them as with la Padoana. We all left rather gay and on very good terms. Without returning to these girls' home, three or four days afterward I went to dine at M. de Jonville's whom I had not seen again since then, and who gave me the welcome I have told. Since I could not imagine another cause for it than some misunderstanding relative to this supper and since I saw that he did not want to explain himself I made my decision and ceased to see him: but I continued to send him my works; he often had his compliments paid to me, and one day when I met him in the Chauffoir [71] of the Comedy, he made me some obliging reproaches over the fact that I no longer went to see him which did not bring me back. Thus this business had more the appearance of pouting [72] than of a rupture. Nevertheless, since I had not seen him again and had no longer heard him spoken of since that time, it was too late to go back after an interruption of several years. This is why M. de Jonville does not enter my list here, although I frequented his house for a rather long time.

I will not inflate the same list at all with many other less familiar acquaintances or those who had ceased to be so through my absence, and whom I did not fail to see sometimes in the country both at my home and in my neighborhood, such, for example, as the Abbés de Condillac, de Mably, Messieurs de Mairan, de la Live, de Boisgelou, Vatelet, Ancelet,[73] and others it would take too long to name. I will also pass lightly over M. de Margency,[74] Gentleman ordinary of the King, former member of the Holbachic coterie which he had left as I had, and former friend of Mme d'Epinay from whom he had detached himself as I had, and his friend Desmahis, the celebrated but ephemeral author of the Play *The Impertinent Man*. The former was my country neighbor, since his estate of Margency was near Montmorency. We were old acquaintances; but the neighborhood and a certain conformity of experiences brought us more closely together. The latter died a little later. He had merit and intelligence: but he was a bit the model for his comedy, a little foppish around women, and was not extremely regretted.

But I cannot omit a new correspondence from that time which has influenced the rest of my life too much for me to neglect to call attention to its beginning. This was M. de Lamoignon de Malesherbes, First President of the Court of Excise, charged at that time with book dealing, which he governed with as much enlightenment as gentleness, and to the great satisfaction of literary people.[75] I had not seen him a single time at Paris; nevertheless, I had always experienced the most obliging readiness on his part with regard to censorship, and I knew that on more than one occasion he had handled the people who wrote against me extremely roughly. I had some new proofs of his kindness on the subject of the printing of Julie; for—because it was extremely costly to have the proof-sheets of such a large work sent from Amsterdam by the post—he permitted them to be addressed to him since he had a franking privilege and he sent them to me franked also under the counter signature of his father M. the Chancellor. When the work was printed he permitted the sale in the Kingdom only after an edition he had made for my profit in spite of me: since this profit would have been a theft on my part made from Rey to whom I had sold my manuscript, I not only did not want to accept the present intended for me without Rey's assent, which he very generously granted; but I also wanted to share with him the hundred pistoles to which this present amounted and which he did not accept. For these hundred pistoles I had the nuisance, about which M. de Malesherbes had not warned me, of seeing my work horribly mutilated, and of hindering the sale of the good edition until the bad one was gone.[76]

I have always regarded M. de Malesherbes as a man of an unassailable uprightness. Nothing that has happened to me has ever made me doubt his probity for a moment: but because he is as weak as he is decent, he sometimes injures the people in whom he takes an interest as a result of wanting to preserve them. Not only did he have more than a hundred pages cut out of the Paris edition;[77] but in the copy of the good edition which he sent to Mme de Pompadour he made a cut that could bear the name of a breach of faith. Somewhere in that work it says that the wife of a Charcoal-burner is more respectable than the mistress of a Prince.[78] This sentence had come to me in the heat of composition without any application, I swear it. Upon rereading the work, I saw that this application would be made. Nevertheless, out of the very imprudent maxim of not removing anything out of respect to the applications that could be made when I had the witness in my conscience of not having made them while writing, I did not want to remove this sentence, and I satisfied myself by substituting the word *Prince* for the word *King* which I had put at first. This softening did not appear sufficient to M. de Malesherbes: he cut out the entire sentence in a sheet he had expressly printed and glued as cleanly as possible in Mme de Pompadour's copy. She was not unaware of this sleight-of-hand trick. Some good souls were found who informed her of it. As for me, I did not learn about it until a long time afterward, when I was beginning to feel its consequences.

Is this not the first origin of the open but implacable hatred of another Lady who was in a similar position without me knowing anything about it, nor even being acquainted with her when I wrote this passage?[79] When the Book was published the acquaintance had been made and I was very anxious. I said so to the Chevalier de Lorenzy,[80] who made fun of me and assured me that the Lady was so little offended by it that she had not even paid attention to it. I believed him, a little lightly, perhaps, and I calmed myself extremely inappropriately.

At the beginning of winter I received a new mark of M. de Malesherbes's kindness for which I was extremely grateful, although I did not judge it appropriate to take advantage of it. A position was vacant on the *Journal of the Learned*. Margency wrote to me to propose it as if on his own initiative. But it was easy for me to understand from the course of his letter (Bundle C. #33) that he had been instructed and authorized; and he notified me himself later on (Bundle C. #47)[81] that he had been given the commission of making me this offer. The work for this position was a very small thing. It was only a question of two summaries a month of books which would be brought to me, without me ever being obliged to make any trip to Paris, not even to make a visit of thanks to the Magistrate. By means of this I would enter a society of literary people of the first merit, Messieurs de Mairan, Clairaut, de Guignes, and the Abbé Barthelemi, with the first two of whom I was already acquainted, and with the two others it would be very good to become so.[82] Finally for such hardly troublesome work which I could do[83] so conveniently, there was an honorarium of eight hundred francs attached to this position. I deliberated for several hours before deciding, and I can swear that the [only thing that made me hesitate was the][84] fear of getting Margency angry, and of displeasing M. de Malesherbes. But finally the unbearable bother of not being able to work at my own pace and of being commanded by time; much worse still, the certainty of fulfilling badly the functions with which I had to burden myself, overshadowed everything, and made me decide to refuse a position for which I was not fit. I knew that all my talent came only from a certain warmth of soul about the matters I had to treat,[85] and that it was only the love of the great, the true, the beautiful that could animate my genius, and what would the subjects of the majority of the books I had to summarize, and the books themselves, have mattered to me. My indifference for the thing would have frozen my pen and stupefied my mind. They imagined that I could write as a trade as all the other literary people did, instead of which I could never write except out of passion. That was assuredly not what was needed at the *Journal of the Learned*. Thus I wrote a letter of thanks to Margency phrased with all possible politeness, in which I gave him the particulars of my reasons so well that neither he nor M. de Malesherbes could believe that either ill humor or pride entered into my refusal. Also both approved of it without giving me a less warm welcome, and the secret of this business was so well kept that the public never had the slightest wind of it.

This proposition did not come at a favorable moment for making me accept it. For some time, I had been forming the plan of leaving literature altogether and above all the trade of Author. Everything that had just happened to me had absolutely disgusted me with literary people, and I had felt that it was impossible to follow the same career without having some relations with them. I was hardly less disgusted with society people and in general with the mixed life I had just been leading, half for myself and half for social circles for which I was not at all made. I felt more than ever and from a constant experience that every unequal association is always disadvantageous to the weak party. Living with opulent people from another station than the one I had chosen, I was obliged to imitate them in many things even though I did not maintain a house like them, and tiny expenses that were nothing for them were as ruinous as they were indispensable for me. If another man goes to a country house, he is served by his lackey, both at table and in his room; he sends him to look for everything he needs: having nothing to do directly with the people of the house, not even seeing them, he gives them tips only when and as it pleases him: but I, alone, without a servant, was at the mercy of those of the house whose good graces I had to win so as not to have to put up with a lot, and since I was treated as the equal of their master, I also had to treat the people the same way and even do more than anyone else for them, because in fact I needed them much more.[86] I could let this pass when there were few servants; but in the houses into which I went there were many, all very arrogant, very roguish, very alert, I mean for their own interest, and the scoundrels knew how to act in such a way that I needed them all one after the other. The women of Paris, who are so intelligent, have no accurate idea on that point, and as a result of wanting to spare my purse they ruined me. If I supped in the city a little distant from my home, instead of allowing me to send for a cab, the Lady of the house had her horses brought out to bring me back; she was extremely glad to spare me the twenty-four sous for the cab: as for the écu I gave the lackey and the coachmen, she did not dream of it.[87] Did a woman write to me from Paris to the Hermitage or at Montmorency? since she was sorry about the four sous of post that her letter would have cost me,[88] she sent it to me by one of her people who arrived on foot, bathed in sweat, and to whom I gave something to eat and an écu that he had assuredly well earned. Did she propose that I go spend a week or two with her in her country home, she said to herself, "This at least will be an economy for that poor chap; during this time his nourishment will cost him nothing." She did not dream that also during this time I was not working at all, that my housekeeping and rent and my linen and clothes did not go on any less, that I paid my barber double, and he did not fail to cost me more in her home than he would have in mine. Although I limited my little gifts only to the houses in which I lived customarily, they did not fail to be ruinous for me.[89] I can assure you that I spent a good twenty-five écus at Mme d'Houdetot's house at Eaubonne where I slept only four or five times, and more than a hundred pistoles both at Epinay and at la Chevrette during the five or six years that I was there the most assiduously. These expenses are unavoidable for a man of my disposition who does not know how to provide himself with anything nor to improvise anything, nor to put up with the appearance of a Valet who is growling, and who serves you while looking sullen. Even at Mme Dupin's, where I was a part of the house and where I rendered a thousand services to the servants, I never received their services except at the point of my money. Afterward I had to renounce completely these little liberalities which my situation no longer allowed me to make and then I was made to feel even more harshly the disadvantage of frequenting people from another station than one's own.[90]

Still if that life had been to my taste, I would have consoled myself for an onerous expense dedicated to my pleasures: but to ruin oneself in order to be bored was too unbearable, and I had felt the weight of this style of life so much that, taking advantage of the freedom in which I found myself at that time, I was determined to perpetuate it, to renounce totally high society, the composition of books, all literary dealings, and to close myself up for the rest of my days in the narrow and peaceful sphere for which I felt myself born.

The proceeds from the *Letter to d'Alembert* and *La Nouvelle Héloïse* had restored my finances which had been extremely drained at the Hermitage. I found myself with around a thousand écus in hand. *Emile*, which I had set myself to in earnest when I had finished *Héloïse*, was extremely far along, and its proceeds were supposed at least to double that sum. I formed the plan of placing this fund so as to make a little life annuity for myself which along with my copying could make me subsist without writing any more. I still had two works in progress. The first was my *Political Institutions*. I examined the condition of this book, and I found that it still required several years of work. I did not have the courage to pursue it and wait until it was finished to execute my resolution. Thus, renouncing this work, I resolved to extract from it what could be detached, then to burn all the rest, and pushing this work with zeal, without interrupting that on *Emile*, in less than two years I put the finishing touches on the *Social Contract*.

There remained the *Dictionary of Music*. It was unskilled research that could be done at any time, and which had no other object than pecuniary proceeds. I waited to abandon it or to finish it at my ease, according to whether my other assembled resources would make it necessary or superfluous. With regard to *The Sensitive Morality* the undertaking of which had remained in outline, I abandoned it totally.

Since, if I could dispense with copying altogether, my ultimate plan was to get far away from Paris where the abundance of chance arrivals rendered my subsistence costly and deprived me of time to provide for it; in order to forestall the boredom in my retirement into which they say an Author falls when he has abandoned the pen, I reserved an occupation for myself that could fill the void of my solitude without tempting me to have anything published in my life. I do not know what whim made Rey press me for a long time to write the memoirs of my life.[91] Although they might not have been extremely interesting up to that time from the facts, I felt that they could become so by the frankness I could put into them, and I resolved to make them into a unique work by means of a truthfulness without precedent, so that at least once a man could be seen as he was inside. I had always laughed at the false naiveté of Montaigne who, while making a pretence of admitting his flaws, takes great care to give himself only amiable ones: while I, who always believed myself to be and who still believes myself to be, taking everything into account, the best of men, felt that there is no human interior as pure as it can be, that does not harbor some odious vice. I knew that I was depicted in public under features so little like my own and sometimes so deformed that in spite of the evil, about which I wanted to hold back nothing, I could still only gain by showing myself as I was. Moreover, since it was not possible to do this without letting other people be seen as they were also, and consequently since this work could not appear until after my death and that of many others, that emboldened me further to make my confessions which I would never have to blush about in front of anyone. Then I resolved to dedicate my leisure to executing this undertaking well, and I began to collect letters and papers that could guide or awaken my memory, extremely regretting all that I had torn up, burnt, lost up to then.[92]

This project of absolute retirement, one of the most sensible I had ever made, was strongly stamped in my mind, and I was already working toward its execution, when Heaven—which was preparing another destiny for me—threw me into a new whirlwind. Montmorency, that old and beautiful patrimony of the illustrious house of that name, does not belong to it any more since the confiscation. Through Duc Henri's sister it passed into the house of Condé, which changed the name of Montmorency into Anguien, and this Duchy has no Chateau other than an old Tower where the archives are kept and where the homages of vassals are received.[93] But at Montmorency or Anguien one sees a private house built by Croisat[94] (called "the poor") which, since it is as magnificent as the most superb chateaux, deserves and bears the name of one.[95] The imposing aspect of this beautiful edifice, the terrace on which it is built, its view, perhaps unique in the world, its vast drawing room painted by an excellent hand, its garden planted by the famous Le Nôtre;[96] all this forms a whole whose striking majesty nevertheless has an indefinable something simple that sustains and nourishes admiration. Twice every year, M. the Maréchal Duc de Luxembourg, who occupied this house at that time, came into this country where formerly his fathers were the masters to pass five or six weeks, as a simple inhabitant, but with a lustre that did not degenerate at all from the former splendor of his house.[97] On the first trip he made there after my establishment at Montmorency, M. and Mme the Maréchale sent a valet-de-chambre to pay me a compliment on their behalf and to invite me to sup with them whenever I might please. Each time they returned they did not fail to repeat the same compliment and the same invitation. That reminded me of Mme de Beuzenval sending me to dine in the servants's hall.[98] Times had changed; but I had remained the same. I did not want to be sent to dine in the servants's hall, and cared little about the table of grandees. I would have preferred them to leave me as I was without making much of me and without demeaning me. I answered M. and Mme de Luxembourg's acts of politeness decently and respectfully; but I did not accept their offers at all, and both my indispositions and my timid mood and perplexity at speaking made me shudder so much at the mere idea of presenting myself in an assemblage of people from the Court that I did not even go to the Chateau to pay a visit of thanks, although I understood well enough that that was what they were looking for, and that all this eagerness was an affair of curiosity rather than of benevolence.

Nevertheless, the advances continued and even kept increasing. When Mme the Comtesse de Boufflers,[99] who was strongly connected with Mme the Maréchale, came to Montmorency, she sent for news about me and to propose that she come to see me. I answered as I should, but I stayed put. On the Easter trip of the following year 1759, the Chevalier de Lorenzy, who was in the Court of M. the Prince de Conti and in Mme de Luxembourg's social circle, came to see me several times; we struck up an acquaintance; he urged me to go to the Chateau: I did nothing about it. Finally one afternoon when I least expected it, I saw M. the Maréchal de Luxembourg arrive followed by five or six people. This time there was no longer any way get out of it and I could not avoid, under pain of being an arrogant and ill-bred person, returning his visit and going to pay my Court to Mme the Maréchale, on whose behalf he had loaded me with the most obliging messages. Thus under baneful auspices there began relations from which I could no longer defend myself, but which a too well-founded [100] presentiment made me dread until I was committed to them.

I feared Mme de Luxembourg excessively. I knew that she was amiable. I had seen her several times at the Theater and at Mme Dupin's, ten or twelve years before, when she was the Duchesse de Boufflers, and when she was still shining with her first beauty.[101] But she passed for wicked, and in such a great Lady this reputation made me tremble. No sooner did I see her than I was subjugated. I found her to be charming with that charm that is proof against time, all the more fit to act on my heart. I expected to find in her a mordant conversation full of epigrams. That was not at all the case; it was much better. Mme de Luxembourg's conversation does not sparkle with wit. It is not sallies and it is not even exactly finesse: but it is an exquisite delicacy that is never striking and that always pleases. Her flatteries are all the more intoxicating since they are very simple; one would say they are escaping her without her thinking about it, and that it is her heart that is pouring itself out, solely because it is too full. From the first visit, I believed I noticed that, in spite of my awkward manner and my heavy phrases, I did not displease her. All the women of the Court know how to persuade you of that when they want to, true or not, but not all know—as Mme de Luxembourg does—how to make this persuasion so sweet for you that you no longer take it into your head to want to doubt it. From the first day my confidence in her might have been as complete as it became before long, if her daughter-in-law, Mme the Duchesse de Montmorenci [102] (a rather malicious young fool, and I think a bit of a busybody), had not taken it into her head to tackle me, and all through her mother's many praises and the feigned teasing on her own account made me suspect they might be bantering with me.

Perhaps it would have been hard to reassure me about that fear with regard to the two Ladies, if the extreme kindness of M. the Maréchal had not confirmed to me that theirs was serious. Nothing could be more surprising, given my timid character, than the promptness with which I took him at his word about the footing of equality upon which he wished to put himself with me, unless perhaps it is the promptness with which he took me at my word himself about the absolute independence in which I wanted to live. Since both of us were persuaded that I was right to be content with my station and not to want to change it, neither he nor Mme de Luxembourg appeared for an instant to want to give their attention to my purse or my fortune; although I could not doubt the tender interest both of them took in me, they never proposed a position to me and never offered me their influence, except the one time that Mme de Luxembourg appeared to desire that I enter the French Academy. I brought up my Religion as mitigation: she told me that it was not an obstacle, or that she took it upon herself to remove it. I answered that whatever honor it might be for me to be a member of such an illustrious body, after having refused M. de Tressan's and in a way the King of Poland's offer for me to enter the Academy of Nancy, I could no longer decently enter any. Mme de Luxembourg did not insist and we did not speak about it again. This simplicity of dealings with such great lords who could do everything in my favor, since M. de Luxembourg was and well deserved to be the King's particular friend, contrasts very singularly with the continuous— and both tiresome and officious—concerns of the protector friends I had just left, who sought less to serve me than to demean me.

When M. the Maréchal had come to see me at Mont Louis, I had received him and his retinue with difficulty in my single room, not because I was obliged to make him sit down in the middle of my dirty dishes and my broken pots; but because my rotten floor was falling in ruins, and I was afraid that the weight of his retinue might make it collapse completely. Less occupied with my own danger than with the one which this good Lord's affability was making him run, I hastened to take him out of there in spite of the cool weather we were still having in order to lead him to my Turret which was completely open and had no fireplace. When he was there, I told him the reason that had required me to lead him there: he told Mme the Maréchale, and each of them pressed me to accept a lodging in the Chateau while I was waiting for my floor to be redone, or, if I preferred it, in the isolated building that was in the middle of the park, and which was called the Petit-Chateau. This enchanting residence deserves to be spoken about.

The park or garden of Montmorency is not in a plain like that of la Chevrette. It is uneven, hilly, mixed with hillocks and low-lying places, which the skillful artist used to vary the groves, the ornaments, the waters, the viewpoints, and, by virtue of art and genius, to multiply, so to speak, a space that was rather confined in itself. This Park is crowned at the high point by the terrace and the chateau; in the low point it forms a gorge that opens and widens toward the valley and the angle of which is filled up by a big sheet of water. The Petit Chateau about which I have spoken is between the orangery which occupies this widening space and this sheet of water which is surrounded by knolls well decorated by groves and trees. This building and the terrain that surrounds it formerly belonged to the celebrated Le Brun, who took pleasure in building and decorating it with that exquisite taste for ornaments and architecture with which this great Painter was well supplied.[103] Since then this chateau has been rebuilt, but always based on the design of the first master. It is small, simple, but elegant. Since it is in a hollow, between the pond of the orangery and the big sheet of water, and is consequently subject to humidity, it has been split in the middle by an open peristyle between two stories of columns, through which air flowing through the whole building keeps it dry in spite of its position. When one looks at this building from the opposite high point which gives a perspective on it, it appears absolutely surrounded by water, and one believes one is looking at an enchanted

Island or the prettiest of the three Borromean Islands called *Isola Bella* in Lake Magiore.

It was in this solitary edifice that I was given the choice of one of the four complete apartments it contained, aside from the ground floor composed of a ballroom, a billiard, room and a kitchen. I took the smallest and the simplest, above the kitchen which I also had.[104] It was of a charming cleanliness, its furnishings were white and blue. It is in this profound and delightful solitude in the middle of the woods and waters, of concerts from birds of every sort, of the scent of orange blossoms that, in a continuous ecstasy, I composed the fifth book of *Emile*, whose rather fresh coloring I owe in large part to the lively impression of the locality in which I was writing it.

With what eagerness did I run to breathe the fragrant air on the peristyle every morning at sunrise! what good café au lait did I take there tête-à-tête with my Therese! my cat and my dog gave us company. This retinue alone would have been enough for me for my whole life, without ever experiencing a moment of boredom. There I was in the terrestrial Paradise; I lived there just as innocently, and I tasted the same happiness.

On the trip in July, M. and Mme de Luxembourg showed me so many attentions and gave me so many endearments that, being lodged with them and loaded with their kindnesses, I could do no less than to respond to them by seeing them assiduously. I hardly left them at all: in the morning I went to pay my Court to Mme the Maréchale; I dined there, in the afternoon I went to take a walk with M. the Maréchal; but I did not sup there, because of the many people, and because they supped too late for me. Up to that point everything was suitable, and there was no harm in it yet if I had been able to keep myself there. But I have never been able to keep a mean in my attachments and simply fulfill the duties of society. I have always been everything or nothing; soon I was everything, and seeing myself feted, spoiled, by persons of that consideration, I exceeded the limits and acquired a friendship for them that one is allowed to have only for one's equals. I put all its familiarity into my manners, while they never relaxed the politeness to which they had accustomed me in theirs. Nevertheless, I was never very much at ease with Mme the Maréchale. Although I was not perfectly reassured about her character, I feared it less than her wit. Above all she impressed me with that. I knew that she was demanding in conversations, and that she had the right to be so. I knew that women and above all great Ladies absolutely want to be amused, that it would be better to offend them than to bore them, and from her commentaries about what the people who had just left had said, I judged about what she must think of my gaffes. In order to save myself from the embarrassment of speaking in front of her I ventured a supplement, this was to read. She had heard Julie spoken of; she knew that it was being published: she showed some eagerness to see this work; I offered to read it to her; she accepted. Every morning I made my way to her at ten o'clock: M. de Luxembourg came in; the door was closed. I read beside her bed, and measured out my readings so well, that there would have been some for the whole trip, even if it had not been interrupted.* The success of this expedient exceeded my expectation. Mme de Luxembourg was crazy about Julie and its Author; she talked about nothing but me, was interested in nothing but me, said sweet things to me all day long, kissed me ten times a day. She always wanted me to have my place at table beside her, and when some Lords wanted to take that place, she told them it was mine and had them put elsewhere. One can judge what impression these charming manners made on me, who is overcome by the slightest marks of affection. In fact I became attached to her in proportion to the attachment she bore witness of for me. When I saw this infatuation and felt so little attractiveness in my mind for maintaining it, my only fear was that it might change into distaste, and unfortunately for me this fear was only too well founded.

There must have been a natural opposition between her turn of mind and mine, since—independently of the crowds of gaffes that escaped me at each instant in conversation, even in my letters and when I was on the best terms with her—there were things that displeased her without me being able to imagine why. I will cite only one example and I could cite twenty of them. She knew that I was making a copy of *Héloïse* for Mme d'Houdetot at so much a page. She wanted to have one on the same terms. I promised it to her, and when I set her down in the number of my customers because of that,[106] I wrote her something obliging and decent on this subject, at least such was my intention. Here is her answer which fell on me out of the blue.[107]

From Versailles this Tuesday (Bundle C. #43)

I am delighted, I am content; your letter gave me an infinite pleasure and I am hurrying to tell you so in a letter and to thank you for it.

Here are the very words of your letter. *Although you are surely a very good customer, I have some trouble taking your money: in accordance with regular order it would be up to me to pay for the pleasure that I have in working for you.* I say no more about it to you. I am sorry that you never speak to me about your health. Nothing concerns me more. I love you with all my heart, and I assure you that I am very sad to

---

*The loss of a great battle, which afflicted the King very much, forced M. de Luxembourg to return to Court hurriedly.[105]

be writing to you about it, for I would be very happy to tell you so myself. M. de Luxembourg loves you and embraces you with all his heart.

When I received this letter I hastened to answer it while waiting for a more ample examination, to protest against every disagreeable interpretation, and after having occupied myself with this examination for several days with the anxiety one can conceive, and always understanding nothing of it, here is at last what my final answer was on this subject.

From Montmorency December 8, 1759

Since my last letter I have examined the passage in question hundreds of times. I have considered it in its proper and natural meaning; I have considered it in all the meanings that can be given to it, and I admit to you, Mme the Maréchale, that I no longer know whether it is I who owes you an apology, or whether it is not you who owes me one.

It is now ten years since these letters were written. I have often thought them over since that time; and my stupidity still is such on this article today, that I cannot succeed in feeling what she could have found in that passage, I do not say offensive, but even that could displease her.

In connection with this manuscript copy of the *Héloïse* that Mme de Luxembourg wished to have, I ought to say here what I imagined for giving it some marked advantage that could distinguish it from all others. I had written separately *The Adventures of Lord Edouard*,[108] and I had hesitated for a long time over inserting them either in their entirety or abridged in this work where they appeared out of place to me. I finally decided to cut them out altogether because they would have spoiled its touching simplicity since they did not have the same tone as all the rest. I had another, much stronger reason when I became acquainted with Mme de Luxembourg. It is that in these adventures there was a Roman Marquessa of a very odious character, several features of which, even though they were not applicable to her, could have been applied to her by those who knew only her reputation. Thus I congratulated myself very much about the decision I had made, and was confirmed in it. But in my ardent desire to enrich her copy with something that was not in any other, did I not think of these unfortunate adventures and form the project of making an abridgement of them to add to it. A crazy plan whose extravagance can be explained only by the blind [109] fatality that was dragging me to my ruin.

Quos vult perdere Juppiter dementat.[110]

I was stupid enough to make this abridgement very carefully, with much labor and to send her this piece as if it were the finest thing in the world; at the same time telling her, as was true, that I had burned the original, that the extract was for her alone and would never be seen by anyone unless she showed it herself; which, far from proving my prudence and my discretion to her, as I believed I was doing, only warned her about the judgment I myself bore about the application of the features with which she might have been offended. My imbecility was such that I did not suspect that she was not enchanted with my proceeding. She did not make me the great compliments about it that I expected, and never, to my very great surprise, did she speak to me about the notebook I had sent her. As for me, always being charmed by my conduct in this affair, it was only long afterward that I judged about the effect it had produced based on other indications.

I had still another, more reasonable, idea on behalf of her manuscript, but which was hardly less harmful[111] to me through more remote effects; so much does everything conspire toward the work of destiny when it calls a man to misfortune! I thought of adorning this manuscript with the drawings for the Engravings of Julie, which drawings happened to be in the same format as the manuscript. I asked Coindet for these drawings, which belonged to me by every sort of title, and all the more so since I had given over to him the proceeds from the plates, which were big sellers. Coindet is as wily as I am the opposite. As a result of being asked for these drawings, he succeeded in finding out what I wanted to do with them. Then, under the pretext of adding some ornament to these drawings, he caused them to be left with him, and ended by presenting them himself.

Ego versiculos feci, tulit alter honores.[112]

That put the finishing touch on introducing him to the hôtel de Luxembourg on a definite footing. Since my establishment at the Petit Chateau, he had come to see me there very often, and always in the morning, above all when M. and Mme de Luxembourg were at Montmorency. That made it so that in order to pass the day with him I did not go to the Chateau. I was reproached for these absences: I told the reason for them. I was pressed to bring M. Coindet along: I did so. That was what the rascal had been looking for. Thus, thanks to the excessive kindness they had for me, one of the clerks of M. Thelusson,[113] who sometimes wanted to invite him to his table when he had no one to dine with, found himself admitted all at once to that of a Maréchal of France with Princes, Duchesses, and everyone great who was at Court. I will never forget that one day when he was obliged to return to Paris early, M. the Maréchal said to the company after dinner, "Let us take a walk on the road to St. Denis, we will accompany M. Coindet." The poor boy could not stand it; he lost his head completely from it. As for me my heart was so moved that I could not say a single word. I followed behind weeping like a child, and dying from the desire to kiss this good Maréchal's footprints: but the sequel of this story of the copy made me run ahead of the time here. Let us take it up again in order, as much as my memory will permit me to.

As soon as the little house at Mont Louis was ready for me, I had it furnished cleanly, simply, and went back to establish myself there;[114] since I could not give up always having my own lodging as required by that law I had made when I left the Hermitage; but I could not resolve to give up my apartment at the Petit Chateau either. I kept its key and, since I was so fond of the pretty breakfasts on the peristyle, I often went to sleep there and sometimes passed two or three days there as in a country house. At that time I was perhaps the best and most agreeably lodged private man in Europe. My landlord M. Mathas, who was the best man in the world, had left the direction of the repairs for Mont Louis absolutely up to me, and wanted me to dispose of his workers without even getting mixed up in it himself. I thus found the way of making out of a single room on the second floor a complete apartment for myself, composed of a room, an antechamber, and a wardrobe. On the ground floor was the kitchen and Therese's room. The Turret served me as a study by means of a good windowed partition and a fireplace they had built there. When I was there I amused myself by adorning the terrace which was already shaded by two rows of young lime trees; I had two more added to them to make a study out of greenery; I had a table and stone benches put there; I surrounded it with lilacs, syringa, honeysuckle, I had a beautiful flower bed put there parallel to the two rows of trees; and that terrace, which was more elevated than the Chateau's, from which the view was at least as fine, and on which I had tamed multitudes of birds,[115] served me as a country room to receive M. and Mme de Luxembourg, M. the Duc de Villeroy, M. the Prince de Tingry, M. the Marquis d'Armentiéres, Mme the Duchesse de Montmorency, Mme the Duchesse de Boufflers, Mme the Comtesse de Valentinois, Mme the Comtesse de Boufflers, and[116] other people of that rank who did not disdain to make the pilgrimage from the chateau to Mont Louis by means of a very tiring climb.[117] I owed all these visits to the favor of M. and Mme de Luxembourg; I felt it, and my heart paid them much homage for it. In one of these transports of emotion, I once said to M. de Luxembourg while embracing him, "Ah, M. the Maréchal, I hated Grandees before I knew you, and I hate them even more, since you make me feel so much how easy it would be for them to make themselves adored."

Moreover, I put the question to everyone who saw me during that epoch, whether they ever noticed that this splendor dazzled me for an [118] instant, whether the vapor of that incense went to my head; whether they saw me less plain in my bearing, less simple in my manners, less responsive with the people, less familiar with my neighbors, less prompt to do a service to everyone when I was able to, without ever balking at the innumerable and often unreasonable importunities with which I was ceaselessly loaded. If my heart drew me to the Chateau of Montmorency out of my sincere attachment for its masters, it brought me back to my neighborhood the same way to taste the sweetness [119] of that even and simple life, outside of which there is no happiness whatsoever for me. Therese had struck up a friendship with the daughter of my neighbor, a mason named Pilleu: I did the same with the father, and after having dined at the Chateau in the morning, not without bother, but in order to please Mme the Maréchale, with what eagerness did I return in the evening to sup with the good man Pilleu and his family, sometimes at his home, sometimes at mine.

Aside from these two lodgings, I soon had a third one at the Hôtel de Luxembourg, whose masters pressed me so strongly to go to see them there sometimes that I agreed to it in spite of my aversion for Paris, where I had not been since my retirement to the Hermitage, except only for the two times about which I have spoken.[120] Again I did not go except on the days agreed upon, solely to sup and to return from there the next morning. I entered and left through the garden that adjoined the boulevard, so that I could say with the strictest truth that I had not set foot on the pavement of Paris.

In the bosom of this transient prosperity the catastrophe that was to mark its end was being prepared from afar. A short time after my return to Mont Louis I made, and very much in spite of myself as usual, a new acquaintance which again is epoch-making in my story. In what follows one will judge whether it is for good or for bad. It is my neighbor, Mme the Marquise de Verdelin,[121] whose husband had just bought a country house at Soisy near Montmorency. Mademoiselle d'Ars, the daughter of the Comte d'Ars, a man of rank but poor, had married M. de Verdelin, old, ugly, deaf, harsh, brutal, jealous, scarred, one-eyed, for the rest a good man if you knew how to take him, and possessor of fifteen to twenty thousand livres of income for which she was married to him. This darling, who swore, shouted, scolded, stormed, and made his wife weep all day long, ended by always doing what she wanted, and did so in order to make her angry, since she knew how to persuade him that it was he who wanted it and that it was she who did not want it. M. de Margency, about whom I have spoken, was Madame's friend and became Monsieur's. For several years he had rented his chateau at Margency near Eaubonne and Andilly to them, and they were there precisely during my love for Mme d'Houdetot. Mme d'Houdetot and Mme de Verdelin knew each other through their common friend, Mme d'Aubeterre,[122] and since the garden of Margency was in Mme d'Houdetot's path for going to her favorite walk, Mont Olympe, Mme de Verdelin gave her a key to pass through. By the favor of this key I often passed through it with her; but I did not like unforeseen encounters at all, and when we chanced upon Mme de Verdelin while we were passing through, I left them together without saying anything to her, and I always went ahead. This not very gallant action must not have put me in a good category with her. Nevertheless, when she was at Soisy she did not fail to seek me out. She came to see me several times at Mont Louis without finding me, and, seeing that I did not return her visit, in order to force me to do so she took it into her head to send me pots of flowers for my terrace. It was very necessary to go to thank her: that was enough. There we were bound together.

This relationship began by being stormy like all the ones I made in spite of myself. A true calm never reigned in it. Mme de Verdelin's turn of mind was too antipathetic to mine. Malicious strokes and epigrams come out of her with such simplicity that one needs a continuous—and for me very tiring—attention in order to feel when one is being bantered with. One bit of nonsense that comes back to me will be sufficient for one to judge about it. Her brother had just had the command of a frigate on a voyage against the English. I was talking about the manner of arming this frigate without harming its nimbleness. "Yes," she said with a completely even tone; "they take only as many cannons as they need for fighting." I rarely heard her speak well of any of her absent friends, without slipping in some word at their expense. What she did not see as bad, she saw as ridiculous, and her friend Margency was not excepted. Yet what I found unbearable in her was the continuous bother of her little dispatches, her little gifts, her little notes which I had to wear myself out to answer, and always new perplexities about thanking or refusing. Nevertheless, as a result of seeing her, I ended by becoming attached to her. She had sorrows as I did. Reciprocal confidences made our tête-à-têtes interesting for us. Nothing ties hearts together so much as the sweetness of weeping together. We sought each other out in order to console ourselves, and this need made me let many things pass. I had put so much harshness into my frankness with her that, after having sometimes shown so little esteem for her character, I really needed to have a lot of it to believe that she could sincerely pardon me. Here is a sample of the letters that I sometimes wrote to her, and about which one should note that she never appeared irritated in any fashion in any of her answers.

From Montmorency November 5, 1760

You tell me, Madame, that you have not explained yourself very well in order to make me understand that I explain myself badly. You speak to me about your supposed stupidity in order to make me feel mine: You vaunt yourself for being nothing but a simple-minded woman,[123] as if you were afraid of being taken at your word, and you make excuses to me in order to teach me that I owe them to you. Yes, Madame, I know it well; it is I who am stupid, a simple-minded man, and even worse if that is possible: it is I who chooses my terms poorly to the taste of a fine French Lady, who pays so much attention to words, and who speaks as well as you do. But consider that I take them in the common meaning of the language, without knowing all about or caring about the decent acceptation they are given in the virtuous social circles of Paris. If my expressions are equivocal [124] sometimes, I try to make my behavior determine the meaning" etc.

The rest of the letter is just about in the same tone. See the answer Bundle D. #41,[125] and judge of the unbelievable moderation of the heart of a woman who can have no more resentment at such a letter than she lets appear in that answer and which she never showed to me. Coindet, enterprising,[126] bold to the point of effrontery, and who kept himself on the lookout for all my friends, did not take long to introduce himself in my name at Mme de Verdelin's, and, unknown to me, was soon more familiar than myself there. What an odd fish that Coindet was! He presented himself on my behalf at the homes of all my acquaintances, established himself there, ate there without any ado. Carried away with zeal for my service, he never spoke about me except with tears in his eyes: but when he came to see me he kept the most profound silence about all these relations and about everything he knew ought to concern me. Instead of telling me what he had learned or said or seen that concerned me, he listened to me, even interrogated me. He never knew anything about Paris except what I informed him about it: in sum, although everyone talked to me about him, he never talked to me about anyone: he was secretive and mysterious only with his friend; but let us leave Coindet and Mme de Verdelin for the present. We will come back to them later on.

Some time after my return to Mont Louis, the Painter La Tour came to see me there, and brought me my portrait in pastels which he had exhibited at the Salon several years before.[127] He had wanted to give me this portrait, which I had not accepted. But Mme d'Epinay, who had given me hers and who wanted to have that one, had urged me to ask him for it again. He had taken some time in order to touch it up. My rupture with Mme d'Epinay came during that interval, I returned her portrait to her, and since there was no longer any question of giving her mine, I put it in my room at the Petit Chateau. M. de Luxembourg saw it there and found it to be good; I offered it to him, he accepted it, I sent it to him. He and Mme the Maréchale understood that I would be very glad to have theirs. They had them done in miniature by a very good hand, had them set in a rock crystal candy box mounted in gold, and made me a gift of it in a very gallant fashion with which I was enchanted. Mme de Luxembourg would never consent to having her portrait occupy the top of the box. Several times she had reproached me for preferring M. de Luxembourg to her, and I had not denied it at all, because it was true. By that way of placing her portrait she testified to me very courteously but very clearly that she did not forget that preference.

At about this same time I committed a stupidity that did not contribute to keeping me in her good favor. Although I did not know M. de Silhouette at all,[128] and I was hardly inclined to like him, I had a great opinion of his administration. When he began to bring his hand down heavily on the financiers I saw[129] that he was not beginning his operation at a favorable time; I did not make less ardent wishes for its success because of that, and when I learned that he had been removed from office, in my intrepid thoughtlessness I wrote him the following letter, which assuredly I am not undertaking to justify.

From Montmorency December 2, 1759

Deign, Sir, to receive the homage of a solitary man who is unknown to you, but who esteems you for your talents, who respects you for your administration, and who did you the honor of believing that it would not be left to you for long. Not being able to save the State except at the expense of the Capital which ruined it, you have braved the shouts of the money-makers. When I saw you crush these wretches I envied you for your position; when I see you leave it without acting inconsistently I admire you. Be satisfied with yourself, Sir; it leaves you an honor which you will enjoy for a long time without a rival. The curses of rogues are the just man's glory.

Mme de Luxembourg, who knew that I had written this letter, spoke to me about it during the Easter trip; I showed it to her; she wanted a copy of it; I gave it to her: but when I gave it to her I did not know she was one of those money-makers who was concerned with the under-farms and who had had Silhouette removed from office. From all my blunders, one might have said that I was acting deliberately to excite the hatred of a lovable and powerful woman, to whom, in truth, I was becoming more attached day by day, and from whom I was very far from wanting to attract disfavor to myself, although as a result of clumsiness I did everything necessary for doing so. I believe that it is rather superfluous to inform you that the story about M. Tronchin's opiate, about which I spoke in my first part,[130] relates to her: the other Lady was Mme de Mirepoix. Neither of them has ever spoken to me about it again or given the slightest appearance of remembering it; but it appears to me very difficult to presume that Mme de Luxembourg could have really forgotten it, even if one knew nothing about subsequent events. As for me, I tried to forget the effects of my stupidities, by means of the witness I rendered to myself of not having done any of them deliberately to offend her: as if a woman could ever pardon such things, even with the most perfect certainty that one's will did not have the slightest part in them.

Nevertheless, although she did not appear to see anything or feel anything, and I still did not find either a diminution in her eagerness or a change in her manners, the continuation, even the increase of a too well-founded presentiment, made me tremble ceaselessly that boredom might soon succeed this infatuation. Could I expect a constancy proof against my little skill at maintaining it from such a great Lady? I did not even know how to hide from her this dull presentiment which made me anxious, and made myself only more sullen. One will judge this from the following letter, which contains a very singular prediction.

(N. B.: This letter, without a date in my rough draft, is from the month of October 1760 at the latest.) [131]

How cruel your kindnesses are! Why trouble the peace of a solitary man who renounced the pleasures of life in order not to feel its worries any longer. I have passed my days by vainly looking for solid attachments. I was unable to form them in the ranks I could reach; should I look for them in yours? Neither ambition nor self-interest tempts me: I am not very vain, not very fearful; I can resist everything aside from blandishments. Why do you both attack me by means of a weakness I must overcome, since in the distance that separates us the outpourings of sensitive hearts ought not to bring mine near you. Will gratitude be enough for a heart that does not know two ways of giving itself, and does not feel itself capable only of friendship. Friendship, Mme the Maréchale! Ah! there is my misfortune! It is fine for you, for Monsieur the Maréchal to use this term: but I am mad to take you at your word. You are playing, I am becoming attached, and the end of the game is preparing new regrets for me. How I hate all your titles and how I feel sorry for you for bearing them! You seem to me so worthy of tasting the charms of private life! If only you lived in Clarens! [132] I would go there to seek the happiness of my life: but the Chateau of Montmorency, but the hôtel de Luxembourg! Is it there that Jean Jaques should be seen? Is it there that a friend of equality should bring the affections of a sensitive heart who—paying in this way for the esteem one bears witness of to him—believes he returns as much as he receives. You are good and sensitive also; I know it, I have seen it; I regret that I could not believe it earlier: but in the rank you are in, in your way of living, nothing can make a durable impression, and so many new objects efface each other mutually that none remain. You will forget me, Madame, after you have made it impossible for me to imitate you. You will have done much to make me unhappy and to be inexcusable.

I joined M. de Luxembourg to her in this so as to make the compliment less harsh for her; for besides, I felt myself so sure of him that not a single fear about the continuance of his friendship had even come to me. Nothing that intimidated me with regard to Mme the Maréchale extended to him for a moment. I never had the slightest mistrust about his character, which I knew was weak but reliable. I did not fear a cooling off on his part any more than I expected a heroic attachment from him. The simplicity, the familiarity of our manners with each other showed how much we reciprocally counted on each other. We were both right: I will honor, I will cherish the memory of that worthy Lord as long as I live, and whatever might have been done to detach him from me, I am as certain that he died my friend as if I had received his last sigh.

On the second trip to Montmorency of the year 1760, since the reading of Julie was finished, I had recourse to that of *Emile* to maintain myself with Mme de Luxembourg; but that did not succeed as well; either because the material was less to her taste,[133] or because so much reading bored her in the end. Nevertheless, since she reproached me for letting myself be duped by my publishers, she wanted me to leave her the care of having this work printed, so as to turn it to better account. I agreed to this under the express condition that it would not be printed at all in France, and we had a long dispute about that: I claimed that tacit permission[134] was impossible to obtain, even imprudent to ask for, and I did not at all want to allow printing in the Kingdom without it; she maintained that, in the system the Government had adopted, this would not even cause a difficulty to the censorship. She found the way to make M. de Malesherbes participate in her intentions and he wrote me a long letter on this subject entirely in his own hand, to prove to me that the profession of faith of the Savoyard Vicar was precisely a piece made to have the approval of the human race everywhere, and that of the Court in the existing circumstances.[135] I was surprised to see this Magistrate, always so fearful, become so accommodating in this business. Since the printing of a book of which he approved was made legitimate by that alone, I no longer had any[136] objection to make against that of this work. Nevertheless, out of an extraordinary scruple, I still required that the book be printed in Holland, and even by the Publisher Neaulme, whom I was not satisfied to indicate, but whom I informed of my intention, consenting, moreover, that the Edition be made for the profit of a French book dealer and that when it was made it would be sold either at Paris, or wherever they wanted, considering that this sale had nothing to do with me.[137] That is exactly what was agreed between Mme de Luxembourg and me, after which I handed over my manuscript to her.

On this trip she had brought along her granddaughter, Mademoiselle de Boufflers, today Mme the Duchesse de Lauzun.[138] She was called Amelie. She was a charming person. She truly had a virginal countenance, sweetness, timidity. Nothing was more lovable and more interesting[139] than her countenance, nothing was more tender and more chaste than the feelings she inspired. Besides she was a child; she was not eleven years old. Mme the Maréchale, who found her to be too timid, was making efforts to animate her. Several times she allowed me to give her a kiss; which I did with my usual glumness. Instead of the gracious things that someone else might have said in my place, I stood there speechless, bewildered, and I do not know which of us was the more bashful, the poor little girl or I. One day I met her alone in the stairway of the Petit Chateau: she had just seen Therese whom her Governess was still with. For lack of knowing what to say to her, I proposed a kiss which in the innocence of her heart she did not refuse, since she had received one the same morning at her grandmama's order and in her presence. The next day, when I was reading *Emile* at Mme the Maréchale's bedside, I fell precisely on a passage in which I correctly censure what I had done the day before.[140] She found the reflection to be very just, and said something extremely sensible about it that made me blush. How I cursed my unbelievable stupidity which has so often given me a low and guilty manner when I was only foolish and perplexed! a stupidity that is even taken for a false excuse in a man who is known not to be unintelligent. I can swear that in this so reprehensible kiss as well as in the others, Mlle Amélie's heart and senses were no more pure than mine were, and I can even swear that if at that moment I could have avoided meeting her, I would have done so; not that it did not give me great pleasure to see her, but out of the perplexity at finding some pleasant word to say to her in passing. How can it be that even a child intimidates a man who has not been frightened by the power of Kings. What decision should be made? How can one behave when one is devoid of all presence of mind? If I force myself to speak to the people I meet, I infallibly make a blunder: if I say nothing, I am a misanthrope, a wild animal, a Bear. A total imbecility would have been very much more favorable to me: but the talents I lacked in the world have made the talents that did belong to me into the instruments of my ruin.

At the end of this same trip Mme de Luxembourg did a good deed in which I had some part. Diderot had very imprudently offended Mme the Princesse de Robeck, M. de Luxembourg's daughter;[141] Palissot, who was her protégé, avenged her by means of the comedy the *Philosophers*, in which I was turned to ridicule, and Diderot treated extremely badly. The Author handled me more gingerly, less I think because of the obligation he had to me, than out of fear of displeasing his protector's father by whom he knew I was liked. The publisher Duchesne,[142] whom I did not know at all at that time, sent me this play when it was printed, and I suspect that this was by the order of Palissot, who perhaps believed that I would be pleased to see a man with whom I had broken torn apart. He was extremely mistaken. In breaking with Diderot, whom I believed[143] to be less wicked than indiscreet and weak, I always preserved in my soul some attachment for him, even esteem, and some respect for our former friendship, which I know had been as sincere on his part as on mine for a long time. It is a completely different thing with Grimm, a man false by character, who never loved me, who is not even capable of loving, and who, out of gaiety of heart, without any subject of complaint, and solely to satisfy his black jealousy under his mask made himself my cruelest calumniator. The latter is no longer anything for me: the former will always be my former friend. My innermost emotions were stirred at the sight of that odious Play: I could not bear reading it, and without finishing it, I sent it back to Duchesne with the following letter.

From Montmorency May 21, 1760

Sir, while skimming over the play you sent me I shuddered at seeing myself praised in it. I do not accept this horrible present at all. I am persuaded that you did not want to pay me an insult by sending it to me; but you do not know or you have forgotten that I had the honor of being the friend of a respectable man, undeservedly slandered and calumniated in this libel.

Duchesne showed this letter.[144] Diderot, who should have been touched by it, was annoyed at it.[145] His amour-propre could not pardon me for the superiority of a generous action, and I knew that his wife was venting her rage everywhere against me with a peevishness that affected me little, since I was aware that everyone knew her to be a fishwife.

Diderot in his turn found an avenger in the Abbé Morrellet, who composed a little writing against Palissot imitating the *Little Prophet* and entitled *The Vision*.[146] In this writing he very imprudently offended Mme de Robeck, whose friends had him put in the Bastille: as for her, naturally hardly vindictive and at that time dying, I am persuaded that she was not mixed up in it.[147]

D'Alembert, who was extremely closely tied with the Abbé Morrellet, wrote to me to induce me to ask Mme de Luxembourg to solicit his freedom,[148] promising her in gratitude some praise in the *Encyclopedia*.* Here is my answer.

Sir, I did not wait for your letter to testify to Mme the Maréchale de Luxembourg about the pain the Abbé Morrellet's detention caused me. She knows the interest I take in it, she will learn the interest that you take in it, and knowing that this is a man of merit will be enough for her to take an interest in it herself. What is more, although she and M. the Marêéchal honor me with a benevolence that makes up the consolation of my life, and although the name of your friend might be a recommendation for the Abbé Morrellet with them, I do not know how far it suits them to employ the influence attached to their rank and the consideration due to their persons on this occasion. I am not even persuaded that the vengeance in question concerns Mme the Princesse de Robeck as much as you appear to believe it does, and if it did, one ought not to expect the pleasure of vengeance to belong exclusively to philosophers, and that when they would like to be women, the women will be philosophers.

I will give you an account of what Mme de Luxembourg says to me when I have shown her your letter. While waiting, I believe I know her well enough to be able to assure you in advance that if she does have the pleasure of contributing to the Abbé Morrellet's release she would not accept the tribute of gratitude that you promise her in the *Encyclopedia*, although she considers herself honored by it; because she does not do what is good in order to get praise, but in order to satisfy her good heart.

I spared nothing to excite Mme de Luxembourg's zeal and commiseration in favor of the poor captive, and I succeeded. She made a trip to Versailles expressly to see M. the Comte de St. Florentin, and this trip cut short the one to Montmorency which M. the Maréchal was obliged to leave at the same time in order to proceed to Rouen, where the King was sending him as Governor of Normandy, concerning some movements of the Parlement which they wished to restrain.[149] Here is the letter that Mme de Luxembourg wrote to me two days after her departure.[150]

From Versailles this Wednesday (Bundle D. #23)

M. de Luxembourg left yesterday at six o'clock in the morning. I do not know yet whether I will go. I am waiting for news from him, because he does not know himself how long he will be there. I have seen M. de St. Florentin, who is very well disposed for the Abbé Morrellet; but he finds some obstacles over which he nevertheless hopes to triumph at his first work with the King, which will be next

---

*Along with several others, this letter disappeared from the Hôtel de Luxembourg when my papers were deposited there.

week. I also beseeched them not to exile him, because there is some question of it: they want to send him to Nancy. There, Sir, is what I have been able to obtain: but I promise you that I will not leave M. de St. Florentin in peace unless the affair is concluded as you desire. Now let me tell you at present how sorry I was to leave you so soon, but I flatter myself that you do not doubt this. I love you with all my heart, and for my whole life.

Some days afterward, I received this note from d'Alembert which gave me genuine joy.

This August 1 (Bundle D. #26)

Thanks to your efforts, my dear Philosopher, the Abbé has left the Bastille, and his detention will not have any other consequences at all. He is leaving for the country and gives you, as I do, a thousand thanks and compliments. "*Vale et me ama.*[151]

Some days afterward the Abbé wrote me a letter of thanks (Bundle D. #29) [152] which did not appear to me to betoken an unquestionable effusiveness of heart, and in which in some measure he seemed to belittle the service I had rendered him; and some time after that I found that d'Alembert and he had in some measure, I will not say, supplanted, but succeeded me with Mme de Luxembourg, and that I had lost as much as they had gained with her. Nevertheless, I am very far from suspecting the Abbé Morrellet of having contributed to my disgrace; I esteem him too much for that. As for M. d'Alembert I say nothing about it here; I will talk about him again in what follows.

At the same time I had another affair which occasioned the last letter I wrote to M. de Voltaire, a letter against which he has let out loud shouts as an abominable insult, but which he has never shown to anyone. I will make up here for what he did not want to do.

The Abbé Trublet, whom I knew a little but whom I had seen very little, wrote to me on June 13, 1760 (Bundle D. #11),[153] to inform me that his friend and correspondent M. Formey had printed in his Journal my letter to M. de Voltaire on the disaster at Lisbon. The Abbé Trublet wanted to know how this printing could have taken place, and in his very subtle and Jesuitical turn of mind asked me my opinion about reprinting this letter, without wanting to tell me his own. Since I supremely hate artful dodgers of this sort, I gave him the thanks I owed him, but I put into them a harsh tone which he felt and which did not keep him from wheedling to me again in two or three letters, until he knew everything he wanted to know.

I understood very well, whatever Trublet might have said, that Formey had not found this letter printed, and that the first printing of it had come from him. I knew him to be a barefaced pilferer who made a revenue for himself from the works of others without any ado, although he had not yet put into it the unbelievable impudence of removing the name of the Author from an already published Book in order to put his own on it, and to sell it for his own profit.[154]* But how had this manuscript come to him? That was the question, which was not hard to resolve, but over which I had the simplicity to be perplexed.[156] Since in the end, in spite of his dishonest proceedings, Voltaire might have grounds for complaint if I had had the letter printed without his approval—even though he was lavishly honored in it—I decided to write to him on this subject. Here is that second letter, to which he made no response, and by which he made a pretence of being irritated to the point of rage so as to put his brutality more at ease.

From Montmorency June 17, 1760

I did not think, Sir, that I would ever find myself in correspondence with you. But learning that the letter I wrote you in 1756 has been printed at Berlin, I ought to give you an account of my behavior in this regard, and I will fulfill this duty with truth and simplicity.

Since this letter was actually addressed to you, it was not intended for publication at all. I circulated it under conditions to three persons to whom the rights of friendship did not permit me to refuse anything of that sort, and who were even less permitted by the same rights to abuse their trust by violating their promise. These three persons are Mme Dupin's daughter-in-law Mme de Chenonceaux, Mme the Comtesse de Houdetot, and a German named M. Grimm. Mme de Chenonceaux wished this letter to be printed, and asked me for my consent. I told her that it depended on yours. You were asked for it; you refused it, and there was no longer any question of it.

Nevertheless M. the Abbé Trublet, with whom I have no sort of connection, just wrote to me out of a thoughtfulness full of decency that, having received the sheets of a journal by M. Formey, he had read this same letter, with a notice in which, under the date of October 23, 1759, the Editor says that he found it several weeks before in the Book Dealers of Berlin, and that—since it is one of those loose sheets that soon disappear without return—he believed he ought to give it a place in his journal.

There, Sir, is everything I know about it. It is very certain that until now they have not even heard this letter spoken of in Paris. It is very certain that the copy, either in manuscript or printed, that fell into M. Formey's hands could only have come from you, which is not likely, or from one of the three persons I just named.

---

*This is how he appropriated *Emile* for himself later on.[155]

Finally it is very certain that the two Ladies are incapable of such an infidelity. I am not able to learn any more about it in my retirement. You have some correspondents by means of which it would be easy, if the thing were worth the trouble, to get to the source, and to verify the fact.

In the same letter M. the Abbé Trublet notifies me that he is holding the sheet in reserve and will not impart it without my consent which assuredly I will not give. But this copy might not be the only one in Paris. I wish, Sir, that this letter not be printed there, and I will do my best for that: but if I cannot avoid that, and am informed in time so that I can have the preference; then I would not hesitate to have it printed myself. That appears just and natural to me.

As for your reply to the same letter, it has not been communicated to anyone, and you can count on it never being printed without your permission for which I assuredly will not be so indiscreet as to ask you, knowing very well that what a man writes to another, he does not write for the public. But if you would like to write one to be published and to address it to me, I promise you to join it faithfully to my letter and not to answer a single word to it.

I do not like you at all Sir; you have done me—your disciple and enthusiast—wrongs which could have been most palpable to me. You have ruined Geneva as the reward for the refuge you have received there; you have alienated my fellow citizens from me as the reward for the applause that I lavished on you among them: it is you who makes staying in my country unbearable for me; it is you who will make me die in a foreign land, deprived of all the consolations of the dying, and thrown on a garbage heap as my only honor, while all the honors that a man can expect will accompany you in my country. In sum, I hate you because you wanted it so; but I hate you as a man still more worthy of loving you if you had wished it. Of all the feelings with which my heart is permeated for you, there remains only the admiration that one cannot refuse to your beautiful genius and love for your writings. If I cannot honor in you anything but your talents, it is not my fault. I will never fail in the respect that is due to [157] them nor in the actions required by this respect.[158]

In the middle of all these little literary fusses which confirmed me more and more in my resolution, I received the greatest honor that letters have drawn to me, and for which I was most grateful, in the visit that M. the Prince de Conti deigned to pay me two times, one at the Petit Chateau, and the other at Mont Louis. Both times he even chose the period when Mme de Luxembourg was [159] not at Montmorency so as to make it more manifest that he was coming only for me. I have never doubted that I owed this Prince's first kindnesses to Mme de Luxembourg and to Mme de Boufflers: but I do not doubt, either, that I owe the ones with which he has not ceased to honor me since then to his own feeling and to myself.*

* Notice the perseverance of that blind and stupid confidence in the midst of all the treatment that should have disabused me of it the most. It did not cease until my return to Paris in 1770.

Since my apartment at Mont Louis was very small and the position of the Turret was charming, I led the Prince there, who for the acme of favors wanted me to have the honor of playing a game of chess with him. I knew that he beat the Chevalier de Lorenzy, who was a stronger player than I was. Nevertheless, in spite of signs and grimaces from the Chevalier and the onlookers, which I made a pretence of not seeing, I won the two games that we played. Upon finishing I said to him in a respectful but serious tone, "My Lord, I honor Your Most Serene Highness too much not to beat him at chess always." This great Prince, full of intelligence and enlightenment and so worthy of not being fawned upon, felt in fact—at least I think so—that I was the only one there who was treating him like a man, and I have every grounds for believing that he was very grateful to me for it.

Even if he had been annoyed with me for it, I would not have reproached myself for not having wanted to deceive him in anything, and I assuredly did not have to reproach myself with having responded badly in my heart to his kindnesses either, but I did have to reproach myself very much for having sometimes responded to them ungraciously, while he himself put an infinite grace in the manner he showed them to me. A few days afterward he had me sent a basket of game, which I received as I ought to. Some time later he had me sent another one, and one of his Officers of the hunt wrote from his orders that this was from His Highness's Hunt and from game shot by his own hand. I accepted it again, but I wrote to Mme de Boufflers that I would not accept any more. This letter was generally blamed, and deserved to be. To refuse presents of game from a Prince of the Blood who moreover put so much politeness in sending it is less the delicacy of a proud man who wants to preserve his independence, than the rusticity of an ill-bred person who forgets what he owes to others. I have never reread this letter in my collection without blushing over it, and without reproaching myself for having written it. But in the end I have not undertaken my confessions to be silent about my foolish acts, and this one revolts me too much myself for me to be allowed to cover it up.

If I did not commit the foolish act of becoming his rival, I came very close to it: for at that time Mme de Boufflers was still his mistress, and I did not know anything about it. She came to see me rather often with the Chevalier de Lorenzy. She was beautiful and still young, she affected the Roman spirit, and I have always had the Romantic one; that was close enough. I almost got caught; I believe she saw it: the Chevalier saw it also; at least he talked to me about it, and in a manner so as not to discourage me. But this time I was wise, and it was time for it at fifty years of age. Full of the lesson that I had just given to graybeards in my letter to d'Alembert,[160] I was ashamed of taking advantage of it so poorly myself: moreover, once I learned what I had not known, my head would have had to be[161] turned to carry my pretensions so high. Finally, perhaps still being poorly cured of my passion for Mme d'Houdetot, I felt that nothing could replace her in my heart any longer, and I bade farewell to love for the rest of my life. At the moment I am writing this I have just had some very dangerous flirting from a young woman who had her intentions and very disturbing eyes:[162] but if she has made a pretence of forgetting my[163] twelve lustres,[164] I have remembered them. After extricating myself from this step, I no longer fear any falls, and I answer for myself for the remainder of my days.

Having noticed the emotion she had given me, Mme de Boufflers might also have noticed that I had triumphed over it. I am not either foolish enough or vain enough to believe I could have inspired her with an inclination at my age; but based on certain remarks she made to Therese I believed I had inspired some curiosity in her: if that is true, and she did not pardon me for that frustrated curiosity, it must be admitted that I was certainly born to be the victim of my weaknesses, since conquering love has been so fatal to me, and conquered love has been even more so.[165]

Here ends the collection of letters that has served as my guide in these two books. I can no longer proceed except in the track of my remembrances: but they are such in this cruel epoch, and the strong impression of it has remained with me so well, that, lost in the immense sea of my misfortunes, I cannot forget the details of my first shipwreck, although its consequences no longer offer me anything but confused remembrances. Thus I can still proceed in the following book with enough assurance. If I go farther, it will no longer be except by groping.[166]

Book XI[1]

Although Julie, which had been in press for a long time, had not yet appeared at the end of 1760, it began to cause a great commotion. Mme de Luxembourg had spoken about it at Court, Mme d'Houdetot at Paris. This latter had even obtained permission from me for St. Lambert to have it read in manuscript to the King of Poland who had been enchanted by it. Duclos, whom I had also had read it, had spoken about it at the Academy. All of Paris was impatient to see this novel; the booksellers of the rue St. Jaques and at the Palais Royal were besieged by people who were asking for news about it. It finally appeared and, contrary to what usually happens, its success lived up to the eagerness with which it had been expected.[2] Mme the Dauphine,[3] who had been among the first to read it, spoke about it to M. de Luxembourg as a ravishing work. Feelings were divided among the literary people,[4] but in society there was only one opinion, and above all women were intoxicated by both the Book and the author, to the point that there were hardly any, even in the highest ranks, whose conquest I might not have made if I had undertaken it. I have proofs of this that I do not want to write, and which authorize my opinion without requiring the experiment. It is peculiar that this book succeeded better in France than in[5] the rest of Europe although the French, both men and women, are not treated extremely well in it.[6] Completely contrary to my expectation, its least success was in Switzerland and its greatest in Paris. Do friendship, love, virtue reign at Paris more than elsewhere then? No, without a doubt; but that exquisite sense which thrills the heart at their image, and which makes us cherish in others the pure, tender, decent feelings that we no longer have does still reign there.[7] Henceforth corruption is the same everywhere: neither morals nor virtues exist in Europe any more; but if some love for them still exists, one must look for it in Paris.*

Through so many prejudices and factitious passions one must know how to analyze the human heart well in order to disentangle the true feelings of nature in it. One must have a delicacy of tact, which one acquires only in the education of high society, in order to feel—if I dare to

---

* I wrote this in 1769.

speak this way—the subtleties of heart with which this work is full. I put its fourth part next to[8] the Princesse de Cleves without fear,[9] and I say that if these two pieces had been read only in the Provinces, their whole value would never have been felt.[10] Thus one must not be surprised if this Book's greatest success was at Court. It abounds in lively but veiled features which ought to please there because the people at Court are more practiced at penetrating them. Nevertheless, one must make another distinction here. This reading is assuredly not fit for that sort of witty people who have only guile, who are subtle only for penetrating evil, and who see nothing at all where there is only good to see. If, for example, Julie had been published in a certain country I am thinking of,[11] I am sure that no one would have finished reading it, and that it would have died at birth.

I have gathered together the majority of the letters that were written to me about this work in a bundle that is in the hands of Mme de Nadaillac.[12] If this collection ever appears, very peculiar things will be seen, and an opposition of judgment that shows what it means to have anything to do with the public. The thing that people have noticed least in it and which will always make it a unique work is the simplicity of the subject and the chain of interest which—being concentrated among three people—is maintained for six volumes without episode, without romantic adventure, without wickedness of any sort, either in the characters, or in the actions. Diderot has paid great compliments to Richardson about the prodigious variety of his tableaux and about the multitude of his characters.[13] In fact Richardson deserves them for having characterized all of them well: but as for their number, he has that in common with the most insipid novelists who make up for the sterility of their ideas by virtue of characters and adventures. It is easy to wake up attention by incessantly presenting both unknown events and new faces which pass like the figures of the magic lantern: but it is certainly more difficult always to maintain this attention on the same objects and without miraculous adventures, and if, everything being equal, the simplicity of the subject adds to the beauty of the work, Richardson's Novels—superior in so many other things[14]—cannot enter into comparison with mine on that score. It is dead, nevertheless, I know it, and I know the cause; but it will rise from the dead.[15]

My only fear was that as a [result of simplicity my][16] development might be boring, and that I might not have been able to nourish enough interest to maintain it up to the end. I was reassured by a fact that has flattered me more by itself than all the compliments this work has been able to draw to me.

It was published at the beginning of Carnival. The peddler brought it to Mme the Princesse de Talmont* one day when there was a ball at the Opera. After supping she had herself dressed to go to it, and she began to read the new Novel while waiting for the time. At midnight she ordered them to get the horses ready and continued to read. They came to tell her that her horses were ready; she gave no answer. Seeing that she was forgetting herself, her people came to notify her that it was two o'clock. "There is no rush yet," she said, still reading. Some time afterward, because her watch had stopped, she rang to know what time it was. They told her that it was four o'clock. "Since that is so," she said, "it is too late to go to the ball, put up my horses." She had herself undressed and passed the rest of the night reading.

Ever since this action was recounted to me I have desired to see Mme de Talmont, not only to learn from her herself if it is precisely true; but also because I have always believed that one could not take so lively an interest in the *Héloïse*, without having that sixth sense, that moral sense with which so few hearts are endowed, and without which no one can understand my own.

What made women so favorable to me was their persuasion that I had written my own story and that I myself was the Hero of this novel. That belief was so well established that Mme de Polignac[18] wrote to Mme de Verdelin to beg her to induce me to let her see Julie's portrait. Everyone was persuaded that one could not express so vividly feelings that one had not experienced at all, nor depict the raptures of love this way except after one's own heart. In this they were right and it is certain that I wrote this novel in the most burning[19] ecstasies; but they were wrong when they thought that real objects were needed to produce them; they were far from conceiving to what extent I can catch fire for imaginary beings. Aside from some reminiscences of youth and Mme d'Houdetot, the loves that I felt and described were only with the Sylphides. I did not want either to confirm or to destroy an error that was advantageous to me. One can see in the preface in dialogue form that I had printed separately how I left the public in suspense about that.[20] Rigorists might say[21] that I should have declared the truth entirely explicitly. As for me, I do not see what could oblige me to do so, and I believe that there would have been more stupidity than frankness in that declaration made unnecessarily.

At about the same time appeared *Perpetual Peace*, the manuscript of which I had given up the preceding year to a certain M. de Bastide,[22] Author of a journal called *The World*, in which he wanted to stuff all my

---

* It was not she, but another Lady whose name I do not know.[17]

manuscripts whether I liked it or not. He was an acquaintance of M. Duc-los, and came in his name to press me to help him fill up *The World*. He had heard Julie spoken of and wanted me to put it[23] in his journal: he wanted me to put *Emile* in it; he would have wanted me to put *The Social Contract* in it if he had suspected its existence.[24] Finally, being exasperated by his badgering,[25] I made the decision to give up to him my *Abridgment of the Perpetual Peace* for twelve Louis. Our agreement was that he would print it in his journal; but as soon as he was the owner of this manu-script, he judged it appropriate to have it printed separately, with some cuts which the Censor demanded.[26] What might have happened if I had joined to it my judgment on that work, about which I very fortunately did not speak at all to M. de Bastide, and which did not enter at all into our bargain! This judgment is still in manuscript among my papers. If it ever sees the light, people will see[27] how much Voltaire's jokes and con-ceited tone on this subject must have made me laugh, since I saw so well this poor man's range in the political matters that he involved himself in speaking about.[28]

In the midst of my successes with the public and in the favor of the Ladies, I felt myself losing ground at the Hôtel de Luxembourg, not with regard to M. the Maréchal, who even seemed to redouble kindnesses and friendship for me each day, but with regard to Mme the Maréchale. Since I no longer had anything to read to her, her apartment had been less open to me, and, although I offered myself punctually enough during the trips to Montmorency, I hardly saw her any more except at table. Even my place next to her was no longer as strongly reserved. Since she no longer offered it to me, since she spoke to me very little, and since I did not have much to say to her either, I liked just as much to take another place where I was more at my ease, above all in the evening; for little by little I unconsciously acquired the habit of placing myself closer to M. the Maréchal.

Concerning the evening, I remember having said that I did not sup at the Chateau,[29] and that was true at the beginning of the acquaintance; but since M. de Luxembourg did not dine at all and did not even sit at the table, it thereby happened that, at the end of several months and already being very familiar in the house, I had never yet eaten with him. He had the kindness to take note of it. That decided me to sup there sometimes when few people were there, and I felt very comfortable about it, given that they dined almost in the open air, and as they say at the edge of the bench; whereas the supper was very long, because they rested there with pleasure after returning from a long walk, very good, because M. de Luxembourg was a gourmand, and very pleasant, because Mme de Luxembourg did the honors charmingly. Without this explanation it would be hard to understand the end of one of M. de Luxembourg's letters (Bundle C. #36)[30] in which he tells me that he recalls our walks with delight; "*above all*," he adds, "when we did not find any tracks of carriage wheels when we went back into the Courtyard in the evening"[31]; that is, since they raked the sand in the Courtyard every morning in order to erase the ruts, I judged the number who had arrived unexpectedly in the afternoon from the number of these tracks.

That year 1761 added the finishing touches to the continual losses that happened to this good Lord since I had the honor[32] of seeing him; as if the evils that destiny was preparing for me should have begun through the man for whom I had the greatest attachment and who was the most worthy of it. The first year he lost his sister Mme the Duchesse de Villeroy;[33] the second he lost his daughter Mme the Princesse de Robek; the third he lost his only son, the Duc de Montmorency, and his grandson, the Comte de Luxembourg, the only and last props of his branch and his name.[34] He bore all these losses with an apparent courage, but all the rest of his life his heart did not stop bleeding inside and his health no longer did anything but decline. He must have felt the unforeseen and tragic death of his son all the more keenly since it happened precisely at the moment when the King had just granted him for his son and promised him for his grandson the reversion of his duty as Captain of the Body Guard. He had the pain of seeing this last child, object of the greatest hopes, pass away little by little[35] from his mother's blind confidence in the Doctor who caused this poor child to starve to death, with medicines as his only nourishment. Alas! if I had been believed, the grandfather and grandson would both still be alive. What did I not say, what did I not write to M. the Maréchal, how many representations did I not make to Mme de Montmorency about the more than austere regimen that she made her son follow based on the faith of her Doctor. Mme de Luxembourg, who thought as I did, did not wish to usurp the mother's authority; M. de Luxembourg, a gentle and weak man, did not like to contradict at all. Mme de Montmorency had a faith in Bordeu[36] which her son ended by being the victim of. How glad this poor child was when he could obtain permission to come to Mont-Louis with Mme de Boufflers to ask Therese for a snack, and put some food in his famished stomach! How much did I deplore within myself the miseries of greatness, when I saw this sole heir of such great property, of such a great name, of so many titles and dignities devour a poor little piece of bread with the eagerness of a beggar. In sum, I might well speak and act, the Doctor triumphed, and the child died of hunger.

The same confidence in charlatans that caused the grandson to perish dug the grandfather's grave, and in addition he joined to it the pusillanimity of wanting to conceal the infirmities of age from himself. At intervals M. de Luxembourg had had some pain in his big toe; he had an attack at Montmorency, which gave him insomnia and a slight fever. I dared to pronounce the word gout; Mme de Luxembourg scolded me. M. the Maréchal's Valet-de-chambre Surgeon[37] maintained that it was not gout, and began to soothe the suffering part with some tranquilizing balm. Unfortunately the pain was calmed and when it came back, they did not fail to use the same remedy that had calmed it: his constitution was impaired, the ills increased, and the remedies in the same ratio. Mme de Luxembourg, who finally saw very well that it was gout, was opposed to this senseless treatment. They hid from her, and after several years M. de Luxembourg perished by his own fault for having wanted to persist at being cured. But let's not anticipate misfortunes from so far away; how many others do I have to narrate before that one!

It is peculiar with what fatality everything I could say and do seemed made to displease Mme de Luxembourg, even though I had preserving her benevolence most at heart. The afflictions that M. de Luxembourg experienced blow upon blow only made me more attached to him, and consequently to Mme de Luxembourg: for they always appeared to me to be so sincerely united that the feelings I had for the one necessarily extended to the other. M. the Maréchal was growing old. His assiduousness at Court, the cares it occasioned, the continual hunts, above all the fatigue of serving during his quarter of a year[38] would have demanded the vigor of a young man, and I no longer saw anything that could maintain his vigor in that course. Since his ranks were to be dispersed and his name dead after him, it mattered little to him to continue a laborious life, whose principal object had been[39] to husband the Prince's favor for his children. One day when the three of us were alone, and he was complaining about the fatigues of the Court as a man who had been disheartened by his losses, I dared to speak of retirement, and to give him the advice that Cyneas gave to Pyrrhus;[40] he sighed, and did not answer decisively.[41] But at the first moment Mme de Luxembourg saw me in private she started up again in a lively way about this advice which it appeared to me had alarmed her. She added something whose justness I felt, and which caused me to renounce touching the same cord again; it is that the long habit of living at Court became a true need, that at that moment it was even a distraction for M. de Luxembourg, and that the retirement I was advising to him would be less a repose for him than an exile, in which idleness, boredom, sadness would soon finish consuming him. Although she might have seen that she had persuaded me, although she should have counted on the promise I made her and which I kept, she never appeared very well calmed in that regard, and I recall that after that my tête-à-têtes with M. the Maréchal were more rare and almost always interrupted.

While my loutishness and my bad luck were acting in concert to harm me with her, the people she saw and liked the most did not serve me. Above all, the Abbé de Boufflers;[42] a young man who was as brilliant as could be, never appeared to me to be well-disposed toward me, and not only is he the only one of Mme the Maréchale's social circle who never showed me the slightest attention, but I believed I noticed that on all the trips he made to Montmorency I lost something with her, and it is true that, without him even wanting it, his presence alone was enough for this to happen: so much did the favor and the salt of his engaging manners made my heavy *spropositi*[43] even duller. The first two years, he had almost never come to Montmorency, and I had maintained my position passably by means of Mme the Maréchale's indulgence, but as soon as he appeared a little afterward, I was irreversibly trampled. I would have wanted to take refuge under his wing, and behave so that he might acquire a friendship for me; but the same sullenness that made me need to please him kept me from succeeding in it, and what I did unskillfully to gain his friendship completely ruined me with Mme the Maréchale without being useful to me with him. With so much intelligence, he could have succeeded at anything, but the impossibility of applying himself and his taste for dissipation did not allow him to acquire anything but half-talents in every field. On the other hand, he has many of them, and that is all one needs in high society where he wants to shine. He writes little poems very well, writes little letters very well, dabbles a little on the zither, and daubs a little in painting pastels. He took it into his head to want to paint Mme de Luxembourg's portrait; this portrait was horrible. She claimed that it did not resemble her at all and that was true. The treacherous Abbé consulted me, and, like a fool and a liar, I said that the portrait did resemble. I wanted to cajole the Abbé, but I did not cajole Mme the Maréchale, who entered this stroke in her records, and, after he had struck his blow, the Abbé made fun of me. From the success of my belated first try I learned not to get mixed up any longer in wanting to toady and flatter when Minerva is unwilling.

My talent was to tell men useful but harsh truths with sufficient energy and courage; I should have stuck with that. I was not at all born, I do not say to flatter, but to praise. The clumsiness of the praises I wanted to give did me more harm than the sharpness of my censures. I have an example of this to cite here that is so terrible that its consequences have not only caused my destiny for the rest of my life, but will perhaps decide my reputation among all posterity.

During the Montmorency trips M. de Choiseul[44] sometimes came to sup at the Chateau. He came there one day as I was leaving. They spoke about me. M. de Luxembourg told him my story about Venice with M. de Montaigu. M. de Choiseul said that it was a shame that I had abandoned that career, and that if I wanted to return to it he asked for nothing better than to employ me. M. de Luxembourg repeated this to me; I was all the more grateful for it since I had not been accustomed to being spoiled by Ministers, and it is not certain that I would have avoided[45] committing the folly all over again in spite of my resolutions, if my health had allowed me to think of it; with me ambition has never had anything but short intervals when every other passion left me free; but one of those intervals might have been enough to re-engage me. By giving me an affection for him, this good intention of M. de Choiseul increased the esteem I had conceived for his talents based upon some of his ministry's operations, and the family compact in particular appeared to me to announce a statesman of the first rank.[46] He gained even more in my mind from the low estimation that I made of his predecessors without excepting Mme de Pompadour whom I regarded as a sort of prime Minister, and when the rumor circulated that, of her or him, one of the two would drive out the other, I believed I was praying for the glory of France by praying for M. de Choiseul's triumph. At all times I had felt some antipathy for Mme de Pompadour, even before her fortune when I had seen her at Mme de la Popliniére's when she still bore the name of Mme d'Etiol. Since then I had been discontent[47] with her silence on the subject of Diderot and with all her actions with regard to me, both on the subject of the *Ramirro's Festivals* and *The Gallant Muses*, and on the subject of the *Village Soothsayer*, which by any measure of proceeds had not been worth advantages to me proportionate to its success, and on all occasions I had always found her very little disposed to oblige me; which did not keep the Chevalier de Lorenzy from proposing that I write something in praise of that Lady, while insinuating that it might be useful to me. This proposal made me all the more indignant since I saw very well that he was not making it out of his own initiative, knowing that this man thinks and acts only through someone else's impulsion[48] because he is nothing through himself. I know too poorly how to constrain myself to have been able to hide either from him my disdain for his proposal, or from anyone my slight penchant for the favorite; she knew it, I am sure of it, and all that mixed my own interest to my natural inclination in the prayers I made for M. de Choiseul. Being predisposed by esteem for his talents, which were the only things I knew about him,[49] full of gratitude for his good will, otherwise being totally ignorant in my retirement about his tastes and his manner of living, I regarded him in advance as the public's avenger and mine; and while I was putting the final touches on the *Social Contract* at that time, in a single stroke I noted what I thought about the preceding ministers and about the one who was beginning to eclipse them.[50] On that occasion I did not live up to my most constant maxim, and moreover, I did not dream that when one wishes to praise and blame strongly in the same item without naming the people, one must adapt the praise so much to the people whom it regards that the most skittish amour-propre cannot find any misunderstanding. On that point I was in such a foolish security that it did not even enter my mind that someone could be led astray. It will soon be seen whether I was right.

One of my pieces of luck was always to have some woman authors among my connections. I believed that at least among the Nobility I would avoid that piece of luck. Not at all: it followed me again. Nevertheless, as far as I know Mme de Luxembourg was never struck by that mania; but Mme the Comtesse de Boufflers was. She wrote a tragedy in prose which was first read, tried out, and extolled in the social circles of M. the Prince de Conti, and which—not being satisfied with so many encomiums—she also wanted to consult me about so as to have mine. She had it, but moderately, as the Work deserved. Moreover, I notified her, as I believed I owed her to do, that her Play entitled *The Generous Slave* bore a very close relation to a rather little known, but nonetheless translated, English play entitled *Oroonoko*.[51] Mme de Boufflers thanked me for the notice while nevertheless assuring me that her play did not at all resemble the other. I never spoke about this plagiarism to anyone in the world except to her alone, and did that to fulfill a duty she had imposed on me; that has not kept me from recalling often since then the result of the duty fulfilled by Gil-Blas with the Preaching Bishop.[52]

In addition to the Abbé de Boufflers who did not like me, in addition to Mme de Boufflers with whom I had committed wrongs that neither women nor authors ever pardon, all of Mme the Maréchale's other friends always appeared little disposed to be mine, among others M. the President Henault,[53] who—being enrolled among the authors— was not exempt from their flaws; among others also Mme du Deffand and Mlle de Lespinasse, both in close relations with Voltaire and intimate friends of d'Alembert with whom the latter even ended by living (with nothing untoward taking place, of course).[54] I had begun at first by being extremely interested in Mme du Deffand, whose loss of her sight made her an object of commiseration in my eyes; but her manner of living—

so contrary to mine that the time for getting up of the one was almost that for going to bed of the other—her limitless passion for trifling fine wit, the importance she gave—either for good or evil—to the slightest rags that appeared, the despotism and the fury of her oracles; her extravagant infatuation for or against everything, which did not allow her to talk about anything except with convulsions, her unbelievable prejudices, her invincible stubbornness, the enthusiasm of unreasonableness to which the obstinacy of her passionate judgments carried her; all that soon wearied me with the efforts I wanted to make on her behalf; I neglected her, she noticed it: that was enough to put her in a rage, and although I felt well enough how much a woman of that character could be feared, I still preferred to expose myself to the scourge of her hatred than to that of her friendship.

As if it were not enough to have so few friends in Mme de Luxembourg's social circle, I also had some enemies in her family. I only had one, but one who is worth a hundred in the position in which I find myself today. This was certainly not her brother, M. the Duc de Villeroy; for not only had he come to see me, but several times he had invited me to go to Villeroy, and since I had responded to this invitation with as much respect and decency as I could, taking that vague response as a consent, he had arranged with M. and Mme de Luxembourg a trip of two weeks in which I was to go along, and which was proposed to me. Since the cares that my health demanded did not allow me to move about without risk at that time I asked M. de Luxembourg to release me. One can see from his response (Bundle D. #3)[55] that this was done with the best grace in the world, and M. the Duc de Villeroy did not bear witness to me of any less kindness than before. His nephew and his heir the young Marquis de Villeroy[56] did not share the benevolence with which his Uncle honored me, nor also I admit in the respect I had for him. His feather-brained manners made him unbearable to me, and my cool manner attracted his aversion to me. One night at table he even made a wounding remark from which I extricated myself badly because I am stupid, without any presence of mind, and because anger, instead of sharpening the little I have, deprives me of it. I had a dog that had been given to me when it was very young, almost at my arrival at the Hermitage, and whom I had called *Duc* at that time. This dog, not beautiful, but of a rare breed, whom I had made into my companion, my friend, and who certainly deserved this title more than the majority of those who have taken it, had become famous at the Chateau de Montmorency from his loving, sensitive natural disposition and from the attachment we had for each other; but out of an extremely foolish pusillanimity I had changed his name to *Turk*, as if there were not multitudes of dogs who were called *Marquis* without any Marquis getting angry about it. The Marquis de Villeroy, who knew about this change of name, pushed[57] me so much about it that I was obliged to recount openly at table what I had done. What was offensive in this story was not so much that I had given the name *Duc* to him as[58] that I had taken it away. The worst thing was that there were several Ducs there; M. de Luxembourg was there, his son was there; and the Marquis de Villeroi—born to become one and who is one today—enjoyed with a cruel joy the perplexity into which he had put me, and the effect this perplexity produced. I was assured the next day that his Aunt had scolded him about it in a very lively way; and one can judge whether this reprimand—supposing it to be real—must have mended my affairs with him very much.

As a support against all this, both at the Hôtel de Luxembourg and at the temple[59] I had only the Chevalier de Lorenzy who professed to be my friend; but he was even more the friend of d'Alembert, in whose shadow he passed among the women for a great Geometer. He was moreover the Sigisbee[60] or rather the obliging servant of Mme the Comtesse de Boufflers, herself very friendly with d'Alembert, and the Chevalier de Lorenzy did not exist and did not think except through her. Thus, far from me having any outside counterweight to my ineptitude to sustain me with Mme de Luxembourg, everyone who came near her seemed to cooperate in harming me in her mind. Nevertheless, besides *Emile* which she had wanted to take charge of, at the same time she gave me another mark of interest and benevolence, which made me believe that, even while she was becoming bored with me, she preserved and would always preserve the friendship which she had promised so many times would last for her whole life.

As soon as I believed I could count on this feeling on her part, I had begun by lightening the burden of my heart with her by the admission of all my faults, having for an inviolable maxim with my friends of showing myself to their eyes exactly as I am, neither better nor worse. I had declared my relations with Therese to her, and everything that had resulted from them, without omitting the manner I had disposed of my children. She had received my confessions very well, even too well, while sparing me the censures I deserved, and what touched me deeply above all was to see the kindnesses she lavished on Therese, giving her little gifts, sending to look for her, exhorting her to come to see her, receiving her with a hundred caresses and embracing her very often in front of everyone. That poor girl was carried away with joy and gratitude which I certainly shared very much, since the acts of friendship which M. and Mme de Luxembourg loaded on me through her touched me much more deeply even than the ones they did for me directly.

For rather a long time things stayed there: but finally Mme the Maréchale pushed kindness to the point of wanting to take back one of my children. She knew that I had had a cipher put in the oldest one's swaddling clothes; she asked me for the duplicate of that cipher; I gave it to her. For this search she used La Roche, her Valet-de-Chambre and confidential servant, who made vain searches and found nothing, even though at the end of only twelve or fourteen years, if the records of the foundling hospital had been very much in order, or if the search had been well made, this cipher should not have been undiscoverable. However that might be, I was less upset about this poor success than I would have been if I had followed[61] that child from its birth. If, with the aid of the information, they had presented some child to me as my own, the doubt whether it was so in fact, whether they had not substituted another for it would have shut my heart as a result of the uncertainty, and I would not have tasted the true feeling of nature in all its charm: in order to sustain itself it needs to be propped up by habit at least during childhood. The long separation from a child one does not yet know weakens, finally reduces paternal and maternal feelings to nothing, and one will never love the one whom one has sent out to nurse as much as the one whom one has nursed under one's own eyes. The reflection that I make here can extenuate my wrongs in their effects, but only by aggravating them in their source.[62]

It is perhaps not useless to remark that through Therese's mediation, this same La Roche made the acquaintance of Mme le Vasseur, whom Grimm continued to keep at Deuil at the gate of la Chevrette, and very close to Montmorency. When I left it was through M. la Roche that I continued to have the money that I did not stop sending to her delivered to that woman, and I believe that he also often brought her presents on behalf of Mme the Maréchale; thus she surely had nothing to complain about, although she was always complaining. With regard to Grimm, since I do not at all like speaking about people I ought to hate, I never spoke about him to Mme de Luxembourg except in spite of myself: but several times she put me onto that subject without telling me what she thought about him, and without letting me ever discern whether this man was one of her acquaintances or not. Because reserve with people one likes and who do not have any with us is not to my taste above all in matters that concern them, I have sometimes thought about this since then; but only when other events have made this reflection natural.

After having gone for a long time without hearing *Emile* spoken of, after I had turned it over to Mme de Luxembourg, I finally learned that the deal for it was concluded at Paris with the Publisher Duchesne, and through him with the Publisher Neaulme at Amsterdam. Mme de Luxembourg sent me the two duplicate copies of my contract with Duchesne to sign. I recognized the writing as being of the same hand as that of M. de Malesherbes's letters when he did not write to me in his own hand. This certainty that my contract was made with the approval and under the eyes of the magistrate made me sign it confidently. Duchesne gave me six thousand francs for this manuscript, half in cash, and I believe a hundred or two hundred copies.[63] After I had signed the two duplicates I sent both of them to Mme de Luxembourg, who had desired me to do so: she gave one to Duchesne, she kept the other instead of sending it back to me, and I never saw it again.

While making some diversion in my project of retirement, the acquaintance with M. and Mme de Luxembourg had not made me renounce it. Even at the time of my greatest favor with Mme the Maréchale I had always felt that it was only my sincere attachment for M. the Maréchal and for her that could make the people close to them bearable for me, and my whole perplexity was to reconcile this very attachment with a sort of life more in conformity with my taste and less contrary to my health, which was continually undermined by that bother and those suppers, in spite of all the efforts they made not to expose me to upsetting it; for on this point as on all others they pushed attentiveness as far as possible, and for example, every evening after supper M. the Maréchal, who went to bed early, never failed to lead me away willy-nilly so I could go to bed also. It was only some time before my catastrophe that he ceased, I do not know why, paying this attention.

Even before I noticed Mme the Maréchale's cooling off, I desired to execute my old plan so as not to expose myself to it; but since I lacked the means to do so, I was obliged to wait for the conclusion of the contract for *Emile*, and while waiting I put the finishing touches on the *Social Contract*, and sent it to Rey, setting the price of this manuscript at a thousand francs, which he gave me. Perhaps I should not omit a little fact that regards the said Manuscript. I delivered it, well sealed to Duvoisin, a minister from the Pays de Vaud[64] and Chaplain of the Hôtel of Holland, who sometimes came to see me, and who took it upon himself to send it to Rey with whom he had connections. This manuscript, written in tiny characters, was extremely small and did not fill his pocket. Nevertheless upon passing the gate his package somehow or other fell into the hands of the clerks who opened it, examined it, and returned it to him afterward when he reclaimed it in the name of the Ambassador; which put him in a position to read it himself, as he naively informed me he had done, with strong praises for the work, and not a word of criticism or censure, doubtless waiting for the opportunity to be the avenger of Christianity when the work appeared. He sealed up the manuscript again and sent it to Rey. In substance such was the narrative he made to me in the letter in which he gave me an account of this affair, and that is all I knew about it.

In addition to these two books and my *Dictionary of Music* on which I still kept working from time to time, I had some other writings of lesser importance, all in a condition to appear and which I still intended to give, either separately, or with my general collection if I ever undertook it. The principal one of these writings, the majority of which are still in manuscript in Du Peyrou's hands,[65] was an *Essay on the Origin of Languages*[66] which I had read to M. de Malesherbes and to the Chevalier de Lorenzy, who said some good things to me about it. I counted on all these productions put together to be worth at least a capital of eight to ten thousand francs after all expenses were paid,[67] which I wanted to place in a life annuity on both my head and Therese's; after which we would go, as I have said, to live together in the depths of some Province without occupying the public with me any more, and without occupying myself any more with anything except peacefully ending my career, by continuing to do all the good I could around me, and to write at leisure the memoirs I was meditating.

Such was my plan the execution of which was facilitated by a generous deed by Rey about which I ought not to remain silent. This publisher, about whom they told me so many bad things at Paris, is nevertheless the only one of all those with whom I had dealings with whom I have always had reason to be satisfied.* In truth we often quarreled about the execution of my works; he was careless, I was touchy. But in matters of interest and the proceedings that relate to it, I have always found him full of exactitude and probity even though I have never made a formal contract with him. He is even also the only one who has admitted to me frankly that he did good business with me, and he has often told me that he owed his fortune to me, while offering to share it with me. Since he could not exercise his gratitude directly with me, he wanted to bear witness of it to me at least through my housekeeper, to whom he gave a life pension of three hundred francs, expressing in the act that this was out of gratitude for the advantages I had procured for him. He did that from him to me without ostentation, without pretentiousness, without a commotion, and no one would have known anything about it if I had not spoken

---

*When I wrote this I was still very far from imagining, conceiving, and believing the frauds I discovered later in his printings of my writings, and which he has been forced to acknowledge.

about it first to everyone. I was so touched by this proceeding that since then I have attached myself to Rey with a genuine friendship. Some time afterward he wanted me as Godfather of one of his children, I agreed to it, and one of my regrets in the situation to which I have been reduced is that I have been deprived of all means of rendering my attachment useful to my god-daughter and her parents from now on. Why, since I am so grateful for the modest generosity of this Publisher, am I so little grateful for the noisy forwardness of so many high society swells who pompously fill up the universe with the good they say they wanted to do for me and from which I have never felt anything? Is it their fault, is it mine? Are they only vain, am I only an ingrate? Sensible reader, weigh, decide; as for me I remain silent.

This pension was a great resource for Therese's upkeep, and a great relief for me. But moreover I was very far from drawing a direct profit for myself from it, nor from all those gifts that were given to her. She has always disposed of everything herself. When I kept her money I kept a faithful account of it for her, without ever putting a liard of it to our common expense, even when she was richer than I was. "*What is mine is ours,*" I told her; "*and what is yours is yours.*" I have never ceased to conduct myself in accordance with this maxim which I have often repeated to her. Those who have the baseness to accuse me of receiving from her hands what I refused with my own doubtlessly judge about my heart from their own, and know me very poorly. I would willingly eat with her the bread she earned, never that which was given to her. I call on her testimony on this point, both for the present and when, in the course of nature, she will have survived me. Unfortunately she is hardly well versed in economy in any regard, hardly careful and extremely prodigal, not out of vanity or gluttony, but solely out of negligence. Nothing is perfect here below, and since her excellent qualities must be counterbalanced, I prefer that she have flaws rather than vices; although perhaps her flaws cause the two of us even more harm. The efforts I made for her, as formerly for mamma, to accumulate some advance that might one day serve her as a resource are unimaginable: but they were always wasted efforts. Neither one of them ever called herself to account, and in spite of all my efforts every-thing always left as fast as it arrived. However simply Therese dresses, Rey's pension has never been enough to rig her out without me having to supplement it from mine each year. Neither she nor I were made ever to be rich, and I assuredly do not count that among our misfortunes.

The *Social Contract* was being printed rapidly enough. It was not the same with *Emile*, whose publication I was waiting for in order to execute the retirement I was meditating. At one time or another Du Chesne sent me models of typesetting to choose; when I had chosen, instead of beginning he sent me still others. When we had finally completely settled the format, the type, and he already had several sheets printed, based on some slight change that I made on a proof he began everything over again, and after six months we found ourselves less advanced than the first day. During all these attempts I saw very well[68] that the work was being printed in France as well as in Holland, and that he was making two editions of it at the same time. What could I do? I was no longer master of my manuscript. Far from having had a hand in the French edition I had always opposed it; but in the end, since that edition was being done whether I wanted or not, and since it was serving as a model for the other, it was very necessary to cast my eyes on it and see the proofs, so as not to let my book be maimed and disfigured. Besides, the work was being printed so completely with the Magistrate's permission that he was directing the undertaking in some manner. He wrote to me very often, and he even came to see me on this subject, on an occasion about which I am going to speak presently.

While Duchesne was advancing at a tortoise's pace, Neaulme, whom he was holding back, was advancing even[69] more slowly. He believed he perceived some bad faith in the maneuvering of Duchesne, that is to say of Guy who was acting for him, and seeing that the contract was not being performed, he wrote letter upon letter to me full of complaints and grievances, which I could remedy even less than the ones I had on my own account. His friend Guerin, who saw me extremely often at that time, talked to me incessantly about this book, but always with the greatest reserve. He knew and did not know that it was being printed in France, he knew and did not know that the Magistrate was taking a hand in it: when sympathizing with me about the trouble this book was going to give me, he seemed to accuse me of imprudence, without ever wanting to say what it consisted in; he shuffled and beat around the bush incessantly; he seemed to talk only to get me to talk. My feeling of assurance was so complete at that time that I laughed at the circumspect and mysterious tone he put into this business, as a quirk contracted from Ministers and Magistrates, whose offices he visited rather frequently. Since I was certain of being in proper order in every respect on this work, strongly persuaded that it had, not only the Magistrate's approval and protection, but even that it deserved and that it had the minister's favor, I congratulated myself for my courage at doing good, and I laughed at my pusillanimous friends who appeared to be anxious for me. Duclos was among this number, and I admit that my confidence in his uprightness and his enlightenment could have alarmed me in imitation of him, if I had had less confidence in the usefulness of the work and the probity of its patrons. He came to see me from M. Baille's home,[70] while *Emile* was in press; he spoke to me about it: I read him the profession of faith of the Savoyard Vicar. He listened to it very quietly and, it seemed to me, with great pleasure. When I had finished he said to me, "What, Citizen? Is this part of a book that is being printed at Paris?" "Yes," I said to him, "and they ought to print it at the Louvre by order of the King;" "I agree," he said to me, "but give me the pleasure of not telling anyone that you have read me this piece." This striking manner of expressing himself surprised me without frightening me. I knew that Duclos saw M. de Malesherbes a lot. I had trouble conceiving how he thought so differently from him on the same subject.

I lived in Montmorency for more than four years without having had a single day of good health there. Although the air is excellent there, the water is bad, and that might very well be one of the causes that contributed to making my habitual ills worse. At the end of autumn 1761 I fell completely sick, and I passed the entire winter in sufferings almost without respite. The physical illness, increased by a thousand anxieties, made them all the more palpable to me. For some time cloudy and sad presentiments troubled me without me knowing what they were all about. I received rather peculiar anonymous letters, and even signed letters that were hardly less so. I received one of them from a Counsellor of the Parlement of Paris who, discontent with the present constitution of things and not auguring well for the sequel, consulted me on the choice of a refuge at Geneva or in Switzerland in order to withdraw there with his family. I received one from M. de . . . Président *à Mortier* at the Parlement of . . . which proposed that I draw up some memoranda and remonstrances for this Parlement which was on bad terms with the Court at that time, offering to furnish me all the documents and materials I would need to do so.[71] When I am suffering I am subject to bad moods. I was in one when I received these letters, I put it into the answers I made to them, flatly refusing what they asked me for: I assuredly do not reproach myself for this refusal; since these letters might have been traps from my enemies,* and what they were asking me for was contrary to principles from which I wanted to depart less than ever. But I refused harshly when I could have refused gracefully, and that is where I was in the wrong.

The two letters about which I have just spoken will be found among my papers. The one from the Counsellor did not absolutely surprise me, because I thought, as he and many others did, that the failing constitution

---

* I knew, for example, that the Président de . . . was strongly tied to the Encyclopedists and the Holbackians.

was menacing France with a near breakdown. The disasters of an unfortunate war[72] which all came through the fault of the Government; the unbelievable disorder of finances; the continuous friction of the administration which until then was divided between two or three Ministers in open war with each other, and who cast the Kingdom into an abyss in order to harm each other; the general discontentment of the people and of all the orders of the State; the stubbornness of an obstinate woman[73] who, always sacrificing her enlightenment (if she had any) to her tastes, almost always dismissed the most capable employees in order to place the ones who pleased her the most; everything joined together to justify the Counsellor's foresight and the public's and mine. This foresight even made me hesitate several times about whether I would not look for a refuge outside the Kingdom myself before the troubles that seemed to menace it; but being reassured by my insignificance and my peaceful disposition, I believed that no storm could penetrate to me in the solitude in which I wanted to live; upset only because in this state of things M. de Luxembourg was lending himself to compromising actions that would make him less well liked in his Government,[74] I would have wished that he prepare a retreat for himself there ready for any eventuality in case the great machine happened to founder, since that appeared reasonable to fear in the existing state of things, and at present it still seems to me indubitable that if all the reins of the government had not finally fallen into a single hand,[75] the French Monarchy would now be at its last gasp.

While my condition was growing worse, the printing of *Emile* slowed down and was finally completely suspended, without my being able to learn the reason for it, without Guy deigning any longer to write me or answer me, without my being able to get news from anyone or know anything about what was going on, since M. de Malesherbes was in the country at that time. Never does misfortune trouble me and pull me down whatever it might be provided I know what it consists of; but my natural inclination is to be afraid of obscurities, I dread them and I hate their black air, mystery always makes me anxious, it is far too antipathetic to my natural character which is open to the point of imprudence.[76] The sight of the most hideous monster would frighten me little, it seems to me, but if in the night I catch a glimpse of a figure under a white sheet, I will be afraid. Behold my imagination, having been kindled by this long silence, occupied by tracing out phantoms for me. The more I had the publication of my last and best work at heart, the more I tormented myself by seeking what might be holding it up, and always carrying everything to the extreme, during the suspension of the printing of the Book I believed I saw suppression[77] in it. Nevertheless, not being able to imagine either its cause or its manner, I remained in the cruelest uncertainty in the world. I wrote letter upon letter to Guy, to M. de Malesherbes, to Mme de Luxembourg, and since answers did not come at all or did not come when I was expecting them, I became entirely confused, I was raving. Unfortunately I learned at the same time that Father Griffet,[78] a Jesuit, had spoken about *Emile* and had[79] given an account of some passages from it. Instantly my imagination went off like a flash of lightning and unveiled the entire iniquitous mystery to me: I saw its course as clearly, as surely as if it had been revealed to me. I fancied[80] that, being furious at the scornful tone about which I had spoken of the colleges,[81] the Jesuits had laid hands on my work, that they were the ones who were holding up the edition, that—informed by their friend Guérin about my present condition and foreseeing my impending death, which I did not doubt— they wanted to delay the printing until then, with the plan of mutilating, distorting my work, and attributing to me sentiments different from my own in order to fulfill their own aims. It is surprising what a crowd of facts and circumstances came into my mind to trace themselves based on this madness, and to give it an air of likelihood, what do I say, to show me the evidence and the demonstration for it. Guerin had totally surrendered to the Jesuits, I knew it. I attributed to them all the advances of friendship he had made me; I persuaded myself that it was out of their instigation that he had[82] urged me to make a contract with Neaulme, that they had received the first sheets of my work from the said Neaulme, that afterward they had found the means to stop its printing with Duchesne, and per- haps to lay hands on my manuscript so as to work on it at their ease, until my death left them free to publish it travestied in their fashion. In spite of Father Berthier's wheedling,[83] I had always felt that the Jesuits did not like me, not only as an Encyclopedist, but also because all my principles were even more opposed[84] to their maxims and their influence than the incredulity of my colleagues were; since Atheistic fanaticism and pious fanaticism—touching each other through their shared intolerance—can even unite with each other, as they have done in China,[85] and as they have against me, whereas reasonable and moral Religion, by removing all human power over consciences, no longer leaves any resources to the arbiters of this power.[86] I knew that M. the Chancellor[87] was also a strong friend of the Jesuits: I feared that the son, having been intimidated by the father, might see himself as forced to abandon to them the work he had protected. I even believed I saw the effect of that abandonment in the quibbling that began to be stirred up for me over the first two volumes in which revised proofsheets were required over trifles; whereas the two other volumes were—as was not unknown[88]—full of things so strong that I would have had to recast them entirely if they were censored as the

first two. I knew furthermore, and M. de Malesherbes told it to me himself, that the Abbé de Grave, whom he had charged with the inspection
of this edition, was yet one more partisan of the Jesuits. I saw nothing but
Jesuits everywhere, without dreaming that, since they were on the eve of
being destroyed and were entirely occupied by their own defense, they
had something else to do other than to be bothered with the printing of a
book in which they were not at issue.[89] I am wrong to say *"without dreaming"*; for I certainly did dream it, and this is even an objection that M. de
Malesherbes was careful to make to me as soon as he was informed of my
vision: but out of another of those eccentricities of a man in the depths
of his retirement who wants to judge the secret of big affairs about which
he knows nothing, I never wanted to believe that the Jesuits could be in
danger, and I regarded the rumor that spread about it as a decoy on their
part in order to put their adversaries to sleep. Their past successes, which
were never interrupted, gave me such a terrible idea of their power, that
I already was lamenting the debasement of Parlement. I knew that M. de
Choiseul had studied with the Jesuits, that Mme de Pompadour was not
at all on bad terms with them, and that their league with favorites and
Ministers had always appeared advantageous to both sides against their
common enemies. The Court appeared not to be getting mixed up in anything, and since I was persuaded that if the society one day received some
rude check, it would never be the Parlement that was strong enough to
give it, from this inactivity of the Court I drew the foundation for the
society's confidence and the augury of their triumph. In sum, seeing in
all the rumors of the day only a trick and some traps on their behalf, and
believing them to have time to attend to everything in their security, I
did not doubt that soon they would crush Jansenism and the Parlement,
and the Encyclopedists, and everyone who would not have borne their
yoke, and that, if they finally let my book appear, it would only be after
having transformed it to the point of making it into a weapon by availing
themselves of my name in order to deceive my readers.[90]

I felt that I was dying; I have trouble understanding why this extravagance did not finish me off: the idea of my memory being dishonored
after me in my worthiest and best book was so frightening to me. Never
have I feared dying so such, and I believe that if I had died[91] in those
circumstances, I would have died in despair. Even today when I see the
blackest, the most dreadful plot that has ever been schemed against the
memory of a man proceeding to its execution without any obstacle, I will
die much more calmly, since I am certain of leaving in my writings a testimony of myself, which will sooner or later triumph over the plots of
men.

M. de Malesherbes, the witness and confidant of my agitations, made efforts to calm them that prove his inextinguishable goodness of heart. Mme de Luxembourg cooperated in this good deed, and went to Duchesne's several times to learn what condition this edition was in. Finally the printing was begun again and proceeded more briskly without my ever having been able to find out why it had been suspended. M. de Malesherbes took the trouble to come to Montmorency to calm me down; he succeeded in doing so, and my perfect confidence in his uprightness, which had prevailed over the disorder in my poor head, made everything he did to bring me round from it efficacious. After what he had seen of my anguishes and my delirium, it was natural that he found me very much to be pitied. So he pitied me. The incessant remarks repeated over and over again by the philosophic cabal which surrounded him came back to his mind. When I went to live at the Hermitage, they announced, as I have already said, that I would not stay there very long. When they saw that I persevered, they said that it was out of obstinacy, out of pride, out of shame at taking back what I had said, but that I was bored to death and that I lived very unhappily there. M. de Malesherbes believed this and wrote to me. Being sensitive to that error in a man for whom I had so much esteem, I wrote four consecutive letters to him in which—exposing the true motives for my behavior to him—I faithfully described my tastes, my inclinations, my character, and everything that passed in my heart. These four letters, written without a rough draft, rapidly, with the stroke of a pen, and without even having been reread, are perhaps the only thing that I have written with ease in my whole life, which is very surprising in the midst of my sufferings and of the extreme dejection I was in. While feeling myself faltering, I moaned to think that I was leaving so unjust an opinion of myself in the mind of decent people, and by means of the sketch traced hastily in these four letters, I sought to substitute in some measure for the Memoirs that I had projected. These letters, which pleased M. de Malesherbes and which he has shown in Paris, are in some way the summary of what I am exposing here in more detail and deserve to be preserved by that title. The copy he had made of them at my request, and which he sent me some years afterward, will be found among my papers.[92]

From then on the only thing that afflicted me in the opinion of my imminent death was that I did not have any trustworthy literary man into whose hands I could deposit my papers to sort them out after me. Since my trip to Geneva, I had become linked by friendship with Moultou; I had some inclination for this young man and I would have desired for him to come to close my eyes; I notified him of this desire and I believe that he would have performed this act of humanity with pleasure if his

business and his family had permitted it. Deprived of this consolation, I
wanted at least to notify him of my trust by sending him the profession
of faith of the Vicar before publication. He was satisfied with it, but in
his answer he did not appear to me to share the security with which I
was waiting for its effect at that time. He desired to have some piece from
me that no one else had. I sent him a *Funeral Oration for the Late Duc
d'Orléans* which I had written for the Abbé Darty, and who did not deliver it because, contrary to his expectation, he was not the one charged
with it.[93]

After having been begun again, the printing continued, even finished
calmly enough, and I noticed this peculiar thing in it, that, after the revised proofsheets which had been severely demanded for the first two
volumes, the last two were passed without anything being said, and without their contents making any obstacle to its publication. Nevertheless, I
still had some anxiety which I should not let pass in silence. After having
been afraid of the Jesuits, I was afraid of the Jansenists and the philosophers. As an enemy of everything that is called party, faction, cabal, I
have never expected anything good from people who are in them. The
"Godmothers"[94] had left their former residence some time before and
had established themselves right beside me, so that from their room one
heard everything that was said in mine and[95] on my terrace, and from
their garden one could very easily climb over the little wall that separated
it from my Turret. I had made this Turret into my working study, so that
I had a table in it covered with proofs and sheets from *Emile* and the *Social
Contract*, and stitching these sheets as they were sent to me, I had all my
volumes a long time before they were published. My carelessness, my negligence, my trust in M. Mathas, in whose garden I was enclosed, made it
so that, forgetting to close my Turret at night, I often found it wide open
in the morning; which would hardly have made me anxious if I had not
believed I noticed some disorder in my papers. After I had noticed this
several times, I became more careful to close the Turret. The lock was bad,
the key only closed a half turn. Now that I had become more attentive,[96]
I found an even greater disorder than when I left it completely open.
Finally one of my volumes was found to have suddenly disappeared for a
day and two nights, without my being able to learn what had become of
it until the morning of the third day when I found it on my table again.
I did not have and never have had any suspicion of M. Mathas, nor of
his nephew M. Du Moulin,[97] since I knew that they both liked me, and I
trusted them completely. I began to have less trust in the "Godmothers."
I knew that although they were Jansenists they had some connection with
d'Alembert and lodged in the same house. That made me somewhat anx-

ious, and made me more attentive. I took my papers back into my room, and I completely stopped seeing those people, having learned moreover that in several houses they had shown off the first Volume of *Emile* which I had had the imprudence to lend them. Although they continued to be my neighbors until my departure, from that time on I no longer had any communication with them.

The *Social Contract* appeared a month or two before *Emile*.[98] Rey, whom I had always demanded never to introduce any of my books furtively into France, addressed himself to the Magistrate to obtain permission for this one to enter through Rouen where he made his shipment by sea. Rey did not get any answer: his bales stayed at Rouen for several months, at the end of which they sent them back to him after having tried to confiscate them, but he made so much commotion that they returned them to him. Some curious people brought several copies from Amsterdam which circulated with little commotion. Mauleon,[99] who had heard it spoken of and who had even seen[100] some of it, spoke to me about it in a mysterious tone that surprised me, and which might even have made me anxious, if—certain of being in proper order in every respect and of having no reproach to make to myself—I had not calmed myself by means of my great maxim.[101] I did not even doubt that M. de Choiseul would sustain me against Mme de Pompadour's malevolence on this occasion since he was already well-disposed to me and would be grateful for the praise that my esteem for him had made me put in this work.

At that time I certainly had good grounds for counting as much as ever on M. de Luxembourg's kindness and on his support if it was needed: for he never gave me more frequent or more touching marks of friendship. Since my sad condition did not allow me to go to the Chateau during the Easter trip, he did not fail to come to see me a single day, and finally, seeing me suffer without a respite, he suffered so much that he induced me to see Brother Côme, sent for him, brought him to me himself, and had the courage, rare, to be sure, and meritorious in a great lord, to stay with me during the operation which was cruel and long.[102] Nevertheless, it was only a question of being probed, but I had never been able to be probed, even by Morand who undertook to do it several times, and always unsuccessfully. Brother Come, who had a hand of unequaled skill and lightness, finally succeeded in introducing a very small probe after having made me suffer very much for more than two hours, during which I struggled to hold back my moans so as not to rend the good Maréchal's sensitive heart. At the first examination Brother Côme believed he found a large stone, and told me so; at the second he no longer found it. After having begun again a second and[103] a third time with a care and exactness that caused me to find the time extremely long, he declared that there was no stone there at all, but that the prostate was scirrhous and supernaturally large; he found the bladder large and in good condition, and ended by declaring to me that I would suffer a lot and that I would live for a long time. If the second prediction comes true as accurately as the first has, my ills are not ready to end.

It is thus that, after having been treated successively for so many years for twenty illnesses that I did not have, I ended by learning that my malady, since it was incurable but not mortal, would last as long as I would. Being repressed by this knowledge, my imagination no longer made me see in prospect a cruel death of suffering from stones. I stopped fearing that the tip of a catheter which had broken in the urethra a long time before had formed the kernel of a stone. Freed from imaginary ills more cruel for me than real ills, I endured these latter more peacefully. It is certain that since that time I have suffered much less from my malady than I had until then, and I never recall that I owe this relief to M. de Luxembourg without being moved anew at his memory.

Having returned to life so to speak, and more occupied than ever with the scheme upon which I wanted to pass the rest of it, I was waiting only for the publication of *Emile* in order to execute it. I thought about Touraine where I had already been and which pleased me very much, for the mildness of both the Climate and the inhabitants:

> *La terra molle lieta e dilettosa*
> *Simili a se gli abitator*[104] *produce.*[105]

I had already spoken about my plan to M. de Luxembourg, who had wanted to dissuade me from it; I spoke to him about it again for a second time as a settled thing. Then he proposed to me the Chateau of Merlou, fifteen leagues from Paris, as a refuge that might suit me and in which they would both take pleasure in establishing me. This proposal touched me and did not displease me. Before deciding anything it was necessary to see the place; we agreed on the day when M. the Maréchal would send his Valet-de-Chambre with a carriage to drive me there. That day I found myself extremely ill; it was necessary to put off the party, and the mishaps that arrived unexpectedly kept me from executing it. Having learned since that the land of Merlou was not M. the Maréchal's but Madame's, I consoled myself more easily for not having gone there.

Emile finally appeared without my hearing any more about Revised Proofsheets or about any difficulty.[106] Before its publication M. the Maréchal asked me for all of M. de Malesherbes's letters that related to this work. My great trust in both of them, my profound sense of security kept me from reflecting on what was extraordinary and even disquieting in this request. I returned the letters, aside from one or two which remained in some books out of an oversight. Some time previously M. de Malesherbes had informed me that he would withdraw the letters I had written to Duchesne during my alarms on the subject of the Jesuits, and it must be admitted that these letters did not do great honor to my reason. But I informed him that I did not wish to pass as better than I was in anything and that he could leave the letters with him. I do not know what he did.

The publication of this book did not occur with that burst of applause that followed the publication of all my writings. Never did a work have such great private praise, but so little public approbation. What was said to me about it, what was written to me about it by the people most capable of judging it, confirmed to me that this was the best of my writings, as well as the most important. But all this was said with the most bizarre precautions, as if it were important to keep secret the good one thought about it. Mme de Boufflers, who informed me that the Author of this book deserved statues and the homage of all humans, asked me off-handedly at the end of her letter to send it back to her. D'Alembert, who wrote to me that this book settled my superiority and ought to put me at the head of all the literary people, did not sign his letter at all, although he had signed all those he had written me until then. Duclos, a reliable friend, a staunch man, but circumspect, and who made much of this book, avoided speaking to me about it in writing: La Condamine [107] threw himself on the profession of faith, and beat around the bush: Clairaut [108] limited himself to the same piece in his letter; but he was not afraid to express the emotion that his reading had given him and informed me in so many words that this reading had rekindled his old soul: out of everyone to whom I had sent my book, he was the only one who said loudly and freely to everyone all the good he thought about it.

Mathas, to whom I had also given a copy before it was on sale, loaned it to M. de Blaire, Counsellor at Parlement, father of the Intendant of Strasbourg. [109] M. de Blaire had a country house at St. Gratien, and his old acquaintance Mathas sometimes went there to see him when he was able to go. He had him read *Emile* before it was published. Upon returning it to him, M. de Blaire said to him these very words which were brought back to me the same day: [110] "M. Mathas, here is an extremely fine book, but which in a short time will be spoken of more than would be desirable for the Author." When he reported this remark [111] to me, I only laughed at it, and in it I saw only the self-importance of a man of the robe who puts some mystery into everything. All the disquieting remarks that came back to me did not make any more of an impression on me, and, far from foreseeing in any manner the catastrophe I was reaching, certain of the usefulness, of the beauty of my work, certain of being in proper order in all respects; certain as I believed I was of all Mme de Luxembourg's influence and of the Minister's favor, I applauded myself for the decision I had made to retire in the midst of my triumphs, and when I had just crushed all those people who were envious of me.

A single thing alarmed me in the publication of this book, and that, less for my safety than for the peace of my heart. At the Hermitage, at Montmorency, I had seen close up and with indignation the vexations that a jealous care for the pleasures of Princes has inflicted on the unfortunate peasants, who are forced to suffer the devastation that the game causes in their fields, without daring to defend themselves except by virtue of noise, and are forced to spend nights among their beans and their peas with cauldrons, drums, bells in order to keep the wild boars away. Since I had been the witness of the barbarous harshness with which M. the Comte de Charrolois[112] had his poor people treated, I had written a diatribe on this cruelty near the end of *Emile*.[113] Another infraction of my maxims which did not remain unpunished.[114] I learned that M. the Prince de Conti's Officers made hardly less cruel use of them on his land;[115] I trembled that this Prince for whom I was filled with respect and gratitude might apply to himself what aroused humanity had made me say about his uncle and might take offense at it. Nevertheless, since my conscience fully reassured[116] me on this score, based on its testimony I calmed myself and I did well. At least I have never learned that this great Prince has paid the slightest attention to this passage, written a long time before I had the honor of being known by him.

A few days before or after the publication of my book; for I do not recall the exact time very well, another work appeared on the same subject taken word for word from my first volume, aside from some platitudes that were mixed into this extract. This book carried the name of a Genevan called Balexert, and it was said in the title that he had won the prize of the Academy of Harlem. I understood easily that this Academy and this prize were of an entirely new creation in order to disguise the plagiarism from the public's eyes; but I also saw that there was some prior intrigue in this about which I understood nothing; either from the communication of my manuscript without which this theft could not have been made, or to build up the story of this so-called prize, for which it had been very necessary to give some foundation. It is only many years later on a word that d'Ivernois let slip out that I penetrated the mystery and caught a glimpse of those who had put the said Balexert into play.[117]

The dull roar that preceded the storm began to make itself heard and all slightly perceptive people saw very well that some plot was brewing over the subject of my book and myself that would not take long to burst out. As for me, my feeling of security, my stupidity was such that, far from foreseeing my misfortune, I did not even suspect its cause after I felt its effect. They began by rather skillfully circulating the idea that since they had dealt severely with the Jesuits they could not show a partial indulgence for books and authors who attacked Religion.[118] They reproached me for having put my name on *Emile*, as if I had not put it on all my other Writings, about which nothing had been said.[119] It seemed that they feared seeing themselves forced to some steps they would make regretfully, but which circumstances made necessary and for which my imprudence had given grounds. These rumors reached me and hardly made me anxious: it did not even enter my mind that there could be the slightest thing in all this business that regarded me personally, I who felt myself so perfectly irreproachable, so well supported, in such proper order in every regard and who did not fear that Mme de Luxembourg would leave me in trouble over a wrong which, if it existed, was entirely hers alone. But knowing how things happen in such a case, and that the practice is to deal severely with the publishers while sparing the authors, I was not without anxiety for poor Duchesne, if M. de Malesherbes happened to abandon him.

I remained calm. The rumors increased and soon changed their tone. The public and above all the Parlement seemed to be irritated by my calmness. After several days the fermentation became terrible, and, changing their object, the threats became addressed directly at me. Members of Parlement were heard to say quite openly that nothing was accomplished by burning books, and that it was necessary to burn the authors:[120] as for the publishers, they were not spoken of at all. The first time that these remarks—more worthy of an inquisitor from Goa[121] than of a senator—came back to me, I did not at all doubt that this was an invention of the Holbachians to seek to frighten me and to incite me to flee. I laughed at this puerile ruse, and while making fun of them I said to myself that if they had known the truth about things, they would have sought some other way of scaring me: but the uproar finally became such that it was clear that it was entirely true. That year M. and Mme de Luxembourg had put forward their second[122] trip to Montmorency so that they were there at the beginning of June. There I heard my new books spoken about very little in spite of the commotion they were causing at Paris, and the masters of the house did not speak to me about them at all. One morning, nevertheless, when I was alone with M. de Luxembourg, he said to me, "Have you spoken ill of M. de Choiseul in *The Social Contract*?" "I!"

I said to him drawing back from surprise, "No, I swear to you; but on the contrary I have written in it, and from a pen which is not flattering,[123] the finest praise that a Minister has ever received"; and right away I brought the passage to him. "And in *Emile?*" he resumed. "Not a word," I answered, "there is not a single word in it that concerns him." "Ah!" he said with more liveliness than he usually had, "You should have done the same thing in the other book, or have been clearer!" "I believed I was clear," I added, "I esteemed him enough for that." He was going to begin speaking again; I saw him ready to confide; he held himself back and kept silent. Unfortunate policy[124] of a courtier, which dominates friendship even in the best hearts!

This conversation, although brief, enlightened me about my situation, at least in certain respects, and made me understand that it was very much me they were after. I deplored this unheard of fatality that turned everything good I said and did to my disadvantage. Nevertheless, feeling that I had Mme de Luxembourg and M. de Malesherbes as a breast-plate in this affair, I did not see how they could set about pushing them aside and reaching me: for moreover I felt very well from that time that there would no longer be any question of equity or of justice and that they would not trouble themselves with examining whether I was really in the wrong or not. The storm, nevertheless, rumbled more and more.[125] In the diffuseness of his chattering, even Neaulme showed me regret at having been mixed up with this work and he appeared to be certain about the fate that menaced the book and the author. Nevertheless, one thing always reassured me: I saw Mme de Luxembourg so calm, so content, even so cheerful that she must have been sure of her fact in order not to have the slightest anxiety on my score, in order not to have said a single word of commiseration or excuse to me, in order to see the turn this business was taking with as much coolness as if she was not at all mixed up in it and she had not taken the slightest interest in me. What surprised me was that she said nothing at all to me: it seemed to me that she should have said something. Mme de Boufflers appeared less calm. She came and went with an air of agitation, making herself very active, and assuring me that M. the Prince de Conti was also making himself very active to ward off the blow that was being prepared for me and which she always attributed to the present circumstances in which it was important to Parlement not to let itself be accused by the Jesuits of indifference on Religion. She appeared, nevertheless, to count little on the success of the steps of the Prince and his people. Her conversations, more alarming than reassuring, all tended toward inducing me to withdrawal, and she always[126] counseled England to me where she offered me many friends, among others the famous Hume, who had been her friend for a long time. Seeing that I persisted in remaining calm, she took a course more capable of disturbing me. She made me understand that if I was arrested and interrogated, I was putting myself in the necessity of naming Mme de Luxembourg and that her friendship for me very much deserved that I not expose myself to compromising her. I answered that in such a case she could remain calm and that I would not compromise her at all. She replied that this resolution was easier to make than to execute, and in that she was right, above all for me, since I was very determined never to perjure myself nor to lie in front of the Judges, whatever risk there might be in telling the truth.

Seeing that this reflection had made some impression on me, although I could not [127] resolve to flee; she spoke to me about the Bastille for several weeks as a means of escaping the jurisdiction of the Parlement which did not meddle with State prisoners. I made no objection against this singular favor, as long as it was not solicited in my name. Since she did not speak to me about it any more, I judged afterward that she had proposed this idea only to sound me out, and that they had not wanted an expedient that would finish everything.

A few days later M. the Maréchal received from the Curate of Deuil, a friend of Grimm and Mme d'Epinay, a letter containing the warning which he said he had from a good source that Parlement was to proceed against me with the ultimate severity, and that on a certain day, which he noted, a warrant would be issued for my arrest. I judged this warning to be of Holbachian fabrication; I knew that the Parlement was very attentive to legal formalities, and that to begin on this occasion with a warrant of arrest, before knowing juridically whether I acknowledged the book [128] and whether I was really its author, was to violate all of them. "It is only," I said to Mme de Boufflers, "crimes that violate public security [129] for which they issue a warrant for the arrest of the accused out of fear that they might escape Punishment. But when one wants to punish an offense such as mine, which deserves honors and recompense, one proceeds against the book and avoids finding fault with the author as much as one can." To this she made me a subtle distinction which I have forgotten, to prove to me that they were issuing a warrant for my arrest as a favor, instead of subpoenaing me to be heard. The next day I received a letter from Guy, who notified me that, when he was at M. the Procurator General's that very day, he had seen on his Desk the draft of an Indictment against *Emile* and its Author. Note that the said Guy was the partner of Duchesne who had printed the work; who, extremely calm on his own account, was giving this warning to the author out of charity. One can judge how believable all this appeared to me! It was so simple, so natural, that a Publisher admitted to an audience by the Procurator General calmly read the manuscripts and drafts scattered on this Magistrate's Desk! Mme de Boufflers and others confirmed the same thing to me. Based on the absurdities that were incessantly dinned into my ears, I was tempted to believe that the entire world had gone mad.

Since I felt very well that underneath all this there was some mystery which they did not want to tell me, I calmly awaited the event, counting upon my uprightness and my innocence in this whole business, and only too happy, whatever persecution was to await me, to be called to the honor of suffering for the truth. Far from being afraid and keeping myself hidden, every day I went to the Chateau and in the afternoons I took my usual walk. On June 8, the eve of the Warrant, I took it with two Oratorian Professors, Father Alamanni and Father Mandard.[130] To Champeaux we brought a little snack which we ate with great appetite. We had forgotten glasses: we substituted for them with some straws of rye, with which we sucked the wine in the bottle, priding ourselves for choosing very large tubes to see who could suck the hardest. I have never been so gay in my life.

I have recounted how I lost the ability to sleep in my youth. Since then I had acquired the habit of reading in my bed every night until I felt my eyes growing heavy. Then I put out my candle and I tried to doze off for several moments that barely lasted. My usual reading at night was the Bible, and I have read it through at least five or six times in a row in this manner. That night, finding myself more awake than usual, I prolonged my reading longer, and I read the entire book that ends with the [131] Levite of Ephraim and which, if I am not mistaken, is the book of Judges, for I have not seen it again since then.[132] This story affected me very much, and I was occupied with it in a sort of dream, when all at once I was snapped out of it by some noise and light. Therese, who was carrying it, lit the way for M. la Roche who, when he saw me sit up brusquely, said to me, "Do not be alarmed; I come on behalf of Mme the Maréchale who writes to you and sends you a letter from M. the Prince de Conti." In fact, in [133] Mme de Luxembourg's I found the one that an Express Messenger from that Prince had just brought her, carrying the warning that in spite of all his efforts they were determined to proceed against me with all severity. "The fermentation," he noted to her, "is extreme; nothing can ward off the blow, the Court demands it, Parlement wishes it; at seven o'clock in the morning a warrant will be issued for his arrest, and they will send to arrest him on the spot; I have obtained assurances that they will not pursue him if he gets away; but if he persists in wanting to let himself be arrested, he will be arrested." La Roche besought me on behalf of Mme the Maréchale to get up and go to confer with her. It was two o'clock; she had just gone to bed: "She is waiting for you," he added, "and does not want to go to sleep without having seen you." I hastily got dressed and I ran to her.

She appeared troubled to me. That was the first time. Her agitation touched me. In this moment of surprise in the middle of the night,[134] I was not exempt from emotion myself: but when I saw her I forgot myself in order to think only about her and about the sad part she was going to play if I let myself be taken: for while I felt that I had enough courage never to say anything but the truth, even if it must harm me and ruin me, I did not feel that I had either enough presence of mind, or enough skill, or perhaps enough firmness to avoid compromising her if I was sharply pressed. That made me decide to sacrifice my glory to her tranquillity, to do for her on this occasion what nothing would have made me do for myself.[135] The moment my resolution was made I declared it to her, since I did not want to spoil the value of my sacrifice by making her purchase it. I am certain that she could not have been mistaken about my motive; nevertheless, she did not say a[136] word to me that showed that she was grateful for it. I was so shocked[137] by this indifference that I hesitated over retracting: but M. the Maréchal happened to arrive; Madame de Boufflers arrived from Paris several moments later. They did what Mme de Luxembourg should have done. I let myself be flattered; I was ashamed to retract what I had said, and there was no longer any question except about the place for my withdrawal and of the time for my departure. M. de Luxembourg proposed that I stay in his home for several days incognito to deliberate and take my measures more at leisure; I did not consent to this at all, nor to the proposition to go secretly to the Temple.[138] I persisted in wanting to leave as early as the same day rather than to remain hidden in any place whatsoever.

Feeling that I had secret and powerful enemies in the Kingdom, I judged that, in spite of my attachment for France, I ought to leave it to ensure my tranquillity. My first impulse was to withdraw to Geneva; but an instant of reflection was enough to dissuade me from performing this stupid act. I knew that, if he had resolved to torment me, the Minister of France, even more powerful at Geneva than at Paris, would not leave me in peace in one of these cities any more than in the other. I knew that the *Discourse on Inequality* had excited a hatred against me in the Council which was all the more dangerous since it did not dare to show itself. In the last place I knew that when *La Nouvelle Héloïse* appeared, the Council had been pressed to prohibit it by Doctor Tronchin's solicitation; but seeing that no one was imitating it, not even at Paris, it became ashamed of this stupidity and withdrew the prohibition. I did not doubt that, upon finding the occasion more favorable here, it would make great efforts to take advantage of it. I knew that in spite of all the fine appearances a secret jealousy reigned against me in all Genevan hearts which was only waiting for the occasion to satisfy itself. Nevertheless, love of the fatherland called me back to my own, and if I had been able to flatter myself that I could live there in peace, I would not have hesitated; but, since neither honor nor reason allowed me to take refuge there like a fugitive, I decided only to draw near it and to go to Switzerland in order to wait for what they might decide to do with regard to me in Geneva. It will soon be seen that this uncertainty did not last very long.

Mme de Boufflers very much disapproved of this resolution, and made new efforts to induce me to go to England. She did not shake me. I have never liked England or the English, and far from overcoming my repugnance, all of Mme de Boufflers's eloquence seemed to increase it, without me knowing why.

Once I had decided to leave the same day, from the morning on everyone was told I had left, and la Roche, whom I sent for my papers, did not want to tell even Therese whether I had left or not. Since I had resolved to write my memoirs someday, I had accumulated many letters and other papers, so that several trips were necessary. One portion of these papers, which had already been sorted, was put aside, and for the rest of the morning I occupied myself with sorting the others in order to take away only what might be useful to me and to burn the rest. M. de Luxembourg wanted very much to help me in this labor, which took so long that we were not able to finish in the morning, and I did not have time to burn anything. M. the Maréchal offered to take charge of the rest of this sorting, of burning the scraps himself, without referring to anyone whatever, and of sending me everything that would have been set aside. I accepted the offer, very glad to be freed from this effort, to be able to pass the few hours I had left with such dear persons, whom I was going to leave forever. He took the key of the room in which I left these papers, and at my earnest entreaty he sent to find my poor aunt who was consumed in mortal perplexity about what had become of me and about what was going to become of her, and waiting for the Process-servers at any moment, without knowing how to behave and how to answer them. La Roche brought her to the Chateau without telling her anything, she believed that I was already very far away; when she noticed me she pierced the air with her cries and threw herself into my arms. Oh friendship, harmony of hearts, habit, intimacy! In this sweet and cruel moment were gathered together so many days that we had passed together in happiness, tenderness, and peace, in order to make me feel better the wrench of a first separation, after having hardly lost each other from sight a single day in almost seventeen years. Witnessing this embrace, the Maréchal could not hold back his tears. He left us. Therese did not want to leave me. I made her feel the inconvenience of her following me at that moment, and the necessity for her to remain in order to liquidate my effects and collect my money. When a warrant is issued for a man's arrest, the practice is to seize his papers, to place a seal on his effects or to make an inventory of them, and to name a guardian for them. It was very necessary for her to stay to watch over what happened and turn it all to the best account possible. I promised her that she would rejoin me in a little while: M. the Maréchal confirmed my promise; but I never wanted to tell her where I was going so that she could truthfully protest her ignorance on this score when she was interrogated by the people who would come to arrest me. When I embraced her at the moment we left each other, I felt a very extraordinary movement inside myself, and I told her in an outburst, alas only too pro-phetic, "My child, you must arm yourself with courage. You have shared the prosperity of my good days; it remains for you to share my miseries, since you wish it so. In following me, do not expect anything but affronts and calamities any longer: the fate that begins for me on this sad day will pursue me until my final hour."

There was nothing left for me to do except think about leaving. The Process-servers should have come at ten o'clock. It was four in the after-noon when I left, and they had not yet arrived.[139] It had been decided that I would take the post. I had no carriage at all, M. the Maréchal made me the present of a cabriolet, and loaned me some horses and a postilion until the first post where no difficulty was made about furnishing me some horses because of measures he had taken.

Since I had not dined at table and had not shown myself in the Cha-teau, the Ladies came to bid me farewell in the mezzanine where I had passed the day. Mme the Maréchale embraced me several times with a rather sad appearance; but in these embraces I no longer felt the pressure of the ones she had lavished on me two or three years before. Mme de Boufflers also embraced me and said some extremely fine things to me. An embrace that surprised me more was Mme de Mirepoix's; for she was also there. Mme the Maréchale de Mirepoix is an extremely cold, decorous, and reserved person, and to me did not appear entirely exempt from the natural haughtiness of the house of Lorraine.[140] She had never given evi-dence of much attention to me. Either because I was seeking to increase the value of an honor that flattered me and which I did not expect; or because she in fact put a little of that commiseration natural to generous hearts into this embrace, I found a certain energetic quality in her move-ment and her look that pierced me. Often when thinking about it again later on, I have suspected that, since she was not ignorant of the fate to which I was condemned, she could not protect herself from a moment of emotion over my destiny.

M. the Maréchal did not open his mouth; he was as pale as a dead man. He absolutely wanted to accompany me to my carriage which was waiting for me at the watering place. We crossed the whole garden without saying a single word. I had a key for the park which I used to open the gate, after which, instead of putting the key back in my pocket, I held it out to him without saying a word. He took it with a surprising promptness, which I have not been able to keep myself from thinking about often since that time. I have hardly had a more bitter moment in my life than the one of this separation. The embrace was long and mute: both of us felt that this embrace [141] was a last farewell.

Between La Barre and Montmorency I encountered four men in black in a hired carriage who saluted me while smiling. Based on what Therese reported to me later on about the appearance of the Process-servers, about the hour of their arrival, and about the manner in which they com-ported themselves, I did not doubt at all that it was they; above all when I learned later on that instead of the warrant having been issued for me at seven o'clock as had been announced to me, it had not been done until noon. I had to cross all of Paris. One is not extremely hidden in a com-pletely open cabriolet. In the streets I saw several people who saluted me with an air of acquaintance, but I did not recognize any of them. The same night I detoured to pass Villeroy. At Lyon post travelers were supposed to be taken to the commandant. That might be embarrassing for a man who did not want either to lie or to change his name. I went with a letter from Mme de Luxembourg to ask M. de Villeroy to get me exempted from this irksome duty. M. de Villeroy gave me a letter which I did not use because I did not pass through Lyon.

This letter has remained still sealed among my papers. M. the Duc pressed me very much to sleep at Villeroy; but I preferred to take to the highway again, and I did two more posts the same day.

My carriage was rough, and I was too ill to be able to walk long stages. Moreover, I did not have an imposing enough air to get myself served well, and it is known that in France the post horses feel the rod only on the postilion's shoulders. By paying the guides liberally I believed I was compensating for appearance and speech; this was even worse. They took me for a bumpkin who was going on orders and who was taking the post for the first time in his life. From that time I no longer had anything but sorry nags and I became the postilions' plaything. I ended, as I should have begun, by acquiring patience, saying nothing, and going along as they pleased.

By abandoning myself to reflections that presented themselves about everything that had just happened to me, I had enough resources not to be bored on the road; but that was neither my turn of mind nor the inclination of my heart. It is surprising how easily I forget past evil, however recent it might be. As soon as it has happened its remembrance returns to me weakly and passes away without difficulty every bit as much as its foresight frightens me and troubles me as long as I see it in the future. My cruel imagination, which ceaselessly torments itself by foreseeing evils that do not yet exist, diverts my memory and keeps me from recalling the ones that do not exist any longer. There are no longer any precautions to take against what is done, and it is useless to be concerned about it. In some manner I consume my unhappiness in advance. The more I have suffered by foreseeing it, the easier it is for me to forget it; while, on the contrary, since I am ceaselessly occupied with my [142] past happiness, I recall it and ruminate, so to speak, to the point of enjoying it all over again when I want to. I feel that I owe it to this fortunate inclination that I have never known that spiteful mood that ferments in a vindictive heart, from the continual remembrance of offenses received, and which torments itself with all the evil it would like to do [143] to its enemy. Being naturally quick-tempered, I have felt anger, even rage in the first impulses, but a desire for vengeance has never taken root inside of me. I occupy myself too little with the offense to occupy myself very much with the offender. I think about the evil I have received from him only because of the evil I might still receive from him, and if I were sure that he no longer is doing me any, the one he has done me would be instantly forgotten. Pardoning offenses is preached to us very much. That doubtless is an extremely fine virtue, but one that I do not practice. I do not know whether my heart would be able to dominate its hatred, for it has never felt it, and I think too little about my enemies to have the merit of pardoning them. I will not say to what point they torment themselves in order to torment me. I am at their mercy, they have all the power, they make use of it. There is only one thing beyond their power, and I defy them to attain it: that is, by tormenting themselves with me, to force me to torment myself with them.

From the day after my departure I so perfectly forgot everything that had just passed, Parlement, and Mme de Pompadour, and M. de Choiseul, and Grimm, and d'Alembert, and their plots, [144] and their accomplices, that I would not even have thought about them again on my whole trip, except for the precautions I was obliged to take. A remembrance that came to me in the middle of all this was my last reading on the eve of my departure. I also recalled the *Idylls* by Gessner which his translator Hubner had sent me some time before.[145] These two ideas came back to me so well and mingled to such an extent in my mind that I wanted to try to bring them together by treating the subject of the *Levite of Ephraïm* in Gessner's manner. This rustic and naive style hardly appeared appropriate for such an atrocious subject, and it was hardly to be presumed that my present situation furnished me with very cheerful ideas to lighten it. Nevertheless, I attempted to do it, solely to amuse myself in my coach and without any hope of success. I had hardly tried when I was astonished by the attractiveness of my ideas, and by the facility I experienced at rendering them. In three days I composed the first three cantos of this little poem which I finished later on at Môtiers, and I am sure that I have not written anything in my life in which there reigns a more moving gentleness of morals, a fresher coloring, more naive depictions, a more precise description of local color, a more antique simplicity in everything, and all that, in spite of the horror of the subject, which at bottom is abominable; so that in addition to everything else I also had the merit of the difficulty overcome. If it is not the best of my works, *The Levite of Ephraïm* will always be the dearest.[146] Never have I reread it, never will I reread it without feeling inside the applause of a heart without bile which, far from being embittered by its misfortunes, consoles itself for them with itself and finds enough to compensate it within itself. Gather together all those great philosophers, in their books so superior to the adversity they have never experienced, put them in a position similar to mine, and give them a similar work to write in the first indignation of outraged honor: one will see how they will acquit themselves.

When I left Montmorency for Switzerland, I had made the resolution to stop at Yverdon, at the home[147] of my good old friend M. Roguin, who had retired there several years before, and who had even invited me to go there to see him. En route I learned that Lyon required a detour; that prevented me from passing through it. But, as a result, it was necessary to pass through Besançon, a fortified city, and consequently subject to the same inconvenience. I took it into my head to turn aside and pass through Salins, under the pretext of going to see M. de Miran, M. Dupin's nephew, who had a position in the Saltworks, and who had formerly given me many invitations to go there to see him.[148] The expedient succeeded; I did not find M. de Miran, and being extremely glad of being dispensed from stopping, I continued my way without anyone saying a word to me.

Upon entering the territory of Bern I had the coach stop; I got out, I prostrated myself, I hugged, I kissed the earth, and shouted out in my rapture, "Heaven, protector of virtue, I praise you, I touch a land of freedom." It is thus that, blind and confident in my hopes, I am always filled with enthusiasm for what must cause my misfortune. My surprised postilion believed I was mad: I got back into my coach and a few hours afterward, I had the joy, as pure as it was lively, of feeling myself pressed into the arms of the respectable Roguin. Ah, let us catch our breath for several moments in the home of this worthy host! I need to take up courage and strength again; I will soon find cause to use them.

It is not without reason that I enlarged upon all the circumstances I could recall in the account I just gave. Although they do not appear[149] extremely luminous, once one catches the thread of the scheme, they can throw some light on its course, and for example, although they do not give the foremost idea of the problem I am going to propose, they help very much to resolve it.

Let us assume that my withdrawal was absolutely necessary for the execution of the plot whose object I was, in order to bring this about everything should have occurred just about as it did occur; but if I had continued to keep firm, as I had begun, without[150] letting myself be scared by Mme de Luxembourg's nocturnal embassy and troubled by her alarms, and if I had returned to my bed to sleep tranquilly until the early morning instead of staying at the Chateau, would the warrant have been issued for me all the same? A big question upon which depends the solution of many others, and for whose examination it is not useless to take note of the time of the comminatory Warrant and the real Warrant. A rough but palpable example of the importance of the slightest details in the exposition of facts whose secret causes one seeks, in order to discover them by means of induction.[151]

Book XII [1]

Here begins the work of darkness in which I have found myself enshrouded for the past eight years without having been able to penetrate its frightening obscurity no matter what I might try to do about it. In the abyss of evils in which I am submerged, I feel the contact of the blows that are aimed at me, I perceive their immediate instrument, but I cannot see either the hand that directs it, or the means it puts into operation. Opprobrium and misfortunes fall upon me as if by themselves and without being seen. If my torn-up heart lets some moans escape, I have the appearance of a man who is complaining for no reason, and the authors of my ruin have found the inconceivable art of making the public into an accomplice of their plot without the public suspecting it and perceiving the effect. Thus as I narrate the events that concern me, the treatment I have suffered and everything that has happened to me, I am in no position to go back to the impelling hand, and to fix the causes as I state the facts. These primitive causes are all marked out in the three [2] preceding books; all the interests relative to me, all the secret motives are exposed there. But to say how these diverse causes combined to bring about the strange events of my life; this is what I am unable to explain, even by conjecture. If any of my readers are generous enough to want to get to the core of these mysteries and to discover the truth, let them reread the three [3] preceding books with care, then let them take the information that will be in their grasp for each fact they will read in the following ones, let them go back from intrigue to intrigue and agent to agent up to the prime movers of everything; I know with certainty at what terminus their research will come to an end, but I get lost in the obscure and tortuous route of the underground passages that will lead them there.

During my stay at Yverdon I made the acquaintance of M. Roguin's entire family, and among others his niece Mme Boy de la Tour and her daughters, whose father, as I believe I have said, I had formerly known at Lyon. [4] She had come to Iverdon to see her uncle and sisters; her oldest daughter, who was about fifteen years old, enchanted me with her great sense and her excellent character. I became attached to the mother and daughter with the most tender friendship. This latter had been [5] destined by M. Roguin to his nephew the Colonel, [6] already advanced in age, and who also bore witness of the greatest affection for me; but although the uncle was enthusiastic for this marriage, although the nephew desired it extremely also, and although I took a very lively interest in the satisfaction of both of them, the great disproportion of age and the extreme repugnance of the young person made me cooperate with the mother in discouraging this marriage, which did not take place. Subsequently the Colonel married his relative Mademoiselle Dillan who has a character and beauty in accordance with my heart, and who has made him the happiest of husbands and fathers. In spite of that M. Roguin has not been able to forget that I interfered with his desires on this occasion. I have consoled myself for it with the certainty of having fulfilled, both toward him and toward his family, the duty of the most holy friendship, which is not to make oneself always agreeable, but always to counsel for the best.

I was not left in doubt for very long about the welcome that was waiting for me at Geneva in case I wanted to return there. My Book was burned and a warrant issued[7] on June 18, that is to say nine days after the one was issued in Paris. So many unbelievable absurdities were accumulated in this second warrant, and the Ecclesiastical Edict[8] was so absolutely violated in it that I refused to give faith to the first news that came to me about it, and when it was well confirmed, I trembled that such a manifest and flagrant infraction of all laws, beginning with the law of good sense, might turn Geneva upside down: I might have had reason to be reassured; everything remained calm. If some uproar stirred up the populace it was only against me, and all the babblers and prigs publicly treated me as a Schoolboy whom one would threaten with the rod for not having said his catechism well.

These two Warrants were the signal for the shout of malediction that was raised against me throughout Europe with an unprecedented fury. All the gazettes, all the journals, all the pamphlets rang the most terrible alarms! Above all the French—those people so gentle, so polite, so generous, who pride themselves so extremely on decorum and consideration for the unfortunate—suddenly forgot all their favorite virtues and distinguished themselves by the number and the violence of the outrages with which they vied with each other in heaping on me. I was an impious person, an atheist, a wild man, a madman, a wild beast, a wolf. The continuator of the Journal of Trévoux made a flight on my supposed Lycanthropy which showed his own well enough.[9] In sum, you might have said that at Paris they were afraid of getting embroiled with the authorities, if they failed to sprinkle in some insult against me when they published a writing on any subject whatsoever. While I vainly sought the cause of this unanimous animosity, I was ready to believe that the whole world had gone mad. What! the editor of *Perpetual Peace* stirs up discord, the publisher of the Savoyard Vicar is an impious man, the author of *La Nouvelle Héloïse* is a wolf, that of *Emile* is a madman. Oh my God, what would I have been then if I had published the book *On the Mind*[10] or some other similar work? And nevertheless in the storm that was raised against the Author of that book, the public, far from joining its voice to that of his persecutors, avenged him from them by its praises. Compare his book and mine, the different welcome they received, the treatment given to the two Authors in the different States of Europe; find some causes for these differences that can satisfy a sensible man; this is all I ask, and I am silent.

I found myself so well off from the stay at Yverdon that, at the lively solicitation of M. Roguin and of his whole family, I formed the resolution to stay there. Through his kindness, M. de Moiry de Gingins,[11] the Bailiff of that city, also encouraged me to stay under his government. The Colonel urged me so strongly to accept the habitation of a little lodge that he had between the courtyard and the garden of his house that I consented to it, and he immediately hurried to furnish and stock it with everything my little household needed. Roguin the Banneret,[12] among the most eager around me, did not leave me all day long. I was always very grateful for so many blandishments, but I was sometimes very pestered by them. The day of my moving in was already set, and I had written to Therese to come to join me, when suddenly I learned that a storm was being raised against me at Berne which was attributed to the pious, and whose first cause I have never been able to penetrate. The Senate, having been excited without it being known by whom, appeared not to want to leave me tranquil in my retirement. At the first warning that M. the Baillif had of this fermentation, he wrote to several members of the Government in my favor, reproaching them for their blind intolerance, and making them ashamed of wanting to refuse to an oppressed man of merit the refuge that so many Bandits found in their States. Sensible people presumed that the warmth of his reproaches had more sharpened than softened minds. However that might be, neither his influence nor his eloquence could ward off the blow. Upon being informed of the order he was supposed to notify me of, he warned me in advance, and so as not to wait for this order I resolved to leave as early as the next day. The difficulty was to know where to go, seeing that Geneva and France were closed to me, and foreseeing very well that in this business each would rush to imitate his neighbor.[13]

Mme Boy de la Tour proposed that I go to establish myself in an empty but completely furnished house which belonged to her son in the village

of Môtiers in the Val-de-Travers Comté of Neuchâtel. I only had to cross
a mountain to make my way there. The offer came all the more appropri-
ately since I ought naturally to be sheltered from persecutions in the King
of Prussia's States, and at least Religion could hardly serve as a pretext.[14]
But a secret difficulty that it was not suitable for me to state had made me
hesitate very much. This innate love of justice, which always devoured my
heart, joined to my secret inclination for France, had inspired me[15] with
aversion for the King of Prussia who, by his maxims and his conduct,
appeared to me to trample underfoot all respect for natural law and for
all human duties. Among the engravings with which I had decorated my
Turret at Montmorency was a portrait of this Prince underneath which
was[16] a couplet that ended this way:

He thinks like a philosopher, and behaves like a King.

This verse, which might have made a fine enough praise from any other
pen, had a sense that was not equivocal from mine, and which moreover
explained the preceding verse only too clearly.[17] This couplet had been
seen by everyone who came to see me which was not a small number.
The Chevalier de Lorenzy had even written it down in order to give it to
d'Alembert, and I did not doubt that d'Alembert had taken the trouble
to pay my Court to this Prince with it. I had even aggravated this first
wrong with a passage from *Emile* in which one saw well enough whom
I had meant under the name of Adrastus King of the Daunians, and the
remark had not escaped the cavillers, since Mme de Boufflers mentioned
this subject to me several times.[18] Thus I was very sure of being inscribed
in red ink on the King of Prussia's records, and if it were assumed moreover that he did have the principles which I had dared to attribute to him,
from that alone my writings and their Author could only displease him:
for it is known that the wicked and Tyrants have always acquired the most
mortal hatred for me, even without knowing me, and solely upon reading
my writings.

Nevertheless, I dared to put myself at his mercy, and I believed I was
running little risk. I knew that base passions subjugate only weak men,
and have little hold on souls of a strong temper, as I had always recognized
his to be. I judged that it was part of his art of ruling to show himself to be
magnanimous on similar occasions, and that it was not beyond his character to be so in fact. I judged that a vile and easy vengeance would not
counterbalance love of glory in him for a moment, and—putting myself
in his place[19]—I did not believe it impossible that he might avail himself
of the circumstance to overwhelm with the weight of his generosity the
man who had dared to think badly of him. Thus I went to establish myself

at Môtiers with a confidence the value of which I believed he was made to feel, and I said to myself, "When Jean-Jaques raises himself up next to Coriolanus will Frederic be beneath [20] the General of the Volscians." [21]

Colonel Roguin absolutely wanted to cross the mountain with me and to come to install me at Môtiers. One of Mme Boy-de-la-Tour's sisters-in-law called Mme Girardier, for whom the house I was going to occupy was very convenient, did not see me arrive with very much pleasure: nevertheless, she put me in possession of my lodging with a good grace, and I ate at her home while waiting until Therese had come and my little household was set up.

Since my departure from Montmorency, I hesitated to permit her to come to join me and share the wandering life to which I saw myself condemned, because I felt very much that from then on I would be a fugitive on the earth. I felt that our relations were going to change because of that catastrophe, and that what had been a favor and benefit on my part up to then would be one on hers from then on. If her attachment remained proof against my misfortunes, she would be torn apart by them, and her suffering would add to my ills. If my disgrace cooled her heart, she would make me value her constancy as a sacrifice, and instead of feeling the pleasure I had in sharing my last crust of bread with her, she would feel only the merit she had in wanting to follow me everywhere fate forced me to go.

Everything must be said: I have concealed neither my poor Mamma's vices nor mine; I ought not to do any greater favor for Therese, and whatever pleasure I take in doing honor to a person who is so dear to me, I do not want to disguise her wrongs either, if an involuntary change in the affections [22] of the heart is a true wrong. For a long time I had been noticing that hers was cooling off. I felt that she no longer was for me what she was during our fine years, and I felt it all the more since I was still the same for her. I fell back into the same inconvenience whose effect I had felt with Mamma, and this effect was the same with Therese: Let us not seek perfections beyond nature; it would be the same with any woman whatsoever. However well reasoned the decision I had made with regard to my children might have appeared to me, it had not always left my heart tranquil. While meditating on my treatise on education, I felt that I had neglected duties from which nothing could dispense me. Finally remorse became so lively that it drew from me the almost public admission of my fault at the beginning of *Emile*, and the reference itself is so clear that after such a passage it is surprising that anyone has had the courage to reproach me for it. [23] Nevertheless, at that time my situation was the same, and even worse because of the animosity of my enemies, who sought only to catch me at fault. I feared the possibility of a recurrence, and not wanting to run the risk of it, I preferred to condemn myself to abstinence rather than to expose Therese to seeing herself in the same position once more. Moreover, I had noticed that intercourse with women made my condition sensibly worse.[24] This double reason had caused me to form some resolutions which I have sometimes kept rather badly; but in which I had persisted with more constancy for three or four years; it was also during this epoch that I had noticed the cooling off in Therese: she had the same attachment for me out of duty, but no longer had it out of love. That necessarily threw less pleasure into our relations, and I imagined that, being sure of the continuation of my care wherever she might be, she would perhaps prefer to stay in Paris rather than to wander with me. Nevertheless, she had shown so much suffering at our separation, she had demanded such positive promises from me to reunite us, she had expressed the desire for it since my departure in such a lively way to both M. the Prince de Conti and M. de Luxembourg that, far from having the courage to speak to her about separation, I hardly had enough to think about it myself, and after having felt in my heart how impossible it was for me to do without her, I no longer thought of anything but recalling her at once. Thus I wrote to her to leave; she came: it had been barely two months since I had left her; but it was our first separation in so many years.[25] We had both felt it very cruelly. What a thrill when we embraced each other. How sweet are the tears of tenderness and joy! How my heart drinks them in! Why have I been made to shed so few of them?

Upon arriving at Môtiers I had written to Lord Keith, Marshal of Scotland and Governor of Neuchâtel, to give him notice of my withdrawal into his Majesty's States, and to ask him for his protection. He answered me with the generosity for which he is known and which I expected from him. He invited me to go to see him. I went there with M. Martinet,[26] the Châtelain of Val-de-Travers, who was in great favor with his Excellency. The venerable aspect of the famous and virtuous Scot powerfully moved my heart, and from the very instant there began that lively attachment between him and me which on my part has always remained the same, and which would always have been so on his if the traitors who have deprived me of all the consolations of life had not taken advantage of my absence to abuse his age and disfigure me in his eyes.[27]

George Keith, the hereditary Marshal of Scotland, and brother of the famous General Keith who lived gloriously and died in the bed of honor,[28] had left his country in his youth and was proscribed from it for having been attached to the house of Stuart, with which he was soon disgusted by the unjust and tyrannical spirit he noticed in it and which was always its dominant character. For a long time he resided in Spain, the climate of which pleased him very much, and ended as his brother did by attaching himself to the King of Prussia, who is a good judge of men and welcomed[29] them as they deserve. He was well paid for this welcome by the great services that Marshal Keith rendered him, and by an even much more precious thing, the Lord Marshal's sincere friendship. That worthy man's great soul, entirely republican and proud, could submit only under the yoke of friendship but it submitted so perfectly to it that—even with very different maxims—he no longer saw anything but Frederic from the moment he became attached to him. The King charged him with important business, sent him to Paris, to Spain, and finally seeing that, being old already, he needed rest, gave him the government of Neuchâtel for his retirement with the delightful occupation of passing the remainder of his life there by making this little people happy.

When the Neuchâtelois, who like only ridiculous affectation and tinsel, who are not at all good judges of genuine material, and attribute intelligence to long sentences, saw a cold man without much ado, they took his simplicity for haughtiness, his frankness for rusticity, his laconism for stupidity, and kicked against his beneficent efforts, because—wanting to be useful and not a cajoler—he could not flatter people he did not esteem. In the ridiculous business of the Minister Petitpierre, who was dismissed by his colleagues for not having wanted them to be eternally damned, His Lordship, who was opposed to the Ministers' usurpations, saw the whole country whose side he was taking rise up against him, and when I arrived there this stupid murmuring was not yet dead.[30] He passed at least for a man who let himself be predisposed, and of all the imputations with which he was charged that was perhaps the least unjust. My first emotion upon seeing this venerable old man was to be moved by the thinness of his body already emaciated by the years; but when I raised my eyes to his animated, open, and noble physiognomy, I felt myself seized by a respect mixed with confidence that swept aside every other feeling. To the very short compliment which I paid him as I approached him, he answered by speaking of something else as if I had been there for a week. He did not even tell us to sit down. The stiff Châtelain remained standing. As for me I saw in His Lordship's piercing and subtle eye an indefinable something so affectionate that—feeling myself at my ease from the first—without any ado I went to share his sofa and sat down beside him. From the familiar tone he instantly took, I felt that this liberty pleased him, and that he said to himself inside, "This one is not a Neuchâtelois."

Peculiar effect of great conformity of characters! At an age when the heart has already lost its natural warmth, that of this good old man warmed up for me in a manner that surprised everyone. He came to see me at Môtiers under the pretext of shooting quails, and passed two days there without touching a rifle. Such friendship, for that is the word, was established between us that we could not do without each other. The Chateau of Colombier in which he lived in the summer was six leagues from Môtiers; at least every two weeks I went to pass twenty-four hours there; then I returned on foot like a pilgrim, my heart still full of him. The emotion that I formerly experienced in my walks from the Hermitage to Eaubonne was assuredly very different, but it was not sweeter than the one with which I drew near Colombier. How many tears of emotion I often shed on my route while thinking about the paternal kindness, about the lovable virtues, about the gentle philosophy of this respectable old man. I called him my father, he called me his child. These sweet names in part give the idea of the attachment that united us, but they do not also give that of the need we had for each other and of the continuous desire to come together. He absolutely wanted to lodge me at the Chateau of Colombier, and for a long time urged me to take the apartment I occupied there as a residence. Finally I told him that I was freer in my home, and that I preferred to pass my life by coming to see him. He approved of this frankness and did not speak to me about it any more. Oh my good Lord! oh my worthy father! how moved my heart still is in thinking about you! Ah the barbarians! what blow did they strike me by detaching you from me! But no, no, great man, you are and will always be the same for me who am always the same. They have fooled you, but they have not changed you.

The Lord Marshal is not flawless: he is a wise man, but he is a man. Even with the most penetrating mind, with the subtlest tact one can have, with the most profound knowledge of men, he lets himself be deceived sometimes, and does not recover from it. He has a peculiar disposition, something bizarre and strange in his turn of mind. He appears to forget the people he sees every day, and remembers them at the moment they least expect it: his attentions appear inappropriate: his gifts are whimsical and not suitable. He gives or sends instantly what enters his head, of great value or of no worth indifferently. A young Genevan desiring to enter the King of Prussia's service presents himself to him. Instead of a letter His Lordship gives him a little [31] bag full of peas which he orders him to deliver to the King. Upon receiving this peculiar recommendation the King instantly places the one who carries it. These elevated geniuses have a language between them that vulgar minds will never understand.[32] These little peculiarities, similar to the caprices of a pretty woman, only made the Lord Marshal more interesting to me. I was very sure and later on I very much experienced that they did not influence the feelings or the efforts that friendship prescribed to him on serious occasions. But it is true that he still put the same peculiarity in his way of obliging as he did in his manners. I will cite only a single stroke about a trifle. Since the journey from Môtiers to Colombier was too much for me, I ordinarily divided it by leaving after dinner and sleeping at Brot half-way there. When the Landlord, called Sandoz, had to solicit a favor at Berlin that was extremely important to him, he begged [33] me to ask His Excellency to ask it for him: gladly. I bring him with me; I leave him in the antechamber and I speak about his business to His Lordship, who does not answer anything to me. The morning passes; upon crossing the room to go to dine, I see poor Sandoz who was cooling his heels waiting. Believing that His Lordship had forgotten him, I speak to him about him again before sitting down at table; not a word, as before. I found this manner of making me feel how much I was badgering him to be a little harsh and I kept quiet while silently feeling sorry for poor Sandoz. Upon returning the next day I was very surprised at the thanks he gave me for the good welcome and the good dinner he had had at His Excellency's, who furthermore had accepted his paper. Three weeks later His Lordship sent him the rescript he had asked for, expedited by the Minister and signed by the King, and did so without ever having wished to tell either me or him or to answer a single word about this business, with which I believed he did not want to burden himself.

I do not want to stop talking about George Keith: it is from him that my final happy remembrances come; all the rest of my life has been nothing but afflictions and heartaches. The memory of it is so sad and comes to me so confusedly that I cannot put any order in my accounts: henceforward I will be forced to arrange them by chance and as they present themselves.

It was not long before I was relieved of anxiety about my refuge by the King's response to the Lord Marshal, in whom I had found a good advocate as can be believed. Not only did His Majesty approve of what he had done, but he charged him, for everything must be said, with giving me twelve Louis. The good Lord, embarrassed at such a commission, and not knowing how to perform it decently, attempted to extenuate the insult by transforming this money into provisions, and notifying me that he had been ordered to furnish me with wood and coal to begin my little household; [34] he even added, and perhaps on his own authority, that the King would willingly have a little house built to my liking for me if I wanted to choose the site. This last offer touched me extremely and made me forget the stinginess of the other one. Without accepting either of the two I regarded Frederic as my benefactor and my protector, and I attached myself so sincerely to him that from that time I took as much interest in his glory as I had found injustice in his successes until then. I testified to my joy for the peace he made a little time afterward by a very tasteful illumination: it was a chain of garlands with which I adorned the house I inhabited, and on which I had, it is true, the vindictive pride of spending almost as much money as he had wanted to give me.[35]

When the peace was concluded, I believed that, since his military and political glory was at its peak, he was going to give himself one of another sort by revivifying his States, by making commerce, agriculture reign in them, by creating a new soil, by covering it with a new people, by maintaining the peace among all his neighbors, by making himself the arbiter of Europe after having been its terror. He could put away the sword without risk, very sure that he would not be obliged to pick it up again. Seeing that he was not disarming, I feared that he might make poor use of his advantages, and that he might be only half great. I dared to write to him on this subject and, taking the familiar tone made to please men of his stamp, to bring to him that holy voice of truth, which so few Kings are made to understand. It was only in secret and from me to him that I took this liberty. I did not even make the Lord Marshal a participant in it and I sent him my letter to the King sealed up. His Lordship sealed the letter without being informed of its contents. The King made no response to it, and some time after, when the Lord Marshal had gone to Berlin, he told him only that I had given him a good scolding. I understood from this that my letter had been poorly received, and that the frankness of my zeal had passed for the rusticity of a pedant. At bottom that might very well be true; perhaps I did not say what had to be said and did not take the tone that had to be taken. I can only answer for the feeling that put the pen into my hand.

A little time after my establishment at Môtiers-Travers, since I had all possible assurances that I would be left tranquil there, I put on Armenian dress. This was not a new idea. It had come to me several times in the course of my life, and it often came back to me at Montmorency where the frequent usage of catheters, which often condemned me to stay in my room, made me feel all the advantages of the long garment better. The convenience of an Armenian tailor, who often came to see a relative he had at Montmorency, tempted me to take advantage of it to take up this new outfit at the risk of what people will say about it, about which I cared very little. Nevertheless, before adopting this new adornment I wanted to have the advice of Mme de Luxembourg, who strongly counseled me to take it up. Thus I had a little Armenian wardrobe; but the storm excited against me made me put off its use to calmer times, and it was only several months later, that, being forced to have recourse to catheters again by new attacks, I believed I could take up this new form of dress at Môtiers without any risk, above all after having consulted the Pastor of the place who told me that I could even wear it to the Temple without scandal. Thus I put on the coat, the caftan, the fur cap, the belt, and after having assisted at the divine service in this outfit, I did not see any unsuitability at all in wearing it to the Lord Marshal's. Seeing me dressed this way, His Excellency said to me as his only compliment, "*Salamaleki*,"[36] after which everything was settled, and I no longer wore any other clothes.

Since I had given up literature completely, I no longer thought of anything but leading a tranquil and sweet life as far as it depended on me. Alone I have never known boredom, even in the most perfect inaction: by filling up all the voids, my imagination was enough to occupy me all by itself. It was only the inactive chatting in a room, each sitting across from the others moving nothing but their tongues, that I could never bear. When one walks, when one takes a stroll, it is tolerable; at least the feet and eyes do something: but to stay there with arms crossed, talking about the weather and the flies that are flying around, or what is worse by paying each other compliments; that is an unbearable torture to me. So as not to live like a savage, I took it into my head to learn to make laces. I brought my cushion on my visits, or I went to work at my door like the women and chatted with passersby. That caused me to bear the inanity of babbling and pass my time without boredom at the homes of my neighbors, several of whom were rather amiable and did not lack intelligence. One among others called Isabelle d'Ivernois,[37] daughter of the Procurator General of Neuchâtel, appeared to me estimable enough to bind me to her with a particular friendship, from which she did not find herself badly off, because of the useful advice I gave her, and because of the efforts I made for her on essential occasions, so that now, as a worthy and virtuous mother of a family, she perhaps owes me her reason, her husband, her life, and her happiness. On my side I owe her some very sweet consolations, and above all during a very sad winter in which—at the peak of my illnesses and my pains—she came to pass long evenings with Therese and me which she knew how to make very short for us by the pleasantness of her mind and by the mutual effusions of our hearts. She called me her papa, I called her my daughter, and I hope these names, which we still give each other, will not cease to be as dear to her as to me. To make my laces good for something I gave them as a present to my young female friends upon their marriages on the condition that they nurse their children; her elder sister had one of them on this title and deserved it. Isabelle had one in the same way, and has not deserved it any less from intention. But she did not have the happiness of being able to do her will. In sending them these laces, I wrote both of them letters the first of which has circulated in the world; but the second did not receive so much commotion; friendship does not walk with such great noise.

Among the connections I made in my neighborhood, and into the details of which I will not enter, I ought to note that of Colonel Pury,[38] who had a house on the mountain where he came to pass the summers. I was not eager for his acquaintance, because I knew that he was on very bad terms with the Court and with the Lord Marshal whom he did not see at all. Nevertheless, since he came to see me and performed many polite acts for me, I had to go see him in my turn; that continued and we sometimes ate in each other's home. At his house I made the acquaintance of M. du Peyrou, and afterward too intimate a friendship for me to be able to dispense with speaking about him.

M. du Peyrou[39] was an American, the son of a Commandant of Surinam whose successor, M. le Chambrier of Neuchâtel, married the widow. Having become a widow for a second time she came with her son to settle in her second husband's country. Du Peyrou, an only son, extremely rich, and tenderly loved by his mother, had been raised carefully enough, and his education had profited him. He had acquired much half-knowledge, some taste for the arts, and he prided himself above all for having cultivated his reason: his Dutch, cold, philosophic manner, his bronze complexion, his quiet and reserved disposition favored this opinion very much. He was hard of hearing and gouty although still young. That made all his motions extremely solemn, extremely serious, and although he liked to dispute, sometimes even at a little length, generally he spoke little, because he did not hear. All this exterior made an impression on me. I said to myself, "Here is a thinker, a wise man, the sort one would be happy to have as a friend." To complete winning me over he often addressed his words to me without ever paying me any compliment. He spoke little about me, little about my books, very little about himself; he was not deprived of ideas, and everything he said was accurate enough. This accuracy and this equanimity attracted me. He did not have either the elevation or the subtlety of the Lord Marshal in his mind, but he did have his simplicity; thus in some respect he represented him. I did not become infatuated, but I attached myself out of esteem, and little by little[40] this esteem led to friendship. With him I totally forgot the objection I had made to the Baron d'Holback that he was too rich, and I believe that I was wrong to do so. I have learned to doubt whether a man who enjoys a great fortune, whoever he might be, can sincerely love my principles and their author.

For a rather long time I saw little of Du Peyrou, because I did not go to Neuchâtel at all, and because he came to Colonel Pury's Mountain only once a year. Why didn't I go to Neuchâtel at all? This is a childishness about which I must not be silent.

Although I was protected by the King of Prussia and by the Lord Marshal, if at first I avoided persecution in my refuge, I did not avoid at least the muttering of the public, the municipal magistrates, the Ministers. After the impulse given by France, it was not good form not to give me at least some insult: one would have been afraid of appearing to disapprove of my persecutors if one did not imitate them. The Classis[41] of Neuchâtel, that is to say, the company of Ministers of that city, gave the impulse by attempting to excite the Council of State against me. When this attempt did not succeed, the Ministers addressed themselves to the municipal magistrate, who quickly had my book prohibited, and, by treating me in a hardly decent manner on every occasion, made it understood and even said that if I had wanted to settle in the city I would not have been allowed to. They filled their *Mercury*[42] with nonsense and the most insipid[43] hypocritical calumnies, which—while they made sensible persons laugh—did not fail to excite the people and animate it against me. All that did not prevent it from being the case that, to listen to them, I ought to be very grateful for the extreme favor they were doing of letting me live at Môtiers, where they had no authority; they would have willingly measured me out air by the pint, on condition that I pay very dearly for it. They wanted me to be obliged to them for the protection the King granted me in spite of them, and which they worked without respite to deprive me of. Finally, not being able to succeed, after having done me all the wrong they could, and having disparaged me with all their power, they made a merit of their impotence, by making the most to me of the kindness they had of putting up with me in their country. I should have laughed in their faces as my only answer, I was stupid enough to be offended, and I was foolish enough not to want to go to Neuchâtel at all, a resolution which I kept for almost two years, as if it were not to give too much honor to that kind of people to pay attention to their proceedings, which—good or bad—could not be imputed to them, because they never act except by impulsion. Moreover, minds without cultivation and without enlightenment, who know no other object for their esteem but influence, power, and money, are very far even from suspecting that some regard is owed to talents and that it is dishonorable to insult them. A certain Mayor of a Village, who had been dismissed for his malversations, said to my Isabelle's husband, the Lieutenant of Val-de-Travers, "They say this Rousseau is very smart; bring him to me so I can see whether it is true." Certainly the dissatisfaction of a man who takes such a tone[44] ought to anger very little those who experience it.

From the way I was treated at Paris, at Geneva, at Berne,[45] even at Neuchâtel I did not expect more discretion from the Pastor of the place. I had nevertheless been recommended to him by Mme Boy de la Tour and he had made me very welcome; but in this country where everyone is equally flattered, blandishments mean nothing. Nevertheless, after my solemn reuniting with the reformed Church, while I was living in a reformed country I could not neglect the public profession of the worship into which I had returned without failing in my engagements and my duty as a Citizen: thus I assisted at divine service. On the other hand, I was afraid that I might be exposing myself to the affront of a refusal by presenting myself at the communion table, and it was by no means probable that, after the uproar raised at Geneva by the council and at Neuchâtel by the Classis, he would wish to administer Communion to me tranquilly in his Church. Thus, when I saw the time for communion drawing near I reached a decision to write to M. de Montmollin,[46] that was the Minister's name, to perform an act of good will and to declare to him that at heart I had always been joined to the Protestant Church; in order to avoid quibbles over the articles of faith, I told him at the same time that I did not wish any individual explanation over dogma. Having thus put myself in proper order on this side, I stayed calm, not doubting that M. de Montmollin would refuse to admit me without the preliminary discussion which I did not want and that everything might be finished this way without it being my fault. Not at all. At the moment when I least expected it M. de Montmollin came to declare to me, not only that he was admitting me to the communion under the condition I had put, but furthermore that he and his elders conceived it a great honor to have me in his flock. In all my life I have not had such a surprise nor a more consoling one. To me it appeared to be a very sad destiny always to live isolated on the earth, above all in adversity. In the midst of so many proscriptions and persecutions I found an extreme sweetness in being able to say to myself, "At least I am among my brothers," and I went to communion with an emotion of heart and tears of tenderness which were perhaps the most agreeable preparation for God that one could bring.

Some time afterward, His Lordship sent me a letter from Mme de Boufflers, which had come—at least I presumed so—through d'Alembert, who knew the Lord Marshal. In this letter, the first that this Lady had sent me since my departure from Montmorency,[47] she scolded me sharply for the one I had written to M. de Montmollin and above all for having gone to communion. I understood all the less what her object was with her remonstrance because I had always loudly declared myself to be Protestant since my trip to Geneva and I had gone very publicly to the Hôtel of Holland without anyone in the world having found it bad.[48] It seemed humorous to me that Mme the Comtesse de Boufflers wanted to meddle in directing my conscience in matters of Religion. Still, since I did not suspect that her intention was not the best in the world, I was not at all offended by this peculiar sally, although I did not understand it at all, and I answered her without anger by telling her my reasons.

Nevertheless, the printed insults went on their course, and their benign authors reproached the powers for treating me too gently. This concurrence of carping, the motors for which continued to act under the veil, had something sinister and frightening in it. As for me I let them talk without getting alarmed. I was assured that there was a censure at the Sorbonne; I believed nothing of the sort. How could the Sorbonne get mixed up in this business. Did it want to make sure that I was not a Catholic? Everyone knew it. Did it want to prove that I was not a good Calvinist? What difference did this make to it?[49] That was taking on a very peculiar care; that was making itself the substitute for our Ministers. Before I had seen this writing, I believed that someone was making it circulate under the Sorbonne's name in order to make fun of it; I believed this even more after I read it. Finally when I could not doubt its authenticity any longer, all I was resolved to believe was that it was necessary to put the Sorbonne into the madhouse.[50]

Another Writing affected me more, because it came from a man whom I always esteemed and whose constancy I admired while I pitied his blindness. I am speaking of the mandate of the Archbishop of Paris against me.[51] I believed that I owed it to myself to answer it. I could do so without debasing myself; it was a case just about similar to that of the King of Poland.[52] I have never loved brutal disputes in Voltaire's manner. I could fight only with dignity and, for me to deign to defend myself, I wanted the one who attacks me not to dishonor my blows. I did not doubt at all that this Mandate was of the Jesuits' making, and, even though they were themselves in misfortune at that time, in it I still recognized their old maxim of crushing the unfortunate. Thus I could also follow my old maxim of honoring the titular Author and striking down the work, and I believe[53] I did this rather successfully.[54]

I found the stay in Môtiers extremely pleasant, and in order to determine me to end my days there I lacked only an assured subsistence; but it is rather expensive to live there, and I had seen all my old plans turned upside down from the dissolution of my household, from the setting up of a new one, from the sale or dispersion of all my furnishings, and from the expenses I had had to incur since my departure from Montmorency. Daily I saw the little capital I had in front of me diminishing. Two or three years were enough to consume the remainder of it, without my seeing any way of renewing it, short of beginning to write books again; a disastrous trade which I had already renounced.

Persuaded that everything would soon change with regard to me, and that, having returned from its frenzy, the public would make the powers blush for it; I sought only to prolong my resources until that fortunate change, which would leave me more in a position to choose among the ones that might offer themselves. For that I took up my *Dictionary of Music* again, which ten years of work had already advanced extremely, and which lacked only the final touches and being put into a fair copy. My books, which had been sent to me a short time before, furnished me with the means to finish this work: my papers, which were sent to me at the same time, put me in a position to begin undertaking my memoirs, with which I wanted to occupy myself solely from then on. I began by transcribing some letters in a collection which could guide my memory in the order of facts and of times. I had already made the choice of the ones I wanted to preserve for that effect, and their succession was not interrupted at all for almost the last ten years. Nevertheless, upon arranging them in order to transcribe them, I found a gap that surprised me. That gap was of almost six months from October 1756 until the month of March following.[55] I remembered perfectly having put into my selection a number of letters from Diderot, from De Leyre, from Mme d'Epinay, and Mme de Chenonceaux, etc., which filled up this gap, and which were no longer to be found. What had become of them? Had someone put a hand on my papers during the several months they had stayed at the Hôtel de Luxembourg? That was not conceivable and I had seen M. the Maréchal[56] take the key of the room in which I had deposited them. Since several letters from women and all those from Diderot had no date, and since in order to arrange these letters in their order I had been forced to fill in these dates from memory and feeling my way, at first I believed I had made errors in dates, and I passed all the letters in review which did not have any or to which I had supplied one, to see whether I would not find the ones that should fill in this void. This attempt did not succeed at all; I saw that the void was very real, and that the letters had very certainly been removed. By whom and why? That is what was beyond me. These letters, prior to my great quarrels, and from the time of my first intoxication with Julie, could interest no one. There was at most some teasing from Diderot, some banter from Deleyre, some testimonies of friendship from Mme de Chenonceaux and even from Mme d'Epinay, with whom I was on the best possible terms at that time. To whom could these letters matter? what did they want to do with them?[57] It is only seven years afterward that I suspected the horrible object of this theft.[58]

Once this deficit was well authenticated, it made me look among my rough drafts to see whether I would discover any other. I found some which, given my lack of memory, made me suppose that there were others in the multitude of my papers. Those I noticed[59] were the rough draft of *The Sensitive Morality*, and that of the extract from the *Adventures of Lord Edward*. This latter, I admit it, gave me some suspicions about Mme de Luxembourg. It was her Valet-de-Chambre La Roche who had forwarded these papers to me, and she was the only one in the world who I imagined could take an interest in this rag; but what interest could she take in the other and in the removed letters of which, even with bad designs, one could not made any use which could harm me, unless they were falsified. As for M. the Marechal, whose invariable uprightness and the truth of his friendship for me I knew, I could not suspect him for a moment. I could not even fix this suspicion upon Mme the Maréchale. After having fatigued myself for a long time in seeking the Author of this theft, the most reasonable thing that came to my mind was to impute it to d'Alembert who, since he had already wormed his way in with Mme de Luxembourg, could have found the means of nosing through these papers and of removing from them what had pleased him, both in manuscripts and letters; either to try to stir up some worries for me, or to appropriate what might suit him. I assumed that, deceived by the title of *The Sensitive Morality*, he had believed he found the framework of a true treatise in materialism which he would have used against me as one can well imagine. Certain that he would soon be disabused by the examination of this rough draft, and determined to give up literature completely, I did not make myself very anxious about these pilferings which were not the first by the same hand* that I had endured without complaining about them.[60] Soon I thought no more about this faithlessness than if none had been done to me, and I began to gather together the materials that had been left to me, in order to work on my confessions.

For a long time I had believed that in Geneva the company of Min-

---

* In his *Elements of Music* I had found many things taken from what I had written about that art for the Encyclopedia, and which was handed over to him several years before the publication of his Elements. I do not know what part he might have had in a book entitled *Dictionary of the Fine Arts*; but in it I found Articles transcribed from mine word for word, and this a long time before these same articles were published in the Encyclopedia.

isters, or at least the Citizens and Bourgeois would protest against the infraction of the Edict in the Warrant brought against me. Everything stayed calm, at least on the outside; for there was a general discontentment that was only waiting for an occasion to manifest itself. My friends or self-proclaimed ones wrote me letter upon letter to exhort me to come put myself at their head, assuring me of a public reparation on the part of the Council. The fear of disorder and troubles that my presence might cause kept me from acquiescing in their entreaties, and faithful to the Oath I had previously made of never being a party to any civil dissension in my country,[61] I preferred to let the offense continue to exist and banish myself from my fatherland forever than to return there by violent and dangerous means. It is true that I had expected some legal and peaceful protests on behalf of the Bourgeoisie against an infraction that interested it extremely. There were none. The people who led it sought less the true redress of grievances than the opportunity to make themselves necessary. They formed cabals but they kept silent, and they allowed the babblers and the sanctimonious people or self-proclaimed such—who were put forward by the Council to make me odious to the populace and to get its insult attributed to zeal for religion—to chatter.

After having waited vainly for more than a year for someone to protest against an illegal procedure, I finally made my decision, and, seeing myself abandoned by my Fellow Citizens, I decided to renounce my ungrateful fatherland where I had never lived, from which I had not received either property or service, and by which—as reward for the honor I had tried to give it—I saw myself so unworthily treated by unanimous consent, since those who should have spoken had said nothing. Thus I wrote to the first Syndic of that year who I believe was M. Favre,[62] a letter by which I solemnly abdicated my right of Bourgeoisie, and in which moreover I observed the modesty and moderation that I have always put into the acts of pride which the cruelty of my enemies have often wrenched from me in my misfortunes.[63]

This step finally opened the Citizens' eyes; feeling that they had injured their own interest when they abandoned my defense, they took it up when it was too late. They had other grievances which they joined to that one, and they made them the subject of several very well reasoned protests which they extended and reinforced as the harsh and rebuffing refusals of the Council, which felt itself supported by the minister of France, made them feel better the plan formed to subjugate them. These altercations gave birth to several pamphlets which decided nothing, until there suddenly appeared the *Letters Written from the Country*, a work written in favor of the Council with infinite art, and by which the protesting party was reduced to silence and crushed for a time. This piece, a durable monument of the rare talents of its Author, was by the Procurator General Tronchin, an intelligent man, an enlightened man, very well versed in the laws and the Government of the Republic. *Siluit terra.*[64]

Having recovered from their first dejection, the Remonstrators[65] undertook an answer and came off passably in time. But all eyes were cast on me as the only one who could enter into the lists against such an adversary with any the hope of overthrowing him. I admit that I thought the same, and, pushed by my former Fellow Citizens who made it a duty for me to aid them with my pen in a difficulty for which I had been the occasion, I undertook the refutation of the *Letters Written from the Country*, and I parodied its title by that of the *Letters Written from the Mountain* which I gave to mine. I wrote and I executed this undertaking so secretly that in a meeting I had at Thonon with the leaders of the Remonstrators to speak about their business, and in which they showed me the sketch of their answer, I did not tell them a word about mine, which was already written, fearing that some obstacle to its publication might crop up if the slightest wind of it came either to the magistrates or to my private enemies.[66] Nevertheless, I did not keep this work from being known in France before its publication; but they preferred to let it appear rather than to make me understand too well how they had discovered my secret. I will tell below what I have learned, which is limited to very little; I will keep quiet about what I have conjectured.

At Môtiers I had almost as many visits as I had had at the Hermitage and at Montmorency, but the majority of them were of an extremely different sort. Those who had come to see me up to then were people who, since they had some talents, tastes, maxims in common with me, alleged them as the cause of their visits, and immediately introduced matters about which I could converse with them. At Môtiers that was no longer true, above all with regard to France. It was officers or other people who had no taste for literature, who even for the most part had never read my writings, and who did not fail, according to what they said, to have traveled thirty, forty, sixty, a hundred leagues to come to see and admire the famous, celebrated, very celebrated man, the great man etc. For from that time they have not stopped throwing in my face the most impudent toadyisms from which the esteem of the people who accosted me had protected me until then. Since the majority of these unexpected arrivals did not deign either to give their names nor tell me their station, since their knowledge and mine did not fall on the same objects, and since they had neither read nor leafed through my works, I did not know what to talk to them about: I waited for them to talk, since it was up to them to know and to tell me why they came to see me. One feels that this did not make for very interesting conversations for me, although they might have been so for them, depending on what they wanted to know: for since I was not mistrustful I expressed myself without reserve about all the questions they judged it appropriate to ask me, and they usually went back as knowledgeable as I was about all the details of my situation.

For example, in this manner I had M. de Feins, Equerry of the Queen and Captain of cavalry in the Queen's Regiment, who had the persistence to pass several days at Môtiers, and even to follow me on foot as far as La Ferrière,[67] leading his horse by the bridle, without having any other meeting point with me than that we both knew Mlle Fel and that we both played cup-and-ball. Before and after M. de Feins I had another much more extraordinary visit. Two men arrive on foot each leading a mule loaded with his small baggage, lodge at the inn, rub down their mules themselves, and ask to come to see me. From their outfit, these muleteers were taken for smugglers, and the news circulated immediately that some smugglers were coming to pay me a visit. Only their manner of accosting me informed me that they were people of another stuff; but although they were not smugglers they might be adventurers, and this doubt kept me on guard for some time. They did not take long to calm me. One was M. de Montauban, called the Comte de la Tour Dupin, a Nobleman from the Dauphiné; the other was M. Dastier from Carpentras,[68] a former soldier, who had put his cross of St. Louis in his pocket since he was not able to display it.[69] These Gentlemen, who were both very likable, both had a good deal of intelligence; their conversation was pleasant and interesting; their manner of traveling, so much to my taste and so little to that of French Noblemen, gave me a sort of attachment to them which their company could only make more solid. This acquaintance did not even end there, since it still persists and they came back to see me several times—no longer on foot however, that was good for the beginning; but the more I saw these Gentlemen the less I found in common between their tastes and mine, the less I felt that their maxims were mine, that my writings were familiar to them, that there was any genuine sympathy between them and me. What did they want from me then? Why come to see me in that outfit? Why stay several days? Why return several times? Why desire so extremely to have me as Host? I did not take it into my head to ask myself these questions then. I have asked them to myself sometimes since then.

Touched by their advances, my heart surrendered itself, above all to M. Dastier, whose more open manner pleased me more. I even remained in correspondence with him, and when I wanted to have the *Letters from the Mountain* published, I thought of addressing myself to him to put off the track the people who were waiting for my package on the route to Holland. He had spoken to me very much, and perhaps on purpose, of the freedom of the press at Avignon; he had offered me his efforts if I had something to have published there: I availed myself of this offer and I addressed my first notebooks to him one after the other by the post. After having kept them for a rather long time he sent them back to me, notifying me that no Publisher had dared to take them on, and I was constrained to go back to Rey, taking care to send him my notebooks only one after the other, and not to let the following one go until after having been notified of the reception of the first. Before the publication of the work, I knew that it had been seen in the offices of the Ministers, and d'Escherny of Neuchâtel spoke to me about a book of *The Man of the Mountain* which d'Holback had told him was by me. I assured him, as was true, that I had never written any book that had that title. When the letters appeared he was furious, and accused me of lying, although I had only told him the truth. That is how I became assured that my manuscript was known. Sure of Rey's faithfulness I was forced to bring my conjectures elsewhere, and the one at which I preferred to stop was that my packages had been opened in the post.

Another acquaintance from about the same time, but which was at first made only through letters, was that of a M. Laliaud from Nîmes, who wrote me from Paris to ask me to send him my profile in silhouette which he said he needed for my bust in marble which he was having made by Le Moyne[70] to put in his Library. If this was a cajolery invented to tame me, it fully succeeded. I judged that a man who wanted to have my bust in marble in his library was filled with my works, consequently with my principles, and that he loved me because his soul was in the same key as mine. It was hard for me not to be seduced by this idea. I saw M. Laliaud later on. I found him very zealous to do me many small services, to meddle very much in my little affairs. But beyond that I doubt that any of my writings has been in the small number of books he has read in his life. I do not know whether he has a library, and whether it is a room he uses; and as for the bust, he limited himself to a bad figure in clay made by Le Moyne[71] based on which he had a hideous portrait engraved, which did not fail to circulate under my name, as if it bore some resemblance to me.[72]

The only Frenchman who appeared to come to see me out of taste for my feelings and for my works was a young Officer of the Regiment of Limousin called M. Seguier de St. Brisson, who has been seen and who perhaps is still seen to shine at Paris and in society by means of rather pleasing talents, and of pretensions to fine wit. He had come to see me at Montmorency the winter that preceded my catastrophe. In him I found a liveliness of feeling that pleased me. He subsequently wrote to me at Môtiers, and either because he wanted to cajole me, or because his head was really turned by *Emile*, he informed me that he was leaving the service to live independently, and that he was learning the trade of carpenter. He had an older brother who was a Captain in the same regiment, who had all the predilection of their mother, an extravagantly pious woman— directed by some abbé Tartuffe or other—who badly treated the younger son whom she accused of irreligion, and even of the unforgivable crime of having relations with me. These are the grievances based on which he wanted to break with his mother and make the decision about which I have just spoken; all to play the little Emile.

Alarmed by this petulance, I hastened to write to him in order to make him change his resolution, and I put all the strength I could into my exhortations: they were heard. He returned to his duty with regard to his mother, and he took back from his Colonel's hands his resignation which he had given him, and which the latter had been prudent enough to make no use of, so as to leave him time to reflect about it better. Having returned from his follies, St. Brisson committed one that was a little less shocking, but which was hardly more to my taste; this was to make himself an Author. One after the other he gave two or three pamphlets, which heralded a man not without talent; but as for the pamphlets I will not have to reproach myself for having given him praise that would encourage him very much in pursuing that career.[73]

Some time afterward he came to see me and together we made the pilgrimage to the Island of St. Pierre.[74] On this trip I found him different from what I had seen him to be at Montmorency. There was something affected about him that did not shock me very much at first, but which has often come back to my memory since that time. He came to see me one more time at the hôtel de St. Simon upon my passage through Paris to go to England. I learned there what he had not told me, that he was living in high society, and that he saw Mme de Luxembourg rather often. He did not give me any sign of life at Trye and had nothing said to me by his relative Mlle Seguier, who was my neighbor and who never appeared very well disposed toward me. In a word, M. de St. Brisson's infatuation ended suddenly like the connection with M. de Feins: but the latter owed me nothing, and the former owed me something,[75] unless the foolish acts I had kept him from committing had only been a game on his part: which, at bottom, might very well be the case.

I also had any number of visits from Geneva. The De Lucs, father and son,[76] chose me successively for their nurse: the father fell sick en route; the son was so upon leaving Geneva; both came to get well with me. Ministers, relatives, bigots, fellows of all sort came from Geneva and from Switzerland, not like those from France to admire me and to banter with me, but to scold me and catechize me: the only one who pleased me was Moultou, who came to pass three or four days with me and whom I would have very much wanted to keep for longer; the most constant of all, the one who was the most stubborn and who subjugated me by dint of importunities, was a M. d'Ivernois, a Merchant from Geneva,[77] a French refugee and relative of the Procurator General of Neuchâtel. This M. d'Ivernois from Geneva passed through Môtiers twice a year expressly to come to see me there, stayed with me from morning to night several days in a row, came on my walks, brought me a thousand sorts of little gifts, insinuated himself into my confidence in spite of me, meddled in all my affairs, without there being any communion of ideas or of inclinations or of feelings or of knowledge between him and me. I doubt that he has read an entire book of any sort in his whole life, and that he even knows what mine are about. When I began to botanize he followed me in my walks on botany, without having any taste for that amusement and without having anything to say to me or I to him. He even had the courage to pass three whole days with me tête-à-tête in a tavern in Goumoens from where I had believed I would get rid of him as a result of boredom and by making him feel how much he bored me; and all that without me ever having been able to rebuff his unbelievable constancy, or to penetrate the motive for it.

Among all these connections which I made and kept up by force only, I ought not to omit the sole one that was pleasant for me, and into which I put a genuine interest of heart: that is the one with a young Hungarian who came to settle at Neuchâtel and from there to Môtiers several months after I settled there myself. In the country he was called the Baron de Sauttern, the name under which he had been recommended from Zurich. He was tall and well formed, with an agreeable appearance; with an amiable and gentle society. He said to everyone and made me understand myself that he had come to Neuchâtel only because of me, to form his youth to virtue by my company. His physiognomy, his tone, his manners appeared to me to agree with his speeches, and I would have believed I was failing in one of the greatest duties if I sent packing a young man in whom I saw nothing but pleasing things, and who sought me out from such a respectable motive. My heart cannot abandon itself half-way. Soon he had all my friendship, all my confidence; we became inseparable. He went on all my pedestrian outings, he acquired a taste for them. I brought him to the

Lord Marshal's, who gave him a thousand blandishments. Since he could not yet express himself in French, he spoke to me and wrote to me only in Latin, I answered him in French, and this mixture of the two languages did not make our conversations either less flowing or less lively in every respect. He spoke to me about his family, about his business, about his adventures about the Court of Vienna the intimate details of which he appeared to be well acquainted with. In sum, during the almost two years we passed in the greatest intimacy, I found in him only a sweetness of character proof against everything, not only decent but elegant morals, a great cleanliness in his person, and extreme modesty in all his speeches, in sum, all the marks of a well-born man, which rendered him too estimable not to render him dear to me.[78]

At the height of my relations with him, d'Ivernois from Geneva wrote to me to watch out for a young Hungarian who had come to settle near me, that he had been assured that he was a spy whom the Minister of France had put near me. This warning could appear all the more disquieting since in the country where I was everyone was warning me to keep myself on my guard, that I was being watched, and that they were seeking to lure me on to the territory of France in order to do me a bad turn there.

To close the mouths of these inept givers of advice once and for all, I proposed to Sauttern a pedestrian outing to Pontarlier without giving him any warning; he agreed to it. When he arrived at Pontarlier I gave him d'Ivernois's letter to read, and then embracing him with ardor, I said to him, "Sauttern does not need me to prove my trust to him; but the public needs me to prove that I know how to place it well." This embrace was very sweet; it was one of those pleasures of the soul that persecutors cannot know or take away from the oppressed.[79]

I will never believe that Sauttern was a spy, or that he betrayed me; but he did deceive me. While I opened my heart to him without reserve, he had the courage to close his to me constantly and to impose upon me with lies. He concocted some story or other that made me judge that his presence was needed in his country. I exhorted him to leave as quickly as possible; he left, and when I believed he was already in Hungary, I learned that he was at Strasbourg. This was not the first time he had been there. He had thrown disorder into a household there: knowing that I saw him, the husband had written to me. I had omitted no effort to bring the young woman back to virtue, and Sauttern to his duty.[80] When I believed they were perfectly separated from each other, they had come back together and the husband even was obliging enough to take the young man back into his house; from that point I had nothing more to say. I learned that the so-called Baron had imposed upon me with a heap of lies. He was not called Sauttern, he was called Sauttersheim. With regard to the title of Baron which he was given in Switzerland, I could not reproach him for it, because he had never taken it; but I do not doubt that he was really a Nobleman, and the Lord Marshal who knew men and who had been in his country always looked at him and treated him as such.

As soon as he was gone, the serving girl of the inn in which he ate at Môtiers declared herself to be pregnant by him. She was such a nasty-looking slut, and Sauttern, who was generally esteemed and given consideration in the whole country from his behavior and his decent morals, prided himself so extremely on cleanliness that this impudence shocked everyone. The most lovable women of the country, who had uselessly lavished their flirting on him, were furious: I was exasperated with indignation. I made all my efforts to make this brazen hussy stop, offering to pay all the expenses and to answer for Sauttersheim. I wrote to him in the strong persuasion not only that this pregnancy was not of his doing but that it was faked, and that all this was only a game played by his enemies and mine: I wanted him to return to the country in order to confound this minx and those who were making her speak. I was surprised by the tameness of his answer. He wrote to the Pastor whose parishioner the slut was, and acted so as to stifle the business, seeing which I stopped meddling in it, extremely astonished that such a crapulous man could have been sufficiently master of himself to impose upon me, by his reserve in the most intimate familiarity.

From Strasbourg Sauttersheim went to Paris to seek his fortune and found only misery there. He wrote to me saying his peccavi.[81] My innermost emotions were stirred at the remembrance of our former friendship; I sent him some money. The following year when I passed through Paris I saw him again in just about the same condition, but a great friend of M. Lalliaud, without me being able to find out how this acquaintance came to him and whether it was old or new. Two years afterward Sauttersheim returned to Strasbourg from where he wrote to me and where he died. Here is the abridged story of our relations and what I know about his adventures: but while deploring the fate of this unfortunate young man, I will never cease to believe that he was well-born, and that all the disorder of his conduct was the effect of the situations in which he found himself.

Such were the acquisitions I made at Môtiers as regards connections and acquaintances. How many similar ones would I have needed to compensate for the cruel losses I had at the same time.

The first was that of M. de Luxembourg who, after having been tormented by Doctors for a long time, was their victim at last, being treated for the gout, which they did not want to recognize at all, as for an illness which they could cure: if the relation on this subject[82] that was written to me by La Roche, Madame the Maréchale's confidential man, ought to be relied on, this was an example—as cruel as it is memorable—of how very much the miseries of greatness must be deplored.

I felt the loss of that good lord all the more since he was the only true friend I had in France, and the sweetness of his character was such that it had made me completely forget his rank in order to become attached to him as to my equal. Our relations did not cease after my withdrawal and he continued to write to me as before. I nevertheless believed I noticed that absence or my misfortune had cooled off his affection. It is very difficult for a courtier to keep the same attachment for someone whom he knows to be in disgrace with the powerful. I judged moreover that the great ascendancy Mme de Luxembourg had over him had not been favorable to me and that she had taken advantage of my distance to harm me in his mind. As for her, in spite of several affected demonstrations which became less and less frequent, she hid her change with regard to me less from day to day. She wrote to me four or five times in Switzerland at one time or another, after which she no longer wrote to me at all; and it required all the prepossession, all the trust, all the blindness I still had, not to see in her anything more than some cooling off toward me.

The publisher Guy, Duchesne's partner, who frequented the Hôtel de Luxembourg very much after me, wrote to me that I was in M. the Maréchal's will. There was nothing in that but what was very natural and very believable; thus I did not doubt it. That made me deliberate in myself how I would behave toward this legacy. All things considered, I resolved to accept it whatever it might be, and to render that honor to a decent man who, in a rank into which friendship hardly penetrates, had had a genuine one for me.[83] I was dispensed from this duty, since I did not hear anything more about this true or false legacy, and in truth I would have been distressed to wound one of the great maxims of my morality by profiting from the death of someone who had been dear to me. During the final illness of our friend Mussard,[84] Lenieps proposed to me to take advantage of the gratitude he was showing for our care for him to insinuate some arrangements in our favor from him. "Ah, dear Lenieps," I said to him, "let us not soil the sad but sacred duties we are rendering to our dying friend with ideas of self-interest; I hope I will never be in anyone's will, and at least never in that of any of my friends." It was at about the same time that the Lord Marshal spoke to me about his, about what he planned to do for me in it, and that I gave him the answer I spoke about in my first part.[85]

My second loss, even more painful and much more irreparable, was that of the best of women and mothers who—already burdened with years and overburdened with infirmities and miseries—left this Vale of tears to pass into the abode of the good, where the lovable remembrance of the good one has done here below forms the eternal recompense for it. Go, sweet and beneficent soul, among Fénelon, Bernex, Catinat,[86] and those who in a more humble station have, as they did, opened their hearts to genuine charity, go taste the fruit of yours and prepare for your student the place he hopes to occupy one day near you. Fortunate in your woes that by ending them Heaven has spared you the cruel spectacle of his! Since I was afraid of saddening her heart by the narrative of my first disasters, I had not written to her at all since my arrival in Switzerland: but I wrote to M. de Conzié to inform me about her, and he was the one who notified me that she had ceased to comfort those who suffered and to suffer herself. Soon I also will cease to suffer, but if I believed I would not see her again in the other life, my weak imagination would not accept the idea of perfect happiness that I promise myself there.[87]

My third and last loss, for since then there are no more friends left for me to lose, was that of the Lord Marshal. He did not die, but being tired of serving ingrates, he left Neuchâtel, and I have not seen him again since then. He is alive and will survive me, I hope: he is alive, and thanks to him all my attachments are not broken on the earth, there still remains one man worthy of my friendship; for one's true worth is even more in the friendship one feels than the friendship one inspires; but I have lost the sweetness which he lavished on me, and I can no longer put him anywhere but in the rank of those whom I still love, but with whom I no longer have any connection. He went to England to receive his pardon from the King and buy back his property[88] which formerly had been confiscated. We did not separate from each other without plans for a reunion which appeared almost as sweet for him as for me. He wanted to establish himself at his Castle of Keith Hall near Aberdeen and I was supposed to make my way there near him; but this plan flattered me too much for me to be able to hope for its success. He did not stay in Scotland at all. The tender solicitations of the King of Prussia called him back to Berlin, and it will soon be seen how I was prevented from going there to join him.[89]

Foreseeing the storm that was beginning to be stirred up against me, before his departure on his own initiative he sent me letters of naturalization, which seemed to be a very secure precaution to keep me from being driven out of the country. The Community of Couvet in the Val de Travers imitated the governor's example, and gave me letters of *communal status* free, as the first were. Thus having become a Citizen of the country in every respect, I was sheltered from every legal expulsion, even on the part of the Prince: but it has never been by legitimate routes that they have been able to persecute the one of all men who has always most respected the laws.

I do not believe I should count among the number of losses I had at this same time that of the Abbé de Mably. Because I had resided in his brother's home I had had some[90] connections with him but never very intimate ones, and I have some grounds for believing[91] that his feelings in my regard had changed their nature since I had acquired more fame than he. But it was upon the publication of the *Letters from the Mountain* that I had the first sign of his ill will for me. A letter to Madame Saladin was circulated in Geneva that was attributed to him and[92] in which he spoke about that work as the seditious clamors of an unruly Demagogue. The esteem I had for the Abbé de Mably and the value I set on his enlightenment did not allow me to believe for a moment that this extravagant letter was his. I made the decision about it that my frankness inspired in me. I sent him a copy of the letter while notifying him that it was being attributed to him. He gave me no answer.[93] This silence surprised me: But judge my surprise when Madame de Chenonceaux wrote to me that the letter really was from the Abbé, and that mine had embarrassed him extremely! For in sum, even if he was right, how could he excuse a striking and public step made out of gaiety of heart without obligation, without necessity, for the sole end of weighing down a man who was at the greatest height of his misfortunes[94] and to whom he had always shown benevolence, and who had never forfeited his esteem. Some time afterward appeared the *Dialogues of Phocion*[95] in which I saw only a compilation of my writings made without restraint and without shame. Upon reading this book I felt[96] that the author had taken his stand with regard to me, and that from then on I would have no worse[97] enemy. I believe that he did not forgive me either for *The Social Contract*, which was too much beyond his strength, nor for *Perpetual Peace*, and that he had appeared to desire me to make an abridgment of the Abbé de St. Pierre only because he assumed that I would not pull it off so well.[98]

The farther I advance in my account, the less order and sequence I can put into it. The agitation of the rest of my life has not left events time to arrange themselves in my head. They have been too numerous, too mixed up, too unpleasant, to be capable of being narrated without confusion. The only strong impression they have left me is that of the horrible mystery which covers their cause and of the deplorable condition into which they have reduced me. My account can no longer proceed except at random and as the ideas come back into my mind. I recall that at the time about which I am speaking, being entirely occupied with my *Confessions*, I imprudently spoke about them to everyone, not even imagining that anyone might have an interest, or the will, or the power to put an obstacle to this undertaking, and if I had believed it, I would hardly have been more discreet because of the total impossibility my natural disposition gives me of keeping anything I feel or think hidden. That this undertaking was known was, as far as I can judge about it, the genuine cause of the storm that was stirred up to expel me from Switzerland and to deliver me into hands that might keep me from executing it.

I had another undertaking that was hardly seen with a better favor by the people who feared the first; that was a general edition of my writings. This Edition appeared necessary to me to certify which of the books[99] bearing my name were genuinely by me, and to put the public in a condition to distinguish them from those pseudonymous Writings which my enemies attributed to me in order to discredit and demean me. Aside from that, this edition was a simple and honest means of assuring me of bread, and it was the only one; considering that, because I had renounced writing books (since my memoirs could not appear during my life), and because I was not earning a sou in any other manner and was always spending, I saw the end of my resources in the end of the proceedings from my last writings. This reason had pressed me[100] to give my *Dictionary of Music* still unpolished.[101] It had been worth a hundred Louis cash and a hundred écus of life annuity; but one must soon see the end of a hundred Louis when one spends more than sixty annually, and a hundred écus of annuity was the same as nothing for a man upon whom beggars and others ceaselessly came to swoop like Starlings.

A company of Merchants from Neuchâtel presented themselves for the undertaking of my general edition, and a printer or Publisher from Lyon called Reguillat[102] somehow or other stuck himself among them to direct it. The agreement was made on a[103] reasonable footing, and was enough to fulfill my object well. In printed works and in pieces still in manuscript, I had enough to furnish six volumes in Quarto; in addition I committed myself to supervising the edition.[104] At the middle of which they were supposed to make me a life pension of sixteen hundred French livres and a downpayment of a thousand écus.

The contract was concluded, not yet signed, when the *Letters Written from the Mountain* appeared. The terrible explosion that was made against that infernal work and against its abominable author appalled the company and the undertaking disappeared. I would compare the effect of this last work to that of the *Letter on French Music* if that letter had not at least left me consideration and esteem while attracting hatred to me and exposing me to peril. But after this last work they appeared to be astonished at Geneva and at Versailles that [105] a Monster such as myself was allowed to breathe. Stirred up by the Resident of France and directed by the Procurator General, the Little Council issued a declaration on my work by which, with the most atrocious qualifications, it declares it unworthy of being burned by the Hangman, and adds with a skill that belongs to burlesque that one cannot answer or even make any mention of it without dishonoring oneself.[106] I would like [107] to be able to transcribe this curious Piece here, but unfortunately I do not have it and do not remember a single word of it.[108] I ardently desire that one of my readers, animated by zeal for truth and equity, might please reread the *Letters Written from the Mountain* in full: he will feel, I dare to say it, the stoic moderation that reigns in that work, after the palpable and cruel outrages which they vied with each other over heaping upon the author. But since they could not respond to insults, because there were not any in it, nor to the reasoning, because it was unanswerable, they decided to appear too incensed to wish to respond; and it is true that if they took invincible arguments for insults, they should have considered themselves extremely insulted.

Far from making any complaint about this odious declaration, the Remonstrators followed the route it traced out for them, and instead of making a trophy of the *Letters from the Mountain* which they veiled in order to make it into a shield for themselves, they had the cowardice to render neither honor nor justice to this writing [109] which had been written for their defense and at their solicitation; they neither cited it nor named it, although they tacitly drew all their arguments from it, and the exactitude with which they followed the advice on which this work ended was the sole cause of their salvation and their victory. They had imposed this duty on me; I had fulfilled it; I had served the fatherland and their cause to the end. I asked them to abandon mine and not to think of anything but themselves in their contentions. They took me at my word, and I no longer meddled in their affairs except by ceaselessly exhorting them to peace, not doubting that if they persisted they would be crushed by France. That did not happen; I understand the reason for it, but this is not the place to tell it.

At first the effect of the *Letters from the Mountain* at Neuchâtel was very peaceful. I sent a copy of it to M. de Montmollin; he received it well, and read it without objection. He was sick, as I was;[110] he came to see me amicably when he recovered and did not say anything to me. Nevertheless, the uproar was beginning; the book was burned somewhere or other.[111] From Geneva, from Berne, and from Versailles perhaps, the focus of the effervescence soon passed to Neuchâtel and above all into the Val-de-Travers, where even before the Classis had made any apparent movement, they had begun to rouse the people by underhanded practices. I dare say I ought to have been loved by the people of that country, as I was in all those where I have lived, pouring out alms with an open hand, not leaving any indigent around me without assistance, not refusing to any-one any service I could render and that was within justice, familiarizing myself perhaps too much with everyone, and concealing any distinction that could excite jealousy with all my power. All that did not prevent the populace [112]—secretly stirred up by someone unknown to me—from being animated against me gradually up to the point of rage, from insult-ing me publicly in the full light of day, not only in the country and in the paths, but in the open road. Those for whom I had done the most good were the most relentless, and even the people for whom I continued to do it (although they did not dare to show themselves) stirred up the others, and seemed to want to avenge themselves this way for the humiliation of being obliged to me. Montmollin appeared to see nothing, and did not yet show himself. But since a communion time was drawing near, he came to my house to advise me to abstain from presenting myself, assuring me moreover that he had nothing at all against me, and that he would leave me in peace. I found the compliment bizarre; it recalled Mme de Bouf-flers's letter to me, and I could not conceive to whom it thus mattered so extremely whether I received communion or not. Since I regarded this condescension on my part as an act of cowardice, and since moreover I did not want to give the people this new pretext for shouting at the im-pious man, I flatly refused the Minister, and he went back dissatisfied, making me understand that I would be sorry for it.

He could not forbid me communion on his authority alone: he re-quired that of the Consistory which had admitted me, and as long as the Consistory had said nothing, I could present myself boldly without fear of refusal. Montmollin had the Classis give him the commission of sum-moning me to the Consistory to give an account of my faith there, and to excommunicate me in case of refusal. This excommunication moreover could not be made except by the Consistory and by the plurality of votes. But the peasants who under the name of elders made up that assembly, presided over and, as is well understood, governed by their Minister, ought naturally not to be of any other opinion than his, principally on theological matters, which they understood even less than he did. Thus I was summoned, and I resolved to appear before them.

What a fortunate occurrence and what a triumph for me if I had known how to speak, and if I had had, so to speak, my pen in my mouth? With what superiority, with what ease I would have floored that poor Minister in the midst of his six peasants! Since avidity for dominating had made the Protestant Clergy forget all the principles of the Reformation, in order to remind him of them and to reduce him to silence, I had only to comment on my first *Letters from the Mountain,* upon which he had the stupidity to censure me. My text was ready made, I had only to extend it, and my man was confounded. I would not have been foolish enough to keep myself on the defensive; it was easy for me to become the aggressor without him even noticing it or being able to protect himself against it.[113] Since they were as thoughtless as they were ignorant, the Little Preachers of the Classis had themselves put me in the most fortunate position I could have desired for crushing them at my pleasure. But what? I had to speak, and to speak on the spot, to find ideas, turns of phrase, words at the moment of need, always to have presence of mind, always to be cool, never to be upset for a moment. What could I hope from myself, who felt so well my inaptitude for expressing myself impromptu? I had been reduced to the most humiliating silence at Geneva in front of an assembly entirely in my favor and already resolved to approve everything. Here it was entirely the opposite; I had to deal with a harasser who put wiliness in the place of knowledge, who would set a hundred traps for me before I noticed one of them, and was totally determined to put me at fault whatever the cost might be. The more I examined this position, the more perilous it appeared to me, and, feeling the impossibility of getting myself out of it successfully, I imagined another expedient. I meditated a speech to pronounce in front of the Consistory to challenge it and to dispense myself from responding: the thing was very easy. I wrote this speech and I began to study it by heart with an unrivaled ardor. Therese made fun of me while listening to me ceaselessly mutter and repeat the same phrases to try to stuff them into my head. In the end I hoped to retain my speech. I knew that the Châtelain would attend the Consistory as an Officer of the Prince, that in spite of Montmollin's maneuvers and his bottles the majority of the elders were well disposed toward me. In my favor I had reason, truth, justice, the protection of the King, the authority of the State Council, the wishes of all good patriots who were concerned about the establishment of this inquisition;[114] everything contributed to encouraging me.

On the eve of the designated day I knew my speech by heart; I recited it faultlessly. I called it to mind all night long in my head; in the morning I no longer knew it; I hesitate at each word, I already believe myself to be in the illustrious assembly, I get upset, I stutter, I lose my head; finally, almost at the moment for going, courage totally fails me; I stay at home, and make the decision to write to the Consistory hastily telling my reasons, and using as a pretext my ailments which genuinely would have made it difficult for me to endure the entire session in the condition I was in at that time.

Perplexed by my letter, the Minister put off the business to another session. In the interval, through himself and his dependents, he made a thousand movements to seduce those of the elders who, following the inspirations of their conscience rather than his, did not form their opinions at his whim and that of the Classis. However powerful his arguments[115] drawn from his wine cellar might have been on these sorts of people, he could not win any more than the two or three who were already devoted to him and who were called his lost souls. The Officer of the Prince and Colonel Pury, who comported himself with much zeal in this business, supported the others in their duty, and when this Montmollin wanted to proceed to the excommunication, his consistory flatly refused it by the plurality of votes. Reduced then to the final expedient of rousing the populace, along with his colleagues and other people, he began to work openly on it, and with such a success, that in spite of the strong and frequent rescripts of the King, in spite of all the orders of the State Council, I was finally forced to leave the country, so as not to expose the Officer of the Prince to having himself assassinated while defending me.

I have only such a confused remembrance of all this business that it is impossible for me to put any order, any connection in the ideas that come back to me about it, and I can render them only sparsely and in an isolated way, as they present themselves to my mind. I recall that there had been some sort of negotiation with the Classis of which Montmollin had been the go-between. He had pretended that it was feared that I might trouble the repose of the country with my writings for which they would blame my freedom of writing.[116] He made me understand that if I pledged myself to give up the pen[117] they would be accommodating about the past. I had already made this pledge with myself; I did not hesitate at all about making it with the Classis, but conditionally, and only as to matters of religion. He found means of having this written in duplicate, based on some change he required:[118] when the condition was rejected by the Classis, I asked for my writing back: he returned one of the duplicates to me and kept the other, on the pretext that he had misplaced it.[119] After that, being openly excited by the ministers, the people mocked the King's Rescripts, the orders from the State Council, and no longer knew any brake. I was preached from the pulpit, named the antichrist, and pursued in the countryside like a Werewolf. My Armenian outfit served as an indication to the populace; I cruelly felt its inconvenience; but to give it up in these circumstances seemed to me an act of cowardice. I could not resolve to do it, and I calmly walked in the country with my caftan and my fur cap surrounded by the hoots of the rabble and sometimes by its stones. Several times while passing in front of some houses, I heard the people who lived in them say, "Bring me my rifle, so I can shoot at him." I did not go any faster; they were only more enraged by this; but they always kept themselves to threats; at least on the score of firearms.

During all this fermentation I did not fail to have two extremely great pleasures for which I was extremely grateful. The first was to be able to perform an act of gratitude through the medium of the Lord Marshal. Being indignant at the treatment I was suffering and the maneuvers of which I was the victim, all the decent people of Neuchâtel held the Ministers in execration; they felt very well that the Ministers were following foreign impulsions and that they were only the satellites of other people who hid themselves while making them act, and were afraid that, as a consequence, my example might result in the establishment of a genuine inquisition. The Magistrates and above all M. Meuron,[120] who had succeeded M. d'Ivernois in the office of Procurator General, made every effort to defend me. Colonel Pury made even more and succeeded better even though he was merely a private citizen. He was the one who found the means to make Montmollin cry uncle in his consistory by keeping the elders in their duty. Since he had some influence he used it as much as he could to stop the sedition; but he had only the authority of the laws, of justice and of reason to oppose that of money and wine; the contest was not equal and in this point Montmollin triumphed over him. Nevertheless, grateful for his efforts and his zeal, I would have wished to be able to return him a good service for a good service and to be able to repay him in some way. I knew that he strongly coveted a position as State Councillor; but since he had behaved badly to the taste of the Court[121] in the business of the Minister Petitpierre,[122] he was in disfavor with the Prince and the Governor.[123] I nevertheless risked writing in his favor to the Lord Marshal: I even dared to speak of the employment he desired, and so fortunately that it was conferred on him by the King almost immediately contrary to everyone's expectation.[124] It is thus that fate, which has always put me too high and too low at the same time, continues to toss me from one extremity to the other, and while the populace was covering me with mire, I appointed a State Councillor.

My other great pleasure was a visit that Mme de Verdelin had just paid me along with her daughter whom she had brought to the baths of

Bourbonne, from where she pushed on as far as Môtiers and lodged with me for two or three days. As a result of attentions and efforts she had finally overcome my long repugnance, and, having been conquered by her blandishments, my heart returned to her all the friendship she had born witness of for me for so long. I was touched by this trip, above all in the circumstance in which I found myself, and in which I greatly needed the consolations of friendship in order to sustain my courage. I feared that she might be grieved by the insults that I was receiving from the populace, and I would have wanted to hide the spectacle of it from her so as not to afflict her heart: but I could not, and although her presence restrained the insolent people a little on our walks, she saw enough to judge about what happened at other times. It was even during her stay at my house that I continued to be attacked at night in my own residence. One morning her chambermaid found my window covered by rocks that had been thrown at it during the night. A very massive bench, which was in the street beside my door and strongly attached, was detached, lifted up and positioned upright against the door; so that if it had not been noticed, the first person who opened the entrance door to go out should naturally have been knocked down. Mme de Verdelin was ignorant of nothing that happened; for aside from what she saw herself, her servant, a trustworthy man, moved about very much in the village, approached everyone there, and was even seen in conference with Montmollin. Nevertheless, she did not appear to pay any attention to anything that happened to me, did not speak to me either about Montmollin or about anyone, and answered very little to what I told her about him sometimes. Only, since she appeared persuaded that a stay in England would suit me more than anything else, she talked to me very much about M. Hume who was then in Paris, about his friendship for me, about the desire he had to be useful to me in his country. It is time to say something about this M. Hume.[125]

He had acquired a great reputation for himself in France and above all among the Encyclopedists from his treatises on Commerce and Politics, and in the last place from his history of the House of Stuart, the only one of his writings of which I had read something, in the Abbé Prevost's translation.[126] For lack of having read his other works, I was persuaded, based on what I had been told about him, that M. Hume associated a very republican soul with the English paradoxes in favor of luxury.[127] Based on this opinion, I looked at his whole apology for Charles the First as a prodigy of impartiality and I had as great an idea of his virtue as of his genius. The desire to become acquainted with this rare man and to obtain his friendship had very much increased the temptations to go into England which were given to me by the solicitations of Mme de Boufflers, M. Hume's intimate friend. After I arrived in Switzerland I received an extremely flattering letter from him by the way of that Lady, in which to the greatest praises of my genius he joined the pressing invitation to go over to England, and the offer of all his influence and of all his friends to make my stay pleasant.[128] In the place I found M. Hume's fellow citizen and friend, the Lord Marshal, who confirmed to me all the good I thought about him, and who even informed me of a literary anecdote about him which had struck him very much and which struck me the same way. Wallace, who had written against Hume on the subject of the population of the ancients, was absent while his work was being printed. Hume took it upon himself to review the proofs and to oversee the edition.[129] This conduct accorded to my turn of mind. In the same way I had sold copies of a song that had been written against me at six sous apiece. I thus had every sort of prejudice in favor of Hume, when Mme de Verdelin came to speak in a lively manner about the friendship he said he had for me and about his eagerness to do me the honors of England; for that is the way she expressed herself. She urged me very much to take advantage of this zeal and to write to M. Hume. Since I did not naturally have any inclination for England and since I did not want to come to this decision except in the extremity, I refused to write and to promise:[130] but I left her the mistress of doing everything she judged appropriate to maintain Hume in his good inclinations. Upon leaving Môtiers, she left me persuaded by everything she had told me about this illustrious man that he was one of my friends, and that she was even more one of his friends.

After her departure Montmollin pressed on with his maneuvers, and the populace no longer knew any restraint. I nevertheless continued to take walks calmly in the midst of hoots, and the taste for botany which I had begun to acquire with Doctor d'Ivernois[131] gave a new interest to my walks and made me scour the country while botanizing without being alarmed by the outcries of all that rabble, whose rage was only irritated by this coolheadedness. One of the things that affected me most was to see the families of my friends* or people who bore that name enter rather

---

*That fatality had begun as early as my stay at Yverdon: for when the Banneret Roguin died a year or two after my departure from that city, old papa Roguin had the good faith to point out to me with sorrow that some proofs had been found in this relative's papers that he had entered into the plot to expel me from Yverdon and from the State of Berne. That proved very clearly that this plot was not, as they wished to have it believed, an affair of sanctimony; since, far from being a pious man, the Banneret Roguin pushed materialism and disbelief to the point of intolerance and fanaticism. Moreover no one at Yverdon had so extremely monopolized me, had so lavished me with blandishments, with praise and with flattery as the said Banneret Roguin. He faithfully followed my persecutors' favorite plan.[132]

openly into the league of my persecutors; like the d'Ivernois, without excepting even my Isabelle's father and brother, Boy de la Tour,[133] the relative of the friend at whose house I was lodged, and her sister-in-law Mme Girardier. This Pierre Boy was so loutish, so stupid and behaved so brutally that I allowed myself to poke fun at him so as not to get angry, and in the style of the *Little Prophet* I wrote a little pamphlet of several pages, entitled *The Vision of Pierre of the Mountain called the Seer*,[134] in which I found the means to let fly [135] at miracles, which formed the great pretext for my persecution at that time. Du Peyrou had this rag printed at Geneva, which had only a mediocre success in the country, since with all their wit the Neuchâtelois hardly feel Attic salt,[136] or joking as long as it is a little subtle.

I put a little more care into another writing from the same time the manuscript of which will be found among my papers and whose subject it is necessary to tell here.

In the greatest furor of warrants and persecution, the Genevans had particularly distinguished themselves by raising a hue and cry with all their strength, and, with a truly theological generosity, my friend Vernes among others chose precisely this very time to publish some letters against me in which he claimed to prove that I was not a Christian. These letters, written with a tone of self-conceit, were not the better for it, although I was assured that the naturalist Bonnet had set his hand to them; for the said Bonnet, although a materialist, does not fail to be of a very intolerant orthodoxy as soon as I am concerned. I was assuredly not tempted to respond to this work: but since the *Letters from the Mountain* presented an occasion to say a word about it, I inserted a rather disrespectful little note into it that put Vernes into a rage.[137] He filled Geneva with shouts of his outrage, and d'Ivernois notified me that he was beside himself. Some time afterward there appeared an anonymous sheet, which seemed written with Phlegethon water instead of ink.[138] In this letter I was [139] accused of having exposed my children in the streets, of dragging after me an army slut, of being worn out from debauchery, rotten with pox, and other similar obliging things.[140] It was not difficult for me to recognize my man. My first idea when I read this libel was to put at its true worth everything that is called renown and reputation among men, in seeing treated as a Bordello chaser a man who was never in one in his life, and whose greatest flaw was always to be as timid and bashful as a virgin, and in seeing myself held as being rotten with pox, I, who not only has not had the slightest attack of any illness of that sort in my whole life, but whom experts have even believed conformed in a manner so as not to be able to contract it. Everything considered I believed I could not refute this libel better than by having it printed in the city where I had lived the most, and I sent it to Duchesne to have it printed as it was, with a foreword in which I named M. Vernes, and some short notes for the clarification of the facts.[141] Not satisfied at having had this sheet printed, I sent it to several people, and among others to M. the Prince Louis of Wirtemberg,[142] who had made very decent advances to me, and with whom I was then in correspondence. This Prince, Du Peyrou, and others appeared to doubt that Vernes was the author of the libel, and blamed me for having named him too inconsiderately. Based on their remonstrances scruples were aroused in me and I wrote to Duchesne to suppress this sheet. Guy wrote to me that he had suppressed it; I do not know whether he did it; I have found him a liar on so many occasions that one more would not be a miracle, and since then I have been enveloped by this profound darkness through which it is impossible for me to penetrate to any sort of truth.

M. Vernes bore this imputation with a moderation that was more than astonishing in a man who did not deserve it, after the rage he had shown previously.[143] He wrote me two or three very measured letters whose goal appeared to me to be to seek to fathom how well informed I was by means of my answers, and whether I had any proof against him. I made him two short answers that were dry and harsh in their meaning, but without any rudeness in their expression and about which he did not get at all angry. At his third letter, seeing that he wanted to strike up a sort of correspondence, I no longer answered: he had d'Ivernois speak to me. Mme Cramer wrote to Du Peyrou that she was sure that the libel was not by Vernes.[144] All that did not shake my persuasion at all. But since in the end I could be mistaken, and since in that case I owed an authentic reparation to Vernes, I had d'Ivernois tell him that I would give him one that would satisfy him, if he could indicate the genuine author of the libel to me or at least prove to me that it was not he. I did more; feeling very well that, if he was not guilty after all, I did not have the right to demand that he prove anything to me, I made the decision to write the reasons for my persuasion in a rather ample Memorandum and to submit them to the judgment of an arbiter that Vernes could not challenge. One would not guess which one was the arbiter I chose? [The Council of Geneva.][145] I declared at the end of the memorandum, that if, after having examined it, and having made the investigations it might judge necessary[146] and which it was in a very good position to make successfully, the Council pronounced that M. Vernes was not the author of the memorandum, from that instant I would sincerely cease to believe that he was, I would leave to go to throw myself at his feet and ask him for pardon until I obtained it. I dare to say it, never has my ardent zeal for equity, never have the uprightness, the generosity of my soul, my confidence in that love of justice innate in all hearts shown themselves more fully, more palpably [147] than in that wise and touching memorandum, in which, without hesitating, I took my most implacable enemies as arbiters between the calumniator and me. I read this writing to Du Peyrou: his advice was to suppress it, and I suppressed it. He advised me to wait for the proofs that Vernes promised, I waited for them and I am still waiting for them: he advised me to keep silent while waiting, I kept silent and I will keep silent the rest of my life, blamed for having charged Vernes with a serious false imputation without proof even though I remain inwardly persuaded—as convinced as I am of my own existence—that he is the author of the libel. My memorandum is in M. du Peyrou's hands: if it ever sees the light my reasons will be found in it, and the soul of J.-J., which my contemporaries have wanted so little to know, will be known from it I hope. [148]

It is time to move on to my catastrophe at Môtiers, and to my departure from Val-de-Travers, after two-and-a-half years of residence, and eight months of an unshakable constancy in suffering the most undeserved treatment. [149] It is impossible for me to recall the details of that disagreeable epoch distinctly, but they will be found in the relation that du Peyrou published of them, and about which I will have something to say below. [150]

After Mme de Verdelin's departure the fermentation became more lively, and in spite of repeated Rescripts from the King, in spite of the frequent orders of the State Council, in spite of the efforts of the Châtelain and the Magistrates of the place, the people finally appeared to want to proceed to action since they seriously regarded me as the Antichrist and saw all their uproar to be useless; already in the streets, the stones were beginning to roll after me, although they were still being thrown from a little too far away to be able to reach me. Finally on the night of the fair of Môtiers, which is at the beginning of September, I was attacked in my residence in a manner that put the lives of the people who lived in it into danger. [151]

At midnight I heard a loud noise in the gallery that ran along the back of the house. A hail of stones thrown against the window and the door which gave access to this gallery fell with such a crash that my dog, who was sleeping in the gallery and who had begun by barking, became silent out of fright and took refuge in a corner, gnawing and scratching the boards to try to flee. I got up because of the noise, I was starting to leave my room to pass into the kitchen, when a stone thrown by a vigorous hand crossed the kitchen after having broken its window, opened the door to my Room and fell at the foot of my bed, in such a way that if I had been a second earlier, the stone would have hit me in the stomach. I judged that the noise had been made to draw me in, and the stone thrown to welcome me on my exit.[152] I leap into the kitchen. I find Therese who had also gotten up and who ran up to me trembling. We stand aside against a wall away from the direction of the window to avoid the range of the rocks, and to deliberate about what we had to do: for to leave in order to call for help was the way to get ourselves knocked down. Fortunately the servant of a good old man who lodged below me got up because of the noise and ran to call M. the Châtelain who lived next door. He leaps from his bed, hastily puts on his dressing gown, and instantly comes with the guard who were making the rounds that night because of the fair and were close by. The Châtelain was so frightened when he saw the damage that he blanched at it, and when he saw of the stones with which the gallery was full, he cried out, "My God! It's a quarry!" Upon visiting the outside, we found that the door of a little Courtyard[153] had been forced, and that they had tried to break into the house by means of the gallery. When he investigated why the guard had not noticed or prevented the disorder, he found that the ones from Môtiers had insisted on making up this guard out of their ranks, even though it was another village's turn. The next day the Châtelain sent his report to the State Council, which two days afterward sent him the order to gather information about this affair, to promise a reward and secrecy to anyone who would denounce the guilty, and, while waiting, to put guards, at the expense of the Prince, on my house and on the Châtelain's which touched it.

The next day Colonel Pury, Procurator General Meuron, Châtelain Martinet, Receiver Guyenet,[154] Treasurer d'Ivernois, and his father, in a word all the distinguished people there were in the country, came to see me and united their solicitations to induce me to give way to the storm, and to leave, at least for a time, a parish in which I could no longer live in safety or with honor. I even noticed that, frightened by the furies of this frenzied people, and fearing they might extend all the way to him, the Châtelain would have been very glad to see me leave as quickly as possible so as not to have the trouble of protecting me any longer, and to be able to leave himself, as he did after my departure. Thus I gave way and even without much trouble, for the spectacle of the people's hatred caused me a heartache which I could not bear.

I had more than one retreat to choose from. Since Mme de Verdelin's return to Paris she had spoken to me in several letters about a M. Walpole, whom she called His Lordship, who—because he had acquired a great zeal in my favor—proposed a refuge in one of his estates of which she gave me the most pleasant descriptions, entering into details with relation to lodging and subsistence that showed how far the said Lord Walpole was engaged with her in this plan.[155] The Lord Marshal had always recommended England or Scotland to me, and also offered me refuge in his estates; but he offered me one that tempted me much more near him at Potsdam. He had just informed me of a conversation the King had engaged in with him about me, and which was a sort of invitation to go there, and Mme the Duchesse de Saxe-Gotha [156] was counting so much [157] on this trip that she wrote to me to urge me to go see her on the way, and to stop with her for some time; but I had such an attachment for Switzerland that I could not resolve to leave it as long as I could live there, and I took this occasion to execute a plan with which I had been occupied for several months, and about which I have not been able to speak yet in order to avoid cutting the thread of my narrative.

This project consisted in going to establish myself on the Island of St. Pierre, property of the Hôpital of Berne in the middle of the Lake of Bienne. On a walking pilgrimage I had made with Du Peyrou the preceding summer, we had visited that Island, and I was so enchanted by it that, since that time, I had not ceased to dream of ways of making my residence there. The greatest obstacle was that the Island belonged to the Bernese who had basely driven me away three years earlier and, aside from the fact that my pride suffered from returning among people who had received me so poorly, I had grounds for fearing that they would not leave me any more in peace on that Island than they had done at Yverdon. On that point I had consulted the Lord Marshal who—thinking as I did that the Bernese [would be] [158] very glad to see me banished to that [159] Island and to keep me as a hostage there for the writings I might be tempted to undertake—had had their inclinations [160] sounded out on this point by a M. Sturler,[161] his former neighbor at Colombier. M. Sturler addressed himself to [162] the leaders of the State, and based on their answer assured the Lord Marshal that, since they were ashamed of their past behavior, the Bernese did not ask for anything better than to see me domiciled on the Island of St. Pierre and to leave me there tranquilly. Before I risked going there to reside, as an additional precaution I had new information acquired by Colonel Chaillet [163] who confirmed the same things to me, and when the Receiver [164] of the Island received permission from his masters to lodge me there, I believed that I was not risking anything by going to establish myself in his home with the tacit approval from both the sovereign and the owners; for I could not hope that the Gentlemen of Berne would openly acknowledge the injustice they had done me, and in that way sin against the most inviolable maxim of all sovereigns.[165]

The Island of St. Pierre, called the *Island of the Hillock* at Neuchâtel, in the middle of the Lake of Bienne, is about a half-league in circumference; but in this little space it furnishes all the principal products necessary for life. It has fields, meadows, orchards, woods, vineyards, and—thanks to a varied and mountainous terrain—all form an arrangement that is all the more pleasant since its parts (which are not all visible at the same time) set each other off and make one judge [166] the Island to be bigger than it is in fact. An extremely elevated terrace forms the western part which looks toward Gleresse and Bonneville. This terrace has been planted with a long tree-lined lane which has been divided in half by a trellised enclosure where people from all the neighboring shores gather on Sundays during the grape harvest to dance and amuse themselves. There is only a single house on the Island, but a huge and commodious one in which the Receiver is lodged and which is situated in a hollow that shelters it from the winds.

At five or six hundred feet from the Island on the south side, is another much smaller uncultivated and deserted Island, which appears to have been detached from the large one by storms some time ago and produces only willows and Persicaria in its gravel, but on which nevertheless there is an elevated mound that is well turfed and very pleasant. The shape of this lake is an almost perfect oval. Its banks, less rich than those of the lakes of Geneva and Neuchâtel, nonetheless form a rather beautiful decoration, above all on the western side which is very populated, and is bordered by vineyards at the foot of a chain of mountains, just about like Côte-rotie,[167] but which do not yield as good a wine. When one goes from the South to the North one finds the Bailiage of St. Jean, Bonneville, Bienne, and Nidau at the far end of the lake. All this is interspersed with very pleasant villages.

Such was the refuge I had arranged for myself, and where I resolved to go to establish myself when I left the Val-de-Travers.* This choice conformed so well to my pacific taste, to my solitary and lazy mood that I count it among the sweet reveries for which I have had the most lively passion. It seemed to me that on this Island I would be more cut off from men, more sheltered from their outrages, more forgotten by them, in a word more abandoned to the sweetness of inactivity and the contemplative life: I would have wished to be so confined to that Island that I would no longer have any dealings with mortals, and it is certain that I

---

*It is perhaps not useless to note that I left a particular enemy there in a M. de Terreaux, the Mayor of Les Verriéres, who is held in very mediocre esteem in the country, but who has a brother in M. de St. Florentin's Offices who is said to be a decent man.[168] The Mayor had gone to see him some time before my adventure. Little comments like this one, which are nothing by themselves, can lead to the discovery of much underground dealing later on.[169]

took every measure imaginable to remove myself[170] from the necessity of having to maintain any.

There was the question of how to live. Because of both the expensiveness of commodities and the difficulty of transportation, it is expensive to live on that Island where, besides, one is at the discretion of the Receiver. This difficulty was removed by an arrangement that Du Peyrou was willing to make with me by substituting himself for the company that had undertaken and abandoned my general edition. I handed over to him all the material for that edition. I put it in order and organized it. To this I joined the pledge to hand over the memoirs of my life to him, and I made him generally the depositary of all my papers, with the express condition that he not make use of them until after my death, since I had it at heart to finish my career peacefully, without making the public remember me any longer. By means of this, the annual life pension which he took it upon himself to pay me was enough for my subsistence.[171] When the Lord Marshal recovered all his property, he had offered me one of Twelve hundred francs which I had accepted only after reducing it by half. He wanted to send me the capital for it which I refused, because of the trouble of placing it. He passed this capital over to Du Peyrou, in whose hands it has remained, and who pays me the income in accordance with the terms agreed upon with the grantor.[172] Thus combining my agreement with Du Peyrou, the pension from the Lord Marshal (two-thirds of which was to revert to Therese after my death), and the income of 300 francs I had from Duchesne, I could count on a decent subsistence both for me and after me for Therese, to whom I was leaving seven hundred francs of income, from Rey's pension and the Lord Marshal's: thus I no longer had to be afraid that she would lack bread any more than I would. But it was written that honor would force me to decline[173] all the resources which fortune and my labor put within my reach, and that I would die as poor as I have lived. One will judge whether, unless I were the worst of disgraceful men, I could keep up arrangements that they have always been careful to render ignominious for me, by carefully depriving me[174] of any other resource so as to force me to consent to my dishonor. How could they doubt what choice I would make, given these alternatives?[175] They have always judged my heart from their own.[176]

At ease on the side of subsistence[177] I had no care on any other side. Although I was leaving the field free to my enemies in the world, in the noble enthusiasm that had dictated my writings and in the constant uniformity of my principles, I was leaving behind a testimony about my soul that corresponded to the one which all my behavior gave about my natural disposition.[178] I did not need any other defense against my[179] calumniators. They could depict another man under my name, but they could deceive only those who wanted to be deceived. I could leave them my life to censure from one end to another, I was sure that through my faults and my weakness, through my inability to bear any yoke, one would always find a man who was just, good, without bile, without hatred, without jealousy, prompt to acknowledge his own wrongs, more prompt to forget those of someone else; who sought his whole felicity in loving and gentle passions, and who in everything pushed sincerity to the point of imprudence, up to the point of the most unbelievable disinterestedness.

Thus, in a way I took leave of my Century and of my contemporaries, and I bade farewell to the world by confining myself on this Island for the remainder of my days; for that was my resolution, and it was there that I counted on finally executing the great project of that idle life to which until then I had uselessly devoted all the little activity which Heaven had assigned me. For me this Island was going to become Papimania, that blessed country where one sleeps.

Where one does more, where one does nothing.[180]

This more was everything for me; for I have always hardly missed sleep;[181] idleness is enough for me, and as long as I am doing nothing, I prefer to dream while awake than while asleep. Now that the age for romantic plans had passed and the fumes of vainglory had made me dizzy more than they had flattered me, only living without bother in an eternal leisure remained as my last hope.[182] That is the life of the blessed in the other world, and henceforward I made it my supreme happiness in this one.

Those who reproach me for so many contradictions will not fail to reproach me for still one more here. I have said that the idleness of social circles makes them unbearable for me, and here I am seeking out solitude solely to abandon myself to idleness. Nevertheless, that is the way I am; if there is any contradiction there, it is of nature's making and not mine; but there is so little contradiction that it is precisely because of it that I am always myself. The idleness of social circles is killing because it is from necessity. That of solitude is charming, because it is free and from the will. In company it is cruel for me to do nothing, because I am forced to do it. I have to stay there nailed down on a chair or standing up stuck in like a stake, without shifting either a foot or a leg, daring neither to run, nor to leap, nor to sing, nor to shout, nor to make a gesture when I want to, not daring even to dream; having all the boredom of idleness and all the torment of constraint at the same time; obliged to be attentive to all the foolish remarks that are said and to all the compliments that are paid, and to fatigue my Minerva ceaselessly, so as not to miss my turn for putting in my quip and my lie.[183] And you call that idleness? That is forced labor.

The idleness I love is not that of a do-nothing who stays there with his arms crossed in total inactivity and thinks no more than he acts. It is both that of a child who is ceaselessly in motion while doing nothing and, at the same time, that of a dotard who strays when [184] his arms are at rest. I love to occupy myself [185] by doing trifles, beginning a hundred things and finishing none of them, going and coming as the fancy comes into my head, changing plans at each instant, following a fly in all its flying about, wanting to uproot a rock to see what is under it,[186] undertaking a labor of ten years with ardor, and abandoning it without regret after ten minutes, in sum, musing all day long without order and without sequence, and following only the caprice of the moment in everything.

Botany, as I have always considered it and as it began to become a passion for me, was precisely an idle study, suited to filling up the whole void of my leisure, without leaving room for the delirium of the imagination, or for the boredom of total inactivity. To wander nonchalantly in the woods and in the country, here and there to take up mechanically, sometimes a flower, sometimes a branch;[187] to graze on my fodder almost at random, to observe the same things thousands of times, and always with the same interest because I always forgot them, was enough for me to pass eternity without being bored for a moment. However elegant, however admirable, however diverse the structure of plants might be, it does not strike an ignorant eye enough to interest it. That constant analogy and nevertheless prodigious variety that reigns in their organization carries away only those who already have some idea of the vegetal system. Others have only a stupid and monotonous admiration at the sight of all these treasures of nature. They see nothing in detail, because they do not even know what they need to look at, and they do not see the ensemble [188] either because they have no idea of that chain of relations and combinations which overpowers the mind of the observer with its marvels. I was, and my lack of memory ought to have always kept me, at that fortunate point of knowing little enough about it so that everything was new to me and enough so that I was able to feel everything. The diverse soils into which the Island was divided in spite of its smallness offered me a sufficient variety of plants for my whole life's study and amusement.[189] I did not want to leave a leaf of grass without analysis,[190] and I already was settling down to write the *Flora Petrinsularis* [191] with an immense collection of curious observations.

I had Therese come with my books and my effects. We started boarding with the Receiver of the Island. His wife had sisters in Nidau who took turns coming to see her, and who gave Therese some company. There I tried out a sweet life in which I would have wished to pass my own, and the taste I acquired for it there served only to make me feel better the bitterness of the one that was to succeed it so promptly.

I have always loved the water passionately, and the sight of it throws me into a delightful reverie, although often without a settled object. When the weather was good, when I got up I did not fail to run onto the terrace to breathe in the morning's salubrious and fresh air, and to let my eyes slide over the horizon of that beautiful lake, whose banks and mountains which bordered it enchanted my sight. I find no more worthy homage to the divinity than this mute admiration excited by the contemplation of its works and which is not at all expressed by amplified actions. I understand how it is that the inhabitants of cities who see only walls, streets, and crimes have little faith; but I cannot understand how country folk and above all solitary people can have none whatsoever. How is it that their soul does not raise itself with ecstasy a hundred times a day to the author of the marvels that strike them? For me, it is above all when I get up, worn down by my insomnia, that a long habit carries me to those elevations of heart which do not impose any of the fatigue of thinking. But that requires that my eyes be struck by the ravishing spectacle of nature. In my room I pray more rarely and more stiffly: but at the sight of a beautiful countryside, I feel myself moved without being able to say what is causing it. I have read that when a wise [192] Bishop visited his diocese and found an old woman who could say nothing but, "Oh," as her only prayer: he said to her, "Good mother, continue to pray that way always; your prayer is worth more than ours." That better prayer is also mine.

After breakfast, I hastened to write some wretched letters while looking sullen, ardently aspiring to the happy moment of no longer having any more to write at all. For several moments I fidgeted around my books and papers, to unpack and organize them rather than to read them; and this organizing, which became the work of Penelope for me,[193] gave me the pleasure of musing for several moments, after which I got bored with it and left it to pass the three or four hours of the morning I had left in the study of botany and especially Linnaeus's system, for which I acquired a passion which I have not been able to cure myself of completely, even after having felt its gap.[194] To my taste, along with Ludwig,[195] this great observer is the only one up to now who has seen botany as a naturalist and as a philosopher; but he has studied it too much in herbaria and in gardens and not enough in nature itself. As for me who took the entire Island as my garden; as soon as I needed to make or verify some observation, I ran into the woods or the meadows, my book under my arm: there

I lay down on the earth next to the plant in question to examine it on the spot, entirely at my ease.[196] This method served me very well for understanding plants in their natural state, before they had been cultivated and denatured by the hand of men. They say that Fagon, the Premier Doctor of Louis XIV, who named and knew perfectly all the plants in the royal garden, was so ignorant in the country that he no longer knew anything there.[197] I am precisely the opposite. I know something about nature's work, but nothing about the gardener's.

As for the periods after dinner, I abandoned them totally to my idle and nonchalant mood and to following the impulsion of the moment without any rule. Often, when the air was calm, immediately after leaving the table I went to throw myself alone into a little boat which the Receiver had taught me to guide with a single oar; I went forward into open water. The moment when I left the shore gave me a joy that reached the point of shivering and whose cause I am unable to state or understand very well, unless it was possibly a secret self-congratulation at being out of reach of the wicked in this position.[198] Next I wandered alone on the lake sometimes drawing near the banks, but never touching them. Often letting my boat drift at the mercy of the air and water I abandoned myself to reveries without object and which were no less sweet[199] for being stupid. Every so often I cried out with emotion, "Oh nature, oh my mother, here I am under your protection alone; here there is no clever and deceitful man who comes between you and me." In this way I went as far as a half a league from land; I would have wished this lake to be the ocean.[200] Nevertheless, to gratify my poor dog who did not like such long stays on the water as much as I did, I ordinarily followed a goal for the excursion; that was to land on the little island, to take a walk there for an hour or two or to stretch myself out on the grass on the summit of the mound, to satiate myself with the pleasure of admiring this lake and its surroundings, to examine and dissect all the grasses that were within my reach, and, like another Robinson, to build an imaginary residence for myself on this little Island.[201] I became very attached to this knoll. When I was able to bring Therese with the Receiver's wife and her sisters to take a walk there, how proud I was to be their Pilot and their guide! In pomp we carried Rabbits there to colonize it. Another festival for J.-J. This colony[202] made the little Island even more interesting for me. From then on, I went there more often and with more pleasure to look for traces of the progress of the new inhabitants.

To these amusements, I joined one that recalled to me the sweet life at les Charmettes, and to which the season particularly invited me. This was the occupation of rustic tasks of the vegetable and fruit harvest, which

Therese and I made into a pleasure[203] of sharing with the Receiver's wife and her family. I remember that a Bernese named M. Kirkebergher,[204] who had come to see me, found me perched in a big tree, a sack attached around me by a belt and already so full of apples that I could no longer move. I was not upset by this encounter and some other similar ones. I hope that when the Bernese witnessed how I used my leisure, they would no longer dream of disturbing its tranquility and would leave me in peace in my solitude. I would have much preferred to be confined there by their will than by my own: I would have been more assured that I would not see my repose disturbed at all.

Here again is[205] one of those admissions about which I am sure in advance of the incredulity of my readers, obstinate in always judging me from themselves, although in the whole course of my life they have been forced to see a thousand internal affections which did not resemble theirs at all. What is more bizarre is that while they deny that I have all the good and indifferent feelings they do not have, they are always ready to lend me ones that are so bad that they could not even enter a man's heart: then they find it entirely simple to put me into contradiction with nature and to make me into such a monster as could not even exist. Nothing absurd appears unbelievable to them as soon as it tends to blacken me, nothing extraordinary appears possible to them as soon as it tends to honor me.[206]

But whatever they might be able to believe or say, I will nonetheless continue to set forth[207] faithfully what J.-J. Rousseau was, did, and thought, without explaining or justifying the singularity of his feelings and his ideas, or looking for whether others have thought as he did. I acquired so much taste for the Island of St. Pierre, and the stay there suited me so extremely, that as a result of inscribing all my desires on that Island I formed the desire of not leaving it at all.[208] The visits I had to pay in the neighborhood; the errands I had to run to Neuchâtel, Bienne, Yverdon, Nidau already tired out my imagination. A day to spend off the Island appeared to me to be a day subtracted from my happiness, and to leave the enclosure of this lake was for me to leave my element. Besides, the experience of the past had made me fearful. It was enough for some good to flatter my heart for me to expect to lose it, and the ardent desire to end my days on this Island was inseparable from the fear of being forced to leave it. I had acquired the habit of going in the evenings to sit on the shore, especially when the lake was agitated. I felt a singular pleasure in watching the waves break at my feet. Out of them I made the image of the tumult of the world and the peace of my habitation, and I was sometimes so moved by this sweet idea that I felt tears flow from my eyes. This repose which I enjoyed with passion was disturbed only by anxiety about losing it, but this anxiety went far enough to spoil[209] its sweetness. I felt my situation to be so precarious that I did not dare to count on it. I said to myself, "Ah how willingly I would trade the freedom to leave here, which I do not care about at all, for the assurance of being able to stay here always. Instead of being tolerated here as a favor why am I not detained here by force. Those who only tolerate me can drive me away at any moment and, can I hope that, when my persecutors see that I am happy here, they will allow me to continue to be so. Ah it is little enough that they permit me to live here, I would like them to sentence me to stay here and I would like to be constrained to stay here so as not to be constrained to leave."[210] I cast an envious eye on the fortunate Micheli Du Cret who, tranquil at the Chateau of Arberg, had only to wish to be happy in order to be so.[211] In sum, as a result of abandoning myself to these reflections and to disquieting presentiments about new storms always ready to burst upon me, I came to desire with an unbelievable ardor that, instead of only tolerating my habitation on this Island, they might give it to me as a perpetual prison, and I can swear that if had been up to me alone to be sentenced there, I would have done it with the greatest joy, for I preferred a thousandfold the necessity of passing the rest of my life there to the danger[212] of being expelled from it.[213]

This fear did not remain idle for long. At the moment I expected it least, I received a letter from M. the Bailiff of Nidau who had the governance of the Island of St. Pierre;[214] by means of this letter he notified me on behalf of Their Excellencies of the order to leave the Island and their States. When I read it I thought I was dreaming. Nothing could be less natural, less reasonable, less foreseen than such an order: for I had looked at my presentiments more as the anxieties of a man frightened by his misfortunes, than as a foresight that might have the slightest foundation. The measures I had taken to assure myself of the tacit agreement of the sovereign, the tranquillity with which I had been allowed to establish myself, the visits of several Bernese and of the Bailiff himself who had loaded me with acts of friendship and consideration: the rigor of the season, in which it was barbaric to expel an invalid, everything made me believe—along with many other people—that this order was based on a misunderstanding, and that people with bad intentions had deliberately taken the time of the harvest and of poorly attended sessions of the Senate to inflict this blow on me brusquely.[215]

If I had listened to my first indignation I would have left on the spot. But where to go? What would become of me at the beginning of winter, without a goal, without preparations, without a driver, without a carriage? Unless I were to leave everything in confusion, my papers, my effects, all my business, I needed time to provide for them, and the order did not say whether they were leaving me any or not. The continuation of misfortunes began to make my courage sink.[216] For the first time I felt my natural pride bend under the yoke of necessity, and I had to lower myself to asking for a delay in spite of the murmuring of my heart. In order to get the order interpreted, I addressed myself to M. de Graffenried, who had sent it to me. His letter contained a very sharp disapproval of this same order of which he notified me only with the greatest[217] regret, and the testimonies of sorrow and esteem with which it was full seemed to be so many very gentle invitations to speak to him with an open heart; I did so. I did not even doubt that my letter would open the eyes of these iniquitous men to their barbarity, and that, even if they did not revoke such a cruel order, they would at least grant me a reasonable delay and perhaps the entire winter to prepare myself for the withdrawal and to choose the place.

While waiting for the answer I began to reflect about my situation and to deliberate about the decision I had to make. I saw so many difficulties from all sides, affliction had affected me so strongly, and my health was so bad at that moment that I let myself be completely subdued, and the effect of my discouragement was to deprive me of the few resources I could have left in my mind for making the best possible use of my sad situation. No matter what refuge I might want[218] to take shelter in, it was clear that I could not protect myself against either of the two ways that had been used to expel me. The one by raising the populace against me by means of subterranean maneuvers; the other by driving me out by open force, without giving any reason for it. Thus I could not count on any assured retreat, unless I went to look for it farther away than my strength and the season seemed to permit me to go. Since all this brought me back to the ideas I had just been occupied with, I dared to desire and propose that they would prefer to dispose of me in a perpetual captivity over making me wander ceaselessly on the earth by expelling me successively from all the refuges I would have chosen. Two days after my first letter I wrote a second one to M. de Graffenried to ask him to make this proposal to Their Excellencies. The answer from Berne to both of them was an order conceived in the most categorical and[219] harshest terms to leave the Island and all the mediate and immediate territory of the Republic in the space of twenty-four [hours][220] and never to return to it under the most grievous penalties.[221]

This moment was horrible. Since then[222] I have found myself in worse anguish, but never in a greater quandary. But what afflicted me most was being forced to renounce the plan that had made me desire to pass the winter on the Island. It is time to report the fatal anecdote which put the finishing touch on my disasters and which dragged into my ruin an unfortunate people whose nascent virtues were already promising to equal those of Sparta and Rome one day.

I had spoken about the Corsicans in *The Social Contract* as a new People, the only one in Europe that was not too worn out for legislation, and I had made note of the great hope one should have for such a people if it had the good fortune to find a wise founder.[223] My work was read by some Corsicans who were grateful for the honorable manner in which I spoke about them, and the circumstance in which they found themselves of working for the establishment of their Republic made their leaders think of[224] asking me for my ideas about this important work. A M. Buttafoco from one of the leading families of the country and a Captain in the Royal Italian Regiment in France wrote to me on this subject and furnished me with several[225] pieces for which I had asked him to inform myself about the history of the nation and the condition of the country.[226] M. Paoli[227] wrote to me several times, and although I felt that such an undertaking was beyond my strength, I believed I could not refuse to cooperate in such a great and fine work when I had acquired all the information I needed. I responded to both of them to this effect, and this correspondence continued until my departure.

At precisely the same time I learned that France was sending troops into Corsica and that it had made a treaty with the Genovese.[228] This treaty, this dispatch of troops made me anxious, and, although I did not yet imagine that all this was related to me in any way, I judged it to be impossible and ridiculous to labor on a work that requires as deep repose as the founding of a people does, at the moment at which it was perhaps going to be subjugated.[229] I did not hide my anxieties from M. Buttafoco, who reassured me with the certainty that, if there were anything in this treaty contrary to the freedom of his nation, such a good citizen as he would not remain in the service of France as he was doing. In fact his zeal for legislation for the Corsicans and his close connections with M. Paoli could not leave me any suspicion on his account; and when I learned that he was making frequent trips to Versailles and to Fontainebleau and that he had relations with M. de Choiseul, I did not conclude anything from it, except that he had assurances about the genuine intentions of the Court of France which he allowed me to understand, but about which he did not want to explain himself openly in letters.

All that partially reassured me. Nevertheless, since I did not understand anything about this dispatch of French troops; since I could not reasonably think that they were there to protect the freedom of the Corsicans who were in a very good position to defend themselves against the Genovese by themselves, I could not calm myself perfectly or completely involve myself in the proposed legislation, until I had solid proofs that all this was not a joke in order to banter with me.[230] I very much desired an interview with M. Buttafoco; that was the true[231] way to draw the enlightenment I needed from him. He made me hope for it[232] and I waited for it with the greatest impatience. As for him, I do not know whether he genuinely planned to do it; but even if he did, my disasters would have kept me from taking advantage of it.

The more I meditated about the proposed undertaking, the farther I advanced in the examination of the pieces I had in my hands,[233] and the more I felt the need to study from close at hand the people to found[234] and the ground it inhabited and all the relations required for adapting this founding to them. Each day I understood[235] more that it was impossible for me to acquire from far away all the enlightenment I needed to guide me. I wrote this to Buttafoco; he felt it himself. And if I did not precisely form the resolution of going to Corsica, I occupied myself very much with the means for making this trip. I spoke about it to M. Dastier, who should have been acquainted with it because he had formerly served on that Island under M. de Maillebois.[236] He spared nothing to dissuade me from this plan, and I admit that the horrible depiction he made me of the Corsicans and their country very much cooled the desire I had to go to live in their midst.

But when the persecutions at Môtiers made me think of leaving Switzerland, this desire came to life again from my hope of finally finding among these islanders that rest which they did not want to leave me anywhere. Only one thing frightened me about this trip; it was the ineptitude and the aversion I have always had for the active life to which I was going to be condemned. Made to meditate at leisure in solitude, I was not at all made to speak, act, deal with business among men. Nature, which had given me the former talent, had refused me the latter. Nevertheless, I felt that as soon as I was in Corsica, without[237] directly taking part in public affairs, I would be constrained to abandon myself to the urging of the People and to confer with the Leaders very often. The very object of my trip required that instead of looking for retirement, I would be looking for the enlightenment I needed in the bosom of the nation. It was clear that I would no longer be able to dispose of myself, and that—dragged in spite of myself into a whirlwind for which I was not at all born—I would be leading a life completely contrary to my taste there and would only show myself at my disadvantage. I foresaw that, because my presence would poorly maintain the opinion my books might have given them of my capacity, I would discredit myself with the Corsicans, and would lose, both to their disadvantage and to [mine],[238] the confidence they had given me, and without which I could not successfully do the work they expected of me. I was sure that by leaving my Sphere this way I would become useless to them and would make myself unhappy.

Tormented, beaten by storms of every sort, fatigued by trips and persecutions for several years, I keenly felt the need for the rest of which my barbaric enemies made a game of depriving me; I sighed more than ever[239] after that lovable idleness, after that sweet quietude of mind and body which I had coveted so much, and to which my heart limited its supreme felicity now that it had returned from the chimeras of love and friendship. It was only with fright that I envisaged the labors I was going to undertake, the tumultuous life to which I was going to abandon myself, and if the greatness, the beauty, the usefulness of the object enlivened my courage, the impossibility of successfully running risks absolutely deprived me of it. Twenty years of profound meditation by myself would have cost me less than six months of active life in the midst of men and business, and with the certainty of succeeding poorly in it.

I took into my head an expedient that seemed to me suitable for reconciling everything. Pursued in all my refuges by the subterranean intrigues of my secret persecutors, and no longer seeing anywhere but Corsica where I could hope in my old age for the rest they did not wish to leave me anywhere, I resolved to make my way there with Buttafoco's directions as soon as I could; however, in order to live there peacefully, I would renounce the labor of legislation, at least in appearance, and would limit myself to paying my hosts in some way for their hospitality by writing their history on the spot, even while acquiring without commotion the information I needed to become more useful to them,[240] if I saw the opportunity to succeed in doing so. In beginning this way by not committing myself to anything, I hoped to be in a position to meditate in secret and more at my ease over a plan that might suit them, and to do so without renouncing much of my dear solitude or submitting to a type of life that was unbearable to me and for which I did not have the talent.[241]

But in my situation this trip was not an easy thing to execute. From the manner in which M. Dastier had spoken to me about Corsica, I would not find the simplest conveniences of life there aside from the ones I would bring along: linen, clothes, dishes, kitchen equipment, paper, books, one had to bring everything along with one. In order to transplant myself there with my housekeeper, I had to cross the Alps, and to drag an entire baggage in my train on a journey of two hundred leagues; I had to cross[242] the States of several sovereigns, and, from the tone set by all of

Europe after my misfortunes, I naturally ought to expect to find obstacles everywhere and to see each sovereign make it an honor for himself to burden me with some new disfavor and to violate all the rights of nations and of humanity with me. The immense expense, the fatigues, the risks of such a trip obliged me to foresee in advance and to weigh well all the difficulties. The idea of finding myself alone in the end without resource at my age[243] and far from all my acquaintances at the mercy of this barbaric and wild people, as it was depicted to me by M. Dastier, was very suited to making me ponder such a resolution before executing it. I passionately[244] desired the interview that Buttafoco had made me hope for and I awaited its effect to make up my mind completely.

While I was hesitating this way, along came the persecutions at Môtiers which forced me to withdraw. I was not ready for a long trip and above all[245] for the one to Corsica. I waited for news from Buttafoco; I took refuge on the Island of St. Pierre from where I was dismissed at the beginning of winter as I have said above. Since they were covered with snow at that time, the Alps made this emigration impracticable for me, above all with the precipitateness that was being prescribed to me. It is true that the extravagance of such an order made it impossible to execute: for—closed up in the middle of the water in the midst of that solitude and having only twenty-four hours from the intimation of the order to prepare myself for the departure, to find boats and carriages, to leave the Island and the whole territory—if I had wings it would have been hard for me to be able to obey. I wrote that to M. the Bailiff of Nidau when I answered his letter, and I rushed to leave that land of iniquity.[246] That is how it became necessary for me to renounce my favorite plan, and how,[247] since in my discouragement I had not been able to prevail upon them to dispose of me, I decided on the trip to Berlin based on the Lord Marshal's invitation, leaving Therese to winter on the Island of St. Pierre with my effects and my books and depositing my papers[248] in Du Peyrou's hands.[249] I made such haste that as early as the morning of the next day I left the Island and made my way to Bienne before noon. My trip was nearly ended by an incident the narration of which should not be omitted.

As soon as the rumor had spread that I had been ordered to leave my refuge, I had an influx of visits from the neighborhood, and above all from Bernese who came with the most detestable falseness to fawn on me, to assuage me, and to protest to me that someone had taken the moment of vacation and the Senate's having infrequent sessions for drafting and notifying me of that order against which, they said, the whole Two Hundred was indignant. Among this heap of consolers, there came several from the city of Bienne, a small free State enclosed inside that of Berne, and among others a young man called Wildremet[250] whose family held the first rank and had the principal influence in that small city. In the name of his fellow citizens Wildremet entreated me in a lively way to choose my retreat in their midst, assuring me that they eagerly desired to receive me there, that they would make it into a glory and a duty for themselves to make me forget the persecutions I had suffered, that I did not have to be afraid of Bernese influence among them, that Bienne was a free city that did not receive laws from anyone, and that all the citizens were unanimously determined not to listen to any solicitation that was against me.

Seeing that he was not impressing me, Wildremet had himself supported by several other persons both from Bienne and its environs and from Berne itself, and among others by the same Kirkeberguer about whom I have spoken, who had sought me out after my withdrawal into Switzerland and whose talents and principles made him interesting to me. But less foreseen and weightier solicitations were those of M. Barthès, the secretary of the Ambassador of France,[251] who came to see me with Wildremet, strongly exhorted me to accept his invitation, and astonished me with the lively and tender interest he appeared to take in me. I did not know M. Barthès at all; nevertheless, I saw him put into his speeches warmth, the zeal of friendship, and I saw that he had it genuinely at heart to persuade me to settle at Bienne. He made me the most pompous praise of that City and its inhabitants with whom he showed himself so intimately connected that several times in front of me he called them his patrons and his fathers.

This step from Barthès disconcerted me in all my conjectures. I had always suspected M. de Choiseul of being the hidden author of all the persecutions I experienced in Switzerland. The conduct of the Resident of France at Geneva, that of the Ambassador at Soleure confirmed these suspicions only too well; I saw France secretly influencing everything that happened to me at Berne, at Geneva, at Neuchâtel, and I did not believe I had any powerful enemy in France except for the Duc de Choiseul alone. What could I think then about the visit from Barthès and about the tender interest he appeared to take in my fate. My misfortunes had not yet destroyed that trust natural to my heart, and experience had not yet taught me to see traps everywhere under blandishments. With surprise I looked for the reason for that benevolence from Barthès; I was not foolish enough to believe that he was taking this step on his own initiative: in it I saw a publicness and even an affectation that showed a hidden intention, and in all these little subaltern agents I was always very far from finding that generous intrepidity which had often made my heart seethe when I was in a similar post.

I had formerly known the Chevalier de Beauteville[252] a little at M. de

Luxembourg's house; he had born witness to some benevolence for me; since his appointment to the embassy he had again given me some signs of remembrance, and had even had me invited to go see him at Soleure; an invitation by which I had been touched even though I did not accept it, since I was not accustomed to being treated so decently by people in positions. Thus I presumed that, although he was forced to follow his instructions in what concerned the affairs of Geneva, but nevertheless feeling sorry for me in my misfortunes, M. de Beauteville had arranged this refuge of Bienne for me by his private efforts so that I could live tranquilly there under his auspices. I was grateful for this attention, but did not want to take advantage of it, and, being completely determined to make the trip to Berlin, I aspired with ardor to the moment of rejoining the Lord Marshal, since I was persuaded that I would no longer find true peace and lasting happiness anywhere but with him.

Upon my departure from the Island, Kirkeberguer accompanied me as far as Bienne. There I found Wildremet and several other Biennois who were waiting for me as I alighted from the boat. We all dined together at the inn, and my first effort upon arriving there was to have them look for a carriage since I wanted to leave as early as the morning of the next day. During the dinner these Gentlemen again took up their solicitations to keep me among them, and did so with such warmth and such touching protestations that in spite of all my resolutions, my heart—which has never been able to resist blandishments—let itself be moved by theirs: as soon as they saw me weakened they redoubled their efforts so much that I finally let myself be overcome and consented to stay at Bienne, at least until the next Spring.

Immediately Wildremet rushed to provide me with lodging and praised to me as a lucky find a nasty little room at the rear of the third story opening on a courtyard where, as a treat, I had the display of the stinking pelts of a Chamois Worker. My host was a little man, base looking and passably roguish, whom I learned the next day was a debauched fellow, a gambler, and in very bad repute in the Neighborhood; he had neither wife nor children nor servants and, sadly cloistered in my solitary room, in the most cheerful country in the world, I was lodged in a manner that would have made me perish of melancholy within a few days. What affected me most, in spite of everything I had been told about the eagerness of the inhabitants to receive me, was that while passing in the streets I did not notice anything with regard to me that was decent in their manners or obliging in their looks. I had nevertheless completely determined to stay there, when I learned, saw, and even felt beginning the next day that there was a terrible fermentation in the city with regard to me; several busybodies obligingly came to warn me that as early as the next day I was to be notified as harshly as possible of an order to leave the State, that is to say the town, on the spot. I had no one in whom to confide; all those people who had kept me there had scattered, Wildremet had disappeared, I no longer heard Barthès spoken of, and it did not appear that his recommendation had put me in great favor with the patrons and fathers he had attributed to himself in front of me. A M. de Vau-Travers,[253] a Bernese who had a pretty house near the city, nevertheless offered me a refuge there, hoping, he told me, that I would be able to avoid being stoned there. To me the advantage did not appear flattering enough to tempt me to prolong my stay among this hospitable people.

Nevertheless, since I had lost three days in this delay, I had already considerably exceeded the twenty-four hours the Bernese had given me to leave all their States, and, knowing their harshness, I did not fail to be in some difficulty over how they would let me cross them, when M. the Bailiff of Nidau came to extricate me from this perplexity in the nick of time. Since he had loudly disapproved of Their Excellencies' violent proceeding, in his generosity he believed he owed me a public testimonial that he was not taking any part in it, and was not afraid to leave his jurisdiction to come to pay me a visit at Bienne. He came on the eve of my departure, and far from coming incognito he even assumed some ceremony, came *in fiocchi*[254] in his carriage with his secretary and brought me a passport in his name to cross the State of Berne at my ease and without fear of being challenged. The visit touched me more than the passport. I would have been hardly less grateful for it if someone other than myself had been its object. I do not know of anything so powerful over my heart as an act of courage done opportunely in favor of the weak who are unjustly oppressed.

Finally, after having procured a carriage with difficulty, I left that homicidal land the next morning, before the arrival of the deputation with which I was to be honored, even before I had been able to see Therese again, whom I had notified to come join me when I had believed I would be stopping at Bienne, and which I barely had the time to countermand by a word in a letter notifying her of my new disaster.[255] If I ever have the strength to write it, in my third part one will see how, while I believed that I was leaving for Berlin, I was in fact leaving for England, and how, after they had dismissed me as a result of intrigues from Switzerland where I was not sufficiently in their power, the two Ladies[256] who wanted to dispose of me[257] succeeded in handing me over to their friend.[258]

I added what follows in the reading I made of this writing to M. and Mme the Comtesse d'Egmont, to M. the Prince Pignatelli, to Mme the Marquise de Mesme, and to M. the Marquis de Juigné.[259]

I have told the truth. If anyone knows some things contrary to what I have just set forth, even if they are proven a thousand times, he knows lies and impostures, and if he refuses to get to the bottom of them and clear them up with me while I am alive he does not love either justice or truth. As for me, I declare it loudly and without fear: Anyone who, even without having read my writings, will examine with his own eyes my natural disposition, my character, my morals, my inclinations, my pleasures, my habits, and will be capable of believing that I am a dishonest[260] man, is himself a man fit to be stifled.

I completed my reading this way and everyone was silent. Mme d'Egmont was the only one who appeared moved; she visibly trembled; but she very quickly recovered and kept silent as did the whole company. Such was the fruit I drew from this reading and from my declaration.

Appendix I

Letters referred to in the text of the *Confessions*[1]

From Rousseau to Mme de Francueil (p. 301)[2]

From Paris, April 20, 1751

Yes, Madame, I have put my children into the Foundling Hospital. I have entrusted the establishment made for that purpose with their support. If my poverty and my illness deprive me of the power of carrying out such a dear care, it is a misfortune about which I must feel sorry, and not a crime for which I must reproach myself. I owe them sustenance, I have procured it for them better or at least more securely than I would have been able to give it to them myself. This point is above everything else. Next comes the consideration of their mother who must not be dishonored.

You are acquainted with my situation, I earn my bread from day to day with difficulty enough, how would I feed a family in addition, and if I was constrained to have recourse to the profession of author, how would domestic cares and the worry of children in my garret leave me the tranquillity of mind necessary to do a lucrative work? Writings dictated by hunger hardly bring in anything and that resource is soon exhausted. Thus it would be necessary to have recourse to protection, to intrigue, to tricks, to court some low employment, to turn it to account by the ordinary means, otherwise it will not feed me and will soon be taken away from me, in sum to abandon myself to every infamy for which I am filled with such a just horror. To feed myself, my children, and their mother from the blood of the poor! No madame, it would be better for them to be orphans than to have a rogue for a father.

Overpowered by a painful and mortal malady, I can no longer hope for a long life. If, during my life, I was able to support these unfortunate people who are destined to suffer one day, they would pay dearly for the advantage of having been kept up a little more delicately than they could be where they are. Their mother, a victim of my indiscreet zeal, burdened by her own shame and her own needs, almost as valetudinary as myself and even less in a condition to feed them than I, will be forced to abandon them to themselves, and I do not see anything for them but the alternative of making themselves into bootblacks or bandits, which soon comes down to the same thing. At least if their status were legitimate, they could find resources more easily, but since they have to carry the dishonor of their birth and that of their poverty at the same time, what will become of them?

Why am I not married, you will say to me? Ask your unjust laws, madame. It did not suit me to enter into an eternal commitment, and one will never prove to me that any duty obliges me to do so. What is certain is that I have done nothing of the sort and that I do not want to do anything of the sort. One must not have children if one cannot feed them. Excuse me, madame, nature wants one to have them because the earth produces enough to feed the whole world, but it is the social station of the rich, it is your station that steals my children's bread from mine; nature also wants one to provide for their sustenance, that is what I have done; if a refuge for them did not exist, I would do my duty and resolve to die of hunger myself rather than not feed them.

Does this expression Foundling Hospital give you the impression that they found these children in the streets exposed to perish if chance does not save them? Rest assured that you would not have any more horror than I would for the unworthy father who could resolve upon that barbarism; it is too far from my heart for me to deign to justify myself for it. There are established rules, inform yourself about what they are and you will learn that the children leave the hands of the midwife only to pass into those of a nurse. I know that these children are not brought up delicately, so much the better for them, they become more robust for it, they are not given anything superfluous but they have what is necessary, they are not made into gentlemen but peasants or workers, I do not see anything in that manner of bringing them up that I would not choose for my own if I were the master of doing so. I would not at all prepare them by means of softness for the maladies that fatigue and the inclemency of air give to those who are not made for them, they would not learn either how to dance or to get on a horse but they would have good indefatigable legs. I would not make them into either authors or office people. I would not train them to handle the pen but the plough, the file, or the plane, instruments that make one lead a healthy, laborious, innocent life which one never abuses in order to do evil and which does not attract enemies when one does good. That is what they are destined to by the rustic education they are being given. They will be happier than their father.

I am deprived of the pleasure of seeing them and have never savored the sweetness of paternal embraces, alas; I have already told you that I do not see anything in this but something to feel sorry about and I am delivering them from poverty at my expense; in his republic Plato wanted all the children to be brought up in such a way that each would remain unknown to his father and all would be children of the state. But this education appears low and base, there is the great crime, it impresses you as it does other people and you do not see that by always following the prejudices of high society you take for the dishonor of vice what is only the dishonor of poverty.

From Chouet to Rousseau (p. 331) [3]

[From Geneva, June 18, 1755]

Sir

Following your intention, M. the Syndic Saladin has given me the new work that you just had published. As you desired, I have made the report about the Epistle Dedicatory to the Magnificent Council. It has seen with pleasure the Feelings of Virtue and Zeal for the Fatherland that you express with so much elegance. It is always with a great deal of satisfaction that the Fathers of the Fatherland learn that their Fellow Citizens are finding fame as you are by means of works which can only be the fruit of a rare merit and distinguished talents. Recognize, Sir, that in my private capacity I testify to you how much I have been touched by the beauties of this piece, and receive assurances that I am with all the esteem that you deserve

Sir

> Your very humble and very obedient servant
> Chouet

From the Comte de Tressan to Rousseau (p. 335) [4]

> From Toul, December 20, 1755

Sir you will know, from the letter from the King of Poland that I am sending to M. d'Alembert, how indignant this prince is over the Said Palissot's outrage. It is completely straightforward, it is very certain that you would have despised Palissot too much to be moved by the stupidity he has just committed, but the King of Poland deserves to have devoted servants, and I am too jealous of his glory not to have fulfilled duties so dear to my heart on this occasion.

I do not have the honor of having made your acquaintance, Sir, but I am bound with your fellow citizens by a tender friendship. I regard Geneva as the city in Europe where the young receive the most excellent education. I always have many young Genevan officers under my orders; I do not see any of them leave his family without proving that he has morals and literature. If the old friendship with which several of your friends honor me, if the love I have for the sciences and letters which you enrich every day, can be a title for me with you, I will be very eager, Sir, to form a connection with you on the first trip I will make to Paris, and I beg you to receive with pleasure and friendship the assurances of the high esteem with which I have the honor of being

Sir

> Your very humble and very obedient servant
> De Tressan

From Rousseau to the Comte de Tressan (p. 335) [5]

> [December 27, 1755]

Sir, I honored you as we all do; it is sweet for me to join gratitude to esteem, and I would willingly thank M. Palissot for having procured for me—without thinking about it—the testimonies of your kindness which permit me to give you those of my respect. If this author has been lacking in the respect he owed and which the whole earth owes to the Prince he wanted to amuse, who ought to find him more inexcusable than myself? But if his whole crime is to have exposed my absurdities, that is the theater's right, I do not see anything reprehensible in that for the decent man and for the author I see the merit of having known how to choose a very rich subject. Thus I beg you, Sir, not to listen to the zeal inspired in M. d'Alembert by friendship and generosity on this point, and not to distress for this trifle a man of merit who has not caused me any pain, and who would painfully bear the King of Poland's disfavor and yours.

My heart is moved by the praises with which you honor those of my fellow citizens who are under your orders. Indeed the Genevan is naturally good, he has a decent soul, he does not lack sense and he needs only good examples in order to be turned entirely to the good. Permit me, Sir, to exhort those young officers to take advantage of your example, to make themselves worthy of your kindness, and under your eyes to perfect the qualities which they perhaps owe to you and which you attribute to their education. For myself I will willingly take the advice I am giving them when you come to Paris. They will study the man of war, I the philosopher: Our common study will be the good man, and you will always be our teacher.

Sir, I am with respect your very humble and very obedient servant

JJ Rousseau

From the Comte de Tressan to Rousseau (p. 335) [6]

From Lunéville, January 1, 1756

Sir, receive the reward for the purest virtue! Your works make us love it by depicting its charms in their first simplicity; you have just taught it at this moment by means of the action that is most generous and most worthy of you.

Sir, having been softened and edified by your letter, the King of Poland believes that he cannot give you a more striking mark of his esteem than by agreeing with the clemency that you alone are capable of pronouncing today.

M. Palissot will not be expelled from the Society of Nancy, but this literary anecdote is to remain inscribed in its records, and you cannot blame us for preserving in the memory of men the excesses that can debase them, the acts of virtue that honor them. Enchanted by your works, Sir, and desiring to solidify in my heart the feelings that are so natural in yours, on this occasion I have done only what I ought to do, and without the order from the King of Poland who has charged me with passing his letter on to you, I would not have dared to make you acquainted with all my zeal.

Sir, you promise me to receive me when I come to Paris, and I promise to listen to you with trust, and to work in good faith to make myself worthy of being your friend.

Forgive me for having given away several copies of the letter that you did me the honor of writing me; in spite of the too honorable esteem for me to which you testify in it, I feel that people must forget me while they are reading this letter, and pay attention only to the great man who shows himself entirely in it in order to make vice blush and for the triumph of virtue.

I have the honor of being with the highest esteem and the most sincere attachment

Sir

Your very humble and very obedient servant
De Tressan

From Rousseau to the Comte de Tressan (p. 335) [7]

From Paris, January 7, 1756

Sir, whatever danger there might be of making myself tiresome, I cannot keep myself from joining some remarks about the recording of the affair of M. Palissot to the thanks I owe you, and at first I will take the liberty of telling you that even my admiration for the virtues of the King of Poland does not allow me to accept the testimonial of the kindness with which His Majesty honors me on this occasion except on condition that everything be forgotten. I dare to say that it does not become him to grant an incomplete clemency, and that only a pardon without reservation is worthy of his great soul. Besides, is it to grant clemency to make the punishment eternal and should not the records of an academy extenuate rather than call attention to its members' little faults. Finally, however little esteem I hold my contemporaries in, may it not please God that we debase them to this point of inscribing as an act of virtue what is only one of the simplest actions, which any man of letters would not have failed to do in my position.

Sir, complete the good work which you have begun so well, so as to make it worthy of you. Let there be no more question of a trifle which has already caused more commotion and given more grief to M. Palissot than the affair deserves. What will we have done for him if the pardon costs him as dearly as the penalty?

Permit me not to respond to the extreme praises with which you honor me; these are severe lessons from which I will draw a profit; for I am not unaware, and this letter is evidence of it, that one praises soberly the people whom one esteems perfectly. But, Sir, we must put off these clarifications to our meetings; I eagerly await the pleasure that you promise me, and one way or another you will see that you will not praise me any more once we have gotten to know each other.

I am with respect etc.

From the Comte de Tressan to Rousseau (p. 335) [8]

From Lunéville, January 11, 1756

You will be obeyed, Sir, it is very just for you to enjoy the ascendancy that you are acquiring over minds. Nevertheless I admit to you that perhaps I would still have hesitated to grant you everything for M. Palissot, were it not for a letter that I received from Paris at the same time as the one you did me the honor of writing to me. He begins by assuring me of a friendship proof against everything, and it is in consequence of this feeling that he warns me that he has just left a numerous and brilliant gathering where they have let fly against me on the subject of the affair of M. Palissot and that they even whispered to each other an epigram composed against me.

This letter made me decide on the spot, Sir, to follow your example. Today I too find myself in the position of having to pardon M. Palissot; I do so without any restriction, only too happy that he is procuring me this opportunity to prove to you that I love to profit from your lessons.

I have answered this person with all the plainest truth. I wrote to him what has happened, what I had done and what you have kept me from completing; thus let us not talk about it anymore and may M. Palissot be fortunate enough never to throw rocks except at wise men. If I am wise at this moment, he and I equally owe it to you. With all my heart I consent not to praise you anymore until I enjoy the happiness of seeing you and listening to you. Then my manner of applauding you will be useful to me and will correspond to your views; until that moment allow me to tell you again that my admiration for your works and for your heart equals the attachment that I vow to you for the rest of my life.

I have the honor of being, Sir,

Your very humble and very obedient servant
De Tressan

From Rousseau to the Comte de Tressan (p. 335) [9]

From Paris, January 23, 1756

Sir, I learn with a keen satisfaction that you have entirely concluded the affair of M. Palissot, and I thank you for it with all my heart. I will not say anything to you about the little displeasure it might have occasioned for you; for the ones of this sort are hardly discernible to the wise man, and moreover you know better than I do that in the griefs that can follow a good action the value always blots out the pain. After having finished this one happily, there is nothing left for you and me to desire other than not to hear it spoken about again.

I am with respect etc.

From Voltaire to Rousseau (p. 361) [10]

Les Délices, September 12, 1756

My dear philosopher, we are able you and I, in the intervals of our ills, to reason in verse and in prose. But at the present moment, you will pardon me for leaving there all these philosophical discussions which are only amusements. Your letter is very beautiful, but I have with me one of my nieces who for three weeks has been in rather great danger; I am her sick-nurse and very sick myself. I shall wait to get better before daring to think with you.[11] Monsieur Tronchin has told me that you will finally come into your fatherland. Monsieur d'Alembert will tell you what a philosophical life one leads in my little refuge. It would deserve the name it bears, if it could possess you sometimes. It is said that you hate to stay in cities; I have that in common with you; I would like to resemble you in so many things that this conformity could determine you to come to see us. My condition does not permit me to say more to you about it. Be assured that of all those who have read you, no one esteems you more than myself, despite my bad jokes, and that of all those who will see you, no one is disposed more to love you tenderly.

I begin by suppressing all ceremony.

From Doctor Théodore Tronchin to Rousseau (p. 361) [12]

September 1, 1756

My worthy friend, I have received your letter with the eagerness that precedes and follows everything that comes from you and with the pleasure that accompanies everything that is good. I would like to be able to answer you to the same effect about our friend, but what can one expect from a man who is almost always in contradiction with himself, and whose heart has always been the dupe of his mind. Since his earliest childhood his moral condition has been so unnatural and so impaired that his present being makes up an artificial whole that does not resemble anything. Of all the men who co-exist, the one with whom he is least acquainted is himself. All of his relations with other men and of other men with him are unbalanced. He has wanted more happiness than he could lay claim to, the excessiveness of his claim has led him insensibly to that sort of injustice which the laws do not condemn but of which reason disapproves. He has not carried off his neighbor's grain, he has not taken his ox or his cow, but he has committed other plundering in order to give himself a reputation and a superiority that the wise man disdains because its cost is always too high. Perhaps he has not been fastidious enough about the choice of means. The praise and cajolery of his admirers completed what his immoderate claims had begun and, while believing he was their master, he has become the slave of his admirers; his happiness depended on them. This deceptive foundation has left immense voids in his happiness; he has become accustomed to praises and to what does one not become accustomed? Habit has caused them to lose an imaginary value. Vanity has caused them to be esteemed, and then it counts for nothing what it has taken possession of, and for too much what has been refused to it, from which it finally happens that la Baumelle's insult [13] causes more pain, than the pit's acclamations have ever caused pleasure, and what is the consequence of this? Fear of death, for one quakes at it, does not prevent one from complaining about life, and not knowing with whom to quarrel, one complains about providence, when one ought to be dissatisfied only with oneself.

How unjust men are, my dear Rousseau, and how they are to be pitied. After all the changes that have happened to their natural state, happiness is no longer made for them. I shrug my shoulders while pitying them, at seeing them run breathlessly after a shadow that flees from them, and it is God who made them who is in the wrong. No, He is not in the wrong, for I am satisfied, and if I am others can be. I have children who will be, if I can take several more steps with them. They will not need at all the Arts that put the sick heart to sleep, but which do not cure it. Their perfections proves the excessiveness of the illness; no Lute would have been necessary for Saul if he had been healthier.[14]

To judge the future from the past, our friend will stiffen himself against your reason. When he finished his poem, I entreated with him to burn it. I left for Paris; our mutual friends joined together to obtain the same favor. All the ground that could be gained from him was to soften it; you will see the difference by comparing the second poem to the first. Our friend Gauffecourt was a witness of the scene, from what I was told afterwards. Nevertheless, I hope he will read your fine letter attentively. If it produces no effect whatsoever, it is because ills that begin at eighteen are hardly ever cured at sixty. He has been spoiled, many others will be spoiled. Let us pity him and preserve ourselves.

I have not lost our last conversation from sight for an instant. Do you still think the same way? I flatter myself that Cardinal de la Rochefoucault will grant me what his predecessor had promised me.[15] I embrace you tenderly, my worthy friend, your friendship forms one of the great charms of my life.

T. Tronchin

From Diderot to Rousseau (p. 383) [16]

[March 10, 1757]

You see very well, my dear fellow, that it is not possible to go to find you in this weather, whatever desire, even whatever need I might have to do so. Previously, everyone in my home was sick, first myself, who had been tormented by stomach-aches and diarrhea because of having taken some bad milk; afterwards my child with a chest cold, which made her mother frantic, and which was so dry and hoarse that it made me anxious. We are all better, but the weather does not permit anything. Do you know what you should do? You should come here and stay for two days incognito. I would come to pick you up on Saturday at St. Denis where we would dine, and from there we would come back to Paris in the cab that brought me. And do you know what we would use those two days for? For seeing each other, then for conversing about your work; we would discuss the places I have underlined and about which you would understand nothing if we were not face to face with each other. At the same time you would finish the business of the Baron's manuscript either with Pissot or with Briasson.[17] You would make arrangements for your own; and perhaps you would arrange a third business which I am saving to talk to you about when you come. See then if you want me to come to pick you up.

I am very glad that my work has pleased you, that it has touched you! You do not share my opinion about Hermits; say as much good about them as you please, you will be the only one in the world about whom I will think it. Still there would be a lot to say about this, if one could talk to you without getting you angry. An eighty-year-old woman! Etc. . . . Someone told me a phrase from a letter from Mme d'Epinay's son which must have distressed you very much or I know the bottom of your soul poorly. I salute you, I embrace you, I am waiting for your answer to go pick you up at St. Denis and even all the way to the park at Montmorency. See. Farewell. I also embrace Mme Levasseur and her daughter. I feel very sorry for you in this weather.

Thursday

I ask your forgiveness for what I said to you about the solitude in which you are living. I had not [18] spoken to you about it again at all. Forget what I said, and be certain that I will not speak to you about it anymore.

Farewell Citizen! Nevertheless a hermit makes a very peculiar citizen.

From Diderot to Rousseau (p. 385) [19]

[March 14, 1757]

It is true that for fifteen years I have had a wife, child, servant, no fortune, and my life has been so full of difficulties and pains that often I cannot even enjoy the several hours of happiness and relaxation that I promise myself. My friends make this into a subject of joking or of insult in accordance with their character. After that, what would I have to complain about?

I no longer want to go to Paris. I will not go any longer. For this time, I have resolved upon it.[20] It is not absolutely impossible that this is the tone of reason.

You do not know what the business I have to propose to you can be. Nevertheless you refuse it and thank me for it. My friend, I have never proposed to you anything that was not honest, and I have not changed what I am.

It has hardly been two weeks since the time when I should have talked to you about your work has expired. It was necessary for us to confer about it together. It is necessary. You do not want to come to Paris. Very well, Saturday, in the morning, whatever the weather might be, I will leave for the hermitage. I will leave on foot. My difficulties have not allowed me to go sooner. My fortune does not allow me to go in any other way, and it is very necessary for me to avenge myself for all the harm you have done me for four years.

Whatever harm my letter could have done you, I do not repent having written it to you. You are too satisfied with your answer.

You will not reproach heaven for having given you friends. Let heaven pardon you for their uselessness.

I am still frightened about the danger for Mme Levasseur, and I will not recover from it until I have seen her (I will whisper to you that the reading you made to her of your letter might be a very inhumane sophistry). But at present she owes you her life, and I keep silent.

The *Scholar* must have written to you that on the rampart there were twenty poor people who were dying of hunger and cold, and who were waiting for the liard that you used to give them. That is a sample of our little babble, and if you heard the rest, it would entertain you the same way.

It would be better to be dead than a rogue; but bad luck to whoever is alive and does not have any duties whose slave he is.

Scipio had as his friends everyone who was great in the republic, and I suspect very much that the road from Rome to Liternum and from Liternum to Rome was often encumbered with litters.[21] But the most opulent of your friends cannot pay the rental fee for a cab without inconveniencing themselves, and that is why one will not find on the road from the hermitage to la Chevrette anything but some philosophers on foot, reaching the country with a staff in their hand, soaked to the bones and covered with mud up to their backs.

Nevertheless in whatever spot in the world you might like to save yourself from them, their friendship and the interest they take in Mme Levasseur would follow you. Live, my friend, live, and do not be afraid that she will die of hunger.

Whatever success my work might have had; and although you tell me so, I have hardly garnered anything but trouble from it, and do not expect anything but grief.

Farewell. Until Saturday.

This Monday in the evening.

From Mme d'Epinay to Rousseau (p. 396) [22]

[Around September 26, 1757]

If you were in your natural state I would leave you to reflect all by yourself. But my friend I see only too well how much the bitterness of your situation has torn apart and saddened your soul. I repeat it to you I am inside your heart and I read in it better than you do yourself, but that is not enough, I want always to be at your side to keep the balance between your natural disposition and the mood that your condition gives you. Thus I beg you to reflect with this paper in your hand. The step that I am asking you to take is dictated by your heart, why don't you want to listen to it. You have been softened for an instant; that is enough for me to judge you. Does a man like you harden himself in his wrongs by means of his sophisms? You cannot be the dupe of the accusations that you make against our friend for a moment. If you were in the right to suspect him of them, you would necessarily have the right to despise him, and would not be the master of not doing so. Oh, certainly nothing could have softened you toward him, and you would be enjoying that indifference that you believe you desire with regard to him, and which I answer to you that you would be very sorry to have. But let us examine your situation with regard to him and his with regard to you a little. You have known him to be, you say, the most amiable man in the world because of his qualities of heart, but always with a cold exterior:—that is in him, thus one must not demand demonstrativeness from a man who cannot have any. You have loved him that way for three years, and you agree that he is the man in the world whom you have loved most tenderly. At the end of three years since your situation has filled your soul with bitterness, you have seen some wrongs in him. Wrongs! but I do not know what one wants to say to me when one cries out, "he has committed many wrongs toward me! There he has lacked confidence,—here he has preferred a certain thing to an attention he owed me . . . he should have made such a sacrifice for me,—and then comes a sulking which would still be nothing if it had been followed by an explanation." Let us leave, let us leave this commerce of misery to all those hearts void of feelings and to those heads without ideas. It goes only with those little vulgar lovers who have only agitated senses, and who put in the place of that confidence and those delightful effusions—which in decent and strong souls such as yours increase feelings by means of virtue and even philosophy— little quarrels that shrink the mind, sour the heart, and make morals empty when they do not make them vicious. Would you like your ill-humor to overbear your feelings and your reason and make you run the same course as those weak and limited devout people who put so many little superstitious practices in the place of the genuine love of God? All the true facts you had to articulate against him nevertheless bear only on miseries of that sort which your gloom has taken care to accumulate very carefully. As for the great grievance I do not speak about it at all, it does not exist, it cannot exist, that was demonstrated at the beginning of the other page, and was so in your heart and in mine much earlier; but as chimerical as this grievance is, it has been articulated by you, and to many people other than him, or to state it better to all your friends except him for four months. Thus he is the offended party and he is all the more so since for two years you have done nothing to make up for that offence, on the contrary. The feelings of your heart aside, see my friend whether you have any choice in what you have to do? Oh how much should this act of justice not only not cost you, but be sweet to you because it must reunite you to a friend you love who loves you and who is waiting for only the slightest mark of what he has a right to demand in order to draw tighter a friendship that is dear to you and precious to both of you. Above all consider that in the impossibility of isolating itself and holding onto nothing that exists for a soul as tender as yours, the only consolation left for it in your horrible situation is to multiply its supports, or at least to enjoy all those it has chosen for itself. Thus I will not be saying too much when I say to you that honor, your heart, and consequently your amour-propre oblige you to what I am inducing you to do. I cite amour-propre because it necessarily has a very big role to play in all this. It can bring you to do it only if it is well understood, it would keep you from it if it was poorly understood; but begin by seeing things coolly and I am not at a loss about the decision you will allow yourself to make.

At present, let us see what concerns him. His soul is truthful and upright, naturally a little reserved, and has been made even more so by the different misfortunes it has experienced. He is extremely sensitive, although calm; he was born melancholy, which gives him an unconcerned exterior, about which however only those who do not know him can be mistaken. You know that he is incapable of feigning a feeling or even an opinion, you see him carefully flee all the people he does not like, or maintain silence if he is forced to stay where he is displeased to be. On the contrary, he is at his ease with the people he likes, he brings frankness, freedom, and everything that proves he is content. These are the only external demonstrations that must be expected from him in the course of life. Next let some occasions be presented in which someone needs him, if they are only people who are of no consequence to him, his benevolence and his natural civility will be very capable of making him desire to oblige them, but often his laxness will prevent him from succeeding. If, on the contrary, it is a question of those he likes, his laziness changes into an activity that makes him foresee everything, do everything, and which leaves nothing to be desired. Since it is less his portrait that I claim to be making, than to be establishing your position to both of you; this sketch is enough to show you his behavior toward you clearly, and far from friendship finding itself offended by the behavior he has maintained with you, you see how he has the right to complain about the offence that you have committed against him. His feelings for you have not left his heart at all. I have heard him say twenty times that if he could have believed for an instant that he would be so strongly attached to you, he would have avoided making your acquaintance, so much does your situation affect him. Those are not the feelings of an indifferent man. Even 20 times since you have not been seeing each other any longer, he has conversed with me of his own accord about the means that could be found to make your position bearable for you, by means of the compensations that friendship can offer, either by seeking to procure an establishment for you that would keep up the mean between your present retreat where your friends cannot reach you in the Winter; and Paris which you flee or by other efforts which I would not enumerate so quickly, and which prove a heart occupied with you.

With this I am acquitting myself of what my friendship owes to both of you. Since it is my heart that is dictating all this to me, I have not watched out for the terms I used. In any case you are well enough acquainted with my soul and my manner of thinking to be sure that I want neither to offend you nor to spare you. I believe I ought to tell you again my dear friend, that I believe so strongly that your duty and your well being are engaged in all this, that it is for your sake much more than for him and for me that I am speaking to you. You are in the wrong; and if it is in the most perfect humanity to be so; it is unworthy of a man like you not to know how to atone for it. That is to fall from your character; and I who love you for yourself and with all my soul, I would be acting against my heart, and against my principles, if I did not induce you to it with all my power. My friend, it is enough to tell you that I would believe myself obliged to demand it of you, if I did not prefer to leave you the merit for it; a merit that you will not fail to have if you want to be cool for a moment, and keep away those unfortunate sophisms which in fact would be extremely convenient if they could always take the place of the truth. But their reign never lasts very long.

Yes, I will follow into your reverie all the way to the smallest of your thoughts. You will hear me cry out to you in accord with your conscience, "*I enjoin it!*" It is right, and then you will say, "But what does it want from me! That I reconcile with a friend whom I have offended, and who in spite of that is waiting with open arms for me to return to him!" That idea alone will soften you; and you will say in spite of yourself, "She is right my heart tells me so." Moreover will you also envisage without interest the sweet, the inextinguishable satisfaction of having fulfilled a duty, and the recompense for which is in the happy and tranquil days that we will all pass here? Think about the happiness that must necessarily follow this step. For a moment I am assuming that at first you might not find again that same tenderness that you had for each other. Do you count it for nothing to have destroyed that constraint that puts all three of us ill at ease: but that is not the only advantage you will have from it, I answer to you for that.

My dear friend, this is what the rapidity of conversation and the emotion I often experience when I talk about the things that keep close to my heart have kept me from telling you coherently. Moreover I carry out my plan better by writing to you because I want always to be like a lucky shadow around you which drags you to happiness in spite of yourself.

From Saint-Lambert to Rousseau (p. 401) [23]

Wolfenbuttel, October 11, 1757

My dear friend, I received your letter of September 15 only on the tenth of this month and I have the misfortune of having been in the wrong with regard to you for longer than I would have been if I had received your letter sooner. Do not accuse our friend either of flightiness or of cooling off, she is capable of neither of them. What she has loved she loves forever and more and more, and she would not begin to know inconstancy for a friend such as you. I alone am the one who must be blamed for her behavior, her heart has not changed at all toward you, she loves you, she honors you, but she has seen you less because she wanted to spare me the pains that you should not have done to me but that you did nonetheless and through my own fault. I am the one who sought to tie you to each other and I certainly do not reproach myself for that. In my heart there is a constant desire to unite and bring together what I love and esteem the most and I have always made for myself a charming image of the manner I would pass my life at Aubonne between her and you if we could induce you to live in her home. This is where all the harm comes from, here are my blunders. On my last trip I believed I saw some change in her. I love her too much to lose anything in her heart without noticing it right away and without feeling it cruelly. I admit to you that I believed you were the cause of what I imagined I had lost. Do not think, my dear friend, that I believed that you were either faithless or a traitor, but I knew the austerity of your principles, people had spoken to me about them, she herself spoke to me about them with a respect that did not conform with love. Nothing more was needed to alarm me about an intimacy which I had so strongly desired and you feel very well that once my head became anxious all the false scruples and all the blunders possible must have passed through it. I have made three people unhappy, I am the only one for whom pains remain because I am the only one who can have remorse. I have already had time to seek to redress my injustice towards her, I want to redress my injustice toward you. Neither of us has ceased to esteem or love you. Excuse us and love us, we deserve your heart and you will be content with ours. Nevertheless I reserve the word that you give me never to speak to her against our bonds. Believe that it is not these bonds alone that attach me to her, and even if there were nothing between her and me of what you condemn, she would still be what I would love the most. I had imagined hearts like hers, but I have never found any of her sort except her and it is enough to be well acquainted with her character to love her for all one's life. The deplorable state my health is in forces me to go to the waters at Aix-la-Chapelle. I am paralyzed in one arm and one leg and my weak nerves have succumbed to the fatigues of this campaign. Give me news about you at Aix-la-Chapelle. Speak to me about your health and your occupations. Tell me that you forgive me and that you love me. I do not know what there is between Grimm and you, but I owe it to you to tell you that he has spoken to me about you, as a man whom he respected, whom he loved, but whose injustice caused his unhappiness. Regard me and treat me as your friend and be assured that this friendship will make up one of the greatest charms of my life.

From Mme d'Epinay to Rousseau (p. 406) [24]

From Geneva, November 12 [1757]

I received your letter of the 29th only upon my arrival here, that is to say on the 9th. I found it hard to believe that it was from you and that it was for me. It is not from a man who swore to me on the eve of my departure that he would not have enough time in his life to redress the insults he had given me. This manner of redressing is entirely new. I have no answer to make to it at all. You make me pity you. If you are cool your behavior makes me fear for you, for I do not find it above-board. It is not natural to pass one's life suspecting and insulting one's friends. There are incomprehensible things in doing so. What I can say to you again is that you are abusing the patience that my friendship for you has given to me up to now.

From Deleyre to Rousseau (p. 412) [25]

Paris, February 28, 1758

I left dismayed over your situation, dear citizen of a world where you are treated very badly, alas! David composed the psalms of penitence in a state of malady like you, and I can propose him as an example to you, since you are reading the Bible. Behold you alone struggling with fortune and infirmities. To resemble Job you are lacking only a wife; yet you do not lack her. When one speaks about you to your friends, they always say that you have left them. If you wanted to test them I fear the result of that test for you and for them. But I am calling only afflicting ideas to your mind. The spring is reborn and brings back joy and health. Look at all of nature reviving around you. Would you be the only one to languish? No, citizen, you will taste happy moments again. The nightingale will resume its most tender tunes, in order to sweeten your insomnia. You will go into those deep groves, to dream about Julie again. If she were alive, perhaps she would be fickle and faithless like the others. But her image cannot flee you or betray you. She will embellish your days, your thoughts, and will take the place of all friends for you.

I saw the philosopher [26] tonight, always absorbed by work or distracted by pests. Nevertheless he thinks about you, and even tenderly. But I do not know what has taken place between you two. Forgive each other mutually for what is too firm or too weak in your character. Foreigners, a man and woman, are still visiting him. Moreover that cursed chemistry always keeps him chained up, and the *Father of the Family*, and the encyclopedia, and the worries that all that gives; there are certainly several motives for indulgence. Ah! who does not need it? We are full of nothing but wrongs. But it is so sweet to forgive each other among friends, that it would almost be sad never to have any wrongs.

Since you are the one who makes up the moments of your life for yourself, take care to put all the little pleasures into them that your painful existence allows. Reserve a part of your extreme sensitivity for pleasant objects. Do not exhaust your soul and your life in suffering, in regrets. Read Seneca, imitate Petronius. You are walking on flowers, do not crush all of them. Border your black hair with violets while you wait for the roses. compose now an article and then a tune of music. If I had your resources I would know how to while away the time. Whatever the void of reputation might be, amuse yourself nevertheless with the pleasure that people have in paying attention to you. Send serious pronouncements on morality back to the city in order to disturb those wicked people who shudder at recognizing themselves and at finding themselves to be so small. The wolves are in Paris, my dear friend, they are howling in the pulpits, in the schools, and the innocent doe and the peaceful buck are wandering in your forests. In the illnesses you suffer, count those you do not see as a good.

Farewell, dear citizen, here is a letter from M. Rey that I have had since Saturday. But I wanted to talk to you about M. Diderot when I sent it to you. He is anxious, as I am, about the resources you have left for living. He is afraid that you might be running short at present. You would be the cruelest man of all to hide your needs.

Farewell, good day, I will go to see Mme Levasseur tomorrow.

From Mme d'Houdetot to Rousseau (p. 416) [27]

Eaubonne, May 6 [1758]

You have not heard me spoken of for a long time, it is just to tell you the reasons for it, and those for the way I must behave toward you in the future. I have grounds for complaint in your indiscretion and that of your friends. For you, I would have kept the secret of your unfortunate passion for me for my whole life, and I hid it from the one I love in order not to give him an aversion for you. You have spoken about it to people who have made it public; and who have caused likelihoods to be seen against me which can harm my reputation. Some time ago these rumors reached my lover who has been distressed that I made a mystery to him of a passion that I never indulged and that I kept quiet about to him in the hope that you would become reasonable and that you could become our friend. I have seen a change in him that I thought would cost me my life. The justice that he is finally doing me about the honesty of my soul and his return to me have brought back my repose, but I do not want to risk troubling it any more and I owe it to myself not to expose myself to that. I also owe it to my reputation to break off all dealings with you, I cannot preserve any that would not be dangerous for it. You know that almost everyone who makes up my social circle displeases you and that you have never sought to see me with my friends. Since it has been established in the world that you are in love with me, it would not be decent for me to see you in private. I did so at a time when I believed that your passion would remain hidden and when you were asking my friendship to help you to cure yourself. You can be calm about the manner in which we think of you, my love and I. In the first moments that he learned about your passion and what you had caused to be done, for an instant he stopped seeing in you the virtue he was looking for and which he believed was there. Since then he feels sorry for you about your weakness more than he reproaches you for it, and we are both extremely far from joining you with the people who wish to slander us. We dare and we will always dare to talk about you with esteem; moreover, you feel that you owe it to me not to have either confidence or explanation on this point and that you must allow both your passion and the pains it has caused me to be perfectly forgotten. All you must do is to remain calm, certain that my repose has been reestablished, that my innocence which you might wish to defend is acknowledged, and that we do not think at all badly of you, and that we will not let anything bad be said. I will send to know news about you with interest and be persuaded that I will never cease to be concerned about you in spite of the decision that my reputation, concern for my happiness and my repose obliges me to make. If you want to continue the copies of Julie for me I will be obliged to you for them, if not I will send back to you what I already have but for which it is just to pay you. Farewell.

From Saint-Lambert to Rousseau (p. 419) [28]

Eaubonne, October 9, [1758]

We have been here for two days, sir, and both of us have the most tender friendship for you, I will come to assure you of it if you want to tell me at what time you are usually found in. Mme d'Houdetot is very impatient to see what new things you have done on Julie and I have the same eagerness for that work that I will always have for everything that comes from you. If the weather were not so bad you would have seen me today. I have been told that you are well. You know how much your health concerns me. give us some news about you by means of this messenger. I embrace you with all my heart.

St. L.

From Margency to Rousseau (p. 429) [29]

[From Paris, November 15, 1759]

My good neighbor or rather my very amiable friend; for I have very quickly accepted that glimmer of friendship that you have offered me. I am writing to you for a matter which appeared to me to suit you and which would suit the public much more. It suits you because it puts you in the position to be useful; it suits the public because it will be only too happy for you to instruct it. This is what it is about. There is a vacant place on the Journal of Scholars. These are the functions that it imposes. That is every month to give two summaries of books which would be brought to your home very punctually. These books would never turn on anything but history, philosophy and literature. It would not cost you eight days of work a month to read, to summarize, and to compose. I must tell you everything. There is an honorarium of eight hundred livres attached to this place. If that suits you, I believe I have enough influence with M. de Malesherbes from my friends to get it for you on the spot.

I can even assure you that it will not cost you any step, any displacement, any visit; at most a letter of thanks if you accept. You will not be at all in the position of seeing the people who make up that Society because you will not be in the position of coming to Paris except as much as it suits you. Moreover if you did want to see them, you would find only people who all have the greatest consideration and the most perfect esteem for you. These decent people are Messieurs de Mairan, Clairaut, Deguignes, and the Abbé Barthélemy. Do me the friendly action of writing to me what you think about my proposal as soon as you receive my letter. There are a thousand people who are asking for this place and I believe that this place is asking for you. Once again, if you do accept you will not get mixed up in anything, and I will do everything. Doubtless you will not tell me as an excuse that, since the Journal of Scholars is invested with public approbation, that approbation would bother you. I would answer you that, in addition to the genius that characterizes your works, all sensible people have found in them all the decency that can be desired for what concerns the state, religion, and morals. I am obliged to set out for the court. Without that obstacle I would go to Montmorency today to tell you all this. I will wait for your answer at Versailles. I will be staying there until Saturday the 24th, but I beg you, write to me as soon as you can. My address is to M. de M . . . gentleman ordinary to the King.

At the Court

Good day my good friend. I embrace you with all my heart. my friend Desmahis[30] begs me to say a thousand things for him. I very much want to because he is a very sensitive and very honest friend. I forgot to tell you that, if you do not accept, the most profound secrecy will be kept about it. You will not be spoken to about it anymore and I will not love you any less. Nevertheless I cannot hide from you that I would desire you to accept with all my heart.

De Margency

From Margency to Rousseau (p. 429) [31]

From Paris, January 9, 1760

My dear neighbor, I want very much to write to you; but on condition that you not answer me. You have very much else to do and I do not want to disturb you at all. You judge very well that I do not want to interrupt you by speaking to you about the new year either. There would be so many things in the wishes I could make for you that I would never finish enumerating them all to you. Thus it is solely to chat with you because I cannot see you. I was sorry about your refusal; but I was not at all surprised by it. I did not even need to reflect very much in order to feel that you were right. Thus I did not find any obstinacy in the decision you have made; but solely that constancy which every sensible and steady man puts into and keeps in his behavior. Besides do not be obliged to me at all for what I have done. I would have been paid enough by the pleasure of being useful to you. But nothing came from me. I was given the commission of offering you that place by those upon whom it depended. That is all. You see very well that you do not owe me any sort of gratitude. M. Desmahis commissions me with thanking you for your feelings for him. He deserves them because of the esteem and attachment he has for you. His health is still extremely impaired. His blood goes too rapidly; it is a dragon that gnaws on him. We are waiting until he gets better and the days are longer to come to see you. Truly we prefer the hermit very much to the courtier and we like the simplicity of your food and the freshness of your dairy products very much better than all the luxury of our modern Luculluses.[32] That is where we are. From time to time I turn my eyes toward that charming valley. Ah my neighbor how much that life that you are leading, how very much that pleasant and sweet life would have been mine; if I had been the master of arranging one for myself. They were right to call me Shepherd, *Ipsi me fontes ipsa haec arbusta vocabant*.[33] By the way, our friend[34] told me that you had written to her that you do not love her any more. Without examining the affair, I have decided that she was wrong and that you were right. I forgot to tell you that, based on the advice of that lovable friend, I went to see our former Infanta two months ago.[35] I found her decked out like the fiancee of the King of Garbe.[36] She received me as if she had seen me the day before and I treated her as if I was to come back the next day. It is true that I have not set foot there again and that I have never heard her spoken about since. I received a visit from her son and his tutor at the beginning of the year. But not a word from her and de Caron.[37] Mme de V. claimed that I would not escape the wand; but the charm ended a long time ago and I no longer fear *tristis Amaryllidis iras*.[38] I am free Lord and I want to be so always. I conclude out of fear of boring you. Truly if I wished to speak to you about my attachment for you, you would not be rid of me so cheaply.

De M.

Here is M. Thierry[39] who gives me the commission of telling you a thousand things, he is in front of my fire, and I am well.

From the Marquise de Verdelin to Rousseau (p. 444) [40]

[From Soizy, November 8, 1760]

Sir, if I was at my own disposal and I was mistress of my moments, I would arrive tomorrow at your breakfast with the desire and the hope of making you acknowledge that my manner of thinking in regard to you deserves a different judgment than the one you passed. I was wrong, sir, to send a cake to M. Coindet, but acknowledge at least that this is one of those wrongs that one does not commit with one's acquaintances. In my view one can give them presents. Amour-propre profits from it, but that a piece of steeped squash with a glass of milk from my cow might be found to be good or bad by them, that they might say something good about my dear Saintonge cake, love it or hate it, I feel that I would not care about it in the least, and I do care about whether M. Rousseau's friend acquires a poor opinion of my cake. I can do nothing to change that way of thinking, but I promise you very much, my neighbor, that I certainly will keep myself on guard against it, for I am very far from finding pleasure in displeasing you. My neighbor, you judge me poorly if you believe that I claim to be anything better than a good woman.[41] I set a lot of store by that quality, I limit my entire ambition to deserving it and to finding someone truthful enough to tell me the things that keep me from being one.

Sir, I believe I wrote you that I wanted to lose the title of acquaintance with you; you did me the honor of telling me that you waited years to test your friends. I have had the honor of being acquainted with you for so few of them, and I am so little in the habit of obtaining the things that I desire, that I have not dared to give myself any name but that of your acquaintance. It is not that I do not date my attachment from long ago, you inspired me with it, Sir, before I saw you, and whatever you might say, you do not lose anything in company. It is not the charm of your mind, which I am not worthy of appreciating, that made me desire it, it was the qualities of your soul, and they have attached me to you in an unchanging way. Good night, Sir, your letter has afflicted me extremely. I beg you to find it good that I am going to take leave of you. I strongly exhort you not to leave your fire.

From the Abbé Morellet to Rousseau (p. 451) [42]

From St. Just Near Chambly [August 4, 1760],

Sir, upon recovering freedom, I learn that you have taken much interest in my little misfortunes and that in great part I owe to you that interest that Mme de Luxembourg has been willing to take in them. I thank you with all my heart for that mark of your esteem, I would like to be able to say of your friendship but I do not profane such a beautiful name by applying it to the hardly continuous connection I have had with you. Nevertheless I feel that I would have acquired and deserved that friendship, if your remoteness from the country where I live did not forbid me a company which appeared very sweet to me and which I would renew with the greatest pleasure in the world if the obstacles that interrupted it could cease. I would not dare to blame your retirement but when I ponder what has been lost by a small number of philosophers who might have been worthy of living with you I am genuinely afflicted by it.

I, too, have retired from the world for the rest of the Autumn and I am writing to you from the country. I am addressing my letter to M. d'Alembert, who will make it reach you. Since my hermitage is only 4 or 5 leagues from yours, please expect to see me come to pass several hours with you before the end of the month. I ask your permission to do this.

I had the honor of seeing Madame de Luxembourg before my departure, she received me with the greatest kindness. I ask you to take it upon yourself to express my gratitude to her. You would please me very much if you would write her a word assuming that you might not see her for some time.[43] What is more, after the conversation I had with Madame the Maréchale I understand extremely well that she can be excepted from the renouncement that you have made of the world and its pomp. I embrace you with all my heart, without prejudice to the respect and the esteem that you have so many different claims to deserve. I cannot resolve to use any other formulas with you.

Abbé Morellet

From the Abbé Trublet to Rousseau (p. 451) [44]

Paris, June 13, 1760, Rue Guenegaud

Sir, perhaps you are unaware of at least a part of what I am going to tell you, and it might be useful for you to know it. Thus here it is. By informing you of it, I believe I am giving you a new proof of the feelings that I have had for you for a long time, since I have been acquainted with you, and the date we made each other's acquaintance is very old. Perhaps you do not even recall it. It was M. the Abbé de Mably who procured for me the pleasure of seeing you for the first time, when we were both at M. the Cardinal de Tencin's. It concerned your first opera,[45] a part of which you read to me etc. But let us come to the subject of this letter.

You wrote one to M. de Voltaire in August 1756 on his two poems, *Natural Law* and the *Disaster at Lisbon*. This letter has been printed in M. Formey's journal, entitled; *Letters on the Present State of the Sciences and Morals*, at Berlin, 1759; and contains about 30 pages in octavo; it is M. Formey himself who sent me this Journal, because he sends me almost all his works. I received the two sheets which contain your *Letter to M. de V.* only a short time ago, and in the one that M. Formey had added to his package he does not enter into any detail, and does not give me any clarification about your writing. But #1 In introducing it in his *Journal*, he says, after having dated from October 23, 1759, *That he found it, several weeks ago, in the book stores of Berlin, and that, since it is one of those loose sheets that soon disappear never to return, he believed that he ought to give it a place in his journal.*

#2 He has added several notes in which he takes turns praising and criticizing you. M. Formey is very religious, or if you wish, a religionist, and does not find you to be enough of one. Thus he raises a protest against what you say about suicide, which you appear to permit, and about the eternity of punishment, which you expressly deny.

From the fact that M. Formey found your *Letter to M. de V.* in the book shops of Berlin, I conclude that it was printed in Holland, and that it is from there that the book dealers of Berlin have taken it. But when was it printed there? That is what M. Formey does not say at all.

I had never heard this writing spoken about, and it is the same for all the people to whom I have spoken about it here, among whom several are friends of yours, among others Messieurs Duclos and d'Alembert. I have a good literary correspondence in Holland. It is with M. de Loches, the Pastor of the Walloon Church at Rotterdam, and formerly chaplain of the Ambassador of Holland to our Court. I believe that he has seen you sometimes, during the stay he made in Paris. At least he is one of your most zealous admirers, and you have often been the subject of our philosophic conversations. Now M. de Loches has never written to me nor spoken about your *Letter to M. de V.* Nevertheless it is very suited to cause a commotion; it is by you, to the most famous author, and very worthy of both of you. Thus I am lost in the enigma of this incognito, and I dare to ask you for the key to it. While waiting, I did not want to lend my copy to anyone; I made an exception for Father Berthier[46] who sent it back to me the next day. He is a man of perfect probity, and if you have read the articles in the *Journal of Trévoux* in which he has reviewed your works, you know how much he esteems you. I will also admit to you that I read the letter said to be yours to two or three of our philosophers, and you can believe very much that they strongly begged me to lend it to them. I refused them, and it will not leave my hands at all, unless you give me permission. One of them tells me that, "that would be good to reprint under the circumstances;" yes and no; but it would be curious, and from then on very much sought after. What do you think about it?

I will not talk to you at all about everything that is happening on the subject of M. Pompignon's Discourse to the Academy,[47] about his *Memorandum* presented to the King,[48] about the comedy *The Philosophers* and about the writings for and against. You have friends who do not let you remain unaware about anything in all that, or if they do not write it to you, it is because they know that you do not care about knowing it, or even that you do not want to. That is well done; you would learn horrors, and you would bewail them. I will tell you only, because the news is recent enough that no one might yet have had the time to write it to you, that some peddlers and your colleague on the *Encyclopedia*, M. the Abbé Morellet have been arrested. This is on the subject of the writing entitled: *The Vision of Charles Palissot*.

I am with the most perfect esteem and consideration, Sir, your very humble and very obedient servant

Trublet

From the Duc de Luxembourg to Rousseau (p. 460) [49]

From Paris, May 1, 1760

Sir, you have given me the commission of a negotiation which is not difficult, because it is a only question of getting Mme de Luxembourg to approve of something you desire, thus there is no more question of the trip to Villeroy, nonetheless we are sorry to be deprived of the pleasure of being with you during that time, but we have no other will than yours, and you give us the hope of coming to make an outing here when we return from the trip to Villeroy where we will be going next week; when I have returned you will have news from me to remind you what you said about that in your last letter. My poor daughter's health is still getting worse, every day some new illness crops up without her being rid of the old ones. Her thinness is so great that she does not know what posture to keep in. I assure you that I also find the period from now to the month of July very long because of the desire I have to find myself with you again.

From the Duc de Luxembourg to Rousseau (p. 465) [50]

From Versailles, November 30, 1759

I am very obliged to you, Sir, for writing to me that you are satisfied enough about your health for the season we are in. I would like us to have a continuous springtime, it seems to me that it is the season when you are most well. I believe that my son is on the way and I imagine that he will be able to arrive around the middle of next week. My health is good enough, but it would be much better if I found myself brought to make the walks you spoke about to me and which I always recall with delight above all when we did not find any tracks of carriage wheels when we went back into the courtyard in the evening.

Four Letters to M. the Président de Malesherbes Containing the true picture of my character and the true motives for all my behavior (p. 477) [51]

I

To M.

From Montmorency, January 4, 1762

Sir, I would have delayed less in thanking you for the last letter with which you honored me if I had proportioned my diligence in responding to the pleasure it gave me. But in addition to the fact that it pains me very much to write, I thought that it was necessary to give several days to the importunities of these times in order not to overburden you with my own. Although I do not console myself at all for what just happened, I am very satisfied that you were informed about it considering that it has not deprived me at all of your esteem, it will belong to me all the more if you do not believe me to be better than I am.

The motives to which you attribute the decisions I have been seen to make since I have borne a sort of name in the world perhaps do me more honor than I deserve but they are certainly closer to the truth than the ones attributed to me by those men of letters who, giving everything to reputation, judge my feelings by their own. I have a heart that is too sensitive to other attachments to be so strongly attached to public opinion; I love my pleasure and my independence too much to be a slave to vanity to the point they assume. The person for whom fortune and the hope of succeeding never outweighed a meeting or a pleasant supper should not naturally sacrifice his happiness to the desire of making himself talked about, and it is not at all believable that a man who feels some talent in himself and who delays making it known until the age of 40 would be foolish enough to go to bore himself for the rest of his life in a wilderness, solely to acquire the reputation of a misanthrope.

But Sir, even though I hate injustice and wickedness sovereignly, this passion is not dominant enough to determine me to flee the society of men by itself, if I had some great sacrifice to make by leaving them. No, my motive is less noble and closer to myself. I was born with a natural love for solitude which has done nothing but increase in proportion as I have gotten to know men better. I find my advantage better with the chimerical beings that I assemble around me than with the ones I see in the world, and the social circle for which my imagination pays the expenses in my retirement completely disgusts me with all the ones I have left. You assume that I am unhappy and consumed with melancholy. Oh! Sir how wrong you are! It is in Paris that I was so; it is in Paris that a black bile gnawed at my heart, and the bitterness of that bile made itself felt only too much in all the writings I published as long as I stayed there. But Sir, compare those writings with the ones I have written in my solitude; either I am mistaken, or you will feel in these latter a certain serenity of soul which is not at all pretence and based on which one can bring a sure judgment about the author's internal state. The extreme agitation I just experienced has been able to make you pass a contrary judgment; but it is easy to see that this agitation did not have its principle in my present situation but in a disordered imagination, ready to take fright over everything and to carry everything to the extreme. Continuous successes have made me sensitive to glory, and there is no man who has some loftiness of soul and some virtue who could think without the most mortal despair that, after his death, under his name they would substitute for a useful work a pernicious one, capable of dishonoring his memory and of doing a lot of harm. It might be that such an upheaval accelerated the progress of my illnesses, but in the assumption that such an onset of madness had taken me in Paris, it is not at all certain that my own will would not have spared nature the rest of the work.

For a long time I deceived myself about the cause of this invincible disgust that I have always experienced in the company of men; I used to attribute it to sorrow at not having enough intelligence ready to hand to show what little I had in conversation, and, by after-effect, the sorrow of not occupying the place in the world that I believed I deserved. But when, after having scribbled on some paper, I was very certain of not being taken for a stupid person even when I said stupid things, when I saw myself sought after by everyone, and honored by much more consideration than my most ridiculous vanity would have dared to claim, and since in spite of this I felt this same disgust increased more than diminished, I concluded that it came from a different cause, and that these sorts of enjoyments were not at all the ones I needed.

Finally what is that cause then? It is nothing other than that indomitable spirit of freedom which nothing has been able to overcome, and before which honors, fortune, and even reputation are nothing to me. It is certain that this spirit of freedom comes to me less from pride than from laziness; but this laziness is unbelievable; everything makes it take fright; the slightest duties of civil life are unbearable to it. A word to say, a letter to write, a visit to make, as soon as it is necessary to do, are tortures for me. That is why, although the ordinary company of men is odious to me, intimate friendship is so dear to me, because there are no more duties for it. One follows one's heart and everything is done. That is also why I have always been unable to stand benefits. For every benefit demands gratitude; and I feel my heart to be ungrateful from the very fact alone that gratitude is a duty. In a word the sort of happiness I need is not so much to do what I want, as it is not to do what I do not want. The active life has nothing that tempts me, I would a hundred times rather consent to never doing anything than to doing something in spite of myself; and I have thought a hundred times that I would not have lived too unhappily at the Bastille, since I would not be restricted to anything at all except to staying there.

Nevertheless in my youth I made several efforts to succeed. But these efforts never had anything but retirement and rest in my old age as their goal, and since they were only by jolts like those of a lazy man, they never had the slightest success. When illnesses came they furnished me with a fine pretext for abandoning myself to my dominant passion. Finding that it was a folly to torment myself for an age I would not reach, I threw everything down there, and I hurried to enjoy. There, Sir, I swear to you, is the genuine cause of that retirement for which our literary people have been looking for motives of ostentation which assume a constancy, or rather an obstinacy in holding to what pains me, directly contrary to my natural character.

You will say to me Sir that this supposed indolence accords badly with the writings I have composed in the last ten years, and with that desire for glory that must have incited me to publish them. That is an objection to resolve which obliges me to prolong my letter and which consequently forces me to end it. I will come back to it Sir, if my familiar tone does not displease you, for in the effusion of my heart I do not know how to take another one, I will depict myself without disguise and without modesty, I will show myself to you as I see myself, and as I am, for since I pass my life with myself I ought to know myself and, from the manner in which those who think they know me interpret my actions and my behavior, I see that they do not know anything about it. No one in the world knows me except myself alone. You will judge about it when I have said everything.

Do not send me back my letters Sir, I entreat you. Burn them, because they are not worth the trouble of keeping but not out of consideration for me. Do not think either about taking back the ones that are in Duchesne's hands. If it was necessary to wipe the traces of all my follies out of the world there would be too many letters to take back, and I would not move the tip of my finger for that. Charged or defended, I do not fear at all being seen as I am. I know my great flaws, and I feel all my vices keenly. With all that I will die full of hope in the Supreme God, and very persuaded that of all the men I have known in my life, none was better than I.

2

To M. de Malesherbes

From Montmorency, January 12, 1762

Sir, I continue to give you an account of myself, since I have begun; for what can be most unfavorable to me is to be known halfway, and since my faults have not deprived me of your esteem at all, I do not presume that my frankness ought to deprive me of it.

A lazy soul that gets frightened at every effort, a temperament that is ardent, bilious, easily affected and excessively sensitive to everything that affects it do not seem capable of being joined together in the same character, and nevertheless these two opposites make up the basis of mine. Although I cannot resolve this opposition by means of principles, it exists nevertheless, I feel it, nothing is more certain, and at least I can give a sort of historical account of it by means of facts which can serve for conceiving it. I was more active in childhood, but never like another child. Very early on this boredom with everything threw me into reading. When I was six years old Plutarch fell into my hands, at eight I knew him by heart; before the age at which the heart takes an interest in novels, I had read them all, they had made me shed buckets of tears. From this was formed in my heart that heroic and romantic taste which has done nothing but increase up to the present, and which ended by disgusting me with everything, aside from what resembled my follies. In my youth, since I believed I found in the world the same people I had known in my books, I abandoned myself unreservedly to anyone who knew how to make an impression on me by means of a certain jargon of which I have always been the dupe. I was active because I was foolish; to the extent that I was undeceived I changed tastes, attachments, projects, and in all these changes I always wasted my effort and my time because I was always looking for what did not exist. In becoming more experienced, little by little I lost the hope of finding it, and consequently the zeal for looking for it. Soured by the injustices I had suffered, and by those I had been the witness of, often afflicted by disorder where example and the force of things had dragged me, I acquired a disdain for my century and my contemporaries and, feeling that in their midst I would not find a situation that could satisfy my heart, little by little I detached it from the society of men, and I made myself another one in my imagination which charmed me all the more since I could cultivate it without effort, without risk, and always find it reliable and as I needed it to be.

After having passed forty years of my life this way, dissatisfied with myself and with others, I fruitlessly sought to break the bonds that were keeping me attached to that society which I esteemed so little, and which chained me to occupations that were least to my taste through needs that I considered to be those of nature, and which were only those of opinion. Suddenly a fortunate chance happened to enlighten me about what I had to do for myself, and to think about my fellows about whom my heart was ceaselessly in contradiction with my mind, and whom I still felt myself brought to love along with so many reasons to hate them. Sir, I would like to be able to depict that singularly epoch-making moment in my life and one that will always be present to me if I live eternally.

I was going to see Diderot, at that time a prisoner in Vincennes; I had in my pocket a *Mercury of France* which I began to leaf through along the way. I fell across the question of the Academy of Dijon which gave rise to my first writing. If anything has ever resembled a sudden inspiration, it is the motion that was caused in me by that reading; suddenly I felt my mind dazzled by a thousand lights; crowds of lively ideas presented themselves at the same time with a strength and a confusion that threw me into an inexpressible perturbation; I feel my head seized by a dizziness similar to drunkenness. A violent palpitation oppresses me, makes me sick to my stomach; not being able to breathe anymore while walking, I let myself fall under one of the trees of the avenue, and I pass a half-hour there in such an agitation that when I got up again I noticed the whole front of my coat soaked with my tears without having felt that I shed them. Oh Sir, if I had ever been able to write a quarter of what I saw and felt under that tree, how clearly I would have made all the contradictions of the social system seen, with what strength I would have exposed all the abuses of our institutions, with what simplicity I would have demonstrated that man is naturally good and that it is from these institutions alone that men become wicked. Everything that I was able to retain of these crowds of great truths which illuminated me under that tree in a quarter of an hour has been weakly scattered about in my three principal writings, namely that first discourse, the one on inequality, and the treatise on education, which three works are inseparable and together form the same whole.[52] All the rest has been lost, and only the prosopopeia of Fabricius was written on the very spot.[53] That is how when I was thinking about it least, I became an author almost in spite of myself. It is easy to conceive how the attraction of a first success and the criticism of scribblers threw me completely into the career. Did I have some true talent for writing? I do not know. A lively persuasion has always taken the place of eloquence for me, and I have always written in a cowardly manner and badly when I was not strongly persuaded. Thus perhaps it is a hidden return of amour-propre that made me choose and deserve my motto,[54] and attached me so passionately to the truth, or to everything I have undertaken for it. If I had written only to write, I am convinced that I would never have been read.

After I had discovered or believed I discovered the source of their miseries and their wickedness in the false opinions of men, I felt that it was only these very opinions that had made me unhappy myself, and that my ills and my vices came to me very much more from my situation than from myself. Since at the same time a malady whose first attacks I had felt as early as childhood had been declared to be absolutely incurable in spite of all the promises of false healers whose dupe I had not been for a long time, I judged that if I wanted to be consistent and shake the heavy yoke of opinion from my shoulders once and for all, I did not have a moment to lose. I abruptly made my decision with enough courage, and I have kept it up well enough until now with a firmness whose value is felt by me alone, because I am the only one who knows what obstacles I had and I still have to combat every day in order to hold out ceaselessly against the current. Nevertheless I feel very well that I have gone a little off course for ten years, but if I only estimated that I still had four left to live, one would see me give a second jolt and reascend at the very least to my first level hardly to descend from it again at all. For all the great tests have been made and henceforth it has been demonstrated for me by experience that the state in which I have put myself is the only one in which man can live as good and happy, since it is the most independent one of all, and the only one in which one never finds oneself in the necessity of harming someone else for one's own advantage.

I admit that the name my writings has made for me has very much facilitated the execution of the decision I have made. One must be believed to be a good author in order to make oneself into a bad copyist with impunity, and not to lack work because of it. Without that first title, they would be able to take me too much at my word about the other, and perhaps that would have mortified me; for I face ridicule easily, but I would not bear scorn so well. But if some reputation gives me a little advantage in that regard, it is very much compensated by all the inconveniences attached to that same reputation, when one does not want to be its slave, and if one wants to live isolated and independent. In part it is these inconveniences that chased me away from Paris, and which—still pursuing me into my refuge—would very certainly chase me farther away if my health ever happened to be restored. Another of my scourges in that great city was those crowds of so-called friends who laid hold of me, and who, since they judged my heart by theirs, absolutely wanted to make me happy in their fashion and not in my own. Out of despair at my retirement they have pursued me there in order to draw me out of it. I have not been able to maintain myself in it without breaking off everything. I have been truly free only since that time.

Free! No, I am not free at all yet. My last writings have not yet been printed, and given the deplorable state of my poor machine I no longer hope to live until the printing of the collection of them all: but if, contrary to my expectation, I can go until then and take leave of the public once and for all, believe Sir that then I will be free or never will a man have been so. Oh *utinam!*[55] Oh thrice happy day! No, it will never be granted to me to see it.

I have not said everything, Sir, and perhaps you will have at least one more letter to bear. Fortunately nothing obliges you to read them, and perhaps you would be very much at a loss to do so. But for mercy's sake forgive me; in order to recopy these long hodge-podges it would be necessary to compose them over again, and in truth I do not have the courage to do it. I certainly have much pleasure in writing to you, but I do not have less in resting and my condition does not allow me to write for very long in succession.

3

To M. de Malesherbes

From Montmorency, January 26, 1762

Sir, after having exposed to you the true motives for my behavior, I would like to talk to you about my moral condition during my retirement; but I feel that it is very late; my soul, alienated from itself, belongs entirely to my body. The breakdown of my poor machine holds it more attached to it from day to day, and until it finally suddenly separates itself from it. I would like to talk to you about my happiness, and one talks about happiness poorly when one is suffering.

My ills are the work of nature but my happiness is my own. Whatever one might say about it, I have been wise, since I have been as happy as my nature has permitted me to be: I have not looked for my felicity far away, I have looked for it near me and I have found it there. Spartian says that Trajan's courtier, Similis, who had left the Court and all his employments without any personal dissatisfaction in order to go to live peacefully in the country, had these words put on his tomb: *I dwelt on the earth for seventy-six years and I lived for seven.*[56] That is what I can say in some respect, even though my sacrifice might have been smaller. I began to live only on April 9, 1756.[57]

I would not know how to tell you, Sir, how touched I was to see that you consider me the unhappiest of men. Doubtless the public will judge about this as you have, and that is still what distresses me. Oh if only the fate I have enjoyed were known by the whole universe! Everyone would want to make a similar one for himself; peace would reign on the earth; men would no longer think about hurting each other, and there would no longer be any wicked people when no one had an interest in being wicked. But, finally, what did I enjoy when I was alone? Myself, the whole universe, everything that is, everything that can be, everything that is beautiful in the perceptible world, and that is imaginable in the intellectual world: I assembled around me everything that could gratify my heart, my desires were the measure of my pleasures. No, the most voluptuous people have never known similar delights, and I have enjoyed my chimeras a hundred times more than they have enjoyed realties.

When my sufferings make me sadly measure off the length of the nights, and the agitation of fever keeps me from tasting a single moment of sleep, often I distract myself from my present condition by pondering the various events of my life, and the things I repent, the sweet remembrances, the regrets, and the emotion share the effort of making me forget my sufferings for several moments. What times, Sir, would you believe that I recall most often and most willingly in my dreams? They are not at all the pleasures of my youth, they were too rare, too mixed with bitterness, and are already too far away from me. They are those of my retirement, they are my solitary walks, they are those quickly passing but delightful days that I have passed entirely alone with myself, with my good and simple housekeeper, my well-loved dog, my old cat, the birds of the country, and the does of the forest, with all of nature and its inconceivable author. Upon getting up before the sun in order to go to see, to contemplate its rising in my garden, my first wish when I saw a fine day beginning was that neither letters nor visits might come to disturb its charm. After having given the morning to various concerns all of which I fulfilled with pleasure, because I could have put them off to another time, I hastened to dine in order to escape tiresome people, and to arrange a longer afternoon for myself. Even on the most scorching days, before one o'clock, at the height of the sun, I left with the faithful Achates[58] hurrying the pace in the fear that someone might come to seize hold of me before I could elude him; but once I had been able to turn a certain corner, with what beating of the heart, with what sparkling of joy did I begin to breathe when I felt that I was saved, saying to myself, "Here I am master of myself for the rest of this day!" Then I went at a calmer pace to look for some wild spot in the forest, some deserted spot where, since nothing showed the hand of men, it did not announce servitude and domination, some refuge where I could believe I was the first to penetrate and where no tiresome person might come to put himself between nature and me. It was there that nature seemed to spread out an ever new magnificence to my eyes. The gold of the broom and the purple of the heather struck my eyes with a luxury that touched my heart, the majesty of the trees that covered me with their shadow, the delicacy of the shrubs that surrounded me, the astonishing variety of the grasses and flowers that I trod underfoot kept my mind in a continuous alternation between observation and admiration: the conjunction of so many interesting objects which disputed for my attention, ceaselessly attracting me from one to the other, favored my dreamy and lazy mood, and often made me say within myself again, "No, Solomon in all his glory was not arrayed like one of these."[59]

My imagination did not leave the earth, adorned this way, deserted for very long. I soon peopled it with beings in accordance with my heart, and driving opinion, prejudices, all factitious passions very far away, into these refuges of nature I transported men worthy of inhabiting them. From them I formed a charming society for myself of which I did not feel myself to be unworthy. I made myself a golden age at my whim and filling these fine days with all the scenes of my life which had left me sweet remembrances, and with all those my heart could still desire, I became tender to the point of tears over the true pleasures of humanity, pleasures so delightful, so pure, and which now are so far from men. Oh if in these moments some idea of Paris, of my century and of my little author's vainglory came to disturb my reveries, with what disdain did I instantly drive it away in order to abandon myself without distraction to the exquisite feelings with which my soul was full! Nevertheless, in the midst of all that, I admit, the nothingness of my chimeras sometimes suddenly came to sadden it. If all my dreams had been turned into realities they would not have been enough for me; I would have imagined, dreamed, desired again. I found an inexplicable void in myself that nothing could fill; a certain yearning of the heart toward another sort of enjoyment the idea of which I did not have and the need for which I felt nonetheless. Very well, Sir, even that was enjoyment, since from it I was penetrated by a very lively feeling and an attractive sadness that I would not have wanted not to have.

Soon I raised my ideas from the surface of the earth to all the beings of nature, to the universal system of things, to the incomprehensible being who embraces everything. Then with my mind lost in that immensity, I did not think, I did not reason, I did not philosophize; with a sort of sensual pleasure I felt myself weighed down with the weight of that universe, with rapture I abandoned myself to the confusion of these great ideas, I loved to lose myself in imagination in space; confined within the limits of beings my heart found itself too constrained, I was smothered in the universe, I would have wanted to throw myself into the infinite. I believe that if I had unveiled all the mysteries of nature, I would have felt myself to be in a less delightful situation than that stupefying ecstasy to which my mind abandoned itself without reserve, and which sometimes made me cry out in the agitation of my raptures, "Oh great being! Oh great being," without being able to say or think anything more.

Thus flowed away in a continuous delirium the most charming days that a human creature has ever passed, and when the setting of the sun made me think about retiring, astonished at the rapid passing of the time, I believed I had not put my day to enough profit, I thought I could still enjoy it further and to make up for the lost time, I said to myself, "I will come back tomorrow."

I returned with short steps, my head a little fatigued, but my heart content, I rested pleasantly on my return, abandoning myself to the impression of the objects but without thinking, without imagining, without doing anything else but feeling the calm and the happiness of my situation. I found my place set on my terrace. I supped with great appetite in my little household, no image of servitude and dependence disturbed the benevolence that united us all. My dog himself was my friend, not my slave, we always had the same will but he never obeyed me. My gaiety during the whole evening testified that I had lived alone all day long; I was very different when I had seen company, I was rarely satisfied with others and never with myself. In the evening I was a grumbler and taciturn: this remark is from my housekeeper, and since she told it to me, I have always found it to be just when I observed myself. Finally, after having made several more turns in my garden or sung several tunes on my spinet, in my bed I found a rest of body and soul a hundred times sweeter than sleep itself.

Those are the days which have formed the true happiness of my life, happiness without bitterness, without boredom, without regrets, and to which I would have willingly limited all the happiness of my existence. Yes, Sir, may similar days fill eternity for me, I ask for nothing else, and do not imagine that I am much less happy in these rapturous contemplations than the celestial intelligences are. But a body that is suffering deprives the mind of its freedom; henceforth I am no longer alone, I have a guest who pesters me, I must free myself of him in order to belong to myself, and the trial I have made of these sweet enjoyments no longer serves for anything but making me wait with less fright for the moment of tasting them without distraction.

But here I am already at the end of my second sheet. Nevertheless I would need one more. Thus one more letter and then no more. Excuse me, Sir. Although I like to talk about myself too much, I do not like to talk about myself with everyone, that is what makes me abuse the opportunity when I have it and when it pleases me. There is my wrong and my excuse. I beg you to be willing to put up with it.

4

To M.

From Montmorency, January 28, 1762

Sir, in the secret of my heart I have shown you the true motives for my retirement and of all my behavior; motives that are doubtless much less noble than you assumed them to be, but nevertheless the sort that make me content with myself, and inspire me with the pride of soul of a man who feels himself well-ordered, and who, having had the courage to do what was necessary to be so, believes he can ascribe the merit for it to himself. It was up to me, not to make a different temperament for myself, or a different character, but to turn mine to account, in order to make me good for myself and in no way wicked to others. That is a lot, Sir, and few men can say as much. Also I will not disguise from you that, in spite of the feeling of my vices, I have a high esteem for myself.

Your literary people have shouted as much as they could that a man by himself is useless to everyone and has not fulfilled his duties in society. I myself consider the peasants of Montmorency to be members of society more useful than all those heaps of idlers paid by the fat of the people to go six times a week to chatter in an academy, and I am more content to be able to give some pleasure to my poor neighbors when the opportunity presents itself than to help those crowds of petty intriguers with which Paris is full to succeed, who all aspire to the honor of being rogues in place, and who, for the public good as well as their own, should all be sent to plow the earth in their provinces. It is something to give men the example of the life they should all lead. It is something when one no longer has either strength or health to work with one's arms, to dare to make the voice of truth heard from one's retirement. It is something to warn men about the madness of the opinions that are making them miserable. It is something to have been able to contribute to preventing or at least putting off the pernicious establishment in my fatherland that d'Alembert wanted them to make among us in order to pay his court to Voltaire. If I had lived in Geneva I would not have been able either to publish the dedicatory epistle of the *Discourse on Inequality*, or even to speak against the establishment of the theater in the tone that I did. I would be much more useless to my fellow citizens if I lived in their midst than I can be from my retirement when the opportunity presents itself. What does it matter what spot I live in if I act where I ought to act? Moreover, are the inhabitants of Montmorency less men than the Parisians are, and if I can dissuade someone from sending his child to be corrupted in the city, am I doing less good than if I could send him back to the paternal hearth from the city? Would not my indigence alone keep me from being useless in the manner that all those fine speakers understand it, and since I eat only as much bread as I earn, am I not forced to labor for my sustenance and to pay society for all the need I might have for it? It is true that I have declined occupations that are not fit for me; since I did not feel the talent in myself that could make me deserve the good that you wanted to do for me, accepting it would have been stealing from some man of letters as indigent as I am and more capable of that labor; by offering it to me you assumed that I was in a condition to make a summary, that I could occupy myself with matters that were of no concern to me, and since that is not so, I would have deceived you, I would have made myself unworthy of your kindness by behaving differently from the way I did,[60] it is never excusable for one to do badly what one does voluntarily: I would now be dissatisfied with myself, and you also; and I would not be tasting the pleasure that I take in writing to you. In sum, in so far as my strength has allowed me to do it, by working for myself I have done everything I could for society in accordance with my reach; if I have done little for it, I have demanded even less, and I believe I am so clear with it in the position I am in, that if I could henceforth rest completely and live for myself alone I would do so without scruple. At least I would keep the importunity of the public commotion away from myself with all my strength. If I lived another hundred years I would not write a line for the press, and would not believe I had truly begun living again until I was completely forgotten.

I admit nevertheless that it depended on very little for me to find myself re-engaged in the world, and that I might have abandoned my solitude not out of distaste for it, but out of a no less keen taste that I almost preferred to it. Sir, in order to judge the impression their advances and their blandishments made on my afflicted heart, you would have to know the state of desertion and abandonment by all my friends in which I found myself, and the profound suffering with which my soul was affected by it when M. and Mme de Luxembourg desired to become acquainted with me. I was dying; without them I would have infallibly died of sadness, they brought me back to life, it is very just that I use it to love them.

I have a very loving heart, but which can suffice for itself. I love men too much to need to choose among them; I love them all, and it is because I love them that I hate injustice; it is because I love them that I flee them, I suffer less from their evils when I do not see them. That interest for the species is enough to nourish my heart; I do not need particular friends, but when I have them, I greatly need not to lose them, for if they break away, they tear me apart. All the more guilty in that, since I do not ask them for anything but friendship, and as long as they love me, and I know it, I do not even need to see them. But in the place of feelings they always wanted to put efforts and services that the public saw and which did nothing for me. If I loved them, they wanted to appear to love me. For me, who disdains appearances in everything, I was not satisfied with them, and finding nothing but that, I took it as settled. They did not exactly stop loving me, I discovered only that they did not love me.

Thus, for the first time in my life I suddenly found my heart to be alone, and besides, I was also alone in my retirement, and almost as sick as I am today. It is in these circumstances that this new attachment began which has so much compensated for all the others and for which nothing will compensate me, for I hope it will last as long as my life, and whatever happens it will be the last. I cannot dissimulate to you, Sir, that I have a violent aversion for the social stations that dominate the others, I am even wrong to say that I cannot dissimulate it from you, for I have no trouble admitting it to you, to you born of an illustrious blood, son of the Chancellor of France, and First Président of a Sovereign Court; yes Sir to you who have done a thousand good things for me without knowing me and to whom in spite of my natural ingratitude, it does not pain me at all to be obliged. I hate the great, I hate their status, their harshness, their prejudices, their pettiness, and all their vices, and I would hate them even more if I despised them less. It is with this feeling that I was almost dragged to the Chateau of Montmorency; I saw its masters, they loved me, and I, Sir, I loved them and will love them as long as I live with all the strength of my soul: I would give for them, I do not say my life, the gift would be weak in the state I am in, I do not say my reputation among my contemporaries about which I hardly care; but the sole glory that has ever touched my heart, the honor that I expect in posterity and which it will render to me because it is due to me, and posterity is always just. My heart, which does not know how to attach itself by halves, has given itself to them unreservedly and I do not repent it, it would even be useless for me to repent it, for it would be too late to contradict myself. A hundred times in the heat of the enthusiasm they have inspired in me I have been on the point of asking them for a refuge in their house in order to pass the rest of my life near them there, and they would have granted it to me joyfully, except that I must even look at myself as having been anticipated by their offers because of the way they have gone about it. This project is certainly one of those that I have meditated for the longest time and with the greatest willingness. Nevertheless, in spite of myself, in the end I had to feel that it was not good. I was thinking only about the attachment of the people without thinking about the intermediaries who would have kept us apart, and there were so many types of them, especially in the discomfort attached to my illnesses, that such a project is excusable only because of the feeling that inspired it. Moreover the manner of living that it would have been necessary to take on shocks all my tastes, all my habits too directly, I would not have been able to hold out for even three months. In sum we might have brought our habitation as close as we could, that delightful intimacy which makes up the greatest charm of a close society would always have been lacking in ours, since the distance between the social stations always remained the same. I would have been neither the friend nor the servant of M. the Maréchal de Luxembourg; I would have been his guest; when I felt myself away from my own home, I would have often sighed after my former refuge and it is a hundred times better to be apart from people one loves and to desire to be close to them, than to be exposed to making an opposite wish. Several degrees nearer might perhaps have caused a revolution in my life. A hundred times in my dreams I have assumed M. de Luxembourg to be not a Duc, but a Maréchal of France, but a good Country Gentleman living in some old chateau, and J.-J. Rousseau not an author, not a writer of books, but having an average mind, and a few accomplishments, presenting himself to the Lord of the Manor, and to the Lady, pleasing them, finding the happiness of his life near them, and contributing to theirs; if, in order to make the dream more pleasant, you would allow me to push the chateau of Malesherbes a half league away from there with a nudge of the shoulder, it seems to me, Sir, that when I dream in that manner I would not desire to wake up for a long time.

But it is done; nothing remains for me but to end the long dream; for the others are henceforth all out of season and it is a lot if I can still promise myself some of those delightful hours that I have passed at the chateau of Montmorency. However that may be, here I am as I feel myself affected, judge me based on all this hodge-podge if I am worth the trouble, for I cannot put more order into it and I do not have the courage to begin all over again. If this too veracious picture deprives me of your benevolence I will have ceased to usurp what did not belong to me; but if I preserve it, it will become dearer to me, as belonging to me more.

Appendix II

Fragments

The Neuchâtel Preface to The Confessions of J.-J. Rousseau

Containing the detailed account of the events of his life, and of his secret
feelings in all the situations in which he has found himself.

P. 3[1]

I have often remarked that, even among those who pride themselves the most
for knowing men, each hardly knows anyone but himself, if it is even true that
anyone knows himself; for how can a being be defined by means of the relationships that are inside itself alone, without being compared with anything? Nevertheless, this imperfect knowledge that one has of oneself is the only means one
uses for knowing others. One makes oneself into the rule of everything, and this
is precisely where the double illusion of amour-propre is waiting for us; either
by falsely attributing to those we are judging the motives that would have made
us act as they do in their place; or—in that same assumption—by deceiving ourselves about our own motives for lack of knowing well enough how to transport
ourselves into a different situation from the one in which we are.

I have made these observations in relation to myself above all, not in the judgments that I have delivered about others, since I soon felt that I was a separate
sort of being, but in the ones that others have delivered about me; judgments
that are almost always false in the reasons they give for my behavior, and usually
all the more false the more intelligent those who delivered them were. The farther
their rule was extended, the farther they were pushed from the object by the false
application they made of it.

Based on these considerations, I have resolved to cause my readers to make
an additional step in the knowledge of men by pulling them away, if possible,
from that unique and faulty rule of always judging someone else's heart by means
of their own; whereas, on the contrary, even to know one's own it would often
be necessary to begin by reading in someone else's. In order for one to learn to
evaluate oneself, I want to attempt to provide at least one item for comparison,
so that each can know himself and one other, and this other will be myself.

Yes, myself, myself alone, for I do not know any other man up to now who
has dared to do what I am proposing. Histories, lives, portraits, characters! What
are all those? Ingenious novels constructed upon a few external actions, upon a
few speeches that relate to them, on some subtle conjectures in which the Author
seeks much more to shine than to find out the truth. One grabs hold of conspicuous features of a character, one links them by means of invented features, and as

long as the whole makes up a physiognomy, what difference does it make whether it resembles? No one can judge about that.

In order to know a character well one would have to distinguish the acquired from what is by nature, to see how it was formed, what occasions have developed it, what chain of secret affections have made it the way it is, and how it changes, sometimes in order to produce the most contradictory and most unexpected effects. What shows itself is only the smallest part of what is; it is the apparent effect whose internal cause is hidden and often very complicated. Each one guesses in his manner and portrays at his whim; he is not afraid that someone might confront the image with the model, and how would we make known this internal model, which the one who portrays it in someone else does not know how to see, and which the one who sees it in himself does not want to show?

No one can write the life of a man except himself. His internal manner of being, his genuine life is known only to him; but he disguises it when he writes it; under the name of his life he makes his apology; he shows himself as he wants to be seen, but not at all as he is. At most, the most sincere are truthful in what they say, but they lie by their reticence, and what they keep silent about changes what they pretend to admit so much, that by saying only a part of the truth they do not say anything. I put Montaigne at the head of these false sincere people who want to deceive while speaking truthfully. He shows himself with his flaws, but he gives himself only agreeable ones; there is no man at all who does not have odious ones. Montaigne portrays himself in a good likeness but in profile. Who knows whether some scar on the cheek or an eye put out on the side he hides from us might not totally change his physiognomy. A man who is more vain but more sincere than Montaigne is Cardan.[2] Unfortunately this same Cardan is so mad that one cannot draw any instruction from his reveries. Moreover who would want to go fish for such rare instruction in ten volumes in folio of extravagances?

Thus it is certain that if I fulfill my pledges well I will have done a unique and useful thing. And do not object that, since I am only a man of the people, I have nothing to say that deserves the attention of readers. That might be true of the events of my life: but I am writing less the story of these events in themselves than that of the state of my soul as they happened. Now souls are not more or less illustrious except according to whether they have more or less great and noble feelings, more or less sharp and numerous ideas. Here the facts are only precipitating causes. In whatever obscurity I might have lived, if I have thought more and better than Kings, the history of my soul is more interesting than that of theirs.

I say more. Counting experience and observation for something, in that regard I am perhaps in the most advantageous position in which a mortal has ever found himself, since, without having any social station myself, I have known all stations; I have lived in every one from the lowest up to the highest, except the throne. The Great do not know anything except the Great, the small do not know anything except the small. The latter see the former only through admiration for their rank and are seen by them only with an unjust scorn. In these too distant relations, the being common to both of them, the man, escapes them equally. As for me, careful to set aside the mask, I have recognized him through everything. I have weighed, I have compared their respective tastes, their pleasures, their prejudices, their maxims. Admitted everywhere as a man without pretensions and without consequence, I examined them at my ease; when they stopped disguising themselves I could compare man to man, and status to status. Being nothing, wanting nothing, I did not trouble or bother anyone; I entered everywhere without holding on to anything, sometimes dining in the morning with Princes and supping in the evening with peasants.

If I do not have the celebrity of rank and birth, I do have another one which is more my own and which I purchased more dearly; I have the celebrity of misfortunes. The commotion from mine has filled Europe; wise people have been astonished by it, good ones have been afflicted by it: all have finally understood that I had known this learned and philosophic century better than they did: I had seen that the fanaticism which they believed to be destroyed had only been disguised; I had said it before it threw off the mask,* I did not expect that I would be the one who would make it throw it off. The history of these events, worthy of the pen of Tacitus, ought to have some interest under mine. The facts are public, and everyone can know them; but the issue is to find their secret causes. Naturally no one should have seen them better than myself; to show them is to write the history of my life.

Its events have been so varied, I have felt such lively passions, I have seen so many types of men, I have passed through so many sorts of social stations, that in the space of fifty years I have been able to live several centuries if I have known how to profit from myself. Thus, in both the number of the facts and in their type, I have everything I need to make my narratives interesting. In spite of that, perhaps they will not be, but that will not be at all the subject's fault, it will be the Writer's. The same flaw could be found in the life that is most brilliant in itself.

If my undertaking is singular, the position that causes me to do it is no less so. Among my contemporaries there are few men whose names are more known in Europe and whose person is more unknown. My books wandered around the cities while their Author wandered around nothing but forests. Everyone read me, everyone criticized me, everyone spoke about me, but in my absence; I was as far away from the speeches as I was from the men; I did not know anything about what they were saying. Each drew me according to his whim, without fear that the original might come to give him the lie. There was a Rousseau in high society, and another in retirement who bore no resemblance to him.

It is not that, taking everything into consideration, I have anything to complain about in the public speeches with regard to me;† if they have sometimes vilified me without discretion, they have often honored me the same way. That depended on the diverse inclinations the public had with regard to me, and, in accordance with its favorable or contrary predispositions, it did not keep any more proportion in the good than in the bad. As long as they judged me only from my books, in accordance with the interest and the taste of the readers, they made

---

* See the Preface of my First Discourse printed in 1750.[3]

† I wrote this in 1764 already fifty-two years old, and very far from foreseeing the fate that was waiting for me at that age. Now I would have too much to change on that score; I will not change any of it.

me into only an imaginary and fantastic being, who changes his face with each writing I publish. But as soon as I had personal enemies they formed systems in accordance with their intentions, based on which in concert they have settled my reputation, which they cannot destroy entirely. In order not to appear to play an odious role, they do not accuse me of true or false bad actions, or if they do accuse me of them, it is by attributing them to my unruly head, always in a manner so that people believe that they are being misled as the result of geniality, and so that their heart is honored at the expense of mine. But by pretending to excuse my faults, they accuse me for my feelings, and, while they appear to see me in a favorable light, they know how to expose me in a very different light.

Such a skillful tone becomes easy to adopt. With the most good natured manner they kindly slandered me; by means of the effusiveness of friendship they rendered me hateful, while pitying me they vilified me. It is thus that, while having been spared in my actions, I was treated cruelly in my character, and they succeeded in making me odious while they were praising me. Nothing was more different from me than this depiction: I was not better, if one wishes, but I was different. They did not do me justice either in the good or in the bad: while granting me virtues that I did not have they made me into a wicked man, and on the contrary along with vices that are not known to anyone I felt myself to be good. By being better judged I might have lost among the vulgar, but I would have gained among the wise, and I never aspired to any approbation except from the latter.

These are not only the motives that have caused me to do this undertaking, but also the guarantee of my faithfulness in executing it. Since my name must endure among men, I do not want it to bear a fallacious reputation; I do not want to be given virtues or vices that I do not have, or to be depicted under features that are not my own. If I have some pleasure in thinking that I will live in posterity, it is by means of things that adhere to me more closely than the letters of my name; I prefer to be known with all my flaws and that it be myself, than with spurious qualities, under a character that is alien to me.

Few men have acted worse than I have done, and never has a man said about himself what I have to say about myself. There is no vice of character whose admission is not easier to make than that of a black or base action, and one can be assured that whoever dares to admit such actions will admit everything. That is the harsh but certain proof of my sincerity. I will be truthful; I will be so without reserve; I will say everything; the good, the bad, in sum, everything. I will carry out my title rigorously, and never has the most fearful devout woman made a better examination of her conscience than the one for which I am preparing myself; never has she spread out all the innermost recesses of her soul to her confessor more scrupulously than I am going to spread out all of mine to the public. Only begin to read me based on my word; one will not go far without seeing that I want to keep it.

For what I have to say it would be necessary to invent a language as new as my project: for what tone, what style does one adopt in order to unravel this immense chaos of feelings so diverse, so contradictory, often so low and sometimes so sublime, with which I am ceaselessly agitated? What trifles, what miseries do

I not need to expose, into what revolting, indecent, puerile, and often ridiculous details must I not enter in order to follow the thread of my secret inclinations, in order to show how each impression that has left a trace on my soul entered into it for the first time. While I blush only to think about the things I must say, I know that harsh men will still treat the humiliation of the most painful admissions as impudence; but I must make these admissions or disguise myself; for if I keep silent about something one will not know me about anything, so much does everything depend on everything else, so much is everything one in my character, and so much does this bizarre and peculiar assemblage need all the circumstances of my life to be well unveiled.

If I want to compose a carefully written work like the other ones, I will not be depicting myself, I will be disguising myself. The issue here is my portrait, not a book. I am going to work in the camera obscura, so to speak; no other art is necessary than to follow exactly the features I see marked. Thus I decide the style as I do the things. I will not tie myself down to making it uniform; I will always have the one that comes to me, I will change it according to my mood without scruple, I will tell each thing as I feel it, as I see it, without refinement, without bother, without troubling myself about motley. By abandoning myself at the same time to both the remembrance of the received impression and to the present feeling, I will depict the state of my soul doubly, namely at the moment when the event happened to me and at the moment when I described it; my uneven and natural style, sometimes sharp and sometimes diffuse, sometimes wise and sometimes foolish, sometimes serious and sometimes gay, will itself form a part of my story. In sum, in whatever manner this work might be written, by its object it will always be a precious book for philosophers: I repeat, it is an item of comparison for the study of the human heart, and it is the only one that exists.

This is what I have to say about the spirit in which I am writing my life, about the one in which it should be read, and about the use that can be drawn from it. The connections I have had with several people force me to speak as freely about them as about myself. I can make myself known well only if I make them known also, and it should not be expected that—by dissimulating in this case what cannot be kept silent without harming the truths I must tell—I will make use of precautions for others that I do not make use of for myself. Nevertheless, I would be very sorry to compromise anyone at all and the resolution I have made not to let these memoirs appear during my lifetime is an effect of the consideration I want to have for my enemies in everything that does not concern the execution of my design. I will even take the most reliable measures so that this writing will not be published except when the passage of time makes the facts that it contains inconsequential to everyone, and I will deposit it only into reliable enough hands so that no indiscreet use might ever be made of it. As for me, I would be punished very little if it did appear even in my lifetime, and I would hardly miss the esteem of anyone who could despise me after having read it. I say some very odious things about myself in it, for which I would be horrified to want to excuse myself; but also it is the most secret history of my soul, these are my confessions in the strictest sense. It is just that my reputation atone for the evil which the desire to preserve it has caused me to commit. I expect public speeches, the severity of

render nature without
distorting it?

judgments pronounced out loud, and I submit to them. But let each reader imitate me, let him go back into himself as I have done, and let him say to himself at the bottom of his conscience if he dares, "*I am better than that man was.*"

P. 42 [5]

Just as Mlle Lambercier was giving us the cares of a mother, she also excercised the authority of one. This right sometimes put her in the position of inflicting the ordinary chastisement of children on us. Before I received it, I dreaded this correction more than death. Upon the experience I did not find it to be so terrible, and although it never occurred to me to do anything on purpose to deserve it, I had more of an inclination to desire it than to fear it. Having doutless perceived from some sign that this chastisement was not serving its purpose, the modest Mademoiselle Lambercier declared that she was abandoning it because it tired her too much, and, without knowing why, I had some regret at seeing her keep her word.

This behavior in an unmarried woman of thirty who is the only one who knows her motive appears noteworthy to me. Another thing that is almost as noteworthy is the date. This took place in 1721 and I was not yet nine.

I do not know the reason for this precocious sensuality; perhaps the reading of novels accelerated it; what I do know is that it had an influence on the rest of my life, on my tastes, on my morals, on my behavior. I see the thread of all that; it is useful to follow its track; but how can I mark it down on these sheets without soiling them?

This first emotion of the senses impressed itself so much on my memory that, when it began to warm up my imagination after several years, it was always under the form that had produced it, and when the sight of young and beautiful persons made me uneasy, the effect of it was always to set them to work in idea, and to make so many Mademoiselle Lamberciers out of them.

The obstinacy with which these images returned on the slightest occasion, the ardor with which they inflamed my blood, the extravagant acts I was brought to by the desire to see them realized, were not the strangest things that happened in me. A modest and severe education had filled my heart with decent feelings and with an invincible horror for debauchery; all the ideas that related to it inspired me with aversion, disgust, fright. The mere thought of the union of the sexes appeared to me to be so disgraceful that it would have stifled my lascivious imaginings, if it had come to me at the same time.

From this peculiar contrast which separated such closely related things in my mind, an effect resulted that was no less peculiar. What should have been my ruin saved me from myself for a long time. At the age of puberty the object with which I was occupied made a diversion from the one that I had to fear. One idea sidetracking the other heated me up without corrupting me; my agitations, which did not lead to anything, were only more tormenting because of that, but they did not inspire me with any shame except that of playing the child for so long. That reason alone made me discreet about my whims; I found them puerile, but not libertine. One could not be more chastely lustful.

It is from this bizarre diversion of ideas that, along with an imagination inflamed with love and a blood burning with sensuality almost from childhood, I nevertheless escaped from the precocious going astray that exhausts and causes the ruin of most young people. Later, far from overcoming my disgust, the example of my comrades' sullying increased it. I envisaged street walkers only with horror, and thanks to the efforts of the prudent people who had brought me up, the instinct of nature was so well hidden in my whims that after having already made rather long journeys and lived among all sorts of people, I had reached my nineteenth year before I was well acquainted with my sex.

Upon being better informed, I always kept my first reserve with women. Love alone led me astray, never debauchery; my senses were always directed by my heart: shame, the preserver of morals, never abandoned me, and as far as I can proceed to the deepest seeds of my secret passions, this shame was still in part the work of my earliest tastes, continuing to exist. What good would it be to become enterprising in order to obtain the desired pleasures only halfway? Only the ones about which I did not dare to speak could give all their worth to the others. Those that one ought to share were fit to propose; but who would not have disdained the ridiculous pains which, in order to please too much the one who received them, often harmed the one who deigned to give them?

Then, did I have regular morals only because I had depraved tastes? This conclusion would be unjust and exaggerated. A timid natural disposition, a tender heart, a romantic imagination mixed love and reserve into all my desires: a constant taste for honesty, decency, an aversion for impudence, for debauchery, for all excesses, were the fruits in me of an always modest and sound—although otherwise extremely mixed and extremely inconsistent—education; but in a gentle character that was sensitive to shame, the desires it hid left less strength to the others. Already disposed to attach myself to individuals more than to their sex, already fearful because of the danger of displeasing, I developed an affection for acts of submissiveness; this way I found the means to draw near the object of my covetousness in some way by mingling the attitude of a suppliant lover with that of a penitent schoolboy. To be on my knees with an imperious mistress was the sweetest of favors for me. One feels that this manner of making love does not lead to very rapid progress, and does not put the virtue of those who are its object into great peril.

If I did not feel the difficulty of getting so many puerile details tolerated, how many examples would I not give of the strength that the slightest facts of childhood often have for branding the greatest features of the character of men. I dare to say that one of the most deeply engraved features in mine is an indomitable aversion for injustice. The sight of an iniquitous action, even without me taking any personal interest in it, makes me indignant to the point of fury, to such a point that in such a case I have never known either greatness or power that could keep me from showing that indignation. I dare to add that it is so disinterested and so noble that it acts less against the injustices of which I am the victim than against the ones of which I am the witness. Who would believe that this invincible feeling originally came to me from a broken comb?

P. 63[6]

But I did not know that when I was devouring her this way with my heart and eyes, she herself saw me in a mirror which I had not thought about. She turned around and surprised me in a rapture that made me sigh while I was extending my two arms toward her. Nothing can be imagined equal to the sudden fright with which I was seized when I saw myself discovered in that posture: I blanched, I trembled, I felt myself swoon. She reassured me while looking at me with a gentle enough eye and with a finger showed me a better place at her feet. One can judge that I did not make her tell me twice. Up to here everything was perhaps simple enough, but the sequel to this little trick appeared stranger to me: as is seen that was a hardly equivocal declaration on both our parts, and it seemed that nothing more of the familiarity of two declared lovers should be lacking between us. Not at all, on my knees before her, I found myself in the most delightful situation it is true, but the most constrained one in which I have been in my life; I did not dare either to breathe or to raise my eyes and if I had the temerity to put my hand on her knee several times, it was so gently that in my simplicity I believed that she did not feel it. On her side, being attentive to her embroidery, she did not speak to me or look at me. We did not make the slightest motion; a profound silence reigned between us; but how many things the heart says and feels! This situation will appear very tame to many readers; nevertheless I have grounds for thinking that it was not displeasing to the young person, and as for me, I would have passed my entire life in it, I would have passed eternity in it without desiring anything more.

P. 549[7]

It is important to me that the details of my life be known to someone who loves justice and truth and who is sufficiently young that he ought to outlive me.[8] After long periods of uncertainty, I have decided to pour out the secrets of my heart to the small but select number of good men who are listening to me. I will make them my confessions, and I beg them to receive the deposit of them in their memory without any other condition than to make use of them during my life to verify, when there are opportunities, what I have told them, and, after my death, to render the justice they believe they owe to my memory, without favor and without partiality.

Ten years ago,[9] I undertook to write my confessions in the strictest sense of the term. After I had pushed the execution of this undertaking rather far, I saw myself forced to renounce it or at least to suspend it; but there is enough done for one to be able to make an enlightened judgment both about me and about the people with whom I have dealt, for, unfortunately, along with my own confessions, I have been forced to make those of other people, without which mine would not be understood: this disadvantage had made me take measures so that my memoirs would not be seen until a long time after my death and after that of the people who can take an interest in them. My misfortunes have rendered these measures insufficient, and there are no other reliable means left for preserving my deposit except to place it in virtuous and honest hearts who preserve its remembrance.

In order to judge my behavior well, it would be important to know to the bottom my temperament, my natural disposition, my character, which, by a peculiarity of nature, do not at all resemble those of other men; by persisting in judging all my motives from the ones that would have determined themselves, in such a case they have always been mistaken in the interpretation of my intentions. But these details, which it would be necessary to pick up from my earliest childhood, are too extensive to be capable of being done in a day. And it is important to me to begin with what is most essential for me to say, so that if obstacles crop up to other sessions, the fruit of this one might not be lost. Thus today I will limit myself, sirs, to giving you the faithful narrative of everything that has happened to me, and if I dare to speak this way, the history of my soul from my arrival in France until my departure from Montmorency, at the time of the warrant issued against me, aside from returning to the part that I have been forced to omit, when the opportunity presents itself, if you are not too bored by this one.[10]

Sirs, I entreat you to try to listen to me with an attentiveness worthy, not of the importance of the things that I have to tell you and which are hardly worthy of it by themselves, but of the employment with which I dare to burden you; the most noble employment that mortals can fulfill on the earth, because it is a question of deciding, on behalf of all posterity, whether my name, which must live, must be passed down to it with opprobrium or glory. The most astonishing measures have been taken to hide from me forever both my base accusers and their underhanded deceptions, which they will make public as soon as I am no longer alive. Feeling their secret blows without seeing either the instrument or the hand that strikes them, by what means can I defend myself, since I do not know either by whom or of what I am accused? Only one, that is to expose naively and faithfully the good, the evil, and all the details of my life, and then to let someone compare and judge. You are the first, you will probably be the only ones to whom I will make this narrative, consequently the only ones who, since they have heard the two parties, will be competent judges of the truth.

I beg the ladies who have the goodness to listen to me to try to ponder very well that one cannot take upon oneself the function of confessor without exposing oneself to the disadvantages that are inseparable from it, and that, in that austere and sublime employment, it is up to the heart to purify the ears. As for myself, I have put myself into the necessity of faithfully fulfilling my function, which is not only always to be faithful and truthful, but also to overcome shame and sacrifice it to the truth.

Notes

Bloom Jean-Jacques Rousseau. *Emile*. Edited by Allan Bloom. New York: Basic Books, 1979.

Collected Writings, I Jean-Jacques Rousseau. *Rousseau, Judge of Jean-Jacques: Dialogues. Collected Writings of Rousseau*, Vol. I. Edited by Roger D. Masters and Christopher Kelly. Hanover, N.H.: University Press of New England, 1991.

Collected Writings, II Jean-Jacques Rousseau. *First Discourse and Polemics. Collected Writings of Rousseau*, Vol. II. Edited by Roger D. Masters and Christopher Kelly. Hanover, N.H.: University Press of New England, 1992.

Collected Writings, III Jean-Jacques Rousseau. *Discourse on the Origins of Inequality (Second Discourse), Polemics, and Political Economy. Collected Writings of Rousseau*, Vol. III. Edited by Roger D. Masters and Christopher Kelly. Hanover, N.H.: University Press of New England, 1992.

Collected Writings, IV Jean-Jacques Rousseau. *Social Contract, Discourse on the Virtue Most Necessary for a Hero, Political Fragments, and Geneva Manuscript. Collected Writings of Rousseau*, Vol. IV. Edited by Roger D. Masters and Christopher Kelly. Hanover, N.H.: University Press of New England, 1994.

Cranston, I Maurice Cranston. *Jean-Jacques: The Early Life and Work of Jean-Jacques Rousseau, 1712–1754*. Chicago: University of Chicago Press, 1990.

Cranston, II Maurice Cranston. *The Noble Savage: Jean-Jacques Rousseau, 1754–1762*. Chicago: University of Chicago Press, 1991.

Kelly Christopher Kelly. *Rousseau's Exemplary Life: The "Confessions" as Political Philosophy*. Ithaca, N.Y.: Cornell University Press, 1987.

Launay Jean-Jacques Rousseau. *Oeuvres complètes*, Vols. 1–2. Edited by Michel Launay. Paris: Editions du Seuil [Collection L'Intégrale], 1967–1971.

Leigh	Jean-Jacques Rousseau. *Correspondance complète*. Edited by R. A. Leigh. Geneva: Institut et Musée Voltaire, 1965ff.
Pléiade	Jean-Jacques Rousseau. *Oeuvres complètes*, Vols. 1–4. Paris: NRF-Editions de la Pléiade, 1959ff.
Voisine	Jean-Jacques Rousseau. *Les Confessions*. Edited by Jacques Voisine. Paris: Garnier, 1964.

NOTES TO THE EDITORS' INTRODUCTION

1. On Rousseau's readings from the *Confessions* and their consequences, see Pléiade, I, 1611–1614.

2. The *First Discourse* and the polemical writings about it can be found in *Collected Writings*, II.

3. On this point, see 3.

4. Letter to Rey, November 16, 1762 (Leigh, XIV, 55).

5. See Book VIII, 303–304.

6. Letter to Rey, April 27, 1765 (Leigh, XXV, 189).

7. Rousseau's most important discussion of different types of truth occurs in the Fourth Promenade of the *Reveries* where he discusses the truthfulness of the *Confessions* in particular. For a discussion of the relation between general, philosophic truth and particular, factual truth, see Kelly, 1–47.

8. See, for example, the beginning of Book VII, 233.

9. The best of these biographies is Cranston, I and II.

10. On this point, see *Emile*, IV (Bloom, 237–240).

11. Even the confessional religious literature that existed before Rousseau and with which his title links his book is extraordinarily different because of its emphasis on the glorification of God. There is nothing in Rousseau's *Confessions* that vaguely resembles the concluding book of Augustine's *Confessions* with its turn away from Augustine to focusing attention on God's creation. Some indication of the difference between Rousseau and Augustine is given below. In addition, one should consult the excellent account given by Ann Hartle in *The Modern Self in Rousseau's "Confessions": A Reply to St. Augustine* (Notre Dame, Ind.: University of Notre Dame Press, 1983).

12. See Appendix II, 586.

13. The best account of Rousseau, which uses the account of his feelings, or psychological development, as the key to his entire literary career is Jean Starobinski's *Jean-Jacques Rousseau: Transparency and Obstruction* trans. Arthur Goldhammer [Chicago: University of Chicago Press, 1988]).

14. For an interpretation of the *Confessions* that develops this argument, see Kelly.

15. For an excellent account of the working out of this principle in Rousseau's political thought, see Arthur M. Melzer, *The Natural Goodness of Man: On the System of Rousseau's Thought* (Chicago: University of Chicago Press, 1990). For the assertion that this is the fundamental principle of Rousseau's system, see *Rousseau, Judge of Jean-Jacques* (*Collected Writings*, I, 212–214).

16. See Book I, 5.

17. See Pléiade, IV, 938.

18. Ibid., 939.

19. Rousseau gives a comparable account on a more general level and from a historical perspective in Part Two of the *Second Discourse*.

20. See Kelly, 84–100.

21. This point has been made by Hermine de Saussure, *Rousseau et les manuscripts des "Confessions"* (Paris: Editions E. de Boccard, 1958), 277–281. The following discussion is an elaboration of her argument.

22. See the *Discourse on the Origin of Inequality* (*Collected Writings*, III, 38).

23. See Book II, 47.

24. See Book VI, 218.

25. The word translated as "fault" is the French "*faute*," which can also have the even more innocent connotation of "mistake."

26. See Book II, 71–72; Book III, 108; and Book VIII, 288, Rousseau does not call his discussion of the last of these an "admission," probably because the fact was generally known before he wrote the *Confessions*.

27. The word translated as "wrong," is the "*tort*." There are only a few cases in the *Confessions* in which Rousseau admits that we was guilty of a wrong, but there are numerous cases in which he admits he was guilty of a fault. He does admit that he had committed wrongs toward Saint-Lambert when he fell in love with Sophie d'Houdetot (Book IX, 397). In the case of the abandonment of his children he vacillates between calling it a wrong and a fault.

28. See Book VI, 193.

29. See Book IX, 393.

30. See *Second Discourse* (*Collected Writings*, III, 43).

31. The case of compassion or pity complicates this because compassion is both pleasant to feel and leads directly to helping others. However, Rousseau is well aware that very frequently compassion is at odds with the strict demands of justice. Anything but the most generalized compassion for the entire human race can lead to the same sort of faults that come from any other form of weakness. See *Emile*, IV (Bloom, 252–253).

32. The complex interplay between reality and appearance is the major theme of Starobinski's book.

33. See Books VIII and IX, 310 and 391.

34. Pléiade, IV, 966.

35. For these examples, see Books III and IV, 105, 117, and 137.

36. The encounter with Zulietta is in Book VII, 269–271.

37. See Book VIII, 294.

38. See *Letter to Beaumont* (Pléiade, IV, 966).

39. On the different diagnoses that have been given of Rousseau's physical and emotional disorders, see the excellent discussion in Starobinski, 365–377. For different interpretations of the role of the conspiracy in the *Confessions*, see Hartle, 118–125, and Kelly, 210–221. The work in which the conspiracy is most prominent is *Rousseau, Judge of Jean-Jacques*, not the *Confessions*. For a brief examination of the role of the conspiracy in that work, see *Collected Writings*, I, Introduction.

40. That these notes were added can be shown by a number of factors. At times Rousseau mentions how much time had passed between his writing of the original passage and his addition of a footnote. Sometimes it is possible to date a particular footnote because of the ink with which it is written. De Saussure has shown that many scholarly disputes can be resolved by paying close attention to colors of ink and types of paper used in a manuscript.

41. See Book X, 410–411. The passage in which this assertion occurs is largely a recapitulation of the situation described in Book IX. The precise moment of the formation of the idea of the plot in Grimm's mind is indicated in Book IX, 401. Again, the footnotes tell a different story. See Book VIII, 312n.

42. See Book VIII, 325.

43. There has not yet been a comprehensive examination of the intellectual relationship between Rousseau and Diderot, to say nothing of other major figures in the French Enlightenment such as Duclos and Condillac. Very broadly it is reasonable to say that over a wide range of political, philosophic, and artistic issues Diderot and Rousseau shared a view of the inadequacies of the tradition they had inherited, but that they took increasingly diverging directions as they looked for solutions to the problems they observed.

44. See Book IX, 364.

45. See Book I, 13–17 and Book II, 46–47.

46. See Appendix II, 588.

47. See André Wyss, *La Langue de J.-J. Rousseau* (Geneva: Editions Slatkine, 1989).

48. See Book V, 159.

EDITORS' NOTES TO THE NOTE ON THE TEXT

1. The most detailed account of the composition of the *Confessions* is in Hermine de Saussure's *Rousseau et les manuscrits des "Confessions"* (Paris: Editions E. de Boccard, 1958). The account given here relies on the information in de Saussure's book.

2. See Book X, 433.

3. The best account of the early publications of the *Confessions* and their relations to the manuscripts can be found in R. A. Leigh, *Unsolved Problems in the Bibliography of J.-J. Rousseau* (Cambridge: Cambridge University Press, 1990), 114–146.

EDITORS' NOTES TO BOOK I

1. In the N. the title is given as *The Confessions of J.-J. Rousseau, Containing the Circumstances of the Events of His Life, and of His Secret Feelings in All the Situations in Which He Found Himself.*

2. This foreword appears opposite the first page of Book I in G. It does not appear in either of the other two manuscripts.

3. "Inside and under the skin" (Persius, *Satires*, III. 30). The line is applied to a man who is pining away because he has lost virtue. This epigraph is not in N.

4. Material placed in brackets is in P. and not in G. In addition to the numbering of paragraphs in G., P. contains numbering of the groups of paragraphs or chapters. This introductory chapter occurs only in G. and P. For the preface to N., see Appendix II, 585–590.

5. P. reads simply, "and which will have," rather than "and the execution of which will have."

6. This statement indicates that one of the purposes of the *Confessions* is to make it possible for readers to judge Rousseau properly. The sequel to the *Confessions, Rousseau, Judge of Jean-Jacques* was undertaken in part because Rousseau had lost confidence in the ability of readers to act as impartial judges. See *Collected Writings*, I, xvii and 5–7.

7. This appeal to the "Sovereign Judge" parallels the beginning of St. Augustine's *Confessions*. For the most fully elaborated treatment of the relation between Rousseau's work and that of Augustine, see Ann Hartle, *The Modern Self in Rousseau's "Confessions": A Reply to St. Augustine* (Notre Dame, Ind.: University of Notre Dame Press, 1983).

8. P. reads, "let them shudder at my woes," with the addition of "let them blush at my unworthiness" in the margin.

9. In Geneva at the time of Rousseau's birth, only about 1,500 adult males of the total population of approximately 20,000 had the status of citizen. See Cranston, I, 13–29 for a detailed account of Rousseau's family and their status in Geneva. His parents were Isaac Rousseau (1672–1747) and Susanne Bernard (1671–1712).

10. In fact, she was the niece of the Minister Samuel Bernard, who brought her up after the death of her father and his brother Jacques, a watchmaker.

11. N. adds a note concerning the Treille: "Name of a public promenade."

12. In fact Gabriel Bernard married Théodora Rousseau in 1699 shortly before the birth of their first child, while Isaac Rousseau married Suzanne Bernard in 1704. See Cranston, I, 19.

13. N. reads, "Belgrade, and at the arrival of peace returned to his fatherland to work on the fortifications."

14. The poem can be translated, "These two Gentlemen who are absent are dear to us in many ways; They are our friends, our lovers; They are our husbands and our brothers, And the fathers of these children." The spelling of the French is Rousseau's. A theorbo is a sort of lute that was popular in the seventeenth century.

15. This was the title of the senior French diplomat in Geneva. Pierre Cadiot de la Closure (1663–1748) was Resident from 1698 to 1739. De la Closure would no longer have had his official position at the time Rousseau says he talked with him.

16. N. reads, "forty years later."

17. P. reads, "loved her husband passionately."

18. Rousseau was born on June 28, 1712. His mother died on July 7.

19. N. reads, "thirty years."

20. N. reads, "leaves only very short respites.* One of my father's sisters." The * refers to a note at the bottom of the page that reads, "A retention of urine originating from a vice in the conformation of the urethra and in the bladder."

21. Suzanne Rousseau (1682–1775), who married Isaac Henri Gonçerut in 1730.

22. Jacqueline Faramond (1695–1777).

23. N. reads, "I do not know how I learned to read: it seems to me that I have always known. I remember."

24. In *Emile* Rousseau delays the use of this "dangerous method" that awakens the imagination until the student is between the ages of twelve and fifteen (*Emile*, III). Until then he experiences only real things; consequently, he does not undergo either the strange disproportion between feelings and knowledge or the tendency to turn into other people described by Rousseau here. On this point and further comparisons between Jean-Jacques and Emile, see Kelly, 76–84.

25. P. reads, "felt everything, and the imaginary misfortunes of my heroes drew from me a hundred times more tears in my childhood than my very own have ever made me shed. These emotions which."

26. Jean Le Sueur (or Lesueur) (c. 1602–1681) was a Protestant minister. Jacques-Bénigne Bossuet (1627–1704) wrote the *Discourse on Universal History*. Plutarch (first century A.D.), frequently mentioned by Rousseau as his favorite author, wrote lives of Greek and Roman statesmen. Giovanni Battista Nani (1616–1678) was Venetian ambassador to France. Rousseau used Ovid (43 B.C.–A.D. 16) as the hero of one of the acts of his opera *The Gallant Muses* (see Book VII 247–248). He also used the line "*Barbarus hic ego sum, quia non intelligor illis*" (Here I am the barbarian because no one understands me) from *Tristia* as the epigraph of both the *First Discourse* and *Rousseau, Judge of Jean-Jacques: Dialogues*. Jean de La Bruyère (1645–1696) is author of *Characters*. Bernard Le Bovier de Fontenelle (1657–1757) wrote *Conversations on the Plurality of Worlds* and many other literary and scientific works; he was one of the leading participants in the so-called quarrel between the ancients and the moderns at the end of the seventeenth and beginning of the eighteenth century. Molière (1622–1673) was the preeminent French comic playwright.

27. N. reads, "during his work. It is from this little collection that were formed so to speak the first features of my soul, and the ones that have been least effaced. There I developed a taste that was rare and perhaps unique for that age. Plutarch above all had the preference. The pleasure"

28. N. reads, "Novels; Amyot's style disgusted me with that of La Calprenède." Jacques Amyot (1513–1593) was the translator of Plutarch into French. Gauthier de Costes La Calprenède (1610–1663) was the author of novels including *Cassandre*, *Cléopatre*, and *Faramond*.

29. Agesilaus, Brutus, and Aristides are written about by Plutarch. Orondates and Juba are characters in La Calprenède's *Cassandre* and *Cléopatre*, respectively. Artamenes is the hero of Madeleine de Scudéry's *Artamène ou le Grand Cyrus*, written in the middle of the seventeenth century.

30. The phenomenon of living outside of oneself, or of identifying with someone else, is a crucial part of Rousseau's understanding of what it means to be

a social human being. For a discussion of this in relation to the *Confessions*, see Kelly, 19–30.

31. Having failed in his attempt to assassinate the Etruscan king Porsenna, Gaius Mucius Scaevola was threatened with death or torture by the Etruscans. He held his own right hand in a fire until it was burned off. As a consequence of this display of steadfastness, Porsenna made peace with the Romans.

32. N. concludes the paragraph, "to represent his deed with more energy."

33. François Rousseau was born in 1705 and apprenticed to a watchmaker in 1722. No evidence concerning him has been found to add to the account in the *Confessions*.

34. It should be noted that this account shows clearly that Rousseau does not regard natural goodness as involving a spontaneous obedience to a standard of rigorous unselfish behavior.

35. P. reads, "surrounded."

36. The 1839 edition of the *Confessions*, edited by Petitain, gives the conclusion of this song:

> *Un coeur s'expose*
> *A trop s'engager*
> *Avec un berger:*
> *Et toujours l'épine est sous la rose.*

The entire lyric can be translated "Thyrcis, I dare not listen to your pipe under the elm; for they are already gossiping about it in our hamlet. A heart runs too high a risk in getting involved with a shepherd: and the thorn is always under the rose." The lyrics remembered by Rousseau are very close to some that appear near the end of his opera, *The Village Soothsayer*. See Voisine, 11–12, note 2.

37. For the details of this incident, which took place in 1722, see Cranston, I, 28.

38. Rousseau's cousin Abraham Bernard was born December 31, 1711. For a rather different account of the two boys' relations at Bossey, which began in October of 1722, see *Emile*, II (Bloom, 135–136).

39. Jean-Jacques Lambercier (1676–1738). His sister Gabrielle Lambercier was born in 1683 and thus was ten years older than Rousseau indicates below.

40. In P. the numbering of paragraphs is discontinued after this paragraph.

41. P. omits, "for although little sensitive to praise I always was very much so to shame."

42. For somewhat contrasting interpretations of the two examples of spanking that follow, see Jean Starobinski, *Jean-Jacques Rousseau: Transparency and Obstruction*, trans. Arthur Goldhammer (Chicago: University of Chicago Press, 1988), 6–11, and Kelly, 84–98. For the very different version of the first example that appears in N., see Appendix II, 590–591.

43. As indicated in editorial note 39, Mlle Lambercier was forty at this time. Rousseau was eleven, and not eight.

44. The word translated as "decent" is "*honnête*." In Rousseau's use this word most frequently has the connotation of decency and honesty, but in earlier French usage *honnêteté* frequently applied only to people at court and had the connotation of good breeding. These different connotations indicate profound differences in

what it means to be honorable. There is much literature on this word and its subtle shifts of meaning. For a useful brief discussion, see Peter France, *Politeness and Its Discontents* (Cambridge: Cambridge University Press, 1992), 56–58. We would like to thank Ruth Grant for calling the importance of Rousseau's democratization of this term to our attention.

45. Little Sacconex is a village to the west of Geneva.

46. P. omits, "in the extravagant acts to which they sometimes carried me."

47. P. reads, "her mistress's," rather than "Mlle Lambercier's."

48. The idea of finding at least a partial remedy for an evil within the evil itself is a recurring theme in Rousseau's work. See, for example, *First Discourse* (*Collected Writings*, II, 19); "Preface to *Narcissus*" (*Collected Writings*, II, 196); and "Letter to Voltaire of September 10, 1755" (*Collected Writings*, III, 106). Rousseau also uses virtually the exact phrase in the Geneva Manuscript of the *Social Contract* (see *Collected Writings*, IV, 82). For an excellent discussion of this theme, see Jean Starobinski's essay, "The Antidote in the Poison: The Thought of Jean-Jacques Rousseau," in *Blessings in Disguise; or the Morality of Evil*, trans. Arthur Goldhammer (Cambridge, Mass.: Harvard University Press, 1993), 118–168.

49. P. reads, "head," rather than "brain."

50. *Carnifex* is the Latin term for the public executioner. It is also used as a general term of reproach for a tormentor.

51. P. reads, "feeling," rather than "remembrance."

52. For the importance of the first experience of injustice in a child's education, see *Emile*, II (Bloom, 98–100), and Kelly, 91–98.

53. See Genesis 3:7–23.

54. P. reads, "little angry over," rather than "regretting little."

55. King Victor Amadeus passed through Bossey on August 23, 1724.

56. P. omits, "the gate to."

57. P. reads, "where there was a bench where."

58. "Persevering labor conquers all." This is a version of Virgil's *Georgics*, Book I, 145–146: *Labor omnia vicit Improbus*. The context is the description of the obstacles to human existence and the need for labor that enter the world under the reign of Jupiter. The passage praises the role of the arts (in the sense of skills and inventions) in human life. Both the exalted context and the fact that it involves praise of those things condemned by Rousseau in the *First Discourse* increase the humor of Rousseau's use of a Latin motto for the description of his childish prank.

59. N. reads, "made a triangular conduit, whose joints we carefully coated with clay, and at whose entrance we planted."

60. The word translated "toad-catcher," is "*crapaudine*," which is a sort of lead grating at the end of a pipe from a pond or reservoir. See Pléiade, I, 1245.

61. For Emile's first experience of vanity, see *Emile*, III (Bloom, 172–175).

62. See Book VIII, 327–331.

63. P. reads, "old, and which ought now, if it still exists, to be about half of one."

64. In fact, it must have been only several months.

65. N. reads, "for drawing; since my reason was not well enough formed for

Geometry; I learned the demonstrations by heart, my cousin did the same; we learned nothing more: but we did not stop always advancing." The paragraph ends here, although a portion of what follows occurs several pages later in N.

66. N. reads, "my aunt, in order to console herself for her husband's infidelities, made herself devout and became a sort of pietist." The word, pietist, covers a range of meanings, but generally indicates an emotional or affected piety and attachment to the literal meaning of scripture.

67. Rousseau is referring to his grandfather David Rousseau (1641–1738) who was a watchmaker.

68. In Genevan dialect this means "bridled ass." It involves a play on the name Bernard which is the name of the ass in the *Roman de Renard* from the twelfth and thirteenth centuries. See Pléiade, I, 1247.

69. One of the members of the Twelve Peers of Charlemagne, in other words, a knight of medieval romances.

70. N. reads, "nothing in common, although both are very violent: the one sensuous, or from temperament, and the other Platonic or from opinion. The whole."

71. Coutance is a neighborhood named after a street in Geneva.

72. Most commentators regard the expression "tic tac" as a direct reference to the spanking, but Voisine connects it to numerous provincial expressions used to tease lovers, none of which have any connection to spanking. See Voisine, 29.

73. Charlotte de Vulson was married to Jean-Pierre Christin in the Fall of 1724.

74. The preceding paragraph is not found in N. Instead it reads,
Returning to Geneva I soon forgot Mlle Goton, although the girls of St. Gervais sometimes reminded me of her. But as for Mlle de Vulson I remembered her all the better since I often received news from her, even without counting the eternal fidelity that we had sworn to each other when we separated. In order to ratify this oath in person, she came to Geneva herself, we saw each other twice at my Aunt Bernard's. Nothing is as tender as my mistress's caresses, nothing is so lively as her declarations, we separated melting in tears. Several days later I learned that she had married a M. Christin who had been extremely badly treated during my triumphs, and that her trip to Geneva with which she had had the kindness to do me the honor was to buy her wedding clothes. Young though I was, the adventure appeared more humorous than tragic to me; my love went as it had come, and the vanity that kindled it extinguished it effortlessly. I did not write any insults to the perfidious one, I was not going to reproach her for her infidelity; but I swore not to speak to her again in my life, and I kept this oath so well, that when I went to see my father almost twenty years later and was boating with him on the lake, I saw some Ladies in a boat near ours. I asked who they were. "What," my father said to me laughing and showing me one of them, "Doesn't your heart tell you? It is Madame Christin, your former mistress, it is Mademoiselle de Vulson." I judged that it was not worth the trouble to renew the quarrel with a woman of forty, and making a sign to our boatmen to change direction, I turned my back without saying anything.
The next paragraph begins, "Nevertheless they deliberated about whether they

would make me into an artisan, Procurator, or Minister. I had enough taste for the ministry, as do all children who find preaching to be a fine thing, but the small revenue from my mother's property, to be divided between my brother and myself, was not enough to push forward my studies. They decided to place me with Masseron, the registrar at the City Hall, to learn under him."

75. P. reads, "a secret horror."

76. Rousseau's contract of apprenticeship with Abel Ducommun was signed April 26, 1725.

77. Laridon is a dog in La Fontaine's *Fables* VIII, Fable XXIV. Although descended from a noble breed, he ends up as a kitchen dog "for lack of cultivating nature and its gifts."

78. N. reads, "orders of chivalry for myself and my comrades, for the romantic spirit still mixed its color in my games a little."

79. The As was a Roman copper coin that was progressively devalued over the history of the Republic. A sou was worth one-twentieth of a livre or slightly more than one-twentieth of a franc.

80. Apprentices were not entitled to dessert. See Pléiade, I, 1249, n 3 to p. 31.

81. P. reads, "almost a year."

82. The Molard was the location of a market in Geneva.

83. N. reads, "fidelity, while the one who made me do it was corrupting a child out of the vilest self-interest. Nevertheless."

84. The garden of the Hesperides is the site of one of the twelve labors of Hercules. The golden apples in this garden are guarded by the daughters of the Night and a hundred-headed dragon. Thus, Rousseau is playfully comparing himself to Hercules in his effort to steal the apples. This incident also has an important parallel in the *Confessions* of St. Augustine. In Book II Augustine discusses his own childhood theft of some pears and gives it as an example of the human tendency toward sinfulness; whereas Rousseau's example is a comic discussion of the corruption of a naturally good boy by the ill treatment he suffers from his master. For discussions of this parallel, see Kelly, 103–108, and Hartle, 24–25.

85. P. reads, "did I put."

86. This discussion of money and pure pleasures should be compared with the comparable discussion in *Emile*, IV (Bloom, 344–354), where Rousseau discusses how he would behave if he were rich.

87. P. reads, "a long time if I can without."

88. P. reads, "instrument," rather than "the one."

89. On Charles-Louis Dupin de Francueil (1716–1780), see Book VII, 245–246. This event probably took place sometime around 1750 when Rousseau was employed by the Dupin family.

90. P. reads, "my togs as security."

91. P. reads, "almost thirty years old."

92. P. omits, "she says."

93. The lady was apparently Marie-Anne de Bourbon, 93, Louis XIV's granddaughter. See Voisine, 43.

94. This apparently occurred on Sunday, March 14, 1728.

95. N. reads, "before the others: it amused him to make the walkers sleep out-

side: this was known, but it was not always known which day and at which gate he was waiting for them. One unfortunate Sunday at the beginning of Spring, seduced by the fine weather, we had prolonged our walk a little and two of my comrades and I were returning just about on time. Half a league."

96. The Bernard family lived in the more fashionable upper city, whereas, after the death of his wife, Rousseau's father began living in the working-class neighborhood of St. Gervais.

97. In other words, Rousseau sold the sword in order to buy food. However, in N. he indicates that the sword was taken from him by M. and Mme Sabran. See Book II, below, 50.

98. P. adds here, "End of First Book."

EDITORS' NOTES TO BOOK II

1. In P. this book begins, "The Confessions of J.-J. Rousseau/First Part/Second Book."

2. P. reads, "sail," rather than "fly."

3. Benoît de Pontverre who welcomed Rousseau in fact was not descended from the Pontverre who was the first leader of the "Gentlemen of the Spoon," a group of Savoyard nobles founded in the first half of the sixteenth century who wore spoons around their necks to commemorate their oath to eat the Calvinist Genevans with a spoon.

4. N. reads, "Ministers. Without having studied as M. de Pontverre had, I was less but better informed than he. But although he did not tell me anything to which I did not believe I had a solid answer, I was too good a guest."

5. N. reads, "I felt or I believed I felt the superiority of my cause, I did not want."

6. P. reads, "even if I had the desire to do so."

7. P. and N. both read, "delicate mouth, with bad teeth, black eyebrows."

8. N. reads, "to excite Mme de Warens's commiseration."

9. Such a railing was placed on this spot on the two hundredth anniversary of Rousseau's meeting with Mme de Warens. For another account of this first meeting, see the Tenth Walk of the *Reveries of the Solitary Walker*.

10. Françoise-Louise de la Tour was born at Vevey in the Pays de Vaud on March 31, 1699, not 1700 as Rousseau says. She was married to Sebastien-Isaac de Loys in 1713. Vuarens, or Warens, is the name of an estate possessed by de Loys. She made her flight to see Victor Amadeus in 1726 and therefore had been in Annecy for about eighteen months when Rousseau arrived, not five or six years as he says. Her husband divorced her in 1727. For more information about her life before meeting Rousseau, see Cranston, I, 47–49, 69–77.

11. P. omits, "her husband."

12. Slightly under 1,900 French Francs.

13. P. reads, "five or six years."

14. N. reads, "radiance, and even when she was old she was always beautiful. She had."

15. N. reads, "a little from her husband," rather than "a little from her teachers."

16. Etienne-Sigismond de Tavel, a former army officer, born in 1687.

17. Empirical medicine is medicine based on what has been observed to work in previous similar cases rather than medicine based on a knowledge of why a particular treatment works. It can have the connotation of quackery.

18. The Duchesse de Longueville (1619–1679) was a leading literary patron and an instigator of the revolt known as the first Fronde. She was the daughter of Henri de Bourbon, Prince de Condé, and, for a time, the mistress of the Duc de la Rochefoucauld, author of the *Maxims*.

19. François de Sales (1567–1622), like Michel-Gabriel de Rosillon, Marquis de Bernex (1657–1734), was Bishop of Geneva. Along with Jeanne-Françoise de Chantal (1572–1641) he founded the Order of the Visitation. François de Sales was canonized in 1665 and Mme de Chantal in 1767.

20. N. reads, "a lovable, beautiful, dazzling woman." P. reads, "a cultured, lovable, dazzling woman."

21. N. reads, "I had unknown ones."

22. N. reads, "fire of my childhood, which." P. reads, "fire that Mlle de Vulson had inspired in me and which."

23. N. and P. read, "with," rather than "for."

24. Turin was the capital of Savoy.

25. N. reads, "at my age in order to play the little Hannibal so to speak, and to raise."

26. Antoine Houdar de La Motte (1672–1731) was a member of the French Academy. In his "The Orchard of Madame de Warens," published in 1739, Rousseau mentions the "too sweet La Motte" along with the "touching Voltaire" as his favorite contemporary poets. See Pléiade, II, 1129.

27. David Rival (1696–1759) was a watchmaker and wrote poetry; his son Jean became an internationally famous actor.

28. N. reads, "lost several years before by."

29. P. reads, "father, and above all." N. reads, "father, above all for me who represented a cherished spouse. He loved me."

30. In the *Second Discourse* Rousseau identifies this as a "maxim of natural goodness." He formulates it as, "Do what is good for you with the least possible harm to others," and argues that it is more useful than the golden rule because it is more deeply rooted in natural feelings. See *Collected Writings*, III, 38. A central part of Rousseau's indictment of society is his claim that social life creates new circumstances and develops new passions that make it virtually impossible for people to seek their own good without harming others. As a result, social life requires more than natural goodness; it also requires virtue, or the ability to refrain from seeking what is good for oneself. On the centrality of this issue for Rousseau's thought, see Arthur M. Melzer, *The Natural Goodness of Man: On the System of Rousseau's Thought* (Chicago: University of Chicago Press, 1990). With this digression on the subject of the maxim of natural goodness, Rousseau shows the way reflection on his own experience led him to discover this maxim and the way he attempted to apply it in practice. The digression also illustrates how Rousseau uses the *Confessions* to convey the principles of his thought in concrete form.

31. P. adds in the margin, "In 1763."

32. On Lord Marshal George Keith (1686–1778), see Book XII, 498–501.

33. Rousseau never finished the sequel to *Emile*, entitled *Emile and Sophie, or the Solitaries*. What he did complete can be found in Pléiade, IV, 881–924.

34. Peter the Hermit (c. 1050–1115) preached for the First Crusade.

35. P. (evidently mistakenly) omits, "less."

36. Hannibal crossed the Alps with his Carthaginian army at the beginning of the Second Punic War in 218 B.C.

37. In all probability the trip took around three weeks, rather than seven or eight days. See Voisine, 63, note 1.

38. On Rousseau's relations with Grimm and Diderot, see Part II of *The Confessions*.

39. For an account of the events recorded up to this point in Book II, see Cranston, I, 42–51.

40. N. reads, "even the sword stayed in their hands; they had faithfully." Note that in the final version Rousseau indicates that he managed to keep the sword until he sold it for food.

41. N. reads, "the Hospice of the catechumens where I was expected, to be instructed there."

42. The French word is *vilaine* which has numerous connotations, including nasty, mean, filthy, ugly, shabby, and unpleasant. As a substantive it can also mean a miser or a rogue. Originally it meant low-born. In the *Confessions* Rousseau seems to use it to express a combined moral and physical disgust. Where possible it will be translated as nasty or nasty-looking.

43. P. omits, "here." N. reads, "why dissimulate my."

44. Rousseau said this in *Emile*, IV (Bloom, 257).

45. N. reads, "Sometimes one takes away from it, one never adds to it, or that addition, if one makes it, is only for other people: it is only vanity or self-interest that dictates it: it does not penetrate inside at all. Dogmatic faith."

46. P. reads, "peculiar to our city at that time."

47. N. reads, "of the city, it was only at the Church that they scared me, I very much liked to see them at the rectory. At the same time."

48. P. reads, "living in it without difficulty, but not with that of entering it; that idea had offered itself to me." N. reads, "in a distant future which disguised its horror from me. At that moment."

49. N. reads, "the genuine," and P., "the good," rather than, "the true."

50. See Book I, editors' note 26.

51. P. reads, "objections," rather than "difficulties." N. reads, "I stopped him on everything that appeared to me to be subject to dispute, and I did not spare him."

52. P. reads, "shocking," rather than "filthy."

53. N. reads, "tossing about, without respect for the altar and the crucifix which were behind him, I saw."

54. This is Piedmontese dialect for, "Cursed, filthy beast!"

55. A slang term for pederasts.

56. P. reads, "comparison. The ideas that it caused to be born in me changed into desire and charm the disgust that I had felt until then for possessing them. It seemed to me that."

57. P. and N. read, "rebaptize," rather than "baptize."

58. It has been suggested that Rousseau is referring to a ceremony in which two cardinals, representing Henri IV, submitted to the Pope at the end of the sixteenth century. See Voisine, 75, note 1.

59. N. reads, "the monk gave no answer, but I heard him mumble something or other between his teeth, in an extremely poorly satisfied manner.

All the ceremonies having ended, at the moment."

60. N. reads, "for almost three months," with "more than two months" having been corrected. P. reads, "for almost two months." Rousseau entered the hospice on April 12, abjured on the April 21, visited the Inquisitor the next day or the day after, and was baptized on April 23. There is considerable disagreement about when he finally left the hospice. The man identified as the Slav who accosted Rousseau was baptized on May 1. The attractive Jewish girl Rousseau mentions left on June 13. Since Rousseau refers to her departure, he probably left sometime afterwards. He probably entered the service of Mme de Vercellis service toward the end of July. On these points, see Voisine, 65, note 1; Pléiade, I, note 3 to p. 69; and Cranston, I, 52–53. For another account of the events at the hospice and afterwards, see Book IV of *Emile* (Bloom, 260–266).

61. *Amour-propre* is one of Rousseau's key technical terms and is not easily translated. It is the sort of preference for oneself over others that is the root of both a healthy pride and an unhealthy vanity. For Rousseau's accounts of the term, see *Rousseau, Judge of Jean-Jacques* (*Collected Writings*, I, 9); and *Second Discourse* (*Collected Writings*, III, 91–92, note 12).

62. N. reads, "looked at myself, if not exactly as the master, at least as one of the residents, and that appeared extremely fine to me. At last."

63. *Giuncà* is Piedmontese for curds and *grisse* is a long, slender loaf of bread from the Piedmont.

64. Gianbattista Somis (1676–1763) was a violinist and student of Corelli and Vivaldi. The Bezozzi (not Bezuzzi) family were well-known musicians during this period; Alexandre (1722–1775) and Paolo Girolamo (1704–1778) were in Turin after Rousseau's stay. Felici De'Giardini (Desjardins) (1716–1796) was a student of Somis.

65. P. reads, "sound," rather than "playing."

66. N. reads, "passable wine and freedom."

67. N. reads, "further. In a word, I pleased this young lady enough to come back to her shop with a sort of familiarity, which did not depend on my taste, nor perhaps on hers, which increased further. But."

68. The Pléiade edition mistakenly fails to begin a new paragraph here.

69. N reads, "touching, her manner was obliging without being tender; at first sight it seemed that the friendship was already made, and that nothing more could happen. She was called."

70. When Agamemnon sailed to fight the Trojan War, he left his wife Clytem-

nestra to be looked after by Aegisthus, who became her lover and accomplice in the murder of her husband.

71. P. reads, "feel," rather than "consider."

72. For an early draft of this passage, see Appendix II, ooo. For a comparison of the different versions (including a report of yet another version told by Rousseau at the end of his life), see Starobinski, *Jean-Jacques Rousseau*, 153–155.

73. P. reads, "sign from," rather than "motion of."

74. N. reads, "surmount it. A remnant of uncertainty made me tremble at incurring her indignation and at having myself dismissed from her home; her position as a woman and five or six."

75. P. reads, "delights," rather than "sweetness."

76. N. reads, "from her, and perhaps she wanted to anticipate her husband's return. Our mute declarations."

77. P. omits "only." N. reads, "added only a hat, some stockings, and some linen."

78. Thérèse de Chabod Saint-Maurice, later the Comtesse de Vercellis (1670–1728), was in fact from Savoy as Rousseau guessed.

79. Mme de Sévigné (1626–1696) was famous for her letters, which were published after her death.

80. N. reads, "effort to disguise herself. Although she did not depart at all from her role as a woman, she bore the pain with a constancy that was so natural to her that she did not even suspect that in this there might be philosophy, and this word, less in fashion at that time than today, was barely known to her. That." In both versions, this passage is a slap at Rousseau's former friends the so-called *philosophes*, and particularly at Diderot, whose nickname was "philosopher."

81. N. reads, "unfortunate, it was less out of a genuine commiseration than out of the greater and more noble motive of doing what was good in itself. I."

82. N. reads, "since, especially in Paris, that."

83. Giuseppe-Ottaviano della Rocca.

84. N. reads, "for them; they did not at all like to leave me in a tête-à-tête with her. They saw."

85. In giving Rousseau the thirty *livres*, the Comte was merely following the terms of the will, which left that amount to each of the domestic servants.

86. For another account of the incident that follows, see the Fourth Walk of the *Reveries of the Solitary Walker*.

87. N. ends this paragraph, "come true. But my punishment is not entirely inside, and today David Hume does nothing but return to me what I formerly did to the poor Marion." Rousseau is referring to *A Concise and Genuine Account of the Dispute between Mr. Hume and Mr. Rousseau*, published in 1766 by Hume and presenting his version of the quarrel between the two of them during Rousseau's stay in England. Since N. is the earliest of the three manuscripts, this gives some indication of the date Rousseau wrote, or copied for the first time, this part of the *Confessions*.

88. N. reads, "making her more disreputable than she would have been without me."

89. N. reads, "as if it had just been committed. A hundred times I have believed I heard her say to me at the bottom of my heart, 'You play the honest man, and you are only a scoundrel.' I cannot say how many praises that I have received have been poisoned by this idea, and how often it makes the esteem of men tormenting inside me. Sometimes that goes to the point of making me regard it as a confirmation of my crime that I am well thought of. Nevertheless."

It has been suggested that the work to which Rousseau refers in the text is the *Confessions* itself. See Book IV, 111n3. Another possibility is in the discussion of conscience near the end of the first half of the Profession of Faith of the Savoyard Vicar in *Emile*.

90. N. reads, "consisted in, for if I knew someone who had committed one that was similar in all its circumstances, I feel that it would be impossible for me not to acquire a horror for him. Thus this weight."

91. N. reads, "would fulfill my goal only halfway, if." P. reads, "would not fulfill my task either, if."

92. P. reads, "shame," rather than "fear."

93. N. reads, "'admit it to me,' I am perfectly sure that at the instant I would have admitted it. Never, either at that fatal moment, nor at any other, did deliberate crime draw near my heart. It is."

94. N. reads, "as I dare to believe it is, it must have been by the misfortunes of my life, which I have often endured with more patience, by regarding them as its just chastisement. This is what."

95. P. adds here, "End of the Second Book."

EDITORS' NOTES TO BOOK III

1. N. gives the title as "*The Confessions*/of J.-J. Rousseau/First Part/Book III." P. gives it the same way except that it says, "Third Book" rather than "Book III."

2. N. reads, "of enjoyment in the feeling of need."

3. N. reads, "hardly cared, and if the whim of holding me back had taken them, as long as the man and the sword did not become mixed up in the game, I was very certain, lusty and vigorous as I was, of easily saving myself from both their cudgels and them."

4. N. concludes the paragraph, "that adventure cured me of the bizarre taste that produced it."

5. Jean-Claude Gaime (1692–1761). Pierre de Mellarède (1659–1730) was a Savoyard diplomat.

6. N. reads, "sometimes a hero, sometimes a good-for-nothing, never a man." In the *Iliad*, Thersites is presented as base and insolent. He is a sort of foil for the nobility of the Homeric heroes.

7. P. reads, "merit," rather than "natural disposition."

8. The "Profession of Faith of the Savoyard Vicar" appears in Book IV of *Emile*.

9. Ottavio-Francesco Solaro, Comte de Gouvon (or Govone), was born in 1648.

10. The Marquise was the wife of the Comte de Gouvon's oldest son, the Mar-

quis de Breil (Giuseppe-Roberto Solaro). The Abbé de Gouvon (Carlo Vittorio di Govone) was the Comte's second son.

11. N. reads, "I already knew customary practices well enough to know that so much fuss."

12. Carlo-Giuseppe Solaro, Comte de Favria.

13. P. reads, "mansion," rather than "house."

14. N. reads, "relax so that they might not notice this difference too much, if they were accustomed to my first efforts. 'Your.'"

15. N. reads, "an agitation that hardly permitted thinking about me, even if they had in my favor all the fine projects upon which I had counted a little too much. Nevertheless, up to then I had relaxed very little, I had not given the slightest subject for complaint, and the lack of attention they had for me surely did not come from my fault. One thing."

16. Pauline-Gabrielle de Breil was born around 1712.

17. The mourning was because of the death of the queen of Sardinia in August of 1728. Rousseau's stay with the Gouvon family appears to have taken place roughly from February into the summer of 1729.

18. N. reads,

I did not forget myself at all; I kept to my place, and even my desires did not get out of control, perhaps because I did not know very well what to settle them on. I liked to see Mlle de Breil, to hear her make some remarks that showed intelligence, sense, decency; my ambition did not go at all beyond the pleasure of serving her, but I felt an extreme passion for this pleasure of my station. At table I was attentive in seeking occasions for making them worthwhile. If her lackey left her chair for a moment, instantly I was seen standing there: otherwise I kept myself across from her; I sought in her eyes for what she was going to ask, I spied out the moment for changing her plate. I would have done everything in the world for her to deign to order me to do something, to look at me, to say a single word to me. All that did not succeed for me at all, and I had the mortification of seeing that I was nothing for her; she did not even notice I was there. Nevertheless when her brother—who sometimes addressed a word to me at table—said something or other to me that was not very gracious, I gave him an answer so sharp and well turned that she paid attention to it and cast her eyes upon me, with a little smile that was not ungracious. This glance.

19. For a story told by the Solar family that Rousseau not only explained the *t*, but also interpreted the motto by explaining that it was love that wounds but does not kill, see Voisine, 103.

20. N. reads, "then she looked at her grandfather with an affectionate eye, as if to excite the praise that I had the right to expect from him and that in fact he gave me. But although I was not insensitive to it, I enjoyed this praise much less than the secret applause Mademoiselle de Breil gave to it.

The next day at dinner she finally paid attention to the fact that I was there, and during her lackey's absence she asked me for something to drink in an extremely sweet tone. I trembled and flew to serve her. I had filled the glass too full: upon presenting it to her I spilled."

21. The similarity between this "romance" or novel and the romance between Mlle de la Mole and Julien Sorel in Stendhal's *The Red and the Black* has been noted frequently. For the most extensive comparison between the two accounts and a useful general treatment of Stendhal's response to Rousseau, see Raymond Trousson, *Stendhal et Rousseau: Continuité et ruptures* (Cologne: DME-Verlag Georg Molich, 1986).

22. P. reads, "two times passing by with her daughter and finding me in her antechamber."

23. Cruscantism, from the Accademia della Crusca in Florence, represents a sort of purism in speaking Italian. Louis de Courcillon, the abbé de Dangeau (1643–1723), was an author of numerous works on grammar.

24. See Book I, 33.

25. N. reads, "who, because I was the youngest, affected treating me as their inferior, and who, seeing me."

26. This is, perhaps, François-Robert Mussard (1713–1775), a well-known painter of miniatures.

27. This is probably either Etienne or Pierre Bâcle, two brothers who were contemporaries of Rousseau.

28. N. reads, "agreeable. Nothing more was necessary. Behold me."

29. P. reads, "justify to myself in that way a decision."

30. The Hiero-fountain was invented by Hiero of Alexandria (second century A.D.). Consisting of two chambers one of which is filled with wine and the other with water, it makes use of air pressure to present the illusion of causing water to turn into a fountain of wine. See Voisine, 110. Using similar examples, Rousseau presents the temptation to use the knowledge of science to dupe the credulous in *Emile* (Bloom, 172–175 and 182–183).

31. P. reads, "in order to begin, the life of a true vagabond, attracted by a chimera." N. reads, "in order to begin the way of life of a true vagabond under the most extravagant auspices."

32. It has not been possible to date Rousseau's return to Annecy exactly. It was probably in the early summer of 1729, but possibly either somewhat earlier or later.

33. N. reads, "consulted her chambermaid, less, I think, in order to have her advice, about which she hardly cared, than in order to win her approval. I did not dare"

34. *Julie*, Pléiade, II, 421. St. Preux says that he was "almost breathlessly overjoyed at seeing that they were taking possession of me."

35. "Precipitating causes" translates "*causes occasionelles*." As the context makes clear, Rousseau uses the term here to indicate circumstances that allow the development of something that has a more fundamental underlying cause the precise nature of which might not be known. This is a technical term used by followers of Descartes, most notably Malebranche. In the precise technical sense, "*causes occasionelles*," are not genuine causes. Rather they are something more like correlations between events.

36. N. reads, "Mme de Warens', but what I have never seen joined with mag-

nificence either at Turin or elsewhere: cleanliness, modesty, and a patriarchal abundance that the stinginess of ostentation never knows. She had."

37. In Littré's *Dictionnaire de la langue française*, this passage from the *Confessions* is used to illustrate the word "patriarcal" in the sense of the simplicity of ancient times.

38. P. reads, "drinking in accordance with the old Swiss practice."

39. Anne-Marie Merceret (c. 1710–1783).

40. Claude Anet (1706–1734) left Vevey and converted to Catholicism at the same time as Mme de Warens. He was the nephew of her husband's gardener and became apprenticed to a carpenter at Annecy.

41. N. reads, "began hers. While reacquiring her appetite, she cheered herself up and cheered me up. I began."

42. N. reads, "familiarity or rather the habit of that familiarity was established."

43. Much has been made of these nicknames, given the sexual relations that later arose between Rousseau and Mme de Warens. This fact is indeed noteworthy, but it is also worth noting that in Savoy it was common for everyone to refer to the mistress of a house as Mamma. Diderot also used this as a nickname for his fiancée. See Pléiade, I, 1280, note 2 to p. 106, and Voisine, 116, note 1. Voltaire also gave one of his mistresses the same nickname.

44. N. reads, "painful. I was always afraid that someone might speak to her, that someone would give her a distaste for me, that something might be done or said that would separate us. My need."

45. For the accomplishment of this dream, see Book VI, 204–205.

46. On the theme of the "dangerous supplement" in Rousseau, see Jacques Derrida, *Of Grammatology*, trans. Gayatri Chakravorty Spivak (Baltimore: Johns Hopkins University Press, 1976), 141–164.

47. N. reads, "found several books in my room, the *Spectator*, the *Duties of Man and Citizen*, the *Henriade*: although." P. reads, "in the room I occupied: Pufendorf, the *Spectator*, the *Henriade*." *The Spectator Papers* by Addison and Steele were translated into French in 1714. Marivaux published an imitation, *The French Spectator*, in 1722. Emile gives a copy of *The Spectator* to Sophie. See *Emile* (Bloom, 450). Samuel Pufendorf (1632–1694) was a German jurist of modern natural law. Among his books is *The Law of Nature and Nations*, translated into French by Jean Barbeyrac in 1718 in an abridged version under the title *Duties of Man and Citizen*. He is one of the modern natural law theorists criticized by Rousseau in the *Second Discourse*. See *Collected Writings*, III, 21. Charles Marguetel de Saint-Denis, Seigneur de Saint-Evremond (1610–1703) was forced to leave France and settled in Holland and then England. Voltaire's poem *The Henriade* was published in 1723.

48. "Perhaps some ancient respect for the blood of their masters still spoke for him in the heart of these traitors." *Henriade*, II, 337–338.

49. All the manuscripts read this way, although *parla* is from the *passé simple*, rather than the present.

50. N. reads, "flower. She had not read any more than I had, but she had read better. Numerous."

51. Pierre Bayle (1647–1706) was a French Protestant and skeptic who took refuge in Holland. His most important work is the *Historical and Critical Dictionary*, first published in 1697.

52. Jean de La Bruyère (1645–1696) was the author of *Characters*. François de La Rochefoucauld (1613–1680) was the author of *The Maxims*.

53. Contrary to the manuscripts, the Pléiade edition begins a new paragraph here.

54. Paul-Bernard d'Aubonne.

55. André-Hercule, Cardinal de Fleury (1654–1743).

56. N. reads, "with him believing that he was so with me. The result."

57. P. reads, "could," rather than "ought to."

58. See Book I, 25.

59. P. reads, "one ought to feel."

60. N. reads, "Two almost inalienable [sic] things come together and are joined in me."

61. P. reads, "head," rather than "mind."

62. Literally the insult would be, "By your throat" (*A votre gorge*), as in being held by the throat. The Duke of Savoy had offered a ridiculously low price for some merchandise in Paris and was stunned by the coarse reply of the merchant who did not know who he was. The Duke had made it all the way back to Savoy before turning around and responding with the same coarse insult the merchant had given him. See Pléiade, I, 1284–1285, note 1 to p. 111.

63. P. reads, "devoid of all verbal memory."

64. N. reads, "I do not end at all, I always repeat the same old thing; an appalling disorder reigns in my letter, and barely intelligible."

65. N. reads, "I have studied men, I have had only too many occasions to do so: I have profited from them, and I believe myself to be a rather good observer."

66. P. reads, "know all their histories." N. reads, "know their whole history, guess everything they have in their soul in order to be sure."

67. N. reads, "talking on the spot. That troubles me to the point of losing my head over the slightest things: I feel an anguish, a cold sweat, dark clouds trouble my brain, I become nervous, I become perplexed, and I must only."

68. N. reads, "One evening I was at Mme the Maréchale de Luxembourg's; Mme the Maréchale de Mirepoix and M. the Duc de Gontaut were there: no one else was there." In Book X, 446, Rousseau confirms the identities of the participants in this conversation. On the Duchesse de Luxembourg, see Book X, 434–435. On Anne-Marguerite-Gabrielle, Duchesse de Mirepoix, see Book XI, 488. The other participant was Charles-Antoine-Armand, Duc de Gontaut (1708–1783).

69. Théodore Tronchin (1709–1781) was a Genevan doctor. His "opiate" was a well-known treatment for venereal disease and was also thought to induce miscarriages. Rousseau's remark is difficult to translate because when he first mentions the "opiate" he gives a masculine article to what was usually a feminine noun. The word translated "it" here is a feminine pronoun which could conceivably refer to the lady. If this were the case the remark would be "I believe that she hardly is worth any better." In either case Rousseau's remark could be taken as implying that the lady is being treated for venereal disease.

70. N. reads, "difficulty keeping themselves from bursting out, but People of the Court know how to contain themselves and nothing at all was apparent. This is."

71. N. reads, "my animated physiognomy and my eyes full of fire promise."

72. P. reads, "was," rather than "is."

73. On Mme Dupin, see Book VII, 244–245.

74. Aimé Gros (1677–1742). The Lazarists were a religious order founded by St. Vincent de Paul in the seventeenth century for the religious instruction of the common people.

75. N. reads, "occupation that did not appear to displease the good man. While."

76. N. reads, "fee being filled with the idea of one day having a new convert among his priests. Nevertheless he permitted."

77. Rousseau probably entered the seminary in the Fall of 1729.

78. Louis Clérambault (1676–1748).

79. N. reads, "barbaric and harsh," rather than "sardonic."

80. N. reads, "three weeks," rather than "two months."

81. Jean-Baptiste Gatier (or Gattier) (1703–1760).

82. N. reads, "from the only two Priests whom I found truly worthy of attachment and esteem I made the original."

83. In a Castillian proverb the gardener's dog will not eat his dog food, but gets angry when the cows eat it.

84. Lazare Corvesi and Apolline-Catherine Corvesi. The term *ultramontane tastes* refers to homosexuality, which the French regarded as characteristically Italian.

85. N. reads, "by several years, but it is certain that I was not twenty-two, and there is nothing in it in which that is not apparent." For the "Preface" to *Narcissus, or the Lover of Himself,* see *Collected Writings,* II, 186–198.

86. N. reads, "the others. Almost at the same time the wind."

87. N. reads, "Two or three years later." The order of St. Anthony was established in the eleventh century. The Bishop de Bernex died in 1734. The fire took place on October 16, 1729. It was, in fact, in 1742, eight years after the bishop's death, that Rousseau gave his testimony about the alleged miracle.

88. Father Claude Boudet (1705–1774) was the Bishop de Bernex's biographer.

89. Elie-Catherine Fréron (1719–1776), an ardent opponent of the Enlightenment, published Rousseau's testimony in the *Année littéraire* in 1765. In the *Letters Written from the Mountain* (published at the end of 1764) Rousseau wrote against miracles. See especially Letter Three, Pléiade, III, 727–754.

90. N. reads, "and at the end of two or three months they sent me."

91. N. reads, "for this art, which she loved very much herself, gave her the idea of making me into a musician for lack of anything better."

92. Jacques-Louis-Nicholas Le Maître.

93. N. reads, "good man, amusing when he was not boring, and whom she called kitten because of his monkeyshines. Mamma."

94. N. reads, "chambermaid was the daughter of an organ-maker and knew."

95. N. reads, "everything keeps its place and nothing is indifferent in the imaginary recollections of these times of innocence and happiness that often."

96. A *parlement* is mainly a law court, not a legislative body like an English parliament.

97. N. reads, "against that seduction. Moreover his maxims of pleasure and debauchery appeared to me to be very good for him, but I felt."

98. N. reads, "he was a good chap, sweet, accommodating, and whose gaiety when he was cooled off was worth more than his gaiety when he was sodden. Unfortunately."

99. Joseph-Auguste Vidonne de Saint-Ange.

100. Easter was on April 9 in 1730.

101. Louis-Emmanuel Reydellet (1692–1743).

102. P. reads, "favor," rather than "support," and the clauses of the sentence appear in a slightly different order.

103. On Philibert Caton, see Book V, 155–157. The Comte de Lyon was probably Jean-François de Dortan.

104. P. omits, "as will soon be seen."

105. In N. Book III ends at this point. Book IV begins with the next paragraph.

106. As Rousseau indicates in his article on the subject in his *Dictionary of Music*, diapason is a term from Greek music equivalent to an octave. It is also used to describe the proper range for an instrument or voice. Thus, here it means out of pitch or proper range.

107. In N., this paragraph ends, "for Paris, and perhaps I had met her on the road without knowing anything of it."

108. P. reads, "present and the future, my." N. (in which this passage is a part of Book IV) reads, "his friends' secrets, above all with regard to things already past. Solely occupied with the present and sometimes with the future with those I love, my heart."

109. For what is known about Mme de Warens's trip to Paris see Cranston, I, 85–87. There is reason to believe that M. d'Aubonne was involved in a conspiracy to stir up a revolt in the Pays de Vaud with the aim of bringing it under the control of the King of Sardinia. At this point P. concludes, "End of the third book."

EDITORS' NOTES TO BOOK IV

1. P. reads, "The Confessions of J.-J. Rousseau/First Part/Fourth Book."

2. In N. the paragraph concludes, "thus lost the labor of twenty-five years."

3. N. reads, "die out at all: time erases all the other feelings, but it sharpens remorse and makes it more unbearable; above all when one is unhappy, one says to oneself that one deserves to be so, and instead of finding the consolation one looks for in oneself, one finds only a new torment. I believe that happy people have little remorse; but the one who commits the wrong must be assured of having it his whole life; otherwise he does not know what future he is preparing for himself in his unhappiness.
The only decision."

4. N. reads, "no longer there, and I was not curious to see my former teacher. I saw."

5. N. reads, "Madame the wife of the Intendant for whom I felt some inclination but I never dared."

6. P. omits, "admiring, coveting his rare talents."

7. N. reads, "took it into her head to fall in love with me. That girl always." Like Rousseau and Mme de Warens, Esther Giraud (1702–1774) was a convert to Catholicism from a Protestant country. She was, in fact, ten years younger than Rousseau indicates below.

8. N. reads, "near my face, it was as if she wanted to bite me. But I was patient."

9. N. reads, "I did not take it into my head, and I do not know that anything of the sort has ever fallen into my mind in the whole course of my life, even though I have sometimes been rather provoked by women. Moreover."

10. P. reads, "Each has his whims: that has always been mine. Nevertheless it is not vanity, it is sensual delight that attracts me; it is." N. reads, "However, it is not precisely vanity of status and rank that attracts me, but it is." In *Satires*, I, ii, 75–85 Horace expresses a preference for freedwomen who are prostitutes over respectable women because the former do not disguise themselves.

11. This dawn was probably on July 1, 1730.

12. P. adds a note in the margin, "At Wooton, in Staffordshire."

13. Mlle de Graffenried's first name is not known. She died in 1748. The mother of Claudine Galley (1710–1781) owned a chateau at Thônes, which Rousseau spells "Toune" below.

14. N. reads, "heart beat with a strange force while I looked at."

15. P. reads, "the poor cook's helper ate his bread without saying a word at the smoke from the roast." Rousseau uses this colloquial expression (indicating standing by helplessly at the sight of delights being received by someone else) again in Book VI, 210.

16. N. reads, "the two little chicks sitting on benches on the two sides of the long table and the little rooster above between the two of them."

17. P. reads, "added some value to that of the slight favor."

18. The *juge mage*, a magistrate charged mainly with civil cases.

19. Jean-Joseph Mouret (1682–1738) composed numerous operas and ballets.

20. Jean-Baptiste Simon (Simond, or Symond) was named civil magistrate or president of the tribunal of Annecy in 1730. He died in 1748. When Rousseau met him he would have been about 38 years old.

21. The incident occurs in Chapter VII of the *Roman comique* by Paul Scarron (1610–1650).

22. P. reads, "three feet tall," with "two" crossed out.

23. N. reads, "M. Simon would not be adequately depicted, even as to his figure, if I did not add to all this that he was extremely gallant."

24. N. reads, "insulted by a woman, gets angry in his turn, blurts out some coarse words, says to him."

25. *Anas* are collections of sayings by famous people. The expression is derived from Latin, as in *dicta Virgiliana* for the sayings of Virgil. In the eighteenth century the suffix was used as a generic term to indicate a sort of literature.

26. N. reads, "playing the love-sick Spaniard."

27. N. reads, "Merceret, who, I think, also had a bit of a taste for me, found this very well imagined. They."

28. N. reads, "without playing the conceited fellow."

29. In fact Rousseau was eighteen and Merceret about twenty.

30. N. reads, "a good woman, but both mealy-mouthed and a scold at the same time, pretended."

31. M. Merceret was an organist.

32. A kreutzer (or creutzer) was worth a little more than one-tenth of a French franc.

33. A batz was worth four creutzers, or around one-half a French franc.

34. P. omits, "with thanks."

35. A white écu was worth three French francs.

36. N. reads, "advances not only with the best heart, but with the best grace in the world."

37. François-Frédéric de Treytorrens (1687–1737).

38. "What a caprice! What an injustice! What! Would your Clarice betray your love?"

39. N. and P. read, "two or three beats."

40. Rousseau's distaste for French opera is shown most clearly in the *Letter on French Music*, which concludes with the assertion that there is no such thing as French music and that it would be so much the worse if there were.

41. The *Hôpital des Quinze-Vingt*, a hospital for the blind in Paris. It seems clear that Rousseau means that the noise would rupture the ears of a deaf man, not a blind man.

42. N. reads, "and all his Court your music would excite murmurs of surprise and admiration, and that all around you the greatest princesses and the most beautiful ladies would say in a low voice, 'What delightful songs! what enchanting music! there is not a sound in it that does not go to the heart.'" For an additional account of this performance of *The Village Soothsayer*, see Book VIII, ooo–ooo.

43. N. reads, "told him everything that was least necessary for him to know, taking, it is true, the useful precaution of asking him for secrecy."

44. This sentence is not found in P.

45. N. reads, "My heart tenderly leapt at a thousand ideal felicities."

46. N. reads, "into that water, no less pure than they were!"

47. Vevey is the setting for *Julie*, and Julie and St. Preux are its protagonists. Claire is Julie's confidante.

48. N. reads, "a good son if ever there was one. He loved."

49. David de Crousaz (1656–1733).

50. The new market was on the Ile de la Cité in Paris. No scholar has been able to identify what was remarkable about it.

51. Manuscript N. breaks off at this point in mid-sentence.

52. The so-called Archimandrite claimed to be Athanasius-Paulus of the order of Saints Peter and Paul in Jerusalem. Archimandrite is the title of a brother superior in a monastery. It is the Greek Orthodox equivalent of an abbot. The fake Archimandrite and Rousseau were in Fribourg in April 1731.

53. Lingua franca was an uninflected jargon made up of some French, Spanish, and mainly Italian used in the Middle East for communication between people who did not speak the same language.

54. "Admire, Gentlemen, this is Pelagian blood." Voisine suggests that this is a

play on words that refers to the Pelagian heresy and the Pelages who were held to be the ancient inhabitants of Greece.

55. This sentence and the one preceding it are written in the margins of both G. and P. The repetition and slight variation from the preceding paragraph may represent a copying error on Rousseau's part.

56. The gift was presented on June 16, 1764. Rousseau visited the city a few days later, but it was a year later that he stayed with his friend Daniel Roguin (1691–1771).

57. P. reads, "muddled," rather than "perplexed."

58. Jean-Louis d'Usson, Marquis de Bonac (1672–1738).

59. The Marquis had been French Ambassador to Constantinople from roughly 1716 to 1724.

60. Laurent-Corentin La Martinière (d. c. November 1732).

61. The poet Jean-Baptiste Rousseau (1671–1741) was banished from France in 1712. For several years at the beginning of his banishment, he lived at the embassy in Soleure, where the Comte Du Luc was ambassador.

62. P. concludes the paragraph, "completely and probably I would have had little success."

63. Antoine Marianne had been the Marquis de Bonac's secretary in Constantinople and was chargé d'affaires of the embassy at Soleure until Jacques-Dominique Barberie, Marquis de Courteille, became ambassador in 1738. On M. de Malesherbes, see Book X. A letter, now judged to be apocryphal, purporting to be the one referred to by Rousseau has been published.

64. P. reads, "a copy of this letter with which he is acquainted. If I obtain it."

65. For an account of what is known about the Marquis de Bonac's assistance to Rousseau at this time, see Cranston, I, 97.

66. David-François Merveilleux (not *de* Merveilleux).

67. Jean-François Gaudard.

68. Armand-Frédéric, Duc de Schomberg (1615–1690), served in the armies of a number of European countries and finally died at the Battle of the Boyne in the service of William of Orange.

69. On the identity of this M. de Surbeck see Voisine, 1073–74. There were many officers with this name in the French military in the eighteenth century.

70. On the identities of Mme Merveilleux and her nephew, see Voisine, 1039.

71. In P. Rousseau originally wrote, "attractiveness, a sensitive heart, a very pleasant wit," and then struck out "a sensitive heart."

72. On the nephew, or great-nephew, see Voisine, 177–178, note 2.

73. Mme de Warens had, in fact, left Paris in July of 1730, although it is not impossible that she had returned for a short time.

74. "Decrepit old man, you thought that a foolish madness would inspire me with the desire to bring up your nephew."

75. Rousseau is referring mainly to the writings in defense of the *First Discourse*. See *Collected Writings*, II.

76. This note was added to the margin in both P. and G.

77. The peasant is referring to the pre-Revolutionary French system of taxation.

78. The pastoral novel *Astrée* by Honoré d'Urfé (1568–1625) is set in Forez. Its heroes are Astrée and Céladon. Diane and Sylvandre are also characters in the novel.

79. No more is known for certain about Mlle du Chatelet. It appears that she was a boarder at the convent of Chazottes or Chazeaux.

80. This other trip may have taken place in 1732.

81. As André Wyss points out (*La Langue de J.-J. Rousseau*, [Geneva: Editions Slatkine, 1989], 155), this is a rather ambiguous construction. Although it seems reasonable to assume that Rousseau is referring to one of the daughters as pretty, it is not impossible that he is referring to the mother.

82. P. reads, "instant or ever made a worker come twice for his money. I have."

83. P. reads, "passageway," rather than "blind door."

84. P. reads, "saw the sun, the water."

85. Blancs were pieces of small change. Rousseau is indicating that he had about two and a half sous.

86. Batistin (c. 1680–1750), a French composer of German origin, wrote four books of cantatas. *The Baths of Thoméry* is based on a poem by Jean-Baptiste Rousseau.

87. Nothing more is known about M. Rolichon. On the Antonines, see Book III, 101, editors' note 87.

88. On Rousseau as a music copyist, see *Rousseau, Judge of Jean-Jacques (Collected Writings*, I, 138–145).

89. P. reads, "collating and correcting my scores."

90. A petit écu was worth three francs.

91. P. reads, "reduce," rather than "oblige."

92. *Gil Blas*, by Alain-René Lesage (1668–1747), appeared in installments between 1715 and 1735.

93. Suzanne Serre (1720–1755) was eleven, not fourteen, when Rousseau first met her. On his later fondness for her, see Book VII, 237. Hermine de Saussure has suggested and given some evidence for the hypothesis that at one time Rousseau planned to end Part One with a longer account of his romance with her. See *Rousseau et les manuscrits des "Confessions"* (Paris: Editions E. de Boccard, 1958), 113–116.

94. Rousseau lived in Môtiers from 1762 to 1765 after his flight from France at the time of the condemnation of *Emile*. See Book XII, 496.

95. P. omits, "mountains."

96. The Pas de l'Echelle is, in fact, near Bossey. Rousseau is evidently thinking of the village of Echelles, which is on the way from Lyon to Chambéry. This trip probably took place in September 1731. Rousseau entered the survey in October.

97. P. reads, "crows and sparrow-hawks that flew."

98. Don Antoine Petitti was the Intendant General of Finances for Savoy.

99. P. reads, "equality," rather than "equity."

100. P. reads, "reader," rather than "public."

101. At this point P. adds, "End of the Fourth Book."

EDITORS' NOTES TO BOOK V

1. P. reads, "The Confessions of J.-J. Rousseau/*First Part*/*Fifth* Book."

2. In fact, it was at the end of September or beginning of October 1731.

3. P. reads, "began to work on."

4. P. reads, "paid for," rather than "purchased."

5. Victor-Amédée Chapel, Comte de Saint-Laurent (1682–1756).

6. A sort of medicinal herb tea.

7. Richard Davenport was Rousseau's landlord at Wootton, Staffordshire, when he was in England in 1766–67. His own estate was Davenport Park.

8. P. omits, "While I was writing down my numbers."

9. P. reads, "I had acquired as sort of disdain and disgust for it: I looked at it, as all ignorant people do, as a sort of Apothecary's study."

10. For a more detailed account of Rousseau's view of botany, see Book XII, 537. See also the Seventh Walk of the *Reveries*.

11. P. reads, "a pretty duet."

12. War between France and the Empire was declared in October 1733. The dispute was over the candidates that were supported for the elective monarchy of Poland. In exchange for his support of the French candidate and their annexation of Savoy, the King of Sardinia was promised rule over Milan. The candidate supported by the French was Stanislaus Leczinski (1677–1766), who had previously been King of Poland from 1704 to 1709 and was Louis XV's father-in-law. After renouncing his claim to the throne as a result of the French defeat, he retained the title of King of Poland while living in France. Stanislaus wrote a "Response" to Rousseau's *First Discourse*. See *Collected Writings*, II, 28–36, and Book VIII, 307.

13. Charles-Armand-René de la Trémoille (1708–1741). His ancestor Louis de la Trémoille is written about in *Lives of the Illustrious Men and Great Captains of France* by Pierre de Bourdeilles de Brantôme (1540–1614), to which Rousseau refers below.

14. P. reads, "among them made despising them into a duty for himself."

15. For part of the time Rousseau was at Wootton he believed that the British government would not give him permission to leave.

16. These are all figures in Brantôme.

17. Rousseau refers to the Seven Years War.

18. The French term is "*gobe-mouche*," which is a fly-catcher, a bird of the sparrow family. In slang it is applied to gullible people who believe anything that is told to them. Its equivalent in American slang would be a sucker or perhaps a pigeon. We have chosen to render it as "gull" to give both senses of easily duped and a flock of birds.

19. La Fontaine, *Fables*, VI, Fable 8.

20. On September 14, 1734, the Comte de Broglie was surprised by the imperial forces and barely escaped being made prisoner. King Charles-Emmanuel came to the aid of the French forces.

21. Jean-Philippe Rameau (1683–1764) was the leading French composer of the eighteenth century. His opera *Hippolyte et Aricie* was first presented in 1732. His *Treatise on Harmony* was published in 1722. For his relations with Rousseau, see Book VII, 280. Although Rousseau was an admirer of Rameau's genius as a com-

poser, he developed both his own style of composition and his theories of music in express opposition to Rameau's. For a careful account of Rousseau's response to and debates with Rameau, see Robert Wokler, *Social Thought of J.-J. Rousseau* (New York: Garland Publishing, 1987), 235–378.

22. Nicolas Bernier (1664–1734) composed seven books of cantatas. Rousseau makes a very unfavorable remark about them in Chapter XV of the *Essay on the Origin of Languages*.

23. On Clérambault, see Book III, 99.

24. Apparently Jean-Antoine Palais, or Palazzi.

25. P. reads, "I dreamed about nothing else."

26. P. reads, "draw up the parts, lead the rehearsals, etc."

27. P. reads "Canavas, a relative of Mme Van Loo, who." Gianbattista Canavas, or Canavazzo, became related by marriage to the singer Anne-Antoinette Christine Van Loo. For more information on her see, Book VIII, 314. No one has identified Roche or his son.

28. This expression for the conductor's baton comes from Grimm's pamphlet *The Little Prophet*. See Book VII, 322. In the eighteenth century it was customary for the conductor actually to beat out the tempo by striking the baton against a block.

29. See Book III, 108.

30. Jean-François Noyel de Bellegarde, Marquis de la Marche and Comte (not Marquis) d'Entremont (1661–1742), the Sardinian Ambassador to France.

31. From a golden chain worn by members of the order.

32. This is one of the places in the *Confessions* for which Rousseau has been accused of complete fabrication. However, his account has been shown to be substantially correct. See G. Daumas, "En marge des Confessions," *Annales J.-J. Rousseau* XXXIII (1953–1955), 211–219.

33. P. reads, "for my whole life."

34. See Book III, 94.

35. Records show that he left the Surveyor's Office on June 7, 1732, after about eight months.

36. P. omits the words "sweat" and "smell" from this sentence.

37. P. reads, "the most amiable people."

38. See Plutarch, *Life of Pyrrhus*. Cineas asks Pyrrhus what he will do after all his conquests have been accomplished. When Pyrrhus answers that he will then be able to relax and converse with Cineas, Cineas replies that they can do that immediately without conquering any place.

39. Marie-Anne de Mellarède, born around 1718.

40. Thought to be Françoise-Sophie de Menthon, who was born in 1719. She was the daughter of the Comtesse de Menthon, whom Rousseau discusses below.

41. Gasparde-Balthazarde de Challes, who was born in 1702.

42. P. reads, "if unfortunately her hair were not a little too blonde." Mlle de Challes's sister, whose name was either Anne-Catherine or Catherine-Françoise, was married to the Comte de Charlier. Their daughter, Françoise-Catherine, was born in 1725.

43. Péronne Lard, daughter of Jean and Marie Lard.

44. P. reads, "almost always found."

45. P. omits, "the flirting and."

46. Mme de Menthon was perhaps involved in getting the Comte de Belle-garde, a member of the d'Entremont family, to write posters insulting the deputy of police. He had to leave the country to escape a prison sentence but went on to have a very successful diplomatic career. See Pléiade, I, 1324, note 2 to p. 192.

47. One of the names of Apollo.

48. P. reads, "sense," rather than "feeling."

49. P. omits, "the thirst for."

50. See Book IX, 374–375.

51. P. omits, "and it was for that reason that she was not a mistress."

52. Perret was the pastor of Vevey. As the indefiniteness of Rousseau's statement suggests, there is no evidence that he was, in fact, the lover of Mme de Warens.

53. Aspasia was the mistress of Pericles. In the Platonic dialogue *Menexenus* Socrates says that he took lessons in rhetoric from her. Rousseau's immediate source on this point is probably Plutarch's *Life of Pericles*.

54. On this type of relation of union or wholeness among three people, see Kelly, 141–147.

55. This originally read, "When everyone is doing something, one speaks only when one should; but." Rousseau struck it out and replaced it with what now appears.

56. P. reads, "who, distributing fortune and hopes by the millions, needed an écu while they were waiting."

57. P. reads, "always favored one project."

58. François Grossi, or Grossy (1682–1752), became the Premier Doctor of Savoy in 1727. He moved to Chambéry in 1735.

59. The new pistole, which had recently come into use at this time, was worth about 28 francs.

60. Joseph Picon, or Piccone.

61. P. reads, "died in our arms after."

62. Claude Anet died in March of 1734. The fact that he died so early in the year has caused some critics to doubt the story about the Genipi, on the grounds that the mountains would still have been covered with snow. Based on this and the earlier story about Anet's suicide attempt, they suggest that Anet committed suicide, presumably out of jealousy of Rousseau. The lack of any evidence whatsoever aside from what is said in the *Confessions* makes any conclusion contrary to what Rousseau says highly speculative.

63. A louis was worth a little under 25 francs.

64. P. reads, "removed what I had put there."

65. P. reads, "misfortune I foresaw than."

66. Esprit-Joseph-Antoine Blanchard, or Blanchar, was dismissed as music master of the cathedral at Besançon at the end of 1732 and became music master at Amiens in 1735. In February of 1734 he was in Paris. This makes it quite unclear as to exactly when Rousseau went to study with him. There is a letter to Mme de Warens from Rousseau written from Besançon dated June 29, but without a

year and critics have placed this letter in each of the years between 1732 and 1735. Cranston accepts 1732 as the date of this visit (Cranston, I, 105), which would place it shortly after Rousseau's decision to leave the survey office and become a music teacher; but 1733 is not impossible if the Abbé Blanchard remained in Besançon for a while after his dismissal. Either 1732 or 1733 would place Rousseau's visit before Claude Anet's death. See Pléiade, I, 1329–1330, notes 1 and 2 to p. 208, and Voisine, 239–240, note 1, for summaries of the dispute over the dating.

67. The term *"torche-culs"* is a slang term for pamphlets useful only as toilet paper.

68. Racine's *Mithridates* was first performed in 1673.

69. Claude-Marie d'Entremont (1700–1755).

70. Jean-Baptiste-François d'Entremont (1701–1778).

71. P. reads, "voices convenience, and for which the transposition rendered a different bass necessary. I answered."

72. This passage also indicates some problems of chronology. The preliminaries of peace were concluded in October of 1735, but the Orléans Regiment did not cross the mountains until the end of 1736. Furthermore, the Comte de Lautrec (Daniel-François, Comte de Voisins d'Ambres, Viscomte de Lautrec, 1686–1762) was not with that regiment and was promoted from the rank of colonel in August 1734. Rousseau's suggestion that his acquaintance with the comte occurred around the same time as his trip to Besançon, coupled with the difficulties in setting the date of that trip, have led commentators to suggest that this acquaintance began at the beginning of the war (in 1733) rather than at the end.

73. P. reads, "at just about the same time." Jean-Charles de Sennectere, or Saint-Nectaire (1714–1785).

74. *Jephtha*, by the Abbé Pellegrin and Monteclair, was first performed in 1732. This is one further indication that the events reported here may have occurred in 1733 rather than 1735.

75. "The earth, Hell, even Heaven, all tremble before the Lord."

76. Jean-Vincent (or Jean-Victor) Gauffecourt (1691–1766).

77. See Book I, 6, note 15.

78. P. reads "he could have his choice, he chose them all, and did what he wanted."

79. See Book VII, 272.

80. See Book VIII, 327–328.

81. François-Joseph de Conzié, Comte de Charras and des Charmettes, Baron d'Arenthon (1707–1789).

82. In the margin of P. is the following remark, which was added later: "I have seen him since and I have found him totally transformed. Oh what a great magician M. de Choiseul is! Not one of my old acquaintances has escaped his metamorphoses." On de Choiseul, see Book XI, 463–464.

83. P. reads, "King," rather than "Crown Prince." Frederick the Great began his correspondence with Voltaire in 1736, after the publication of the *Philosophic Letters*.

84. In 1717 Voltaire had been imprisoned in the Bastille for writing satires against the regent. In 1725–26 he was beaten, imprisoned in the Bastille for a second time, and exiled to England after a dispute with a nobleman. He returned to

France in 1729 and four years later published the *Philosophic Letters*, based on his experiences in England.

85. P. reads, "a slightly fickle inclination."

86. Camille Perrichon (1678–1768) was a government official and member of the Academy of Lyon. Gabriel Parisot (1680–1762) was a surgeon and member of the Academy of Lyon. For more about Rousseau's relations with him, see Book VII, 236.

87. The precise identification of both of these women is uncertain. The first could be either of two Mmes. d'Eybens. The second could be either Elisabeth de Bardonanche or her daughter-in-law Marie.

88. Jacques Barillot and his son, also named Jacques Barillot, were book dealers and published the first edition of Rousseau's *First Discourse*.

89. See Book XII, 509–511, for Rousseau's account of the disturbances in Geneva in 1763–64 after the censoring of the *Social Contract*.

90. Gabriel Bernard worked on the fortifications of Charleston, where he died in July 1737.

91. P. omits, "nosing about and."

92. Jacques Rohault (1620–1675) was a mathematician and editor of the works of Descartes.

93. P. reads, "in the chateau of Arberg."

94. Jacques-Barthelemy Micheli du Crest (1690–1766) worked as an engineer in Geneva and was an important republican opponent of the government. For an account of the significance of Rousseau's possession of this document, see Cranston, I, 126–127.

95. The baptism took place in April of 1737.

96. Adrien Baillet (1649–1706) wrote intellectual history, and Paul Colomiès (1638–1692) was a Protestant polemicist. In Book IV, 119, Rousseau comments on M. Simon's tendency to report old events as if they had just happened; therefore it is not surprising that he would use fifty-year old sources of news.

97. P. reads, "From his example, and aided by Ozanam's *Mathematical Recreations*, I wanted to make." Jacques Ozanam (1640–1717) wrote numerous works on mathematics. His *Mathematical and Physical Recreations* was published in 1694.

98. Invisible ink, which becomes visible when heated or put into contact with a "sympathetic" chemical.

99. This accident happened June 27, 1737.

100. P. reads, "devoured me even in."

101. P. omits, "in their fullness."

102. *The English Philosopher or History of Mr. Cleveland, the Natural Son of Cromwell, Written by Himself and Translated from the English*, by Antoine-François Prévost (1697–1763), was published in successive volumes between 1732 and 1739. The Abbé Prévost was the translator of Rousseau's favorite novelist, Samuel Richardson, and compiled the *Histoire générale des voyages*, which Rousseau cites in the *Second Discourse*. See *Collected Writings*, III, 72.

103. Gabriel Bagueret.

104. P. reads, "nastiest-looking men, in spite of his handsome appearance, and greatest fools."

105. P. reads, "this man did not fail to seize hold of."

106. The Calabrian is a treatise on chess written by Gioachino Greco, who was called the Calabrian. He made a fortune winning chess matches in the second half of the seventeenth century.

107. François-André Danican, or d'Anican, called Philodor (1726–1795), became famous as a chess player by the time he was eighteen. He was from a family of musicians and helped Rousseau a bit with the *Gallant Muses*. See Book VII, 279–280. He published his *Analysis of the Game of Chess* in 1748. Philippe Stamma was the author of the *Essay on the Game of Chess*, published in 1737.

108. The vapors were referred to frequently in the eighteenth century to denote a depression that could have either a physical or psychological cause. They came to be considered as a manifestation of hypochondria.

109. P. reads, "and perhaps she alone could have saved me."

110. P. reads "invincible nature would."

111. P. omits, "a short and precious interval."

112. Claude-François Noeray.

113. For some time this was one of the most disputed statements in the *Confessions* because of a lease showing that Mme de Warens took possession of M. Noeray's house in 1738. If it were true that she and Rousseau moved to the country only then, the period of happiness described in Book VI would not have taken place. Research by Hermine de Saussure and others has confirmed, however, that Rousseau and Mme de Warens lived in at least two houses in the valley of les Charmettes, beginning no later than 1737 and perhaps as early as 1736, as Rousseau says. For an account of the results of this research, see Cranston, I, 119–120. It is also worth noting that the final lease that allowed Mme de Warens to begin farming was signed shortly after Rousseau received his inheritance and that, therefore, he made a genuine financial contribution to their household.

114. Here P. adds, "End of Fifth Book."

EDITORS' NOTES TO BOOK VI

1. In P. the title is given as, "The Confessions of J.-J. Rousseau/*First Part*/Sixth Book."

2. "This is what I prayed for: a piece of land not so large, a garden, a stream of running water near the dwelling, and a very little grove of trees besides." This is the opening of Horace, *Satires*, II, vi, although Rousseau makes the grove very little rather than merely little as in the original and also makes a slight omission in the quotation. The continuation, which Rousseau gives immediately below, is, "More and better than this have the Gods done for me."

3. P. omits, "but tasted."

4. P. omits, "I left her and I was happy."

5. Pierre-Alexandre Du Peyrou (1729–1794) was born in Dutch Guiana and settled in Neuchâtel. Rousseau entrusted him with many of his papers and at one time was going to give him the *Confessions*. Their friendship underwent a crisis in November of 1767, when Rousseau's suspicions were at their height after his return from England. Subsequently, their relations were distant, but Du Peyrou did act as one of Rousseau's literary executors. For more on Du Peyrou, see Book XII, 504–505.

6. "In the worthless soul [or life]," that is, working on the living body rather than on the immortal soul.

7. P. reads "providence," rather than "nature."

8. On the issue of accepting the necessity of death for attaining happiness, see Kelly, 147–160.

9. On Mme de Warens's religious education, see Pléiade, I, 1345–46, note 2 to p. 228.

10. François de Salignac de la Mothe-Fénelon, Archbishop of Cambrai (1651–1715), was condemned by Rome for unorthodoxy. He was the author of *Telemachus*, a novel of education. This novel plays an important part in Emile's education. See *Emile*, V (Bloom, 404). In *Rousseau, Judge of Jean-Jacques*, Fénelon is mentioned as one of the very few examples of virtuous men in modern times. See *Collected Writings*, I, 158.

11. P. reads, "are not extremely scrupulous."

12. Jean-Baptiste Salomon (1683?–1757).

13. P. reads, "them," rather than "him."

14. The Oratory and Port-Royal were the centers of Jansenist scholarship in Paris. The Jansenists were opponents of the Jesuits. Blaise Pascal was among their leading thinkers.

15. Bernard Lamy (1640–1715) was the author of many books, especially on mathematics and sciences. He was censured because of his Cartesianism.

16. P. reads, "flatter," rather than "entice."

17. P. reads, "cooling," rather than "lessening."

18. Jean-Baptiste Bouchard (1707?–1747).

19. P. omits, "the best I could."

20. P. reads, "carry me under an oak."

21. P. reads, "cannot encompass all."

22. The *encyclopedia* in this sense is the whole of the sciences considered in their relations to each other.

23. In *Emile* Rousseau discusses the relative merits of the synthetic and analytic method of study. See *Emile*, III (Bloom, 171, and especially the editor's note to this passage). It should be kept in mind that Emile's education differs from Rousseau's in that it excludes books altogether, while at this point Rousseau's relies on books supplemented by occasional experiments like the one on sympathetic ink in Book V (p. 183).

24. P. reads, "and did not tire myself out at all."

25. P. reads, "pleasure," rather than "delight."

26. The *Logic* of Port-Royal is one of the Jansenist books referred to above. Locke's *Essay* is the *Essay on Human Understanding* by John Locke (1632–1704), which was translated into French in 1700. Nicholas de Malebranche (1638–1715) was a follower of Descartes. For an account of his influence on Rousseau, see Patrick Riley, *The General Will before Rousseau: The Transformation of the Divine into the Civic* (Princeton: Princeton University Press, 1986). Gottfried-Wilhelm Leibniz (1646–1716) is most famous for his claim that this is the best of all possible worlds. For Rousseau's discussion of this claim, see his letter to Voltaire of August 18, 1756 (*Collected Writings*, III, 108–121). In the *Responses* on the *Meditations*, René Descartes (1596–1650) discusses the synthetic and analytic methods

alluded to by Rousseau above. For a more complete list of authors studied by Rousseau at this time, as well as an account of his daily life, see *Le Verger de Madame la Baronne de Warens* (The Orchard of Madame la Baronne de Warens) in Pléiade, II, 1123–1129. This poem was first published in 1739 shortly after the period described here.

27. "In the words of the master." This is a reference to ancient Pythagoreans who attempted to preserve Pythagoras's teachings verbatim.

28. On Father Lamy, see editors' note 15 above.

29. Charles Reyneau (1656–1728) was an Oratorian like Father Lamy and Malebranche.

30. On Emile's study of geometry, which follows the spirit of this passage, see *Emile*, II (Bloom, 145–146).

31. P. reads, "feel," rather than "taste."

32. Denis Pétau (1583–1652) was a Jesuit, who wrote an *Abridged Chronology of Sacred and Profane Universal History*.

33. Emile also studies astronomy. See *Emile*, III (Bloom, 167–172). Rousseau consistently attributed his failure to study astronomy to his nearsightedness and to the necessity of using an instrument. See the Seventh Walk of the *Reveries*.

34. P. reads, "sky," rather than "stars."

35. See Letter III (Pléiade, III, 738), where Rousseau discusses his own performances of magic tricks as part of his argument against miracles.

36. Charles Hemet died in May 1738.

37. François Couppier (1679–1768).

38. For a discussion of this incident, see Jean Starobinski, *Jean-Jacques Rousseau: Transparency and Obstruction*, trans. Arthur Goldhammer (Chicago: University of Chicago Press, 1988), 166–167.

39. August 25.

40. P. reads, "chapel belonging to the house."

41. See Book III, 90.

42. Giovanni-Andrea Bontempi-Angelini (c. 1630–c. 1704) wrote a *Historia Musica* in which he discusses the question of whether the principles of harmony were practiced in ancient music, a subject that Rousseau is concerned with in the *Essay on the Origin of Languages*. Adriano Banchieri (1567–1634?) was the author of the *Cartella di Musica*, also called *Cartella Musicale*, which was published near the beginning of the seventeenth century. It was a sort of compendium of methods of composition and musical notation along with biographies of composers.

43. Rousseau reached the age of majority for Geneva on June 28, 1737, the day after the explosion of his chemistry experiment. See Book V, 183. He went to Geneva and concluded his legal business concerning his inheritance by July 31.

44. Rousseau is referring to the virtual civil war that broke out in Geneva in 1737, which he describes in Book V, 181.

45. The estate, which consisted in the house in which Rousseau was born, amounted to more than 30,000 florins in 1717. Because of Isaac Rousseau's debts, it was reduced to 13,000 florins at the time Rousseau took possession of his half. This share would have amounted to about 3,000 French francs. Rousseau received his brother's share after the death of his father in 1747. See Book VII, 284–285.

46. For a list of the books, see Pléiade, I, 1356, note 1 to p. 247.

47. P. reads, "and the good condition of one almost always spoils the other."

48. P. omits, "the decay of years and."

49. A similar case of the "vapors" plays an important role in *Julie*. Near the end of the novel Julie complains of a similar "distaste for well-being." See Pléiade, II, 686–702, and Voisine, 286, note 2.

50. M. Sauvages is probably Pierre-Augustin Boissier de la Croix de Sauvages (1710–1795). M. Fizes is Antoine Fizes (1690–1765).

51. P. omits this sentence.

52. See Book IV, 117, and note.

53. Mme du Colombier is thought to be the former Justine de Chabrière de La Roche who had been married in February of 1736. The meeting with Rousseau took place in September 1737.

54. Suzanne-Françoise de Larnage (1693–c. 1755). At the time of her relations with Rousseau, she was 44 and he was 25.

55. Rousseau uses a slang expression here, *"Faire un tour de casserole."*

56. The expression *femmes galantes* normally has the sense of "kept women," but Rousseau evidently uses it here in the older sense of women who enjoy socializing with men.

57. A supporter of the deposed Stuart monarchy living in exile. This is not quite as preposterous a masquerade as it might appear, for many Jacobites lived in Provence after the Stuart court was moved from St. Germain to Rome in 1715. This fact also explains Rousseau's fear of detection in the masquerade. See Voisine, 289, note 1.

58. Joseph Louis-Bernard de Blégiers, Marquis de Taulignan, was seventy-one at this time.

59. Anthony Hamilton (1646–1720) wrote the *Memoirs of the Life of the Count de Grammont*, about the Stuart Court.

60. P. reads, "I went with her. I behaved as I always did at church; that almost spoiled my business. From my."

61. *The Legacy* is a comedy by Marivaux in which a Marquis hesitates interminably between two women. He loves one, but he must pay a portion of his legacy to the other if he does not marry her. The play was first produced in 1736, not long before the events Rousseau is discussing here.

62. Céladon is the romantic hero of *Astrée*. See Book IV, 138.

63. P. reads, "bore," rather than "overcome."

64. P. reads, "evening," rather than "day."

65. This is probably Thomas Fitzmaurice, an Irishman who studied medicine at Montpellier and then remained there for the rest of his life.

66. P. reads, "several," rather than "most of."

67. P. reads, "amusing," rather than "pleasant."

68. Since Rousseau wrote a letter to Mme de Warens dated December 4 saying that he would be staying in Montpellier until February, his departure must have been somewhat later.

69. P. reads, "suppressed while I was coming. While."

70. P. omits, "dishonor."

71. P. reads, "this resolution," rather than "it."

72. This is an example of a virtuous, rather than merely, good action. In the latter, one would be following a personal inclination while performing a good deed, whereas in this case, Rousseau is overcoming a personal inclination in order to perform a less pleasant good deed. It should also be noted that Rousseau leaves open the possibility that virtue and a certain sort of pride are indistinguishable both in practice and in principle.

73. P. reads, "firm," rather than "good."

74. Jean-Samuel-Rodolphe Wintzenried de Courtilles (1712–1772) was, in fact, the son of a member of the gentry from the Pays de Vaud. Like Mme de Warens and Rousseau, he was a convert to Catholicism. As Rousseau says, Wintzenried had become part of the household before his departure for Montpellier. There is good reason to believe that Rousseau was aware of the newcomer's relations with Mamma long before his return to Chambéry. See Cranston, I, 132–135.

75. Spelling based on the provincial pronunciation of Leander, a stock name for a handsome rustic swain.

76. P. reads, "friendship," rather than "attachment."

77. The use of the plural for an abstract noun like "adoration" is as unusual in French as it is in English. See André Wyss, *La Langue de J.-J. Rousseau* (Geneva: Editions Slatkine, 1989), 99–100, for a discussion of this example.

78. On Mme Deybens (or d'Eybens), see above, Book V, 180. Jean Bonnot de Mably was chief of gendarmerie for several provinces. He was the father of François-Paul-Marie Bonnot de Mably (Sainte-Marie) and Jean-Antoine Bonnot de Mably (Condillac). The older of the two boys was under six and the younger under five when Rousseau became their tutor in April of 1740. He remained with the Mably household until May of 1741. On Rousseau's plans for the education he was to give the boys see "Mémoire presenté à Monsieur de Mably sur l'éducation de M. son fils" and "Projet pour l'éducation de Monsieur de Sainte Marie" (Pléiade, IV, 3–51).

79. P. reads, "*Condillac*, from the name of his uncle who has since become so famous." The uncle is Etienne Bonnot de Condillac (1715–1780), the author of the *Essay on the Origin of Human Knowledge* and *Treatise on Sensations*. On Rousseau's relations with him, see Book VII, 291. In the *Second Discourse* Rousseau relies on and corrects Condillac's account of the origin of language. See *Collected Writings*, III, 29–33.

80. These are precisely the instruments against which Rousseau argues in *Emile*. See, for example, Bloom, 89–90, 96–97, and 168–69. The passage at p. 90 is a particularly good example of how a child can be incapable of understanding a certain level of reason and yet be extremely reasonable at the same time.

81. P. reads, "thought I could soften him."

82. P. reads, "soon even I was discouraged seeing."

83. Compare this with the passage in Book I, 27, where Rousseau argues that once one has acquired the inclination to steal, whether one does so or not will depend on the circumstances in which one is placed. For example, all apprentices acquire such inclinations but cease stealing when circumstances give them property of their own.

84. This passage is frequently cited to show that Marie-Antoinette was not the

original source for this remark. See Voisine, 310. The word translated as "cake" is *brioche*.

85. P. reads, "see," rather than "find."

86. P. reads, "eyes," rather than "welcome."

87. P. reads, "would not fail to be seized and perhaps."

88. On the Hiero-fountain, see Book III, 85. Rousseau left Savoy in the Summer of 1742.

89. Here P. reads, "End/of the Sixth Book, and of the First Part." Rousseau temporarily gave up his plan of continuing the *Confessions* in November of 1767, shortly after his quarrel with Du Peyrou.

EDITORS' NOTES TO BOOK VII

1. Etienne-François Duc de Choiseul (1719–1785) became minister of Foreign Affairs in 1758 and subsequently was also minister of War and of the Navy. He was the virtual head of the French government until his fall from power in 1770. For Rousseau's relations with him, see Book XI, 482–483.

2. Marie-Charlotte-Hippolyte de Campet de Saujon, Comtesse de Boufflers (1724–1800), and Marie-Madeleine, Marquise de Verdelin (1728–1810), were responsible for persuading Rousseau to accept Hume's invitation to seek refuge in England. See Books XI and XII.

3. This note occurs only in the Geneva manuscript, at the beginning of the second notebook that contains Part Two of the *Confessions*. In the Paris manuscript, Book VII is contained in the first notebook, although it is still designated as belonging to the second part. The part of this note in brackets was scratched out by Rousseau, presumably after Choiseul's fall from power at the end of 1770 and Rousseau's partial reconciliation with Mme de Verdelin in 1771. See Voisine, 317, note 1, and Pléiade, I, 1369, note 1 to p. 273.

4. On this epigraph, see Book I, editors' note 3.

5. In addition to numbering paragraphs, P. gives chapter numbers beginning here with 1.

6. Rousseau began writing Part Two in November of 1769, two years after deciding not to continue the *Confessions*.

7. P. reads, "draw," rather than "develop."

8. Since in general virtue requires (and is almost identical to) strength, Rousseau is not suggesting much here beyond the claim that he has preserved his goodness.

9. P. reads, "with as much simplicity as innocence, left."

10. In P. the remainder of this paragraph reads,
succession of my being, and whose impression is not at all erased from my heart. These feelings remind me of the events which caused them to be born enough to enable me to claim that I am narrating them faithfully, and if there is found some omission, some transposition of facts or dates, which can take place only in immaterial things which have made little impression on me, enough monuments for each fact remain to put it in its place easily in the order of the ones I will have indicated. The particular object of my confessions is to make my interior known exactly in all the situations of my life. It is the history

of my soul I have promised, and henceforward this history becomes all the more interesting, since it is the key to a web of events that are well-known to the whole world, but which will never be explained reasonably without this.
This version of the paragraph was originally in G. also, but was crossed out and replaced with the version in the text.

11. This collection originally was intended to form a part of the *Confessions*. In Appendix I, we have included translations of the letters from this collection to which Rousseau makes specific references in the text.

12. Argus was a giant with eyes all over his body who was used as a watchman by Hera.

13. P. reads, "some enlightenment about the truth of the facts, either."

14. Apology in the sense of vindication or defense, as in Plato's *Apology of Socrates*.

15. P. reads, "but, after the exposition of my project, he ought not."

16. Rousseau stayed at the Chateau of Trye, which belonged to the Prince de Conti, after his return from England. He was there from June of 1767 until June of 1768.

17. P. reads, "enjoyments for me."

18. P. reads, "hastily and furtively throw."

19. This extreme passage gives a good indication of Rousseau's emotional state when he began writing Part Two. It should be kept in mind that his fears were not delusional in every respect. From the time he first let it be known that he was writing the *Confessions* and that it would contain his version of his quarrels, many people (including Hume and Diderot) were concerned to find out what he was saying or to preempt his account by publicizing their own versions of events. The culmination of this occurred in 1771 when Mme d'Epinay sought government intervention to prevent Rousseau from giving readings from the *Confessions* even in private homes.

20. In G. the numbering of paragraphs is omitted for the next eight paragraphs. We have reproduced the numbering in P. in brackets.

21. There is some controversy over the date of this visit to Lyon and Rousseau's departure for Paris, but some grounds exist for accepting Rousseau's account.

22. Gabriel Bonnot, Abbé de Mably (1709–1785), was a member of the ministry of foreign affairs, an historian, and an economist.

23. On Fontenelle, see Book I, 8. Anne-Claude-Philippe, Comte de Caylus (1692–1765), was an archeologist, art critic, and translator.

24. P. reads, "showing me goodwill and friendship."

25. Charles Bordes (1711–1781). For his later relations with Rousseau, see Book VIII, 280–284.

26. The Pléiade edition neglects to begin a paragraph here.

27. On the Duc de Richelieu, see Book VII, 280–284.

28. P. reads, "which I did several times, as will be said below. Nevertheless that high acquaintance, which did not fail to have consequences, was never useful to me for anything."

29. Jacques David (1683–c. 1750) was music master for the Academy of Fine Arts at Lyon.

30. P. reads, "He had loaned me a cap and some stockings which he has never

asked me to give back and which I have never given back to him. However, later on."

31. On Perrichon and Parisot, see Book V, 180, editors' note 86. The poet Pierre-Auguste Barnard (1710–1775) was given the nickname "the noble Bernard" (*"Gentil Bernard"*) by Voltaire.

32. In P. this note has the word "principle," rather than "consequence" in the second sentence. The shrewish character of Socrates' wife, Xanthippe, is famous. Dion, who was a friend of Plato, was assassinated by Calippus. Rousseau married Thérèse Levasseur in 1768 in a sort of civil ceremony. Since he had reconverted to Protestantism at the time, it would have been impossible for them to be legally married in France.

33. P. reads, "witness to it assiduously and exactitude in writing has always been beyond my strength. Thus I have been."

34. See Book IV, 143.

35. P. reads, "tradesman," rather than "merchant."

36. Jean-Victor Genève (1715–c. 1778) signed the marriage contract with Mlle Serre in 1742. The religious ceremony did not take place until 1745 after the birth of their son.

37. In fact, she was still alive in 1755.

38. The numbering of paragraphs resumes here in G. The chapter number is only in P.

39. Poet and playwright Jean-Baptiste-Louis Gresset (1709–1777).

40. Jean-Baptiste-Louis Vulliet de la Saunière, Comte d'Amézin (1704–1793), who later married Rousseau's former pupil Mlle de Menthon; Anne-Thérèse Princesse de Carignan (1717–1745); Claude Gros de Boze (1680–1753); and Louis-Bertrand Castel (1688–1757). Father Castel's ocular clavichord attempted to produce the effect of music by using colors rather than sounds. Rousseau criticizes it in the *Essay on the Origin of Languages*. Father Castel wrote attacks on the *Letter on French Music* and *Second Discourse*.

41. P. omits this last sentence of the paragraph.

42. Antoine-Alexandre de Gasq (1712–1781) and Louis-August de Chabot, Abbé de Léon then Vicomte de Rohan, then Vicomte de Chabot (1722–1753). The title President *à Mortier* refers to the cap or mortar board worn by some presidents of the parlements as a mark of dignity.

43. René-Antoine Feschault de Réaumur (1683–1757), geometrician, naturalist, and inventor of the Réaumur thermometer.

44. The memorandum is entitled, *Project Concerning New Signs for Music*.

45. Jean-Jacques Dortous de Mairan (1678–1771) was a mathematician; Jean Hellot (1685–1766) was a chemist; and Jean Paul de Fouchy was an astronomer.

46. Jean-Jacques Souhaitti, or Souhaitty, wrote a *New Elements of the Plain Chant, or Essay on a New Discovery That Has Been Made in the Art of Singing*, in 1677. As Rousseau says, it applies numbers only to the plain chant.

47. P. reads, "but they are bad in that for each interval they demand an operation of the mind."

48. P. reads, "at first glance I see that one is joined to the other by conjoined degrees."

49. The *Dissertation on Modern Music* was published in January of 1743 by

Gabriel-François Quillau. The "privilege" is the exclusive right of publication granted to the bookseller by the government. It is somewhat comparable to a copyright.

50. A liard was 1/80th of a franc.

51. Pierre-François Guyot, Abbé Desfontaines (1685–1745), was a leading literary critic. He wrote a generally favorable review of the *Dissertation on Modern Music* that appeared in *Observations on Modern Writings*, February 1, 1743. Rousseau wrote a response to the review that appeared in the *Historical Journal*, March 1743.

52. P. reads, "gain a lot of time."

53. P. reads, "not extremely burdened."

54. P. reads, "I was thirty years old, I was a grown man, and I found myself."

55. See Book VII, 266–267.

56. P. reads, "I had for someone to look after me was."

57. P. omits, "almost."

58. See Book VIII, 294–295.

59. P. reads, "prisoners," rather than "captives."

60. This story is in Plutarch's life of Nicias, although it involves Euripides rather than Homer.

61. P. reads, "at the Café Maugis."

62. In P. this paragraph is numbered 14.

63. Mme de Besenval, or Bezenval, was of Polish origin and married to Jean-Victor de Besenval de Bronstatt, de Soleure. Rousseau's spelling of her name varies, especially in this and the following paragraphs.

64. In P. this paragraph is numbered 4.1.

65. P. reads, "After having put off the performance of this terrible conscripted labor for a long time, at last I."

66. Guillaume de Lamoignon, Seigneur de Blancmesnil and de Malesherbes (1683–1772), held a number of important government positions. He was the father of Chrétien-Guillaume de Lamoignon de Malesherbes, who was director of publishing for all of Rousseau's literary career.

67. In P. this paragraph is numbered 14.

68. This letter can be found in Pléiade, II, 1136–1143.

69. *The Confessions of the Comte de* *** was written by Charles Pinot de Duclos (1704–1772). It had just been published when Mme de Broglie gave Rousseau a copy. Duclos's best-known work is *Considerations on the Morals of This Century*, published in 1751. He became Royal Historian and Permanent Secretary of the French Academy.

70. P. reads, "sometimes," rather than "often."

71. Instead of this note, P. gives one that reads, "That is what I would always have thought if I had not returned to Paris."

72. Françoise-Thérèse de La Touche (1712–1767) was the wife of Nicolas Vallet, Seigneur de La Touche, and became the mistress of the Duke of Kingston. Her sister, Marie-Louise de Fontaine d'Arty or Darty (1719–1765?), was the wife of Antoine-Alexis Paneau and became the mistress of the Prince de Conti (1717–1776). Rousseau's statement that she was "sole and sincere friend" of the Prince

tacitly suggests that the Comtesse de Boufflers (another of the Prince's mistresses) was not a sincere friend. Louise-Marie-Madeleine Dupin (1706 or 1708–1799) was the wife of Claude Dupin (1681–1769), who was a wealthy tax farmer.

73. P. reads, "with her nevertheless."

74. P. reads, "In sum, her house."

75. The insignia of the order of knights of the Holy Spirit.

76. The Princesse de Rohan (1725–1781) was the former Marie-Louise-Henriette-Jeanne de la Tour d'Auvergne. Marie-Françoise de Forcalquier, also born in 1725, was nicknamed *Bellissima* in the salons she frequented. Anne-Marguerite-Gabrielle de Mirepoix is discussed in Book XI, 488. Mme *de* Brignole (not Brignolé) was probably Anna Balbi (1702–1774), the Marquise de Brignole-Sale who was sister-in-law of the Doge of Venice. Mary Lady Hervey (1700–1768) was the wife of Lord Hervey of Ickworth, first Count of Bristol. Charles Castel de Saint-Pierre (1658–1743) was most famous as the author of the *Project of Perpetual Peace* that Rousseau edited. See Book IX, 342–343. Claude Sallier (1685–1733) was a philologist and member of the French Academy. There are three members of the Fourmont family, each of whom was an orientalist. See Voisine, 995. François-Joachim de Pierres de Bernis (1715–1794) was a poet and Minister of Foreign Affairs. George-Louis Leclerc de Buffon (1707–1788) was the Intendant of the King's Garden. His *Natural History* began to be published in 1749. Rousseau frequently refers to him with admiration, particularly in the *Second Discourse*. On Voltaire's influence on Rousseau, see Book V, 179.

77. On M. de Francueil, see Book I, 32, editors' note 89.

78. P. reads, "only the desire to obey."

79. Jacques-Armand Dupin de Chenonceaux (1730–1767) lived a dissolute life and, after being sent on a long ocean voyage by his father, died on Mauritius, not Réunion (Isle de Bourbon). Rousseau gives a version of their few days together in Book II of *Emile*. See Bloom, 121–124.

80. Guillaume-François Rouelle (1703–1770) was a famous chemistry teacher and demonstrator at the King's Garden.

81. Joseph Royer (c. 1700–c. 1795) was a musician and composer. In 1743 his opera, *The Power of Love*, was being performed.

82. P. reads, "dream," rather than "think."

83. P. reads, "I composed verses, songs, duos."

84. Rousseau devotes an article to this Italian musical term in his *Dictionary of Music*. In this article he says "An Air, a piece *di prima intenzione*, is the one that is formed, suddenly, completely and with all its Parts in the mind of the Composer, just as Pallas emerged entirely armed from the brain of Jupiter. Pieces *di prima intenzione* are from these rare strokes of genius, all of whose ideas are so closely connected that they make up, so to speak, only a single one, and cannot be present to the mind except together." In a way Rousseau's sudden inspiration with his system of thought could be considered a piece *di prima intenzione*. See Book VIII, 294–295.

85. P. reads, "I had formerly written."

86. Nicolas-Charles-Joseph, Abbé Trublet (1697–1770), was a man of letters and was later employed as a government censor.

87. Rousseau, in fact, did not destroy these works. For *Iphis and Anaxeretes* and *The Discovery of the New World*, see Pléiade, II, 797–842. Giovanni Battista Buononcini (1672–1748?) was a successful composer and was a rival of Handel in London in the early eighteenth century.

88. For the text of the final version of *The Gallant Muses*, see Pléiade, II, 1049–1078.

89. Oestrus is derived from the Greek and Latin words for gadfly. It is used to describe the frenzy into which one is driven by the gadfly's stings and, by extension, to any sort of frenzy.

90. P. reads, "in the arms of the foremost beauty of the universe."

91. Pierre-François-Auguste, Comte de Montaigu (1692–1764).

92. Barjac was the confidential servant of the Cardinal de Fleury.

93. P. reads, "he very assiduously."

94. Louis-Gabriel-Christophe, the Chevalier de Montaigu, was a member of the group of companions for the Dauphin, called gentlemen of the sleeve. They were given this name because they were not allowed to hold the young prince by the hand. See Voisine, 345, note 2.

95. P. reads, "the new Ambassador."

96. Rousseau demanded the equivalent of 1,200 francs and was offered 1,000.

97. P. reads, "a little Abbé."

98. In fact, it does appear that Rousseau made a side trip to Chambéry from Lyon, but Mme de Warens may not have been there. He left Paris July 10 and arrived at Venice September 4, 1743.

99. P. reads, "at Toulon for Genoa, as much for reasons of economy as to acquire."

100. The plague killed half the population of Messina, about 40,000 people. The French and British navies were cooperating in the quarantine operation to prevent a spread of the plague.

101. A felucca is a small ship with both oars and sails.

102. P. reads, "a long and tiring crossing."

103. A lazaretto is a quarantine station.

104. P. reads, "like another Robinson."

105. Rousseau had a great fondness for *Robinson Crusoe*. It is the first book Emile is allowed to read. See *Emile*, III (Bloom, 184–188).

106. P. reads, "to that poor man," rather than "to such a man."

107. Charles-François, Comte de Froulay, or Froullay (1683–1744), had been Ambassador to Venice from 1733 to 1738.

108. P. reads, "although he understood nothing about it himself."

109. The word "Conferent" does not correspond to any title at Venice. It is also not used in French outside of Rousseau's letters and the *Confessions*. In a letter he explains that a conferent is a senator appointed by the Republic of Venice to carry on negotiations with a foreign ambassador. See Voisine, 350, note 2.

110. France joined Spain in the War of the Austrian Succession just after Rousseau's arrival in Venice in 1743. For a useful discussion of the political situation faced by the embassy, see Cranston, I, 168–171. The whole of Cranston's chapter on Rousseau's stay in Venice is extremely useful.

111. A sequin was worth between 11 and 12 francs.

112. P. omits, "and that a single Frenchman paid it."

113. P. reads, "he would gain."

114. P. reads, "ribbon and all the rest without him."

115. P. omits, "and which I dressed up."

116. Amelot was secretary of state for Foreign Affairs; Maurepas, secretary of state for the Navy; the Marquis de Lanmary (not M. Havrincourt, who was appointed in 1749), ambassador to Sweden; and the Marquis de La Chétardie, ambassador to the Czar.

117. P. reads, "tempted me to."

118. This note is not in P.

119. "A masked Lady." This was a formula for the introduction of a masked person, male or female. See Voisine, 357, note 1. A Domino is a short cloak used along with a mask.

120. P. omits, "I have forgotten the name of the Vessel."

121. This incident took place on July 6, 1744.

122. P. omits, "and hardly wanted to sign the statement after me."

123. P. reads, "Carrio, a man of merit and."

124. P. omits, "which is notable for a man as negligent and as heedless as I am."

125. P. omits, "on a receipt."

126. Rousseau did not finally settle the bill until 1749. The three sequins he offered would have been about 20 per cent of the full amount.

127. Rousseau mistakes or exaggerates the importance of the event. The notification from Vincent was received October 26, 1743, and forwarded immediately by Montaigu. The military events Rousseau refers to did not happen until the Spring of 1744.

128. The French version of *Bailo*, the title of the Venetian ambassador.

129. P. reads, "necessity," rather than "position."

130. P. reads, "Vitali who kept the keys was not there."

131. P. reads, "and above all about himself."

132. Montaigu, who himself had not been paid his salary by the Foreign Ministry, had not paid Rousseau any of his salary or travel expenses.

133. P. reads, "rascals," rather than "bandits."

134. P. reads, "good," rather than "upright."

135. For Montaigu's version of this story, see Cranston, I, 188.

136. P. reads, "about it more moderately."

137. P. reads, "asked him only to."

138. P. reads, "I never in my life saw him."

139. P. reads, "between you and me."

140. For Montaigu's version of this story, see Cranston, I, 189–190.

141. Songs sung by gondoliers as they row their boats.

142. P. reads, "of its enormous length."

143. "Protect me the beautiful one for whom my heart burns so much." The work within which these lines occur has not been found.

144. P. reads, "Even ugliness."

145. P. reads, "rather often in the winter."

146. P. reads, "I have always had an aversion for prostitutes."

147. P. reads, "entrance to the good houses of the country."

148. P. reads, "I knew that when one does not have a well-furnished purse one ought not to get mixed up in making love, especially in Venice."

149. P. reads, "sad," rather than "fatal."

150. P. reads, "One evening at table."

151. P. reads, "sensible," rather than "wise."

152. P. reads, "that I do not understand myself."

153. "So as not to appear too much of a blockhead." "*Coglione*" literally means "testicle."

154. Apparently Giustina Padoana, a courtisan who had been involved in a scandal in 1742.

155. P. reads, "La Padoana had a good enough appearance."

156. A ducat was the equivalent of 3 to 4 French francs.

157. P. reads, "that I experienced for more than three weeks, although no incommodity, no apparent sign authorized it."

158. P. reads, "deserve it from their rank as much as."

159. P. reads, "it was out of vanity rather than greed."

160. "In intimate dress."

161. P. reads, "character," rather than "natural disposition."

162. P. reads, "felt," rather than "known."

163. The term translated as "malformed nipple" is "*téton borgne*." *Borgne* is usually used to describe someone with an eye missing as on p. 265. Consequently some commentators have assumed that Zulietta was severely deformed. Rousseau's close examination revealing that one nipple is formed differently from the other suggests that the malformation was rather small. Perhaps it is his bizarre concern with precise measurement that inspires Zulietta's remark, "Zanetto, leave the Ladies alone, and study mathematics."

164. In fact, not quite twelve. Rousseau left Venice on August 22, 1744.

165. This had been an established practice in Venice for some time.

166. P. reads, "I became less."

167. P. reads, "my behavior and demand justice. From Venice."

168. M. de la Closure had not been French Resident in Geneva since 1739.

169. P. omits, "nothing more."

170. A quintal is 50 kg, or about 110 pounds.

171. P. reads, "would be worth the effort," rather than "deserved."

172. This note does not occur in P.

173. P. reads, "Everyone privately agreed."

174. This could be translated "society," rather than "the society," but the full name for the Jesuits is the Society of Jesus, which was frequently referred to as "the society." Furthermore, in Book XII Rousseau refers to the Jesuits' "old maxim of crushing the unfortunate." See Book XII, 507.

175. See Book VI, 203.

176. Guillaume-François Berthier (1704–1782) was a professor of philosophy and theology. Montesquieu's *Spirit of the Laws*, published in 1748, contains criticism of the French system of tax-farmers. M. Dupin, who was a tax-farmer, wrote

a response to Montesquieu along with Father Berthier. Rousseau also worked on this book. *Reflections on Some Parts of a Book Entitled: On the Spirit of the Laws* was published in 1749. On this book and a sequel to it, see Cranston, I, 213–215.

177. P. reads, "of the high sciences. Nothing."

178. P. omits, "bigot."

179. P. omits, "or put up with bother."

180. P. reads, "to join him in Azcoitia."

181. Don Manuel-Ignacio Altuna Portu was married in 1749 and died in 1763.

182. Rousseau probably met Thérèse Levasseur (1721–1801) in 1745. She was the daughter of François and Marie Levasseur. Rousseau's spelling of Thérèse's name is not consistent.

183. See Book VII, 237.

184. P. omits, "I was ready not to know what to think about her any more."

185. P. omits, "of joy."

186. P. reads, "never learned how to."

187. P. reads, "always," rather than "often."

188. P. reads, "this quiet and domestic life was so advantageous."

189. Alexandre-Jean-Joseph Le Riche de la Pouplinière (not Popliniére) was a wealthy tax farmer and patron of the arts.

190. P. reads, "for Singers, Berard, La Garde, and Mlle Boubonnois." They were all leading singers at the Opera.

191. On the Duc de Richelieu, see Book VII, 235.

192. The *Menus Plaisirs* were the royally sponsored ceremonies, festivals, and entertainments.

193. François Francoeur (1698–1787) was inspector of the Royal Academy of Music and later on director of the Opera.

194. In fact Rousseau's letter asks for Voltaire's approval to changes he had already made.

195. Voltaire's letter actually read, "counting either upon."

196. Both Voltaire's original and P. read, "that you have filled in the gaps and compensated for everything."

197. Voltaire's original reads, "I feel very well."

198. Voltaire's original reads, "it is rather beneath a thinking being to make a serious business for himself out of these bagatelles;"

199. "Oh Death! Come end the misfortunes of my life."

200. P. reads, "words," rather than "verses."

201. P. reads, "until the performance before the King, he did."

202. It appears that Voltaire was not named either.

203. To assist Prince Charles, the Stuart pretender to the British throne.

204. Rousseau's father died on May 9, 1747, at the age of 75.

205. See Book VIII, 328–329.

206. P. omits, "Le Duc."

207. Pierre de Jelyotte (1713–1787 or 1797) was a famous singer and director at the Opera.

208. François Rebel (1701–1775) was a violinist, composer, and conductor and co-director of the Opera along with Francoeur.

209. P. reads, "they had grafted my talents onto theirs."

210. In fact, Rousseau was extremely busy at this time. For Mme Dupin he made thousands of pages of extracts for a book she was writing on the rights of women and wrote a 330-page draft of this book under her dictation. He also wrote a manuscript on the *History of the Emperors of Constantinople*. He also worked on the refutation of Montesquieu's *Spirit of the Laws*. See Pléiade, I, 1413–1414, note 2 to p. 342.

211. They wrote a manuscript of over 1,200 pages called *Chemical Institutions*. This work can be found in the *Annales J.-J. Rousseau* (1918–1919 and 1920–1921).

212. P. omits, "if I ever write one."

213. See Pléiade, II, 875–932.

214. This was published in the *Mercury* in 1750, shortly after Rousseau won the prize for the *First Discourse*.

215. P. reads, "I had put into progress more."

216. P. reads, "anecdotes," rather than "news."

217. For *The Prisoners of War*, see Pléiade, II, 843–874. It was probably begun in 1743 before Rousseau went to Venice.

218. Rousseau is quite correct to refer to "the practice of the country." The foundling hospitals were founded in the Seventeenth Century by Saint Vincent de Paul. In 1750 roughly 20 per cent of the children baptized in Paris were admitted to the foundling hospitals. Baptisms would account for a very high percentage of the births aside from the infants who were simply abandoned to die. By the 1770s the figure was over 40 per cent. Rousseau himself made note of the figures for 1758 which included 5,082 children admitted to the foundling hospitals out of 19,148 baptisms (slightly over 25 per cent). See *Collected Writings*, IV, 53. The mortality rate for infants in the hospitals was somewhere around 70 per cent. For other children in France the mortality rate varied widely based on locality and other circumstances. For example, in Normandy the infant mortality rate was 15 per cent, in provincial cities it was more typically 35 to 40 per cent. Among children in Paris who were put out to nurse (i.e., children of parents who were well-off), it was over 50 per cent and by some estimates considerably higher. See Pléiade, I, 1415–1416, note 3 to p. 344; Leigh 2, 145–146 and especially Pierre Goubert, "Historical Demography and the Reinterpretation of Early Modern French History: A Research View," in *The Family in History*, ed. by Theodore K. Rabb and Robert I. Rothberg (New York: Harper & Row, 1971), 16–27. For discussions of the significance and truth of Rousseau's admission that he had his children given to the foundling hospital, see Pléiade, I, 1416–1422, note 1 to p. 345, and Voisine, 405–407, note 1. Rousseau's frequent denials that he had abandoned his children were based on the precise but strained distinction between abandoning (for example, leaving on church steps as had happened to d'Alembert), and placing them in the hospitals. On this distinction, see Rousseau's letter to Mme de Francueil in Appendix I, 551–552.

219. P. reads, "to la Gouin's at the Pointe St. Eustache to have her."

220. One of these secrets is the fact that Mme d'Epinay gave Francueil a case of venereal disease which she had contracted from her husband. She tells the story, herself, in her pseudo-memoirs, *The History of Madame de Montbrillant*.

Another secret, which she attempted to cover up, was that her second daughter was Francueil's child rather than her husband's.

221. Elisabeth-Sophie-Françoise Lalive de Bellegarde (1730–1813) married the Comte d'Houdetot on February 28, 1748.

222. P. reads, "marriage, she had me look at the apartment they were preparing for her; and she chatted."

223. See Book IX, 369–370.

224. P. reads, "My Therese, at least as good-looking."

225. The *Essay on the Origin of Human Knowledge* was published in 1746.

226. P. reads, "appointments even with women never."

227. See Pléiade, I, 1103–1112, for the sketch of the first pamphlet.

228. Ephraim Chambers published his *Cyclopedia: Or an Universal Dictionary of Arts and Sciences* in 1728. Robert James's *Medical Dictionary* was published in 1743.

229. Rousseau worked on this articles from the end of 1748 through the beginning of 1749. His articles were on Cadence, Cantata, Cantabile, Chant, Chiffres, Coeur, Composition, and Consonance.

230. The *Philosophic Thoughts* were burned by a decree of the Paris Parlement in 1746. The *Letter on the Blind for the Use of Those Who See* was published in June of 1749, and Diderot was put in the Keep at Vincennes on July 24, 1749. He was given his final release on November 3, 1749.

231. P. adds, "End of Seventh Book."

EDITORS' NOTES TO BOOK VIII

1. P. reads, "The Confessions of J.-J. Rousseau/Second Part/Eighth Book."

2. Frederick, Crown Prince of Saxe-Gotha (1735–1756), had a tutor named von Thun whose first name is not known.

3. The Abbé Seguy (whose name Rousseau spells correctly immediately below) had published the *Complete Works* of Jean-Baptiste Rousseau in 1743.

4. P. reads, "Fontenay-aux-Roses," rather than "Fontenay-sous-Bois."

5. Emanuel-Christoph Klüpfel, which Rousseau consistently spells Klupffell (1712–1776).

6. Friedrich-Melchior Grimm (1723–1807) had studied philosophy and law in Leipzig. He is best-known for his *Literary Correspondence*, through which he sent news about Parisian intellectual life to a number of German courts and nobility. This sort of private journal began publication in 1753 and continued until 1793, although Grimm played a lesser role in it in the later years. In 1775 Grimm became the government of Saxe-Cobourg-Gotha's minister in Paris.

7. P. reads, "some Italian music."

8. After twenty days in the keep, Diderot admitted his authorship of the *Letter on the Blind* and agreed not to publish anything in the future without its prior submission for censorship. The easier terms of his imprisonment began on August 21, 1749, and Rousseau's visit took place approximately August 25.

9. Jean Le Rond d'Alembert (1717–1783) was a famous mathematician, member of numerous academies, and co-editor of the *Encyclopedia*.

10. P. reads, "after this transport was."

11. The question, "Has the restoration of the sciences and arts tended to purify morals?," appeared in the *Mercury* of October 1749. For his answer, Rousseau altered the question to include the possibility of corruption rather than purification. See *Collected Writings*, II, 4. Here he alters it again, giving precedence to corruption and indicating the progress rather than the restoration of the sciences and arts. This version most accurately reflects the contents of the *First Discourse*.

12. P. reads, "set them down on paper in."

13. See Appendix I, 575–576.

14. See *Collected Writings*, II, 11. A prosopopeia is a rhetorical device in which an absent (in this case, dead) figure is presented as speaking.

15. P. reads, "tree," rather than "oak."

16. There has been some discussion about how much Diderot influenced the substance of the *Discourse*. His own account confirms Rousseau's. It is clear that he encouraged Rousseau very strongly, even though he did not agree with his position fully. See Cranston, I, 235. It has also been shown that Rousseau relied on a translation of Plato's *Apology* that Diderot was working on while he was at Vincennes. On these points, see the introduction to the *First Discourse* in *Collected Writings*, II, xiv, note 10.

17. P. reads, "effect and consequence of."

18. As Rousseau indicates in Book IX, ooo, the period of effervescence ended with his move to the country in April of 1756.

19. Auguste-Henri, Comte de Friese, or von Friesen (1728–1755).

20. Approximately 1,250 francs.

21. *Lieutenant-Criminel* is the title of the magistrate in Paris criminal courts. On the application of this nickname to Thérèse, see Book IX, 404. There Grimm uses only the portion "Criminal."

22. P. omits, "that is to say craftiness."

23. P. reads, "who by agreement did not."

24. This is in *Julie*, Pléiade, II, 294–297.

25. P. reads, "I had fully and freely put."

26. P. reads, "such an extraordinary man."

27. Pope Joan is a legendary character who is said to have been an English-woman who disguised herself as a man in order to study at Rome and was subsequently elected Pope.

28. The prize was announced July 9, 1750.

29. P. reads, "for all my fellows."

30. P. reads, "without innermost emotions, without morals, a denatured."

31. P. reads, "was such, that from then on I no longer looked at my relations with Therese as anything but an honest and healthy engagement, although free and voluntary, and as long as it might last I looked at my faithfulness to her as an indispensable duty, at the infraction that I had made of it a single time as a genuine adultery, and as for my children by abandoning them to public education."

32. P. reads, "to everyone from whom our relations were not hidden; I."

33. Dr. François Thierry.

34. For this letter, see Appendix I, 551–553. It has been suggested that the reasons Rousseau did not mention in this letter concerned fears that the children

would inherit criminal tendencies from the Levasseur family. It is certain that in this letter he is silent about Mme Levasseur's role in persuading Thérèse to give up the children.

35. G. omits the material in brackets, apparently inadvertently. In P. this passage reads, "from the blame I deserve, I would rather be burdened with it than with the blame they deserve themselves."

36. P. omits, "those are not faults;"

37. Louise-Alexandrine-Julie de Rochechouart-Pontville, the daughter of the Vicomte and Vicomtesse de Rochechouart, married Chenonceaux sometime between 1749 and 1751. She later asked Rousseau to set down his thoughts on education, a project that turned into *Emile*.

38. P. reads, "briskly somehow or other. I."

39. P. reads, "for nearly six weeks."

40. Sauveur-François Morand (1697–1773) was a prominent surgeon and member of the Academy of Sciences.

41. Jacques Daran (1701–1784) later became surgeon-ordinary to the king.

42. P. reads, "inserted and in overcoming the obstruction. But."

43. P. reads, "walk proudly and alone."

44. P. reads, "to give an example which they did not want to follow and which seemed to be troublesome to them."

45. When he was forced to leave France after the condemnation of *Emile*, Rousseau was obliged to give up his profession. He resumed it in 1770 and practiced it until close to the end of his life. During this period he estimated that he copied 11,000 pages in seven and a half years.

46. P. omits, "When it had won the prize."

47. The *Discourse* was published in January of 1751.

48. P. omits, "in spite of the internal feeling."

49. This is a nickname given to Thérèse and her mother. The term, "*Gouverneuses*" is almost always used in a jocular way to indicate a sort of governess. Rousseau also refers to Thérèse as his "*gouvernante*," or housekeeper.

50. P. reads, "the principal basis."

51. P. omits, "and finally disappeared completely."

52. Jean Helvétius, the father of Claude-Adrien Helvétius (1715–1771), author of the very controversial *On Mind*.

53. Paul-Jacques Malouin (1701–1778) was a well-known doctor and member of the Academy of Sciences.

54. P. omits, "and without which I did not believe I could live anymore."

55. P. omits, "even in case Daran was not available."

56. P. reads, "I must have used fifty Louis's worth."

57. A character in Molière's *l'Amour médecin* whose name became synonymous with giving self-interested advice. Central to Rousseau's critiques of the role of learning in society is the claim that the vast majority of intellectuals are guided by self-interest rather than a pure devotion to knowledge. See in particular the *Letter to Grimm* (*Collected Writings*, II, 84–92).

58. P. reads, "under my blow, was."

59. See *Collected Writings*, II, 52.

60. See Book VIII, 335 and Book X, 435.

61. See *Collected Writings*, II, 93–129.

62. P. reads, "against me without naming me, and."

63. In fact, Bordes did publish in London works that attacked Rousseau quite viciously. See Voisine, 956.

64. P. omits, "and happily."

65. P. reads, "made me lose. Gifts of all sorts came to seek me out. Soon."

66. This is one of Rousseau's declarations that his thought forms a systematic whole.

67. P. omits, "and to be able to subject myself to it."

68. P. omits, "in order to embolden myself."

69. One of Rousseau's nicknames was "the Bear."

70. P. reads, "a single disagreeable word."

71. P. reads, "clarification," rather than "intelligibility."

72. Paul-Henri Dietrich (or Thiry), Baron d'Holbach (1723–1789), translated numerous scientific works into French and wrote, under other names, works of radical materialism. His house was one of the central meeting-places for partisans of the Enlightenment.

73. P. reads, "was perhaps less."

74. P. reads, "Comte de Schomberg who lodged with him, nor from any of the people." This is probably Gottlob-Louis, Comte de Schomberg (1726–1796).

75. Guillaume-Thomas Raynal (1713–1796) was editor of the *Mercury of France* and wrote, along with others, the *History of the Two Indies*.

76. Marie Fel, or Feel (1713–1794), was a well-known soprano.

77. Louis de Cahusac or Cahuzac (1700–1759) was a librettist and composer.

78. Jean-Baptiste Senac (1693–1770) was the doctor of the Comte de Friese's uncle the Maréchal de Saxe and later became premier doctor to Louis XV.

79. Grimm's "illness" occurred in October of 1751.

80. P. reads, "completely. I was heart-broken by it: for all the."

81. P. reads, "pleasures," rather than "successes."

82. P. omits, "and people of merit."

83. P. reads, "knowledge," rather than "enlightenment."

84. P. reads, "One day he asked me why I was running away from him? I answered him, 'You.'"

85. See Book VII, 244.

86. P. omits, "except his desire to be obliging."

87. Throughout the quarrel over the *First Discourse*, Rousseau reminded his critics that his position was that morality and cultivation of letters could go together in some individuals, but not in society as a whole.

88. P. reads, "less close, but durable, relations."

89. Renée-Caroline, Marquise de Créqui (1704–1803).

90. Actually it was Mme de Créqui's father who preceded Montaigu.

91. P. omits, "and whom I had been to see upon my return from that country."

92. Bernard-Joseph Saurin (1706–1781) was the author of several plays, including *Spartacus*, but he did not write *Barnevelt* (which was adapted by numerous

people in the eighteenth century), although he was the author of a somewhat similar play called *Beverly*. See Voisine, 440, note 1. Saurin's father, Joseph Saurin (1659–1737), had written licentious poems that were attributed to Jean-Baptiste Rousseau and caused his exile.

93. P. omits, "and are for the most part of a very good counterpoint." Phoebe Davenport was the daughter of Rousseau's landlord.

94. See Pléiade, II, 1150–1153.

95. P. reads, "refuge," rather than "resort."

96. François Mussard (1691–1755).

97. P. reads, "elegant," rather than "pleasant."

98. P. reads, "the whole universe."

99. P. omits, "to whom he was dear and."

100. Toussaint-Pierre Lenieps (1697–1774) was a Genevan who had been banished for his radical republican activities.

101. On the Abbé Prévost, see Book V, 184, editors' note 102.

102. Michel Coltelli, called Procope-Couteaux, was a doctor and playwright. He was ugly and a hunchback (like Aesop), but a successful ladies' man.

103. Nicolas-Antoine Boulanger (1722–1759) contributed to the *Encyclopedia*. His *Research on the Origin of Oriental Despotism* was published after his death. His discussion of the age of the world played a significant part in the Enlightenment attack on revealed religion. On this issue, see Frank E. Manuel, *The Eighteenth Century Confronts the Gods* (Cambridge, Mass.: Harvard University Press, 1959), especially 225–226. The connection Rousseau makes between Boulanger's work and the mania of Mussard indicates that this mania is connected with a very serious issue and also may suggest that Rousseau considers the anti-religious passion of his contemporaries to border on mania.

104. Marie-Louise Denis became Voltaire's mistress after the death of her husband. She wrote a number of plays that Voltaire dissuaded her from publishing.

105. Anne-Anoinette-Christine Van Loo was the wife of the famous painter Carle Van Loo to whom Rousseau refers in the *First Discourse*. See *Collected Writings*, II, 16. Before her marriage she had been a singer in Italy. Her brother was Gianbattista Somis who is mentioned in Book II, 60.

106. Classical Italian comic opera.

107. *The Loves of Ragonde* was a comic-opera by Philippe Nericault-Destouches and Jean-Joseph Mouret (see Book IV, 117) that opened in 1742 and was performed again in 1752 and hence was involved in the quarrel over the merits of French and Italian opera.

108. The pieces are "I have lost my servant," "Love grows if it becomes uneasy," and "Forever, Colin, I pledge you."

109. P. reads, "and what was purely filling-in."

110. Rousseau's visit to Mussard, during which these songs were written, probably took place in the Spring of 1752.

111. Jean-Baptiste Lully (1632–1687) was the dominant figure in French music in the reign of Louis XIV. He had his opera *Armide et Renaud* performed privately on February 15, 1686.

112. P. reads, "a similar one for," rather than "that of."

113. In P. this note reads, "That is how Rebel and Francoeur have always been designated."

114. On the *Menus Plaisirs*, see Book VII, 280, editors' note 192. M. de Curtis, not Cury, was the intendant at this time.

115. The Duc d'Aumont was the first gentleman of the king's chamber and was responsible for spectacles performed at Court in 1752.

116. In Rousseau's writings on music he indicates that the recitative is the most crucial part of an opera because it maintains the dramatic illusion that would be destroyed by a jarring, unrealistic juxtaposition between speech and song.

117. Pierre de Jelyotte (1713–1787 or 1797) was one of the most celebrated singers of the period.

118. October 18, 1752.

119. P. omits, "if his lie was recognized."

120. P. reads, "half an hour," rather than "shortly."

121. P. reads, "murmuring," rather than "ridicule."

122. Scene VI, the scene of the lovers' reconciliation.

123. There is an early version of this passage that reads,
As the performance proceeded interest and attention grew; a light murmur enlivened the silence without interrupting it. Noisy applause, outbursts of which were prevented by the presence of the sovereign, did not smother the most pleasing spots, and were changed into a rustling of pleasure and approbation that was a hundred times more flattering. I heard the words *charming* and *delightful* leaving all the boxes in a low voice, and in the king's box I very distinctly noticed an agitation that was not of ill omen. Finally at the moment of the two lovers' interview, at which, in its simplicity, the music genuinely has something inexplicably touching which goes to the heart, I felt the whole spectacle unite in an intoxication which my head could not stand up against.
See Pléiade, I, 1164.

124. See Book IV, 124. A slave whispered reminders of their insignificance into the ear of Roman generals who were receiving a parade of triumph.

125. "I have lost my servant; I have lost all my happiness." This is the opening aria.

126. Diderot's nickname was "the philosopher."

127. Rousseau dedicated the *Second Discourse* to the Republic of Geneva.

128. P. reads, "open to the same spot on."

129. P. reads, "and I would not speak about it here myself, if a rumor had not been spread around Paris some time later, which truly did not last, that I was not the Author of the *Village Soothsayer*."

130. On this issue of Rousseau's knowledge of music and the charge of plagiarism, see *Rousseau, Judge of Jean-Jacques*, in *Collected Writings*, I, 15–22 and 162–164.

131. They made their debut August 1, 1752.

132. *Eglé* by Pierre Lagarde, *Pygmalion* by Rameau. *Le Sylphe* has been identified as either an interlude of that name by Crébillon or *Zélindor, King of the Sylphes* by Rebel and Francoeur.

133. By Giambattista Pergolese (1710–1736).

134. Jean-Joseph Cassanea de Mondonville (1715–1773) was one of the leading French opponents of Italian music.

135. *The Little Prophet of Boemischbroda* was by Grimm. It was published in January of 1753.

136. Rousseau's *Letter on French Music* appeared in November of 1753.

137. A royal order of exile or imprisonment.

138. Marc-Pierre de Voyer, Comte d'Argenson (1696–1764), was in charge of the Opera and later became minister of War.

139. For an excellent discussion of Rousseau's startling claim, see Robert Wokler, "Rousseau on Rameau and Revolution," *Studies in the Eighteenth Century* IV (1979), 251–283. The political situation to which Rousseau refers is well documented. In November of 1753, the month the *Letter* appeared, Paris was close to an uprising over the King's attempt to dissolve the Central Court of the Paris Parlement. For a brief account of the *querelle des Bouffons* over French and Italian music, see Cranston, I, 275–291. This account contains a particularly useful summary of the exchange of pamphlets between Rousseau and Rameau. For a longer account with emphasis on the relations among all of Rousseau's writings from this period, see Robert Wokler, *Social Thought of J.-J. Rousseau* (New York: Garland, 1987), 235–378.

140. P. reads, "imaginable," rather than "possible."

141. As author of both words and music.

142. "Everyone loves justice in someone else's house."

143. P. reads, "granted," rather than "agreed upon."

144. Adrien Quiret (or Cuyret) de Margency was a minor poet and the lover of Mme de Verdelin.

145. For an account of this event, see Cranston, I, 313–314.

146. Compare this to the explanation given of Book VIII, 303.

147. Jeanne-Françoise Quinault (1699–1783) was an actress, who, after leaving the stage, established a salon frequented by Duclos, Marivaux, Diderot, Voltaire, and others. Its sessions alternated between her home and that of the Comte de Caylus.

148. Joseph-Baptiste Sauvé, called La Noue (1701–1761).

149. Jeanne-Catherine Gaussin, or Gaussen (1711–1767), and Marie-Geneviève de Grandval (1714–1784).

150. P. reads, "the end, and taking refuge in the Café de Procope which was directly across, I found."

151. Louis de Boissy (1694–1758) was a playwright who later edited the *Mercury of France*.

152. "I have sinned," the formula for the beginning of confession.

153. P. omits, "or proudly."

154. *Narcissus* was performed December 18, 1752. It was published along with the Preface at the beginning of 1753. For the Preface, see *Collected Writings*, II, 186–198.

155. The question, "What is the origin of inequality among men, and is it authorized by natural law?," appeared in the *Mercury*, in November 1753. For the *Second Discourse* and related works, see *Collected Writings*, III.

156. P. reads, "my soul dared to place itself near."

157. The philosopher who makes rationalizations while blocking his ears can be found near the end of Part One of the *Discourse*. See *Collected Writings*, III, 37. The reference to Clairval is probably to Dorval, the protagonist of Diderot's *Natural Son*, a character who may be based on Rousseau. For this work as a source of the quarrel between Diderot and Rousseau, see Book IX, 382.

158. P. reads, "laboring in secret to corrupt."

159. P. reads, "which my friend should not."

160. P. omits, "even though it was paid punctually."

161. P. reads, "that she would not put a sou of it to her own use."

162. Rousseau left Paris on June 1, 1754, and arrived in Geneva sometime before July 1. The Dedicatory Letter is dated June 12.

163. P. reads, "take that of my country back."

164. P. reads, "the morality of the Gospel."

165. For an elaboration of Rousseau's position on religion and politics, see the letter to Voltaire, August 18, 1756 (*Collected Writings*), III, 108–121, and see Book IV, viii of the *Social Contract* (*Collected Writings*, IV, 216–224).

166. P. omits, "which was outside of the City."

167. Jean or Jacques-Antoine Perdriau (1712–1786) was a minister and Professor of *belles lettres*.

168. The decision to restore Rousseau's rights of citizenship was ratified on August 1, 1754. Pierre Mussard (1690–1767) held the position of Syndic.

169. Jacques-François DeLuc, or Deluc (1698–1780), was a watchmaker who was very active in Genevan politics.

170. Jacob Vernes (1728–1791). On his later relations with Rousseau, see Book XII, 529–531.

171. Jean Jallabert (1712 or 1713–1768).

172. Amedée Lullin (1695–1756) was a minister and professor of ecclesiastical history.

173. Jacob Vernet (1698–1788).

174. Marc Chappuis (1714–1779) handled the Genevan business affairs of both Rousseau and Voltaire.

175. P. reads, "whom he wanted to supplant for the salt franchise for Valais, and who."

176. Isaac-Ami Marcet de Mézières (1695–1763).

177. The Council of the Two Hundred, one of the governing bodies of Geneva.

178. P. reads, "Moultou the son, who during my stay in Geneva was received into the Ministry which he has renounced since: a young man."

179. After numerous hesitations, Rousseau chose Paul Moultou (1725–1787) as his literary executor. He gave Moultou the Geneva Manuscript of the *Confessions*.

180. This work remained incomplete. Rousseau destroyed all of it except for the part that became the *Social Contract*.

181. P. reads, "hope of nothing less than astounding."

182. For the fragments of this play, see Pléiade, II, pp. 1019–1046.

183. See Appendix I, 552–553.

184. Jean-Pierre Crommelin (1716–1768) was Genevan Minister to the Court of

France from 1763 to 1768. He did not hold this position at the time of the dinner Rousseau is discussing.

185. On M. de Mairan, see Book VII, 239, editors' note 45.

186. P. reads, "if it failed in this duty."

187. Rousseau renounced his citizenship in May 1763.

188. P. reads, "works at her house at Epinay with."

189. P. reads, "very little."

190. In February of 1755.

191. For Voltaire's letter and Rousseau's answer, see *Collected Writings*, III, 102–107.

192. Louis, Chevalier de Jaucourt (1704–1779), wrote many articles for the *Encyclopedia*.

193. Several members of the Tronchin family were active opponents of democratic reform in Geneva.

194. P. reads, "on this subject. He answered me decently. This sad event."

195. In P. this note begins, "Here is a very striking example."

196. P. reads, "kept my heart from."

197. P. reads, "fully," rather than "wisely."

198. Charles Palissot (1730–1814) wrote numerous plays. His *The Circle, or the Peculiar People* was performed November 26, 1755.

199. Louis-Elisabeth de La Vergne, Comte de Tressan (1705–1783), was a close confidant of Stanislas and was founder of the Academy of Nancy.

200. P. reads, "was granted at my solicitation and, when he notified."

201. See Appendix I, 553–556.

202. P. reads, "live and reach Posterity, I ought."

203. P. reads, "as his iniquitous enemies."

204. Here P. adds, "End of the Eighth Book."

EDITORS' NOTES TO BOOK IX

1. P. reads, "*The Confessions of J.-J. Rousseau*/Second Part, Ninth Book."

2. As previously, only P. marks chapters in addition to paragraphs.

3. P. reads, "country," rather than "hermitage."

4. P. reads, "who knows how to work."

5. P. reads, "But without repeating what I have said on the same subject, I will add only that writing books in order to have bread."

6. P. reads, "stuck," rather than "plunged."

7. P. reads, "writer," rather than "author."

8. This passage was apparently written before Rousseau's return to Paris in the Fall of 1770.

9. P. reads, "the delightful impression."

10. Latin expression meaning "in the open air," or "under the heavens."

11. P. reads, "often at Mme d'Epinay's house la Chevrette, often badgered."

12. This paragraph is an important statement of Rousseau's aim in the *Social Contract*, the only surviving part of the *Political Institutions*. First, he indicates that he has found a new way of understanding the ancient primary question of

political philosophy: what is the best regime? Rather than focusing on particular types of government, Rousseau focuses on the question of law within any type of government. Second, Rousseau explains the abstract rhetorical character of the *Social Contract*, which differs so much from his other writings, by his desire to "spare the *amour-propre*" of the citizens of Geneva. In other words, he wishes to influence Genevan politics with a discussion of fundamental principles that avoids direct entrance into partisan disputes.

13. Rousseau says, "as they say, *en bonne fortune*." The expression comes from the secrecy necessarily involved in winning the favors of a lady. See Voisine, 481, note 1.

14. P. reads, "did not mean to."

15. P. reads, "never," rather than "not."

16. For Rousseau's attempts to combine publishing what he wanted with obedience to French laws, see Book XI, 471–472.

17. P. reads, "to making me abandon the resolution of going to settle in Geneva and to give way to Mme d'Epinay's entreaties. I felt."

18. See *Emile*, V (Bloom, 474).

19. P. reads, "will be clarified to the liking of certain readers in the continuation of this work."

20. Rousseau is referring to the *Second Discourse*, which was originally published in Amsterdam. On the permission given for it to be sold in France, see Cranston, II, 6–7.

21. P. reads, "unbelievable and which nevertheless is very true, is that the profession."

22. The Profession of Faith of the Savoyard Vicar is in Book IV of *Emile* (Bloom, 266–313). This is the part of *Emile* that caused the most controversy. Julie's profession of faith can be found in Pléiade, II, 703–740.

23. Anne-Charlotte de Crussol-Florensac (1700–1772) married the the Comte d'Agénois who became the Duc d'Aiguillon. She hosted an important literary salon of which the Abbé de St. Pierre was a member.

24. P. reads, "did not fail to be full of excellent things which deserved to be better stated, and it is."

25. P. reads, "men, by putting so little art into getting himself listened to."

26. P. reads, "twenty-three soporific volumes."

27. P. reads, "full of unnecessary repetitions, endless harping on the same thing, little short-sighted."

28. In G. this paragraph and the next three are not numbered. The numbering resumes after them.

29. P. reads, "point out," rather than "look for."

30. P. reads, "our actions," rather than "ourselves."

31. P. omits, "already completely formed."

32. See Book XII, 509. Both *Emile* and the *Confessions* itself illustrate the principles of this work. This passage also gives some indication of the significance of the distinctively human quality of "perfectibility" described in the *Second Discourse*. Rousseau's position entails both the view that humans are profoundly

affected by their environment and the view that they can exercise control over the way they are affected. See *Collected Writings*, III, 26–27.

33. P. reads, "meditate during the daytime except."

34. P. reads, "traced out," rather than "prescribed."

35. See Book VII, 290, editors' note 220.

36. A card game.

37. G. does not number this paragraph.

38. See Book IV, 122.

39. On August 30, 1768, Rousseau declared before witnesses that he considered Thérèse to be his wife. This was not a recognized legal ceremony in France, but was a somewhat common practice in marriages between Catholics (like Thérèse) and Protestants (like Rousseau) who could not be married by a legally recognized ceremony.

40. P. reads, "when I swear to him."

41. On the distinction between purely physical sexual desire that can be satisfied by any partner and moral sexual desire that makes distinctions between individuals, see *Second Discourse* (*Collected Writings*, III, 38–40).

42. Note that Rousseau does not quite say that he believes that Thérèse has been faithful. In fact, James Boswell claimed to have had an affair with her when he accompanied her on her trip to join Rousseau in England in 1766.

43. P. reads, "were a hundred times less deadly. This reason."

44. P. reads, "preferred not to be cleared as much as I could of so serious a blame."

45. P. reads, "new route which threw me into another."

46. G. omits the number of this paragraph.

47. P. reads, "What a stunning change!"

48. P. reads, "accommodating, easy-going, timid."

49. P. reads, "who, furthermore, aside from that became more toadying and more wheedling with me than she had ever been; which did not."

50. The common version of this old expression had the number 2 rather than 10. More than the English, killing two birds with one stone, it implies receiving double (or in this case tenfold) payment for the same thing.

51. P. omits, "false and mysterious."

52. P. reads, "daughter with regard to me? What."

53. P. reads, "thirteen," rather than "twelve."

54. P. reads, "were hers, I was extremely glad of it; when."

55. P. reads, "the immense manuscripts."

56. P. reads, "very few," rather than "some."

57. P. reads, "error," rather than "idea."

58. For Rousseau's view that men must be taken as they are rather than according to an imaginary standard of perfection, see *Social Contract*, I (*Collected Writings*, IV, 131).

59. P. reads, "most honest, most equitable and most useful. It was."

60. In Molière's *Misanthrope* the hero, Alceste, is put in the position of having to give his true opinion of a bad sonnet.

61. In G. the numbering of paragraphs ceases here.

62. The *Abridgment of the Project for Perpetual Peace* was published in 1761. On this work and Rousseau's *Judgment* of it, see Grace G. Roosevelt, *Reading Rousseau in the Nuclear Age* (Philadelphia: Temple University Press, 1990). All of Rousseau's writings on the Abbé de Saint-Pierre can be found in Pléiade, III, 563–634.

63. Louise de Bourbon, Duchesse de Maine (1676–1753), who was the wife of Louis XIV's illegitimate son, and Melchior, Cardinal de Polignac (1661–1741), were enemies of the Regency and defenders of the preceding administration. On the Abbé de St. Pierre's exclusion from the Academy, see Pléiade, III, 667–669.

64. P. reads, "sort of moral preacher."

65. P. reads. "been very different."

66. P. reads, "people, who judge my behavior by my disfavor, would."

67. P. reads, "equity," rather than "truth."

68. P. reads, "at least a single time."

69. See Book IV, 113–116.

70. P. reads, "A hundred times I have regretted."

71. Alexandre Deleyre (1726–1797), a former Jesuit who later collaborated on the *Encyclopedia* and other works and was politically active during the Revolution. He had been introduced to Rousseau by Duclos.

72. P. reads, "discovering," rather than "seeing."

73. The *Poem on the Disaster of Lisbon* and *Poem on Natural Law* were written by Voltaire and published in March 1756. In July Duclos sent copies to Rousseau on Voltaire's behalf.

74. See Book X, 451–453.

75. The core of Rousseau's argument is the claim that, while not every particular thing is good, the whole is. His letter and Voltaire's response can be found in *Collected Writings*, III, 109–122.

76. See Appendix I, 556–558.

77. *Candide* was published in 1759.

78. P. reads, "rare at the same time it is."

79. P. reads, "I absolutely needed."

80. See Book IV, 127.

81. P. reads, "the total majesty of the spectacle which."

82. P. reads, "never," rather than "not."

83. See Book VII, 290.

84. Jean-François, Marquis de Saint-Lambert (1716–1803), was a member of the French army at the beginning of the Seven Years War. The siege of Fort Mahon took place in May and June of 1756, which would place Mme d'Houdetot's visit earlier than Rousseau suggests. Accordingly, several scholars have suggested that she made the visit in January 1757.

85. P. reads, "than his big kitchen-garden at la Chevrette, and furnished his servants' hall and his table almost all year long. So as not."

86. P. reads, "I decided to have his."

87. In P. the following footnote occurs here, "*At this moment I admire my stupidity at not having seen when I wrote this that the spite with which the

Holbachians saw me go to and remain in the country principally concerned the mother le Vasseur whom they no longer had ready to hand to guide them through fixed points of times and places in their systems of imposture. This idea, which comes to me so late, clarifies perfectly the bizarreness of their conduct, which is inexplicable on any other assumption."

88. At the end of this paragraph, P. adds, "Thus those who prompted him wasted their efforts this time, and I did not pass my winter any less tranquilly."

89. P. reads, "heart, naturally turned them."

90. P. reads, "and remain virtuous: whoever."

91. The storm over the *Encyclopedia* did not reach its height until a year or so later. This work began its publication in 1751. After a brief suspension it resumed publication and proceeded fairly smoothly until after the appearance of the seventh volume near the end of 1757. This was the volume that contained the article on Geneva that inspired the *Letter to d'Alembert* (see Book X, 414–415). D'Alembert gave up his part of the editing at the beginning of 1758 and in March of 1759 permission to publish was retracted. It was during this later period that Rousseau was writing the final parts of *Julie*, the parts in which the religious theme is most apparent.

92. P. reads, "in my simplicity of heart, appeared."

93. P. reads, "respect of the whole universe. This."

94. P. reads, "enthusiasm," rather than "zeal."

95. P. reads "made me believe I was succeeding in."

96. Julie, the heroine of Rousseau's novel, is devoutly religious (although not orthodox in her faith), and her husband Wolmar is an atheist.

97. P. reads, "gilt paper for it, drying the writing with azure and silver powder, sewing my notebooks with slender blue ribbon, in sum."

98. P. reads, "whom I was mad about in spite of my greying beard. Every evening."

99. Later Rousseau wrote a lyric scene, *Pygmalion*, about an artist who falls in love with his creation. See Pléiade, II, 1224–1231.

100. Maurice Quentin de La Tour (1704–1788) was the most famous portrait painter of the day. The portrait about which Rousseau is speaking here was exhibited in 1753 and has since disappeared. There are many copies, however, including one by La Tour himself.

101. This word is missing from both manuscripts and has been added by most editors to make sense of this sentence.

102. See Book XII, 508–509.

103. P. reads, "almost," rather than "additionally."

104. P. reads, "the execrable attempt."

105. Rousseau is referring to the unrest in Paris around the time of the attack with a knife made on Louis XV by the valet Damiens. He later came to suspect that efforts were being made to connect him with Damiens.

106. Diderot's play appeared in February 1757.

107. P. reads, "which I dare say feel."

108. See Pléiade, II, 470–488 and 512–522.

109. This visit probably took place in May 1757.

110. P. reads, "Although I do not like these sorts of masquerades at all, I."

111. She was not quite twenty-seven at the time of this visit.

112. P. reads, "conformity of natural disposition contributed."

113. P. reads, "virtues, and the rarest talents. If."

114. P. reads, "for such an attachment."

115. P. reads, "cemented only by virtues."

116. P. reads, "by a new but delightful."

117. P. reads, "she should have avoided. She."

118. P. reads, "remorse that my attire, my gallantry."

119. P. reads, "to my age and to my adornment had debased."

120. See *Julie* (Pléiade, II, 342).

121. P. reads, "I swear to the face of heaven that."

122. Anne-Charlotte-Simonette d'Houdetot had married Nicolas-Charles Dubuisson, Marquis de Blainville.

123. P. omits, "whose just reproaches I was suffering, and."

124. P. reads, "the momentary success."

125. Grimm was the secretary of the Duc d'Estrées, not de Castries, at this time.

126. Different dates have been proposed for this exchange of letters, ranging from Wednesday, June 29, through Wednesday, August 31, 1757. The original version of Mme d'Epinay's first note says August 24, but since she apparently had just returned to la Chevrette from Paris that day or the day before, it is not likely that she would be writing a note complaining about Rousseau not having visited for a week. Her pseudo-memoirs give the date as July 15, although that was not a Wednesday, and give versions of her letters that differ markedly from the originals in her handwriting that Rousseau reproduces faithfully.

127. P. reads, "would always be."

128. P. reads, "with the blame for graver."

129. P. reads, "powerfully," rather than "extremely."

130. The sentence to which Rousseau objects occurs in the play itself, Act IV, Scene 3, rather than in the accompanying *Discussions with Dorval*. As mentioned (see 326, editors' note 157), it has been suggested that the character Dorval, to whom the remark is made, is based on Rousseau.

131. P. reads, "the more, it seems to me, on the part of."

132. P. reads, "who at the time had a friend who had withdrawn into solitude six months before."

133. P. reads, "concerned," rather than "interested."

134. P. reads, "like a child in spite of myself by any means."

135. This is a portion of a letter from Diderot from March 10, 1757. The entire letter can be found in Appendix I, 558. It should be noted that Rousseau is not following chronological order here: the quarrel and reconciliation reported here occurred several months before the quarrel and reconciliation with Mme d'Epinay reported before.

136. P. reads, "to be explained now."

137. P. omits, "even though she was very healthy there."

138. P. reads, "to let elderly people leave Paris."

139. This letter is from March 17, 1757.

140. "The Philosopher" was Diderot's nickname.

141. For this letter, see Appendix I, 559–560.

142. P. omits, "where she was very healthy, where she always had company, and where she lived very agreeably."

143. P. reads, "her very free choice."

144. The rampart was a newly built promenade.

145. P. reads, "entertain," rather than "amuse."

146. P. reads, "I would not so easily find so good a substitute for those."

147. This letter was probably written on March 16, 1757.

148. Carlo Goldoni (1707–1793) wrote numerous plays, one of which, *The True Friend* (*Il Vero Amico*), did serve as a model for Diderot's play, although there was no plagiarism.

149. Françoise de Graffigny (1695–1758) was the author of the *Peruvian Letters* and *Cénie*.

150. Rousseau made his visit to Diderot in July, but Diderot had in fact paid him one at the Hermitage in April. It also appears that Rousseau did not hear about Mme de Graffigny's rumor until August. The accusations of plagiarism were made in June.

151. Diderot published the *Father of the Family* in November of 1758. He was quickly accused of having plagiarized Goldoni's play of the same name. The consultation between Diderot and Rousseau may seem strange given Rousseau's attack on the theater in the *Letter to d'Alembert* that was written less than a year later. However, it should be noted that Rousseau's criticisms are directed toward French classical drama in particular. In Book VIII, 331, he indicates that he was considering writing a new type of play with *The Death of Lucretia*. Ultimately he gave up this plan, and instead wrote his novel *Julie*. In the *Letter to d'Alembert*, Rousseau praises novels in contrast to the theater. Diderot's plays also were based on a rejection of classical drama and were an attempt to create a new sort of drama, bourgeois drama, that would be more effective because it was closer to real life. Thus, it appears that both Rousseau and Diderot were deeply dissatisfied with the traditional French theater and wished to reform it, although their reforms took very different directions.

152. The word is "*feuillu.*" This passage and a letter from Rousseau to Duclos about *Julie* are the only examples in French literature of this particular use of this word.

153. It appears that d'Holbach had arranged to have a translation he had made of a German work on chemistry published through Rousseau.

154. Baron d'Holbach's new wife, Charlotte-Suzanne d'Aine, was the sister of his first wife.

155. Rousseau probably did see Saint-Lambert in Paris in July, but may well also have seen him at the other two places. It should be noted that this visit, or these visits, with Saint-Lambert occurred the month before Rousseau's exchange of notes with Mme d'Epinay narrated earlier in this book. Therefore, it was before Saint-Lambert's letter to Mme d'Houdetot reported on p. 376.

156. P. reads, "still truly love."

157. P. reads, "he often took."

158. It appears that Mme d'Houdetot did keep the letters, but that, after her death, her niece burned most of them. No surviving ones have been discovered.

159. P. reads, "of it, that is not possible. But I."

160. P. reads, "either: she is not capable of it and furthermore I had."

161. P. reads, "it rather sharply several."

162. P. reads, "mistrust," rather than "fears."

163. Rousseau's letter is dated September 4, 1757.

164. This took place on September 15, 1757.

165. Jean de Linant.

166. P. omits "*hic.*" The words mean, "Behold the abode of the one who thunders."

167. The footnote does not occur in P. It is not known whether Rousseau refers to Jean de Santeul (1630–1697), who wrote Latin poetry, or Claude de Santeul, who wrote hymns.

168. P. reads, "airs such as I."

169. The Comte de Tuffière is the hero of the play *The Conceited Man*, by Destouches, which was first performed in 1732. The Comte's valet is named La Fleur, which Rousseau uses in connection with Grimm's valet below.

170. P. reads, "setting. Finally he."

171. P. reads, "former little prig."

172. P. reads, "to lament bitterly at."

173. Maecenus was a Roman statesman and patron of literature in the First Century B.C. His name is synonymous with patronage of literature, and among the writers he assisted were Horace and Virgil.

174. P. reads, "in a way dared to give him."

175. P. reads, "comedy," rather than "farce."

176. This is a pun on the name of the hero of the sixteenth century Castillian novel of chivalry, *Tirant lo Blanch*, one of the novels in Don Quixote's library.

177. For Rousseau's opposition to the so-called esoteric or "interior" doctrine see *Rousseau, Judge of Jean-Jacques* (*Collected Writings*, I, 28) "Observations" (*Collected Writings*, II, 45–46), and the Third Walk of the *Reveries*. For a useful general account of this doctrine (also called the "double doctrine") among Rousseau's contemporaries, see Harry C. Payne, *The Philosophers and the People* (New Haven: Yale University Press, 1976), 65–93.

178. This is probably Louis-Melchior-Armond, Marquis de Polignac.

179. After the death of his employer the Comte de Friese, Grimm had become secretary of the Duc of Orléans, who lived at the Palais Royal.

180. P. reads, "given himself by means of the story of him as a swooning carp after Mlle Fel's cruelty."

181. See Book VIII, 310.

182. Probably really the Hôtel d'Estrées. See Book IX, 377, editors' note 125.

183. P. reads, "several," rather than "other."

184. P. reads, "language, but that was when."

185. P. omits, "or that they certainly wanted to make these two persons serve as an instrument in some hidden plan."

186. P. reads, "judge," rather than "believe."

187. On the term "*en bonne fortune*" translated "in secret," see Book IX, 340, editors' note 13.

188. P. reads, "affected," rather than "feigned."

189. P. reads, "attachment," rather than "bias."

190. P. reads, "oppose," rather than "say."

191. P. reads, "his naturally uncommunicative."

192. See Appendix I, 560–562.

193. Georges Dandin is the hero of the play by the same name by Molière. Dandin is forced to apologize for his accusations of Clitandre who is, in fact, guilty.

194. The term translated as quack is "*jongleur*," which means a juggler or mountebank.

195. That is, that he was following his interior doctrine. See Book IX, 393.

196. P. omits, "Until then I had been in the same circumstance, I had always preserved all my friends, since my most tender childhood I had not lost a single one of them except by death, and nevertheless I had not made a reflection about it until then; it was not a maxim that I would have prescribed for myself. Thus, since this was an advantage common to both of us, why did he plume himself on it then by preference, unless he was thinking in advance of depriving me of it."

197. P. reads, "as he was. The question was to know by what title he had obtained it."

198. Rousseau received this letter on October 24, 1757.

199. "Bear" was one of Rousseau's nicknames.

200. Opinion is divided among scholars about whether Mme d'Epinay really was going to Geneva because of chest problems or because of a pregnancy she wished to conceal.

201. In fact, the letter was addressed, "To Monsieur Rousseau, At the Hermitage or La Chevrette," and it was sealed.

202. This letter was written around October 20, 1757.

203. P. reads, "without almost ever deigning."

204. P. reads, "go too well with."

205. P. reads, "never," rather than "not."

206. See Appendix I, 562–563.

207. P. reads, "high, I dare to say it, in each."

208. October 25, 1757.

209. P. reads, "in peace: that is what I did. Only I."

210. P. reads, "the crude trap."

211. For this letter, see Appendix I, 563–564.

212. P. reads, "it with me for."

213. The visit took place on December 5, 1757, but there is some reason to believe that Diderot had already decided to break with Rousseau. For two contradictory accounts of the visit, given at different times by Diderot, see Cranston, II, 102–103.

214. P. reads, "people that dangerous woman had."

215. Jacques-Joseph Mathas.

216. P. omits, "along with what I already had."

217. P. reads, "find," rather than "believe."

218. Here P. adds, "End of the Ninth Book."

EDITORS' NOTES TO BOOK X

1. P. reads, *"The Confessions of J.-J. Rousseau/2d Part/10th Book."*

2. P. reads, "again in detail."

3. P. reads, "option," rather than "choice."

4. P. uses another word for "compromising" here. In P. he uses *"se compro-mettre,"* while in G. he uses *"se commettre,"* which had the same meaning in the eighteenth century.

5. Cahouet was Mme d'Epinay's superintendent. He was overseer of the Hermitage.

6. In fact, Rousseau did respond to this letter on February 20, saying that he had always paid the gardener from his own money and complaining about rumors that Mme d'Epinay's friends were spreading about him in Paris.

7. Rousseau is referring to the political unrest following the suppression of the *Social Contract* in Geneva.

8. For this letter, see Appendix I, 564–565.

9. P. reads, "expose," rather than "explain."

10. A member of the Mariannas, a chain of islands in the Pacific, discovered by Admiral Anson in 1742. In *Julie,* Saint-Preux makes a trip around the world and visits this island. Voisine has suggested that Rousseau confuses Tinian, which is part of a chain, with the more isolated island, Juan Fernandez. See Voisine, p. 581.

11. P. reads, "plots by themselves; the one."

12. In P. Rousseau adds a note here which says, "I admit that since this book was written, everything I catch a glimpse of through the mysteries which surround me make me fear that I did not know Diderot."

13. P. omits, "truth triumphed, and."

14. P. reads, "ten" rather than "twelve."

15. P. reads, "feels," rather than "fears."

16. Rousseau is referring to the hostility of the government minister Choiseul. See Book XI, 463–464.

17. P. omits, "Above all he needs for me to be surrounded by impenetrable shadows, and for his plot to be always hidden from me, knowing well that with whatever art he has hatched the plot, it would never bear up under my glances. His great skill is to appear to treat me considerately while defaming me, and still to give his perfidy the air of generosity."

18. P. reads, "Diderot told me just about the same thing, and."

19. The article was in the seventh volume of the *Encyclopedia*, which appeared in October 1757. Rousseau received his copy in December.

20. Nicolas de Catinat (1637–1712) was a general under Louis XIV. In *Rousseau, Judge of Jean-Jacques,* Rousseau refers to him as one of the few examples of genuine virtue in modernity. See *Collected Writings,* I, 158.

21. In the *Letter to d'Alembert* there is a lengthy discussion of Molière's play,

The Misanthrope. See *Politics and the Arts: Letter to M. d'Alembert on the Theatre*, trans. Allan Bloom (Ithaca: Cornell University Press, 1960), 34–47. In this discussion it is easy to see that Rousseau identifies himself with the hero, Alceste, with whom he had been compared by Lecat, one of the critics of the *First Discourse* (*Collected Writings*, II, 58 and 146). Grimm is implicitly compared with the character Philinte and Mme d'Epinay with Célimène. See Voisine, 585. In the *Letter* Rousseau also discusses Racine's *Bérénice* involving a love triangle and the opposition between love and duty that could be seen as reflecting the triangle involving Rousseau, Sophie d'Houdetot, and Saint Lambert. One of the major themes of the *Letter* is the unequal contest between love and morality as it is portrayed on the modern French stage.

22. Rousseau was obliged to have the *Letter* cleared by government censors in order to have it published in France. In fact, d'Alembert himself was the censor who approved it.

23. For this letter, written May 6, 1758, see Appendix I, 565–566.

24. Diderot claimed that he had talked to Saint-Lambert about these matters under the assumption that Rousseau himself had already informed Saint-Lambert as he had earlier told Diderot he would. However, there is evidence that Diderot was aware that Rousseau had not informed Saint-Lambert. For a discussion of this, see Cranston, II, 131.

25. P. reads, "ruptures all turned to my prejudice, in that they left my most dangerous enemies with the mask of Friendship."

26. Their break occurred after the publication of *The Persian Letters* in 1721.

27. See *Letter to d'Alembert* (Bloom, 7). The verses from Ecclesiasticus 22: 26–27 are, "Though thou drawest a sword at thy friend, yet despair not; for there may be a returning. If thou has opened thy mouth against thy friend, fear not; for there may be a reconciliation: except for upbraiding, or pride, or disclosing of secrets, or a treacherous wound: for these things every friend will depart." In the first edition of the *Letter* the conclusion of this quotation is absent. It first appeared in the 1764 edition.

28. The *Letter* was published in late July or early August. For the details of its publication, see Cranston, II, 128–137.

29. For this letter written October 9, 1758, see Appendix I, 566.

30. By this point d'Alembert had resigned from the *Encyclopedia* because of the controversy over volume seven. After considerable pressure, in March of 1759, the government withdrew permission to publish subsequent volumes.

31. P. reads, "I admit to you Sir that I cannot dissimulate how much."

32. Rousseau was making a copy of *Julie* for Mme d'Houdetot. He had earlier made a copy of the *Letter* to Voltaire.

33. As mentioned, M. d'Epinay was Mme d'Houdetot's brother.

34. Literally, "while she looked after the mule." In the eighteenth century this was a common expression meaning "wait impatiently out of boredom."

35. P. reads, "one feels well enough that."

36. Megaera was one of the Three Furies. She personified envy and hatred.

37. Ange-Laurent Lalive de Jully (1726 or 1727–1775) was a diplomat. He was also well-known as an engraver and collector of engravings.

38. Jean-François Marmontel (1723–1799) was a poet and member of the French Academy. Rousseau does not exaggerate his hostility, which he manifested frequently in later years.

39. See Book VIII, 324. For an account of this dispute, see Cranston, II, 152–153.

40. Jean-François Sellon (1707–1790) was the Genevan diplomatic resident and then ambassador to France from 1749 to 1764.

41. Louis Phélypeaux, Comte de Saint-Florentin, Duc de La Vrillière (1705–1777).

42. Rebel and Francoeur; see Book VIII, 315.

43. This agreement was made in 1774.

44. P. reads, "society," rather than "freedom."

45. Alexandre-Jerome Loyseau de Mauléon (1728–1771) was a famous lawyer. In 1762 he was the defender of Jean Calas, a Protestant accused of murdering his son to prevent his conversion to Catholicism, whose trial was made famous by Voltaire.

46. P. reads, "did not yet know."

47. Louis, Comte de Portes, had intervened in a case involving the rights of a minor in Nyon.

48. Hippolyte-Lucas Guérin (1698–1765).

49. Jean Néaulme (1694–1780).

50. Antoine Maltor (1689–1767).

51. On Saurin and the other people mentioned here, see Book VIII, 312.

52. On Séguy (whose name Rousseau also gives as Segui), see Book VIII, 293.

53. P. reads, "tender," rather than "ardent."

54. Charles-Gaspard de Vintimille was Archbishop of Paris from 1729 to 1746.

55. Joseph-Etienne Bertier (1702–1783) was a professor of philosophy and physics.

56. Panurge is a character in Rabelais. Rousseau uses this same example in *Rousseau, Judge of Jean-Jacques* to describe the way in which he himself is presented in an engraving. See *Collected Writings*, I, 94.

57. This letter is dated June 26, 1760.

58. I.e., having neither father nor mother. See Hebrews, 7:3.

59. Probably the *Nouvelles ecclésiastiques*, a clandestine Jansenist journal.

60. The term is *commères*, which can also mean gossips.

61. P. omits, "at least I believed he had."

62. François Coindet (1734–1809).

63. P. reads, "people," rather than "society."

64. On the Abbé Trublet, see Book VII, 247.

65. P. omits, "I owe her a place apart here; she will always have a distinguished one in my remembrances."

66. P. reads, "I still found him the same, that is to say, an excellent heart."

67. P. reads, "inexcusable and very shocking wrong."

68. P. reads, "greater," rather than "great."

69. On M. de Jonville, see Book VII, 249.

70. P. reads, "never," rather than "not."

71. A chauffoir is a warming room in the back of a theater.

72. P. reads, "a falling out," rather than "pouting."

73. On Condillac and Mably, see Book VII, 235. On Ancelet, see Book VII, 288. Aside from Mairan and Lalive who are discussed in this book, the others are the composer Paul-Louis Roualle de Boisgelou (1734–1806) and Claude-Henri Watelet (1718–1786), a receiver-general of finances and member of the French Academy.

74. On Margency, see Book VIII, 324. Joseph-François de Corsambleu, known as Desmahis (1722–1761), collaborated on the *Encyclopedia* in addition to writing plays.

75. Chrétien-Guillaume de Lamoignon de Malesherbes (1721–1794) was head of censorship from 1747 until the Revolution, aside from a brief interruption from 1770 to 1774. Thus he was the head of censorship for virtually all of Rousseau's literary career. He was put to death after representing Louis XVI in the trial that led to the King's death. Rousseau had met his father earlier; see Book VII, 243. For a very useful account of Malesherbes's life and thought, see George Armstrong Kelly, *Victims, Authority, and Terror* (Chapel Hill: The University of North Carolina Press, 1982), 213–277.

76. This edition appeared in January of 1761.

77. These cuts mainly concerned the expression of religious opinions by the characters, although some of them concerned anti-monarchical remarks. Rousseau objected to these cuts on the grounds that it was illegitimate to censor for lack of Catholic orthodoxy the expression of opinions of characters who were Protestants. For an excellent account of this edition, see Jo-Ann E. McEachern, "La *Nouvelle Héloïse* et la censure," in *Rousseau and the Eighteeenth Century: Essays in Memory of R. A. Leigh*, ed. Marian Hobson, J. T. A. Leigh, and Robert Wokler (Oxford: The Voltaire Foundation, 1992), 83–100.

78. See Pléiade, II, 633, and *Rousseau, Judge of Jean-Jacques* (*Collected Writings*, I, 204).

79. Rousseau is referring to the Comtesse de Boufflers who was the mistress of the Prince de Conti.

80. Jacques Roland, Chevalier de Lorenzi.

81. For these two letters, dated November 15, 1759, and January 9, 1760, see Appendix I, 566–568.

82. Alexis-Claude Clairaut (1713–1765) was a mathematician and physicist. Joseph de Guignes (1721–1800) was a scholar whose specialty was the Orient. Jean-Jacques Barthélemy (1716–1795) was a scholar of antiquities and later wrote the successful novel *Voyage of the Young Anarchasis in Greece*.

83. P. reads, "work which they would permit me to do so conveniently."

84. G. omits the words in brackets, which are in P. and are necessary for the sense of the sentence.

85. P. reads, "all my talent came from the keen interest I took in the matters I had to treat."

86. P. omits, "and even do more than anyone else for them, because in fact I needed them much more."

87. In other words, Rousseau ended by paying more than twice as much.

88. Postage was paid by the recipient of a letter rather than its sender. This

explains Rousseau's constant complaints about the number of letters he received from people he did not know.

89. P. omits, "Although I limited my little gifts only to the houses in which I lived customarily, they did not fail to be ruinous for me."

90. P. omits, "Afterward I had to renounce completely these little liberalities which my situation no longer allowed me to make and then I was made to feel even more harshly the disadvantage of frequenting people from another station than one's own."

91. Rousseau had first met Marc-Michel Rey during his visit to Geneva in 1754. See Book VIII, 331. It is not known exactly when he began asking Rousseau for his memoirs.

92. This resolution is the origin of the collection of transcriptions of letters that was meant to be an appendix of the *Confessions*.

93. P. reads "where the vassals pay hommage."

94. Pierre Crozat.

95. On this history, see Pléiade, I, 1525, note 1 to 517.

96. André Le Nôtre (1613–1700) was the most famous garden designer of the seventeenth century. He designed the gardens at Versailles.

97. Charles-François-Frédéric de Montmorency, duc de Luxembourg (1702–1764), was one of the King's closest advisors and friends.

98. See Book VII, 243.

99. Marie-Charlotte-Hippolyte de Campet de Saujon, Comtesse de Boufflers (1724–1800).

100. P. reads, "well-founded secret presentiment."

101. Madeleine-Angélique de Neufville-Villeroy (1707–1787) married the Duc de Boufflers in 1721. She became a widow in 1747 and married the Duc de Luxembourg in 1750.

102. Louise-Françoise-Pauline, duchesse de Montmorency, was married to the Duc de Luxembourg's son from his first marriage.

103. Charles Le Brun (1619–1690) was a painter and architect who worked on the decorations of Versailles.

104. Rousseau moved into the Petit-Château on May 6, 1759.

105. The battle was the defeat at Minden on August 1, 1759.

106. P. reads, "that in one of my letters I wrote."

107. This letter was probably written on November 6 in response to Rousseau's letter of October 29, 1759. A number of scholars have suggested that Rousseau simply misunderstood this letter and that the Duchesse was expressing pleasure rather than disapproval. For an account of the exchange of letters over this, see Cranston, II, 200–201.

108. See Pléiade, II, 749–760, for *The Loves of Lord Edouard Bomston*. The title character is one of the secondary characters of *Julie*.

109. P. reads, "invincible," rather than "blind."

110. "Whoever Jupiter wants to ruin he makes mad." This saying usually says "he first makes mad." In its precise form, it seems to come from a seventeenth-century commentary on the Bible and can be traced to an ancient Greek fragment referring to Fortune rather than Jupiter. See Voisine, 618–619, note 1.

111. P. reads, "was hardly more advantageous to me."

112. "I wrote the verses, someone else received the honors for them." This line is attributed to Virgil. See Voisine, 620–621, note 1.

113. Coindet was a clerk in a bank run by the Genevan banker George-Tobie de Thellusson.

114. Rousseau returned to his house in July of 1759.

115. P. omits, "and on which I had tamed multitudes of birds."

116. P. reads, "and many other."

117. The people in this list who are not identified earlier are Louis-François-Anne de Neufville, Duc de Villeroy and de Retz (1695–1765), who was the Duc de Luxembourg's brother; Charles-François-Christian de Montmorency, Prince de Tingry (1713–1787), who later married the Duchesse de Luxembourg's cousin; Louis de Conflans de Brienne, Marquis d'Armentières (1711–1774); Marie-Anne-Philippine-Thérèse de Montmorency, Duchesse de Boufflers, who was the daughter-in-law of the Duchesse de Luxembourg; and Marie-Christine-Chrétienne de Rouvray de Saint-Simon (1728–1774).

118. P. reads, "for a single instant."

119. P. reads, "charms," rather than "sweetness."

120. Rousseau is referring to his visits to Diderot and to Gauffecourt. See Book IX, 386. Actually, he had been to see Gauffecourt twice during the latter's illness.

121. Marie-Madeleine, Marquise de Verdelin (1728–1810).

122. Marie-Rosalie de Scepeau de Beaupréau married the Comte d'Aubeterre.

123. The expression is literally "good woman," and in her response (Appendix I, 568) Mme de Verdelin uses it in the literal sense.

124. P. reads, "expressions have an equivocal turn sometimes."

125. See Appendix I, 568–569.

126. This follows P. There appears to be an error of transcription in G., where this reads, "entering" ("*entrant*") rather than "enterprising" ("*entreprenant*"), and is corrected in a hand other than Rousseau's.

127. See Book IX, 367.

128. Etienne de Silhouette (1709–1767) was Controller General of Finances from March to November of 1759. As Rousseau says, his policies were directed against the tax-farmers.

129. P. reads, "saw very well that."

130. Book III, p. 97 above.

131. The original is dated August 13, 1759.

132. The home of Julie in Rousseau's novel.

133. P. reads, "less interesting for her, or."

134. Legally, all works printed in France had to receive prior permission from the government censors, supervised at this time by Malesherbes. To allow the publication of controversial works, Malesherbes made use of a system of tacit permission that allowed the works to appear, but did not give them the sanction of official approval. Works that appeared with permission, tacit or otherwise, were still subject to action by authorities other than Malesherbes.

135. This letter has been lost along with most of the rest of Malesherbes's letters to Rousseau. See Book XI, 479.

136. P. reads, "any good objection."

137. Rousseau's position was that, once the book was published with permission, only the book dealers were liable to prosecution. It is important to see how cautious he is here to follow a very precise legal course of action. At the same time, he was extremely bold in allowing his name to appear as the author of his books, a practice that was rather uncommon among his contemporaries when there was any danger of controversy.

138. Amélie de Boufflers (1751–1794) was the daughter of the Duc and Duchesse de Boufflers.

139. Interesting, in the eighteenth-century English sense of inspiring benevolent feelings.

140. In Book V of *Emile* (Bloom, 427–428) Rousseau expresses his approval of a suitor kissing his beloved in front of her parents, but censures doing the same in private.

141. Instigated by Diderot, Deleyre published a translation of Goldoni's *Father of the Family* to prove that Diderot's play of the same name was not a plagiarism. The translation was dedicated to "the Princesse de ***," a reference that was understood to poke fun at Mme the Princesse de Robecq (c. 1725–1760), who was an enemy of the Encyclopedists and patroness of Palissot. On Palissot, see Book VIII, 335. On Diderot and the charges of plagiarism, see Book IX, 386.

142. Nicolas-Bonaventure Duchesne (1712–1765) later published *Emile*.

143. P. reads, "knew," rather than "believed." G. originally read the same way, but "knew" is crossed out and replaced with "believed." The corrections were made with a different ink, indicating that they were made some time after the manuscript was first copied.

144. P. reads, "This letter circulated."

145. In June of 1760, the letter was published in a pamphlet attacking Palissot's play.

146. André Morellet (1727–1819) was a contributor to the *Encyclopedia*. He published the *Preface to the Comedy, The Philosophers, or the Vision of Charles Palissot*.

147. Rousseau is correct on this point. Morellet was arrested on Malesherbes's order. Although Malesherbes had considerable sympathy for the Encyclopedists, he was ardently opposed to personal attacks of any kind, especially (although not exclusively) those directed at members of leading families.

148. P. reads, "release," rather than "freedom."

149. The Parlement of Normandy had refused to ratify a new tax and was calling for the convocation of the Estates-General.

150. This letter is dated July 23, 1760.

151. "Be well and love me."

152. For this letter, which is dated August 4, 1760, see Appendix I, 569.

153. For this letter, which is dated June 13, 1760, see Appendix I, 569–571.

154. P. reads, "although he had not yet put into it the unbelievable impudence he employed later on with regard to me. But how."

155. In 1764 Jean-Henri-Samuel Formey (1711–1797) edited a version of *Emile* with a piece of his own substituting for the Profession of Faith. He called his version, *The Christian Emile Dedicated to the Public Utility*.

156. Formey had, in fact, taken it from a pamphlet printed by the Cramer Brothers of Geneva, who were Voltaire's usual publishers.

157. P. reads, "respect that I owe them."

158. Upon receiving this letter, Voltaire wrote to several people that he believed that Rousseau had gone mad.

159. P. reads, "when M. and Mme de Luxembourg were not."

160. See *Politics and the Arts* (Bloom, 50–51).

161. P. reads, "to be completely turned."

162. P. reads, "I have just had some very dangerous flirting from a young and beautiful person with very disturbing eyes."

163. P. reads, "my approximately sixty years, I have."

164. A lustre is a period of five years. The woman referred to here is probably Louise-Rose de Berthier, whom Rousseau met in 1769. She was the wife of the Chevalier de Berthier.

165. P. reads, "since if conquering love has been so fatal to me, conquered love has been even more so."

166. At this point P. reads, *"End of tenth book."* In P. Book XI begins on the same page. This is the only time that one book ends and another begins on the same page of any of the manuscripts.

EDITOR'S NOTES TO BOOK XI

1. P. reads, *"The Confessions of J.-J. Rousseau/Second Part/Eleventh Book."*

2. *Julie* went on sale in Paris at the end of January of 1761, after having gone on sale in London in December of 1760. For an account of the details of its publication and reception, see Cranston, II, 247–277.

3. Marie-Josephe de Saxe (1731–1767) was married to the oldest son of Louis XV.

4. For example, d'Alembert and Duclos admired the book enormously, while Grimm and Voltaire hated it.

5. P. reads, "in all the rest."

6. In fact, *Julie* was phenomenally successful throughout Europe.

7. For Rousseau's judgment of Paris as the place to learn the appreciation of good qualities, as opposed to their practice, see *Emile*, IV (Bloom, 341–342).

8. P. reads, "part in parallel with the."

9. *The Princesse de Clèves*, by Mme de Lafayette (along with the collaboration of several others, including La Rochefoucault), was published in 1678. It is often regarded as the first great modern French novel.

10. P. reads, "have been known. Thus."

11. Rousseau is evidently thinking of Geneva.

12. When Rousseau had made his first decision to abandon work on the *Confessions* in 1768, he entrusted many of his papers, including this collection of letters and possibly a draft of the *Confessions*, to Mme de Nadaillac, the Abbess of Gomerfontaine. The letters are now in the Bibliothèque de Neuchâtel.

13. Samuel Richardson (1689–1761) was the immensely successful author of *Pamela* (1740), *Clarissa Harlowe* (1747), and *The Adventures of Sir Charles Grandison* (1753–1754). All three were quickly translated into French, the latter two by Rousseau's acquaintance, the Abbé Prévost. Diderot published a "Praise of Richardson" in 1761 at least in part to make an unfavorable, but tacit, comparison with

Rousseau. In the *Letter to d'Alembert*, written while he was working on *Julie*, Rousseau says, "In no language whatsoever has a novel the equal of *Clarissa*, or even approaching it, ever been written" (Bloom, 82n.). For a treatment of *Clarissa* that shows its relation to both *The Princesse de Clèves* and *Julie*, see William Ray, *Story and History* (Oxford: Basil Blackwell, 1990).

14. P. reads, "Richardson's Novels—whatever M. Diderot might be able to say about it—cannot enter."

15. P. omits. "It is dead, nevertheless, I know it, and I know the cause of it; but it will rise from the dead."

16. The words in brackets are from P. In G. they are hidden by a rebinding of the manuscript.

17. In P. the note reads, "It was not she, but another Lady whose name I do not know: but I have been assured of the fact." The Princesse de Talmont was the former Marie-Louise Jablonowska.

18. Probably Diane-Marie-Zéphirine-Adélaïde, Marquise de Polignac.

19. P. reads, "most erotic ecstasies."

20. The dialogue, "Preface" to *Julie*, which was published in February of 1761, leaves open the possibility that the novel is based on fact. See Pléiade, II, 28–30.

21. P. reads, "Rigorists will find that."

22. Jean-François de Bastide (1724–1798) founded numerous periodicals.

23. P. reads, "put the whole work in his."

24. P. reads, "if he had known that this work existed. Finally."

25. P. reads, "badgering, in order to free myself from it, I."

26. It was published as a pamphlet in March of 1761. On the details of its publication and Rousseau's response to the attempt to censor parts of it, see Cranston, II, 259–260.

27. P. reads, "people will be able to know how much."

28. Voltaire made fun of this work in his *Emperor of China's Rescript*, published in May of 1761.

29. See Book X, 442.

30. For this letter, dated November 30, 1759, see Appendix I, 571.

31. In P. all the words in quotation marks here are underlined.

32. P. reads, "happiness," rather than "honor."

33. Marie-Renée de Montmorency-Luxembourg (1697–1759) married the future Duc de Villeroy, the brother of Mme de Luxembourg, in 1716.

34. The Duchesse de Villeroy died in December of 1759, the Princesse de Robecq in July of 1760, the Duc de Montmorency in May of 1761, and the Comte de Luxembourg (who was four years old) in June of 1761.

35. P. reads, "little by little under his eyes from."

36. Théophile de Bordeu (1722–1776) was a well-known doctor and contributed to the *Encyclopedia*.

37. P. reads, "Surgeon, named Morlane, maintained."

38. This refers to official duties requiring his presence for a term of three months each year.

39. P. reads, "been only to."

40. P. reads, "Pyrrhus in days gone by; he sighed."

41. See Book V, 158 and editors' note 38.

42. Stanislas-Jean, Abbé de Boufflers (1738–1815).

43. Italian word meaning blunder or gaffe.

44. On Choiseul, see the introduction to Part Two, 229.

45. P. reads, "avoided the temptation of committing."

46. The "family compact," or *pacte de famille*, was an alliance between the Bourbon monarchies of France and Spain made in 1761.

47. P. reads, "I had hardly been content with."

48. P. reads, "through the people who have him at their command, because."

49. P. omits, "which were the only things I knew about him."

50. The *Social Contract*, III, vi, contains the following passage, which was added while the work was in press: "An essential and inevitable defect, which will always place monarchical government below republican, is that in the latter the public voice almost never raises to high positions any but enlightened, capable men, who fulfill them with honor; whereas those who attain them in monarchies are most often merely petty troublemakers, petty rascals, petty intriguers, whose petty talents—which lead to high positions in royal courts—serve only to reveal their ineptitude to the people as soon as these men are in place. The people makes a mistake in its choice much less often than the prince, and a man of real merit is nearly as rare in a ministry as a fool at the head of a republican government. So it is that when, by some lucky chance, one of those men who are born to govern takes control of public affairs in a monarchy that has almost been wrecked by this bunch of fine managers, people are all amazed at the resources he finds, and it is epoch-making for the whole country" (*Collected Writings*, IV, 178).

51. The novel, *Oroonoko or the Royal Slave*, by Aphra Behn (1610–1689), was published around 1688. It was made into a play in 1696. The novel was translated into French in 1745, and the play was translated in 1751. For an account of Rousseau's exchanges with Mme de Boufflers over her play, see Cranston, II, 280–281.

52. In Le Sage's novel, Gil Blas draws the Bishop's enmity by giving his honest opinion of the sermons.

53. Charles-François Hénault (1685–1770), Président of the Paris Parlement, wrote plays, poems, and history.

54. Marie de Vichy-Chambrond, Marquise du Deffand (1679–1780), held a famous literary salon. Julie de Lespinasse (1732–1776) was an orphan who became Mme du Deffand's companion for ten years, after which she set up a rival salon.

55. This letter was not preserved, but see Appendix I, 571, for a letter referring to the same proposed trip.

56. Gabriel-Louis-François de Neufville, Marquis de Villeroy (1731–1794).

57. P. reads, "took it into his head to push me."

58. P. reads, "story was less that I had given it to my dog than that I."

59. The residence of the Prince de Conti.

60. A *sigisbee* is a gentleman escort of a married woman, usually with her husband's consent. The custom was an Italian one that Rousseau would have observed in Venice.

61. P. reads, "followed that child with my eyes from its birth."

62. For an account of this search for Rousseau's child, see Cranston, II, 285–288.

63. P. reads, "copies, I do not remember the number very well. After."

64. Jean-Jacques Duvoisin (1726–1780) was not from the Pays de Vaud, although he had a nephew who was a minister there.

65. On Pierre-Alexandre Du Peyrou (1729–1794), see Book XII, 504–505.

66. For an account of the composition of the *Essay on the Origin of Languages*, see Robert Wokler, *Social Thought of J.-J. Rousseau* (New York: Garland, 1987), 235–378.

67. P. reads, "in addition to my usual expenses," rather than "after all expenses were paid."

68. P. reads, "I discovered that."

69. P. reads, "even much more."

70. It has not been possible to identify this friend of Duclos. It has been suggested that it is, in fact, a M. Abeille, an inspector of manufacturing who was a friend of Duclos.

71. On the office of président *à mortier*, see Book VII, 238. The man was Charles de Brosses of the Parlement of Dijon. For an account of Rousseau's response and his lack of sympathy for either side in the quarrels between the monarch and the provincial Parlements, see Cranston, II, 329–330.

72. The Seven Years War (1756–63), known in the United States also as the French and Indian War, in which the French lost territories in Canada and the West Indies to England.

73. I.e., Mme de Pompadour.

74. That is, in the province of Normandy, for whose government he was responsible.

75. I.e., Choiseul's hand.

76. P. reads, "of heedlessness. The sight."

77. P. reads, "saw destruction in it."

78. Father Henri Griffet (1723–1807) was a professor and then preacher to Louis XV.

79. P. reads, "and had even given."

80. P. reads, "I got it stuck in my mind that."

81. The colleges were schools frequently run by Jesuits.

82. P. reads, "had so strongly urged me."

83. On Father Berthier, see Book VII, 274.

84. P. reads, "all my principles of religion were even much more contrary to their maxims."

85. Voisine (669, note 1) suggests that in this passage Rousseau means not that atheism and piety have joined forces in China, but that the Jesuits and Encyclopedists have joined forces in praising China, since each side sees what it wants there. Nevertheless, in other contexts Rousseau clearly uses this formulation to refer to the situation in China. See André Wyss, *La Langue de J.-J. Rousseau* (Geneva: Editions Slatkime, 1989), 252.

86. For an elaboration of this comparison between the Jesuits and the Encyclopedists, see *Rousseau, Judge of Jean-Jacques* (*Collected Writings*, I, 238–239).

87. That is, Guillaume de Lamoignon de Malesherbes, the father of the head of the censorship.

88. P. reads, "as was very well known."

89. The Parlement of Paris closed the Jesuit colleges in April of 1762 and shortly afterward dissolved the Society and banished its members from France.

90. On Rousseau's fears during this period, see Cranston, II, 315–322.

91. P. reads, "if it had happened to me in those."

92. See Appendix I, 572–583.

93. Alexis-Armand Darty, or d'Arty, was Mme Dupin's nephew. The Duc d'Orléans died in 1752. The funeral oration can be found in Pléiade, II, 1275–1289.

94. See Book X, 424.

95. P. omits, "in mine and."

96. P. reads, "attentive, several times I found."

97. Cyprien-Antoine-Baudoin Dumoulin, or Du Moulin.

98. The *Social Contract* was published in April of 1762 and went on sale in Switzerland and England in May.

99. On Loyseau de Mauléon, see Book X, 422.

100. P. reads, "read," rather than "seen."

101. For this maxim, see Book IX, 341.

102. Jean Baseilhac (1703–1781), who had the name Brother Côme in his religious order, was a famous surgeon. He visited Rousseau in June of 1761.

103. P. omits, "a second and."

104. P. reads, "*Simile a se l'habitator produce.*"

105. "The country is cheerful, pleasant, easy to cultivate, and its inhabitants resemble it in every point." The lines are from Tasso's *Jerusalem Delivered*, I, 62, and in the original context apply to soldiers from Touraine.

106. *Emile* appeared in May of 1762.

107. Charles-Marie de la Condamine (1701–1774) was a famous mathematician and geographer.

108. On Alexis-Claude Clairaut, see Book X, 430.

109. Louis-François de Blair (1687–1764).

110. P. reads, "these very words, which were repeated to me the same day, and which I have not forgotten. 'M.'"

111. P. reads, "these words," rather than "this remark."

112. Charles de Bourbon, Comte de Charolais (1700–1760).

113. See *Emile*, IV (Bloom, 352–353).

114. P. omits, "Another infraction of my maxims which did not remain unpunished."

115. P. reads, "Officers hardly treated them any less cruelly on his land."

116. P. reads, "justified," rather than "reassured."

117. Jacques Balexert, or Ballexserd (1726–1774), in fact did win the prize offered by the Dutch Society of Sciences at Haarlem for his *Dissertation on the Physical Education of Children from Their Birth up to the Age of Puberty*, which was published in 1762. The work agrees with *Emile* on numerous points, but it is not a plagiarism. It is not known what remark by d'Ivernois Rousseau is referring to. On François-Henri d'Ivernois, see Book XII, 515.

118. For a useful account of the increase in religious tensions during the period *Emile* was published, see Cranston, II, pp. 297–301 and 333–335.

119. Rousseau's contemporaries, such as Montesquieu, Voltaire, Diderot, and d'Holbach, regularly published their works anonymously or under pseudonyms to protect themselves from prosecution. Among Rousseau's major works, only the *First Discourse* was published anonymously.

120. P. reads, "that it was necessary to address oneself directly to the authors. The first time that."

121. Goa was a Portuguese colony on the coast of India. In the eighteenth century it was virtually identified with the worst abuses of the Inquisition.

122. P. omits, "second."

123. P. reads, "flattering, perhaps the finest."

124. P. reads, "prudence," rather than "policy."

125. For an account of the events leading up to the warrant for Rousseau's arrest, and particularly to Malesherbes's decision not to risk supporting Rousseau, see Cranston, II, 343–356.

126. P. reads, "strongly," rather than "always."

127. P. reads, "never," rather than "not."

128. P. reads, "the book which bore my name and whether."

129. P. reads, "tranquility," rather than "security."

130. Nothing further is known about Father Alamanni. Father Jean-François Mandar (1732–1803) became prominent and preached before the king and was said to have refused bishoprics from both Louis XV and Napoleon.

131. P. reads, "ends with the story of the Levite."

132. The story is in Judges 19.

133. P. reads, "In fact, upon opening Mme"

134. P. omits, "in the middle of the night."

135. P. reads, "tranquillity, to do for her at this juncture what no human power would have induced me to do for myself."

136. P. reads, "say a single word."

137. P. reads, "indignant," rather than "shocked."

138. The Prince de Conti's residence.

139. For the chronology of the issuing of the warrant and the arrival of the process-servers, see Pléiade, I, 1559–1560, note 1 to p. 583.

140. On Mme de Mirepoix, see Book III, 97.

141. P. omits "embrace."

142. P. reads, "my short past happiness."

143. P. reads, "return," rather than "do."

144. P. reads, "d'Alembert, and their friends and their plots, that I would not."

145. Solomon Gessner (1730–1788) was a poet from Zurich who wrote idylls in prose that praised the simple life. His translator was Jean-Jacques Huber (not Hubner), who was a Genevan who converted to Catholicism, apparently at the same hospice at which Rousseau abjured. Huber had sent Rousseau the translation near the end of 1761.

146. *The Levite of Ephraim* can be found in Pléiade, II, 1205–1223.

147. P. reads, "Yverdon, the fatherland of my good old."

148. Nothing more is known about M. de Miran.

149. P. reads, "Although they might not be, by themselves, extremely."

150. P. reads, "instead of," rather than "without."

151. Here P. adds, "*End of the Eleventh Book.*"

EDITORS' NOTES TO BOOK XII

1. P. reads, "*The Confessions of J.-J. Rousseau/Second Part/*Twelfth Book."

2. P. reads, "two," rather than "three."

3. In P. this originally read "two," but is corrected to "three."

4. On this Pierre Boy de la Tour, see Book VII, ooo. Roguin's niece was Julie-Anne-Marie Roguin (1715–1780). She married Boy de la Tour in 1740. Their oldest daughter was Madeleine-Catherine Boy de la Tour (1747–1816). She married Etienne Delessert in 1766. Later she was the recipient of Rousseau's *Letters on Botany*, which can be found in Pléiade, IV, 1151–95.

5. P. omits, "had been," and the sentence has no verb.

6. Georges-Augustin Roguin (1718–1788) ultimately married Jeanne-Marie-Anne d'Illens in 1766.

7. P. reads, "issued for my arrest on June 18."

8. The *Social Contract* and *Emile* were condemned to be shredded and burned. The Ecclesiastical Edict of 1568 states that anyone who dogmatizes against accepted doctrine should be called in front of the Consistory to explain himself. Rousseau expands on this violation of established procedure in his *Letters Written from the Mountain*. See Pléiade, III, 759.

9. The Jesuit *Journal of Trévoux* continued to be published in spite of the suppression of the order. Lycanthropy was the name of a symptom of mental illness in which the sufferer believes he is a wolf, but in the article in the *Journal of Trévoux* it refers to Rousseau's alleged misanthropy and ferocity.

10. *On the Mind (De l'esprit)*, by Claude-Adrien Helvétius, was published with tacit permission in 1758. Almost immediately the work, which professed materialism, was condemned by the Paris Parlement, the Church, and almost all journals. Helvétius avoided prosecution by making a formal disavowal of his work within a few weeks of its publication. In many respects this case is the closest comparison for the persecution of Rousseau. Rousseau misstates the public response to Helvétius's work, which was almost entirely negative, but he is accurate in his account of Helvétius's personal reception in other European countries.

11. Victor Gingins de Moiry (1708–1776).

12. George-François Roguin (1695–1764). Banneret is an old military title that was transferred to a communal office in the Pays de Vaud.

13. The order was issued on July 1, 1762, and received by the Bailiff on July 3. He obtained a delay until July 9, which is the day Rousseau left for Môtiers. As Rousseau indicates by talking about each state imitating its neighbor, the Bernese condemnation of Rousseau's works was instigated by Geneva.

14. Môtiers was on Prussian territory, and Frederick the Great was well-known for his tolerance and his anti-religious sentiments.

15. P. reads, "me for a long time with."

16. P. reads, "underneath which I had put a couplet."

17. The other verse of the couplet, which apparently was on the back of the engraving, was, "Glory, self-interest, there is his God, his law."

18. Adrastus is a treacherous and impious king in Fénelon's novel *Telemachus*, which figures in Emile's education. The implicit comparison between Adrastus and Frederick is in Book V (Bloom, 467).

19. P. reads, "in his place for a moment—I."

20. P. reads, "Frederick descend lower than."

21. After being exiled from Rome, Coriolanus sought and found refuge among the Volscians against whom he had previously fought.

22. P. reads, "feelings," rather than "affections."

23. In Book I of *Emile* (Bloom, 49) Rousseau says, "He who cannot fulfill the duties of a father has no right to become one. Neither poverty nor labors nor concern for public opinion exempts him from feeding his children and from raising them himself. Readers, you can believe me. I predict to whoever has vitals and neglects such holy duties that he will long shed bitter tears for his offense and will never find consolation for it." In his letter to Mme de Francueil in 1751, Rousseau gave precisely the reasons of poverty, labors, and concern for public opinion as the reasons for giving up his children. See Appendix I, 551–552.

24. P. reads, "sensibly worse; the equivalent vice which I have never been able to cure my self of completely appeared less contrary to it. This double reason."

25. Thérèse left Montmorency on July 10 and rejoined Rousseau on July 20. They had been apart since his departure on June 9.

26. Jacques-Frédéric Martinet (1713–1789). A Châtelain is roughly the equivalent of a mayor.

27. George Keith (1686–1778) was an exiled supporter of the Stuart monarchy who found employment in the service of Frederick the Great. Contrary to what Rousseau says here and to rumor spread by his enemies after his death, Keith never lost his friendship for Rousseau. However, their relations became more distant after Rousseau's quarrel with Hume because Keith did not want to take sides between his two friends.

28. James Francis Edward Keith (1696–1758) fought to restore the Stuart monarchy and later in the Spanish and Russian armies. He became governor of Ukraine and then Russian ambassador to Sweden. Later he became Frederick the Great's governor of Berlin. He was killed at the battle of Hochkirch, October 14, 1758.

29. P. reads, "welcomed both of them."

30. Ferdinand-Olivier Petitpierre had been dismissed in August of 1760 for having preached against the eternity of punishments.

31. P. reads, "little leather bag."

32. On the importance of the language of signs, see Chapter One of the *Essay on the Origin of Languages* and *Emile*, IV (Bloom, 321–322).

33. P. reads, "induced" rather than "begged."

34. In fact, this was Frederick's idea.

35. The Seven Years War ended in February of 1763. The letter to which Rousseau refers in the next paragraph was written in November of 1762, before the conclusion of the peace.

36. Arabic for "Peace be with you."

37. Marie-Isabelle (1735–1797) and Anne-Marie d'Ivernois were the daughters of Guillaume-Pierre d'Ivernois (1701–1775), the procurator general of Neuchâtel.

38. Abraham de Pury (1724–1807) was a retired officer who has served in the Sardinian military.

39. Pierre-Alexandre Du Peyrou (1729–1794) was born in Dutch Guiana. He married Colonel Pury's daughter in 1769.

40. P. reads, "and by the action of time this esteem."

41. As Rousseau indicates, the classis is the name of the body of ministers at Neuchâtel.

42. The former *Swiss Mercury* had the name *Swiss News* (*Nouvelliste suisse*) during this period. Shortly after Rousseau's arrival it ran a series of articles attacking his religious views.

43. P. reads, "idiotic," rather than "insipid."

44. P. reads, "a man with whom one takes such a tone."

45. P. omits, "at Berne."

46. Frédéric-Guillaume de Montmollin (1709–1783) had been a literature professor at Neuchâtel before becoming pastor at Môtiers in 1742.

47. In fact, she had sent him several letters at least two of which he had answered. In this letter of October 2, 1762, she complains about Rousseau writing to Montmollin about his religious opinions rather than about receiving communion.

48. In Paris the Dutch Ambassador's pastor held Protestant services, which were forbidden in France.

49. P. omits, "What difference did this make to it?"

50. The faculty of theology at the Sorbonne published its *Censure of the Faculty of Theology against the Book which Has as Its Title, Emile or On Education* in November of 1762.

51. *The Mandate of Monseigneur the Archbishop of Paris, Containing a Condemnation of a Book which Has as Its Title: Emile or On Education by Jean-Jacques Rousseau, Citizen of Geneva* was published in August of 1762. Christophe de Beaumont (1703–1781) was the Archbishop of Paris.

52. See Book VIII, 306–307.

53. P. reads, "believe in my answer I."

54. Rousseau's *Letter to Beaumont* is dated November 18, 1762, and was published in March 1763. It can be found in Pléiade, IV, 927–1008.

55. This period is covered in the first part of Book IX.

56. P. reads, "Maréchal himself take."

57. In a fragment (Pléiade, I, 1176–1177) Rousseau says that it was not until 1768 that he was struck by this gap. The suspicion he arrived at in 1770 was that the letters had been stolen in order to find a way to implicate him in Damien's attempt to assassinate the King. See Book IX, 368, and editors' note 105.

58. P. omits, "It is only seven years afterward that I suspected the horrible object of this theft."

59. P. reads, "noticed most were."

60. Rousseau also makes this charge in *Rousseau, Judge of Jean-Jacques* (Col-

lected Writings, I, 17). The *Dictionary of the Fine Arts* to which Rousseau refers was probably one published by Jacques Lacombe in 1752. D'Alembert published his *Elements of Theoretical and Practical Music Following the Principles of M. Rameau* in 1752. Aside from a debt to Rameau which he shared with Rousseau, d'Alembert cites Rousseau's articles from the *Encyclopedia*. Although there is no evidence against d'Alembert for the theft of letters and manuscripts discussed here, a surprising number of Rousseau's papers were found in his possession after his death. See Hermine de Saussure, *Rousseau et le manuscript des "Confessions"* (Paris: Editions E. de Boccard, 1958), 206n.

61. See Book V, 181.

62. P. reads, "that year whose name I have forgotten, a letter." The Syndic was Jacob Favre (1690–1775).

63. The letter in which Rousseau renounced his citizenship is dated May 12, 1763. The month before he had been granted naturalized citizenship of Neuchâtel.

64. "The earth was silent," from I Maccabees I:3. Jean-Robert Tronchin, or Tronchin-Boissier (1710–1793), wrote the *Letters Written from the Country*, which were published in September and October of 1763.

65. The word translated as "remonstrators" is "*representans*," or "representatives." It was the name given to the protesting faction in Geneva at this time that had appealed to their traditional right of making a *representation*, or remonstrance, against a government policy.

66. This meeting took place in August of 1764. The *Letters Written from the Mountain* appeared in two parts in October and November of that year.

67. Rousseau made his excursion to La Ferriére in June of 1765.

68. Louis-Henri-Jean-Thomas, Comte de La Tour du Pin de La Charce (1726–1782), and Hyacinthe-Antoine Dastier, or D'Astier (1715–1786), first visited Rousseau in 1763.

69. P. reads, "since he did not want to display it on his mule's tail. These gentlemen."

70. The sculptor Jean-Baptiste Le Moyne (1704–1778) did a bust of Rousseau in marble at Hume's solicitation, probably near the end of 1765.

71. P. omits, "made by Le Moyne."

72. For Rousseau's concern about the various portraits done of him, see *Rousseau, Judge of Jean-Jacques* (*Collected Writings*, I, 89–94).

73. Sidonie-Charles-François Séguier, Marquis de Saint-Brisson (1738–1773), was dissuaded from publishing his "French Idylls" by Rousseau's criticism, but later published a number of works.

74. This trip took place in July of 1765.

75. P. reads, "owed me at least some remembrance, unless."

76. On the De Lucs, see Book VIII, 330.

77. François-Henri d'Ivernois (1722–1778).

78. Ignace Sauttersheim (1738–1767) was the son of an Imperial Councillor. He had gone to Neuchâtel to escape his creditors. Sauttersheim stayed in Môtiers for a little longer than three months.

79. This story can be compared with the story of Alexander the Great's trust of his friend Philip which is told in *Emile* (Bloom, 110–111).

80. P. reads, "to bring Sauttern back to virtue, and the young woman to her duty. When I."

81. The formula for the beginning of a confession. See Book VIII, editors' note 152.

82. P. reads, "on this sad event," rather than "on this subject."

83. P. reads, "honor to the memory of a decent man who had honored me with a sincere friendship. I was dispensed."

84. On Mussard, see Book VIII, 313–315.

85. On this discussion and the maxim referred to in this paragraph, see Book II, 47. There is no record of a will from the Duc de Luxembourg naming Rousseau, but on June 11, 1764, less than a month after the Duc's death on May 18, La Roche informed Rousseau that he had found the acknowledgement of a debt to Rousseau amounting to 1,575 livres as well as some letters and papers belonging to Rousseau.

86. On Fénelon, see Book VI, 192; on Archbishop de Bernex, see Book II, 42–43; and on Catinat, see Book X, 415.

87. In October of 1762 Rousseau was informed of the death of Mme de Warens, which had taken place on July 29.

88. P. reads, "property in Scotland which."

89. Keith left for Scotland in April of 1763. After staying in Scotland for about a year, he returned to Berlin. Keith Hall was in fact near Edinburgh, not Aberdeen.

90. P. reads, "Mably. I had some old connections."

91. P. reads, "presuming," rather than "believing."

92. P. reads, "A letter to Mme Saladin was circulated in Geneva under his name in which."

93. Rousseau's letter to Mably was written February 6, 1765, and Mably did respond on February 11. In his response he expresses admiration for Rousseau and compares him to Socrates, but accuses him of stirring up sedition.

94. P. reads, "without necessity, the effect of which was to weigh down a man who was at the height of all his misfortunes."

95. *The Dialogues of Phocion on the Relation of Morality to Politics* appeared at the beginning of 1763, but Rousseau learned about it in 1764.

96. P. reads, "understood," rather than "felt."

97. P. reads, "no more cruel enemy."

98. P. reads, "only in the hope that I would pull it off badly." In both manuscripts this entire paragraph is added on a separate sheet written in a different ink. On the back of the sheet in P. is a brief passage that has been impossible to decipher completely. For the different possible readings, see Voisine, 931, note a to p. 735.

99. P. reads, "writings," rather than "books."

100. P. reads, "had made me press to give."

101. Rousseau sent the manuscript of the *Dictionary of Music* to Duchesne in February of 1765.

102. Réguillat ultimately was imprisoned and exiled for engaging in the publication of works "against religion, the state, and good morals."

103. P. reads, "on a very reasonable."

104. In a letter to Du Peyrou, Rousseau indicated which works would be included in this edition. This is important because it is Rousseau's statement of which works he wanted to recognize as his own (as of 1765). He indicated: the *Discourse on Inequality*, the *Discourse on Political Economy*, *On the Social Contract*, *Abridgement of the Perpetual Peace*, *Abridgement of the Polysynody*, *Judgment on the Perpetual Peace*, *Judgment on the Polysynody*, the *Translation of the First Book of Tacitus's History*, *Julie*, *Emile*, the *Letter to Beaumont*, the *Letters Written from the Mountain*, the *Letter to d'Alembert*, *On Theatrical Imitation*, the *Discourse on the Virtue of the Hero*, the *First Discourse*, the *Response to an Anonymous Writing in the Mercury of France*, the *Letter on a Response of M. Gautier* (the *Letter to Grimm*), the *Response to the King of Poland*, the *Final Response*, the *Preface to "Narcissus"*, *Narcissus*, *The Reckless Engagement*, *The Gallant Muses*, *The Village Soothsayer*, *Pygmalion*, *Emile and Sophie, or the Solitaries*, *The Levite of Ephraim*, the *Letters to Sara*, *The Queen Fantastic*, the *Translation of Seneca's Apocolokintosis*, the articles "Music" and "Opera" from the *Dictionary of Music*, *Memorandum Read to the Academy of Sciences in 1742*, the *Letter on French Music*, the *Response to M. Rameau*, the *Essay on the Origin of Languages*, *Letters and Memoranda on Various Subjects*.

105. P. reads, "that there was any country in the world where a monster such as."

106. This declaration is dated February 12, 1765. The *Letters Written from the Mountain* had appeared in December of 1764.

107. P. reads, "like with all my heart to."

108. P. reads, "it exactly. I."

109. P. reads, "work," rather than "writing," and omits, "which had been written for their defense and at their solicitation."

110. P. omits, "as I was."

111. It was burned in Holland on January 21, 1765.

112. P. reads, "people," rather than "populace."

113. P. omits, "or being able to protect himself against it."

114. P. reads, "patriots who were concerned about the affair; everything."

115. P. reads, "arguments all drawn."

116. P. omits, "with my writings for which they would blame my freedom of writing."

117. P. reads, "not to write anymore," rather than "to give up the pen."

118. P. omits, "based on some change he required."

119. Rousseau made his offer to cease publishing on religious matters on March 28, 1765, the day before the meeting of the Consistory.

120. Samuel de Meuron (1703–1777).

121. P. omits, "to the taste of the Court."

122. See Book XII, 499.

123. P. reads, "at the court and with the Governor."

124. Rousseau wrote the letter on April 6, 1765, and the position was conferred on June 18.

125. David Hume (1711–1776) was Secretary in the British Embassy in Paris from 1763 to 1765. During this time he became friendly with many of Rousseau's former friends.

126. This translation of a portion of the *History of Great Britain* had appeared in 1760.

127. Rousseau had first gained fame for his argument in the *First Discourse* that luxury was incompatible with any good government. Even before Rousseau, Montesquieu had argued that it was incompatible with traditional republican government.

128. This letter was written from Edinburgh, July 2, 1762.

129. In his *Essays Moral and Political* (1741) Hume had included an essay, "On the Populousness of Ancient Nations." Robert Wallace (1697–1771) had attacked Hume's position in his *Dissertation on the Numbers of Mankind in Ancient and Modern Times* (1753). This dispute on the relative population of Europe was a part of the ongoing dispute about the relative merits of modernity. Hume took the modern side in this dispute, while Wallace (and Rousseau) defended antiquity. For a discussion of this question and its importance to Rousseau's thought, see Arthur M. Melzer, *The Natural Goodness of Man: On the System of Rousseau's Thought* (Chicago: University of Chicago Press, 1790) 288–289.

130. P. reads, "I did not want either to write or to promise."

131. Jean-Antoine d'Ivernois (1703–1764), the brother of the Procurator General, was a famous botanist.

132. In P. the note omits, "Moreover no one at Yverdon had so extremely monopolized me, had so lavished me with blandishments, with praise, and with flattery as the said Banneret Roguin. He faithfully followed my persecutors' favorite plan."

133. Like Rousseau's friend, this Boy de la Tour (1700–1772) was named Pierre.

134. *The Vision* was published in September of 1765. It can be found in Pléiade, II, 1232–1238.

135. P. reads, "fly at the same time at miracles."

136. From Attica, the location of Athens, synonymous with subtle sophistication.

137. The *Letters on the Christianity of Jean-Jacques Rousseau* by Jacob Vernes appeared in July of 1763. Rousseau refers to them in the Third Letter of the *Letters Written from the Mountain*, where, without naming him, he calls Vernes a "public calumniator." See Pléiade, III, 751. Charles Bonnet (1720–1793) was a prominent naturalist and author of works such as *Contemplations on Nature*. He had previously attacked the *Second Discourse* in the "Letter from Philopolis" (*Collected Writings*, III, 123–126).

138. In Greek mythology Phlegethon is one of the rivers of fire that flow into Acheron (the river of woe) in the underworld. Rousseau refers to the *Sentiment of the Citizens* (*Sentiment des Citoyens*) that appeared in December of 1764. The work also made the announcement that Rousseau had abandoned his children. It is almost universally accepted that this work was written by Voltaire, who had become enraged at Rousseau for revealing in the *Letters Written from the Mountain* that Voltaire was the author of the *Sermon of the Fifty* (*Sermon des cinquante*), which is a venomous attack on religion. This was an open secret, but it had never been mentioned in print, and in 1759 Voltaire had claimed that he had not written the work. Thus the personal animosity between Rousseau and Voltaire was connected with their views about the importance of taking personal responsibility for the works one publishes.

139. P. reads, "I was loudly accused."

140. P. reads, "other obliging things in the same tone. It was."

141. Rousseau sent the pamphlet to Duchesne in January of 1765.

142. Louis-Eugène, Duc de Wurtemberg (1731–1795).

143. In fact, in his first letter Vernes vehemently denied having written the pamphlet.

144. Mme Cramer was the wife of one of the brothers who were Voltaire's publishers. She informed Du Peyrou that she knew who the actual author was, but was obliged not to name him.

145. P. reads, "which was this arbiter? The Council of Geneva. I declared." Apparently inadvertently G. omits to name the arbiter. Accordingly the reading from P. has been introduced in brackets.

146. P. reads, "appropriate," rather than "necessary."

147. P. reads, "evidently," rather than "palpably."

148. After Rousseau's death, Du Peyrou published the *Declaration of Jean-Jacques Rousseau Relative to M. the Pastor Vernes*, along with commentary by Vernes. The work argues less that Vernes is the author than that Rousseau cannot be blamed for believing that he is, given the available evidence.

149. These are not overlapping periods. Rousseau lived at Môtiers for three years and two months.

150. Du Peyrou's *Third Letter to M. *** Relative to Monsieur Jean-Jacques Rousseau* is dated September 19, 1765, and was published in the middle of October of that year.

151. This attack took place on the night of September 6–7, 1765. The reports made immediately after the events confirm Rousseau's account.

152. P. omits, "on my exit."

153. P. reads, "a Courtyard in the back."

154. Abraham Guyenet.

155. Horace Walpole, Fourth Earl of Orford (1717–1797), was the son of the Prime Minister, Sir Robert Walpole. He wrote historical and critical works as well as novels, including *The Castle of Otranto* (1764), one of the best-known Gothic romances.

156. Louise-Dorothée de Saxe-Meiningen, Duchesse de Saxe-Gotha (1710–1767), maintained a correspondence with numerous literary people.

157. P. reads, "so much on me taking advantage of this invitation that she."

158. Both P. and G. omit the verb, which is supplied in brackets.

159. P. reads, "that little Island."

160. P. reads, "—had the inclinations of Their Excellencies."

161. Carolus Sturler (1711–1793).

162. P. reads, "to several of the leaders."

163. Jean-Frédéric Chaillet (1709–1778).

164. The Receiver administered the island for the hospital at Berne that owned it.

165. Rousseau arrived at the island between September 10 and September 12 of 1765. The description that follows should be compared with the Fifth Walk of the *Reveries*. See the commentary by Charles Butterworth in *The Reveries of a Solitary Walker* (New York: Harper, 1979), 189–200, and Kelly, 221–235.

166. P. reads, "estimate," rather than "judge."

167. The west bank of the Rhône River south of Lyon.

168. Charles-Auguste Du Terreaux. On M. de Saint-Florentin, see Book X, 421.

169. P. omits, "Little comments like this one, which are nothing by themselves, can lead to the discovery of much underground dealing later on."

170. P. reads, "myself as much as possible from."

171. This was a pension of 1,600 livres.

172. P. omits, "and who pays me the income in accordance with the terms agreed upon with the grantor."

173. P. reads, "would deprive me of all."

174. P. reads, "by depriving me at the same time of."

175. P. reads, "How could they doubt my choice given such alternatives?"

176. At the time Rousseau wrote this passage he had arranged for Du Peyrou to keep the income from Marshal Keith's pension to reimburse him for his expenses. Du Peyrou tried to persuade Rousseau to begin accepting the income again, but Rousseau refused for as long as he believed that he still owed Du Peyrou money.

177. P. reads, "on this side I had."

178. P. reads, "my character. I."

179. P. reads, "my vile calumniators."

180. Rousseau's quotation from La Fontaine's *Devil from the Land of the Heretics* (*Diable de Papefiguière*) is not precise. Where G. says, "*Où l'on fait plus, où l'on fait nulle chose,*" both the original and P. say "*On y fait plus, on n'y fait nulle chose.*" La Fontaine's work is based on passages in Book IV of Rabelais where Papimania is described. The line preceding the one quoted by Rousseau says, "I will see it, this country where one sleeps."

181. P. reads, "for since I have lost sleep I have hardly missed it: idleness."

182. P. reads, "hope anymore. That."

183. P. reads, "my fib. And."

184. P. reads, "as soon as," rather than "when."

185. P. reads, "myself ceaselessly by."

186. P. reads, "wanting to uproot a rock, fearlessly undertaking a labor."

187. P. reads, "sometimes one flower, sometimes another; to graze."

188. In the article *Ensemble* in the *Dictionary of Music* Rousseau says that the term has the general sense of "the suitable relationship of all the parts of a work among themselves and with the whole."

189. P. reads, "study, or rather amusement. I."

190. P. reads, "without a particular examination, and I."

191. *Plants of the Island of Pierre.*

192. P. reads, "holy," rather than "wise."

193. Odysseus' wife Penelope unraveled at night what she had woven during the day because she had promised to decide among her suitors as soon as she had finished weaving a shroud for her father-in-law.

194. Carl von Linne, or Linnaeus (1707–1778), revolutionized the study of botany with his system of classification of plants developed in his *System of Nature* (1735). His system was founded on the analogies between the flowers of plants

rather than their size as had been the traditional method. Rousseau relies heavily on Linnaeus in his *Letters on Botany*. See Pléiade, IV, 1151–1195. He praises Linnaeus in his Introduction to the incomplete *Dictionary of Botany*. See Pléiade, IV, 1205–1209. The gap in Linnaeus's system to which Rousseau refers is its incompleteness in naming even the currently known plants.

195. Christian-Gottlieb Ludwig (1709–1773).

196. P. omits, "to examine it on the spot, entirely at my ease."

197. Guy-Crescent Fagon (1638–1718) was a physician and professor of botany.

198. P. omits, "unless it was possibly a secret felicitation at being out of reach of the wicked in this position."

199. P. reads, "delightful," rather than "sweet."

200. P. omits, "Every so often I cried out with emotion, 'Oh nature, oh my mother, here I am under your protection alone; here there is no clever and deceitful man who comes between you and me.' In this way I went as far as a half a league from land; I would have wished this lake to be the ocean."

201. On Rousseau's fondness for Robinson Crusoe, see Book VII, editors' note 105.

202. P. reads, "This little colony."

203. P. reads, "festival," rather than "pleasure."

204. Nicolas-Antoine Kirchberger (1739–1800) was a former military officer and active Bernese patriot.

205. P. reads, "Here I am again reduced to one of."

206. In P. this paragraph ends, "What is more bizarre is that while they deny that I have all the good and indifferent feelings they do not have, they make no difficulty about lending me ones that are so bad that they could not even enter a man's heart: then they find it entirely simple to put me into contradiction even with nature and to make me into such a monster as could not exist. Nothing absurd appears unbelievable to them provided that it tends to blacken me. They arm themselves with incredulity against what is extraordinary only when it is not criminal."

207. P. reads, "report" rather than "set forth."

208. In P. this sentence reads, "I acquired so much taste for inhabiting the Island of St. Pierre, and the stay there suited me so perfectly, that as a result of inscribing all my desires on that Island I formed the desire of never leaving it."

209. P. reads, "spoil all its sweetness."

210. P. reads, "Instead of being tolerated here only as a favor why am I not here by force. Those who only tolerate me can drive me away at any moment; it is little enough that they permit me to live here, I would like them to sentenced me to stay here and I would like to be constrained to stay here so as not to be constrained to leave.'"

211. On Micheli du Crest, see Book V, 181–182.

212. P. reads, "fear," rather than "danger."

213. Rousseau restates this desire to be imprisoned on the Island in *Rousseau, Judge of Jean-Jacques* (*Collected Writings*, I, 73).

214. This letter was dated October 16, 1765, and was received by Rousseau the next day.

215. In fact, only four Senators had been present at the meeting at which this decision was reached instead of the normal six to eight.

216. P. reads, "deteriorate," rather than "sink."

217. P. reads, "keenest," rather than "greatest."

218. P. reads, "be able," rather than "want."

219. P. omits, "most categorical and."

220. G. omits "hours," which is found in P. It has been supplied in brackets here.

221. In its letter dated October 21, the Senate gave Rousseau three days from the reception of the letter, or until October 26 at the latest, to leave the territory of Berne.

222. P. reads, "Often," rather than "Since then."

223. In the *Social Contract*, II, x (*Collected Writings*, IV, 164), Rousseau says, "In Europe there is still one country capable of legislation; it is the island of Corsica. The valor and perseverance with which this courageous people was able to recover and defend its freedom would well deserve that some wise man should teach them how to preserve it. I have a feeling that some day this little island will astound Europe."

224. P. reads, "ponder," rather than "think of."

225. P. reads, "wrote me several letters on this subject and furnished me with many pieces."

226. Mathieu Buttafuoco (1731–1806) first wrote to Rousseau on August 31, 1764, and maintained a continuous correspondence with him.

227. Pascal Paoli (1725–1807) was a leading Corsican patriot and rebel against the Genovese and their French supporters. He enlisted English aid against the French and Genovese and finally died in exile.

228. On August 7, 1764, the French and Genovese reached an agreement allowing the French to establish garrisons in Corsica. In 1768 the French were given possession of the areas in which their garrisons were placed, and in 1769 they took possession of Corsica after a year of fighting against a rebellion led by Paoli and supported by the British. See Voisine, 771, note 1. In *Rousseau, Judge of Jean-Jacques* (*Collected Writings*, I, 220), Rousseau expresses his opinion that these actions were undertaken by the French as part of the conspiracy to control his movements.

229. In the *Social Contract*, II, viii–x (*Collected Writings*, IV, 157–162), Rousseau discusses the political situation necessary for undertaking a founding. His *Project for a Constitution for Corsica* can be found in Pléiade, III, 901–952.

230. P. reads, "to make fun of," rather than "to banter with."

231. P. reads, "only," rather than "true."

232. P. reads, "it a moment and."

233. P. reads, "I had received, and the more."

234. P. reads, "the people it was a question of founding and."

235. P. reads, "felt," rather than "understood."

236. On Dastier (or D'Astier), see Book XII, 512. The Marquis de Maillebois (1682–1762) had commanded the French forces in Corsica in 1739 when the French suppressed a rebellion against the Genovese.

237. P. reads, "Corsica, even without."

238. G., apparently mistakenly, reads "midst." The reading from P. is in brackets.

239. P. omits, "more than ever."

240. P. reads, " to them, after the departure of the French troops, if I saw."

241. P. reads, "taking on a type of life that put me to the torture for which I did not have the talent."

242. P. reads, "I had to find a free passage across the States."

243. P. omits, "at my age."

244. P. reads, "passionately desired an interview with Buttafuoco to confer with him about all that, and since he had made me hope for one, I was waiting for him to fulfill it to make up my mind completely."

245. P. reads, "trip and very much less still for the one."

246. P. omits,

above all with the precipitateness that was being prescribed to me. It is true that the extravagance of such an order made it impossible to execute: for—closed up in the middle of the water in the midst of that solitude and having only twenty-four hours from the intimation of the order to prepare myself for the departure, to find boats and carriages, to leave the Island and the whole territory—if I had wings it would have been hard for me to be able to obey. I wrote that to M. the Bailiff of Nidau when I answered his letter, and I rushed to leave that land of iniquity. That is how. . . .

The next sentence begins with, "It became."

247. P. omits, "how." There are also some very slight variations in what follows immediately. See Pléiade, I, 1609.

248. P. reads, "and putting my papers in deposit in."

249. P. omits the lengthy passage that begins here. It resumes at the point indicated in editors' note 255.

250. Alexandre Wildermet (1737–1800).

251. Antoine Barthès de Marmorières was the First Secretary of the French Embassy in Switzerland.

252. Pierre de Buisson, Chevalier de Beauteville, was the French Ambassador to Switzerland.

253. Jean-Rodolphe de Vautravers (1723–1815) had recently left a diplomatic career and moved to Bienne.

254. In state, or in official dress, the tassels, or *fiocchi*, on a cardinal's hat.

255. P. resumes after this point.

256. The two Ladies are the Marquise de Verdelin and the Comtesse de Boufflers, and their friend is Hume. After leaving Bienne, Rousseau made his way to Strasbourg, which was outside of the jurisdiction of the Paris Parlement. He stayed there while he was deciding where to go. The two Ladies visited him during this stay and persuaded him to go to England by way of Paris where they would introduce, or "hand him over," to Hume. Rousseau left Strasbourg on December 9, 1765, and eventually arrived in London on January 23, 1766.

257. P. reads, "of me and my reputation finally succeeded."

258. P. ends here saying, "End of the twelfth book/and of the second part."

259. This was the fourth, and apparently last, of the readings Rousseau gave of

the *Confessions* in 1770 and 1771. This one took place near the beginning of May of 1771. For an introduction intended for one of these readings, see Appendix II, 592. The Comte and Comtesse d'Egmont had a very fashionable literary and artistic salon. The Prince Pignatelli is probably Louis-Gonzague-Marie-Ildephonse, Prince de Pignatelli. The other listeners were Anne-Marie, Marquise de Mesme, or Mesmes (1732–1819), and Jacques-Gabriel-Louis Le Clerc, Marquis de Juigné.

260. "*Malhonnête*" has the sense of dishonest, dishonorable, and indecent.

EDITORS' NOTES TO APPENDIX I

1. With the exception of the four letters to Malesherbes (572–583), the following letters are from Leigh. When they are available, Leigh presents the original versions of the letters, noting the changes made in Rousseau's copies. This accounts for variations between the letters as they are found here and some of the quotations or paraphrases from them in the text. Since Rousseau kept both his copied version and the bundles of the originals, we have chosen to rely on the latter when possible.

2. This letter can be found in Leigh, II, 142–146. Rousseau's copy of this letter is written in a very simple code. Given Rousseau's familiarity with complex diplomatic codes, it would appear that he attempted to conceal the contents from anyone casually leafing through his letters, but not to make it impossible for others to read.

3. This letter can be found in Leigh, III, 133–134.

4. Ibid., 234–235.   5. Ibid., 243–244.

6. Ibid., 251–252.   7. Ibid., 256–257.

8. Ibid., 260–261.   9. Ibid., 271–272.

10. This letter can be found in Leigh, IV, 102–103 and in *Collected Writings*, III, 122. The translation is by Terence E. Marshall.

11. Rousseau notes here that "He has no longer written to me since that time."

12. This letter can be found in Leigh, IV, 93–95.

13. Laurent Angliviel de la Beaumelle (1726–1773) had had numerous quarrels with Voltaire, one of which concerned the sale of a version of the manuscript of Voltaire's *Age of Louis XIV*. See *Collected Writings*, III, 103 and editors' note 13.

14. See I Samuel 16.

15. Tronchin is referring to Rousseau's plans to find a place in an institution for the elderly for Mme Levasseur if he decided to move to Geneva.

16. This letter can be found in Leigh, IV, 168–170.

17. Pissot and Briasson were both publishers. Pissot had published the *First Discourse*.

18. The copy Rousseau made of this letter reads, "would not have spoken," which seems to make more sense than the original. Given that Rousseau's copies usually correct grammatical errors made in the originals, it is clear that this is how he understood Diderot's statement.

19. This letter can be found in Leigh, IV, 172–175.

20. This is evidently a quotation from Rousseau's response to Diderot's previous letter. The original of this response has not been preserved.

21. Diderot's reference is to Scipio Africanus the elder (c. 236–183 B.C.), who retired to Liternum after defeating Hannibal.

22. This letter can be found in Leigh, IV, 262–267.

23. Ibid., pp. 281–283.

24. Ibid., p. 354.

25. This letter can be found at Leigh, V, 44–45.

26. That is, Diderot.

27. This letter can be found in Leigh, V, 72–73.

28. Ibid., p. 168.

29. This letter can be found in Leigh, VI, 195–198.

30. On Desmahis, see Book X, 428.

31. This letter can be found in Leigh, VII, 3–5.

32. Lucius Licinius Lucullus (c. 110–156 A.D.) was a Roman general famous for his love of luxury, particularly for his sumptuous and exotic banquets.

33. "Even the springs, even the vineyards call me." Virgil, *Eclogues*, I:39. The original says "you," rather than "me."

34. Mme de Verdelin, who was Margency's mistress.

35. As Leigh indicates, Margency is referring to Mme d'Epinay, who had recently returned from Geneva.

36. As Leigh points out, this is a reference to a story by La Fontaine. In this story the Infanta Alcaciel has relations with eight successive lovers.

37. Leigh suggests that de Caron might be a nickname for Grimm. Caron is an alternate spelling for Charon, the blind boatman who transports the souls of the dead into Hades.

38. "the wrath of sad Amaryllis." Virgil, *Eclogues*, II: 14.

39. On doctor François Thierry, see Book VIII, 300.

40. This letter can be found in Leigh, VII, 306–307.

41. The term translated here as "good woman" is "*bonne femme.*" It usually has the connotation of simplemindedness (see Book X, 444); however, here Mme de Verdelin refers to its literal sense.

42. This letter can be found in Leigh, VII, 203–206.

43. This follows the variant reading given by Leigh.

44. This letter can be found in Leigh, VII, 127–131.

45. *The Discovery of the New World*. This meeting would have taken place in 1742. See Book VII, 247.

46. On Father Berthier, see Book VII, 274, and editors' note 176; also Book XI, 474.

47. Upon being elected to the French Academy in 1760, Jean-Jacques Le Franc, Marquis de Pompignan (1709–1784), delivered an address attacking the Encyclopedists and their allies, especially Voltaire, for irreligion.

48. This memorandum, in which de Pompignan defends himself against attacks made by the Encyclopedists, was published in May of 1760.

49. This letter can be found in Leigh, VII, 77–78.

50. This letter can be found in Leigh, VI, 209–210.

51. These letters can be found in Pléiade, I, 1130–1147.

52. Thus Rousseau indicates that his "system" can be found in the *First* and

Second Discourse plus *Emile*, although he also indicates that this system is not presented in a thoroughly systematic manner there or anywhere else in his works.

53. For the prosopopeia of Fabricius, see *Collected Writings*, II, 11. A prosopopeia is a rhetorical figure in which someone who is absent (or, as in this case, dead) is made to speak.

54. Beginning in 1759 Rousseau used as his motto *"Vitam impendere vero"* (To stake one's life on the truth) from Juvenal's *Satires*, 4.91. It is the epigraph of the *Letters Written from the Mountain* and also occurs in the *Letter to d'Alembert* (Bloom, 131). Rousseau discusses it in the Fourth Walk of the *Reveries*.

55. "Would that it were so!"

56. In the Tenth Walk of the *Reveries* Rousseau tells a different version of this same story, attributing the remark to a Pretorian Prefect who had left the court in disgrace under Vespasian. The story is not in Spartianus and Similis was a prefect under Hadrian. See Pléiade, I, 1831, note 1 to p. 1099. Butterworth has found the source of this quotation in Cassius Dio Cocceianus, *Roman History*, lxix. 22.2 (*Reveries*, ed. Charles E. Butterworth [New York: Harper and Row, 1979], p. 143, note 7).

57. This is the date of Rousseau's move to the Hermitage. This statement should be compared with the account of his happiness in Book VI.

58. The faithful Achates is the companion of Aeneas in the *Aeneid*. It is used here as a nickname for Rousseau's dog Turk.

59. Luke 12: 27.

60. Rousseau is referring to the position on the *Journal of Scholars* that Malesherbes had had Margency offer him. See Book X, 429–430, and the letters from Margency in Appendix I, 566–568.

EDITORS' NOTES TO APPENDIX II

1. This preface can be found in Pléiade, I, 1148–1155. Page numbers in heads in this appendix refer to the present volume.

2. Girolamo Cardano (1501–1576) was an Italian physician, mathematician, scientist, and astrologer. Near the end of his life he wrote an authobiography, *De Vita Propria (On His Own Life)*.

3. In the Preface to the *First Discourse*, Rousseau says, "A man who plays the free Thinker and Philosopher today would, for the same reason, have been only a fanatic at the time of the League" (*Collected Writings*, II, 3).

4. A camera obscura is a primitive ancestor of a modern camera. It consists of a darkened chamber (literally, the camera obscura) with a convex lens and a mirror. When an object is placed between a bright light and the camera obscura, the lens projects its reverse image on the walls of the chamber and the mirror corrects the reversal. The camera obscura was used for making sketches from nature. Simple versions of the camera obscura have been used since antiquity for studying eclipses. Interestingly, one of the earliest treatises describing the addition of the lense and the mirror (which is necessary to prevent the image from appearing in reverse) to the darkened chamber was written by Cardano, to whom Rousseau refers. This treatise is *De Subtilitate Rerum* published in 1551. The issue represented

by the camera obscura of whether it is possible to find a technical or artistic device that can render nature without distorting it is fundamental to Rousseau's thought.

5. This early draft can be found in Pléiade, I, 1155–1158.

6. This early draft can be found in Pléiade, I, 1160–1161.

7. This introductory speech for a reading of the *Confessions*, which may never have been delivered, can be found at Pléiade, I, 1184–1186.

8. In his attempt to find someone to entrust with the manuscript of *Rousseau, Judge of Jean-Jacques*, Rousseau later attempted to distribute copies of a letter with the address, "To all Frenchmen who still love justice and truth" (*Collected Writings*, I, 251–252).

9. This indicates that Rousseau made his decision to write his memoirs sometime around 1760.

10. In other words, Rousseau's reading on this occasion consisted of Books VII through XI with some selections from Part One.

Index

The index includes the names of significant characters referred to in the *Confessions*, but omits names mentioned by Rousseau merely in passing. The spelling of names in the index is in accordance with the way the person is best known. Rousseau's spelling is used for names not well known outside of his book (for example, Mme Charly rather than Charlier). Standard spelling is used for those well known (for example, d'Holbach rather than d'Holback). The important variant spellings of names are given in brackets. Books, musical works, characters, and quotations not by Rousseau are usually indexed under their author. Only important references to places are included. Page numbers with an asterisk refer to Rousseau's footnotes.

Index